n.

Organization Form

Organization Science

Series Editor: Arie Y. Lewin

Books from Sage Publications, *Organization Science*, and the Institute for Operations Research and the Management Sciences

The Sage Publications **Organization Science** book series reprints expanded Special Issues of *Organization Science*. Each individual volume is based on the original Special Issue that appeared in *Organization Science*. It includes all-new introductions by the editors as well as several chapters that did not appear in the original Special Issue. These new chapters may include reprints of papers that appeared in other issues of *Organization Science*, relevant papers that appeared in other journals, and also new original articles.

The book series is published by Sage Publications in partnership with INFORMS (the Institute for Operations Research and Management Sciences) the publisher of *Organization Science*. The Series Editor is Arie Y. Lewin, the Editor in Chief of *Organization Science*.

Organization Science was founded in 1989 as an international journal with the aim of advancing the field of organization studies by attracting, then publishing innovative research from across the social sciences. The term "Science" in the journal's title is interpreted in the broadest possible sense to include diverse methods and theoretical approaches. The editors of *Organization Science* believe that creative insight often occurs outside traditional approaches and topic areas, and that the role of *Organization Science* is to be broadly inclusive of the field by helping to integrate the diverse stands of organizational research. Authors are expected to describe theoretical concepts that give meaning to data, and to show how these concepts are relevant to organizations. Manuscripts that speculate beyond current thinking are more desirable than papers that use tried and true methods to study routine problems.

Initial books in this series:

Longitudinal Field Research Methods: Studying Processes of Organizational Change
Edited by George P. Huber and Andrew H. Van de Ven

Organizational Learning
Edited by Michael D. Cohen and Lee S. Sproull

Cognition Within and Between Organizations
Edited by James R. Meindl, Charles Stubbart, and Joseph F. Porac

Managing in Times of Disorder: Hypercompetitive Organizational Responses
Edited by Anne Y. Ilinitch, Arie Y. Lewin, and Richard D'Aveni

Shaping Organization Form: Communication, Connection, and Community
Edited by Gerardine DeSanctis and Janet Fulk

For information on subscriptions to *Organization Science*, please contact INFORMS at 940-A Elkridge Landing Road, Linthicum, MD 21090-2909, 800-446-3676. For submission guidelines, contact INFORMS at 290 Westminster Street, Providence, RI 02903, 800-343-0062.

Shaping
Organization Form
Communication, Connection,
and Community

Gerardine DeSanctis
Janet Fulk
Editors

Organization Science

SAGE Publications
International Educational and Professional Publisher
Thousand Oaks   London   New Delhi

For information:

SAGE Publications, Inc.
2455 Teller Road
Thousand Oaks, California 91320
E-mail: order@sagepub.com

SAGE Publications Ltd.
6 Bonhill Street
London EC2A 4PU
United Kingdom

SAGE Publications India Pvt. Ltd.
M-32 Market
Greater Kailash I
New Delhi 110048 India

Printed in the United States of America

Library of Congress Cataloging-in-Publication Data

Main entry under title:

Shaping organization form: Communication, connection, and
community / edited by Gerardine DeSanctis and Janet Fulk.
   p. cm. — (Organization science)
  Includes bibliographical references and index.
  ISBN 0-7619-0494-8 (cloth: acid-free paper)
  ISBN 0-7619-0495-6 (pbk: acid-free paper)
  1. Communication in organizations—Technological innovations. 2.
Organizational change. 3. Organizational effectiveness. I.
DeSanctis, Gerardine. II. Fulk, Janet. III. Series: Organization
science (Thousand Oaks, Calif.)
  HD30.3 .S514 1999
  302.3'5—dc21   99-6233

99 00 01 02 03 04 8 7 6 5 4 3 2 1

Acquiring Editor:	Harry Briggs
Editorial Assistant:	MaryAnn Vail
Production Editor:	Wendy Westgate
Production Assistant:	Karen Wiley
Typesetter/Designer:	Danielle Dillahunt
Indexer:	Juniee Oneida
Cover Designer:	Candice Harman

Contents

Introduction

GERARDINE DESANCTIS

JANET FULK

This book is the result of a 5-year effort on the part of researchers, the INFORMS organization, and Sage. Our goal has been to produce a volume that simultaneously provides completed empirical work and contributes to a future research agenda on electronic communication and changing organizational forms. Our efforts began with a special issue of *Organization Science* that presented eight studies addressing the role of electronic communication technology in organizational change. Following the production of the special issue, most of the papers were further edited or updated prior to inclusion in this book. We then selected seven additional papers, some published and some unpublished, to appear in this book. All of the chapters included here were selected for their importance to current organizational scholarship and their significance for future research in the area.

As a result of these efforts, we are pleased to provide the reader with a thought-provoking collection of work that considers the role of new communication technologies in shaping organizations today and in the future. This book considers four key themes: (a) changes in technology, changes in form, and their mutual influence on one another; (b) evolutionary processes in organizations and the ways in which technology can influence these processes; (c) the development of organizational communities and interorganizational relationships that are mediated by electronic communication systems; and (d) important controversies surrounding electronically mediated forms and directions for future research that flow out of these controversies.

Our book provides a range of perspectives on the potential for new organizational forms to emerge in today's economic landscape and on the power of technology to influence their success. Some authors argue that significant, positive changes are made possible due to new communication technologies. Others argue that the real potential for organizational change comes less from technology than from socioeconomic forces and managerial action. Some authors identify commonalities in new forms and new ways of work brought about by technology, whereas others emphasize variations in technology use in relation to organizational structure across groups, firms, and communities. Some authors posit that organizational forms of today are substantively different in structure and function than in prior eras, whereas other authors observe that the new forms embody much of the reality of the past and may not represent the kind of significant change that managers would like. Some authors focus on changes of form that occur "in the small," meaning work groups or dyadic relationships, whereas others observe shifts "in the large," between firms and larger communities. Some authors explore the new connections and work arrangements brought about by communication technology. Others explore the difficulties and dilemmas that new organizational forms can yield.

The chapters in this book consider a wide array of communication technologies from telephones and electronic mail to more sophisticated systems, such as electronic conferencing, discussion databases, news systems, cognitive mapping, and group decision support software. The authors employ a variety of methods, including theory building and theory testing, longitudinal case study, model development and evaluation, controlled survey studies, observational analyses, and historical reviews. Finally, the chapters examine technology and organizational form across a range of settings, including a food services firm, a computer manufacturer, automobile dealerships, a telecommunications firm, a European professional services company, and a Japanese manufacturing firm. The chapters consider both formal work arrangements and self-created "virtual" communities.

Despite the range of viewpoints and approaches taken by these scholars, this book has an important common thread—that the relationship between technology and organizational form is an ongoing dynamic process of mutual influence that is shaped by social context and managerial action. The contributors to this book reflect the advance of the science beyond simplistic, causal models of technology-form relationships. Instead, they introduce rich research models that account for the complexities in technology development and organizational life. Collectively, the chapters in this book move the study of technology and organizations into a broader research territory in which theory is more contextual, empiricism is multivariate, longitudinal, and field based, and the focus is multilevel, ranging from individuals to communities.

More than 150 researchers from throughout the world contributed in some way to making this book possible—through paper submissions, reviewing of manuscripts, editing, and publishing. We thank this community of scholars for their efforts. We particularly thank Gary Dickson, Joey George, Paul Goodman, Lynne Markus, and Carol Saunders, who worked with us on the editorial board of the special issue. We thank Candida Gerzevitz of INFORMS for her assistance in the early stages of compiling chapters. We thank Harry Briggs of Sage for his patience and support through the long publication process required to produce this book. Finally, we thank Arie Lewin for his ongoing intellectual encouragement and for making this book possible.

Contributions to scholarly literature must be viewed within the time frame in which those advances are made. This is particularly true in fields that are technologically bound. The material in this book was written during the period 1994 to 1998. Due to circumstances beyond our control, Sage was unable to publish the book until 1999. Although much of the content remains relevant today, readers should keep in mind the time frame in which the authors developed their ideas. Regarding the sustainability of our contributions to knowledge, only time will tell.

PART I

NEW COMMUNICATION TECHNOLOGIES
AND NEW FORMS OF ORGANIZING

What are organizational forms? What are the "new" forms of the information age? What is the role of technology in these new forms? The first section of this book addresses these fundamental questions from a range of viewpoints. We begin by summarizing key trends in communication technology and organizational form, exploring the ways in which technology and form interact with one another. Chapter 1 presents the literature in the field of technology and organizations from three perspectives: technological, organizational, and emergent. The changes in organizational forms that are linked to electronic communication are described along four dimensions. First are changes in organization size, scope, and product domain; examples include leaner, more responsive firms that produce information-based products and services and rely on a sophisticated technological infrastructure. Second are changes in vertical control, such as flattened hierarchies, reduced middle management, and use of tentative principles rather than fixed rules as mechanisms of control. Third are changes in horizontal coordination, such as electronic workflow, concurrent engineering, cross-functional teams, and stockless production systems. Finally, there are changes in connection between firms, such as strategic alliances, electronic data interchange systems, network relations, and federated organizational structures.

Following this overview, Applegate (Chapter 2) contrasts "hierarchy" and "information age" organizations in terms of their use of technology and other mechanisms of managerial control. In several case studies, Applegate observes that the new forms of the information age are a blend of old and new

1

rather than a radical shift to a unique form of organizing. She observes that organizations today are striving to manage complexity and enable speed and flexibility of response to a highly dynamic marketplace. Core to achieving these capabilities is information technology, but informal systems of communication remain important and powerful to organizational design. Applegate describes new organizational forms in terms of information age forces, and she provides an extensive description of the ways in which companies are currently designing for flexibility and competitive advantage. Today's organizations are relying more heavily than in the past on information-based control, learning, continuous process improvement, and shared understanding and trust among organizational members.

Monge and Fulk (Chapter 3) provide a global perspective on new organizational forms. They emphasize the evolution of networks within and between firms, a trend that yields a "boundaryless" entity in which distinctions between the inside and the outside of a firm, or even an entire industry, can become blurred. The "global network organization" is based on four components: (a) flexible internal communication networks that are emergent rather than imposed, (b) internal networks connected to dynamic networks of external organizations, (c) internal and external networks that are governed by partnerships and teams (rather than hierarchy or ownership), and (d) a sophisticated information technology infrastructure. Monge and Fulk point out that new organizational forms emerge from forces that include more than technology, such as changes in the political and economic landscape. The result is that the organization is embedded in a complex web of interdependencies, and communication and computing systems are used to manage this complex web. At the same time, the new forms require more than technology to manage complexity. Sharing of knowledge, goals, resources, personnel, and finances is vital to the success of global network organizations.

Collectively, the chapters in this section emphasize that technology is but one of a myriad of forces responsible for changes in organizational form. Winter and Taylor (Chapter 4) take this point to the extreme, suggesting that technology may be relatively insignificant as a force in new organizational forms. Their thought-provoking chapter provides a historical review of organizational forms throughout the postindustrial, industrial, and protoindustrial eras. They show that social and cultural changes result from a confluence of forces, of which technology is only one. They argue that the flexible form of organization, which is increasingly popular today and often touted as a new form, is not new at all and does not necessarily require the presence of information technology. They call for research that produces more detailed descriptions of the changes occurring in the evolution of organizational forms. They particularly note the need for clearer, more complete, and less simplistic theories of the causes of change in organizational form.

Together, the first four chapters present important trends in organizational design, outline possibilities for changes in modern organizational design, and reveal the complexity of the technology-form relationship.

1

Articulation of Communication Technology and Organizational Form

JANET FULK

GERARDINE DESANCTIS

A central concern of organization science is the study of organizational form, defined as the structural features or patterns that are shared among many organizations. Researchers have identified a variety of organizational forms beginning with the tribal (McKelvey 1982). Weber (1922/1968) defined the dominant organizational form as bureaucracy, in contrast to the guild form. Two classic forms are markets and hierarchies. An alternative to both markets and hierarchies appears to be emerging—the network form (Miles and Snow 1986, Nohria and Eccles 1992, Powell 1990; see Chapter 3). In addition to the network, other "postbureaucratic" forms have been documented, including the interactive (Heckscher 1994) and virtual (Mowshowitz 1994, Nohria and Berkley 1994; see Chapter 16). Whatever the specific form, the connective mechanism that enables parts of the organization to coordinate with one another and with other organizations is communication (March and Simon 1958). Organizational structures have been designed to meet communication needs inside the organization and between the organization and external

AUTHORS' NOTE: We thank Peter Monge for valuable comments on an earlier version of this chapter.

entities. For example, hierarchical control mechanisms have been implemented to compensate for information asymmetries within and between firms (Williamson 1975), and boundary-spanning units have been created to link uncertainty-reduction activities in the organization to activities within the environment (Galbraith 1973, Thompson 1967, Tushman and Nadler 1978).

With few exceptions (e.g., see Chapter 4), research has proposed that changes in communication technologies are tightly linked with changes in organizations. Three perspectives have arisen to explain the dynamic relationship of communication technology and organizational form. Dutton (see Chapter 16) labels them technological, organizational, and emergent. The *technological* perspective emphasizes ways in which communication technologies have been shown to enable changes in forms. Organizational forms traditionally have been designed to achieve coordination and control in the presence of significant time and distance barriers. Technological developments motivate changes in form to the extent that they offer new capabilities for overcoming such temporal and geographic constraints. For example, early communication inventions, such as the rudimentary file system, interoffice memo, and business meeting, contributed to the development of bureaucracies, enabling coordination and control among organizational components (Yates 1989, Yates and Orlikowski 1992). Later, telephones, telegraph, and mail systems enabled distributed forms of organization and interorganizational communication (Chandler 1977, Pool 1983). Newer electronic communication systems can link disparate business units, firms, and communities, thereby impacting organizational and interorganizational processes (Huber 1990, Lucas 1996; see Chapters 10-12).

The *organizational* perspective emphasizes how new communication technologies are designed or customized to match organizational forms. For example, dual reporting and workflow systems were developed to support matrix organizations. Kling and Zmuidzinas (1994) present a series of case studies showing how workplace visions influenced the computerization process, which in turn transformed organizations. Computer networking tools and collaboration support for dispersed sites have been developed to respond to the significant coordination needs of decentralized structures (see Chapter 7). The organizational perspective focuses on shifts in technology to accommodate organizational form rather than the reverse effect of shifts in form due to changes in technology.

The *emergent* perspective combines technological and organizational views to focus on communication technologies as "occasions" for structuring (Barley 1986). Technology creates new options for organization design, whereas new organizational forms provide new opportunities for technology design (see Chapter 9). Technology and organizational form are viewed as "homologous" (Beniger 1986, 1990), with "the design of information technology and the design of organizations largely becoming the same task" (Lucas and Baroudi 1994, p. 9). In the emergent perspective, not only do communication technology and organizational form dynamically align with each other but also technology users and other organizational members play active roles in shaping the design of this alignment (Karsten 1995, Star and Ruhleder 1996; see Chapters 5 and 8).

This chapter considers all these views as we explore the articulation of technology and organizational form. By articulation, we mean attempts to clarify and explain the complex, reciprocal relationship between technology and form. We recognize that all three perspectives—technological, organizational, and emergent—offer valuable explanation. Each perspective offers insight into how technology and form co-align with one another in the dynamic space of organizational life. Furthermore, each perspective can offer useful guidance to managers as they attempt to design technology or organizations or both for future success.

We begin by summarizing the major advances in communication technology that can bring change to organizational form. Next, we describe in detail the interplay between technology and four dimensions of organizational forms: (a) organization size, scope, and product domain; (b) vertical control; (c) horizontal coordination; and (d) types of connection. Together, these dimensions reveal the ways in which communication technology can affect and, in turn, can be affected by changes in organizational form.

TRENDS IN COMMUNICATION TECHNOLOGY AND IN ORGANIZATIONAL FORM

Communication Technology

Despite considerable discussion of the technology-organization relationship in the research literature, no systematic description exists of the specific mechanisms by which new electronic technologies affect and are affected by organizational form (Henderson and Venkatraman 1994). In general, however, most observers would agree that at least five features of new communication technologies offer important advancements for organizations. The first is the dramatic increase in the speed of communication, with high volumes of data moving from one location to another at rates unimaginable even a decade ago. The second advancement is the dramatic reduction in the costs of communication due to technical developments and to economies of scale achieved through wider penetration of technologies. Third is the sharp rise in communication bandwidth, with more information of multiple fre-

quencies traveling simultaneously on a common communication line. High
bandwidth is facilitating the explosion in multimedia communications, combining text, voice, video, data, and graphics within a broadband communication system. Fourth is vastly expanded connectivity, with literally millions
more people and machines linked together via local, wide-area, and Internet-
based networks than even 5 years ago. Fifth, the integration of communication with computing technologies has permitted communication technology
to offer more than simple connective capabilities. Communication technologies can now store and retrieve information electronically from shared
databases, enabling greater communal information sharing. Furthermore,
integrated technologies can be used to manipulate and change information
or alter communication patterns, providing constructive capabilities (Fulk
and Collins-Jarvis 1998; see Chapter 10).

Organizational Form

Electronic communication technologies could be construed as simply one
more environmental force that contributes to shifts in form (Halal 1994,
Pinder and Moore 1979). New organizational forms enable organizations to
respond to varied environmental pressures, including greater complexity
(Lundberg 1994), global presence (Ghoshal et al. 1994, Mitroff et al. 1994),
severe economic pressures (Halal 1994), innovation demands (Zajac et al.
1991), entrepreneurial pressures (Bartlett and Ghoshal 1993), and incorpo-
ration of social values for more participative, learning-oriented, and diverse
management practices (Heydebrand 1989, Mitroff et al. 1994). Technology-
enabled form is more than reactionary, however. Many organizations actively
design and implement unique electronic communication systems (with varying degrees of success) rather than simply absorb available technology from
the marketplace. As organizations design communication systems to meet
their internal and external coordination needs, organizational form influences electronic communication technology (Thomas 1994; see Chapter 9).
In short, new organizational forms are more than coping mechanisms for
environmental trends. They are both affected by and actively affect communication technologies made available in the marketplace.

What are the new organizational forms? New, electronically based organizations can be described in archetypal form, although variants exist. Heydebrand
(1989) offers a

> general, simplified profile of the typical postindustrial organization . . . small or
> located in small subunits of larger organizations; its object is typically service or
> information, if not automated production; its technology is computerized; its divi-

sion of labor is informal and flexible; and its managerial structure is functionally decentralized, eclectic, and participative. (p. 327)

Hedlund (1986) contrasts new and old forms using opposing metaphors. He describes yesterday's organization as like a tree—with a common trunk of communication linking progressively smaller branches up to a peak representing top management control—and today's organization as like a nervous system—a multicentered entity with governance and operations managed differently at different centers.

New organizational forms have been labeled adhocracy (Malone and Rockart 1991, Mintzberg 1983), technocracy (Burris 1993), the internal market (Malone, Yates, and Benjamin, 1987, Ouchi 1980), heterarchy (Hedlund 1986), knowledge-linked organization (Badaracco 1991), platform (Ciborra 1996), T-form (Lucas 1996), cellular (Miles et al. 1997), postbureaucratic (Heckscher 1994), virtual organization (Davidow and Malone 1992), and network (Biggart and Hamilton 1992, Ghoshal and Bartlett, 1990, Powell 1990, Rockart and Short 1991; see Chapter 3). Progression to new forms has been gradual in most firms, dramatic in some, and nonexistent (or nearly so) in others (Appelbaum and Batt 1994, DiMaggio and Powell 1983, Piore 1994; see Chapter 2). Regardless of the rate of shift to a new form, fundamental to the shift has been a powerful co-alignment between form and communication technology. Four important dimensions of form and their linkages with electronic communication are described in the following section.

FOUR DIMENSIONS OF FORM AND THEIR ARTICULATION WITH COMMUNICATION TECHNOLOGY

Organization Size, Scope, and Product Domain

Researchers have noted a trend toward smaller, more streamlined, information-based organizations supported by advanced coordination technologies. This movement is associated with four dimensions: resizing, rescoping, information production, and technological infrastructure development.

Resizing

Organization and unit size are fundamentally changed by restructuring and reengineering programs designed to reduce overhead, delayer, "right size," divest underperforming businesses, focus more narrowly on core businesses, "do more with less," and redesign core business processes. In these revamped organizations, coordination is accomplished by individuals and teams with cross-functional, computer-mediated jobs (Nohria and Berkley 1994), and new communication and information technologies are employed to manage the "information metabolism" of such coordination-intensive structures. Inevitably, these types of redesign lead to business processes that require a smaller labor force, motivating layoffs and overall reduction in organizational size (see Chapter 12). Indeed, one key criterion for success in the reengineered organization is savings in personnel costs (Hammer and Champy 1993). In a study designed to assess causality, Brynjolfsson, Malone, Gurbaxani, and Kambil (1994) analyzed economy-wide data on information technology investments in a wide variety of manufacturing and service industries. They found that information technology investment led to reductions in firm and unit size in every industry.

One consequence of the move from human to technological control of operations is the associated shift in the level of technological dependency. The costs of technological failure are in direct proportion to the organization's reliance on technology for operations that are central to the firm's core strategy. For example, in an investment firm that relies on instantaneous communication and integration of market information from nodes around the globe, failure of a computer system could result in the end of a business within a matter of hours (Cash et al. 1992; see Chapter 15).

Rescoping

A proliferation of smaller firms is, in part, linked to reductions in scope as information and communication technology developments permit electronically mediated, market-based alliances in lieu of vertically integrated value activities (Malone and Rockart 1991). Management can logically separate abstract business process requirements from the concrete means for their implementation, making rescoping of core activities possible (Mowshowitz 1994). Firms today are outsourcing, spinning off upstream value activities, and replacing backward integration with efforts to improve supplier performance (Cash et al. 1992). Supplier relationships are supported with interorganizational information systems that obviate the need for one firm to fully subsume the other. This strategy can improve not only supplier performance but also the supplier bond with the organization (Miles and Snow 1995).

Governments are beginning to outsource management of schools and prisons, for example, and numerous firms have elected to outsource their key information systems functions and to monitor outsourcing arrangements through information technology linkages (Huber 1993). Outsourcing reduces the size of the core organization and the scope of value activities performed in-house (Cash et al. 1992). Quinn (1992) notes that with outsourcing comes a significant shrinkage in top management, headquarters, and internal overhead groups. Those few at the top need different skills, including "leadership and coordination, rather than order giving" (p. 375).

Malone et al. (1987) use transactions cost theory (Coase 1937, Williamson 1975) to argue that reductions in organizational scope are directly linked to decreased costs of technology-assisted market transactions. Transactions in uncertain markets involve extensive coordination costs, such as gathering information, negotiating contracts, and protecting against opportunistic behaviors. These coordination activities involve communicating and processing information. Hierarchies arise from the decision to control the costs of coordination through internal management rather than use of external markets (Coase 1937, Williamson 1975). Traditionally, hierarchies have been favored over market-based transactions under two conditions: asset specificity and complexity. Asset specificity occurs when knowledge of specific production processes does not readily transfer to other products, contexts, or organizations. Complexity is found when a large amount of information is needed to articulate to potential buyers the features of a particular product.

Malone et al. (1987, p. 489) argue that "databases and high-bandwidth electronic communication can handle and communicate complex, multidimensional product descriptions much more readily than traditional modes of communication," favoring a shift toward markets. Flexible manufacturing technology permits rapid shifts in the organization of production. This flexibility reduces the costs of switchover and coordination between asset-specific technologies, and it permits integration of asset-specific components obtained on the market into products produced internally. The net effect of such technological developments is a greater use of markets rather than hierarchies to coordinate economic activity. Thus, the scope of value activities under hierarchical control can be reduced.

At the same time, scope may increase to reflect new market realities as technologies converge, as has occurred in communication industries. The once-distinct industries of telephone, broadcast, cable, computing, and entertainment are converging. Collis et al. (1997) argue that convergence has fundamentally altered the nature and scope of communications-related industries. The removal of federal policy barriers to free competition through the Telecommunications Act of 1996 has permitted technological developments to be reflected in new industry structures and new cross-industry market opportunities for previously monopolistic firms. Also, the new scope of both firms and industries facilitates development of integrated broadband systems. These systems will integrate voice, video, and data on demand and could also be interactive with the user. Technological integration for the provision of integrated broadband services is also contributing to vertically

integrated firms. Baldwin et al. (1996) summarize their analysis of communication industry convergence as follows:

> Cable operators are already vertically integrated with programmers. Three
> RBOCS [regional Bell Operating Companies] are attempting to form partner-
> ships in Hollywood. Cable and telephone companies are aligning with software
> designers and hardware manufacturers. Broadcast networks are "in play" with
> Hollywood studies, cable MSOs [operators of multiple cable systems], and tele-
> phone companies are all mentioned as prospective buyers. Most of the converg-
> ing industries are also buying into or creating on-line services. (pp. 400-401)

Federal legislative and policy changes are frequently cited as initiating the
current trend toward rescoping. The policy changes are in part a response to
pressure from developments in the technologies of communication and
information processing (Baldwin et al. 1996).

Information Production

With the well-documented shift from manufacturing to services in most
developed economies has come a focus on manipulating information and
symbols rather than physical products. Even traditional product-oriented
organizations such as General Electric now view themselves as being in the
information business. As information products become a more significant
portion of a firm's productive output, information highways replace asphalt
ones for product distribution. Communication rather than transportation
systems become the fundamental constraints for organizational design (see
Chapter 3). Two major concomitant changes are the movement toward global
network organizations and alteration of production systems to process information rather than products.

Heydebrand (1989) notes that evaluation criteria can change radically
when an organization processes information rather than physical products.
When the object of production is physical, the product can be readily
differentiated from the process that created it. When the core product is
service or information, however, "the process itself becomes the product or
is indistinguishable from it, leading to a restriction of evaluation to largely
processual criteria" (p. 326). This trend is evident in efforts to identify the
"best practices" available in an industry and to adapt them for use in multiple
organizations. Likewise, there is a trend toward using client satisfaction as
a key evaluative measure and other customer-based quality metrics that
embed process into product evaluation (Quinn 1992).

Additional opportunities for information-based products arise from organizational change programs that replace sequential work flows across multiple units with integrated processing through a single individual or unit. Convergence of work processes on a single node can offer new opportunities for synergy and the creation of value-added services through such processes as compiling, integrating, and packaging complex information for customers or other interested buyers. For example, large travel agencies compile information from their databases on travel patterns for various segments of the market and then sell this information to travel providers such as airlines and car rental agencies.

Technological Infrastructure Development

Changes in organizational size, scope, and product can affect development and deployment of communication technology. Malone et al. (1987) suggest two ways in which the movement to electronic, information-based markets affects technology. First, it pressures firms to plan and develop the network infrastructure needed to support these transactions. Infrastructure includes agreement on standards and protocols for information encoding and transmission and ensuring that the backbone for electronic exchange is in place. Furthermore, it includes values, attitudes, and behaviors that promote information sharing and commitment by decentralized entities to build compatible technologies (Jarvenpaa and Ives 1994, Star and Ruhleder 1996). It also includes what Fulk et al. (1996) call connectivity and communality. Connectivity is the ability of one node (person, group, organization, etc.) to reach other nodes through the infrastructure. Communality is the availability of a joint depository of information to which nodes contribute and from which nodes can retrieve information. Increasingly, the Internet is serving as this backbone, with the movement toward electronic commerce.

Second, a movement toward electronic markets motivates firms to develop new information processing resources, including "intelligent aids to help buyers select products from a large number of alternatives" (Malone et al. 1987, p. 496) and tools to manage communication load in the leaner organization. With reconfiguration, a firm often finds that fewer resources exist to process the organization's information; a common complaint is the sheer volume of information that needs to be managed. Under a reengineered organization, the information processing demands on a single node will be more complex, requiring computer-based decision tools (Nohria and Berkley 1994). Tools to manage the load, including filtering, searching, and sorting techniques, are developed in response to the needs of the new information-intensive form. Technologies are being developed for filtering, searching, and sorting (Crowston and Malone 1988, Malone et al. 1987), such as the automated information retrieval agent commonly known as "knowbot" (Anthes 1991). The precise nature of effects related to shifts to new structures may vary depending on the degree of complementarity between technology, organization form, and incentive systems (see Chapter 6).

The availability of new convergent streams of information in reengineered organizations can also motivate technological development. Technology applications can be designed to better manipulate and use the information internally or to create an information technology product that can be marketed to others with similar needs. For example, Otis Elevator's Otisline communication system for managing service delivery in elevator repair can be developed for sale to noncompeting businesses that involve the same core process of dispatching service repair technicians.

Vertical Control

From a transactions cost perspective, hierarchical control of value activities is surrendered when they are shifted to the market. Do new organizational forms manifest altered forms of control for value activities that remain within the scope of the organization? If so, how are communication and information technology implicated in altered control systems? Research and theory on centralizing and decentralizing trends associated with technological deployment suggests that there are no simple answers to these questions (see Chapter 2).

The Centralization-Decentralization Debate

Perhaps the most common observation in discussions of new organizational forms is the dwindling ranks of the middle manager and the associated flattening of hierarchies. This change is often attributed to communication and related information technology subsuming the coordination and control roles of managers and staff (Zuboff 1988). Heydebrand (1989) describes this phenomenon as the substitution of technical rationalization for social rationalization. Hierarchical organizations achieve control in part through rationalization of activities via rules, programs, procedures, and goals that standardize information (Weber 1922/1968). Key roles for management include (a) developing and controlling the rationalization protocols and (b) handling "exceptions" that fall outside the parameters of these routines (Galbraith 1973). The flexibility and complexity of newer information and communication technologies offer the ability to handle a greater variety of exceptions with technological rather than managerial solutions. Thus, human-based coordination can be reduced in some parts of the organizational hierarchy. The operative word is "can" because the choices as to whether to deploy such technologies in this fashion are inherently managerial, as Zuboff (1988) and Koppel et al. (1988) note. Technologies can be configured so as not to subsume substantial amounts of traditional managerial roles. Technological configurations are the result of choices made by human designers. Because communication and information systems are malleable, their relationship to organizational form may take many and conflicting shapes. Consider the linkage between technology and levels of centralization and decentralization of control in organizations. Five distinct perspectives are evident in the literature: centralization, decentralization, centralization with decentralization, reinforcement, and context dependent.

Centralization occurs when technology is employed to rationalize tasks and electronically monitor process and output. The prototype of this application is the so-called "electronic sweatshop" (Garson 1988) in which computerized routines track and compile performance details on computer users, such as the number of keystrokes, the number of customers served per time period, and the amount of time per customer. A parallel process is the employment of technology to rationalize tasks that had formerly had a judgmental element, enhancing control through standardization (Zuboff 1988). George et al. (1992) describe executive information systems as monitoring devices for internal operations and industry competition that summarize information for top executives to enhance their communication, planning, and control of the organization. Dutton (see Chapter 16) observes that more centralized control of remote activities is possible through use of personal location devices, wireless telephones, personal communication services, and other communication technologies that permit access to individuals regardless of location.

Decentralization is commonly described in the literature on new organizational forms using such labels as "empowerment" (Malone 1997). For example, Miles and Snow (1995, p. 13) claim that the new "spherical" organizational form is based on "leadership as a shared responsibility among colleagues, not as a superior-subordinate relationship." Communication and information technologies are seen to provide local operators with global data that will permit them to make local decisions consistent with overall organizational goals. For example, local sales personnel can be provided with forecasts calculated from historical and real-time data, thus providing tools and parameters for planning an overall local sales effort. Broadly connected communication networks are seen to rapidly and widely distribute required information for on-the-spot decision making that responds to rapidly changing environmental pressures. These information-intensive firms are described as heavily reliant on lateral communications and "anytime-anyplace" tools, such as computer conferencing, electronic bulletin boards, expert databases, project management software, local area networks, and intranets (Johansen et al. 1991). Sproull and Kiesler (1991) argue from an extensive series of studies, primarily conducted in the laboratory, that use of communication systems such as electronic mail and computer conferencing supports more equal and democratic participation in organizations.

A third perspective argues that organizations no longer must choose between centralized and decentralized modes of organization because new information and communication technologies permit simultaneous centralization with decentralization (Burris 1993, Heydebrand 1989, Keen 1990; see Chapter 2). Using this model, Keen (1990) describes a "federated organization" in which decentralized organizational units act relatively autonomously, but advanced communication technology permits some degree of monitoring and centralized control. Keen cites the example of Toyota of America, which placed microcomputers in dealers' offices to improve local operations and the quality of data employed for local decision making. These computers were also linked to central headquarters personnel who were able to use the information about local decisions to reduce the "information float"—the time gap between a local decision and the central planners' awareness of it. Similarly, Otis Elevator found that the ability to collate data from many localities at a central location permitted the discovery of patterns of problems with company products that at the local level were seen only as isolated incidents.

A fourth perspective argues that designers and users align technology and organizational practices so as to buttress existing structural features rather than change them, an outcome that Dutton (see Chapter 16) refers to as "electronic concrete." Danziger et al. (1982) found that organizational participants manipulated computer adoption and implementation to reinforce the existing power structure. Fulk et al. (1990) and Bikson and colleagues (Bikson and Eveland 1990, Bikson et al. 1989, Eveland and Bikson 1987) similarly found that formal and informal organizational policies regarding use of electronic mail systems constrained usage to existing communication norms. In multicountry studies, Bjorn-Andersen et al. (1986) and Child and Loveridge (1990) found that use of computer-based support systems was more likely to reinforce existing structures rather than change them.

A final perspective views communication and information technology as inherently neutral, and that its relation to structure emerges through complex interactions of people, technology, and organizational processes (Markus and Robey 1988, Zmud 1990). Mantovani (1994, p. 57) argues that computer-mediated communication "does not generally foster democracy in organizations. It depends on the social context, on the history of each organization, and on the regulations ruling the specific network application." Vandenbosch and Ginzberg (1997) similarly argued that their research at a major insurance company supported Orlikowski's (1992) findings that group- ware tools do not increase collaboration in the absence of an extant collabo- rative organizational culture. They asserted that changes depended on the "fit between the technology's underlying premise (e.g., collaboration) and the organization's structure, culture, and policies" (p. 77).

Communication Cultures and Control

An alternative perspective argues that moves to downsize labor and decentralize authority to individuals holding a broader scope of responsibil- ity are not, by themselves, shifts away from basic principles of bureaucracy, which already provide for some degree of autonomy for experts (Heckscher 1994): "Over the long run, indeed, the pattern of bureaucratic evolution is an oscillation between centralizing and decentralizing moves; in recent years it appears this oscillation has speeded up in many companies, because neither solution deals with the essential problems" (p. 30). Heckscher argues that decentralization and other popular techniques such as just-in-time systems do indeed tighten the organization but through bureaucratic means. He contends that they do nothing to accomplish one key requisite of a true postbureaucratic organization: increase the dialogue among the different parts of the organization. A true postbueaucratic form is distinguished by a unique communication culture that overrides hierarchy.

In this view, the drive to rapidly innovate creates organizations that are dominated by communication and influence relationships rather than by hierarchy (Reich 1991). Whereas in traditional bureaucracies consensus is created by individuals' acquiescence to authority and rules, the postbureau- cratic form is derived from "institutionalized dialogue" (Heckscher 1994). Communication and influence are the core features. Heckscher argues that in the postbureaucratic form, influence relationships depend on trust, a high degree of shared vision, and broad communication about corporate strategy. Influence relations are also fluid, unlike fixed positions on an organizational chart. Individuals learn to link with others throughout the organization, many of whom they may never have met. An emphasis on learning and continual improvement can substitute for standardization and supervision as mecha- nisms for ensuring control and movement toward organizational goals (see Chapter 2). Organizationwide electronic mail and discussion systems sup- port "weak ties" among persons who may not even know each other (see Chapter 13). Such ties have been shown to be strongly linked to innovation

(Granovetter 1973, Rogers 1995). Also, because flexibility is critical to innovation and agility, the form is dominated by tentative principles rather than by fixed rules. Indeed, a general lack of expectation of permanence pervades the culture of the postbureaucratic organization (Heckscher 1994).

Horizontal Coordination

A common theme in the literature on new organizational forms is that the reduction in formal vertical control mechanisms is linked to an increase in horizontal coordination mechanisms. Communication and connection become increasingly lateral as the boundaries across units take on increased permeability and flexibility. Cross-functional teams replace functional silos. Increasingly, organizations are seen as communities that dynamically alter in response to organizational needs. Malone and Rockart (1991) describe the new form as a "coordination intensive structure" consisting primarily of patterns and relationships. Several developments in which communication technology is implicated are described in this section: electronic work flow, concurrent engineering, cross-functional and "virtual" teams, stockless production, and collaboration tool development.

Electronic Work Flow

The organization of units into divisions and departments has traditionally been based on the need to collocate activities with high levels of interdependence to reduce the communication costs associated with coordinating activities in the face of uncertainty (Thompson 1967). This collocation involves both physical and organizational proximity. Communication technologies offer electronic proximity as an alternative. Changes in the organization of warehousing and distribution functions are an example. These functions are dependent not simply on movement of product but also on information regarding flow of product into, through, and out of the system to customer premises. Mobile computer-based systems for entering orders and stock-level information, route planning, and other logistics reduce the need for physical proximity to achieve horizontal coordination. Increasingly, distribution systems are changing from centralized warehousing facilities to many smaller, local storage units coordinated through information and communication technology.

Indeed, the design of physical space for organizational activities, labeled "strategic facilities planning" by architectural and engineering firms, is increasingly focused on designing spaces for "virtual teaming" in which work and coordination is conducted independently of shared physical setting (Lipnack and Stamps 1997). Telecommuting from home or satellite centers are traditional examples that have existed for decades (Metzger and Von Glinow 1988). Perhaps the most publicized example of the truly space-independent corporation is Verifone (Cohen 1997), a vendor of security solutions and electronic payment systems with worldwide operations generating annual revenue of $387 million (*http://www.verifone.com*; Verifone was recently acquired by Hewlett-Packard). Verifone is "100% electronic": The entire company, comprising 1,900 employees in 30 worldwide locations, is net-worked and works on-line. Even a $40 billion expenditure for operations in Shanghai is authorized electronically, with electronic signatures and not a single piece of paper generated, according to chief executive officer Hatim Tyabji (1996). The main horizontal coordination mechanism at Verifone is e-mail communication. Shared space in many corporations today is cyber-space, incorporating intranets, extranets, and project Web sites.

In the bureaucratic form, organizational proximity is created for interde-pendent activities by grouping experts by function or alternatively by project or product. Matrix organizations are communication-intensive structures designed to coordinate across both types of grouping simultaneously. Allen and Hauptman (1990) argue that information and communication technolo-gies offer the benefits of coordination across both functions and projects or products without the substantial communication costs of the structurally organized matrix. In essence, electronic technologies support an alternative form of "electronic matrix." Examples of tools that support the electronic matrix include project management software, electronic bulletin boards, expert databases, and electronic conferencing systems. Increasingly common for such coordination are intranets with Web sites maintained by individual units or projects. A searchable site may serve as a key repository for critical information to be shared among members of globally dispersed project teams.

Concurrent Engineering

Changes in horizontal coordination are particularly evident in product design. Traditionally, product design involved sequential processing across functions, with handoffs as each stage was completed. Increasingly, this linear process is being replaced by parallel processing and concurrent engi-neering. Designers, engineers, suppliers, customers, and others who have a stake in a product can be involved simultaneously in design, with coordina-tion assistance from systems such as computer-aided design, computer-aided engineering, and Lotus Notes (Davidow and Malone 1992). Piore (1994) observes that job responsibilities have at least blurred where concurrent engineering has been implemented. Piore uses the label of a multidimen-sional matrix to approximate the form thus enabled in which traditional functions are replaced by teams. These teams may be composed of individuals and units working from many different parts of the world who are linked by telecommunication systems, a hallmark of The Ford Motor Company's global R&D organization (*Business Week* 1994).

Cross-Functional Teams

As team efforts replace serial handoffs across functional silos, members are increasingly cross-trained across functions. Miles and Snow (1995) argue that such cross-functional teams should be self-managing, and the organization should heavily invest in skills for self-management of teams. In this model, teams provide a more flexible alternative for horizontal coordination and offer the responsiveness needed for rapid action and better understanding of total business processes. Nohria and Berkley (1994, p. 115) describe such teams as "holographically equivalent to the organization as a whole." Such teams are also seen as emergent—forming and dissolving as needs wax and wane (DeSanctis and Poole 1997). Nohria and Berkley (1994, p. 120) describe several features of communication and information technologies that support new and more complex forms of interaction. Client-server architectures allow distribution of data in decentralized networks. Relational databases and open architectures assemble and disassemble data in response to personal needs of users. Factory automation systems employ distributed rather than hierarchical control. Nohria and Berkley (p. 123), however, caution that "*cross-functional* can be spoken like a mantra, along with such terms as *teaming* and *empowerment*. Even when this fetish character is refreshingly absent, the compulsion to push an organization to cross-functional extremes has become extremely powerful."

Stockless Production

Actions to reduce or eliminate in-process inventory can have dramatic implications for organizational forms. Common methods of inventory reduction are the Japanese *kanban* method and the American just-in-time systems. Inventory reduction can occur independently or as part of a flexible mass production system. These systems have the capability to produce multiple product designs based on customized programming of generalized equipment. The principle is to have the materials that are needed for an operation delivered to the appropriate workstation at just the right time. When functioning well, these systems eliminate inventories without adding additional downtime due to late or missing parts. Piore's (1994, p. 47) research found that elimination of buffer inventories led to greater interdependence among workstations and "greater lateral communication, less hierarchy, a more broad-based, generally trained labor force, and a greater capacity to respond flexibly to changing market conditions."

Development of Technology for Collaboration

Electronic communication technology is at the heart of current efforts to horizontally integrate the firm. Electronic communication systems have been shown to complement formal work networks and promote more diverse and less formal relationships (Rice 1994, Walther 1995). Simultaneously, a substantial body of research has documented the limitations of communication media for "psychologically involving tasks," such as negotiation and relationship maintenance (Daft and Lengel 1984, Hollingshead and McGrath 1995, Short et al. 1976, Trevino et al. 1987). Media vary in their ability to transmit "rich" information such as nonverbal cues, but in general mediated interaction involves many "process losses" relative to face-to-face communication. These limitations pose important challenges for new organizational forms that are dominated by influence, negotiation, and relationships. As organizations increasingly rely on communication technology for coordination, they confront not only technological advances but also technological limitations.

The need to effectively manage processes in transformed organizations is motivating development of better tools for supporting collaborative relationships (Bostrom et al. 1992, Dennis et al. 1988, Kraut et al. 1990, Marshall and Novick 1995). A variety of collaborative tools have been designed to overcome process losses and to support some process gains in comparison to unmediated interaction (DeSanctis and Gallupe 1987). For example, group support systems permit groups to manage their own structures and processes in productive ways. Four key features are (a) process support, such as anonymous communication and stored collective memory of interactions; (b) process structure, such as Roberts's rules of order or talk queues; (c) decision structure, such as modeling techniques (e.g., Bayesian analysis); and (d) task support, such as access to databases or notes from prior interactions (Nunamaker et al. 1993). Poole and DeSanctis (1990), Poole et al. (1991), and DeSanctis and Poole (1994) argue that such tools are "occasions" for structuring because social processes and technological structures mutually influence each other in an emergent fashion.

Types of Connection

The management of form is increasingly enacted as management of relationships (Bartlett and Ghoshal 1993, Miles and Snow 1995, Ring and Van de Ven 1994; see Chapter 12). Creative new forms of connection are an essential feature of new forms that are "neither market nor hierarchy" (Powell 1990). In the following sections, we describe five such types of connection. Monge and Fulk (see Chapter 3) provide a detailed analysis of connectivity in the context of internal and external firm networks.

Connecting in the Value System

In conjunction with outsourcing and other shifts to more market-like relationships with other firms, new forms of connection may develop through communication technology in what has been termed the electronic integration effect (Malone, Yates, et al. 1987, Venkatraman and Zaheer 1994). For example, a firm may manage its downstream relationships with suppliers by requiring each supplier to adopt a particular form of electronic data exchange, resulting in very tight coupling between buyer and supplier. Upstream, an organization may electronically connect its operations with those of customers, creating a disincentive for customers to seek other suppliers. The classic example of this strategy is American Hospital Supply's direct-order entry system (Cash et al. 1992).

The Internet also has been predicted to significantly impact supplier relations. One argument is that the Internet will permit buyers to bypass intermediaries and purchase directly from the manufacturer (Benjamin and Wigand 1995, Gates 1995). For example, the rise of Web sites such as Expedia (*http://expedia.msn.com*) for airline flight information and direct ticket purchase permits customers to conduct similar search functions to those of travel agents and to purchase tickets on-line. Coupled with on-line discount offers not available to travel agents, considerable incentive exists for customers to bypass travel agents.

A counterargument is that travel agents will thrive to the extent that they can add value by such activities as packing complex flights, collating dispersed information about travel destinations, and selling this information package. The complexity and dispersion of information on the Internet offers greater opportunities for those with the skills to navigate the complex Web to create or collate information with added value. Beyond the travel industry, a whole new breed of "cybermediaries" is arising among those with the skills to add value to the simple searches conducted directly by the customer (Sarkar et al. 1995).

Research and Development Collaboration

Sharing of research and development resources and expertise across firms creates unique interorganizational relationships that can enable learning, product development, and innovation. Such relationships create communities of experts, usually scientists and engineers, that otherwise would not be possible within the realm of one firm. Research collaborations enable firms to leverage expertise in science and engineering without endangering competitive stance in the marketplace. In the United States, for example, research collaborations are possible among firms that would otherwise be viewed as colluding under antitrust laws. Research collaborations are vulnerable to labor turnover and interpersonal difficulties among the parties involved in the collaboration. Their success is dependent on clarity in the communication systems that connect the individual collaborators and their firms at large. Furthermore, a high degree of trust, including organizational cultures that remain receptive to learning from external expertise, is considered vital to successful collaborations (Dodgson 1993).

Lu (1995) argues that engineers need new collaboration tools in several areas of engineering design. First, technology must support sufficing at the individual level while optimizing for the group rather than sufficing for the group while optimizing for the individual. Second, collaboration software must support interval-valued rather than point-valued design specification to permit flexibility. Third, design states should be functionally decomposed and linked to support negotiation. Fourth, software must be based on assumptions of mutual interdependence rather than on linear input-output models. Finally, collaborative negotiation support should also be provided to the customer as part of a product's utilization and refinement. Lu argues that despite the current emphasis on concurrent engineering, most existing engineering support tools do not support a design result based on these types of parameters. New collaboration technology must be designed to meet the needs arising from transformed product design processes.

Strategic Alliances

Strategic alliances are very common today and not just between firms operating along the same value chain. An increasing number of alliances cut across industries and link divergent value chains, supported by electronic communication technology. A popular example is the linkage between major banks and airlines to offer frequent flier miles for bank credit card users. This type of alliance is based on information as a core product, and it would not be possible without the enhanced capability of communication systems to share real-time data between otherwise separate organizations. This linkage of firms across such diverse industries as banking, travel, insurance, and telecommunications is resulting in complex alliance webs in which an organization can serve simultaneously as not only supplier to another but also competitor, customer, and consultant. The result is a circular value chain and new weblike forms of interdependence. Norman and Ramirez (1993) argue that such complexity has transformed value chains into "value constellations." Complex, interconnected value activities illustrate the boundaryless feature of new organizational forms and the importance of relational trust in managing such complex networks of interdependencies.

Hagedoorn and colleagues conducted extensive research on strategic technology alliances. Hagedoorn (1996) investigated trends in strategic technology partnering since the early 1970s. He found that in the past two decades joint ventures, the traditional equity form of partnering, have largely been replaced by contractual agreements that are nonequity based. Although the trend was found across industries, it was particularly evident in high-tech industries (Hagedoorn and Narula 1996). Osborn and Hagedoorn (1997) argue that nonequity forms offer more flexibility and opportunity for reciprocal information exchange. In essence, the form of connection for information technology partnering is toward less hierarchical and more market-oriented forms.

Federations

Federations arise among organizations that are noncompetitively pursuing similar goals (Provan 1983). The strategic mission of the federation is to provide a product or service by linking organizations pursuing similar goals but whose efforts have not been well coordinated. The situation faced by the organization is one of need for collective interorganizational action to achieve shared goals. Examples include international alliances for management of telecommunication services, alliances among health care providers (Provan et al. 1982), and the Japanese *keiretsu*. Communication and information technologies can be important contributors to the development of federations. Monge and Fulk (see Chapter 3) describe the example of "El Centro," a regional information clearinghouse for local, state, and federal law enforcement organizations. The purpose is to provide a mechanism for communication and information sharing among jurisdictions to achieve better interorganizational coordination of enforcement activities for illegal narcotics. El Centro offers technology-based assistance for coordinating action and sharing information. The operations center maintains real-time information on enforcement actions throughout the region so that operations being conducted by different jurisdictions do not conflict. A case management system permits officers from different jurisdictions to share a common electronic case file of shared information regarding specific suspects, operations, locations, and so on. Gateways are available for importing information from other law enforcement databases into the case management files. Cross-jurisdictional teams are created and supported by remote access devices. Electronic mail and conferencing capabilities are also available to officers across jurisdictions. This organization is described in law enforcement circles as the prototype model for coordinating global law enforcement activities in the next century.

Networks

Many scholars have argued that the new network form is less a move to a market-based form than a creation of a new form that resembles neither parent (i.e., neither market nor hierarchy). Powell (1990) describes the following key dimensions that differentiate network forms from both markets and hierarchies: (a) The basis for organizing is complementary strengths rather than the employment relationship; (b) the means of communication is relational rather than routine; (c) conflict is resolved through norms of fair exchange rather than administrative fiat; (d) flexibility is greater than that of the hierarchy but less than that of the market; (e) commitment is relatively similar; (f) the tone is focused on mutual benefits rather than on formality; (g) relationships are governed by interdependency rather than dependence; and (h) multiple hybrid forms exist for both hierarchies and networks.

Multinational corporations have traditionally been viewed as having a central core that connects directly to satellite organizations. This model is hierarchical, with communication and control centrally located. When viewed alternatively as networks, these organizations can be seen to contain both networks and hierarchies in their internal structures as well as external networks whose organizations are interconnected and that transcend national or regional boundaries. Rather than a central core with tentacles, the global network organization is a dense set of interconnected organizations that are embedded in networks that span the globe. The global nature of such enterprises poses at least three important challenges for communication: extensive geographic distances, asynchrony across time zones, and diverse national and regional cultures (see Chapter 3). Currently available electronic communication technology has much to offer for managing the first two challenges as a result of advancements in volume and speed as well as ability to provide rapid but asynchronous interaction. Newer technologies, such as language translators, multimedia networks, and conversational databases, have potential for addressing the third challenge.

Networks across firms rely on the availability of a common information infrastructure. New forms of connection among firms are developing as companies enter precompetitive alliances to jointly develop this common communication infrastructure. Information technology partnering is not simply dyadic. Firms enter complex research networks designed to create the "public good" of the infrastructure necessary for each to compete effectively and individually in product markets (Golden 1993). The types of connection

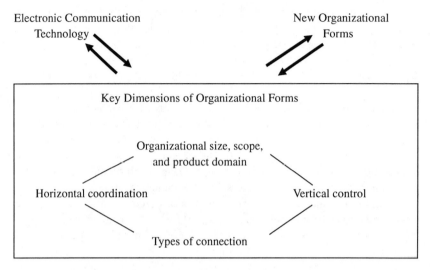

Figure 1.1. Articulation of Communication Technology and Organizational Form

are complex in such forms of "cooperative competition," in which firms may relate to each other as collaborator in some activities or markets and as competitor in others. A classic example is SEMATECH, the alliance among electronic component manufacturers designed to provide a common infrastructure and to improve the strength of the overall industry by cooperative research, development, and testing projects (Browning et al. 1995).

CONCLUSION

Articulation of the interplay between technology and organizational forms requires understanding of communication technology, organizational form, and the causal and reciprocal relationships between technology and form. These relationships are summarized in Fig. 1.1. Communication technology can affect organizational form, and new forms in turn can impact design and use of technology. This interplay takes place via four key aspects of change in organizational form: (a) organization size, scope, and product domain; (b) vertical control; (c) horizontal coordination; and (d) types of connection. By examining these relationships and studying their various components and subcomponents, researchers and managers can advance capabilities for constructively shaping organizational form and communities via design and use of communication technology.

REFERENCES

Allen, T. J. and O. Hauptman (1990), "The Substitution of Communication Technologies for Organizational Structure in Research and Development," in J. Fulk and C. Steinfield (Eds.), *Organizations and Communication Technology,* Newbury Park, CA: Sage, pp. 275-294.

Anthes, G. H. (1991), "Let Your 'Knowbots' Do the Walking," *Computerworld,* 25, 19, 17.

Applebaum, E. and R. Batt (1994), *The New American Workplace: Transforming Work and Systems in the United States,* New York: ILR.

Badaracco, J. L., Jr. (1991), *The Knowledge Link: How Firms Compete Through Strategic Alliances,* Boston: Harvard Business School Press.

Baldwin, T. F., D. S. McVoy, and C. Steinfield (1996), *Convergence: Integrating Media, Information & Communication,* Thousand Oaks, CA: Sage.

Barley, S. R. (1986), "Technology as an Occasion for Structuring: Evidence From Observation of CT Scanners and the Social Order of Radiology Departments," *Administrative Science Quarterly,* 31, 78-108.

Bartlett, C. A. and S. Ghoshal (1993), "Beyond the M-Form: Toward a Managerial Theory of the Firm," *Strategic Management Journal,* 14, 23-46.

Beniger, J. R. (1986), *The Control Revolution: Technological and Economic Origins of the Information Society,* Cambridge, MA: Harvard University Press.

_____ (1990), "Conceptualizing Information Technology as Organization, and Vice Versa," in J. Fulk and C. Steinfield (Eds.), *Organizations and Communication Technology,* Newbury Park, CA: Sage.

Benjamin, R. and R. Wigand (1995), "Electronic Markets and Virtual Value Chains on the Information Superhighway," *Sloan Management Review,* 36, 2, 62-72.

Biggart, N. W. and G. G. Hamilton (1992), "On the Limits of a Firm-Based Theory to Explain Business Networks: The Western Bias of Neoclassical Economics," in N. Nohria and R. Eccles (Eds.), *Networks and Organizations: Structure, Form and Action,* Boston: Harvard Business School Press, pp. 471-490.

Bikson, T. K. and J. D. Eveland (1990), "The Interplay of Work Group Structures and Computer Support," in J. Galegher, R. E. Kraut, and C. Egido (Eds.), *Intellectual Teamwork: Social and Technological Foundations of Cooperative Work,* Hillsdale, NJ: Lawrence Erlbaum.

_____, _____, and B. J. Gutek (1989), "Flexible Interactive Technologies for Multi-Person Tasks: Current Problems and Future Prospects," in M. H. Olson (Ed.), *Technological Support for Work Group Collaboration,* Hillsdale, NJ: Lawrence Erlbaum, pp. 89-112.

Bjorn-Anderson, N., K. Eason, and D. Robey (1986), *Managing Computer Impact: An International Study of Management and Organizations,* Norwood, NJ: Ablex.

Bostrom, R. P., R. T. Watson, and S. T. Kinney (1992), *Computer Augmented Teamwork: A Guided Tour,* New York, Van Nostrand Reinhold.

Browning, L. D., J. M. Beyer, and J. C. Shetler (1995), "Building Cooperation in a Competitive Industry: SEMATEH and the Semiconductor Industry," *Academy of Management Journal,* 38, 113-151.

Brynjolfsson, E., T. W. Malone, V. Gurbaxani, and A. Kambil (1994), "Does Information Technology Lead to Smaller Firms?" *Management Science,* 40, 12, 1628-1645.

Burris, B. H. (1993), *Technocracy at Work,* Albany: State University of New York Press.

Business Week (1994), "Ford: Alex Trotman's Bold Plan," April 3, 94-97, 100-101, 104.

Cash, J. I., Jr., F. W. McFarlan, J. L. McKenney, and L. M. Applegate (1992), *Corporate Information Systems Management,* Boston: Irwin.

Chandler, A. D. (1977), *The Visible Hand: The Managerial Revolution in American Business,* Cambridge, MA: Harvard University Press.

Child, J. and R. Loveridge (1990), *Information Technology in European Services: Towards a Microelectronic Future,* Oxford, UK: Blackwell.

Ciborra, C. U. (1996), "The Platform Organization: Recombining Strategies, Structures, and Surprises," *Organization Science,* 7, 2, 103-118.

Coase, R. H. (1937), "The Nature of the Firm," *Economica,* 4, 386-405.

Cohen, S. (1997), "On Becoming Virtual," *Training and Development Journal,* 51, 5, 30, ff.

Collis, D. J., P. W. Bane, and S. P. Bradley (1997), "Winners and Losers: Industry Structure in the Converging World of Telecommunications, Computing and Entertainment," in D. B. Yoffie (Ed.), *Competing in the Age of Digital Convergence,* Boston: Harvard Business School Press, pp. 159-200.

Crowston, K. and T. W. Malone (1988), "Intelligent Software Agents," *Byte,* 13, 13, 267-271.

Daft, R. L. and R. H. Lengel (1984), "Information Richness: A New Approach to Managerial Behavior and Organization Design," in L. L. Cummings and B. M. Staw (Eds.), *Research in Organizational Behavior,* Greenwich, CT: JAI, Vol. 6, pp. 191-233.

Danziger, J. N., W. H. Dutton, R. Kling, and K. L. Kraemer (1982), *Computers and Politics,* New York: Columbia University Press.

Davidow, W. H. and M. S. Malone (1992), *The Virtual Corporation,* New York: Harper Business.

Dennis, A. R., L. M. Jessup, J. F. Nunamaker, and D. R. Vogel (1988), "Information Technology to Support Electronic Meetings," *MIS Quarterly,* 11, 561 624.

DeSanctis, G. and R. B. Gallupe (1987), "A Foundation for the Study of Group Decision Support Systems," *Management Science,* 33, 589-609.

_____ and M. S. Poole (1994), "Capturing the Complexity in Advanced Technology Use: Adaptive Structuration Theory," *Organization Science,* 5, 121-147.

_____ and _____ (1997), "Transitions in Teamwork in New Organizational Forms," *Advances in Group Processes,* 14, 157-176.

DiMaggio, P. and W. Powell (1983), "The Iron Cage Revisited: Institutional Isomorphism and Collective Rationality in Organizational Fields," *American Sociology Review,* 48, 147-160.

Dodgson, M. (1993), "Learning, Trust, and Technological Collaboration," *Human Relations,* 46, 77-95.

Eveland, J. D. and T. E. Bikson (1987), "Evolving Electronic Communication Networks: An Empirical Assessment," *Office, Technology and People,* 3, 103-128.

Fulk, J. and L. Collins-Jarvis (1998), "Mediated Meetings in Organizations," in F. Jablin and L. Putnam (Eds.), *New Handbook of Organizational Communication,* Newbury Park, CA: Sage.

_____, A. Flanagin, M. Kalman, P. R. Monge, and T. Ryan (1996), "Connective and Communal Public Goods in Interactive Communication Systems," *Communication Theory,* 6, 60-87.

_____, J. Schmitz, and C. Steinfield (1990), "A Social Influence Model of Technology Use," in J. Fulk and C. Steinfield (Eds.), *Organizations and Communication Technology,* Newbury Park, CA: Sage, pp. 117-140.

Galbraith, J. J. (1973), *Designing Complex Organizations,* Reading, MA: Addison-Wesley.

Garson, B. (1988), *The Electronic Sweatshop: How Computers Are Transforming the Office of the Future Into the Factory of the Past,* New York: Penguin.

Gates, W. (1995), *The Road Ahead,* New York: Viking/Penguin.

George, J. F., J. F. Nunamaker, and J. S. Valacich (1992), "ODSS: Information Technology for Organizational Change," *Decision Support Systems,* 8, 307-315.

Ghoshal, S. and C. A. Bartlett (1990), "The Multinational Corporation as an Interorganizational Network," *Academy of Management Review,* 15, 603-625.

_____, H. Korine, and G. Szulanski (1994), "Interunit Communication in Multinational Corporations," *Management Science,* 40, 96-110.

Golden, J. R. (1993), "Economics and National Strategy: Convergence, Global Networks, and Cooperative Competition," *Washington Quarterly,* Summer, 91-113.

Granovetter, M. (1973), "The Strength of Weak Ties," *American Journal of Sociology,* 78, 1360-1380.

Hagedoorn, J. (1996), "Trends and Patterns in Strategic Technology Partnering Since the Early Seventies," *Review of Industrial Organization,* 11, 601-616.

_____ and R. Narula (1996), "Choosing Organizational Modes of Strategic Technology Partnering—International and Sectoral Differences," *Journal of International Business Studies,* 27, 265-284.

Halal, W. E. (1994), "From Hierarchy to Enterprise: Internal Markets Are the New Foundation of Management," *Academy of Management Executive,* 8, 4, 69-83.

Hammer, M. and J. Champy (1993), *Reengineering the Corporation: A Manifesto for Business Revolution,* New York: Harper Business.

Heckscher, C. (1994), "Defining the Post-Bureaucratic Type," in C. Heckscher and A. Donnellon (Eds.), *The Post-Bureaucratic Organization: New Perspectives on Organizational Change,* Thousand Oaks, CA: Sage, pp. 14-62.

Hedlund, G. (1986), "The Hypermodern MNC—A Heterarchy?" *Human Resource Management,* 25, 9-35.

Henderson, J. C. and N. Venkatraman (1994), "Strategic Alignment: A Model for Organizational Transformation via Information Technology," in T. J. Allen and M. S. Scott Morton (Eds.), *Information Technology and the Corporation of the 1990s,* New York: Oxford University Press, pp. 202-220.

Heydebrand, W. (1989), "New Organizational Forms," *Work and Occupations,* 16, 323-357.

Hollingshead, A. B. and J. E. McGrath (1995), "The Whole Is Less Than the Sum of Its Parts: A Critical Review of Research on Computer-Assisted Groups," in R. A. Guzzo and E. Salas (Eds.), *Team Decision and Team Performance in Organizations,* San Francisco: Jossey-Bass.

Huber, G. P. (1990), "A Theory of the Effects of Advanced Information Technologies on Organizational Design, Intelligence, and Decision Making," *Academy of Management Review,* 15, 47-71.

Huber, R. L. (1993), "How Continental Bank Outsourced Its 'Crown Jewels,' " *Harvard Business Review,* January/February, 121-129.

Jarvenpaa, S. L. and B. Ives (1994), "The Global Network Organization of the Future: Information Management Opportunities and Challenges," *Journal of MIS,* 10, 4, 25-57.

Johansen, R., D. Sibbet, S. Benson, A. Martin, R. Mittman, and P. Saffo (1991), *Leading Business Teams: How Teams Can Use Technology and Group Process Tools to Enhance Performance,* Menlo Park, CA: Addison-Wesley.

Karsten, H. (1995), "Converging Paths to Notes: In Search of Computer-Based Information Systems in a Networked Company," *Information Technology & People,* 8, 7-34.

Keen, P. G. W. (1990), "Telecommunications and Organizational Choice," in J. Fulk and C. Steinfield (Eds.), *Organizations and Communication Technology,* Newbury Park, CA: Sage, pp. 295-312.

Kling, R. and M. Zmuidzinas (1994), "Technology, Ideology and Social Transformation: The Case of Computerization and Work Organization," *International Review of Sociology,* 2/3, 28-56.

Koppel, R., E. Applebaum, and P. Albin (1988), "Implications of Workplace Information Technology: Control, Organization of Work, and the Occupational Structure," *Research in the Sociology of Work,* 4, 125-152.

Kraut, R. E., J. Galegher, and C. Egido (1990), "Patterns of Contact and Communication in Scientific Research Collaboration," in J. Galegher, R. E. Kraut, and C. Egido (Eds.),

Intellectual Teamwork: Social and Technological Foundations of Cooperative Work,
Hillsdale, NJ: Lawrence Erlbaum.

Lipnack, J. and J. Stamps (1997), *Virtual Teams: Reaching Across Space, Time and Organiza-*
tions With Technology, New York: John Wiley.

Lu, S. C.-Y. (1995), "Exploring the Total Work Environment of the Future," unpublished paper,
University of Southern California, Impact Laboratory.

Lucas, H. C., Jr. (1996), *The T-Form Organization: Using Technology to Design Organizations*
for the 21st Century, San Francisco: Jossey-Bass.

_____ and J. Baroudi (1994), "The Role of Information Technology in Organization Design,"
Journal of Management Information Systems, 10, 4, 9-23.

Lundberg, C. C. (1994), "Toward Managerial Artistry: Appreciating and Designing Organizations for the Future," *International Journal of Public Administration,* 17, 3/4, 659-674.

Malone, T. W. (1997), "Is Empowerment Just a Fad? Control, Decision Making, and IT," *Sloan*
Management Review, 38, 2, 23-36.

_____, K. R. Grant, F. A. Turbak, S. A. Brobst, and M. D. Cohen (1987), "Intelligent Informa-
tion-Sharing Systems," *Communications of the ACM,* 30, 5, 390-402.

_____ and J. F. Rockart (1991), "Computers, Networks and the Corporation," *Scientific Ameri-*
can, 265, 3, 92-99.

_____, J. Yates, and R. I. Benjamin (1987), "Electronic Markets and Electronic Hierarchies,"
Communications of the ACM, 30, 484-496.

Mantovani, G. (1994), "Is Computer-Mediated Communication Intrinsically Apt to Enhance
Democracy in Organizations?" *Human Relations,* 47, 45-62.

March, J. G. and H. A. Simon (1958), *Organizations,* New York: McGraw-Hill.

Markus, M. L. and D. Robey (1988), "Information Technology and Organizational Change:
Causal Structure in Theory and Research," *Management Science,* 34, 583-598.

Marshall, C. and D. Novick (1995), "Conversational Effectiveness and Multi-Media Communications," *Information Technology & People,* 8, 54-79.

McKelvey, B. (1982), *Organizational Systematics: Taxonomy, Evolution, Classification,* Berkeley:
University of California Press.

Metzger, R. C. and M. A. Von Glinow (1988), "Off-Site Workers: At Home and Abroad," *Cali-*
fornia Management Review, 30, 101-112.

Miles, R. and C. Snow (1995), "The New Network Firm: A Spherical Structure Built on a Human
Investment Philosophy," *Organizational Dynamics,* 23, 4, 5-18.

_____, C. C. Snow, J. A. Mathews, G. Miles, and H. J. Coleman, Jr. (1997), "Organizing in the
Knowledge Age: Anticipating the Cellular Form," *Academy of Management Executive,*
11, 4, 7-20.

Miles, R. E. and C. C. Snow (1986), "Network Organizations: New Concepts for New Forms,"
California Management Review, 28, 62-73.

Mintzberg, H. (1983), *Structure in Fives: Designing Effective Organizations,* Englewood Cliffs,
NJ: Prentice Hall.

Mitroff, I. I., R. O. Mason, and C. M. Pearson (1994), *Framebreak: The Radical Design of*
American Business, San Francisco: Jossey-Bass.

Mowshowitz, A. (1994), "Virtual Organization: A Vision of Management in the Information
Age," *Information Society,* 10, 267-288.

Nohria, N. and J. D. Berkley (1994), "The Virtual Organization: Bureaucracy, Technology, and
the Implosion of Control," in C. Heckscher and A. Donnelon (Eds.), *The Post-Bureau-*
cratic Organization: New Perspectives on Organizational Change, Thousand Oaks, CA:
Sage, pp. 108-128.

_____ and R. G. Eccles (1992), *Networks and Organizations: Structure, Form, and Action,*
Boston: Harvard Business School Press.

Norman, R. and R. Ramirez (1993), "From Value Chain to Value Constellation: Designing Interactive Strategy," *Harvard Business Review,* July/August, 65-77.

Nunamaker, J. F., A. R. Dennis, J. S. Valacich, D. R. Vogel, and J. F. George (1993), "Issues in the Design, Development, Use, and Management of Group Support Systems," in L. M. Jessup and J. S. Valacich (Eds.), *Group Support Systems: New Perspectives,* New York: Macmillan, pp. 123-145.

Orlikowski, W. (1992), "Learning From NOTES: Organizational Issues in Groupware Implementation," *Proceedings of the ACM Conference on Computer-Supported Cooperative Work,* Toronto: ACM Press, October 31-November 4, pp. 362-369.

Osborn, R. and J. Hagedoorn (1997), "The Institutionalization and Evolutionary Dynamics of Interorganizational Alliances and Networks," *Academy of Management Journal,* 40, 261-278.

Ouchi, W. (1980), "Markets, Bureaucracies, and Clans," *Administrative Science Quarterly,* 25, 129-142.

Pinder, C. C. and L. F. Moore (1979), "The Resurrection of Taxonomy to Aid the Development of Middle Range Theories of Organizational Behavior," *Administrative Science Quarterly,* 24, 99-118.

Piore, M. J. (1994), "Corporate Reform in American Manufacturing and the Challenge to Economic Theory," in T. J. Allen and M. S. Scott Morton (Eds.), *Information Technology and the Corporation of the 1990s: Research Studies,* New York: Oxford University Press, pp. 43-60.

Pool, I. de Sola (1983), *Forecasting the Telephone: A Retrospective Assessment,* Norwood, NJ: Ablex.

Poole, M. S. and G. DeSanctis (1990), "Understanding the Use of Group Decision Support Systems: The Theory of Adaptive Structuration," in J. Fulk and C. Steinfield (Eds.), *Organizations and Communication Technology,* Newbury Park, CA: Sage, pp. 173-193.

_____, M. Holmes, and G. DeSanctis (1991), "Conflict Management in a Computer-Supported Meeting Environment," *Management Science,* 37, 926-953.

Powell, W. W. (1990), "Neither Market nor Hierarchy: Network Forms of Organization," *Research in Organizational Behavior,* 12, 295-336.

Provan, K. G. (1983), "The Federation as an Interorganizational Linkage Network," *Academy of Management Review,* 8, 79-89.

_____, J. M. Beyer, and C. Kruytbosch (1982), "Environmental Linkages and Power in Resource-Dependence Relations Between Organizations," *Administrative Science Quarterly,* 25, 200-225.

Quinn, J. B. (1992), *Intelligent Enterprise,* New York: Free Press.

Reich, R. (1991), *The Work of Nations: Preparing Ourselves for 21st Century Capitalism,* New York: Knopf.

Rice, R. (1994), "Relating Electronic Mail Use and Network Structure to R&D Work Networks and Performance," *Journal of Management Information Systems,* 11, 9-29.

Ring, P. S. and A. Van de Ven (1994), "Developmental Processes of Cooperative Interorganizational Relationships," *Academy of Management Review,* 19, 90-118.

Rockart, J. F. and J. E. Short (1991), "The Networked Organization and the Management of Interdependence," in M. S. Scott Morton (Ed.), *The Corporation of the 1990s: Information Technology and Organizational Transformation,* New York: Oxford University Press.

Rogers, E. M. (1995), *Diffusion of Innovation,* 4th ed., New York: Free Press.

Sarkar, M. B., B. Butler, and C. Steinfield (1995), "Intermediaries and Cybermediaries: A Continuing Role for Mediating Players in the Electronic Marketplace," *Journal of Computer-Mediated Communication,* 1, 3. (*http://www.usc.edu/dept/annenberg/vol1/issue3*)

Short, J., E. Williams, and B. Christie (1976), *The Social Psychology of Telecommunications*, New York: John Wiley.

Sproull, L. and S. Kiesler (1991), *Connections: New Ways of Working in the Networked Organization*, Cambridge: MIT Press.

Star, S. L. and K. Ruhleder (1996), "Steps Toward an Ecology of Infrastructure: Design and Access for Large Information Spaces," *Information Systems Research*, 7, 111-134.

Thomas, R. J. (1994), *What Machines Can't Do: Politics and Technology in the Industrial Enterprise*, Berkeley: University of California Press.

Thompson, J. D. (1967), *Organizations in Action*, New York: McGraw-Hill.

Trevino, L. K., R. H. Lengel, and R. L. Daft (1987), "Media Symbolism, Media Richness, and Media Choice in Organizations," *Communication Research*, 14, 5, 553-574.

Tushman, M. and G. Nadler (1978), "Information Processing as an Integrative Concept in Organizational Design," *Academy of Management Review*, 1, 613-624.

Tyabji, H. (1996), "Managing the Virtual Company," in J. Kao (Ed.), *The New Business of Design*, New York: Allworth Press.

Vandenbosch, B. and M. J. Ginzberg (1997), "Lotus Notes and Collaboration: *Plus ça Change*," *Journal of Management Information Systems*, 13, 3, 65-81.

Venkatraman, N. and A. Zaheer (1994), "Electronic Integration and Strategic Advantage: A Quasi-Experimental Study in the Insurance Industry," in T. J. Allen and M. S. Scott Morton (Eds.), *Information Technology and the Corporation of the 1990s*, New York: Oxford University Press, pp. 184-201.

Walther, J. B. (1995), "Relational Aspects of Computer-Mediated Communication: Experimental Observations Over Time," *Organization Science*, 6, 2, 186-203.

Weber, M. (1968), in G. Roth and C. Wittich (Eds.), *Economy and Society: An Outline of Interpretive Sociology*, New York: Bedminster Press. (Original work published 1922)

Williamson, O. E. (1975), *Markets and Hierarchies: Analysis and Antitrust Implications: A Study in the Economics of Internal Organization*, New York: Free Press.

Yates, J. (1989), *Control Through Communication: The Rise of System in American Management*, Baltimore: Johns Hopkins University Press.

_____ and W. Orlikowski (1992), "Genres of Organizational Communication: An Approach to Studying Communication and Media," *Academy of Management Review*, 17, 299-326.

Zajac, E. J., B. R. Golden, and A. M. Shortell (1991), "New Organizational Forms for Enhancing Innovation: The Case of Internal Corporate Joint Ventures," *Management Science*, 37, 2, 170-184.

Zmud, R. W. (1990), "Opportunities for Strategic Information Manipulation Through New Information Technology," in J. Fulk and C. Steinfield (Eds.), *Organizations and Communication Technology*, Newbury Park, CA: Sage, pp. 95-116.

Zuboff, S. (1988), *In the Age of the Smart Machine: The Future of Work and Power*, Oxford, UK: Oxford University Press.

2

In Search of a New Organizational Model

Lessons From the Field

LYNDA M. APPLEGATE

From many quarters we hear that the hierarchical organization must wither away. In this view of the future, middle managers have the life expectancy of fruit flies. Those who survive will not be straw bosses but Dutch uncles dispensing resources and wisdom to an empowered labor force that designs its own jobs. Enabled, to use a trendy term, by information technology, and propelled by the need to gain speed and shed unnecessary work, this flat, information-based organization won't look like the pharaonic pyramid of yore but like—well, like what?

—Stewart (1992, p. 93)

Managers and academics spent the majority of the twentieth century building and perfecting the hierarchical organization. If we are to believe the press, however, they are now busily destroying it, proposing in its stead networked, process-oriented, shamrock, team-based, and fast-cycle organizational models (Bower and Hout 1988, Drucker 1988, Handy 1990, Miles and Snow 1986, Nohria and Eccles 1992, Nolan et al. 1988, Ostroff and Smith 1992, Powell 1990, Reich 1991, Rockart and Short 1991). Although the details of these visions vary, common themes have emerged. The 1990s organization, it is argued, is flat, fast, flexible, and focused on areas of core competency. Inside, empowered interfunctional teams of knowledge workers are reengineering and continuously improving core business processes. Managers— that is, the few who are left—are busy redesigning business processes. They are getting their companies to "think globally and act locally." They are forming strategic alliances and partnerships that will enable them to focus on core competencies while expanding organizational capabilities, scale, and scope. Some are attempting to create virtual corporations, managing a vast network of independent firms that must all work together to deliver products and services to customers. Although the visions are compelling, how, and indeed if, companies can achieve these lofty goals is often unaddressed.

How many firms have actually succeeded in designing a firm that resembles this vision? To answer this question from the viewpoint of managers, in 1992 and 1993 I conducted a survey of more than 500 managers from firms of all sizes located throughout the world (Applegate 1994). The survey identified characteristics of the new organization that had been called for in the business and academic press and compared them with characteristics of the traditional hierarchy. Not surprisingly, most managers stated that their firms were still organized and operated in traditional ways. Standardized procedures and the hierarchical chain of command were still in place but were becoming increasingly less relevant in defining how work was performed. Although most organizations were downsizing and delayering (on average, two layers were removed and the number of direct reports to each manager increased from five to eight), authority and accountability for decisions continued to depend on hierarchical level. Career paths continued to stress vertical movement within functions, and employee progression continued to be managed by current supervisors. Although employees found themselves working within teams and spending a significant portion of their time at meetings, except in small firms (250 million in sales), work and compensation continued to support individual performance and achievement.

Clearly, the hierarchy is not dead. When asked what their firms should look like within the next 5 years, however, many managers expressed strong support for the visions of a new organization that have captured our attention in the literature. In focus groups, many stated that their firms were in the midst of—or were embarking on—organizationwide change initiatives designed to create a more flexible and adaptive organization. The dilemma these managers faced, however, was that they knew they could not lose organizational efficiency and effectiveness in their quest for speed. Similarly, many had learned the hard way that they could not sacrifice control as they empowered employees to make decisions. The environment demanded that they manage both speed and complexity simultaneously, but years of management experience said that this was not possible.

CEO Jack Welch (1988) summarized this dilemma as he discussed the challenges that General Electric faced as it entered the 1990s:

> At the beginning of the decade, we saw two challenges ahead of us, one external
> and one internal. Externally, we faced a world economy that would be charac-
> terized by slower growth, with stronger global competitors going after a smaller
> piece of the pie. Internally, our challenge was even bigger. We had to find a way
> to combine the power, resources, and reach of a large company with the hunger,
> agility, spirit, and fire of a small one.

Percy Barnevik, CEO of Asea Brown Boveri (ABB), echoed Welch's comments: "ABB is an organization with three internal contradictions. We want
to be global and local, big and small, and radically decentralized with
centralized reporting and control. If we resolve those contradictions, we
create real organizational advantage" (as quoted in Simons and Bartlett 1992,
pp. 29-30).

Curiously, as dramatic as it seems, this organization design dilemma is
not new; early descriptions of similar "hybrid" organization models (e.g., the
matrix and adhocracy) emerged in the 1950s and 1960s (Burns and Stalker
1961, Davis and Lawrence 1977, Fouraker and Stopford 1968, Lawrence and
Lorsch 1967, Woodward 1965). In fact, the matrix was originally billed as
the "obvious organizational solution" to the need to manage rather than
minimize environmental complexity while simultaneously enabling flexibility and speed of response. Proponents of these models argued that a flexible,
adaptive, information-intensive, team-based, collaborative, and "empowered" organization was needed. Firms that adopted the hybrid designs of the
1960s and 1970s, however, soon learned that the new structures and systems
bred conflict, confusion, information overload, and costly duplication of
resources. Bartlett and Ghoshal (1991) describe why many firms adopted the
matrix only to abandon it several years later:

> Top-level . . . managers . . . are losing control of their companies. The problem is
> not that they have misjudged the demands created by an increasingly complex en-
> vironment and an accelerating rate of environmental change, nor that they have
> failed to develop strategies appropriate to the new challenges. The problem is that
> their companies are organizationally incapable of carrying out the sophisticated
> strategies they have developed. Over the past 20 years, strategic thinking has out-
> distanced organizational capabilities. (p. 30)

Given such problems, one might legitimately ask, "If the matrix failed in
the past, why are we trying this again?" Interestingly, one of the major
sources of difficulty with complex organization forms such as the matrix and
adhocracy was the dramatic increase in the need for timely information to

successfully manage them (Galbraith 1977, Greiner 1972, Tushman and Nadler 1978). Although the hierarchy managed complexity by minimizing it, these hybrid organization designs were created to deal with complexity directly. Product managers had to coordinate their plans and operations with functional managers. Senior management teams at corporate headquarters, attempting to reconcile overall organization performance and plan corporatewide strategy, faced a dizzying array of conflicting information from functional and business managers.

In the 1960s and 1970s, information moved slowly within organizations, and channels of communication were limited (McKenney 1995). The mainframe computer systems of the day were designed to support centralized information processing and hierarchical communication channels. The microcomputer revolution of the 1980s provided tools to decentralize information processing, which helped improve local decision making, but the technology to support both lateral and vertical information sharing and communication was not adequate to meet the information processing and communication demands of more complex organizational models. Only recently has information technology (IT) become capable of meeting this challenge (Nolan et al. 1988). In the mid-1990s, client-server technologies and the Internet and World Wide Web provided the tools needed to link together disparate information resources, enabling increased vertical and lateral organizational information processing capacity (Applegate et al. 1996, Bauer and Konsynski 1994). Advanced technologies to support information access, packaging, and delivery enable decision makers at all levels of the firm to interactively and intuitively analyze internal and external information (Applegate 1991, Watson et al. 1992). Also, the tools needed to support communication and collaborative work increasingly enable information to be shared any time, any place, and in any form (Bostrom et al. 1992, Johansen 1988). Full realization of the benefits from new distributed IT architectures have been hampered by the immaturity (and instability) of the technology, the cost and difficulty of dealing with the evolution of "legacy" systems, the lack of managerial information literacy, and the need to link IT implementation with organizational and business process redesign (Gartner Group 1994, Ryan 1994). Despite these difficulties, the potential of these new architectures to minimize the information processing crisis engendered by the hybrid organizations offers new hope for the success of the 1990s organization.

Seeking a deeper understanding of how managers were coping with the challenges described previously, I spent the past 8 years conducting a longitudinal field study at firms that had instituted major corporatewide change initiatives during the 1980s and 1990s. The study was designed to address the following questions.

* What organizational change initiatives were implemented by the study firms during the 1980s and 1990s?

* What role did information technology play in enabling (or inhibiting) the change initiatives?

* What was the process by which organizational and IT changes were implemented?

This chapter presents key findings regarding the nature of the organizational change initiatives and the process by which they were implemented. The role of information technology in enabling these changes is also discussed. This chapter is organized as follows: The next section discusses the research methodology. The subsequent section presents the results, and the final section presents concluding thoughts.

RESEARCH DESIGN

A longitudinal, embedded, multiple case study approach was employed to study the previously discussed questions (Yin 1984). This was consistent with the exploratory nature of the research, the inability to control interactions among the multiple constructs of interest, the focus on a contemporary situation in which events are currently unfolding, and the availability of key decision makers for interview.

As recommended by Eisenhardt (1989), case sites were selected on the basis of the research questions and conceptual framework. This permitted what Glaser and Strauss (1967) call "theoretical sampling." The key criterion for case site selection was that companies be in the process of implementing organizational change initiatives that were *organizationwide, radical* in nature, and *led by the CEO.* Consistent with Gersick (1991), radical change was defined as change in the "deep structure" of the organization that fundamentally altered (a) core beliefs and values regarding the organization and its employees and environment; (b) products, markets, technology, and competitive timing; (c) distribution of power relationships; (d) organization structure; and (e) the nature, type, and pervasiveness of management control systems. Because the purpose of this study was to explore IT-enabled organizational change, case sites were also chosen in which the implementation of a new information technology infrastructure was an integral component of the organizational change initiative. Finally, because it was necessary to have full access to the organization during the time frame of the study, firms were sought in which the CEO agreed to sponsor the research project and ensure unrestricted access to written documents and key informants.

The research was conducted in three phases. An exploratory phase was conducted as part of a prior research project on the introduction and assimilation of advanced information technology. It became clear as this early research unfolded that in many companies these technologies were being implemented as one component of an integrated enterprisewide information infrastructure that, in turn, was being developed to support organizational change initiatives similar to those being described in the literature. These early studies clarified the need for the research and provided background data that supported the development of research frameworks and data collection tools.

Using these research methods and tools, Phase 1 of the project was launched in 1989. Two of the companies that had provided the most comprehensive approach to IT-enabled organizational change in my prior research were selected as core case sites for Phase 1. Because these two companies provided a large company perspective, an additional case site was added to provide a small company perspective. The small firm was entering a period of rapid growth and was suffering through the strains of the transition from its simple structure to a more complex organization design. Phase 1 enabled clarification and refinement of the research frameworks. In addition, the research findings from Phase 1 enabled the development of more focused research propositions that formed the basis for Phase 2, which commenced in late 1992 and is still under way. During Phase 2, additional firms were added to the study to enable a broader comparison across industries and geographic locations. The findings from the case research were presented and discussed in small focus groups with more than 500 managers from companies located throughout the world. (See Appendix for a summary of the case sites and a discussion of the data collection and analysis methods.) The study discussed in this chapter focuses specifically on the three companies studied in Phase 1, but the data analysis is based on the findings from all the firms studied.

DISCUSSION OF FINDINGS

In turbulent times, an enterprise has to be managed both to withstand sudden blows and to avail itself of sudden unexpected opportunities. This means that in turbulent times the fundamentals have to be managed, and managed well.

—Drucker (1980, p. 9)

The data from the study suggest that managers have indeed embarked on a process of creating a hybrid organizational model, which I have labeled the *information age organization.* In doing so, they are not abandoning traditional organization design principles but instead are building on and redefin-

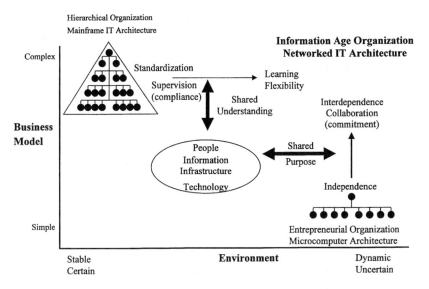

Figure 2.1. Information, Authority, and Control in the Information Age Organization

ing them as they attempt to harness the power of information age technologies in the hands of an information age workforce. As such, the characteristics of the information age organizational model represent an interesting blend of tradition and transformation.

The lessons from the managers in the study suggest that building and sustaining an information age organization requires the adoption of a comprehensive approach to organization change that redefines the nature of control (the integrated set of operating and management processes that enable a firm to define and execute strategy) and authority (the formal and informal structures, coordinating mechanisms, responsibilities, and incentives that define the distribution of power and accountability within a firm) (Figure 2.1). Information processing demands increase dramatically as organizations attempt to cope with greater complexity, uncertainty, and speed of change. Transforming a firm's information infrastructure—formed by the intersection of people and technology—is a critical component that supports and enables organizational transformation.

Achieving Speed and Efficiency in a Complex Environment: Redefining the Nature of Control

The hierarchical organizational model was founded on a fundamental principle of tight control of operating processes (Fayol 1949, Taylor 1911,

Weber 1947). Hierarchical process control begins with a detailed definition of the core operating processes of the firm—the sequence of activities through which an organization designs, produces, markets, delivers, and supports its products and services. To eliminate process complexity, tasks and the people who perform them are segregated within highly specialized units. Detailed procedures, policies, and job descriptions are developed to govern how and by whom activities are to be carried out, and supervisors within the hierarchy ensure that work is performed according to "standard operating procedures."

The hierarchy's action controls were supplemented by input controls, which ensured that (a) the right people are hired for jobs as specified, and that the skills and knowledge needed to perform jobs are developed; (b) the right raw materials are available when needed; (c) the money required to fund operations is available; and (d) managers have access to the information needed to understand the requirements of the outside environment and the effectiveness of the organization in meeting those requirements (Anthony 1988, Merchant 1989). Policies and procedures are communicated through orientation and training programs and written procedure manuals; compliance is controlled through periodic performance evaluations with supervisors. Because tight control of operating processes demands direct supervision, spans of control are limited and deep hierarchies are required (Urwick 1956).

At upper levels of the hierarchy, the ability to standardize and control actions is more difficult. Where management judgment is required, action controls are often replaced by results controls (Merchant 1989). Managers are evaluated in terms of their performance against specified targets (often financial), and no attempt is made to define the activities through which these targets are reached. The success of this traditional control model is founded on a very important principle—the existence of feedback loops that enable managers to understand the linkages among inputs, processes, and outputs. Traditional feedback loops, however, were slow to respond to changes in the environment.

Founded on the concept of simplification and routinization, the hierarchy required ruthless elimination of uncertainty and a very stable environment to operate smoothly (Morgan 1997). Operations needed to be "sealed off" from all nonroutine events and conditions, and requests for changes in standard operating procedure to respond to a change in the local operating environment were pushed up the line for analysis and revision. Frequently, the only place at which there was a complete picture of the entire operating process and its relation to end results was at the very top levels of the firm; the picture from these lofty heights was often incomplete and out-of-date. As market dynamics heated up within industry after industry, traditional controls became increasingly less effective. Figure 2.2 compares the features

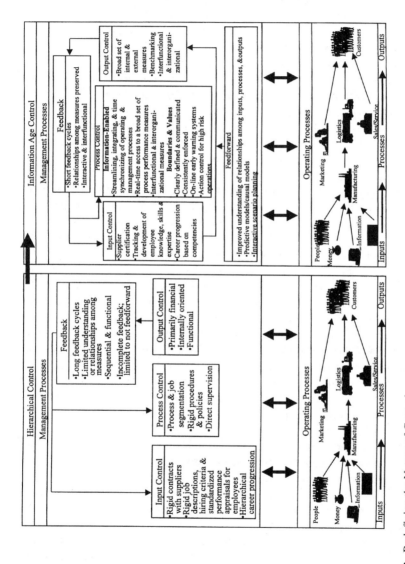

Figure 2.2. Redefining the Nature of Control

Hierarchical Control

Management Processes

Input Control
•Rigid contracts with suppliers
•Rigid job descriptions, hiring criteria & standardized performance appraisals for employees
•Hierarchical career progression

Process Control
•Process & job segmentation
•Rigid procedures & policies
•Direct supervision

Feedback
•Long feedback cycles
•Limited understanding or relationships among measures
•Sequential & functional
•Incomplete feedback; limited to not feedforward

Output Control
•Primarily financial
•Internally oriented
•Functional

Operating Processes

People
Money
Information

Inputs

Marketing
Manufacturing
Logistics
Sales/Service

Processes

Customers

Outputs

Information Age Control

Management Processes

Input Control
•Supplier certification
•Tracking & development of employee knowledge, skills & expertise
•Career progression based on competencies

Process Control
Information-Enabled
•Streamlining, integrating, & time synchronizing of operating & management processes
•Real-time access to a broad set of process performance measures
•Interfunctional & interorganizational measures
Boundaries & Values
•Clearly defined & communicated
•Consistently enforced
•On-line early warning systems
•Action control for high risk operations

Feedback
•Short feedback cycles
•Relationships among measures preserved
•Interactive & interfunctional

Output Control
•Broad set of internal & external measures
•Benchmarking
•Interfunctional & interorganizational

Feedforward
•Improved understanding of relationships among inputs, processes, &outputs
•Predictive models/causal models
•Interactive scenario planning

Operating Processes

People
Money
Information

Inputs

Marketing
Manufacturing
Logistics
Sales/Service

Processes

Customers

Outputs

of a traditional hierarchical control system with the emerging information age control model being adopted by the study firms.

Interestingly, the information age control model, like its hierarchical counterpart, is also founded on tight control of operating processes. Reminiscent of Frederick Taylor's compulsion with efficiency, both models emphasize streamlining and time synchronization of operating processes. The similarity ends here, however. Rather than segregate and structure processes, managers in the study firms sought to integrate and continuously improve them. To do this, detailed, timely information was essential—information that coordinated the flow of activities and provided decision makers at all levels in the organization with a thorough understanding of process dynamics and their relationship to both local and organizationwide performance results.

In all the study firms, significant effort was devoted to analyzing and reengineering operating processes. Company A, for example, dubbed their operating process redesign the "Pipeline Project." An interfunctional middle-management team was charged with integrating, streamlining, and time-synchronizing operations. Efficiency was sought but not at the expense of effectiveness (e.g., customer satisfaction and quality) or flexibility. Overall, cycle time was reduced and process complexity increased; for example, end-to-end product delivery cycle time for key accounts at Company A decreased from 10 to 14 days in 1988 to 1 or 2 days in 1990, whereas the number of products managed with the new integrated process rose from 100 in 1986 to more than 400 by 1990; the number of minor product changes rose from approximately 125 per year in 1986 to more than 500 per year in 1991; and the number of promotions increased from less than 10 per year to more than 500 in 1991. Even as cycle times were shrinking and complexity was increasing, however, productivity benefits improved: Operating costs (excluding head-count reductions) were reduced by more than $150 million per year, the number of customers increased from 300,000 in 1985 to 500,000 in 1992, and revenues increased from $3 billion in 1986 to approximately $6 billion in 1994.

Operating process redesign efforts at Companies B and C were approached in a similar manner. Interfunctional middle-management teams were charged with analyzing and redesigning core operating processes within divisions. The most successful division within Company C reported a 20% improvement in the speed of order fulfillment cycle time. During the same period (1989-1991), the number of defective jobs decreased from 14% to 4%, the number of credits issued to customers decreased from 4% to 0.5%, and late jobs declined from 10% to less than 1%. Head count decreased through attrition by 15%, whereas sales increased 28%. Although Company B has yet to report the results of their integrated operating process redesign efforts on a companywide basis, targeted process improvement in pricing and inventory management in the mid-1980s resulted in productivity improvements of more than $50 million per year. In one division, integrated process improvements enabled managers to decrease the time needed to purchase oil on the commodity market from days to minutes.

Within each firm, improvements in operating processes were enabled by IT that, as predicted by Zuboff (1988), "informated" as it "automated"; the information content was "stripped off" of the physical process, making the dynamics of the process visible. This allowed information-based process control to replace "procedural and action" control (Anthony 1988). Within all three firms, process performance information was available to line managers and employees to enable them to coordinate and control operations locally. Within Company A and some areas of Company B, the information was also made available to managers at all levels of the firm, expanding their understanding of business dynamics and becoming the basis for redefining management processes. Within the study firms, adoption of a more information-intensive approach to control resulted in a shift in emphasis from standardization and supervision to learning.

To achieve control through learning, the study firms created interfunctional operating teams that were "close to the action" and in direct contact with the information. These teams were charged with defining the operating strategy of the firm and managing its execution. (These shifts in structure and authority are discussed in more detail later.) The teams met weekly to debate the meaning of the information they received on operating process performance and its relationships to organizational strategies and business performance. As a result, in all three companies, the cycle time of formal management systems was reduced to match the cycle time of operations and the availability of information. For example, Company A changed its formal planning process from an annual to a triannual cycle and, as mentioned previously, all three companies instituted weekly performance reviews. One manager observed,

> We have a very fast-moving business. When we met only once a month, our thought cycle was once a month and our action cycle extended across several periods. Meeting weekly shortened both our thought and action cycle to be more in pace with changes in the business. The availability of weekly information made those meetings effective.

Across all three firms, responsibility for planning and performance review shifted from corporate headquarters to the operating teams in the field. Although corporate performance targets continued to be developed by senior management, responsibility for defining the operating strategy and the plans to meet performance targets rested with the operating teams.

As operating teams met to review timely and detailed information on the business, management systems also became more integrated and interactive. Team-based planning and performance review replaced functionally oriented systems, and team-based targets replaced functional targets. A manager at Company A described how interfunctional interaction was supported by information technology:

> One of the big improvements in the 1991 planning cycle was that, for the first time, we linked our sales plan with our manufacturing plan. In the past, sales and manufacturing forecasts would be close, but there was no requirement that manufacturing targets link to sales targets. Now that we were organized as teams, the numbers needed to match. When we first reorganized, we all used our own functional information. In a single meeting to plan targets and discuss period results, the manufacturing manager would report that production pounds were down, while the sales manager would discuss the strength of sales. Even though these discrepancies didn't have a major impact on day-to-day decisions, there was a huge disconnect that required endless discussion to understand whose numbers and analyses were correct.

As predicted by Simons (1995), these fast-cycled "interactive" process controls augmented, but did not replace, traditional financial and "diagnostic" controls. See Table 2.1 for a comparison of the methods, measures, and sources of information that were used within the study firms to support varying cycles of management control.

In areas of high risk (e.g., chemical plant operations and securities traders), traditional action controls were still required. These boundary systems defined the limits of authority, decisions, and actions granted to local decision makers. In some instances, physical controls (e.g., security-controlled plant sites, bank vaults, armed guards, and password-protected and encrypted databases) were used.

To be effective, boundaries needed to be clearly defined, consistently enforced, and able to be closely monitored. In some cases, boundary systems were implemented within IT systems that enabled employees to recognize the scope and limits of their authority while IT-enabled early warning systems also notified employees and managers (including senior executives) of decisions made elsewhere that could influence their local operations or overall organization performance.

For example, managers at Company A developed a decision support system to allow key account managers in the field to create customized promotions for local stores. Boundary systems built into the software set upper and lower bounds on the size of the price discount and number of weeks that a promotion could run. Local key account managers were notified

TABLE 2.1 Cycles of Control

Cycle	Information Source	Method	Measure
Cycle A: Slow financial controls	Accounting systems	Planning and budgeting process	Business performance (quarterly and yearly)
Cycle B: Moderate diagnostic controls	Competitor and market scanning Routine operating and variance reports	Business reviews Quality management Structured modeling	Activity-based costs Aggregate process performance statistics (e.g., quality and cycle time)
Cycle C: Fast inter-active controls	Early warning systems Real-time process monitoring systems External scanning and business intelligence systems	Early warning systems Direct observation Ad hoc queries Benchmark comparisons Business simulations	Detailed process performance data Detailed market and competitor data Daily to weekly unit performance data

by the system if they attempted to create a promotion that was outside the limits, and the system prevented them from updating the centralized promotion calendar. Decisions to offer a promotion outside approved limits required face-to-face discussion and agreement by interfunctional management teams. In addition, each time a new promotion was implemented, managers within the plants were notified to ensure that they would be able to meet increased demand; field operating teams were also notified as part of their overall performance management review systems. Managers at Company B created similar IT-enabled boundary systems to define the limits of pricing authority for local field managers.

Company C implemented an interesting IT-enabled boundary system that allowed plant workers to halt production of a product line when a serious design problem or process step (e.g., run speed of a specific machine) would adversely influence product quality or production efficiency. To restart the production line, the appropriate managers and designers were required to meet with the plant worker to discuss the problem and proposed solutions. This boundary system, suggested by a machine operator and approved by the CEO, was designed to ensure that operating employees' voice was heard as the company transitioned to an employee ownership governance model.

Although computer monitoring is an effective means of controlling areas of extremely high risk, it cannot substitute for the more participative, interactive learning model of control described previously. Consider the problems encountered by the founders of Companies J and M—both entrepreneurial start-ups that experienced problems with the transition from a simple, owner-operated firm to a more complex information age organization. In each firm, the founder had worked within the business and perfected firsthand the operating and management processes that led to success when the organization was small. As the firms grew, both founders attempted to automate their personal management approach within IT systems. In one firm—in the fast-food business—the founders developed expert systems that guided 20-year-old store managers through all aspects of running their local storefront (e.g., production and crew scheduling, hiring, and equipment maintenance and repair). These inexperienced "managers" (whose average turnover was 150% per year) were able to step in with minimal training and immediately achieve acceptable levels of performance.

The other firm—a silicon chip manufacturer—could not automate the work of its PhD-level chip designers. Within the product design process, success was based on complex innovation and not on efficiency of routine operations. To achieve tight control, the founder of this firm chose to use IT to track the weekly progress of each employee toward meeting personal goals. Employees were free to define their work and objectives but were closely monitored to ensure that those objectives were met.

In both firms, automated control systems worked well as long as the founder was able to serve as the primary source of expertise and to coordinate and control end-to-end operating processes. Both firms experienced major difficulty, however, as their firms grew and the complexity of the business began to exceed the founder's capabilities.

These examples highlight an important, overarching characteristic of information age controls: The source of organizational learning, innovation, and expertise cannot reside solely at the top of the firm. Computer-based monitoring systems can be highly effective for defining and implementing boundary systems to manage areas of high risk. The essence of information age control, however, must focus on learning and not boundaries—on the commitment that is derived from shared understanding and trust and not compliance.

To achieve control through learning, managers in the study firms found that timely, detailed information on operating processes (inputs, processes, and outputs) must be available to employees at all levels. This is consistent with previous literature on organization learning that states that systems thinking—the ability to view a situation or problem in its totality—is at the heart of learning (Garvin 1993, Senge 1990, Shrivastava 1983, Simon 1991, Walsh and Ungson 1991). As such, for an organization to learn, members of the organization must understand the causal relationships between individual components of a system and the whole.

The majority of the companies in this study were in the process of building vast "data warehouses" to store the detailed information needed to develop this deep understanding of business dynamics. They purchased easy-to-use information packaging and distribution tools that allowed managers and employees with relatively little experience to directly access the information they needed to answer a question or evaluate a specific action. They linked their dispersed operations and employees together using communication networks, and they provided a variety of communication tools to facilitate any time-any place information sharing and communication. Finally, they extended their information and communication infrastructure to include suppliers, business partners, distributors, and customers. Figure 2.3 illustrates the components of the information technology infrastructure that were being developed by the study firms.

Merely having access to data was not enough, however. The path from a hierarchical model to a learning model of control was anything but smooth. Traditionally, computers stored and processed data—not information or knowledge. The analytical frameworks and logic required to convert data to information and then to knowledge needed to be developed by people who interacted directly with the data and with experts who had different perspectives. Experience with using the information to make decisions and take actions was also necessary. Consistent with the findings of Daft and Weick (1984), managers in the study firms found that the process of developing information literacy and the ability to use this information to create new knowledge took much time; data overload was commonly experienced. Initial attempts to create IT systems to support learning produced huge amounts of raw data that needed to be analyzed and interpreted by teams of managers. The experiences of managers at Company A best illustrate the transition.

As mentioned previously, Company A began its transition by forming interfunctional operating teams that were inserted in the middle of the firm and were charged with defining and managing both operating strategy and the processes and systems required to execute it. Team members met for their initial business review meeting during the first week in their new roles. Each functional manager on the team brought a "review book" several inches thick that contained information and reports drawn from its newly implemented data warehouse. The overwhelming conclusion of managers at the meeting was that they were "drowning in data" and "starved for information." One manager complained after the initial meeting,

> Our information is one of our biggest assets and one of our biggest liabilities. There's just too much information coming at us from all sources. We don't know what we're looking for, so we look at everything. We don't know how to use the information to drive business improvement so we spend most of our time just trying to understand and make sense of the data.

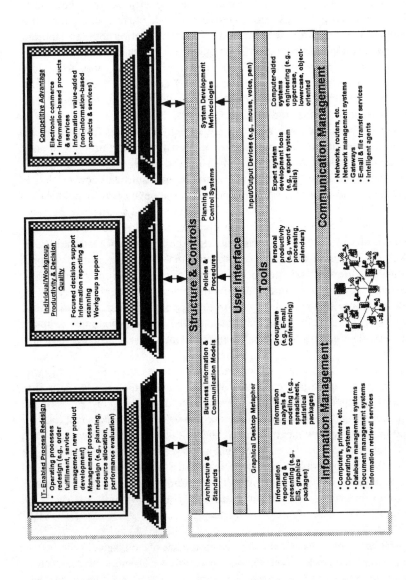

Figure 2.3. Components of the Information Technology Architecture in Study Forms

It became clear that the information system could be used to communicate data (and even predefined information) but not to communicate meaning and perspective. Initially, senior management communicated to the newly formed business teams the knowledge, management skills, and experience needed to use the information to craft business strategy and define and implement action plans. The senior executive responsible for overseeing the organization change initiative explained:

> I needed to help them learn to use information to frame business issues, but I also needed to help them learn to make business decisions, to develop market instincts. I call this making the data actionable rather than just observing it. When we first formed the business teams, the new managers' approach to solving a problem was to tell me about it and say "Boy, am I worried." I had to help them learn you can't just be worried and blame someone else. You need to work together to solve the problem so it goes away. During that first year I met formally with the teams on a monthly basis. But informally, I was on the phone or in their offices on a regular basis.

At the outset, most of the teaching was done by senior management and most of the learning by the new managers. Within the first year, however, roles began to reverse as members of the senior management team began to recognize that the new managers were teaching them a great deal about managing a more real-time, customer-focused business. One of the local business team managers recalled how they began to move from trying to get their "arms around the data" to developing management insight:

> When we first had profit-and-loss data available for our portion of the business, we were like kids with a new toy. That lasted about 1 month—the time that it took us to realize that we were looking at data dumps that gave us no analysis, explanation, or direction. What good is a P&L if you can only observe it as an outcome and do not understand its causes? Now we're attempting to build a path from early warning symptoms that we identify by monitoring our process performance and competitive information to the results that we see on our P&L. We are attempting to develop an understanding of what we call "causals" that allow us to anticipate where and when problems will occur.

As they became more knowledgeable about business dynamics, team members noticed that they were beginning to define key business drivers that helped them frame and structure recurring business decisions. In some cases, the managers captured these insights in spreadsheet computer models that later became the basis for developing more targeted decision support systems. Through this process of exploration and insight, the new management teams at Company A and at other Phase 1 and 2 firms learned to use information to manage much more complex and dynamic businesses. Through frequent face-to-face discussion of timely, detailed information, they developed insights into the nature of the business that were codified in new information reports and decision support systems. The comprehensive, integrated nature of the information infrastructure and the flexibility and ease of use provided by the tools used to package and deliver the information enabled the managers to be in direct contact with the data, which supported the hands-on "trial-and-error" approach required.

Control across organizational boundaries expanded the basic model presented previously to include important business partners (e.g., suppliers, vendors, distributors, and retailers). Supplier certification programs were used at most of the study firms to decrease the total number of suppliers and to ensure that the remainder met quality, cost, and process-performance standards. Electronic linkages were established to enable interorganizational teams to share detailed operating and performance information required to manage integrated operating processes. Also, recognizing that increased uncertainty and speed of change in the business made "ironclad" contracts difficult to achieve, partnerships that depended on shared understanding and trust were used to supplement but not replace formal contracts.

In summary, shifting to a more flexible, adaptive, and locally responsive organization did not imply giving up tight control of operating processes. In fact, the study firms found that the shift to an "empowered," fast-cycle firm demanded even tighter controls that, at the same time, enabled flexibility and fostered innovation. These firms took advantage of the power of a flexible, distributed information and communication infrastructure to design time-sensitive, information-enabled controls that emphasized shared understanding and organizational learning.

Maximizing Independence and Interdependence: Redefining Authority Systems and Structures

The formal authority structure of a firm describes managers' choices about (a) how people are grouped together to enable them to accomplish a "unit of work"; (b) the mechanisms to be used in coordinating work within and across units; and (c) the formal definition of roles, responsibilities, and power among individuals and units (Mintzberg 1983). These formal organization design criteria are complemented by an informal network of roles and relationships.

Grouping people together in formal units of work enables the firm to protect and nurture areas of core expertise (e.g., functional knowledge and

. those working on a
...reaucratic hierarchy was
...ency of a machine (Morgan
...en down into highly specialized
...increasingly smaller units until the
...as specified in detail. This functional
...nented by a clear distinction between the
...e employees: Management did the thinking,
...id line employees were expected to carry out these
...centives, job retention, and supervisory authority
...s to perform repetitive tasks as assigned, and deep
...crarchies were developed to enable direct supervision. These
...authority structures were based on the following important
(Fayol 1949, Taylor 1911, Weber 1947):

...ity of command: No individual should have more than one boss.

Scalar chain of authority: Authority should flow in a clear, unbroken line from
... role of the chief executive to the frontline worker. To achieve this, each
manager—from the first line supervisor to senior management—was granted
specific authority for specific decisions; authority was narrowly defined at the
bottom and more broadly defined at the top. In addition, each boss automatically
inherited the authority level of his or her direct reports.

* Span of control: The number of employees reporting to each manager was limited
by the need to directly supervise actions. When employee tasks were highly
structured and routine, a manager could effectively supervise a greater number
of employees; conversely, when tasks were uncertain and complex, the number
of employees that could be effectively supervised decreased. It was commonly
believed that a manager could not effectively supervise more than four to seven
employees (Urwick 1956). As a result, as the number of employees increased,
deep middle-management chains of command were forged—greatly increasing
administrative costs without contributing directly to bottom-line revenues.

During the past two decades, it has become increasingly obvious that these
costly hierarchical authority structures and incentives cannot cope with the
increasing complexity, speed, and uncertainty of today's business environment (Eccles and Nohria 1992, Heckscher and Donnellon 1994). Decisions
must be made much more quickly and must reflect a more detailed and timely
understanding of local business dynamics.

As they attempted to adopt more flexible and responsive organization
designs, the study firms did not entirely abandon hierarchical design princi-

ples (Figure 2.4). In fact, across all firms, hierarchical reporting and authority structures were maintained, but middle-management layers were removed and spans of control increased. In most of the study firms, downsizing initiatives resulted in spans of control that averaged 15 or more. Corporate headquarters and staff positions were also eliminated as authority for operating strategy and its execution shifted from headquarters to the field. For example, Company A eliminated 1,800 middle-management and corporate staff positions and transferred 60% of remaining corporate staff to the field; the number of organization layers was reduced from eight to five. At Company B, a series of downsizing initiatives reduced middle management and staff by 40% in 1986 and by 24% in 1992. Company C operated with very few middle managers, and there were only 5 people at corporate headquarters. These numbers remained stable despite rapid growth in the number of employees and the complexity of their operations. They eliminated one layer from the organization, which left only one or two layers between the CEO and the frontline workers. This finding is consistent with survey reports that indicate that approximately 50% of all U.S. firms reported workforce reductions that averaged 10% in 1994 (American Management Association 1994). Middle management and staff positions were disproportionately affected by the layoffs. This trend, which started in the 1980s, has continued unabated throughout the 1990s.

Although the functional hierarchy was maintained, a variety of team-based units assumed responsibility for managing operations, designing work, and coordinating processes. The following categories of team-based units were identified within the study firms:

- Operating teams were created at Companies A, B, and C and the majority of Phase 2 firms. At a minimum, these teams were composed of representatives from manufacturing, logistics, marketing, and sales; in many cases, human resources, finance, and management information systems representatives were also included. The teams, which were inserted at the upper-middle-management level, were granted authority for defining, executing, and managing operating strategy. As such, they assumed responsibility for decisions and actions previously performed by the senior management operating committee.

- Work teams, interfunctional teams of line employees, were granted authority for defining, executing, and managing core operating processes. These teams, which were found in Companies B and C and many other Phase 2 firms, assumed responsibility for decisions and actions previously performed at middle-management levels.

- Process management teams, responsible for the coordination, control, and continuous improvement of core operating processes, were established at Companies

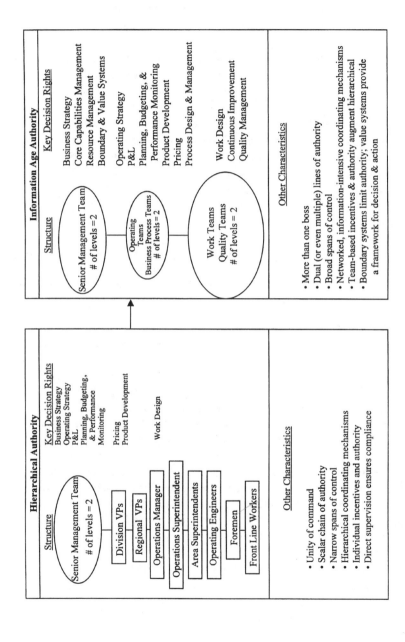

Figure 2.4. Redefining the Nature of Authority

B, D, E, and F. These formally defined, permanent teams were in addition to ad hoc quality teams that were formed and disbanded in response to local operating problems. (Most of the study firms had instituted quality teams.)

- All the study firms maintained functional units to preserve functional expertise despite the shift to team-based operating units. Company C created an interesting variant of the functional unit called functional excellence teams. Composed of representatives from its four plants, these teams were responsible for coordinating and managing functional activities across plants. These teams were formed as an incremental organizational adjustment 5 years after the original redesign. As operations became more efficient and quality and customer satisfaction increased, the company entered into a period of rapid growth in which small, local customers were increasingly being replaced by large, global ones (e.g., Motorola and Hewlett-Packard). Rather than create another layer of hierarchical management or add functional units within corporate headquarters, the CEO created teams that reported directly to the senior management committee. The responsibilities of these teams were surprisingly similar to those found in functional units. For example, the "Blue Sky Engineering" team was responsible for defining engineering standards and ensuring engineering excellence across the plants; the "Inter-plant Sales" and "World Class Customer" teams were responsible for managing existing national accounts and for securing new accounts.

As mentioned previously, within teams, decision authority was vested in the team as a collective unit rather than in one or more individual team members, and incentive and compensation systems recognized team performance. These lateral decision authority and incentive systems served as important coordinating mechanisms within and between units.

At all three case sites, power and authority tended to shift from corporate headquarters to the field and from top to bottom. Even as formal power and authority shifted away from the top, however, senior management became more involved in the business, requesting and reviewing more timely and detailed information that reflected a need to "better understand what's happening in the field." In addition, as mentioned previously, incentives and boundary systems ensured that decisions made in the field were beneficial to the organization. These vertical authority and incentive systems served as important coordinating mechanisms among top, middle, and line managers. Finally, "stretch targets," implemented at Companies A and B and the majority of Phase 2 firms, intensified effort toward achieving team and organizational goals.

The CEO of Company A's parent organization explained the rationale behind adopting stretch targets:

The quest for rapid growth keeps us [innovating]. If your business only grows 2% or 3% and you want it to grow 20%, you have to either redefine your business or get out of that business into a new one. If you don't have that mindset, you'll go along at 3% or 4% like your competitors and someone will come along and redefine the business . . . and *you'll* be left behind.

The head of planning explained how stretch targets were set:

The starting point for stretch targets is often not founded in the fundamental macroeconomic characteristics of the business. It is an art, not a science . . . [We] use benchmarking to get a gut feel for what kind of company [we need] to be. For example, we want to be in the top quartile for performance in our peer group on revenue growth, on margins, on earnings per share growth, and returns to shareholders. We set targets to achieve that performance.

As predicted by Galbraith (1977) and Jensen and Meckling (1991), on-line information reporting systems supported the shared authority and decision-making structures within the study firms. All three Phase 1 firms and many of the Phase 2 firms implemented both vertical and lateral on-line information reporting systems that were used by managers and employees at all levels to provide a shared understanding of the business and to support collaborative decision making and coordinated action. Interestingly, the most extensive systems were those developed for and used by the interfunctional operating team responsible for defining, executing, and managing operating strategy. At Companies A and B, for example, on-line information reporting systems were initially developed to support senior management. As authority for operating strategy was pushed down to middle-management operating teams, however, so too was responsibility for the information reporting systems. Over time, the systems used by the middle-management operating teams became the primary source of corporatewide information. Reflecting its small size, Company C did not initially implement information reporting systems for the senior management team. Instead, information reporting systems were implemented to support operating teams within each plant.

Team-based structures and incentives reflected and reinforced the interdependence within and across organizational units, which in turn greatly increased the need for coordination and collaboration. As mentioned earlier, traditional hierarchical reporting channels were retained, but they no longer served as the primary coordinating mechanism. Instead, they were only one in a network of vertical and lateral relationships that linked organizational and interorganizational units and the individuals within them. Examples of other coordinating mechanisms included matrix reporting structures, team-based structures and incentives, interactive management processes, and IT-enabled information reporting and networked communication systems. A manager at Company D described how information helped to foster collaboration in an environment in which stretch targets and distributed authority forced interdependence:

> We still depend on management judgment and intuition to define our operating strategies and plans, but now our judgment is supported by facts, not just intuition. There is something about a group of managers sitting down with a common set of data that elevates a discussion to the issues and away from personalities. It allows us to put aside our individual interests and differences in interpretation and focus on defining what's best for the business as a whole.

She called this approach "fact-based management."

The development of incentives, rewards, and sanctions that stress team and organizational goals was another mechanism for motivating collaboration. A manager in Company A described how incentives and rewards helped to neutralize the infighting that had been a hallmark of the company's functional hierarchy. He stated,

> I still have a functional boss, and I also have a business team boss. Neither is a dotted line for reporting. The good news is that both bosses are operating under the same profit objectives, so there have been much fewer conflicts. Before the reorganization, my incentives were based on my ability to control functional expenses. [Back then] I would have really fought many of the decisions that I now support because it would have influenced my bottom-line costs.

In addition to defining incentives and rewards that encourage collaboration, some firms also defined boundary and value systems that enforced it. The CEO of Company A noted,

> I talked with each of the functional and business team managers, individually and as a group. I explained that conflict was inevitable as they attempted to meet their individual, team, and organizational goals. I stated that I expected them to work out their difficulties by sitting down with the appropriate parties and negotiating a consensus decision. I explained that they could come to me if they could not reach agreement, but, if they did, they could expect me to favor the [new operating] teams' position. I felt it necessary to provide additional support to the operating teams (as opposed to the functions) to emphasize the shift in power [we were trying to achieve].

Discussions with the managers suggested that the message was clearly communicated and consistently enforced.

The president of Company B preceded face-to-face discussion with newly formed teams with a written memo that described the shared values that he believed would hold their "empowered" organization together. One of these values was collaboration. A recently appointed business team manager recalled his impression of the message that the president was trying to send and the approach he used to send it:

> When [the president] announced the restructuring, he distributed a document in which he described his intent and what would be required of us as general managers in a very concise, uncomplicated way. We knew what would be tolerated and what wouldn't. For example, he stated that, even though we would be working as independent business units, the business was interdependent by nature and demanded cooperation. He made it very clear that he would not tolerate people spending time bickering over prices at the expense of the business. We all knew that, in this organization, you would be considered to be a very poor manager if you took an action that benefited you personally but was not beneficial for the company as a whole. It's obvious to me that to make this kind of structure work you need a strong, knowledgeable, involved senior manager to set the tone. Now it's my job to cascade the values and beliefs he has communicated throughout my organization. To begin the process I took his lead and developed my own document of understanding in which I set down my own policy statement and laid out my values and beliefs about the organization. . . . Many managers believe that verbal explanations of where a company is going and how you need to get there are all that is needed. But verbal explanations don't provide enough guidance to help someone carry that vision forward. Writing it down and then talking about it is a very important tool.

Initially, changes in structure, authority, and incentives destabilized the organization. Confrontation and conflict increased as familiar mechanisms for solving problems, making decisions, and taking action were disrupted. As mentioned earlier, management teams responded by redefining operating and management processes, and frontline work teams redesigned work. As teams and individuals continued to struggle, incremental structural adjustments were also made within many of the study firms. For example, responding to intense pressure to improve margins, the heads of Company B's chemicals and plastics business units, which operated in many of the same global markets, decided to reorganize to share resources. The result was a global matrix organization that spanned the two organizations. The head of the chemicals business explained:

We had been working together informally for years to coordinate our operations since there was strong overlap in our businesses. But as the pressure increased, we decided to formalize our partnership and we split administrative responsibility for worldwide operations. . . . I assumed control of Europe and Africa, and [the head of plastics] assumed control of Asia. We appointed two managers who would share responsibility for global operations: a regional manager and a worldwide business manager. Product line managers reported to both. This has worked extremely well for us but requires intensive communication and information sharing to coordinate. All of our managers communicate regularly, primarily through electronic mail, and we all use a common, on-line business information system that provides daily information needed to manage the business.

A refinery manager at Company B took a different approach:

We were under intense pressure to meet a very ambitious set of performance targets in 1993. We knew that simply downsizing the organization was not the answer. Downsizing is like holding your breath. It doesn't accomplish anything. Instead, we knew we would have to radically change how we did business.

An interfunctional redesign team, composed of middle and line management, was created. On the basis of their recommendations, the refinery was reorganized from a functional hierarchy to four interfunctional area teams. The refinery manager explained:

Each of the area teams was responsible for and contained all the expertise needed to carry out and manage operations start to finish. Levels of management were removed, which greatly decreased the time needed to make a decision and carry it out.

The refinery reorganization reduced head count from 1,569 to 1,345 (mostly middle-management positions were eliminated) and removed two additional layers.

In summary, the managers in the study found that decisions concerning where to locate and how to allocate authority could no longer be viewed through a functional, hierarchical lens. Traditional hierarchical authority systems either centralize decision making at the top of the firm, which slows down response time and limits the ability to respond to local markets, or segregate it within distinct units, which fragments processes, limits understanding of the business, and prevents the company from responding quickly when actions require more than one unit's cooperation. Information age authority systems bring together in teams the expertise and knowledge required to make decisions and manage strategy and processes. Complex, shared authority and incentive systems are designed to ensure both personal and team accountability while simultaneously focusing attention on, and commitment to, organizational priorities. Boundary and value systems that prescribe the limits of authority and the organization's values and ethical principles on which decisions should be based become much more critical in an "empowered" organization in which important corporate decisions are being made far from headquarters and at a much faster pace. Finally, the ability to access a common source of shared information and to debate and discuss the meaning of this information was critical to success.

SUMMARY AND IMPLICATIONS FOR
RESEARCH AND PRACTICE

The organization design challenge has traditionally been thought of as a trade-off between centralization (control) and decentralization (autonomy). Recently, it has been noted that in environments that require organizations to simultaneously manage speed of change and complexity, collaboration becomes a third critical organization design criterion (Astley and Brahm 1989, Floyd and Wooldridge 1992, Keidel 1990, Lawrence and Lorsch 1967/1986). The difficulty of simultaneously balancing all three of these design criteria, however, has rendered previous hybrid designs, such as the matrix and adhocracy, unstable, costly, and conflict-ridden. This study sheds new light on the organization design challenge and suggests the critical role of a flexible, networked information infrastructure for both increasing information processing capacity (Galbraith 1977) and for vertically and laterally aligning the interests and actions of organizational members (Gurbaxani and Whang 1991, Jensen and Meckling 1991).

Through the design of (a) team-based structures, (b) shared authority and incentive systems, (c) networked coordinating mechanisms, and (d) interactive, real-time, information-enabled operating and management processes, the study firms were able to develop a shared understanding of the business and shared purpose that mediated the development of collaboration and became the foundation for defining a new approach to maximizing both autonomy and control (see Figure 2.1). The ability to design a firm that optimizes the flexibility and innovation of an entrepreneurial firm while simultaneously achieving the scale, scope, and efficiency of a traditional hierarchy requires a fundamental shift in the nature of control and authority from standardization and supervision, based on compliance, to a learning model that preserves flexibility and fosters commitment and collaboration (Walton 1988). There is evidence that the study firms were transitioning authority and control systems to foster both learning and collaboration.

As predicted by Zuboff (1988, 1991), the organizational changes were enabled by the automating and "informating" power of IT, captured, stored, and delivered through a distributed but integrated corporatewide information infrastructure. Although it has long been recognized that organizational information processing demands increase with increased environmental and organizational complexity, uncertainty, and speed of change (Galbraith 1977, Tushman and Nadler 1978), only recently has IT progressed to the point where firms can achieve the levels of connectivity, integration, and processing capacity required to support more complex organizational designs. As a result, many organizations remain chained to traditional hierarchical designs and rigid, inefficient processes by rigid, out-of-date information technology. Despite the cost and complexity of "fixing the IT problem," the study firms were all in the process of transitioning toward distributed, client-server architectures. This is consistent with recent surveys (CSC Consulting Group 1994, Gartner Group 1994). McKenney's (1995) study of the emergence of dominant IT architectures from the 1960s to the present found that new IT infrastructures emerged when organizations confronted information processing crises that demanded radically new technological solutions. This study suggests that the emergence of the networked, distributed IT architectures of the 1990s is required to solve the information processing crisis inherent in the transition to more flexible and complex organizational designs. The study provides a view of the coevolution of the organizational and information infrastructure as firms attempt to resolve this crisis.

The research also provides interesting perspectives on the process of change within the study firms. All organizations adapt and adjust on a regular basis (Beer et al. 1990, Hoffman 1989, Kanter et al. 1992, Kelly and Amburgey 1991, Mohman 1989, Nadler and Tushman 1989). Much of this change is incremental, affecting only a single process or function, a subprocess, or the work of a specific individual or work group. Some is radical, however, involving the entire organization in a complex, interdependent set of transitions, many of which may be incomplete and occur over long periods of time. Often, the end state is difficult to predict or understand, requiring that managers begin implementing change before they fully comprehend desired results.

For all the study firms, the transition to an information age organization required radical and comprehensive change. (See Table A1 for a summary of the change sequences within the Phase 1 study firms.) This is not surprising given that, as a precondition for selection, firms were required to have implemented radical change within the previous 10 years. In fact, the specific selection criteria limit generalizability of the study findings; they also provide the foundation for defining future research. Despite these study limitations, it is interesting to note that many of the firms had attempted

incremental adjustments to existing operations, structure, management processes, or authority prior to the decision to implement radical change.
Although these incremental changes often enabled local improvements, they
did not promote the fundamental changes in strategy and the basic operating
model that managers within the study firms believed were necessary to
survive and prosper in the 1990s and beyond. The incremental adjustments,
however, did serve an important role in clarifying the need and vision for
change and in building the required infrastructure for change, including
organization, information, skills, and expertise. A manager at Company B
explained:

> As I look back over the past 3 years, I see three stages of learning that have char-
> acterized our [change] efforts. Phase I, *total quality management,* began in 1988.
> We followed a pretty standard approach to total quality management and devel-
> oped organizational competencies in the areas of strategic quality planning, qual-
> ity management, and team building. We developed a mechanism for identifying
> specific problems and for pulling together an interfunctional group of operating
> people, called *quality action teams,* to recommend improvements. From these
> early efforts, we learned that quality initiatives can lead to major sources of
> improvement at the local level. But we also came to realize that we were viewing
> process innovation too narrowly. This led us to enter Phase 2, *business process
> engineering.* By 1990, we had implemented successful reengineering of our core
> business processes. In late 1992, we began a third phase of activities, which I call
> *business transformation.* This extends our focus even further. We are building on
> the lessons that we learned, the skills that we acquired, and the foundation that
> we built in earlier phases as we throw out all of our old assumptions and chal-
> lenge ourselves to view our business—the way we work, the way we are orga-
> nized, the way we manage, the way we motivate, the way we think—with a clean
> slate. Anyone approaching the task of transforming a company needs to realize
> that change of this magnitude takes time. It's a learning process that can't be ac-
> complished quickly. We wouldn't have had the skills, knowledge, or confidence
> to undertake our most recent radical changes without our earlier efforts.

The previous sentiments were echoed by managers within many of the
other study firms; radical change did not occur as a single "big bang."
Instead, it unfolded as a series of revolutions and evolutions. When not in
crisis, the study firms often began the change process with a series of
incremental changes designed to establish direction and build infrastructure.
In contrast, transformational change often began with a period of revolution
(radical change) during which changes in structure, authority, and incentives
shook up entrenched ways of doing business and "unfroze" the organization
in preparation for the evolutionary changes necessary to institutionalize

change. The radical changes tended to destabilize the organization and increase confrontation and information overload. As teams and individuals struggled to adapt, an evolutionary change process was initiated through which operating and management processes, work, roles, and values were redefined.

Jack Welch's (1995) description of the change initiatives at General Electric during his tenure as CEO (1982-present) is consistent with the revolutionary and evolutionary model of change described previously. He categorized the change activities within three overlapping (and interactive) phases: (a) "change the hardware"—top-down radical change in structure and authority designed to redefine the large company body; (b) "change the software"—incremental change in operating and management processes and work that shifted responsibility for the change agenda to middle and frontline managers and employees; and (c) "change the culture"—incremental change designed to change values and behavior.

CONCLUDING THOUGHTS

Our dream, and our plan, well over a decade ago, was simple. We set out to shape a global enterprise that preserved the classic big company advantages while eliminating the big company drawbacks. What we wanted to build was a hybrid enterprise with the . . . body of a big company and . . . the soul of a small company.

—Welch (1995)

Many companies have spent significant effort during the 1980s reorganizing to meet challenges similar to those faced by the managers in this chapter. As the 1980s drew to a close, however, many were forced to face the grim reality that the 1990s would demand even more radical change. For most, it became clear that despite their efforts to restructure, they were still being asked to respond even more quickly, to deliver even higher quality products and services, and to cut costs even more dramatically. They had cut layers of management and increased spans of control to the point where many worried that control had been lost. They had pushed the hierarchy to the limit, violating many of the major tenets on which it was based.

Thomas Kuhn's (1970) analysis of scientific revolutions suggests that crisis is a necessary precondition to the emergence of a new theory. When presented with crisis, however, most people do not immediately reject the existing paradigm. Instead, they attempt to relate new evidence to their existing theories. They attempt incremental adjustments to theory that, over time, begin to blur its basic tenets. Practitioners are often the first to lose sight of the details of the old paradigm as the familiar rules for solving problems are called into question. At some point, total reconstruction from new fundamental principles is required. During the transition, however, there is frequently an overlap between the problems that can be solved by the old and new paradigms. No matter which paradigm is used, however, there is a decisive difference in the modes of solution.

This appears to be the point at which the companies described in this study find themselves. A crisis, largely driven by a fundamental mismatch between environmental demands and organizational capabilities, has called into question many of the fundamental assumptions of traditional organizational models. Scientific thinking in this area is currently in a state of transition that, as Kuhn (1970) emphasized, is being led by practice. As a result, the nature of the empirical evidence rests in the common patterns of solution that organizations have adopted as they attempt to cope with the problems they face. This chapter provides visions that can help us advance our understanding of the organizational and IT infrastructure required to successfully organize and manage in the information age.

APPENDIX
Data Collection and Analysis

Drawing on prior organization and IT design theory and the research findings from my earlier field study, a conceptual framework and an associated data collection protocol were defined at the outset of Phase 1. The framework and protocol specified that the IT and organizational change initiatives at each firm be analyzed along two dimensions—content and process. (See Table A1 for a summary of the research sites for the study.) The research framework and data collection tools are available from the author.

The content framework, which was based on previous research on organizational and IT design, enabled a detailed exploration of the interplay among the environmental context, organization design, and information infrastructure (Galbraith 1977, Kast and Rosenzweig 1973, Mintzberg 1983, Weick 1977, 1979). The impact on organization effectiveness was also examined. The content framework, however, was unable to capture the sequence of evolutionary and revolutionary changes through which the organizations progressed during the period of the study. A detailed, longitudinal analysis of the change sequences was required to enable a comprehensive understanding of the change process. As a result, a second research framework was added that was used to capture the process of change. The process model traced the relationships among stimuli (Miller 1982, Nadler and Tushman 1989), decision and action sequences (Giddens 1979, Von Hippel 1989), and change mechanisms and outcomes (Argyris 1990, Hoffman 1989, Kanter et al. 1992, Mohman 1989, Petti-

TABLE A.1 Research Sites

Phase No.	Industry	Size (Revenues in $)	Age (Year Founded)	Location	Time Frame Covered by the Study	Stimulus for Change	Change Process
Phase 1 (1989-1993)							
Company A	Consumer products manufacturing	5 Billion	1961	United States	1978-1993	1978-1986: Anticipatory New entrants, increased competition 1987-1988: Leader-initiated Internal organizational dysfunction 1989-1993: Hypercompetition	1978-1984: Incremental change Defining vision and building infrastructure 1985-1986: Radical Failed attempts to change structure, authority, and incentives 1987-1989: Incremental Clarify vision and build infrastructure 1990-1991: Radical/incremental Structural, authority, and incentive change Organizationwide operating and management process change 1992-1994: Incremental Work redesign Culture change
Company B	Petroleum products and chemicals	5 Billion	1917	United States	1984-1993	1984-1985: Crisis Unsuccessful takeover attempts 1986-1990: None Industry and company profitable	1984-1985: Radical Structural, authority, and incentive change 1986-1989: Incremental Returned to pre-takeover structure

						Trigger events	Change actions
						1991-1993: Leader-initiated Severe industry overcapacity	Initiated quality program *1989-1991*: Incremental Business process reengineering *1991-1992*: Radical Structural, authority, and incentive changes Organizationwide operating and management process changes *1992-1994*: Incremental Operating and management process changes within SBU Work redesign Readjust structure and incentives at SBU level
Company C	Manufacturing	19 Million	1947	United States	1985-1993	*1985-1988*: Leader-initiated Increased competition (offshore) *1989-1990*: Leader-initiated Internal organizational dysfunction *1990-1993*: Anticipatory Customer pressure (price, performance, and quality)	*1985-1988*: Radical Structural, authority, and incentive changes *1989-1990*: Incremental Operating and management process changes within divisions Work redesign Culture change *1991-1994*: Incremental Organizationwide structural adjustments to add coordinating mechanisms and expand functional expertise Early process reengineering across divisions

(continued)

TABLE A.1 *Continued*

Phase No.	Industry	Size (Revenues in $)	Age (Year Founded)	Location	Time Frame Covered by the Study	Stimulus for Change
Phase 2 (1992 to present)[a]						
Company D	Computer and electronics manufacturing	18 Billion	1959	United States	1975-1994	Hypercompetition
Company E	Diversified	70 Billion	1892	United States	1982-1996	Leader-initiated strategic repositioning
Company F	Computer and electronics manufacturing	3.2 Billion	1917	United States	1980-1996	Hypercompetition Technological changes
Company G	Consumer products manufacturing	1.6 Billion	1828	Canada	1985-1993	Relaxation of free-trade barriers Increased competition from local competitors and United States
Company H	Agricultural	N/A	1600s	South America	1973-1993	Leader-initiated Desire to expand to global markets
Company I	Transportation	4.6 Billion	1893	United States	1980-1994	Substitute products Technological changes Industry overcapacity
Company J	Retail—snack foods	1.1 Billion	1977	United States	1977-1993	Rapid growth Transition from small entrepreneurial to large multinational
Company K	Financial services	57 Million	1987	Australia	1987-1994	Leader-initiated strategic repositioning
Company L	Government	47.9 Billion (GDP)	1968	Asia	1970-1994	Leader-initiated strategic repositioning
Company M	Semiconductor manufacturing	250 Million	1983	United States	1983-1993	Rapid growth Industry overcapacity Overseas competition

NOTE: In-depth case studies for each of the Phase 1 firms and many of the Phase 2 firms are available (Applegate 1996).
a. Data from these firms were used to validate the findings obtained from the three firms studied in-depth during Phase 1.

grew 1987) to enable detailed mapping of the process through which the organization at time t_1 was converted to the organization at time $t_2 \ldots t_n$. Recognizing that the complexity of the interactions among all elements of the content framework precluded any definite statements regarding causality (Holland 1986), the process model enabled clustering of events into episodes and episodes into sequences (Giddens 1979). It is consistent with Gersick's (1991) punctuated equilibrium theory, which states that periods of revolutionary change are triggered by a key event and interrupt periods of relative stability, and Greiner's (1972) revolutionary and evolutionary change perspective, which states that all organizations pass through cycles of incremental (evolutionary) and radical (revolutionary) change as a normal part of organizational growth and development.

Following the recommendations of Yin (1984) and Van Maanen (1983), data collection and analysis strategies were designed to ensure validity and reliability. A data collection protocol defined at the outset of the study was refined as insights emerged. Because of the longitudinal, on-site nature of the research, refinements could be incorporated across all case sites to ensure comparability of data. When possible, interviews were tape-recorded and transcribed for later content analysis, and most interviews were conducted by more than one interviewer. In many cases, at least one other analyst reviewed the transcripts to provide an additional measure of reliability. Triangulation of data sources, including key informant interviews, company and industry archival analysis, and direct observation, was rigorously pursued. Written case studies were developed and shared with key informants to verify accuracy of facts and interpretations. Divergent interpretations were discussed until insights emerged that explained the phenomenon as fully as possible.

REFERENCES

American Management Association (1994), *Survey on Downsizing and Assistance to Displaced Workers,* New York: Author.

Anthony, R. N. (1988), *The Management Control Function,* Boston: Harvard Business School Press.

Applegate, L. M. (1991), "Executive Information Systems," in G. Davis (Ed.), *Macmillan Encyclopedia of Computing,* New York: Macmillan.

_____ (1994), *Business Transformation Self-Assessment: Summary of Findings (1992-1993),* Boston: Harvard Business School Press.

_____ (1996), *Managing in an Information Age: A Custom Published Case Book,* Boston: Harvard Business School Press.

_____, F. W. McFarlan, and J. L. McKenney (1996), *Corporate Information Systems: Text and Cases,* Homewood, IL: Irwin.

Argyris, C. (1990), *Overcoming Organizational Defenses,* Boston: Allyn & Bacon.

Astley, W. and R. Brahm (1989), "Organizational Designs for Post-Industrial Strategies," in C. Snow (Ed.), *Strategy, Organization Design, and Human Resource Management,* Greenwich, CT: JAI.

Bartlett, C. and S. Ghoshal (1991), *Managing Across Borders: The Transnational Solution,* Boston: Harvard Business School Press.

Bauer, M. and B. Konsynski (1994), "A Distributed System Architecture for a Distributed Application Environment," *IBM Systems Journal,* 33, 3, 399-425.

Beer, M., R. Eisenstat, and B. Spector (1990), *The Critical Path to Corporate Renewal,* Boston: Harvard Business School Press.

Bostrom, R., R. Watson, and S. Kinney (1992), *Computer Augmented Teamwork,* New York: Van Nostrand Reinhold.

Bower, J. and T. Hout (1988), "Fast-Cycle Capability for Competitive Power," *Harvard Business Review,* November/December, 73.

Burns, T. and G. M. Stalker (1961), *The Management of Innovation,* London: Tavistock.

CSC Consulting Group (1994), "Critical Issues of Information Management," in *Seventh Annual Survey of I/S Management Issues,* Cambridge, MA: Author.

Daft, R. and K. Weick (1984), "Toward a Model of Organizations as Interpretive Systems," *Academy of Management Review,* 9, 284-296.

Davis, S. and P. Lawrence (1977), *Matrix,* Reading, MA: Addison-Wesley.

Drucker, P. (1980), *Managing in Turbulent Times,* New York: Harper & Row.

_____ (1988), "The Coming of the New Organization," *Harvard Business Review,* January/February, 45-53.

Eccles, R. and N. Nohria (1992), *Beyond the Hype,* Boston: Harvard Business School Press.

Eisenhardt, K. M. (1989), "Building Theories From Case Study Research," *Academy of Management Review,* 4, 532-550.

Fayol, H. (1949), *General and Industrial Management,* London: Pitman.

Floyd, S. and T. Wooldridge (1992), "Managing Strategic Consensus: The Foundation of Effective Implementation," *Academy of Management Executive,* 6, 27-39.

Fouraker, L. and J. Stopford (1968), "Organizational Structure and Multinational Strategy," *Administrative Science Quarterly,* 13, 47-64.

Galbraith, J. (1977), *Organization Design,* Reading, MA: Addison-Wesley.

Gartner Group (1994), "A Guide for Estimating Client-Server Costs," in *Gartner Group Strategic Analysis Report,* Stamford, CT: Author.

Garvin, D. (1993), "Building a Learning Organization," *Harvard Business Review,* July/August, 83.

Gersick, C. (1991), "Revolutionary Change Theories: A Multilevel Exploration of the Punctuated Equilibrium Paradigm," *Academy of Management Review,* 16, 10-36.

Giddens, A. (1979), *Central Problems in Social Theory: Action, Structure, and Contradiction in Social Analysis,* Berkeley: University of California Press.

Glaser, B. and A. Strauss (1967), *The Discovery of Grounded Theory: Strategies of Qualitative Research,* London: Wiedenfield & Nicholson.

Greiner, L. (1972), "Evolution and Revolution as Organizations Grow," *Harvard Business Review,* 50, 4, 37-46.

Gurbaxani, V. and S. Whang (1991), "The Impact of Information Systems on Organizations and Markets," *Communications of the ACM,* 34, 59-73.

Handy, C. (1990), *The Age of Unreason,* Boston: Harvard Business School Press.

Heckscher, C. and A. Donnellon (Eds.) (1994), *The Post-Bureaucratic Organization: New Perspectives on Organizational Change,* Thousand Oaks, CA: Sage.

Hoffman, R. (1989), "Strategies for Corporate Turnarounds: What Do We Know About Them?" *Journal of General Management,* 14, 3, 46-66.

Holland, P. (1986), "Statistics and Causal Inference," *Journal of the American Statistics Association,* 81, 396, 945-960.

Jensen, M. and W. Meckling (1991), "Specific and General Knowledge, and Organizational Structure," in L. Werin and H. Wijkander (Eds.), *Main Currents in Contract Economics,* Oxford, UK: Blackwell.

Johansen, R. (1988), *Groupware,* New York: Free Press.

Kanter, R., B. Stein, and T. Jick (1992), *The Challenge of Organizational Change,* New York: Free Press.

Kast, F. and J. Rosenzweig (1973), *Contingency Views of Organizations and Management,* Chicago: Science Research Associates.

Keidel, R. (1990), "The Triangular Approach to Organization Design," *Academy of Management Executive,* 4, 4, 21-37.

Kelly, D. and T. Amburgey (1991), "Organizational Inertia and Momentum: A Dynamic Model of Strategic Change," *Academy of Management Journal,* 34, 3, 591-612.

Kuhn, T. (1970), *The Structure of Scientific Revolution,* Chicago: University of Chicago Press.

Lawrence, P. and J. Lorsch (1986), *Organization and Environment,* Boston: Harvard Business School Press. (Original work published 1967)

McKenney, J. (1995), *Waves of Change: Business Evolution Through Information Technology,* Boston: Harvard Business School Press.

Merchant, K. (1989), *Rewarding Results,* Boston: Harvard Business School Press.

Miles, R. and C. Snow (1986), "Organizations: New Concepts for New Forms," *California Management Review,* 28, 3, 62-73.

Miller, D. (1982), "Evolution and Revolution: A Quantum View of Structural Change in Organizations," *Journal of Management Studies,* 19, 2, 131-151.

Mintzberg, H. (1983), *Structure in Fives,* Englewood Cliffs, NJ: Prentice Hall.

Mohman, A. (1989), *Large Scale Organization Change,* San Francisco: Jossey Bass.

Morgan, G. (1997), *Images of Organization,* 2nd ed., Thousand Oaks, CA: Sage.

Nadler, D. and M. Tushman (1989), "Organizational Frame Bending: Principles for Managing Reorientation," *Academy of Management Executive,* 3, 3, 194-204.

Nohria, N. and R. Eccles (Eds.) (1992), *Networks and Organizations: Structure, Form, and Action,* Boston: Harvard Business School Press.

Nolan, R., A. Pollock, and J. Ware (1988), "Creating the 21st Century Organization," *Stage by Stage,* 8, 4, 1-11.

Ostroff, F. and D. Smith (1992), "The Horizontal Organization," *McKinsey Quarterly,* 1, 148-168.

Pettigrew, A. (1987), *The Management of Strategic Change,* Oxford, UK: Basil Blackwell.

Powell, W. (1990), "Neither Market nor Hierarchy: Network Forms of Organization," *Research on Organizational Behavior,* 12, 295-336.

Reich, R. (1991), *The Work of Nations,* New York: Vintage.

Rockart, J. and J. Short (1991), "The Networked Organization and the Management of Interdependence," in M. S. Scott Morton (Ed.), *The Corporation of the 1990s: Information Technology and Organizational Transformation,* New York: Oxford University Press.

Ryan, H. (1994), *Preparing to Implement Client/Server Solutions,* Chicago: Auerbach.

Senge, P. (1990), *The Fifth Discipline,* New York: Doubleday.

Shrivastava, P. (1993), "A Typology of Organizational Learning Systems," *Journal of Management Studies,* 20, 7-28.

Simon, H. (1991), "Bounded Rationality," *Organization Science,* 2, 133.

Simons, R. (1995), *Levers of Control: How Managers Use Innovative Control Systems to Drive Strategic Renewal,* Boston: Harvard Business School Press.

_____ and C. Bartlett (1992), *Asea Brown Boveri,* Boston: Harvard Business School Press.

Stewart, T. (1992), "The Search for the Organization of Tomorrow," *Fortune,* May 18.

Taylor, F. (1911), *The Principles of Scientific Management,* New York: Harper & Row.

Tushman, M. and D. Nadler (1978), "Information Processing as an Integrating Concept in Organizational Design," *Academy of Management Review,* 3, 613-624.

Urwick, L. F. (1956), "The Manager's Span of Control," *Harvard Business Review,* May/June, 39-47.

Van Maanen, J. (1983), *Qualitative Methodology,* Beverly Hills, CA: Sage.

Von Hippel, E. (1989), "Task Partitioning: An Innovation Process Variable," Working Paper No. 2030-88, Cambridge: MIT.

Walsh, J. and G. Ungston (1991), "Organizational Memory," *Organization Science,* 16, 5, 7-91.

Walton, R. (1988), *Up and Running,* Boston: Harvard Business School Press.

Watson, H., R. Rainer, and G. Houdeshel (1992), *Executive Information Systems: Emergence, Development, and Impact,* New York: John Wiley.

Weber, M. (1947), *The Theory of Social and Economic Organization,* New York: Free Press.

Weick, K. (1977), "Enactment Processes in Organizations," in B. Staw and G. Salancik (Eds.), *New Directions in Organizational Behavior,* Chicago: St. Clair.

_____ (1979), "Cognitive Processes in Organizations," *Research in Organizational Behavior,* 1, 41-47.

Welch, J. (1988), "Managing in the 90s," *General Electric Report to Shareholders,* New York: General Electric.

_____ (1995), "Letter From the CEO," *General Electric Annual Report,* New York: General Electric.

Woodward, J. (1965), *Industrial Organization, Theory and Practice,* London: Oxford University Press.

Yin, R. (1984), *Case Study Research: Design and Methods,* Beverly Hills, CA: Sage.

Zuboff, S. (1988), *In the Age of the Smart Machine,* New York: Basic Books.

_____ (1991), "Informate the Enterprise: An Agenda for the 21st Century," *National Forum,* Summer, 3-7.

3

Communication Technology for Global Network Organizations

PETER MONGE

JANET FULK

Global network organizations are an increasingly prevalent organizational form whose diffusion promises to dramatically impact the way business is conducted within and between organizations. Economists posit that globally networked organizations will alter economic and political relationships across nation-states (Golden 1993). Networked organizations are not new to the organizational scene, but their increasing complexity, vastly expanded global scope, and rapid institutionalization as a structural form have brought new forms of organizing to a larger segment of world commerce. This phenomenon and its potential far-reaching impacts on world markets suggests an important need to understand this newly embraced form.

Global network organizations can be conceptualized as having four major components.[1] First, their internal structures are composed of flexible internal communication networks that typically are emergent rather than imposed. These networks emerge from relationships among individuals rather than from formal attributes of organizational position. Thus, communication relationships are not bounded by vertical or horizontal structures. Relationships are also flexible in that the existence of relationships and the volume of communication across them waxes and wanes according to organizational needs.

Second, internal networks are connected to dynamic networks of external organizations through a parallel set of flexible linkages. External ties transcend national boundaries, extending their reach to encompass organizations in various countries throughout the world. External ties are flexible and may develop and disappear in accordance with the duration of joint projects.

Third, both internal and external network linkages are governed by partnerships based on mutual trust and respect and by shared collective outcomes, as contrasted to the traditional dominance of ownership or hierarchy. Internal linkages often encompass self-managing teams. The structure of external linkages can be seen to comprise a value constellation involving a complex network of contributing firms rather than the traditional vertical value chain (Norman and Ramirez 1993). Linkages may include complementary partnerships in which each provides a unique contribution of value but also precompetitive relationships within a value segment in a form of "cooperative competition" (Golden 1993) or "co-opetition" (Brandenburger and Nalebuff 1996).

Finally, global network organizations are based on a sophisticated information technology infrastructure that supports rapid, cost-efficient communication across network linkages. The technology permits the addition and deletion of linkages as relationships emerge and fade and offers common platforms for information sharing across systems, organizations, and nations. The technology assists communication across the vast distances, time zones, and cultures that characterize global network organizations and assists in meeting the coordination challenges that accompany such differentiation.

This chapter describes global network organizations based on the previously discussed four components and contrasts them with traditional forms. Also, changes in the political and economic landscape that undergird the diffusion of the global network form are discussed, and we describe how a network perspective offers special insights on new structures and relationships in the global economy.

INTERNAL NETWORK FORMS

Organizations are composed of structures, the configurations of their parts (McKelvey 1982). *Organizational forms* are structures that share common features among many organizations. The dominant form during the past century has been the bureaucracy. The bureaucratic form includes, among other features, a hierarchical structure of authority relations.

Burns and Stalker (1962) were among the first to identify an alternative internal structural form. On the basis of data collected from British and Scottish firms facing rapidly changing postwar markets, Burns and Stalker argued that the traditional bureaucratic hierarchy, which they labeled a "mechanistic organization," was an effective way to organize only in stable environments. In turbulent environments, a more flexible, adaptive organizational form, which they called the "organic organization," was more effective. Organic organizations were composed of communications networks that transcended the traditional hierarchy. They were seen as temporary, flexible, and adaptive to the problem at hand and focused on lateral rather than vertical communication.

It has become well-known that all organizations contain sets of emergent internal communication networks, the patterns of person-to-person linkages through which information flows within organizations (Monge and Eisenberg 1987). As Kenneth Arrow (1973) persuasively argued, an organization can be viewed as an "incompletely connected network of information flows" (pp. 19-20). Hence, although it is safe to say that almost all organizations contain both hierarchies and emergent networks, the significant increase in the rate of environmental change in recent years has made emergent networks more important. The well-known management technique of matrix organization is based on this insight (Galbraith 1973).

Traditionally, multinational corporations (MNCs), which may have many subsidiaries worldwide, have been viewed from the perspective of a mixed network and hierarchy model. The linkages between the components of MNCs are often represented as a starburst connecting the center, the focal organization, to all the satellite organizations. A similar metaphor is the wheel, in which the hub is the focal organization, the rim contains the external organizations, and the spokes represent the network of connections from the hub organizations to the external organizations. This view is well illustrated in Ghoshal and Bartlett's (1990) representation of the Phillips Corporation (Figure 3.1). They conceptualize MNCs as a "network of exchange relations among different organizational units, including the headquarters and the different national subsidiaries" (p. 604). This definition treats MNCs as a fixed network that connects all its far-flung parts to its central core. This form relies on a single communication center for coordination of a large number of operations. Knowledge lies at either the local node or the centralized communications center; direct lateral interactions among the far-flung nodes are much less important.

Many commentators have noted that advanced economies no longer rely on production of standard commodities in high volumes, the former modus operandi for which the bureaucratic organizational form was well suited (Reich 1991). Instead, firms strive to provide high value for customers

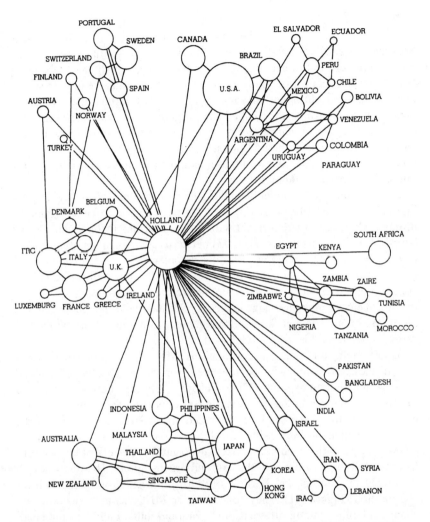

Figure 3.1. Organizational Units and Some of the Interlinkages Within N. V. Phillips (Source: Ghoshal and Bartlett 1990, p. 605)

through differentiated products, customized services, discovering and meeting individual client needs, and rapid response time. Flexible structures offer the opportunity to create customized solutions; close communication among the different parts of the organization permits rapid and effective linkage of solutions with individual customer needs. Networks of relationships unconstrained by rigid functional boundaries or hierarchical layers facilitate the

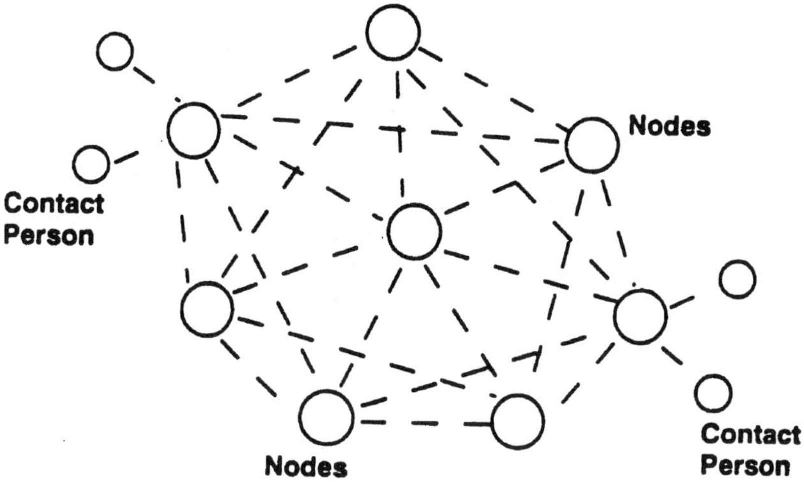

Figure 3.2. Spider's Web Organization (Source: Quinn 1992, p. 121)

rapid flow of information among the various parts of the organization whose activities must be coordinated in the delivery of service and value for the customer. Slow and cumbersome vertical communication up and down a chain of authority is not conducive to the responsiveness required to succeed in an increasingly challenging competitive environment. Filtration of communication through layers of middle management can impede not only speed but also accuracy of information that is passed around the organization. Hence, firms have embarked on the well-publicized shrinkage of middle management in favor of direct coordination among relevant internal parties.

In large firms, semiautonomous divisions may be created that have flexible networked internal structures. These divisions can be loosely coupled through headquarters, which retains information related to scale or scope, creating a network of networks that provides maximum flexibility and responsiveness. Several commentators have referred to such forms as "spider's web" organizations due to their dense interconnections among dispersed nodes and minimal reliance on central hierarchy (Quinn 1992, Reich 1991). A key difference from the MNC model described earlier is the shift from reliance on the central core to creation of multiplex relationships among the individual nodes. Figure 3.2 illustrates such a model.

Miles and Snow (1992) offer a model that adds an additional element of dynamism to the internal network model. Their "spherical network form" envisions an organization in which much of the firm's resources are available on the surface of the sphere. When faced with a problem or opportunity, the sphere rotates to provide access to a wide variety of resources. The rotation brings to the situation the complex of resources (persons, technologies, etc.) that are appropriate to the problem at hand. Spherical networks require autonomous operating units, self-managing teams, and empowerment of participants to assume leadership roles.

Spherical and spider's web organizations may also be embedded in a complex web of external networks. These external networks that cross organizational boundaries reflect an increasing reliance on relationships that are neither subsumed under an organization's own internal boundary nor totally governed by arm's-length market-based transactions. These so-called "mixed mode" (Powell 1990) forms are increasingly made possible by information and communication technology that permits control, collaboration, and coordination of interdependent activities without resorting to the hierarchical mechanisms of the bureaucracy.

EXTERNAL NETWORK FORMS
OF ORGANIZATION

Neoclassical economic theory acknowledges only two forms of economic organization. The first is the free market, in which organizations are seen as independently buying and selling on the basis of self-interest and the best price obtainable. The second is the firm, sometimes called the hierarchy, which seeks to improve efficiency by incorporating parts of market transactions into the firm (Coase 1937, Williamson 1975, 1985). In this case, hierarchical authority and the vested interests of employers are seen to provide a competitive edge over the open marketplace.

Recently, many economists and organizational scholars have argued that a third organizational form has emerged, the network organization (Eccles and Crane 1987, Miles and Snow 1987). Unlike the Burns and Stalker model that centered on internal networks, this new form focuses on the external networks of relations that tie organizations together. These linkages are seen as flexible and adaptive, cutting across traditional organizational boundaries. Powell (1990) provides an interesting comparison of markets, hierarchies, and network forms across eight key features (Table 3.1). The first key feature is the basis for the organization. In the case of hierarchies, organizing is predicated on the employment relationship. In the case of network organizations, the basis is the complementary strengths between the two organizations—what each brings to the other. This shift is important because it changes the focus from one of dominance to one of equality. The second key feature is the means of communication. Hierarchies rely on vertical down-

TABLE 3.1 Stylized Comparison of Forms of Economic Organization

Key Features	Forms		
	Market	Hierarchy	Network
Normative basis	Contract—property rights	Employment relationship	Complementary strengths
Means of communication	Prices	Routines	Relational
Methods of conflict resolution	Haggling—resort to courts for enforcement	Administrative fiat—supervision	Norm of reciprocity—reputational concerns
Degree of flexibility	High	Low	Medium
Amount of commitment among the parties	Low	Medium to high	Medium to high
Tone or climate	Precision and/or suspicion	Formal, bureaucratic	Open-ended, mutual benefits
Actor preferences or choices	Independent	Dependent	Interdependent
Mixing of forms	Repeat transactions (Geertz 1978)	Informal organization (Dalton 1959)	Status hierarchies
	Contracts as hierarchical documents (Stinchcombe 1985)	Market-like features: profit centers, transfer pricing (Eccles 1985)	Multiple partners Formal rules

SOURCE: Powell (1990, p. 300)

ward communication, primarily through routines, orders, and directives. Networks depend on establishing and maintaining communication relationships without regard to direction or dominance. To resolve conflict, the third key issue, hierarchies typically resort to administrative fiat and supervision. Networks use norms of reciprocity (i.e., expectation regarding fair exchange). With regard to the fourth category, flexibility, hierarchies are inflexible and slow to change. Because network forms of organizing attempt to establish stable though not permanent linkages, they tend to be more flexible than hierarchies but not as flexible as the free market.

Feature five, the amount of commitment among the parties, tends to be medium to high for both hierarchies and markets, but the tone or climate, feature number six, is very different. Hierarchies are formal and bureaucratic, whereas networks are open-ended and focused on mutual benefits. The seventh feature is the preferences or choices that govern organizational relations. In pure markets, people are assumed to be independent. In hierar-

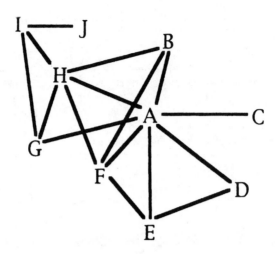

Figure 3.3. Interorganizational Networks

chies, people are clearly dependent on those with authority. In networks, people arc interdependent with each other. The final feature merely notes that hybrid forms exist for all three types of organizations.

The previous analysis of MNCs focused on the relations between a focal organization and its satellite organizations. This notion of a network organization is inadequate because it fails to recognize the network linkages among the external organizations (Eisenberg et al. 1985). Organizations are embedded in entire external networks (Aldrich and Whetten 1981, Ghoshal and Bartlett 1990); many of the organizations to which any organization is connected are also connected to each other (Emery and Trist 1965). These external networks include suppliers, customers, and governmental regulatory agencies. The density of connections among the organizations in these external networks (i.e., the degree to which they are connected to each other) has a major impact on the focal organizations to which they are connected (Emery and Trist 1965, Ghoshal and Bartlett 1990; Figure 3.3). The interrelations among other organizations impact the flow of information to and from competitors and also provide the basis on which other organizations can create exclusive coalitions. One important net effect is barriers to entry into the competitive field.

Of course, this description takes an idiosyncratic view of a single, focal organization. When the view is changed to that of another organization, the picture of the network can change considerably. Furthermore, when we shift the view again to that of the entire set of organizations, to the network as a whole, the picture changes again. From this vantage point, each organization is connected to sets of organizations that are in turn connected to others.

Considerable evidence exists for this embedded form of network organization. In fact, Biggart and Hamilton (1992) argue that networks are the primary organizational forms in most Asian countries. They cite the Japanese *keiretsu* and its predecessor, the *zaibatsu*, the Korean *chaebol*, and the Taiwanese *jituangiye* as network forms of organization. These businesses are organized into groups, often on the basis of family ties and often with people with whom they have had long-standing personal and social relations. As Biggart and Hamilton note, "the crucial economic actor in Asian societies is typically not the individual, but rather the network in which the individual is embedded" (p. 474). In fact, Gerlach (1992) has called this form of Asian network organization "alliance capitalism" to distinguish it from the traditional Western form that typically ignores financial, social, familial, and political ties. Quinn (1992) observed that in practicing this network form of alliance capitalism, "the Japanese generally have been wise enough to practice 'quasi-integration,' not complete vertical integration. Most *keiretsu* operate largely through multiple, carefully interlocked coordination and decision structures based on common interest, rather than on orders from some formal central authority" (p. 233; see also Ju 1994).

Powell (1990) identifies many non-Asian countries in which network forms of organization have also developed, including craft industries, such as construction and publishing, in which people establish long-term contracting relations and regional industrial districts, such as German textiles and the Emilian model centered around Modena in north-central Italy. In the Emilian model, Powell notes, firms are

> grouped in specific zones according to their product, and give rise to industrial districts in which all firms have a very low degree of vertical integration (Brusco 1982). Production is concentrated through extensive, collaborative subcontracting agreements. Only a portion of the firms market final products, the others execute operations commissioned by the group of firms that initiate production. The owners of small firms typically prefer subcontracting to expansion or integration (Lazerson 1988, 1993). The use of satellite firms allows them to remain small and preserve their legal and organizational structure as a small company. Often satellite firms outgrow the spawning firms. Though closely related and highly cooperative, the firms remain strictly independent entities. (p. 310)

As expected, a variety of historical, social, legal, ideological, and other institutional factors support this network form of organizing.

It is interesting to note that each of these examples of network organizations is specific to a different country. In fact, the nature of the networks varies considerably from country to country. For example, Biggart and Hamilton (1992) point out that "the South Korean economy is dominated by networks that on the surface resemble Japan's, but in fact have substantial differences" (p. 475). For example, Korean and Chinese firms are heavily built around family ties, whereas Japanese firms are built around financial ties (although prior to World War II, they were built around family ties). Ju (1994) points out that there are two forms of Japanese *keiretsu*. In the horizontal *keiretsu,* the networks connecting a diverse set of member companies are organized around a core commercial bank such as the Sumitomo group. The vertically organized *keiretsu* are connected "along a supplier chain dominated by a major manufacturer" such as Toyota (p. 76).

It is ironic that these various forms of networked organizations and economies are somewhat isolated from each other in the sense that they do not develop and maintain the same types of external networks beyond their own countries. It is useful to identify these network organizational types that are specific to each country as *national network organizations.*

Global network organizations transcend this national form. Furthermore, to be competitive, global network organizations connect to a variety of different national network organizations. Accordingly, they develop a flexible, adaptive network form capable of integrating with organizations embedded in numerous other national networks. As Quinn (1992) states, most Japanese and other companies throughout the world would "gain greater competitive advantage by jumping beyond the mutual, partial-ownership ties of the *keiretsu* and directly into more flexible contract partnership-oriented structures" (p. 235).

Global network organizations face three difficult challenges not often encountered by more traditional, local organizations: the physical distances that global organizations span, the time asynchronicity encountered, and the diverse cultural differences that comprise the world system (O'Hara-Devereaux and Johansen 1994). Physical dispersion and time displacement makes direct contact and coordination exceedingly difficult, thus necessitating coordination by electronic and other computer-based technologies. As O'Hare-Devereaux and Johansen point out, global organizations require "anytime-anyplace" communication, the ability to communicate across vast distances and diverse time zones, thus maximizing flexibility in global space-time. Finally, global network organizations must address the difficult issues attendant on operating in the different cultures in which their various operating units, alliances, subsidiaries, partners, customers, suppliers, stakeholders, competitors, and governmental agencies reside. Differences in language, values, cultural stereotypes, customs, and management styles must be addressed. Strategies are needed that permit differentiated local responsiveness in the context of overall synergy (Kanter 1995).

Development of Global Network Organizations

The previous analysis provides the foundation of what constitutes the network form of global organizations. It is does not answer the question of why they form as they do, however. Several factors have converged to contribute to the development of global network organizations. First, the increasing rate of globalization of the world economies has opened both new markets and new labor forces. This development has increased the level of competition among firms eager to take advantage of these emerging opportunities. This level of competition requires firms that are responsive and adaptive to new opportunities, a feature that is not characteristic of traditional hierarchies. As Powell (1990) notes,

> A hierarchical structure—clear departmental boundaries, clean lines of authority, detailed reporting mechanisms, and formal decision-making procedures—is particularly well-suited for mass production and distribution. . . . But when hierarchical forms are confronted by sharp fluctuations in demand and unanticipated changes, their liabilities are exposed. (p. 303)

Second, accelerating rates of change, which appear to have become a permanent feature of the contemporary landscape, have dramatically increased the level of uncertainty and risk. Technological advances routinely bring new products to market faster than previously thought possible. Ironically, this same increase in technological productivity has also dramatically shortened the life span of most products, thus increasing competitive pressures. As Quinn (1992) notes, the necessity to generate an ever-increasing number of new products and services requires an organizational form that is knowledge intensive.

Third, computer technology has enabled companies to develop products for "mass customization." This apparent contradiction in terms, which refers to mass-produced products that give the appearance of being customized for each individual, requires highly flexible manufacturing techniques (Miles and Snow 1986). Traditional organizational hierarchies are designed to handle routinization and not customization.

Fourth, a hierarchical organization is one that attempts to deal with its external networks by hierarchical authority. The firm attempts to own and control all aspects of its production process. Historically, as Chandler's (1977) work amply demonstrates, this strategy has led to attempts at vertical integration whereby a company owns all upstream and downstream enterprises needed for the production and distribution of its products. The intent is to provide hierarchical control for all aspects of the process. By contrast, a network organization is one that attempts to deal with its external networks by relational interdependence rather than hierarchical control (i.e., by out-sourcing). The firm attempts to produce its products by establishing and maintaining a set of alliances that preserves the autonomy of the organizations in its networks.

The world industrial environment created by these factors has begun to make organizations based on traditional hierarchies obsolete. Although many traditionally structured organizations still exist, typically they are not at the competitive forefront. Network organizations have developed because they are better suited to operating in this type of challenging and demanding environment. As Nohria and Eccles (1992) point out, they are "fast, flexible, responsive, and knowledge intensive" (p. 290).

NETWORK LINKAGES

There can be little doubt that knowledge and service constitute the bulk of economic output in the developed countries. In fact, Quinn (1992) estimates that service industries, including knowledge and information-generating companies,

> have become the preeminent producers of GNP [gross national product] and new job opportunities in all advanced industrial societies. They now account for 77% of all employment and 74% of all value-added in the U.S. economy and a majority of all GNP in other countries. (p. 30)

The new network organizations are particularly well suited to these intelligent enterprises.

Quinn (1992) argues that successful corporate strategy contains two major components. First, a company must identify its "core competencies," those activities and processes that it does best. The company must strive to become "Best in World" in these core competencies. Second, the company should outsource all other activities required to produce its products or deliver its services, meaning that it should hire, buy, contract, and otherwise obtain all other productive elements other than those that comprise its core competencies. In essence, Quinn is arguing for what we are calling a network form of organization.

Crucial to the creation and maintenance of a network organization are the linkages between the organizations (Eisenberg et al. 1985). Quinn (1992) and others have argued that the core competency of organizations is knowledge—what an organization knows how to do better than any other organization in the world. Badaracco (1991) distinguishes two types of knowledge, migratory and embedded. Migratory knowledge is information that exists in forms that are easily moved from one location to another. Migratory knowledge tends to be contained in books, designs, machines, and individual minds. Blueprints, specifications, formulae, computer programs, engineering plans, and products and machines all encapsulate the knowledge that went into their creation.

Embedded knowledge is more difficult to transfer. As Badaracco (1991) states, "Embedded knowledge resides primarily in specialized relationships among individuals and groups and in the particular norms, attitudes, information flows, and ways of making decisions that shape their dealings with each other" (p. 79). Craftsmanship, unique talents and skills, accumulated know-how, and group expertise and synergy are all difficult to transfer from one place to another and particularly difficult to transfer across firm boundaries.

Badarraco (1991) identifies two forms of linkage—one for each type of knowledge. The first is a product link, which is associated with migratory knowledge. The second is a knowledge link, which is associated with embedded knowledge. A product link is an arrangement whereby a company relies on "an outside ally to manufacture part of its product line or to build complex components that the company had previously made for itself" (p. 11). Knowledge links are alliances whereby companies seek "to learn or jointly create new knowledge and capabilities" (p. 12). These alliances are "organizational arrangements and operating policies through which separate organizations share administrative authority, form social links, and accept joint ownership, and in which looser, more open-ended contractual arrangements replace highly specific, arm's length contracts" (p. 4).

Powell (1990) notes that the network form of organization includes arrangements based on

> joint ventures, strategic alliances, equity partnerships, collaborative research
> pacts of large-scale research consortia, reciprocity deals, and satellite organiza-
> tions. There is no clear-cut relationship between the legal form of cooperative re-
> lationships and the purposes they are intended to achieve. The form of the
> agreement appears to be individually tailored to the needs of the respective par-
> ties, and to tax and regulatory considerations. The basic thrust, however, is quite
> obvious: to pursue new strategies of innovation through collaboration without ab-
> rogating the separate identity and personality of the cooperating partners. (p. 315)

In one sense, network organizations create "boundaryless organizations." Where one organization begins and the other ends is no longer clear. Organizations share knowledge, goals, resources, personnel, and finances. To accomplish this, they must establish collaborative work arrangements because this is the only way to transfer embedded knowledge.

COMMUNICATION AND INFORMATION
TECHNOLOGY IN GLOBAL NETWORKS

The kind of global network organizational form described in this chapter is almost impossible to create without a highly sophisticated communication and information infrastructure (Child 1987). Indeed, new technologies often energize the development of new organizational forms. For example, developments in communication and transportation systems in the late nineteenth century led to the emergence of the current hierarchical organization form. Prior to that time, smaller, regionally based local organizations were the norm (Beniger 1986, Yates 1989). The integration of computing with communication provides the possibility for major changes to these hierarchical organizations.

New communication and computing technologies offer at least three main benefits that impact organizational forms. First, they have greatly reduced transmission time, enhancing the ability of dispersed participants to share information and coordinate their efforts. The decentralization of organizations through the use of local branches was initially made possible by the telephone in the early part of this century (Pool 1983); the decentralization effect has been significantly enhanced by the speed and capabilities of more advanced systems. Not only branch offices but also central core activities may be dispersed widely throughout the globe. Ford's redesigned global research and development organization is an example (*Business Week* 1994).

Second, with new technologies comes a reduction in the costs of communication. As Thompson (1967) noted three decades ago, the costs of communication for coordinating activities are among the highest that organizations face. Thus, organizational structure previously was designed to reduce coordination and communication costs by collocating mutually interdependent activities. With the reduction in coordination costs that accompanies technological developments, organizational structures need not be so closely linked to communication cost-reduction criteria. This decoupling presents opportunities for a greater variety of structures.

Third, the integration of computing with communication has enhanced the complexity of information that can be communicated in a cost-effective and rapid manner. Indeed, it is the enhanced capability for communicating complex information that distinguishes current communication technology developments from those that spawned the hierarchical organization. Older communication technologies such as the telephone served primarily as connective systems, with little capability to modify, enhance, or manipulate the information that was being transmitted. Fulk et al. (1996) note that current integrated communication technologies also have communal properties that permit individuals or organizations or both to share databases and manipulate information.

The ability of these technological developments to foster global network organizations has depended on efforts to develop compatible technical interfaces and standards for information transmission. Compatibility has been substantially enhanced by international standards-setting organizations, governmental policy choices, regulations regarding transborder data flow, and voluntary agreements among vendors during the past decade. In combination, these organizational and political advances have contributed substantially to the ability to network widely across units and organizations.

Communication and information technology are implicated in new network forms through the improvements in connectivity and communality that they provide. *Connectivity* as defined by Fulk et al. (1996) is the ability of members of a defined public to directly communicate with each other. Early examples of connectivity are the universal linkages provided by the postal service and the telephone. *Communality* is the ability of each member of the defined public to contribute to, access, and use a jointly held database. Early examples of communality include public records, libraries, and a company bulletin board. Recent advancements in information and communication technology have provided vastly expanded potential for connectivity and communality within internal networks, within external networks, and across linkages for global network organizations.

Communication and Information
Technology for Internal Networks

Internal networks in the new organizational form are flexible and emergent. A key facilitator for emergent networks is an extensive connective and communal infrastructure for sharing information with all potential partners. When the telephone was introduced in the United States early in the twentieth century, a conscious policy choice was made to provide universal service so that any citizen could reach any other citizen if they chose to do so (Pool 1983). Although no person ever telephoned everyone else, the infrastructure made it possible for individuals to phone persons that they might not otherwise have contacted. Telephone usage illustrates emergent communication whereby a "large number of relatively small, overlapping, and shifting coalitions of users" contact each other directly (Fulk et al. 1996, p. 67). Thus, the telephone and related infrastructures such as the federal postal service facilitated emergent networks and linkages for communication early in the twentieth century.

In a parallel fashion, the advanced infrastructure for connection and communal sharing of information offers possibilities for endless emergent networks within organizations. The mass communication capabilities of these systems permit information to be distributed widely through distribution lists and electronic bulletin boards, extending the reach of internal networks. Because the backbone provides universal access to organization members, communicators need not be able to identify each other prior to interaction. Finholt and Sproull (1990) provided case histories of emergent groups that arose through the use of electronic bulletin boards in one organization. Eveland and Bikson (1987) described the emergence of interest groups through the use of electronic mail in an R&D organization. These groups transcended the existing organization structure, forming a new, overarching layer. Steinfield and Fulk (1988) demonstrated the mass communication effects associated with using distribution lists in an office products firm. Participants were interlinked densely within the organization, and each made new contacts that ultimately paid off for them in the performance of their tasks. Steinfield (1986) demonstrated how the socialization process of new recruits was distributed more broadly throughout the organization through the use of electronic mail. Steinfield (1983) and Kiesler (1986) described how people used electronic mail to send broad requests for information that ultimately reached many individuals previously unknown to the sender and sometimes led to establishing more permanent and intensive dyadic communication linkages.

Even among previously acquainted organizational members, technological support can facilitate more extensive communication and broader network participation. Videoconferences have been shown to facilitate inclusion of more participants in meetings (Dutton et al. 1982), especially when travel budgets are restricted. Huber (1990) proposed that computer-based technology use leads to a larger number and variety of persons involved in making decisions. Asynchronous computer conferences can facilitate participation in meetings by individuals in different time zones. Advanced communication technologies have facilitated more overall communication and not just substituted for other forms (Rice and Bair 1984, Rice and Case 1983).

Because the increased connectivity permits more broadly dispersed communication and more linkages to partners previously unknown to communicators, these systems have been described as promoting more "weak ties" (Granovetter 1973) and more radial communication networks (Fulk et al. 1986). Weak ties and radial networks have been shown to promote more broad dispersion of information and more organizational innovation (Monge and Contractor, in press). The ability of technology-induced radial networks to facilitate innovation is a valuable contribution to the responsiveness that is characteristic of new network forms of organization.

Research by Danowski and Edison-Swift (1985) showed how networks of electronic communication shifted over time in response to an organizational crisis. Volume and dispersion of contacts rose dramatically during the crisis phase and then waned as the crisis began to dissipate. The emergence of extensive networking in response to organizational events may pose challenges to traditional hierarchical control mechanisms in organizations. In traditional hierarchical organizations, key competitive information typically resides in the top management team and does not flow broadly to the organizational community without the acquiescence of top management. The mass communication capabilities of new communication technologies make possible the rapid and blanket dispersion of such information once top management control has been breached. For example, a major aerospace firm literally shut down its electronic mail system in response to concerns about the spread of rumors regarding a potential sale of the firm.[2]

Communication and information technologies are implicated in shifting control away from hierarchical mechanisms. Fulk and DeSanctis (1995) describe this change as a movement from social rationalization (hierarchy) to technological rationalization. Hierarchical arrangements typically arise to deal with information overload and vertical coordination. Hierarchical organizational forms are social structures based on domination and control through rules, programs, procedures, and goals. Communication and information technology can now assume these functions by programmed routines that are built into the technology such that coordination is preprogrammed through technological rationalization. One well-documented effect during the past decade is the significant decline in the number of middle managers—whose traditional jobs are primarily coordinative. Technological rationalization reduces bureaucracy and frees the social form to provide significantly greater flexibility, adaptability, and learning capability—the organicness that characterizes the global network organization. Thus, communication technology can make hierarchy obsolete by subsuming its control and coordination functions. Of course, such an effect depends on political decisions as to how the technology is deployed and employed. Koppel et al. (1988) distinguish between "algorithmic" applications that automate, rigidify, and reinforce existing bureaucracy and "robust" systems that reduce bureaucracy and enhance flexibility. Zuboff (1988) makes a similar distinction between technological systems that "automate" and thus reinforce existing hierarchy versus those that "infomate" by enriching the options for innovation. The choice to automate versus infomate is managerial and political.

The breadth and reach of electronic communication also can help to foster the sense of community and shared goals that are a feature of new organizational forms. Miles and Snow (1992), for example, described the new organization as one in which individuals are committed to the enterprise as a whole rather than their individual functions. Ready electronic access to other organizational members can facilitate a sense of organizational community, as Kling and Gerson's (1977) research demonstrated.

A key feature of global network organizations is the dispersion of functional expertise to cross-functional teams. In traditional hierarchies, functional structures provide experts the ability to share key knowledge within the function and thus keep up-to-date with knowledge in their fields. Advances in computing and database systems offer the opportunity to share information within a function without the requisite of collocating organizationally. Allen and Hauptman (1990) describe three technologies that facilitate knowledge transfer across geographically dispersed functional experts: document search and retrieval systems, expert system-based selective dissemination of information, and bulletin boards for forums for information search. To this list may be added secured videoconferencing links between sites that permit sharing more complex information among R&D personnel (Ruchinskas et al. 1990) and facsimile support for communicating extremely complex diagrams between dispersed functional experts (Fulk et al. 1988).

Information and communication technologies can also support coordination within cross-functional teams. Project management software is a typical illustration. Allen and Hauptman (1990) also describe how hierarchically organized bulletin boards are used for reporting project status and controlling configuration. Lu (1996) provides an advanced communication and software solution through his "engineering as collaborative negotiation" paradigm. He is developing communication and software solutions that support (a) the application of optimizing criteria at the team level in the context of satisficing at the individual level; (b) design specifications that are composed of acceptable ranges for each variable rather than single values in an attempt to facilitate alignment of solutions across functions; (c) functionally decomposed design stages to support negotiation of output across functions; (d) mutual rather than serial interdependence; and (e) involvement of the customer in the design phase.

The penetration of sophisticated electronic mail systems and local area networks in organizations has made it possible to rapidly transmit complex information. One consequence has been that once-isolated databases can now be made available more broadly, contributing to the increased general availability of information reported by Applegate in Chapter 2. Networks of individuals and units linked through these shared, distributed databases are characteristic of new network forms of organization. Finholt (1993) studied a variant of these shared databases that transcended time and current organizational membership. His research on expert databases showed that individuals unknown to each other were linked when experts contributed to a database that was accessible and queriable by other members of the organization. The database accumulated over time such that valuable expertise was captured and retained for use beyond the organizational tenure of the expert. In some cases, queries of the expert database led to personal contacts with individuals that would not have occurred except through the information provided in the database.

Technical compatibility is critical to these processes. Without interoperability, connectivity and communality cannot be achieved. For example, Fulk et al. (1995) describe an R&D site that was somewhat isolated from the rest of the organization because its electronic mail system (DEC architecture) could not link with that of the rest of the organization (IBM architecture). Eventually, the scientists wrote their own code to link the two systems. The historical difficulty of Apple- and IBM-based operating systems to share files is another case in point. Many compatibility issues are being resolved as technologies converge and market mechanisms act to favor one platform over another. One development that speaks directly to this issue is the growth in use of the common platform of the Internet for seamless internal organizational communication, the so-called intranet applications.

Summary

The connectivity and communality offered through advanced communication and information technologies facilitate network structures in a variety of ways. The infrastructure for connectivity offers the technical means for a virtually infinite set of possible emergent networks for direct communication within an organization. The specific sets of networks that emerge will depend on user choices to employ the technology and to select specific sets of communication partners—what Fulk et al. (1996) call *social connectivity*. The research described previously has shown that within the connective infrastructure,

- Mass communication features help to link people with similar interests, leading to emergent, interest-based networks.
- Previously acquainted persons communicate more extensively and may participate in a wider array of interactions.
- Previously unacquainted persons can become acquainted and develop more intensive links.
- More weak ties can be initiated, and more radial and embedded networks can be developed that support the more complex situations faced by organizations today.
- Technological coordination and rationalization can subsume some of the main functions of hierarchy.
- More community building can occur throughout the organization.

The communal capabilities of advanced technologies offer indirect linkages among individuals. Communal features can support

- Complex information sharing among unacquainted parties, across organiza-
  tional subunits, and across time
- Initiation of new communication relationships
- Wide dispersion of information that is characteristic of new forms
- Mechanisms for sharing expertise among functional specialists dispersed to dif-
  ferent teams
- Coordination mechanisms for optimizing team efforts under uncertainty

Connective and communal benefits are optimized when systems are compatible and when consistent support is provided across nodes, whether they be
individuals or units.

Communication and Information Technology
for External Networks

Connectivity and communality pose greater challenges across organizations that lack a common infrastructure for communication and data exchange. Communication and information technologies impact the rise of the
external global network in two major ways. First, some technological improvements facilitate rapid and cost-effective interorganizational exchanges,
including gateways across different electronic mail systems, electronic data
interchange (EDI) standards, proprietary interorganizational systems, and
Internet-based tools. Second, the need for more advanced interorganizational
connectivity and communality motivates alliances designed to help develop
a common infrastructure for information exchange in the marketplace. These
precompetitive alliances typically involve network R&D efforts (Golden
1993).

Technological Support for Interorganizational Exchange

Global network organizations manage external networks through relational interdependence rather than hierarchical control. All but core operations are outsourced, embedding the organization in a complex web of
interdependencies. Communication and information technology are critical
to the ability to monitor and control these interdependencies. For example,
General Motor's (GM) requirement that its suppliers use its own EDI
standard bound the supplier's own internal operations more tightly to those of
GM. Also, American Hospital Supply's (AHS) ASAP system is often described

as a classic example (Vitale 1990). AHS developed inventory management and information systems for its customers (hospitals) that permitted monitoring of supply levels at customer premises and direct order entry into AHS's own internal order-processing system. The system created not only efficiencies but also a high level of dependence of hospitals on AHS—and tremendous switching costs for hospitals to change suppliers.

Computerized reservation systems permit travel agencies to directly book seats in the airlines' computers. This type of system demonstrates how new communication and computing systems can manage complexity. Prior to deregulation of the airline industry, only a small percentage of bookings were made through travel agents. Rates and routes were fixed and manageable because there were few choices. With deregulation, the fares differed not only by airline but also by time of purchase, with as many as a dozen different fares for any one single flight. Passengers needed assistance with this new maze. The travel agency business grew dramatically, and the computerized communication and reservation systems between travel agents and airlines permitted the agencies to manage this information complexity for the traveler. The agency became a critical link in the value chain. Travel agencies also became sellers of information because their reservation systems captured travel patterns, preferences, and other marketable forms of information. Agencies then became a part of more complex networks of relationships, serving simultaneously as customer, competitor, and supplier to airlines, car rental agencies, and other participants in the travel business. The rise of the Internet as an alternative source of up-to-date and comprehensive travel information now offers an alternative to travel agency services. This technological development threatens an industry whose prior success was facilitated by earlier technological developments.

Information systems also facilitate networked organizations in unrelated industries. Consider the alliances between airlines and long-distance companies whereby customers earn frequent flier miles based on volume of long-distance telephone usage. The ability to rapidly transfer information between the disparate organizations is critical to the success of such alliances. In contrast to the outsourcing effects, such arrangements illustrate that technologies may supplement rather than replace or alter existing organizational forms, leaving the core organization intact but expanding their networks to encompass new types of partners.

Organizations also link themselves into new networks through shared proprietary information and communication systems. Examples of this are the regional databases that link law enforcement organizations through sharing communal data. In one such system, officers at state, federal, and local levels can access shared information about criminal activity and can contribute information to the communal database. A computerized monitoring system tracks planned enforcement actions across dozens of agencies and identifies potential conflicts before they occur. The system is designed to assist the organizations to integrate previously separate networked resources rather than to act in isolation. The system also tightly couples the organizations through a communal information repository that replaces the separate databases in the individual agencies.

With the rapid development of the Internet and the World Wide Web, organizations need not rely on proprietary systems to achieve connectivity and communality through a shared infrastructure. Secured Web sites offer options for private exchanges of information between networked firms. Search engines can assist firms in seeking information from previously unknown sources, facilitating new linkages. Newsgroups link individuals and organizations into complex nets. Indeed, the vast information dissemination potential threatens the role of traditional information intermediaries such as travel agencies (Benjamin and Wigand 1995) while offering new linking roles to others, such as producers of information search tools (Sarkar et al. 1995) or information packagers (*The Economist* 1996). The Internet also provides the basic infrastructure on which other networking tools can be built. An example is the recent release of Habenero, a Java-based collaborative tool that permits synchronous conferencing and sharing of complex data through ordinary Internet connections (Webber 1996).

Alliances in Pursuit of Technological Infrastructures for Collaboration

The second form of technology-induced alliances arises from firms linking together to create or enhance the information and communication infrastructure required for interorganizational linkages. A recent example is the alliances among credit card companies and firms that produce Web browsers to craft mechanisms for secured communication of confidential information such as credit card numbers through the Internet. In this case, the alliance hopes to create proprietary software that secures competitive advantage for the alliance firms. The broader goal, however, is to create an infrastructure for secured commercial transactions on the Internet.

Gulati (1995) claims that "the last 15 years have witnessed an unprecedented growth worldwide in the number of interfirm strategic alliances— voluntary arrangements involving durable exchange, sharing, or codevelopment of new products and technologies" (p. 619). A primary thrust is "cooperative competition" in which firms cooperate in R&D to create the communal good of the communication infrastructure needed for global interaction, even though these same firms simultaneously compete with each other in product markets (Golden 1993). The infrastructure is critical because, as Fulk et al.

(1996) assert, a fully connected system provides maximum flexibility for linkages to wax and wane over time, and a firm need not know a priori which specific linkages will be required. Hagedoorn and Schakenraad (1992) draw on a large database of alliances to identify recent international networks of alliances for cooperative R&D in information technology development. Their data show how strategic subnetworks of companies change over time, as do the positions of leading companies within these networks.

Summary

External network forms are facilitated by technologies that specifically support interorganizational exchange:

* Exchanges across stages of the value chain are supported by such developments as EDI standards or by proprietary systems designed to link a constellation of customers to a supplier's own data standards.
* Alliances among unrelated industries may arise through routinely collected information in one industry that can benefit firms in other industries.
* Organizations with common goals can develop coordinated action through information-sharing systems that create jointly held databases that are accessible to all, provided that each participating organization shares relevant information through the database.
* The Internet and World Wide Web provide publicly available infrastructure for exchanges of information between firms.

Global R&D networks also arise to create the basic infrastructure needed for interorganizational exchanges:

* Alliances may be created among previously unrelated firms, each of which is seeking a different part of the new markets that such infrastructure can create (e.g., alliances to develop mechanisms for secured commercial transactions on the Internet).
* Alliances may also be among competing firms in the precompetitive R&D phase— variously called cooperative competition (Golden 1993) or co-opetition (Brandenburger and Nalebuff 1996).

Communication Technology and Network Linkages

With information as the major "product" moving through channels in postindustrial economies, organizations and their component parts need not be linked so much by transportation systems as by communication systems.

Historically, size and location of organizations and their component units have been heavily based on needs to reduce transportation costs. Major industrial areas were located along major transportation routes—rivers, railroads, and oceans—where large consolidated facilities were sited. Advanced information systems are significantly different than transportation systems in that cost of movement through the system is much more weakly tied to distance between points and physical access. As postindustrial organizations focus more on moving information than physical products, dispersion of units is no longer a handicap. As electronic information highways replace asphalt ones, global network organizations that permit local responsiveness through dispersed nodes become the preferred form. Also, as Golden (1993) notes, as exchange of value occurs increasingly through electronic transmission rather than transfer of products, considerable national and international issues arise surrounding the location of the network nodes relative to national boundaries.

Badaracco's (1991) previously described distinction between migratory and embedded knowledge is critical for understanding successful information transfer for global network organizations. Migratory knowledge is easily codified and transmitted electronically. The flow of tacit, embedded knowledge relies heavily on close contact and the development of close working relationships. Although communication and information systems are essential, alliances that network through sharing of personnel and other forms of nontechnological networking are still critical to the success of global network organizations.

Eastman Kodak's (EK) web of relationships for managing their outsourced information services function is an example of the complex interaction of technological and nontechnological linkages through relationship management. EK outsourced its massive information systems function to a web of three different suppliers. Information technology permitted some monitoring of the services. EK also used a second source of control that is commonly described as critical to global network organizations: relationship management and development of trust (Creed and Miles 1996, Handy 1995, Miles and Snow 1992, Yoshiro and Rangan 1995). EK's contracts with its suppliers were explicitly based on trust and shared expectations of each other; EK resisted creating the detailed contract language typical of an arm's-length relationship. Instead, the contracts described broad agreements and shared goals.

Sharing of knowledge, goals, resources, personnel, and finances in boundaryless global networks is nowhere more evident than in the communications industries. "Convergence" is the key buzzword in the business press, indicating the blurring of industry boundaries such that one can no longer tell where one industry begins and another ends. The multitude of alliances across cable, telephone, satellite, cellular, computing, and entertainment providers is the dominant industry form. The race for sole-source provider of bundled services that include terrestrial telephone or satellite, Internet connection, cellular, and entertainment programming has created a heavily interconnected network of organizations from previously discrete industries. Indeed, a new industry has even been spawned from this globally networked "industry"—sales of products designed to help make sense of the linkages. For example, Deloitte & Touche, a consulting company, offers a CD-ROM with information on "convergent industries" of cable, broadcasting, telecommunications, software, and hardware. There is also an increasing number of books on this issue, including *The Red Herring Guide to the Digital Universe* (Red Herring 1996; also a searchable Web site: *http://www.herring.com*) and *Convergence* (Baldwin et al. 1996).

Summary

Changes in network linkages have implications for the form and shape of the global network organization:

* The increasing reliance on information products in international commerce supports more dispersed nodes that are regionally responsive but can be coordinated and monitored via information technology.
* For transferring embedded knowledge, alliances that involve more personal contact and sharing of personnel are required, and these linkages are less susceptible to monitoring via information technology.
* Technological advances in the core knowledge base have brought together previously disparate industries and organizations, as in communications. Complex interconnections among multiple industry partners have become the norm as convergence offers new opportunities for offering complex arrays of bundled services.

CONCLUSION

In this chapter, we have developed a set of ideas that describe a new organizational form: the global network organization. We acknowledged that all organizations contain both hierarchies and networks, although in the network form of organization the networks are far more important than they are in the hierarchy form. A network organization is also embedded in an external network of organizations that are, in turn, connected to each other. To be a global network organization, an organization must transcend its local national network form and interface with various national network forms throughout the world. To do so, it must focus on knowledge linkages, those alliances that enable it to create and share knowledge across a wide variety of organizational partners. This can be accomplished in the contemporary world with the assistance of a wide array of information and communication technology. It is this support that creates the capability for rapid, flexible, and reliable communication, without which global network organizations could not exist.

Global network organizations have emerged in the late twentieth century as the dominant world force, rivaling and sometimes surpassing sovereign nation-states in importance. By dominating the world economy, global enterprises significantly influence the course of political, social, and military events. Furthermore, as more than one observer has commented, global enterprises often capture the minds and loyalties of their executives far more than do their own home countries (Golden 1993). Surely, an organizational form and communication technologies that exert this much power and influence warrant careful study. Also, for those companies that wish to be competitive in the global marketplace, understanding and using this new organizational form has significant long-term potential.

NOTES

1. This section and the subsequent section on linkages draw on an early version of these ideas presented by Monge (1995).

2. This information was provided to the authors by a consultant to the firm. The "public" explanation for the shutdown was "technical problems."

REFERENCES

Aldrich, H. and D. A. Whetten (1981), "Organizational Sets, Action Sets, and Networks: Making the Most of Simplicity," in P. Nystrom and W. Starbuck (Eds.), *Handbook of Organizational Design,* London: Oxford University Press, pp. 385-408.

Allen, T. J. and O. Hauptman (1990), "The Substitution of Communication Technologies for Organizational Structure in Research and Development," in J. Fulk and C. W. Steinfield (Eds.), *Organizations and Communication Technology,* Newbury Park, CA: Sage, pp. 275-294.

Arrow, K. J. (1973), *Information and Economic Behavior,* Stockholm: Federation of Swedish Industries.

Badaracco, J. L., Jr. (1991), *The Knowledge Link: How Firms Compete Through Strategic Alliances,* Boston: Harvard Business School Press.

Baldwin, T., S. McVoy, and C. Steinfield (1996), *Convergence: Integrating Media, Information, and Communication,* Thousand Oaks, CA: Sage.

Beniger, J. R. (1986), *The Control Revolution: Technological and Economic Origins of the Information Society,* Cambridge, MA: Harvard University Press.

Benjamin, R. and R. Wigand (1995), "Electronic Markets and Virtual Value Chains on the Information Superhighway," *Sloan Management Review,* 36, 2, 62-72.

Biggart, N. W. and G. G. Hamilton (1992), "On the Limits of a Firm-Based Theory to Explain Business Networks: The Western Bias of Neoclassical Economics," in N. Nohria and R. G. Eccles (Eds.), *Networks and Organizations: Structure, Form, and Action,* Boston: Harvard Business School Press, pp. 471-490.

Brandenburger, A. M. and B. J. Nalebuff (1996), *Co-opetition,* New York: Doubleday.

Brusco, S. (1982), "The Emilian Model: Productive Decentralization and Social Integration," *Cambridge Journal of Economics,* 6, 167-184.

Burns, T. and G. M. Stalker (1962), *The Management of Innovation,* London: Tavistock.

Business Week (1994), "Ford: Alex Trotman's Bold Plan," April 3, 94-97, 100-101, 104.

Chandler, A. D. (1977), *The Visible Hand,* Cambridge, MA: Harvard University Press.

Child, J. (1987), "Information Technology, Organization, and the Response to Strategic Challenges," *California Management Review,* 29, 33-50.

Coase, R. (1937), "The Nature of the Firm," *Economica,* 4, 386-405.

Creed, W. E. and R. E. Miles (1996), "Trust in Organizations: A Conceptual Framework Linking Organizational Forms, Managerial Philosophies, and the Opportunity Costs of Controls," in R. M. Kramer and T. R. Tyler (Eds.), *Trust in Organizations: Frontiers of Theory and Research,* Thousand Oaks, CA: Sage, pp. 16-38.

Dalton, M. (1959), *Men Who Manage—Fusions of Feeling and Theory in Administration,* New York: John Wiley.

Danowski, J. and P. Edison-Swift (1985), "Crisis Effects on Intraorganizational Computer-Based Communication," *Communication Research,* 12, 251-270.

Dutton, W. H., J. Fulk, and C. Steinfield (1982), "Utilization of Video Conferencing," *Telecommunications Policy,* 6, September, 164-178.

Eccles, R. G. (1985), *The Transfer Pricing Problem: A Theory for Practice,* Lexington, MA: Lexington Books.

Eccles, R. G. and D. B. Crane (1987), "Managing Through Networks in Investment Banking," *California Management Review,* 30, 176-195.

The Economist (1996, March 2), "Facts and Friction," 338, p. 72.

Eisenberg, E. M., R. V. Farace, P. R. Monge, E. P. Bettinghaus, R. Kurchner-Hawkins, K. Miller, and L. Rothman (1985), "Communication Linkages in Interorganizational Systems," in B. Dervin and M. Voight (Eds.), *Progress in Communication Sciences,* New York: Ablex, Vol. 6, pp. 231-261.

Emery, F. and E. Trist (1965), "The Causal Texture of Organizational Environments," *Human Relations,* 18, 21-32.

Eveland, J. D. and T. K. Bikson (1987), "Evolving Electronic Communication Networks: An Empirical Assessment," *Office: Technology and People,* 3, 103-128.

Finholt, T. (1993), "Outsiders on the Inside: Sharing Information Through a Computer Archive," unpublished doctoral dissertation, Carnegie Mellon University, Department of Social and Decision Science, Pittsburgh, PA.

_____ and L. Sproull (1990), "Electronic Groups at Work," *Organization Science,* 1, 41-64.

Fulk, J. and G. DeSanctis (1995), "Electronic Communication and Changing Organizational Forms," *Organizational Science,* 6, 337-349.

_____, A. Flanagin, M. Kalman, T. Ryan, and P. R. Monge (1996), "Connective and Communal Public Goods in Interactive Communication Systems," *Communication Theory,* 6, 60-87.

_____, G. Power, and J. Schmitz (1986, November), "Communication in Organizations via Electronic Mail: An Analysis of Behavioral and Relational Issues," paper presented at the annual conference of the Decision Sciences Institute, Honolulu, HI.

_____, J. Schmitz, and D. Ryu (1988, October), "Communication in R&D via Electronic Mail I: Survey Results for TRC," Technical Report No. 1, CIMS Project, University of Southern California, Annenberg School of Communications, Los Angeles.

_____, _____, and _____ (1995), "Cognitive Elements in the Social Construction of Communication Technology," *Management Communication Quarterly,* 8, 259-288.

Galbraith, J. J. (1973), *Designing Complex Organizations,* Reading, MA: Addison-Wesley.

Geertz, C. (1978), "The Bazaar Economy: Information and Search in Peasant Marketing," *American Economic Review,* 68, 28-32.

Gerlach, M. (1992), *Alliance Capitalism: The Social Organization of Japanese Business,* Berkeley: University of California Press.

Ghoshal, S. and C. A. Bartlett (1990), "The Multinational Corporation as an Interorganizational Network, *Academy of Management Review,* 15, 603-625.

Golden, J. (1993), "Economics and National Strategy: Convergence, Global Networks, and Cooperative Competition," *Washington Quarterly,* Summer, 91-113.

Granovetter, M. (1973), "The Strength of Weak Ties," *American Journal of Sociology,* 78, 1360-1380.

Gulati, R. (1995), "Social Structure and Alliance Formation Patterns: A Longitudinal Analysis," *Administrative Science Quarterly,* 40, 619-652.

Hagedoorn, J. and J. Schakenraad (1992), "Intercompany Cooperation and Technological Developments: Leading Companies and Networks of Strategic Alliances in Information Technologies," *Research Policy,* 21, 163-190.

Handy, C. (1995), "Trust and the Virtual Organization," *Harvard Business Review,* 73, 3, 40-49.

Huber, G. P. (1990), "A Theory of the Effects of Advanced Information Technologies on Organizational Design, Intelligence, and Decision-Making," in J. Fulk and C. Steinfield (Eds.), *Organizations and Communication Technology,* Newbury Park, CA: Sage, pp. 117-140.

Ju, Y. (1994), "Supremacy of Human Relationships: A Japanese Organizational Model," in B. Kovacic (Ed.), *New Approaches to Organizational Communication,* Albany: State University of New York Press, pp. 67-85.

Kanter, R. M. (1995), *World Class: Thriving Locally in the Global Economy,* New York: Simon & Schuster.

Kiesler, S. (1986), "Thinking Ahead: The Hidden Messages in Computer Networks," *Harvard Business Review,* 64, 46-60.

Kling, R. and E. M. Gerson (1977), "The Social Dynamics of Technological Innovation in the Computing World," *Symbolic Interaction,* 1, 11, 132-146.

Koppel, R., E. Applebaum, and P. Albin (1988), "Implications of Workplace Information Technology: Control, Organization of Work, and the Occupational Structure," *Research in the Sociology of Work,* 4, 125-152.

Lazerson, M. (1988), "Organizational Growth of Small Firms: An Outcome of Markets and Hierarchies?" *American Sociological Review,* 53, 330-342.

Lazerson, M. (1993), "Factory or Putting Out? Knitting Networks in Modena," in G. Grabher (Ed.), *The Embedded Firm: On the Socioeconomics of Industrial Networks,* New York: Routledge, pp. 203-226.

Lu, S. C.-Y. (1996), "Exploring the Total Work Environment of the Future," unpublished manuscript, University of Southern California, Engineering Impact Laboratory, Los Angeles.

McKelvey, B. (1982), *Organizational Systematics: Taxonomy, Evolution, Classification,* Berkeley: University of California Press.

Miles, R. E. and C. C. Snow (1986), "Organizations: New Concepts for New Forms," *California Management Review,* 28, 62-73.

_____ (1992), "Causes of Failure in Network Organizations," *California Management Review,* Summer, 53-72.

Monge, P. (1995), "Global Network Organizations," in R. Cesaria and P. Shockley-Zalabak (Eds.), *Organization Means Communication,* Rome: SIPI.

Monge, P. R. and N. S. Contractor (in press), "Emergence of Communication Networks," in F. Jablin and L. Putnam (Eds.), *New Handbook of Organizational Communication,* Thousand Oaks, CA: Sage.

_____ and E. M. Eisenberg (1987), "Emergent Communication Networks," in F. M. Jablin, L. L. Putnam, K. H. Roberts, and L. W. Porter (Eds.), *Handbook of Organizational Communication,* Newbury Park, CA: Sage, pp. 304-342.

Nohria, H. and R. G. Eccles (1992), "On the Limits of a Firm-Based Theory to Explain Business Networks: The Western Bias of Neoclassical Economics," in N. Nohria and R. G. Eccles (Eds.), *Networks and Organizations: Structure, Form, and Action,* Boston: Harvard Business School Press, pp. 471-490.

Norman, R. and R. Ramirez (1993), "From Value Chain to Value Constellation: Designing Interactive Strategy," *Harvard Business Review,* July/August, 65-77.

O'Hara-Devereaux, M. and R. Johansen (1994), *Globalwork,* San Francisco: Jossey-Bass.

Pool, I. (1983), *Forecasting the Telephone: A Retrospective Technology Assessment of the Telephone,* Norwood, NJ: Ablex.

Powell, W. W. (1990), "Neither Market nor Hierarchy: Network Forms of Organization," in B. Staw (Ed.), *Research in Organizational Behavior,* Greenwich, CT: JAI, Vol. 12, pp. 295-336.

Quinn, J. B. (1992), *Intelligent Enterprise,* New York: Free Press.

Red Herring (1996), *The Red Herring Guide to the Digital Universe,* New York: Warner Books.

Reich, R. (1991), *The Work of Nations,* New York: Vintage.

Rice, R. E. and J. H. Bair (1984), "New Organizational Media and Productivity," in R. Rice (Ed.), *The New Media: Communication, Research, and Technology,* Beverly Hills, CA: Sage, pp. 185-216.

_____ and D. Case (1983), "Electronic Message Systems in the University: A Description of Use and Utility," *Journal of Communications,* 33, 131-152.

Ruchinskas, J., L. Svenning, and C. Steinfield (1990), "Video in Organizational Communication: The Case of ARCOvision," in B. Sypher (Ed.), *Case Studies in Organizational Communication,* New York: Guilford, pp. 269-281.

Sarkar, M. B., B. Butler, and C. Steinfield (1995), "Intermediaries and Cybermediaries: A Continuing Role for Mediating Players in the Electronic Marketplace," *Journal of Computer-Mediated Communication,* 1, 3. (*http://www.usc.edu/dept/annenberg/vol1/issue3*)

Steinfield, C. W. (1983), "Communicating via Electronic Mail: Patterns and Predictors of Use in Organizations," unpublished doctoral dissertation, University of Southern California, Los Angeles.

_____ (1986), "Computer-Mediated Communication in an Organizational Setting: Explaining Task and Socio-Emotional Uses," in M. McLaughlin (Ed.), *Communication Yearbook 9,* Beverly Hills, CA: Sage, pp. 777-804.

_____ and J. Fulk (1988, October), "Computer-Mediated Communication Systems as Mass Communication Media," paper presented at the Telecommunications Policy Research Conference, Airlie House, VA.

Stinchcombe, A. L. (1985), "Contracts as Hierarchical Documents," in A. L. Stinchcombe and
    C. A. Heimer (Eds.), *Organization Theory and Project Management: Administering Un-
    certainty in Norwegian Offshore Oil,"* Oslo/London: Norwegian University Press/
    Oxford University Press, pp. 121-171.
Thompson, J. D. (1967), *Organizations in Action,* New York: McGraw-Hill.
Vitale, M. R. (1990), *American Hospital Supply Corporation: The ASAP System,* Cambridge,
    MA: Harvard Business School Press.
Webber, T. E. (1996, May 30), "Will Habanero Be the Next Thing? This Computer Software
    Could Add Hot Dimension to Web: Cooperation," *The Wall Street Journal,* 109, p. B6.
Williamson, O. E. (1975), *Markets and Hierarchies: Analysis and Antitrust Implications,* New
    York: Free Press.
_____ (1985), *The Economic Institutions of Capitalism,* New York: Free Press.
Yates, J. (1989), *Control Through Communication: The Rise of System in American Manage-
    ment,* Baltimore: Johns Hopkins University Press.
Yoshiro, M. Y. and U. S. Rangan (1995), *Strategic Alliances: An Entrepreneurial Approach to
    Globalization,* Boston: Harvard University Press.
Zuboff, S. (1988), *In the Age of the Smart Machine: The Future of Work and Power,* Oxford,
    UK: Oxford University Press.

4

The Role of Information Technology in the Transformation of Work

A Comparison of Postindustrial, Industrial, and Protoindustrial Organization

SUSAN J. WINTER

S. LYNNE TAYLOR

It has become commonplace in the literature on the workplace of the late twentieth century to describe the profound changes occurring as a third revolution and modern society as postindustrial (Bell 1989, Mills 1991). Four recent interrelated changes in the organization of work that seem to mark this third industrial revolution are (a) a flattening of the hierarchy; (b) the disaggregation of functions or outsourcing; (c) an increased use of flexible, dynamic networks or partnerships; and (d) decentralization of the location of work (Huey 1994, Malone and Rockart 1991, Miles and Snow 1986, *Monthly Labor Review* 1992, Nolan et al. 1988, Quinn 1992, Reich 1991, Rockart and Short 1991). This revolution is widely attributed to the increased importance of information in the economy and the attendant rise

This chapter appeared originally in *Information Systems Research, 7,* March 1996. This research was partially supported by grant from the Social Sciences and Humanities Research Council. An earlier version was presented at the National Academy of Management Meetings in 1996 in Vancouver.

in the use of electronics, computing, and telecommunications (Applegate 1994, *Business Week* 1993, Webber 1993). However, the new flattened, flexible, decentralized organization of work bears a striking resemblance to the protoindustrial system found in Europe before the rise of the modern centralized organization (Goodman and Honeyman 1988, Tilly 1981) and to the form of flexible specialization found during early industrialization, both of which were common well before the rise of the information-based economy, electronics, computers, and telecommunications. This similarity calls into question the claim that advances in information technology (IT) are primarily responsible for this form of organization. A comparison between the protoindustrial, industrial, and postindustrial social and economic systems can question existing causal explanations underlying the organization of work in Europe and North America throughout the past 500 years. This historical analysis allows us to incorporate long-term longitudinal data not usually considered in studies of modern IT and organizational structure, thus building on extant research on industrialization and providing a more complete picture of the causal relationship between the two constructs. Adopting a historical perspective also encourages looking beyond the current ideological preferences that characterize the identification of organizational problems and their appropriate solutions (Kieser 1994).

Few researchers in the field of information systems have investigated, at the macro level of analysis, the relationship between the increased use of electronics, computers, and telecommunications and the changes in the way work is organized. Though the structural changes made by several individual companies have been attributed to changes in technology (see, for example, Magnet 1992, Malone and Rockart 1991), few carefully controlled, rigorous, scientific studies have been presented to support these espoused causal relations, to rule out alternative explanations, and to illuminate contributing and inhibiting factors (though see Brynjolfsson et al. 1994, for one notable exception). Without such studies, it is difficult to determine the role of technology, even though managers and informants may state that they believe there is a relationship between IT and the changing organization of work. The perceived relationship may be just a widely held societal myth rather than reflecting the true relationship between IT and structure. Similar gaps between widely held IT myths and objective measures of the results of IT use have been found in previous research. For example, Kling and Iacono (1984) found little objective evidence of IT efficiency and effectiveness claims made by organizational informants and concluded that these claims could be considered ideologically influenced myths.

It is even more tenuous to claim that these same organizational-level causes are acting similarly at higher levels of analysis (e.g., the industry or economy level) causing IT to restructure the postindustrial economy. The relationship between IT and the organization of work is a topic that is important to IS researchers but does not lend itself to the research methods with which most are familiar. It is a topic that would not usually be investigated by economic historians (because it is a contemporary phenomenon) but can best be researched using methods with which they are familiar. This chapter represents a collaborative effort to address the questions: What are the causes of the changing organization of work? Is the shift to a flattened hierarchy, a disaggregation of functions, a decentralized work location, and the use of flexible dynamic networks or partnerships due primarily to the shift to a knowledge-based economy and the increased use of electronics, computers, and telecommunications?

The change to industrialization had a profound impact on organizations and their workers, and the change to postindustrialization will likely have equally profound implications. This chapter investigates this change and considers some possible causes for it using historical analysis. In order to determine the causes of the postindustrial organization of work, we compare it to the industrial organization of work and the protoindustrial system of artisanal and "putting out" manufacturing. We identify strong similarities between postindustrialization, which has been attributed to the use of information technology and an information-based economy; protoindustrialization, which was a goods-based manufacturing economy with little information technology; and certain forms of workplace organization during industrialization. These similarities cast doubt on the argument that the organization of work is solely and causally linked to the technology. We also review the literature on the role of technology in the organization of work in all three eras to outline the support (or lack thereof) for technological determinism in each of them. Alternative causes of organizational structures will be suggested and implications for future research questions and methods will be discussed.

This chapter is organized chronologically. First, we describe the popular version of modern history widely held by laypeople (nonhistorians) and its view of preindustrial society and of the rise of the current centralized industrial organizational form, its history, and the forces that led to its widespread adoption. We then present a critique of this view based on the historical literature and review the evidence regarding the causes of industrialization. Next, we describe the widely held view of the changes associated with the postindustrial organizational form with an emphasis on the role of information technology. Fourth, we present a critique of this view by drawing comparisons between the industrial and postindustrial organization of work in order to illuminate the role of technology in the organization of work and the relevance of other causal agents. Finally, we will discuss the implications of this analysis for future research.

TECHNOLOGICAL DETERMINISM

Technological determinism represents a belief that technological forces determine social and cultural changes. The following discussion of technological determinism and history is informed by Smith and Marx (1994). The causal role of technology has been widely accepted in Western culture, and the role of technology as an agent of change is common in the popular view of modern history where it is usually featured in simple, plausible narratives comparing an aspect of society before and after a technological innovation and inferring causation to the sudden appearance of the technical innovation. For example, Smith and Marx (1994) write,

> The printing press is depicted as a virtual cause of the Reformation. Before it was invented, few people . . . owned copies of the bible; after Gutenberg, however, many individual communicants were able to gain direct, personal access to the word of God, on which the Reformation thrived. (pp. x-xi)

The emphasis of these stories is always on the new machine and the changes it causes, not on the forces that led to the invention of this innovation. This deterministic view of technology is a common theme in the popular discourse on such diverse technologies as the automobile (which created suburbia), the birth control pill (which created the sexual revolution), and the computer (which is restructuring the economy and the workplace). This technologically deterministic view, here called the popular version of workplace organization, will be described below as it applies to industrialization, and, later in the chapter, as it applies to the postindustrial organization of work. For each of these eras, we will present evidence that the popular version is inadequate and argue that social, political, economic, and cultural forces powerfully shape both technological changes and the organization of work.

HISTORICAL PATTERNS OF
ORGANIZING THE WORKPLACE

The Popular Version of Industrialization

The popular version of industrialization commonly accepted among laypersons has it that, over the course of the nineteenth and twentieth centuries, there has been an evolution in the technological and social organization of the workplace from the simple artisanal shop toward large, centralized, bureaucratic places of production structured along the lines of the factory system. The very term "industrialization" is a contentious one, for it can mean many things, but for our purposes industrialization was the process that resulted in the mechanization of manufacturing and the concentration of labor. It has been argued that this process of industrialization was driven by advances in technology and mechanization (Hamerow 1983, Jones 1987, 1992, Landes 1969, Sussman 1973).

The extensive historical literature on the phenomenon of industrialization has branched in a number of ways, including debates concerning changes in the methods of production and the impact of those on the economy and society; the organization of the workplace; the nature and manner of management; the impact of industrialization on workers, both male and, more recently, female; its impact on management; the relationship between industrialization and/or mechanization and labor unrest and organization; and the impact of technology on the workplace, economy, and society. There is much that those interested in understanding the changes in the workplace today could learn from this sizeable body of work, if only to avoid the same pitfalls, as well as to help frame the questions posed of the late twentieth-century workplace.

The study of industrialization began as a study of the industrial revolution, a phrase first coined by Arnold Toynbee in 1884. It was considered, first and foremost, a technological revolution, the application of mechanical power to manufacturing, which revolutionized not only the process of production but also society and the economy as a consequence. It in many ways set the world on the path to modernity, and it began in Great Britain, which became the standard by which other nations' industrial revolutions were measured. This school of thought was masterfully expressed in David Landes' seminal work, *Unbound Prometheus* (1969). In it, he defined the industrial revolution as an interrelated succession of technological changes, with material advances in three areas: the substitution of mechanical devices for human skills; the use of inanimate power, especially steam, instead of human and animal strength; and a marked improvement in the obtaining and working of raw materials, especially in the metallurgical and chemical industries. With these changes came a new form of industrial organization, the factory system, followed by the creation of the middle and working classes and, eventually, the consumer culture and market economy of today. In the words of a nineteenth-century Scottish chemist and economist, Andrew Ure,

(T)he term "Factory," in technology, designates the combined operation of many orders of work-people, adult and young, in tending with assiduous skill a system that is, to substitute mechanical science for hand skill, and the partition of a process into its essential constituents, for the division or graduation of labor among artisans. On the handicraft plan, labor more or less skilled, was usually the most expensive element of production . . . but on the automatic plan, skilled labor gets

progressively superseded, and will, eventually, be replaced by mere overlookers
of machines. (as quoted in Hamerow 1983, pp. 3-4)

The factory system, then, was the predecessor to what Henry Ford introduced in the late nineteenth-century in the United States, continuous flow
production. Essentially, it was the mechanization of production that had
previously been done by hand. The efficiencies, economies of scale and
scope, and improved control over production that resulted from this new
form of organization meant that the traditional artisanal or handicraft form
of production was unable to compete. A classic example of this process, and
of the industrial revolution, is the textile mills of Britain. With the advent of
steam power, textile manufacturers radically rethought the way in which the
manufacture of cloth happened.

They built large textile mills, with huge looms and other machinery, all
powered by steam, in which they would employ hundreds, eventually thousands, of laborers. The locations of these mills were determined first and
foremost by the availability of either running water or coal, the fuels
necessary for the generation of steam power. For the employers, the new form
of workplace organization created tremendous opportunities for reaping
profits hitherto inconceivable. As a result, the traditional form of production
was gradually displaced by the factory system of production, and, by the
twentieth century, supplanted.

Statistical analysis indicated that, beginning in 1780, there was noticeable
improvement in British national production levels, which the statisticians
attributed to the advent of mechanization. Thus, boiled down to its essence,
this school of thought argued that the industrial revolution was technology-
driven, unidirectional (from artisanal to factory production), and a revolutionary event, with a distinct "take-off point." Furthermore, Great Britain,
being the first to industrialize, was the model that all others sought to imitate,
with greater and lesser degrees of success.

Thus, the early historical view of industrialization was that, because of
mechanization, over the course of the nineteenth and twentieth centuries
there was an evolution in the technological and social organization of the
workplace from the simple artisanal workshop toward large, centralized,
bureaucratic places of production providing a division of labor and structured along the lines of the mass-production factory system. Late in the
industrialization process, organizations began to integrate vertically by ac-
quiring their competitors and suppliers and by performing their own distribution (Perrow 1986), thus further increasing their size. They also began
aggressively marketing their products and developed their own sales forces
and research and development functions, which increased both their size and
the degree of differentiation in their structure as departments became more

specialized in their functions (Blau 1970, Blau and Schoenherr 1971, Chandler 1976, Child 1973). Necessarily, there was a dramatic rise in the number of supervisors and managers, often attributed to the application of Scientific Management and the division of labor along skill lines which involved the deskilling of production workers and the use of skilled supervisors and managers to plan and control the work (Edwards 1979, Goodman and Honeyman 1988). Management's control of production and the growth of nonproduction functions within the large firm (e.g., marketing, sales, distribution, personnel, and research and development) meant that nonproduction white-collar employment expanded considerably throughout the industrialization process, beginning in the late nineteenth century and continuing into the twentieth (Edwards 1979). These new, large, bureaucratic firms generally relied on centralized management through a hierarchy for coordination of tasks and extensive use of large, centralized workplaces. Though manufacturing was the first to adopt the centralized, industrial form, companies providing services were also generally organized along these lines.

In summary, the popular version of industrialization argues that there is a steady evolution in the structure of the workplace from that of the simple artisanal shop to the modern factory floor, from small firms to large, from simple to ponderous bureaucracies, structured along the lines of the factory system. It assumes that these organizational changes are the result of technological innovations, and that the new technology required these changes. There is also a sense, in this myth, of the inevitability of progress through industrialization and through factory production, as well as a dismissal of craft or artisanal production as inferior, inefficient, and preindustrial, a hopeless throwback to a bygone era (Edwards 1979, Piore and Sabel 1984). At first glance, this seemed self-evident. Prior to the late eighteenth century, when the industrial revolution began, the European economy was overwhelmingly agrarian in nature with only a small segment of the workforce employed in manufacturing. Mass production and assembly of interchangeable parts as we know it today did not exist. Manufacturing was largely custom and handicraft in nature, done by hand, by skilled artisans, rural and urban, using simple tools, working in small shops, either alone or with a few journeymen and apprentices training with them.

Challenges to the Popular Version

This interpretation has since been challenged on a number of fronts, including arguments that the British model was not the best, evidence that forces other than technology were crucial, and the realization that mechanization was not necessary or sufficient to cause the observed changes in the production process. Each of these challenges will now be discussed in detail.

First, it is now generally accepted by historians that British industrialization was not the only route to industrialization, nor was it a standard against which all others should be measured. Much work has been done investigating the different ways nations have industrialized; these nations emerged with very differently structured, but equally healthy and vibrant, economies as a result. Nations industrialized differently, not because they applied the British model more or less successfully, but because key factors specific to each nation shaped the industrialization process, making each path a unique one, specific to each country. These factors, the second challenge to the technological determinism of the popular view of industrialization, were the environment or context in which the nature of production was changing. They included a wide range of social, political, legal, economic, and cultural forces which either encouraged or constrained change in the workplace. A brief comparison of British and French industrialization may serve to demonstrate the nature of these forces.

Great Britain was the first nation to industrialize due to a favorable confluence of circumstances encouraging mass production and the development of a mass market (Kemp 1985). In Britain, the structure of feudal agrarian relations had broken down much earlier than on the continent, and in the process a class of landless wage-earners was created who were thrust into the cash economy by dint of circumstance. A large portion of the population depended for its material means of existence upon the production and sale of commodities or upon the sale of its labor power. As the standard of living slowly rose over the course of the nineteenth century, these workers became an important market for cheap, mass-produced goods such as cotton textiles. There was also a new emphasis on individual acquisition and on the rights of property. Wealth, not tradition, became the main determinant of social position, and the nature of acceptable wealth changed dramatically, from a landed wealth to include one more fluid, trade-based, and commerce-based. The guild system had disappeared as well, making it easier to pursue innovation, and removing an important barrier to the production of poorer quality, but much less expensive, mass-produced goods. Furthermore, the legal environs facilitated the efforts to engage in mass production and an extensive credit network existed to provide the necessary capital. In addition, the topography of Britain was advantageous, for it had allowed the establishment of a dense transportation and communications infrastructure in the country, which facilitated the movement of goods. Thus, British capitalist entrepreneurs operated in a hospitable environment, where their wealth was deemed socially acceptable.

France developed in a very different manner. It had many of the prerequisites considered necessary for industrialization to flourish, including wealth, a growing population, and a flourishing overseas trade. But certain factors

pushed French industrial development along a path different from that of
Britain. The wealth in France was concentrated in the hands of a very few.
The peasantry, who made up over half of the total population throughout the
nineteenth century, subsisted on small plots of land and functioned largely
outside the cash economy. Any demand for manufactured goods, therefore,
came from groups of nobles, as well as wealthy commoners and a few rich
peasants, all of whom comprised only a small portion of the population. The
remainder of the population primarily consisted of urban servants, artisans,
tradespeople, laborers, and vagrants. They led a hand-to-mouth existence
mostly within the cash economy (though bartering was common) and so did
not have the economic means required to purchase many manufactured
goods. A strong guild system enforced quality standards, preventing mass
production of "substandard" goods. Such a marketplace was not conducive
to the introduction of mass production. The result was an economy special-
izing in the production of a variety of high-quality goods in small shops using
easily reconfigured, labor-intensive (as opposed to capital-intensive), production processes (Sabel and Zeitlin 1985). Also, investment capital was less
available for such a shift, as most of the country's wealth was held in the
form of land, and landowners were loathe to invest in commerce. Finally, the
size of France and the lack of internal waterways on the scale of Britain's
made the creation of national markets difficult. Once the transportation
infrastructure was in place, in which railways played a key role, development
did proceed apace (Kemp 1985). Slowly, then, mass production began to
develop alongside artisanal variants of production. Yet agriculture continued
to dominate the French economy well into the twentieth century. Indeed, the
French industrial sector did not embrace mass production wholeheartedly
until after World War II, and then only with the assiduous encouragement
and assistance of the state, which led the way with the nationalization of
industrial firms such as Renault Motorworks, as well as utilities and major
banks.

So a variety of factors shaped industrialization in these two countries and
ensured that each would industrialize differently. The presence of a large,
landless, wage-earning population facilitated a shift to mass production in
Britain, and its absence in France acted as a brake because such a population
was needed to supply both a labor force and a mass market for mass-produced
goods. The distribution and nature of wealth in each country also shaped the
industrialization process. In Britain, much more wealth was available for
investment purposes, both because it was not sunk into land and because
those with capital were willing to invest in industrialization. The legal
environment and the transportation infrastructure also facilitated this kind of
venture and investment. The opposite was the case in France. Finally, in
Britain, one's social status was not as closely tied to landholding as it was in

France. Unlike in France, trade and commerce were considered respectable endeavors in Britain, and success was well received. This list of factors shaping the development of the two nations' economies is hardly comprehensive. Each of these points is the subject of extensive study and exhaustive debate; however, the overall point is clear. Though the technologies available were the same, the British and French experiences were very different, and they were different because of the confluence of a variety of social, political, economic, and cultural factors.

The third challenge to technological determinism has been the realization that mechanization did not always result in changes to the production process, nor were all changes to the production process the result of mechanization. In his seminal article on mid-Victorian England, Raphael Samuel (1977) convincingly demonstrates that, while mechanical power was extensively applied, it by no means reduced workers to the status of mere hands, nor did it replace human labor. Often, he argues, machinery's role in the production process was ancillary, not primary. In his article, he explores a vast array of different industries, ranging from coal mining to agriculture, food processing, baking, building, railway construction, glass and pottery industries, leather and wood trades, metallurgy, and ironmongering—all of which, while harnessing steam power where practicable, remained, by and large, labor-intensive and often the terrain of a skilled labor force. Ironically, the introduction of machinery often created a demand for new skills on the part of the labor force, as the machinery had to be managed, run, and maintained (Piore and Sabel 1984). Samuel suggests, then, that the organization of work was not greatly altered with the advent of mechanical power and machinery, but instead mechanical power and machinery were adapted to the workplace.

The converse has also proven true in some areas—organizational changes to the production process have occurred without the impetus of mechanization, and even well before the advent of mechanization. Recent research into protoindustrialization in Europe, however controversial the subject may be, has greatly expanded our understanding in this area (Berg et al. 1983, Houston and Snell 1984, Mendels 1972, Mendels and Deyon 1982, Mills 1982). Much of its focus has been on the putting-out system of industrial organization. Merchant-entrepreneurs purchased raw materials to sell to middlemen called factors. The factors, in turn, hired workers to transform the raw materials into a finished product and then sold the transformed product back to the merchant-entrepreneur. The workers were paid by the factor on a piece rate from the proceeds (Goodman and Honeyman 1988). Putting-out typically (but not exclusively) occurred in those rural areas where there was a large landless or land-poor rural population. Those agricultural workers who were unable to earn adequate wages in agriculture (and this was the vast majority of them, due to several reasons including poor wages and the seasonal nature of employment) were the ones available for supplementary employment by the merchant-entrepreneur. Rural industry became an important form of supplementary employment for large segments of rural populations. But protoindustrialization was more than just rural manufacture. It was nascent industrialization, with a complex and rigid division of labor, geared to the international, not local, market and developed in symbiosis with commercial agriculture, or so it was argued. Whether one agrees with the notion of protoindustrialization or not, the literature has brought to light not only the putting-out system but also premechanization innovations in subcontracting, the division of labor, international distribution, cooperative and shared ventures, marketing techniques, credit arrangements, and product innovation. The presence of these innovations, as seen during protoindustrialization, thus defies the assumption that such innovation came only with the advent of mass production processes and the concomitant changes to the structure of management, markets, and marketing (Berg 1993, 1994).

What also has become apparent as historians have explored the process of industrialization is that the stereotypical large mass-production factory was and is far from the only method of organizing work. Small craft-based firms have continued to exist and thrive beside large conglomerates well into the twentieth century (Edwards 1979). Initially, Piore (1980) and others developed the theory of industrial dualism in order to explain the persistence of small firms. This theory holds that a mass-production economy required the presence of a healthy custom or craft-based sector to manufacture the specialized machinery required for mass production of interchangeable parts and to service markets with high rates of fluctuation or low levels of demand. While mass production meant the manufacture of general goods through the use of specialized resources and capital equipment, at the same time that created a need for specialized machines and finely divided and trained labor to build them. Ironically, the special-purpose machinery required could not be mass produced, so on the very fringe of every industry there were small firms to service the large. Yet, the assumption that the backbone of the economy was mass production and the factory system remained intact.

Several historians (Sabel and Zeitlin 1985, Scranton 1991) have objected to this explanation and argued that it does not do justice to the most famous industrial districts of the nineteenth century (such as Lyon, St. Etienne, Solingen, Remscheld, Sheffield, Roubaix, Cincinnati, Philadelphia, and Pawtucket), which operated in a rather different fashion, and very successfully, at least until the world wars. These districts were hives of small firms that practiced an alternate form of industrial organization called "flexible specialization." It was a craft alternative to mass production that rejected a strategy of manufacturing large numbers of any one product and, instead, focused on creating the capacity to manufacture diverse products to fill fluctuating demand.

Those firms that practiced flexible specialization shared common characteristics. They produced a wide range of goods to suit the needs of highly differentiated regional markets at home and abroad, and they could alter the mix of goods to match changing markets and tastes and to take advantage of new opportunities as they arose. This required the flexible use of an increasingly more productive and widely applicable technology and an environment that encouraged permanent innovation. The technology had to be flexible in order to allow quick and inexpensive shifts from one product to another within a family of products, and permit the constant expansion of the range of materials worked and operations performed, facilitating the shift from one family of products to another. These firms banded together in various forms of cooperatives, dependent on the particular characteristics of the regional society, economy, and political structure. The purpose of doing so was threefold: to stabilize the region's industry to the benefit of all; to prevent disastrous competition and, instead, promote judicious cooperation; and to facilitate the promotion of innovation, which would have been much more difficult, if not impossible, for a small shop to do on its own (Best 1990, Piorc and Sabel 1984, Scranton 1991).

Others, notably Maxine Berg (1994), have objected to the stark distinction drawn between small and large firms, and concomitantly, the traditional and modern industrial sectors, even by Piore and Sabel (1984). Berg's concern (similar to that of Williams et al. 1987) is that many manufacturers borrowed techniques from both of these sectors, thus really straddling the divide and rendering it methodologically problematic. Whichever side of the debate one chooses, it is apparent that the nineteenth and twentieth centuries witnessed anything but a unidirectional shift from artisanal to factory production due to advances in technology.

A further implication of protoindustrialization was that the industrial revolution was not a revolution at all. If industrialization had its roots in the cottage manufacturing of the seventeenth century, and if the advent of mechanization and, especially, steam power was not responsible for its "kick-start," then the changes to the structure of the European economy had been a long time in happening and the revolution was not so revolutionary or abrupt after all. This debate was heightened by Crafts (1976) and Wrigley and Schofield (1981), among others, when they reworked the statistical information used by Deane and Cole (1962) to show that there was a marked "kink in the curve" of national production after mechanization. Their conclusion was that overall growth was slower than had been thought and that the story was one of continuity and stability, not dramatic upheaval (Berg

1994, Landes 1991). So the debate continues between those who argue that the numbers deny that anything revolutionary occurred and those, like Landes (1991) and Berg (1994), who argue that, whether the numbers reveal it or not, "there was a break (which) was indeed revolutionary in its import. It consisted in new ways of doing things, supported by new ways of thinking about the problems and tasks of production" (Landes 1991, p. 13)

One conclusion that may be drawn from this brief survey of a complex body of literature is this: If we wish to understand the changes in the workplace of yesteryear or the changes in today's workplace, we must consider not only the impact of technology. We must also consider the roots and enablers of the changes, those social, political, legal, economic, and cultural factors that help to explain why things have changed as they have in the past and are changing in the manner in which they are changing today.

The Emerging Popular Interpretation of Postindustrialization

Because the causal role of technology has been widely accepted in Western popular culture (Smith and Marx 1994), it is not surprising to find that computers are often identified as powerful agents of social and economic change ushering in the new "postindustrial" form of organization (Bell 1989, Bolter 1984, *Business Week* 1993, Davidow and Malone 1992, *Monthly Labor Review* 1992, Sussman 1973). This new story is similar to the industrialization myth in that it emphasizes technology as the causal agent and considers the new flexible, dynamic form of organization the next step in a natural and ever-improving evolution in the organization of work and one that mirrors the evolution of technology and is partly caused by it.

Indeed, many authors, when arguing for a deterministic model of social and cultural change, explicitly draw an analogy between information technology and the causal nature of previous technological innovations. For example, Bolter (1984) claims that IT is a defining technology of our time because it changes our relationship to nature just as the clock and the steam engine were defining technologies in their time. His technologically determinist view of both current and historical changes is clearly shown by his statements that "once the new technology (the clock) was called forth, it proceeded with its own relentless logic and eventually helped to reorder the values of the whole culture" (Bolter 1984, p. 100) and that "the computer is the contemporary analog of the clocks and steam engines of the previous six centuries . . . we will be different people because we live with [computers]" (Bolter 1984, p. 10).

Though the causal agents and mechanisms of change are still debatable, overall the description of the new postindustrial organization of work pre-

sented in the media is fairly consistent. While the early and mid-twentieth
century appeared to be marked by considerable growth in the size of firms
and by the gradual integration and aggregation of business functions, the late
twentieth century seems marked by a trend in the opposite direction. Recently, the large proportion of nonproduction (mostly white-collar, middle-
management, or professional) workers have come to be seen as a drain on
competitiveness in both Western and Japanese companies (*The Economist*
1995d, Thurow 1986, Tomasko 1987). (However, see *The Economist* 1995a
for the opposing view arguing that companies that have dismissed many
middle managers are now coming to realize the value of the knowledge and
perspective they have lost.) Many top management teams have been trying
to create organizations that are leaner, meaner, and more flexible in order to
meet the challenges of rapidly changing technologies and the vagaries of an
apparently more dynamic economy (Best 1990, Labib and Appelbaum 1994).

Thus, in many firms, the traditional organizational structure is now
changing in ways that have purportedly been caused by new advances in
computerized information systems and new information technologies, which
have reduced the demand for labor and lowered the costs of managing
information. As stated in the *Monthly Labor Review* (1992),

> Vital to the new economy are flexible and information-based technologies, the
> most important being the computer. Such technologies permit higher productivity
> and quality and the tailoring of products and services to smaller markets and even
> to individual customers. (p. 44)

Many who study information technology believe that improved telecommunications has reduced the advantages of intrafirm management and performance of professional staff activities (e.g., MIS, personnel, marketing,
and research) and reduced the need for middle managers as conduits for
information (Gurbaxani and Whang 1991, Malone and Rockart 1991, Miles
and Snow 1986, Reddy 1990, Rockart and Short 1989). The advantages of
the large firm, which were seen as rooted in the low costs of intrafirm
communications, are seen as eroded by the rapid decline in the costs of
interfirm communication (Malone et al. 1987, Miles and Snow 1986, Mills
1991, Nilles et al. 1976, Olson 1983, Reddy 1990). According to this school
of thought, because of advances in information technology and the move to
an information-based economy, it is no longer necessary to perform all
aspects of the production, commerce, and distribution processes in-house or
to locate them all in one geographic place (Brynjolfsson et al. 1994). Malone
and Rockart (1991) explicitly reported that, based on their research on the
effect of IT on the cost of information, "information technology should lead

to an overall shift from internal decisions within firms to the use of markets to coordinate economic activity" (p. 131).

Thus, firms in some industries have come to rely on external sources for a larger number of components and for administrative and support services, which often results in the disaggregation or "spinning off" of portions of these activities to other organizations. Some of the production functions and many of the staff functions performed by professionals in large organizations are now being contracted out to smaller, more specialized firms. Increasingly, organizations are dispersing geographically and disaggregating; entire administrative functions and production of components that were previously performed in-house are now contracted out or performed by temporary workers on a contract basis. Now, it is argued, organizations should limit their own operations to a few core areas of competence and engage in partnerships with other firms that have different areas of competence in order to produce a product or provide a service. The new structure has been called the dynamic network organizational form and has been associated with the widespread downsizing of organizations and the firing of many nonproduction, white-collar workers (Best 1990, Malone and Rockart 1991, Miles and Snow 1986, Piore and Sabel 1984, Reddy 1990, Rockart and Short 1989).

Concurrently, much of the work control function formerly performed by supervisors and middle managers is now seen as superfluous—increasingly, these activities are seen as embedded in the ubiquitous computer hardware and software. As Jackson and Humble (1994) write, "Information technology, [sic] is increasingly making information easier to access and share, replacing the middle manager's traditional role as a key link in the communication chain" (p. 16). The number of managerial employees in large firms is shrinking, and scholars have associated this with the use of information technology. Downsizing has become widespread over the last 5 years (Cameron et al. 1991, Freeman and Cameron 1993, Labib and Appelbaum 1994) and has become an accepted, almost routine way of managing; many believe it will remain common during the foreseeable future.

Simultaneously, growth in the geographic dispersion of work, in self-employment, in the business services sector generally, and in the temporary worker industry in particular, has been very rapid (Carey and Hazelbaker 1986, Howe 1986, Pearson 1986). It is difficult to get accurate data on the size of the "contingent" workforce, including part-timers, freelancers, subcontractors, independent professionals, and temporary workers. However, in his widely read book, *The Age of Unreason,* Charles Handy (1989) stated that "less than half of the workforce in the industrial world will be in 'proper' full-time jobs in organizations by the beginning of the twenty-first century" (p. 31) and one recent estimate is that the contingent workforce has already exceeded 28% of U.S. workers (Greenbaum 1994). Many of the workers who have been fired have started their own small businesses or consulting firms competing for contracts in the marketplace. Others have filled a series of temporary positions either through temporary agencies or independently. Concurrently, we have seen a rise in home-based work and telecommuting through the use of information technology. Martino and Wirth (1990) explicitly attribute this growth to the lower cost of information technology. They state that "technological innovation is a leading factor in the development of telework" (p. 534). Future growth of employment in large organizations may well be nonexistent. A large and growing sector of the workforce that would previously have entered a stable long-term employment relationship with a large, hierarchical organization will, instead, likely engage in a series of temporary contractual arrangements to provide a service or product for a limited period of time, much as workers did before the industrial revolution.

It appears, then, that we may be in the midst of yet another industrial revolution or at another "industrial divide" (Piore and Sabel 1984), precipitated by the use of the computer and the shift to a knowledge-based economy and with profound changes being made to the workplace and concomitant changes to society as a whole. IT seems to be restructuring the economy into a more flexible, dynamic, network of organizations with many smaller, leaner, firms narrowly focused on their areas of competence and engaged in temporary partnerships with other firms in order to produce a product or provide a service in response to fluctuating demand. Interestingly, this scenario shares many characteristics of the flexible specialization form of industrial organization found in some manufacturing districts of the nineteenth century and currently seen in such areas as the textile district of Prato and the computer industry in the Silicon Valley of California (Sabel and Zeitlin 1985, Scranton 1991). Some authors (Best 1990, Piore and Sabel 1984) have argued that IT has forced more firms to adopt this form of industrial organization, and so the social, cultural, and economic conditions that arose to support these districts in the past must be established today to support flexible specialization, prevent disastrous competition, and promote innovation.

Challenges to This Popular Version

While the changes currently being made in the organization of work are profound, management researchers are not generally investigating their causes in a comprehensive and systematic fashion. Consequently, an oversimplified and often misleading story is being told about the causes of the shift to the postindustrial form of organization. This new myth is similar to the industrialization myth in that it emphasizes technology as the causal agent and considers the flexible, dynamic form of organization natural and ever-improving evolution in the organization of work, one that mirrors the evolution of technology and is primarily caused by it. However, as we have shown in our historical analysis, this flexible form is not new. It was historically common in many industries, in the forms of flexible specialization and the putting-out system of manufacturing, and has persisted into contemporary times in some (Best 1990, Piore and Sabel 1984, Sabel and Zeitlin 1985, Williams et al. 1987).

Similarly, the myth of technological determinism has been exploded for industrialization (Smith and Marx 1994), and there is no proof of its truth for postindustrialization. Though advances in IT may be affecting the organization of work, other factors may be equally important in explaining the shift away from the typical industrial form (Best 1990, Scranton 1991). Without careful and detailed research, causation is impossible to determine. Several theories have been suggested to explain the changes observed, but none has adequately addressed the questions: Why have these particular changes occurred? Why have these changes occurred now and not earlier or later? Without theories that are sufficiently well developed to address these issues, testable hypotheses cannot be derived, and so the theories are no more useful than tautologies. Several of the causal agents widely accepted in the literature are described below with a critique of the evidence for their relationship to IT and to the organization of work. These agents include flexibility in the location of work, disintegration of the mass market, compression of time and space, the increasing pace of change, and increasing levels of risk, increased flexibility, and global competition.

It has been suggested that the availability of IT has now rendered the location of work more flexible and this has caused the decentralization of work (using satellite offices or working from home) (Martino and Wirth 1990). The popular view of the industrial revolution posits that the location of work became centralized primarily because the new technology required access to a centralized power source (e.g., water power and the steam engine). However, electricity has provided an opportunity for decentralization of the power supply and, therefore, decentralization of the place of work since the early 1890s, but has not appreciably affected the geographic dispersion of workers. No explanation is provided in the literature for why IT has countered this long-standing tradition of a centralized workplace, but electricity did not. Therefore, there is no consistent evidence of the technology as the main driving force for decentralization. There may be other factors associated with IT that were not associated with electricity (such as the ability to closely supervise workers), but these must be illuminated by theory before they can be tested.

Similarly, another reason cited for the change to a flexible work organization is the decline of the mass market and the demand for customized products (Piore and Sabel 1984). One of the critical limits to mass production is the development of a mass market for consumption of standard products (Sabel and Zeitlin 1985, Scranton 1991). However, during industrialization, the mass market was specifically created by mass producers, often through advertising and marketing (Sabel and Zeitlin 1985, Sussman 1973). The literature on IT and the organization of work has not shown that the mass market is substantially disintegrating, explained why it is breaking down now, or explained why producers cannot develop additional mass markets (particularly with the increasingly global marketplace) in Eastern Europe, Africa, and the Far East (Williams et al. 1987). Without evidence of a disintegration of the market and an explanation of why manufacturers were once able to create a mass market to support industrialization, but are no longer able to do so, this claim becomes a tautology, not a testable theory.

Another reason cited for the change to a flexible work organization is the capability of IT to compress time and space. However, IT has been doing so for the past 150 years, in the form of the telegraph and the telephone (Yates and Benjamin 1991). So why are we seeing the change in organizational forms now? Perhaps we have crossed a crucial cost threshold. Only carefully performed studies will be able to answer this question and illuminate where this threshold lies.

The increased pace of change and the increased level of risk experienced by owners of businesses have also been cited as causes of the change to a flexible work organization. However, there has been no objective, quantitative, empirical, economic evidence presented of changes in environmental turbulence over the past 30 years (the period of postindustrialization) (Holbein 1993). Furthermore, there is considerable evidence that perceptions of environmental dynamism (on which changes in organizational structure are based) are not generally related to objective measures of turbulence (Boyd et al. 1993, Holbein 1993, Milliken 1987). Finally, historical analysis shows other economically risky periods (including wars, depressions, and massive unemployment) that did not result in an appreciable increase in the flexible organization form.

Two additional reasons cited for the change are that the technology has become more flexible (i.e., computer-aided design and computer-integrated manufacturing) and multifunctional, and that the marketplace has become increasingly global; therefore, the level of competition has increased (Piore and Sabel 1984). However, Williams and his colleagues (1987) strongly argued that potential flexibility is quite different from flexibility in use and that most "flexible manufacturing systems" in the United States are not used very flexibly and that, indeed, most advanced computer capabilities are not used. Furthermore, they argue that computerized manufacturing technology (with its high capital expense and development costs) does not fundamentally change the scale economies of manufacturers and so does not generally disadvantage mass producers relative to batch producers. Firms selling to a larger market would still be at an advantage because they could spread their fixed costs over more customers (*The Economist* 1995c, Williams et al. 1987). Furthermore, historical evidence has not been presented showing a sharp increase in the level of competition experienced by firms and industries in which changes in the organization of work are occurring. There is, however, some evidence that globalization provides some additional distinct advantages to multinational firms (i.e., global reach, decreasing risk, knowledge management, and economies of time) over smaller firms (*The Economist* 1995c) by opening even larger mass markets. Globalization has been associated with increases in average firm size when other variables were controlled (Brynjolfsson et al. 1994).

Interestingly, these two characteristics (flexibility and globalization) were shared with the artisanal and putting-out manufacturing systems of protoindustrialization and with flexible specialization. The simple hand tools and machine tools used in such systems were more multifunctional, requiring more skill on the part of the worker. In the period of protoindustrialization, strong trading ties existed among the western European nations and among the colonial powers and their colonies, and many of the manufactured goods (particularly those involved in manufacturing cloth) were traded throughout Europe, Asia, and the Americas. Perhaps the change in the organization of work is due more to the potential flexibility of the technology, to the renewed globalization of trade, or to the combination of flexibility and globalization than to the presence of IT, per se. However, so far, there has been insufficient research into this area to draw firm conclusions. Furthermore, what evidence has accumulated casts doubt on the adequacy of these explanations alone (Brynjolfsson et al. 1994, Williams et al. 1987). Future research is needed to understand the roles of flexibility and globalization in the organization of work. In summary, there is insufficient evidence to support the conclusion that IT has caused widespread changes in the organization of work due to its flexibility, compression of time and space, the disintegration of the mass market, or increasing levels of risk or global competition.

Of course, not all researchers investigating the changing nature of work have taken a hard-line technologically determinist position; some have taken more social constructionist positions (Best 1990, Lloyd-Jones and Lewis 1994, Piore and Sabel 1984, Scranton 1991). Social constructionists believe that social and cultural forces give different social meanings to artifacts, and so strongly affect technological changes. These groups are seen to influence the selection of those designs that solve the problems of powerful interest groups and that fill their needs (Hughes 1994). An in-depth treatment of the various arguments surrounding technological determinism versus social construction is not possible here (interested readers may want to investigate Smith and Marx 1994). However, the social construction literature on industrialization and on postindustrialization can illuminate likely nontechnical agents affecting the current changes in the organization of work. The importance of these factors is argued below and a suggestive list of likely agents is reviewed as the first step in developing a theory about the relationship between IT and the organization of work.

The first step in building a more complete and accurate model of the forces affecting the changing organization of work is to determine which types of organizations are changing and which are not. Currently, it is not clear which sectors of the economy in various countries are organized in the industrial form, which have been organized in the flexible form, and how the mix of organizational forms has changed historically. Though some evidence is available regarding the factors associated with changes in the organization of work for specific industries in specific geographic areas, during specific periods of time (see, for example, Lloyd-Jones and Lewis 1994, Scranton 1991), much more work will be needed to illuminate the interaction between technology, society, and the organization of work. Future research should focus on additional detailed descriptions of the mix of structures for various industries and markets, both now and in the past, in order to further develop the search for correlates that may be causally linked to the structure of work. Without such careful, descriptive work, it is too easy to be influenced by a few rare and recent, but memorable, examples of flexible organizations and overestimate the extent of the changes taking place.

Likely conditions affecting the shift to smaller organizations, outsourcing, and downsizing seen in postindustrialization are new configurations of the social, political, and economic factors that affected industrialization. Though this does not represent an exhaustive list, some likely inhibiting or encouraging factors include the following: changing cultural norms, macroeconomic forces, demographics and labor relations, and legal conditions. Each of these will be briefly discussed below.

One possibility is that the societal norms about how efficient and productive organizations should be structured have changed over the past 30 years. In explaining the recent interest in entrepreneurship, Bruce Kirchhoff (1994) suggests that after exposure to the Depression and World War II, American society came to respect and admire large corporations and the public sector because of their demonstrated ability to meet these national challenges, and to see them as the preferred source of employment, as the primary source of wealth creation, and as the best means of wealth distribution. However, this respect and admiration has been greatly eroded recently and replaced by a view of large corporations and government as wasteful and inefficient.

According to the theory of institutionalization, organizations whose structures respond to the pressures of institutions in their environment (regardless of their operational advantages) and, therefore, reflect the norms of society, gain legitimacy and the resources they require for survival. Thus, they are more likely to prosper (DiMaggio and Powell 1983, King et al. 1994, Meyer and Rowan 1977). Consequently, organizations within an institutional environment will become similar to each other. Institutionalization is most likely to be seen in situations where criteria for organizational performance and the best means to achieve these are unclear, companies are highly regulated, and interorganizational relationships are common (DiMaggio and Powell 1983). There is some evidence of the propagation of the factory form of manufacturing throughout the economy due to institutionalization, particularly just after World War I. Some national governments (powerful institutions) actively encouraged the conversion to mass production after World War II (Sabel and Zeitlin 1985) as a form of "modernization." It is equally likely that organizations of today would be strongly influenced by their culture's norms regarding appropriate structure and levels of efficiency.

Previous researchers illuminated the impact of macroeconomic forces on the organization of work in much more detail than can be covered here. However, we will briefly touch on a couple of fundamental issues. One is the use or abandonment of the gold standard with the shift to floating exchange rates (Lloyd-Jones and Lewis 1994, Piore and Sabel 1984), and the relative strength and volatility of various currencies as a determinant of the cost and location of production (*The Economist* 1995d). Another is the rate of inflation, the pursuit of deflationary or inflationary monetary policies, stability and levels of interest rates, the availability of capital for investment and expansion, and the ability to move capital internationally (Best 1990, *The Economist* 1995b, Scranton 1991). All these forces affect a firm's strategy and tactics as it pursues profits and are likely to influence choices about the organization of work through their effects on the costs and availability of capital, labor, and other resources. Many of these effects are simple and immediate, but some may require a specific configuration of influences or may take years to develop.

A related issue is the amount and type of legal regulations and their enforcement. These can include tariff protection and agreements, free-trade treaties, antitrust laws, product and owner liability laws, international commerce and contract law, labor laws, and taxation rates. Japan's relatively closed markets are often cited as a major cause of Japanese companies' economic success (Best 1990). In rejecting the computer as a cause of the current economic restructuring, public policy professor David Howell (1995) suggests that legal restrictions may be a more powerful influence. He explains that in the United States, institutions designed to protect low-skilled workers from wage competition have recently been dismantled, labor-law monitoring has declined, and the real value of the minimum wage has diminished. This change in the legal environment, not IT, has led United States firms to attempt to gain competitive advantage by reducing labor costs through increased use of temporary, part-time, contract, and off-site workers in the United States and abroad. Indeed, lax standards for labor and environmental protection and reduced owner liability are often cited as powerful forces drawing many organizations to move their facilities out of the industrialized countries altogether.

Other issues likely to affect the changing organization of work include demographics and labor relations. Some researchers see computer technology and the new organization of work as an opportunity to reduce the power of labor by replacing it with capital, or fragmenting workers into various categories with divergent interests (i.e., full-time versus part-time, contractual versus permanent, and home-based versus office-based) (Greenbaum 1994). Increases in the unemployment rate certainly improve the bargaining position of employers relative to employees. The current shift in the United States and Canada to an older population may result in a demand for more services and fewer new durable goods, thus shrinking the mass market for these goods.

In summary, IT has been widely accepted as the driving force behind the changing organization of work, which, in turn, has been credited with increasing efficiency, effectiveness, and quality while providing faster time to market, lower overhead costs, increased customization, and, therefore, improved competitiveness (see, for example, Magnet 1992, Malone and Rockart 1991). However, empirical evidence of these benefits has been inconsistent at best (*Business Week* 1993, *The Economist* 1995a) and often nonexistent (Cascio 1993, Labib and Appelbaum 1994). A flattened hierarchy, disaggregation of functions, decentralization of work location, and increased use of partnerships are expected to lead to a renewed reliance on temporary subcontracting and self-employment. Interestingly, this "new" organizational structure of the workplace is strikingly similar to past models, such as protoindustrialization and flexible specialization (Mendels 1972, Mendels and Deyon 1982, Sabel and Zeitlin 1985), which arose without the presence of information technology. The current literature on causes of these recent changes in the organization of work has proven inadequate to account for the shift away from industrialization. To illuminate what is happening to the world of work and to explain why it is happening, we need to concentrate on three areas: (a) producing better, more detailed, descriptive research on the changes occurring; (b) developing clearer, more complete, and less simplistic theories of the causes of the changes from which testable hypotheses can be developed; and (c) performing systematic theory-testing research to illuminate the causes of the organization of work during modern times, recent history, and preindustrial history.

CONCLUSIONS

The similarities between the "new" organizational structure being touted today as industry's salvation and other, older models such as the putting-out system, artisanal production, and flexible specialization are striking. They also warn us against quickly assuming that the new organizational structure is simply the result of recent changes in technology. Instead, we need to consider the possibility of social, economic, political, and cultural causes of this organizational change, while clarifying the role of technology.

It is possible that the similarities between the protoindustrial and postindustrial eras are due to common goals. In each case, the central decision makers sought and seek to reduce their risk, as well as to obtain more flexibility. Such flexibility would, and did, permit a firm to respond more quickly to changing technologies and markets, while minimizing the cost to the firm of adapting to those changing technologies. The flexibility also permits a firm to protect itself from the vagaries of an increasingly unstable economy. Another possibility is that the organizational changes, past and present, came as the result of social movements, macroeconomics, and forces of institutionalization, rather than technology. Though there is considerable evidence of social and economic influence in determining the trajectory of industrialization (Goodman and Honeyman 1988, Jones 1987, 1992, Piore and Sabel 1984, Sabel and Zeitlin 1985, Scranton 1991), little research on postindustrialization has focused on social and economic influences and how they are affecting this transformation of work. It is also likely that institutions are affecting the decisions made by managers to make the changes associated with this new form of organization.

It seems that if the challenge is to try to understand the nature of the changes rocking the workplace today, and, second, to understand and manage the possible consequences of those changes, the historical literature could be useful in helping us identify the questions that need to be asked. It gives us a useful place to start, by identifying factors that shaped the workplace in the past and which may be shaping it today.

REFERENCES

Applegate, L., "Managing in an Information Age: Transforming the Organization for the 1990s," in *Transforming Organizations With Information Technology,* S. Smithson, R. Baskerville, O. Ngwenyama, and J. DeGross (Eds.), Elsevier/North-Holland, Amsterdam, 1994, pp. 15-95.

Bell, D., "The Third Technological Revolution and Its Possible Socioeconomic Consequences," *Dissent,* Spring (1989), 165-176.

Berg, M., "Small Producer Capitalism in Eighteenth-Century England," *Business History,* 35, 1 (1993), 17-39.

_____, *The Age of Manufactures 1700-1820: Industry, Innovation and Work in Britain,* 2nd ed., Routledge, New York, 1994.

_____, P. Hudson, and M. Sonenscher (Eds.), *Manufacture in Town and Country Before the Factory,* Cambridge University Press, Cambridge, UK, 1983.

Best, M. H., *The New Competition: Institutions of Industrial Restructuring,* Polity Press, Cambridge, UK, 1990.

Blau, P. M., "A Formal Theory of Differentiation in Organizations," *American Sociological Review,* 35 (1970), 201-218.

_____ and R. A. Schoenherr, *The Structure of Organizations,* Basic Books, New York, 1971.

Bolter, J. D., *Turing's Man: Western Culture in the Computer Age,* University of North Carolina Press, Chapel Hill, 1984.

Boyd, B. K., G. G. Dess, and A. M. A. Rasheed, "Divergence Between Archival and Perceptual Measures of the Environment: Causes and Consequences," *Academy of Management Review,* 18, 3 (1993), 204-226.

Brynjolfsson, E., T. W. Malone, V. Gurbaxani, and A. Kambil, "Does Information Technology Lead to Smaller Firms?" *Management Science,* 40, 12 (1994), 1628-1644.

Business Week, "The Virtual Corporation: The Company of the Future Will Be the Ultimate in Adaptability," February 8, 1993, 98-103.

Cameron, K., S. J. Freeman, and A. K. Mishra, "Best Practices in White-Collar Downsizing: Managing Contradictions," *Academy of Management Executive,* 5, 3 (1991), 57-73.

Carey, M. L. and K. L. Hazelbaker, "Employment Growth in the Temporary Help Industry," *Monthly Labor Review,* 109, 4 (1986), 37-44.

Cascio, W. F., "Downsizing: What Do We Know? What Have We Learned?" *Academy of Management Executive,* 7, 1 (1993), 95-104.

Chandler, A. D., Jr., *The Visible Hand,* Harvard University Press, Cambridge, MA, 1976.

Child, J., "Predicting and Understanding Organization Structure," *Administrative Science Quarterly,* 18 (1973), 168-185.

Crafts, N. F. R., "English Economic Growth in the Eighteenth Century: A Re-examination of Deane and Cole's Estimates," *Economic History Review,* 29 (1976), 226-235.

Davidow, W. H. and M. S. Malone, *The Virtual Corporation,* HarperCollins, New York, 1992.

Deane, P. and W. A. Cole, *British Economic Growth, 1688-1959: Trends and Structure,* Cambridge University Press, London, 1962.

DiMaggio, P. J. and W. W. Powell, "The Iron Cage Revisited: Institutional Isomorphism and Collective Rationality in Organizational Fields," *American Sociological Review,* 48, April (1983), 147-160.

The Economist, "The Salaryman Rides Again," February 4, 1995a, 64-66.

The Economist, "The Puzzling Infirmity of America's Small Firms," February 18, 1995b, 63-65.

The Economist, "Alive and Kicking: The Death of the Multinational Has Been Much Exaggerated," U.S. edition, June 24, 1995c, S20-S25.

The Economist, "Japan Looks West: Time for a Little Corporate Role Reversal," U.S. edition, June 24, 1995d, S16-S19.

Edwards, R., *Contested Terrain: The Transformation of the Workplace in the Twentieth Century,* Basic Books, New York, 1979.

Freeman, S. J. and K. S. Cameron, "Organizational Downsizing: A Convergence and Reorientation Framework," *Organization Science,* 4, 1 (1993), 10-29.

Goodman, J. and K. Honeyman, *Gainful Pursuits: The Making of Industrial Europe 1600-1914,* Edward Arnold, London, 1988.

Greenbaum, J., "The Forest and the Trees: Defining Labor Skills," *Monthly Review,* 46, 6 (1994), 60-66.

Gurbaxani, V. and S. Whang, "The Impact of Information Systems on Organizations and Markets," *Communications of the ACM,* 34 (1991), 59-73.

Hamerow, T. S., *The Birth of a New Europe: State and Society in the Nineteenth Century,* University of North Carolina Press, Chapel Hill, 1983.

Handy, C., *The Age of Unreason,* Harvard Business School Press, Boston, 1989.

Holbein, G. F., "A Longitudinal Assessment of Environmental Dynamism," presented at the National Academy of Management Meeting, Atlanta, GA, 1993.

Houston, R. and K. Snell, "Proto-Industrialisation? Cottage Industry, Social Change and the Industrial Revolution," *Historical Journal,* 27, 2 (1984), 473-492.

Howe, W. J., "The Business Services Industry Sets Pace in Employment Growth," *Monthly Labor Review,* 109, 4 (1986), 29-36.

Howell, D. R., "Collapsing Wages and Rising Inequality: Has Computerization Shifted the Demand for Skills?" *Challenge,* 38 (1995), 27-35.

Huey, J., "The New Post-Heroic Leadership," *Fortune,* February 21, 1994, 42-50.

Hughes, T. P., "Technological Momentum," in *Does Technology Drive History? The Dilemnia of Technological Determinism,* M. R. Smith and L. Marx (Eds.), MIT Press, Cambridge, 1994, pp. 101-113.

Jackson, D. and J. Humble, "Middle Managers: New Purpose, New Directions," *Journal of Management Development,* 13, 3 (1994), 15-21.

Jones, S. R. H., "Technology, Transaction Costs and the Transition to Factory Production in the British Silk Industry, 1700-1870," *Journal of Economic History,* 17 (1987), 71-96.

_____, "The Emergence of the Factory System in 18th Century England: Did Transportation Improvements Really Matter?" *Journal of Economic Behavior and Organizations,* 19 (1992), 389-394.

Kemp, T., *Industrialization in Nineteenth-Century Europe,* 2nd ed., Longman, New York, 1985.

Kieser, A., "Crossroads. Why Organization Theory Needs Historical Analyses—and How This Should Be Performed," *Organization Science,* 5, 4 (1994), 608-620.

King, J. L., V. Gurbaxani, K. L. Kraemer, F. W. McFarlan, K. S. Raman, and C. S. Yap, "Institutional Factors in Information Technology Innovation," *Information Systems Research,* 5, 2 (1994), 139-169.

Kirchhoff, B. A., "Entrepreneurship Economics," in *The Portable MBA in Entrepreneurship,* W. D. Bygrave (Ed.), John Wiley, New York, 1994, pp. 410-439.

Kling, R. and S. Iacono, "The Control of Information Systems Developments After Implementation," *Communications of the ACM,* 27 (1984), 1218-1226.

Labib, N. and S. H. Applebaum, "The Impact of Downsizing Practices on Corporate Success," *Journal of Management Development,* 13, 7 (1994), 59-84.

Landes, D., *The Unbound Prometheus: Technological Change and Industrial Development in Western Europe From 1750 to the Present,* Cambridge University Press, Cambridge, UK, 1969, pp. 1-29.

_____, "Introduction," in *Favorites of Fortune: Technology, Growth, and Economic Development Since the Industrial Revolution,* P. Higgonet, D. Landes, and H. Rosovsky (Eds.), Harvard University Press, Cambridge, MA, 1991, pp. 1-29.

Lloyd-Jones, R. and M. J. Lewis, "Personal Capitalism and British Industrial Decline: The Personally Managed Firm and Business Strategy in Sheffield, 1880-1920," *Business History Review,* 68 (Autumn 1994), 364-411.

Magnet, M., "Who's Winning the Information Revolution?" *Fortune,* November 30, 1992, 110-117.

Malone, T. W. and J. F. Rockart, "Computers, Networks, and the Corporation," *Scientific American,* 265, 3 (September, 1991), 128-136.

_____, J. Yates, and R. I. Benjamin, "Electronic Markets and Electronic Hierarchies: Effects of New Information Technologies on Market Structures and Corporate Strategies," *Communications of the ACM,* 30 (June 1987), 484-497.

Martino, V. D. and L. Wirth, "Telework: A New Way of Working and Living," *International Labor Review,* 129, 5 (1990), 529-554.

Mendels, F., "Proto-Industrialization: The First Phase of the Process of Industrialization," *Journal of Economic History,* 12 (1972), 241-261.

_____ and P. Deyon, "Proto-Industrialization: Theory and Reality," Eighth International Congress of Economic History, Section A-2: Proto-Industrialization, Budapest, Hungary, 1982.

Meyer, J. W. and B. Rowan, "Institutionalized Organizations: Formal Structure as Myth and Ceremony," *American Journal of Sociology,* 83 (September 1977), 340-363.

Miles, R. E. and C. C. Snow, "Organizations: New Concepts for New Forms," *California Management Review,* 28, 3 (1986), 62-73.

Milliken, F. J., "Three Types of Perceived Uncertainty About the Environment: State, Effect, and Response Uncertainty," *Academy of Management Review,* 12 (1987), 133-143.

Mills, D. Q., *Rebirth of the Corporation,* John Wiley, New York, 1991.

Mills, D. R., "Proto-Industrialization and Social Structure: The Case of the Hosiery Industry in Leicestershire, England." Eighth International Congress of Economic History, Section A-2: Proto-Industrialization, Budapest, Hungary, 1982.

Monthly Labor Review, "The Advent of the New Economy," February 1992, 44-46.

Nilles, J. M., F. R. Carlson, P. Gray, and G. J. Hanneman, *The Telecommunications-Transportation Tradeoff,* John Wiley, New York, 1976.

Nolan, R., A. Pollock, and J. Ware, "Creating the 21st Century Organization," *Stage by Stage,* 8, 4 (1988), 1-11.

Olson, M. H., "Remote Office Work: Changing Work Patterns in Space and Time," *Communications of the ACM,* 26, 3 (March 1983), 182-187.

Pearson, R., "Occupational Trends in Britain to 1990," *Nature,* 323 (1986), 94.

Perrow, C., *Complex Organizations: A Critical Essay,* 3rd ed., Random House, New York, 1986.

Piore, M., "Dualism as a Response to Flux and Uncertainty," in *Dualism and Discontinuity in Industrial Societies,* S. Berger and M. J. Piore (Eds.), Cambridge University Press, Cambridge, UK, 1980.

_____ and C. F. Sabel, *The Second Industrial Divide,* Basic Books, New York, 1984.

Quinn, J., *The Intelligent Enterprise,* Free Press, New York, 1992.

Reddy, R., "A Technological Perspective on New Forms of Organizations," in *Technology and Organization,* P. Goodman, L. Sproull, and Associates (Eds.), Jossey-Bass, San Francisco, 1990, pp. 232-253.

Reich, R., *The Work of Nations,* Vintage Books, New York, 1991.

Rockart, J. and J. Short, "IT in the 1990s: Managing Organizational Interdependence," *Sloan Management Review,* Winter (1989), 7-16.

_____ and _____, "The Networked Organization and the Management of Interdependence," in *The Corporation of the 1990s: Information,* M. S. Scott Morton (Ed.), Oxford University Press, New York, 1991, pp. 189-219.

Sabel, C. and J. Zeitlin, "Historical Alternatives to Mass Production: Politics, Markets and Technology in Nineteenth-Century Industrialization," *Past and Present,* 108 (1985), 133-176.

Samuel, R., "Workshop of the World: Steam Power and Hand Technology in Mid-Victorian Britain," *History Workshop Journal,* 3 (1977), 6-72.

Scranton, P., "Diversity in Diversity: Flexible Production and American Industrialization, 1880-1930," *Business History Review,* 65 (Spring 1991), 27-90.

Smith, M. R. and L. Marx (Eds.), *Does Technology Drive History? The Dilemma of Technological Determinism,* MIT Press, Cambridge, 1994.

Sussman, C., *Understanding Technology,* Johns Hopkins University Press, Baltimore, MD, 1973.

Thurow, L. C., "White-Collar Overhead," *Across the Board,* 23, 11 (1986), 24-32.

Tilly, C., "Protoindustrialization, Deindustrialization, and Just Plain Industrialization in European Capitalism," CRSO Working Paper No. 235, University of Michigan, Ann Arbor, 1981.

Tomasko, R. M., *Downsizing: Reshaping the Corporation for the Future,* AMACOM, New York, 1987.

Webber, A. M., "What's So New About the New Economy?" *Harvard Business Review,* January/February (1993), 24-42.

Williams, K., T. Cutler, J. Williams, and C. Haslam, "The End of Mass Production?" *Economy and Society,* 16, 3 (1987), 405-439.

Wrigley, E. A. and R. S. Schofield, *The Population History of England, 1541-1871: A Reconstruction,* Cambridge University Press, London, 1981.

Yates, J. and R. I. Benjamin, "The Past and Present as a Window on the Future," in *The Corporation of the 1990s: Information Technology and Organizational Transformation,* M. S. Scott Morton (Ed.), Oxford University Press, New York, 1991, pp. 61-92.

PART II

EVOLUTIONARY PROCESSES IN
NEW FORM DEVELOPMENT

Can technology bring about meaningful change in today's organizations? Chapters 5 through 9 explore the role of information and communication technology in the evolution of organizational forms. The authors heed the call from chapters in Part I for more complete and less simplistic theories of the causes of change in organizational form. Using theoretically rich and empirically based analyses, these authors develop important insights into the processes by which connections between groups and individuals evolve in modern, technology-mediated firms.

Orlikowski, Yates, Okamura, and Fujimoto (Chapter 5) observe that the mediation process is a powerful organizing mechanism in today's firms. They observe that organizational forms can be facilitated by explicit and ongoing adaptation of technology to changing contexts of use. The activities of a few individuals ("technology-use mediation") can shape users' interaction with technology, modify features of the technology, and alter the context of use. Technology use practices of a few primary users can shape use practices in the larger community. In this way, changes in organizational form can evolve as a result of technology use practices among a few influential individuals that then become emulated by the larger community.

Barua, Lee, and Whinston (Chapter 6) further consider the interplay between individual and group in the design of organizations. Their analysis focuses on the complementarity effects among incentives, communication technology design, and organization and task characteristics. They show how incentives and technology development approaches for traditional, hierarchical organizations may not be appropriate for the flatter, team-based firm. They call for studies that carefully consider how interactions among reward systems, system design features, and organizational factors determine group behavior and, subsequently, the organizational payoff. The key premise of the perspective presented in this chapter is that for a new organizational form to succeed and technology investments to yield value, managers must consider complementarity effects among incentives, systems design, and organizational and task characteristics. The complexity of the technology-form relationship is again emphasized.

Hinds and Kiesler (Chapter 7) report on a study of the communication patterns of technical and administrative employees within and between departments of a large telecommunications firm. They discover high levels of lateral communication and interdepartmental communication and a notable preference for synchronous technologies to support lateral communication. They observe more boundary-crossing communication in less hierarchical work groups. Their research emphasizes the tight coupling between technology, structure, and communication patterns. As in Chapter 6, this study notes that group processes are affected not only by technology design features but also by reward systems and organizational and task characteristics.

Zack and McKenney (Chapter 8) show how similar groups using similar electronic systems in similar organizations can yield quite different communication patterns due to differences in communication climate, management philosophy, and group philosophy. In this field study, variations in organizational context resulted in different forms of appropriation of communication technology and, ultimately, differential levels of communication and performance effectiveness. The results verify the increasing amount of literature that documents that effects of electronic communication can be socially constructed by the group or firm in which the technology is used.

In Chapter 9, Lea, O'Shea, and Fung describe a 4-year case study revealing the complex relationships between content and context in the design and implementation of technology change. Their study highlights the interplay between a company's electronic mail project and a corporate move from five independent companies to a single, integrated networked organization. Although researchers have been (correctly) enamored with the power of social processes in influencing technology outcomes, these authors remind readers that technology should not be simplified or treated as a black box in studies of electronic communication in organizations. They offer an "actor-network" approach, which they use to describe the coconstruction of the new organizational forms and the new communications systems.

Together, the chapters in this section emphasize the complex and reciprocal interaction between context and action in organizations. Technology and social groups mutually shape each other within the dynamics of organizational life. Although the role of technology in this evolution can be powerful, so too are other forces, such as incentives, reward systems, organizational structure, and, most important, the behavior of people who design and use technology in the course of everyday work.

5

Shaping Electronic Communication

The Metastructuring of Technology in the Context of Use

WANDA J. ORLIKOWSKI

JOANNE YATES

KAZUO OKAMURA

MASAYO FUJIMOTO

A number of commentators have pointed to the profound changes—economic, technological, and social—that contemporary organizations are facing (Drucker 1988, Lewin and Stephens 1993, Malone and Rockart 1991). In response to these changes, many organizations are attempting to transform their structures and processes through teamwork, global intergration, and networking. Underpinning such changes are fast, accessible, and ubiquitous electronic networks that support computer-mediated communication technologies such as electronic mail, computer conferencing, and groupware. Such communication networks are expected to enable organizational members to work more flexibly, to span contexts and boundaries, and to collaborate more effectively. That expectation is widely shared; yet, as Daft and Lewin (1993) point out, we still have much to learn about the interactions among computer-mediated communication technologies, new organizational forms, and changes in work and communication. In this chapter, we offer a framework for thinking theoretically about some of these interactions and their consequences.

This chapter appeared originally in *Organization Science, 6*(4), July/August, 1995.

We suggest that the use of computer-mediated communication technologies in organizations can be facilitated by explicit contextualization of those technologies and their use patterns to particular and changing organizational circumstances over time. Established models of technology implementation, perhaps because they are premised on more stable forms of organization, generally assume that accommodation of the technology to the context of use occurs at the time of a technology's implementation (Leonard-Barton 1988, Rousseau 1989). With the notable exception of work on the "reinvention" of technology in use (Rice and Rogers 1980, Rogers 1983), this literature implicitly assumes that most adaptation will occur initially and later changes will be adequately covered by routine maintenance. This assumption is problematic in the context of more fluid organizational forms that change frequently in response to changing circumstances. In such dynamic contexts, the communication technologies supporting work and interaction will also require frequent adaptation to continue being useful and effective.

Many computer-mediated communication technologies are general-purpose media and hence may facilitate a range of possible interactions. Weick (1990) has referred to such open-ended technologies as "equivoques" to indicate that "they are open to many possible and plausible interpretations." This open-endedness offers benefits of flexibility but also creates the possibility that—without adaptation of the technology to the context and vice versa—the technology will not reflect local conditions or communication norms and hence will be underutilized or inappropriately utilized. Furthermore, the norms for interacting with computer-mediated communication technologies may not be shared by the users, and ambiguity or misaligned expectations may arise around how to use these technologies. In these cases, contextualization can help establish appropriate social protocols for communication in the new electronic media.

In the study we have reported here, we have identified a set of activities—*technology-use mediation*—which we define as deliberate, ongoing, and organizationally sanctioned intervention within the context of use that helps to adapt a new communication technology to that context, modifies the context as appropriate to accommodate use of the technology, and facilitates the ongoing effectiveness of the technology over time. The nature and importance of these activities emerged from a study we conducted into the introduction and use of an asynchronous computer conferencing technology in one R&D project over an extended period. In this study, we found that the effectiveness of the conferencing technology was significantly influenced by the intervention of a few individuals who explicitly engaged in technology-use mediation. Because these activities shaped how primary users structured their use of a technology, we suggest that they may be interpreted more broadly in terms of a process we label *metastructuring.*

Our study and the metastructuring perspective we develop provide an empirically grounded framing of the influential actions taken by individuals when they deliberately adapt computer-mediated communication technologies and their use to particular contexts and change those contexts to accommodate use of the technology. For research, the notion of metastructuring provides a theoretical lens for understanding the nature and influence of activities that intervene in the process of technology use. In practice, the sustained effectiveness of computer-mediated communication technologies in flexible new organizational forms will depend in great part on ensuring that the technologies are relevant to specific contexts of use, and that they continue to be relevant as those contexts change. We argue, thus, that the activities of technology-use mediation constitute a valuable mechanism for locating and providing the ongoing attention and resources needed to contextualize technologies to the shifting conditions and practices represented by dynamic organizational forms.

PRIOR RESEARCH

Technology Intervention

Various studies have looked at the influence of actors who intervene in some aspects of users' use of technologies. For example, some organizational and information systems researchers have suggested that a technological innovation is more likely to succeed when it is vigorously promoted and endorsed by an influential individual, the technology champion (Beath 1991, Howell and Higgins 1990, Maidique 1980, Schön 1963). Training, another form of intervention (e.g., Davis and Olson 1974, Rousseau 1989), is typically conceived of as part of the initial implementation of systems. For example, in a study of groupware use, Bullen and Bennett (1990) found that training was typically offered to users at the point of initial implementation and provided instruction on the mechanics of use, not the rationale behind such systems. More recently, people have recognized the value of continuous training for effective technology use (Johnson and Rice 1987, Strassman 1985) and for focusing training on use of the technology in practice rather than simply on the mechanics of its operation (Orlikowski 1992a).

A number of studies point to ongoing interventions in the use of information technology. For example, Culnan (1983) identifies surrogate users, labeled chauffeurs, who deliver information directly from the technology to individuals. Bullen and Bennett (1990) found that organizations that recognized "the evolutionary nature of a person's use of software" also authorized designated support staff to provide ongoing guidance. In organizations without such sanctioned roles they found that expert users or local gurus emerged to fill this function. Bjørn-Andersen et al. (1986) note the emergence of two roles providing ongoing user support once technology is in place: systems staff (primarily for solving technical problems) and local experts (accessible and proficient users with knowledge of other users' needs). Similar to expert users or local experts are Mackay's (1990) translators and Trigg and Bødker's (1994) tailors, proficient users who shared their software customizations and innovations with less proficient colleagues. Administrative mechanisms for shaping use have also been identified. Sproull and Kiesler (1991) discuss ways of managing computer-mediated communication through the setting of policies and the development of self-policing social norms. In a detailed examination of the IBMPC computer conference over time, Foulger (1990) discussed the actions of conference administrators serving a community of thousands of IBM employees. These administrators established a limited number of conference usage rules initially and modified these over time as issues arose. They then reviewed messages to ensure conformance to these rules.

Our conceptualization of technology-use mediation has both similarities and differences with these existing understandings of the activities and influences of various actors. Champions and trainers typically intervene in the initial stages of technology implementation, establishing its importance and motivating its initial use. While these actors fulfill part of the technology-use mediation activity (discussed below), they rarely play an ongoing role. Chauffeurs do not mediate users' interactions with technology but relieve users of the need to interact directly with the technology. Designated support staff generally work in a reactive mode, rather than proactively facilitating ongoing adaptation to the context of use. Translators, tailors, and local experts or gurus are not organizationally recognized. Thus none of these existing understandings encompass all the activities included in our definition of technology-use mediation, though each refers to actions that can be seen as part of the broader process we identify below as metastructuring.

Technology Structuring

As a set of activities that influence the interaction of users with their technology, mediation can also be viewed from the framework of structuration theory (Giddens 1984), and particularly in terms of how technologies are structured by users in their contexts of use (Barley 1986, Orlikowski 1992b, Walsham 1993, Weick 1990). The structuring of technologies in use

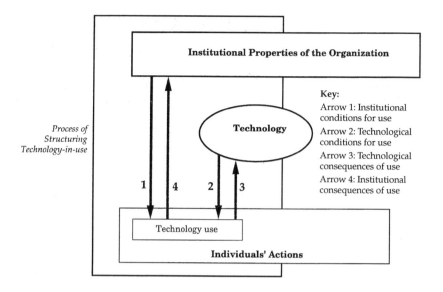

Figure 5.1. Process of Technology Structuring (Adapted From Orlikowski, 1992)

refers to the processes through which users manipulate their technologies to accomplish work, and the ways in which such action draws on and repro-duces (or sometimes changes) the particular social contexts within which they work. Recently, work using the technology structuring perspective has specifically examined the case of computer-mediated communication tech-nologies (e.g., Contractor and Eisenberg 1990, DeSanctis and Poole 1994, Orlikowski and Yates 1994, Poole and DeSanctis 1990, 1992, Yates and Orlikowski 1992).

Technology structuring is influenced by users' interpretations of their work, the organization, and technology; their access to organizational and technological resources; and the normative rules that guide action in their social contexts. Figure 5.1 presents a general outline of the technology structuring process (see Orlikowski [1992b] for a more detailed discussion). Users draw on existing institutional properties of their organization (e.g., division of labor and work procedures; Arrow 1) to use the technological features available to them (Arrow 2). In using technology to accomplish some task, users appropriate technological features (Arrow 3) and enact a set of social practices, which reinforce, adjust, or change the existing institutional prop-erties (Arrow 4). This influence of individuals' technology use on the institu-tional properties is often unintended and unnoticed, just as the influence of the institutional properties on technology use is often unacknowledged.

The research on technology structuring—whether general or specific to communication media—tends to focus primarily on the activities of users who shape their technology as they use it in particular contexts. The research we report below identifies another set of structuring activities that, although carried out by users, are not activities of use. Rather, they involve the shaping of other users' activities of use, a process we designate as metastructuring. The notion of metastructuring allows us to see that interventions in users' use of technology occur frequently over time, in a variety of ways, and are often very influential. In this chapter, we examine a particular type of metastructuring, technology-use mediation, and find that it structures users' use of technology by influencing their interpretations and interactions, by changing the institutional context of use, and by modifying the technology itself. Because technology-use mediation is a sanctioned, explicit, deliberate, and ongoing set of activities, we argue that it is a particularly powerful mechanism in the context of dynamic organizations, enabling rapid and customized adaptations of the technology and its use to changes in circumstances, organizational forms, and work practices. After presenting the findings of our empirical research, we will frame activities of technology-use mediation in terms of the structuring process depicted in Figure 5.1, thus extending it to accommodate metastructuring.

RESEARCH SETTING AND METHODS

Research Setting

We studied the use of computer conferencing in the R&D division of a large Japanese manufacturing firm. The system was used to support communication among the members of a newly formed project group developing a computer product, Acorn (a pseudonym). The history of electronic media use in the R&D division prior to the Acorn project provides essential background to the introduction and use of computer conferencing within the project group. Electronic mail (e-mail) had been introduced into one of the R&D division's labs about 2 years before the Acorn project began, by four young software engineers who were interested in maintaining contact with colleagues outside of the firm. Use of e-mail spread slowly but steadily within the lab so that about half of the Acorn members were e-mail users by the start of the project. The four software engineers were also interested in the worldwide USENET news system (a computer conferencing system publicly available and widely used on a number of electronic networks) and in college had used the Japanese language version created to link several Japanese universities. Seeing its potential for internal use, these engineers decided to create a local news system within their R&D lab a year after introducing electronic mail.

The news-system software is organized hierarchically into topics known as newsgroups. In setting up this local news system, the engineers initially created three parallel newsgroups: *general,* software's default category, and *misc* (miscellaneous) and *rec* (recreational), two of the standard USENET categories. Users could read and respond to messages posted on the newsgroups as well as post their own messages. The software allowed them to include part or all of a previous message embedded within their new message. Normally, messages accumulated within newsgroups until they were automatically purged after 3 months. This news system was initially used only by a very small set of individuals (the engineers and a few friends). As one of these engineers recalled, "At that time we never thought those newsgroups would ever become official communication media in the lab. We were just playing with the software for fun."

Because Acorn was expected to be an innovative product important to the company's competitive position, a new organizational infrastructure, drawing members from three different labs within the R&D division, was formed to develop the Acorn product in late September 1989. The group was composed of about 150 employees, primarily members of the R&D division supplemented by new employees and external contract programmers as needed. The newly formed project group was divided into six teams: four teams for software development, and one each for hardware development and administration. All Acorn project members were experienced computer users and were provided with powerful networked workstations readily supporting electronic communication. The four software engineers who had introduced the news system into one lab were selected to be part of this new project group, and since they all enjoyed using the news system, they set up a similar news system specifically for the Acorn project. Acorn's news system was in operation and accessible by all project members for the full 17 months of the project (from the end of September 1989 to February 1991). Initially, the engineers' news system activities continued to be unofficial and casual, and usage remained restricted in volume and user base in the early days of the Acorn project.

The four engineers soon realized that a large project group such as Acorn would require its own network administration to support communication and data exchange. They explained this need to project managers and volunteered to perform such administration. As a result, the Network Administration Group for Acorn (NAGA), the focus of this study, was created. Its nine members included the original software engineers plus five additional members recruited to ensure that NAGA represented each of the six Acorn teams. Within NAGA, decisions were made primarily by consensus in regular face-to-face meetings. Minutes of these meetings were distributed to all NAGA members via e-mail. E-mail messages were also frequently exchanged among NAGA members to supplement their meeting discussions.

Data Collection and Analysis

We examined the policies and process through which the news system was managed over time by the NAGA members (see Fujimoto [1993] for a more extensive discussion of these policies). Two types of data were collected: extensive textual data supplemented by restrospective interview data. Most of the interview data came from a series of in-depth and unstructured discussions with a key informant, conducted in Japanese, but with later, more focused follow-up interviews in English. These were supplemented by more structured interviews with six other project members, all conducted in Japanese. The interview data, which helped in our interpretation of the textual data, revealed important contextual information about the firm and the Acorn project, as well as details about NAGA activities and use of the news system.

The textual data consisted of computerized records containing two types of messages (all in Japanese): e-mail messages exchanged among the NAGA members and newsgroup messages that were posted on the news system by Acorn participants during the project. We employed qualitative data analysis methods (Eisenhardt 1989, Miles and Huberman 1984), classifying the e-mail messages by common topics and actions, and carefully examining the newsgroup messages around the time of NAGA's administrative actions. This allowed us to trace the process by which decisions were made and implemented over time.

During the 12-month period beginning with NAGA's first discussions of the news system's role and ending after the last major reconfiguration of the news system (see below), 438 e-mail messages were exchanged by the NAGA members, of which 223 concerned the news system rather than the physical computer network. These messages included members' ongoing dialogues about the news system, along with the minutes of their regular face-to-face meetings. We initially classified the contents of the messages into 97 specific topics about the news system (e.g., the addition of a particular newsgroup to the system, or the differences between use of e-mail and of the news system), often with more than one topic per message. We then categorized the topics into four general subjects: definition of the news system (explaining the role and purpose of the news system); promotion of the news system (publicizing and educating users about the news system and about

Number of e-mail messages

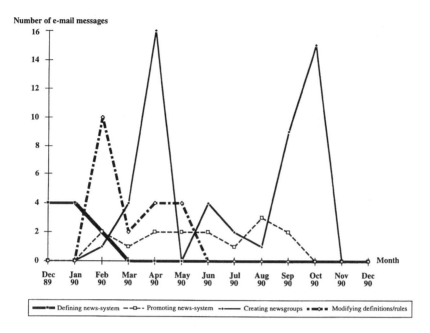

Figure 5.2. Distribution of Four Types of NAGA E-Mail Messages

specific newsgroups); revision of newsgroups (amending definitions and usage rules for existing newsgroups); and creation of new newsgroups (starting new newsgroups, both those suggested by users and those felt by NAGA members to be appropriate). Figure 5.2 shows the distribution of these message types during the period analyzed.

Over the 15 months of the Acorn project for which news-system archives exist, 9,302 messages were posted on the news system. Figure 5.3 shows the distribution of these messages over time. We examined two types of news system messages: messages that were posted by NAGA members in the execution of their administrative activities and messages that were posted by participants. Messages posted by NAGA members as project participants were not considered part of NAGA's administrative messages. NAGA members' administrative messages mostly announced news-system changes or solicited discussion of aspects of the news system. These messages were useful indications of NAGA's administrative activities and policies. Messages posted by participants reflected both the influence of NAGA administrative actions and participants' responses to these actions.

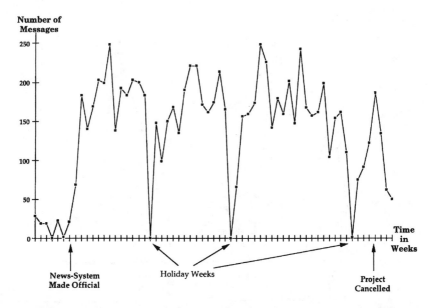

Figure 5.3. Use of the News System During the Project

We analyzed all of these sources of data together and iteratively to get as complete a picture as possible of NAGA's activities. The topics of NAGA e-mail messages could be correlated with NAGA messages posted on the relevant newsgroups (e.g., announcing changes in guidelines or the addition of new newsgroups). Both could be correlated with the dates of first postings on new newsgroups, yielding a time line of NAGA's changes to the news system, shown in Figure 5.4. Data from our interviews were used to elaborate and interpret our findings. Together, these different sources of data allow us to characterize NAGA's activities throughout the Acorn project.

RESULTS

We identified four types of mediating activities that NAGA members performed:

1. *Establishment*: NAGA established its role, determined and built consensus around use of the communication technology, defined the set of newsgroups to be included in the news system, and established guidelines and technical resources for its use.

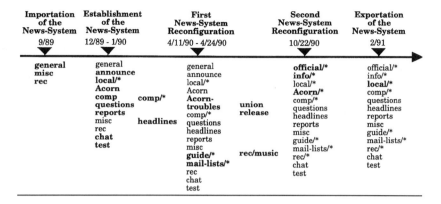

Figure 5.4. Change in news system within the Acorn project over time.

Note: Bold font represents the point at which a newsgroup was first created. Newsgroups followed by "/*" indicate the presence of several newsgroups nested hierarchically within the named newsgroup.

2. *Reinforcement*: NAGA used training, monitoring, and follow-up with members and the group to reinforce the established guidelines.

3. *Adjustment*: On the basis of feedback obtained from members, NAGA adjusted the definitions and usage rules for specific newsgroups and occasionally added new newsgroups on request.

4. *Episodic change*: Twice during the project, NAGA initiated major changes to the news system as a whole.

After discussing each of these, we look at the outcomes of NAGA's activities. We then briefly examine an attempt to transfer the news system after the Acorn project ended, an attempt which highlights the importance of contextualizing technology in use.

Establishment

Establishing its role within the Acorn project was the first essential task NAGA members took on. They prepared a document for their managers in which they articulated the importance of ongoing support for the project's technical and communicative infrastructure, and proposed both that their NAGA activities be recognized as a part of their regular job duties and that they be allowed to hire two contract programmers to do the necessary programming work. Once managers accepted this rationale, NAGA communicated its role to the project in announcements made by the six team leaders at team meetings, in the project's internal biweekly newsletter, and in a news-system message which stated, "Our goal is not only to achieve trouble-free use of the network, but also to increase the productivity of the project by improving communication among members."[1] At this point, NAGA was authorized by Acorn managers and recognized by fellow members of the Acorn project group as the committee responsible for administering the Acorn project's network.

Once its role and initial network infrastructure issues had been settled, NAGA addressed the role of the news system in the project. They believed it could aid communication and coordination and improve morale in their large project group. As one NAGA member indicated in his interview, "We thought it would be nice if everybody communicated and esprit de corps was improved." To encourage such use, NAGA began adding a few new news-groups (e.g., *chat* and *questions*). They also considered whether the news system should be used for official communication (such as announcements in meetings) or for unofficial communication (such as that conveyed via hallway conversations). While NAGA members discussed this issue in their meetings, they also solicited the opinions of project members, as evident in the following message:

Subject: New newsgroups
Date: 6 Dec 89 10:05:48 GMT

Newsgroups: *misc*

We need to discuss the following issues.

(1) The officiality of this news system is unclear. Must everyone read the *general* newsgroup? Will it be just like another bulletin board?

→ Should the news system be used simply according to a person's preference?

The next topic clarifies the relationship between the news system and other media such as meetings, bulletin boards, and e-mail.

(2) The relationship of this news system to bulletin boards organized within each team, and any e-mail mailing lists is unclear.

As long as we use only these closed media, we cannot share useful information among all project members.

→ Should we not gain the advantage of many members working together?

Please continue this discussion by e-mail or the news system.

This message, which triggered a discussion among project members who were already using the news system, reveals NAGA's consensus-building approach. It invited participation of other project members in deciding whether the news system should be official, at the same time that it conveyed

NAGA's view that the news system would offer "the advantage of many members working together." Several participants responded in support of a more official role for the news system.

Because most project members were not yet using the news system, NAGA members also talked individually with many team members, as well as with project managers whose consent was critical to making the news system an official medium for the project. NAGA's inclusive and encouraging but not directive approach enabled it to build general support among other project members, most of whom gradually adopted the view that the news system should be an official communication medium for the project group. NAGA members then deliberated about how best to position the new official medium in relation to the other communication mechanisms in common use: daily lunchtime meetings (required by company policy in each division or group, and including official announcements as well as ceremonial elements such as the singing of the company song), routing slips (used by administrators to circulate information to all members of a group), bulletin boards (used for posting paper-based announcements), and e-mail (used by an increasing number of project members for one-to-one communication and team distribution lists). After NAGA members reflected on and evaluated the current uses of these different mechanisms, they discussed how these should change with the addition of the news system. Their decisions were documented in the following meeting minutes:

To: NAGA@xxx
Subject: Meeting report from December 26, 1989

. . .

Communication media within the division

<principle>
Currently, daily lunchtime meetings, routing-slips, bulletin boards, e-mail, and the news system are used as communication media. Our purpose is to encourage the use of the news system.

<daily lunchtime meetings>
The purpose of the daily lunchtime meeting should be restricted to confirmation of information that has been announced in the news system beforehand. This meeting should not be an official announcement tool.

<routing-slips>
The routing-slip will be terminated. Printed information should be posted on bulletin boards and we should direct project members to use the news system as much as possible.

<bulletin boards>
Bulletin boards can be used only for printed information. However, all information should be provided through the news system and at least summaries have to be posted on the news system.

<e-mail>
Precise e-mail use guidelines should be set. E-mail must be used only for urgent or confidential information.
The definition of "urgent" information: information that should be shared within a day.

As the minutes make clear, NAGA's explicit objective was to encourage news system use by allocating most of the information exchanged within the Acorn project, including all of its official information, to the news system. They also persuaded the six team leaders to require their team members to use the news system, essential support in making the news system an official medium. NAGA also believed that making the new medium official would legitimate its use and, as our key informant noted, "This would increase usage as people wouldn't feel guilty using it." During the daily lunch meeting on January 30, 1990, the project manager announced the new policy requiring project members to use the news system and, in particular, to access two newsgroups—*general* and *announce*—each day.

This authorization of the conferencing system (rather than the lunchtime meeting) as the official communication medium of the project was an important departure from traditional norms and procedures in the firm and the R&D division. NAGA's efforts created a new set of institutional guidelines around what constituted official and legitimate communication in the organization. It diminished the role and centrality of the daily lunchtime meetings, and it made the entire project dependent on the computer conferencing system, requiring all members to become somewhat proficient with this new technology so as to access it daily.

On the day that the manager's announcement made the news system official, NAGA posted on it a usage guide to differentiate and establish guidelines for using e-mail and the news system:

Newsgroups: *announce*
Subject: Guideline for the usage of mail & news
Date: 30 Jan 90 11:03:28 GMT

. . .

(1) Use e-mail and the news system effectively!

If you want to send information to some specific person, e-mail may be useful. However, when you send it to a set of people or to all members in the project group, please use the news system as much as possible.

If you use e-mail all the time, we will receive a huge number of messages and have to read all of them. Remember the difference between a traditional bulletin board posting and a letter. Think again when you send an e-mail message to any mailing list (like all@xxx). You may be able to provide useful information to other project members by using the news system.

The news system will function as an official tool starting in February 1990.

(2) Obligation to access both e-mail and the news system.

NAGA has established a facility allowing all members to use both Mail and News.

We will support it to make sure that everyone is comfortable using these systems.

All members must access Mail/News:

  e-mail: Twice a day both in the morning and afternoon
  News: At least once in the morning to specific newsgroups—the *general* and *announce* newsgroups

*If you want us to send messages on the *general* and *announce* newsgroups by e-mail, NAGA will provide a service to send messages by e-mail automatically.

*You also can post a message by using the e-mail function.

These guidelines promoted usage by assigning to the news system specific functions previously handled by other media and by articulating how the news system would operate as an internal communication mechanism for Acorn. Thus NAGA attempted to remove any ambiguity and uncertainty over the news system's role and expectations for its use to avoid inhibiting usage.

At the same time, NAGA took other actions designed to increase usage. It created *local* newsgroups for each of the six teams within the project, to provide an alternative to their existing e-mail distribution lists. These news-groups, according to our NAGA informant, were also intended to reduce people's apprehension about writing a message to the entire project group. This tactic seems to have had an effect since almost half of all messages on the news system in the early weeks of its official use were on the *local* newsgroups; later, that proportion would drop to about one-third as more discussion shifted to the nonlocal newsgroups. NAGA did not, however, restrict access to the *local* newsgroups because they believed that sharing information across as well as within local teams would ultimately benefit the project as a whole. As they explained in a message posted to announce and define these *local* newsgroups, "It is fine if members of other teams also access the *local* newsgroups. In fact, these newsgroups can even be used as places for public debate." During the entire project, about 33% of the messages in the *local* newsgroups were written by members of other teams. Cross-fertilization across teams occurred via this mechanism, as when someone posted a message on another team's *local* newsgroup saying, "I am an outsider, but I would like to explain my idea about [a certain topic]."

NAGA also attempted to make use of the news system easy and comfortable. For example, they created a *test* newsgroup, which provided a risk-free environment for project members to learn the news system by experimenting with reading and posting messages. NAGA also enhanced the news-system software to deal with the resistance they anticipated from some project members who were uncomfortable with the new conferencing medium. As indicated at the end of the usage guide message shown above, NAGA established a facility allowing members to send and receive news-system items by e-mail, a medium more widely used than the news system at that time. This action allowed NAGA members to avoid possible challenges to their objective of establishing the news system as the primary and official communication medium within the project.

As shown in Figure 5.3, NAGA's activities in establishing the news system generated a dramatic increase in the number of messages posted on the news system. Before the announcement of the new official role for the news system, about 20 messages a week were posted on the news system; after that, the number rose to around 200 messages per week (excluding holiday periods) until the end of the project was announced in February 1991. Thus NAGA's campaign to establish the news system as an official Acorn communication medium and to get project members to use it was clearly successful.

Reinforcement

NAGA members were not content simply to establish the news system in the Acorn project; they were conscious of an ongoing need to promote usage so that the news system would be sustained as an essential part of the project's communication system. In addition to maintaining the operation of the news system, NAGA members wanted to reinforce their vision of how it should be used.

E-mail messages among NAGA members demonstrated a low but fairly consistent level of discussion concerning user education to reinforce and motivate use of the news system during the 8 months following its establishment (see Figure 5.2). For example, an item in the minutes of one NAGA meeting stated, "We will hold a lecture to educate new recruits about the usage of the news system. We will use the companywide network usage guide as a text book and especially explain details about unique issues originating in our news system." NAGA members also posted messages on new newsgroups to encourage and guide other users' use. Such lectures and messages allowed NAGA to promote as well as to shape use of the news system. In addition to reinforcing system use, NAGA maintained the technical integrity of the news system and network, for example, by establishing new user accounts when newcomers joined the project, making regular backups of the system, managing disk space, and keeping the infrastructure operational.

After a high level of usage had been sustained for several months, NAGA shifted its attention from supporting use of the medium to promoting what it saw as its effective and appropriate use. As both users and system administrators, they could easily monitor use. When a project member posted a message on the wrong newsgroup, NAGA first responded with a private explanation. If several participants made the same mistake, NAGA would post a general reminder explanation on the news system. For example, NAGA felt that the mandatory newsgroups should be kept manageable in size. The *general* newsgroup was initially defined as containing "important announcements to all members," and the *announce* newsgroup as containing "information for all project members such as meeting and event schedules." With such broad definitions, many participants were confused about which of these newsgroups, if either, was appropriate for a message. Unimportant messages and discussions sometimes appeared on these newsgroups, especially in *announce*. Thus NAGA kept trying to clarify—both generally and with regard to specific messages—what belonged in the *general* and *announce* newsgroups and what should be posted in the other newsgroups.

Given high usage levels, NAGA was also concerned that people might waste too much time reading and posting messages. As a result, it posted the following general guidelines:

Newsgroups: *general*
Subject: About messages
Date: 5 Oct 90 10:42:26 GMT
Cautions about news-system usage

(1) *Long embedded messages*
There are still many messages that include long embedded parts. As readers can refer to the original message through the automatically embedded "message-ID," please shorten the embedded part as much as possible.

(2) *Choose the proper newsgroup*
What do you do if you cannot find the proper newsgroup for your message? There have been many messages that noted, "This does not fit in this newsgroup . . ."

Please ask NAGA members if you have any question or request. We will respond
to all participants' feedback.
Move to the proper newsgroup when the discussion content changes by using
the follow-up-to command.

(3) *Cross-post*
Please use the cross-post command when you send the same message to several
newsgroups. If you use this command, readers need not read the same messages
several times.
NAGA

This message reflects NAGA's ongoing educational efforts to reinforce
and institutionalize a particular type of news-system usage. NAGA, however, passed up at least one mechanism for ensuring that users followed one
of its guidelines. Responding to managers' concerns about news-system
misuse, NAGA had issued a policy that the *rec* newsgroup was to be used
only outside of regular work hours. When NAGA members observed *rec*
messages posted during work hours, they sent e-mail reminders of this policy
to the transgressors. Although NAGA was not able to eliminate this practice,
it chose not to institute a technical fix that would have prevented violations
of the policy, but focused primarily on attempting to change behavior
through education.

In their ongoing monitoring of the level and nature of news-system usage,
NAGA members paid close attention to direct and indirect user feedback,
attempting to identify and remedy errors, confusion, or ineffective usage,
and to reinforce their vision of appropriate usage. They also maintained
technical aspects of the system to avoid performance deterioration and
system problems. In these reinforcement activities, NAGA members ensured
that the communication technology they had established continued to be used
at a fairly high level and usually in ways that fit their vision of the new
medium's role in the project.

Adjustment

NAGA's objective was not, however, simply reinforcing the structure and
rules it had established for the medium; its members also sought to adjust
and enhance the news system and its use in response to user feedback. In
doing so, they modified newsgroup definitions and usage rules, changed the
news system's software, and created new newsgroups while maintaining
their overall goal of supporting communication within the project.

Revisions to newsgroup definitions and rules were made in response to direct user feedback in the form of questions and statements of problems, as well as indirect user feedback from visible errors in use and statements that suggested confusion about the use of certain newsgroups. Such feedback triggered revisions to the definitions and rules for various newsgroups, such as the *general* and *announce* newsgroups discussed above. When reinforcement did not elicit what NAGA considered appropriate use of these mandatory newsgroups, NAGA members had a series of discussions over several months about how better to define these two newsgroups. They experimented with a number of revisions to the definition and usage rules, but the problem of how to make best use of the mandatory newsgroups was finally resolved during one of the change episodes discussed below.

NAGA also enhanced the software to make the news system easier to use. The news system as established in the project allowed Japanese characters in the body of the messages but required subject lines to be written in English or in Romanized Japanese (Japanese characters represented phonetically in Roman characters). Although such representation was not too difficult for technical language, which was often based on English, it posed problems for administrative messages posted by secretaries and members of the administrative group. Complaints from these users led NAGA to alter the news-system software so that it would accept Japanese subject lines.

Another form of system enhancement was the addition of new newsgroups. In general, NAGA preferred to cluster the addition of newsgroups and changes to news-system structure together (as discussed in the next section). Because NAGA also wanted to be responsive to users' requests, however, it added a few newsgroups at other times. Such adjustments included subdividing the *comp* (computer) newsgroup into various hardware and software categories and creating newsgroups such as *headlines, union,* and *release.* For example, users requested a newsgroup for announcing and discussing company union matters, and *union* was created in response. In another instance, a participant posted the following message on *announce*:

Newsgroup: *announce*

Subject: Subscription to magazines xxx

Date: 13 Feb 90 02:40:16 GMT

Distribution: Acorn

Subscriptions of two magazines were started last month. They are in xxx book-case. Please read them at your convenience.

I would like to send reference messages about new books each month because building B is separated from the main building, so this will be useful for people

who are working in building B. May I post these messages to this newsgroup?
(the *announce* newsgroup)

Or is there any other more proper newsgroup?

This message initiated a dialogue among NAGA and other project members,
and resulted in the addition of the *headlines* newsgroup for the announcement
of newly arrived books and magazines.

Thus in its role as ongoing administrative group in charge of the Acorn
news system, NAGA attempted to respond to both direct and indirect feedback, while keeping in mind its own objectives for the medium. In doing so,
it modified and enhanced the news system socially and technically by
altering definitions and usage rules and by adding new newsgroups. NAGA
thus shaped both users' understandings of the technology and the technology
itself to keep news-system usage more effective and relevant. Some such
refinements were reactive, executed in response to users' requests or on the
evidence of user confusion, while some were proactive, executed opportu-
nistically by NAGA members when they saw a way to improve the system.
Both kinds of adjustments were designed to improve and reinforce existing
conditions of use, rather than to create radical departures from them.

Episodic Change

The adjustments attempted to solve problems as they arose, but sometimes
NAGA either failed to solve the problem with such actions (as with the
confusion about the *general* and *announce* newsgroups) or postponed a full
solution. Periodically, NAGA addressed clusters of such problems and the
larger issue of system configuration. During the news system's official use
in the Acorn project, NAGA conducted two episodes of change involving
significant modifications to the functionality of the news system and to the
structure of newsgroups within it.

The first change episode, in April 1990, introduced three new newsgroups
(see Figure 5.4). Although one of these, *Acorn-troubles* (reporting certain
types of problems with the Acorn product), was similar to existing newsgroups, the other two, *mail-lists* and *guide,* expanded the functionality of the
news system, as well as NAGA's vision of the medium, in new directions.
NAGA had originally envisioned the medium as a coordination mechanism
for internal communication across the six teams making up the Acorn project.
The two new sets of newsgroups significantly expanded this vision by
providing access to external information and long-term archiving of certain
types of reference information.

The *mail-lists* newsgroups were designed to allow Acorn members to access up-to-date technical information available by contract from an outside public network organization. Because the contract required that this external information be kept confidential to the Acorn project group, NAGA created a different social and technical structure for this set of newsgroups. It prohibited participants from posting messages to these external newsgroups, introduced the *mail-lists/discuss* newsgroup for internal discussions about the topics, and named a moderator to monitor and answer questions about these newsgroups. Moreover, NAGA ensured compliance by providing an additional technical feature for automatically transferring to this internal discussion newsgroup any follow-up messages users inadvertently tried to send to the external mail lists.

The other major modification to the news system in this change episode was the addition of the *guide* newsgroups as archival, rather than temporary, sources of shared information. Until this time, the news system automatically deleted a message from a newsgroup after it had been posted for 3 months. But by April 1990 NAGA had identified a need for the retention of some reference information with a longer life span, in essence an organizational memory for the project. Thus by modifying the automatic deletion feature they created a set of moderated *guide* newsgroups to function as repositories of reference documents (e.g., address lists, administrative procedures, and maps). Whenever participants posted messages on these newsgroups, these messages were automatically sent to the moderators, who checked whether or not each message was appropriate for archiving. If it was, the moderator posted the message on the newsgroup. If not, the moderator sent an e-mail message to the participant explaining why it was not appropriate for archiving. NAGA also created a specific format and usage rules for all *guide* newsgroups, explained in a guideline document which each moderator posted on each *guide* newsgroup.

In the second change episode, NAGA attempted to rationalize and restructure the news system and to solve some recurring problems. NAGA members began planning this episode in July 1990, when they posted a message soliciting user requests for new newsgroups and ideas about the structure of the news system. On October 17, 1990, in a very long message posted to the *announce* newsgroup, NAGA announced the schedule and details of this second change episode. One key set of changes was the creation of the *official* newsgroups to solve the ongoing problems with the mandatory *general* and *announce* newsgroups. These latter groups were eliminated and replaced by two moderated newsgroups: *official/secretary* for "important announcements of meetings and events" and *official/general* for "other important announcements." While the definitions were more carefully specified than those for *general* and *announce,* NAGA's real solution for restraining the amount and nature of material posted to the mandatory newsgroups was to put a moderator in charge of each to screen messages before posting them.

Two other major sets of changes involved clustering newsgroups, in one case by priority and in one case by subject. First, several individual newsgroups were organized into a second tier of *info* newsgroups (e.g., *info/lookfor* for lost and found announcements and *info/release* for information related to software releases) that were recommended but not required daily reading. Second, to help project members find information about Acorn previously scattered among several newsgroups, NAGA subdivided the *Acorn* newsgroup, creating new categories and clustering existing Acorn-related newsgroups under it. This second modification tried to reconfigure the news system to improve its clarity, coherence, efficiency, and usefulness as a communication medium supporting the Acorn project.

At the end of the long message announcing the second set of changes, NAGA stated its philosophy about shaping the news system: "NAGA thinks that the news-system schema should be changed depending on the situation. We would like to manage flexibly. This modification is one of those actions." As this statement makes clear, NAGA members viewed the structure of the news system not as fixed and permanent but as context specific. As the situation and the project's needs changed, and as NAGA members refined their concept of what was valuable to the project, they changed the system structure and its rules. Yet NAGA tried to balance the evolving communication requirements of the project organization with a certain amount of stability in the communication medium by undertaking substantial changes only episodically. This approach allowed NAGA to contemplate the changes over a period of time, assessing how they would reshape the news system, and then to institute them together for maximum visibility and minimal disruption. Moreover, NAGA took steps to ease the transition by retaining all the terminated or restructured newsgroups in read-only form, posting a final message on each indicating where messages should now be posted.

Outcomes of NAGA's Mediating Activities

Through its performance of these four activities, NAGA encouraged broad usage of the system in the Acorn project group. Not only did all project members perform the mandatory duty of reading items posted on the *announce* and *general* (later *official/**) newsgroups, but by the end of the project, approximately 95% of the members had also posted messages, an

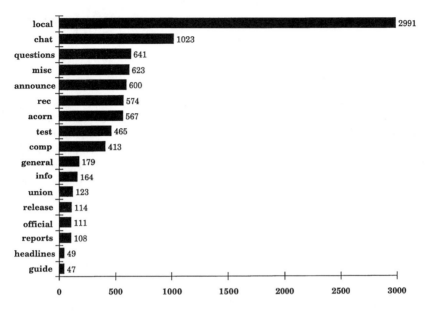

Figure 5.5. Number of Messages per Newsgroup

activity that was not mandatory. Moreover, as Figure 5.5 shows, the messages were distributed over a variety of mandatory and nonmandatory newsgroups. The system's value, however, is suggested not only by its high usage but also by user experiences. For example, one user commented that use had "improved our efficiency," while another noted that "The news system allowed the concentration of information in one place so that everyone could access it." Yet another user saw the news system as improving communication effectiveness: "Because everyone knew what was written in the news system, it reduced explanation time at meetings." In addition, the news system's fostering of cross-team communication was particularly valuable for the coordination of the project as a whole. For example, members noted: "We could share information"; "The news system increased my communication with members of other teams"; and "All teams could know what the other teams were doing." The 33% cross-posting on local newsgroups by members of other teams, noted above, also attests to the system's value in encouraging information-sharing and communication across the six project teams. NAGA itself was recognized by fellow users as improving their news-system usage. As one project member indicated in his interview, "If NAGA hadn't existed, the news system would not have been used properly. They also improved the

level of technical sophistication of many individuals." NAGA's contextualizing activities seem to have been both effective and appreciated.

Epilogue: Transfer of the News System

The importance of these contextualizing activities to the successful ongoing use of the system was underscored by events surrounding the attempted
transfer of the news system after the Acorn project ended. When the planned
February 1991 termination of the Acorn project was announced in January,[2]
system usage began to decline precipitously (see Figure 5.3). At the same
time NAGA began to make plans to transfer the news system into one lab
where many of the Acorn project members, including the founding members
of NAGA, had come from and would return. (This lab still had its old news
system created before the Acorn project began, but usage was quite low.) The
transfer attempt, to the surprise of NAGA, failed. We can draw on our
understanding of mediation activities to suggest some reasons for this outcome.

NAGA members decided to introduce the structure of the successful
Acorn news system into the lab's news system with only two variations:
deleting the set of newsgroups related specifically to the Acorn product and
changing the *local* newsgroups to reflect separate projects in the lab rather
than the six Acorn teams. NAGA assumed that the Acorn news-system
schema would fit this lab with only these minor adjustments because two-
thirds of its members were former members of the Acorn project. While
NAGA members obtained managers' consent for this action and announced
definitions and usage rules for the new *local* newsgroups before introducing
them, they did not obtain consent to continue operating as an official network
administration group in the lab. Each NAGA member belonged to different
product development groups, and news-system administration for the lab as
a whole was not seen by their various project managers as an aspect of their
jobs, in part because the lab already had a technical support group in charge of
the physical network. NAGA thus lost its organizational sanction. As a result,
NAGA's further activities were discouraged and hence were relatively ineffective, being limited in comparison to those performed in the Acorn project.
Not only could NAGA members not effectively establish the role of the news
system within the lab, but they could not pursue the news system's ongoing
reinforcement and adjustment, nor could they initiate change episodes.

Without ongoing contextualization, usage of the recently transferred news
system gradually declined. Only the new *local* newsgroups were popular.
Some of the reasons for the decline were rooted in the lab's structure and its
differences from the structure of the Acorn project group. Because adminis-

trators in the lab were not familiar with the news system and because they used a different type of computer that was not designed to support the news system, none of them posted important official or administrative messages on the news system. In the Acorn project, the administrative group was part of the entire project group and administrators used or had access to the same workstations as other project members. If NAGA had retained its status and resources, its members might have been able to solve this problem as they had solved the problem of reluctant users by setting up forwarding of the mandatory newsgroup messages in e-mail. If that had been accomplished as part of system establishment, the news system might have retained a central role in administrative matters within the lab. Instead, the news system lost its officiality and usage dropped.

Although NAGA succeeded in establishing an effective news system for the Acorn project, the attempt to transfer this system to a different organizational unit was relatively unsuccessful. In interaction with users on the Acorn project, NAGA had contextualized the news-system technology within a specific context. The resulting system, while highly attuned to the Acorn context, did not match the different lab context even with minor adjustments. The technology, customized to one context, supported only limited use within a new context, highlighting the importance of ongoing contextualization to ensure that technologies and their use reflect changing conditions.

TECHNOLOGY-USE MEDIATION AND THE METASTRUCTURING PROCESS

The research study of NAGA described above has provided insights into the actions of organizational actors who significantly and deliberately shaped users' initial and ongoing use of their new communication technology. The above description provides a detailed account of the objectives, activities, and influence of NAGA's role. While intervention in users' technological use happens in many ways—both intended and unintended—we have focused here on a kind of intervention (technology-use mediation) that is deliberate, explicit, ongoing, and organizationally sanctioned. Based on our empirical research we argue that such intervention may serve as a powerful mechanism for contextualizing technologies in use, an issue of increasing importance as more general-purpose communication technologies are used to support dynamic organizational forms and practices. By foregrounding and framing this mediation activity, we can gain insights into how to organize it so as to support the ongoing usefulness of electronic media in conditions of fluidity and change.

In order to provide a theoretical interpretation of the technology-use mediation role, we draw on what we already know about how users structure their technologies (Barley 1986, DeSanctis and Poole 1994, Orlikowski 1992b). As we saw earlier, analyses of technology structuring have tended to focus on users as the key agents whose actions shape and are shaped by their technological and institutional contexts. Yet our study found that others routinely and deliberately intervene in users' structuring activities by influencing users' understandings, altering technological features to ease use, modifying institutional policies to promote particular kinds of communicative practices, and facilitating access to and operation of communication technologies. As such intervening actions are not captured by our current understanding of technology structuring (see Figure 5.1), an extension of this understanding would be useful.

Figure 5.6 depicts the structuring activities of mediators as they intervene in users' structuring of their technology. To allow for the possibility that mediators may also be users (as in the case of NAGA), we distinguish between the actions of use and those of mediation. Like users, mediators are influenced by the institutional context within which they work, and which furnishes them with certain facilities, authority, and job responsibilities (Arrow 5). Technology-use mediation is also constrained (and enabled) by the existing technological configuration within the organization (Arrow 6). In taking action, mediators create policies, procedures, guidelines, templates, access mechanisms, applications, and physical configurations which alter the technology itself (Arrow 7) and change the institutional properties of the organization when used (Arrow 8). In addition, technology-use mediation influences users' interpretations (and hence their actions) by providing them with understandings, images, concepts, knowledge, and heuristics about their specific technology (Arrow 9). In doing so, mediators influence users' work habits around use of the technology, their technological frames (Orlikowski and Gash 1994), and their perceptions of their technology (Fulk et al. 1990). Such action by the mediators, in turn, is influenced by users' existing assumptions, expectations, and knowledge, their level of experience, and their current requirements (Arrow 10).

Technology-use mediation can thus be seen to structure the institutional, interpretive, and technological rules and resources that users draw on when they use their technology (Arrows 1 and 2). In their appropriation by users, these images, concepts, policies, templates, configurations, etc., are accepted, legitimized, and reinforced (Arrows 3 and 4), becoming institutionalized over time. Management's official and/or implicit sanctioning of such policies, configurations, and so on further serves to authorize them as appropriate ways for users to interact with their technology. Where orga-

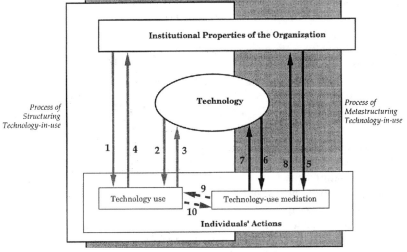

Key:

Arrow 1: Institutional conditions for use   Arrow 6: Technological conditions for mediation
Arrow 2: Technological conditions for use   Arrow 7: Technological consequences of mediation
Arrow 3: Technological consequences for use   Arrow 8: Institutional consequences of mediation
Arrow 4: Institutional consequences of use   Arrow 9: User consequence of mediation
Arrow 5: Institutional conditions for mediation   Arrow 10: User conditions for mediation

Note: Arrows 9 and 10 are dotted to indicate that the interactions are mediated through the institutional properties.
We show a direct relationship for expository convenience.

Figure 5.6. Processes of Technology Structuring and Metastructuring

nizational authorization (Arrow 5) is absent, as in the transfer episode, mediation activities (Arrows 7 and 8) would be significantly limited.

In Figure 5.6, we have depicted technology-use mediation as a process of structuring resembling that engaged in by users when they structure their technologies. Yet, the structuring involved in technology-use mediation shapes users' own structuring of their technologies. Hence, it is a form of second-order structuring, which we refer to as the *metastructuring* of technologies in use. The right-hand side of Figure 5.6 depicts this process of metastructuring engaged in by individuals such as the members of NAGA. More generally, this process can also characterize the interventions of individuals playing roles such as those of champions, trainers, and local experts. Indeed, because use of technology in organizations is a social practice, there will always be other actors who intervene in some way or other in users' structuring of their technologies. Thus, we believe that the process of metastructuring, just like the process of structuring, is always happening, whether interpretively, institutionally, or technically; deliberately or inadvertently; formally or informally. How, by whom, in what situations, and with what intended and unintended consequences remain important empirical questions.

In this chapter, we have characterized one type of metastructuring—technology-use mediation—and our findings about NAGA's activities can begin to explicate the process of metastructuring. In particular, technology-use mediation may be seen to involve at least four types of activities with which technologies and their uses are contextualized over time: establishment, reinforcement, adjustment, and episodic change. This categorization of mediating activities may also be seen as a preliminary classification of metastructuring moves, although metastructuring can take less comprehensive and perhaps quite different forms as well. However, we believe that this categorization serves as a useful starting point to begin thinking more systematically and generally about technology-use mediation and the process of metastructuring. Table 5.1 summarizes these mediating activities and provides illustrative examples from the NAGA story recounted above. Figure 5.7 shows how these four mediating activities might be sequenced in an ongoing process of metastructuring.

Establishment

During establishment of a technology, mediators set up the technology itself (its physical parameters, features, etc.), they articulate the ways in which the technology will initially be adopted by the users in their practices, and they propose modifications to the institutional context and the technology that will facilitate assimilation of the technology into standard operating procedures. In articulating a rationale for use of the technology and motivating its implementation, establishment activities resemble the actions taken by champions in identifying and promoting the adoption of an innovation (Howell and Higgins 1990). Some work has suggested that the initial understandings and routines formed around a new technology congeal fairly rapidly after its implementation (Tyre and Orlikowski 1994), as users reach a plateau of competence (Bullen and Bennett 1990) and are impatient to get on with using the technology to accomplish productive work. Thus, establishing the technology physically in the organization, and establishing it socially in the work habits of its users is a particularly influential mediation activity. NAGA, based on its members' notion of how the news system could serve as a communication vehicle for the whole project, spent almost 2 months discussing ideas, soliciting feedback, articulating a role for the news system, persuading managers to proclaim the news system an official medium, and facilitating a comfortable transition for project members to this new communication technology.

Establishment has the effect of creating a particular set of interpretive, institutional, and technological conditions of use. Depending on whether the intention behind the implementation of the new technology is to improve the existing way of doing business or to change it fundamentally, the establishment process will reinforce, adjust, or replace existing practices. In NAGA's case, both minor improvements and major changes were apparent with the establishment of the news system. For example, NAGA's replacement of e-mail lists with local newsgroups resulted in a change in communication within project teams. On the other hand, when NAGA persuaded project managers to designate the news system as the official medium for the project—in place of the long-standing and traditional daily lunchtime meeting—they occasioned a significant institutional shift in the meaning, privilege, and legitimacy of particular communicative practices within the Acorn project.

Reinforcement and Adjustment

Once a technology has been established, mediators can shift their attention and actions to offering ongoing assistance, encouragement, and support as well as maintaining the technology itself to ensure reliable performance. Shortly after establishment, mediators help users to incorporate the new technology into their work practices, providing advice, demonstration, and hand-holding. In addition, mediators can correct inappropriate or inefficient usage as they encounter it, either through interaction with users or formal/ informal monitoring of technology use. Appropriate use may be promoted through a variety of training and communication sessions. NAGA members had a certain understanding of the role the news system could play in the project, and they advocated this through their actions and their statements in newsletters, news-system messages, lectures, and meeting announcements.

In addition to reinforcing the use of an established technology, mediation also extends or refines particular uses of the technology. By adjusting the technology itself and influencing local norms, mediation may facilitate incremental changes to the use of a technology. As we saw in the Acorn project, mediators may make such adjustments in response to a number of triggers, including user requests, detection of a problem with the existing routine of use, or a perceived opportunity to enhance use. For example,

TABLE 5.1 Activities Constituting Technology-Use Mediation

Mediating Activity	Actions	Examples from NAGA
Establishment	Set up physical parameters and features of the technology	Transferred news system from lab and installed it on project network
		Added new newsgroups, e.g., *local, announce*
		Modified news system to accept and send messages via electronic mail
	Modify institutional properties of the organization to facilitate technology assimilation	Persuaded management to allow use of news system and to sanction technology mediation activities
		Obtained management's authorization to declare the news system the official medium of the project
	Articulate the cognitive and behavioral routines through which the technology may be appropriated by users	Defined role of news system vis-à-vis other media in use in the lab
		Proposed guidelines for news system use
		Communicated the functions, role, and sanctioned use of the news system
		Provided education around use of the news system
Reinforcement	Maintain the operational fidelity of the technology	Maintained the operations of the news system, e.g., new user accounts, backups, network management
	Help users adopt and use appropriate cognitive and behavioral routines to use the technology	Promoted use of the news system
		Engaged in communication of and education in use of the news system
Adjustment	Adjust technical features of the technology to promote use	Added new newsgroups, e.g., *union, headlines*
		Modified news system to accept Japanese characters in the subject line
	Alter usage rules and procedures to facilitate the use of the technology	Modified definition of newsgroups to clarify their purpose and distinguish them from each other
		Modified usage guidelines to ease use

TABLE 5.1 *Continued*

Mediating Activity	*Actions*	*Examples from NAGA*
Episodic change	Redesign the technical functions and features of the technology	Extended functionality of news system through archival newsgroups (e.g., *guide*) and external newsgroups (e.g., *mail-lists*)
		Reconfigured the news system to clarify relations among newsgroups, to aggregate shared newsgroups, and to create greater coherence of the whole
	Modify institutional properties of the organization to facilitate change in technology use	Established moderated newsgroups to monitor and control appropriate use, e.g., *guide, official*
	Redefine cognitive and behavioral routines to facilitate change in users' appropriation of the technology	Redefined usage guidelines and routines for use to accommodate changes in news system configuration
		Communicated the redefined functions, role, and use of the news system
		Provided education for redefined news system

NAGA's modification of the news-system software to allow Japanese subject lines resulted in minor modifications to the technology and its use. Ultimately, however, adjustments have the effect of reproducing the institutional and technological conditions of use, not of challenging them. While the refinements may enhance the technology and its use, the net effect is to increase the effectiveness of the existing system, not to transform it, as may occur with episodic change.

Episodic Change

The fourth type of mediation activity—episodic change—involves a significant reassessment and restructuring of the technology and its routines of use. Unlike adjustments, episodic changes are proactive attempts to create

164

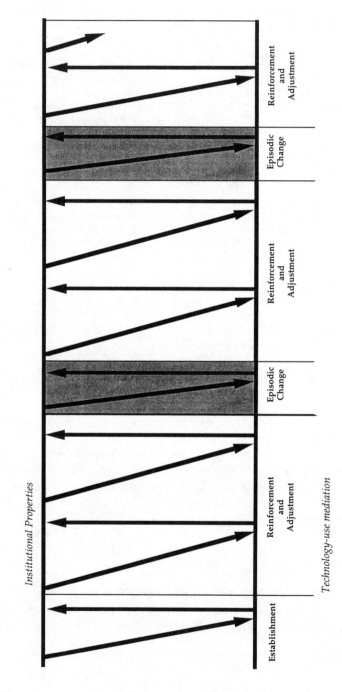

Figure 5.7. Process of Metastructuring Showing Mediated Activities

major improvements in the coherence and performance of a technology, its use, users' understandings, and the institutional context of use. Because change episodes have greater potential to disrupt the established norms and work practices, they tend to be scheduled periodically and require extensive justification to counter user resistance. With episodic change, there is an opportunity to step out of the normal routine of daily use and examine the bigger picture of the technology in relation to its context of use. NAGA, for example, did this when they reconfigured the new system to establish a more logical relationship among the newsgroups. Episodic change may also result from external triggers, such as releases of new versions of technology or action by senior management (Tyre and Orlikowski 1994).

Episodic change resembles Poole and DeSanctis's (1992) notion of "junctural structuring events," which they describe as "episodes during which major determinations are made about which structural features of the [technology] to appropriate, how they will be appropriated, and whether and how they will be reproduced" (p. 28). In their case, the junctural structuring events are precipitated by the primary users of the technology (a group decision support system). In our case, however, it is the mediators, not the primary users, who initiate the structuring event, and this action is more proactive and reflective than that of the primary users whose action is more likely to be unplanned and emergent. Like junctural structuring events, episodic change provides an opportunity for initiating structural transformation. While NAGA's change episodes did not appear to result in significant institutional change, the potential for such transformation was always present in its activities.

CONCLUSIONS

In this chapter, we have identified a level of technology structuring—metastructuring—that influences the structuring activities of technology users within organizations and have outlined the form and general character of the metastructuring process. While such a process occurs with or without conscious planning, our interest has been to articulate a particular kind of metastructuring—technology-use mediation—represented by the deliberate, ongoing, and organizationally sanctioned intervention in the use of a communication technology. This mediation serves as an organizational mechanism for facilitating the ongoing adaptation of technologies, their use, and organizational contexts to each other and to changing conditions. The identification and articulation of the metastructuring process and of technology-use mediation have a number of implications for research and practice.

Implications for Research

On the research side, the notion of metastructuring draws attention to the fact that there may be multiple levels of action and interaction in organizations, and that a process of technology structuring at one level may itself be structured at another level. This suggests that our understanding of the use of new computer-mediated communication technologies should consider these additional levels of structuring, for the intervention of others in technology use exerts a significant influence on the nature and effectiveness of organizational communication via new electronic media. Understanding the effect of different types of metastructuring, from the deliberate and sanctioned technology-use mediation to the relatively inadvertent metastructuring of expert users, is an important goal for future research.

With respect to technology-use mediation, further research is clearly needed to examine its various aspects and their consequences in different organizational contexts and with different communication technologies. For example, NAGA's problematic attempt to transfer the Acorn news system from the project into a lab suggests that the more extensively a technology has been contextualized, the more specific it is to that context, and the more difficult it will be to use that technology directly or with only minor adjustments in a different or changed context. Empirical studies should examine the use of contextualized technologies in different organizational settings to assess the validity of this proposition.

Technology-use mediation probably varies with the type of technology and individuals involved. Technologies that are more specialized and fixed in purpose (e.g., group decision support systems) may need less contextualizing than more generic, open-ended technologies. Although in the case studied here the NAGA members also happened to be users, we do not believe that this is a requirement and suggest that technology-use mediation can be conducted by a range of different organizational actors. Our study suggests that NAGA's effectiveness was facilitated by its members' proximity to the context of use, their understanding of users' practices and norms, their credibility with the users, and their knowledge of users' technical abilities and the technologies at their disposal. Further studies could explore the importance of these specific characteristics to the effectiveness of mediation activities.

By engaging in a deliberate and sanctioned process of metastructuring, mediators are involved in shaping and reinforcing particular forms of meaning, power, and norms. By developing and defining categories of use, disseminating and enforcing rules for use, and allocating resources to certain kinds of contextualizing activities, mediators exert considerable influence over how a particular technology will be established and used in an organization. Whether such influence will be experienced as coercive and controlling or helpful and supportive undoubtedly depends on various contextual factors, including existing norms around help-seeking and help-giving behavior, and how the mediators conduct themselves vis-à-vis their users: as experts dictating or technically precluding particular usage or as facilitators working with users to enable a range of ongoing users. Further research is needed to determine under which conditions such influence will be experienced as constraining and under which as enabling.

Our outline of technology-use mediation is grounded in a single case study in a Japanese R&D lab. In particular, the Japanese cultural setting of this study undoubtedly influenced the use of this conferencing technology. We cannot assume, however, that this study represents typical Japanese use of electronic media, as some studies have suggested that very few Japanese firms use e-mail, much less conferencing technologies (Straub 1994). The Japanese cultural setting, however, undoubtedly shaped aspects of NAGA's mediation role. For example, the careful consensus-building efforts initiated by NAGA during establishment of the communication technology seem to reflect the process of *nemawashi,* described by Ulfhielm (1987, p. 128) as "a tactful (and indirect) sounding out of each group member . . . about his or her thoughts and feelings concerning a certain issue; it also functions as an instrument for subtle persuasion." The process followed by NAGA thus seems to reflect an existing, culturally embedded group process, suggesting one reason that project members responded so rapidly (as reflected in Figure 5.3) to the pronouncement by management and NAGA that the new electronic medium was now to be considered official and mandatory. A similar process might be less effective in a comparable American R&D group. Although details of the mediation activities probably differ in different cultures—both national and corporate—some technology-use mediation probably has value in most contexts where users attempt to appropriate sophisticated communication technologies into work practices and interaction routines. Future studies should examine technology-use mediation and metastructuring under different cultural, organizational, technological, and mediation conditions and validate or elaborate the process as well as the institutional and interpretive influences articulated here.

Implications for Practice

This chapter also has implications for organizations implementing networks and computer-mediated communication technologies. If such electronic media are to be viewed as the backbone of new and fluid organizational forms, the ongoing contextualization performed by mediators adds value by keeping technology usage aligned with user conditions and organizational circumstances. In the particular case study related here, the intervention was initially undertaken casually and without explicit authorization. As NAGA's activities became more deliberate and as its members sought and obtained organizational authorization and resources, thus engaging in activities of technology-use mediation, the effects of their activities became more significant and apparently more effective. The transfer episode discussed above highlights the importance of adequate institutional support—social, monetary, and technical—for mediation to make it as effective as possible. Mediation activities within the Acorn project had enabled NAGA to establish and support the communication technology in one context and organizational form, but when that organizational form dissolved and the context of use shifted, the lack of institutional support for ongoing mediation precluded recontextualizing the technology to new organizational conditions. It also provides further evidence that however good the technology may be, it will not be effective unless the institutional and interpretive conditions facilitate its use (Orlikowski 1992a).

Our study of NAGA's activities suggests that organizations may wish to be more explicit and deliberate about the process of metastructuring. Metastructuring occurs, with or without careful management. Trainers, local experts, and system administrators all intervene in some way in users' interactions with their communication technologies, and hence engage in a type of metastructuring. With reflection and effective distribution of resources, organizations might use this process to advance particular kinds of communication, both initially and over time. For example, organizations wishing to promote innovative use of new electronic media could empower a group of mediators to provide images, procedures, and use guidelines different from those comprising the technology frames, habits, and genres of communication already established in the organization. Because technology-use mediators are interested in the ongoing effective use of the technology by a group as a whole, they are in a much better position to provide the necessary support to a group's use of communication and collaborative technologies than are support staff or local experts who tend to provide stand-alone support to individual users.

Organizations could also use technology-use mediation to occasion and support episodes of experimentation, reflection, and change in technologies and their use, so as to allow for the evolution of technological frames, work habits, and communication routines in conditions of change. Indeed, research by Tyre and Orlikowski (1993) suggests that the effective adaptation of process technologies to their contexts of use requires conscious management of opportunities and resources for improving technology use.

Computer-mediated communication technologies are, by and large, general-purpose tools that help individuals communicate, share information, and make decisions in a broad range of settings. Because these settings are specific and the tools are usually general, customization of the technologies and their use is typically needed to make them relevant to particular contexts of use. In the new fluid organizational forms now emerging in the face of rapidly changing environments, contextualization of technologies will be a critical mechanism for adapting communication norms and work practices. A process of metastructuring shaped by organizationally sanctioned activities of technology-use mediation may thus be a significant element in organizations' adaptation to change.

NOTES

1. All messages and some interview quotes cited in this chapter have been translated from the Japanese.

2. The project was terminated for reasons unrelated to the news system or the internal functioning of the project group.

REFERENCES

Barley, S. R. (1986), "Technology as an Occasion for Structuring: Evidence From Observation of CT Scanners and the Social Order of Radiology Departments," *Administrative Science Quarterly,* 31, 78-108.

Beath, C. M. (1991), "Supporting the Information Technology Champion," *MIS Quarterly,* September, 355-371.

Bjørn-Andersen, N., K. Eason, and D. Robey (1986), *Managing Computer Impact,* Norwood, NJ: Ablex.

Bullen, C. V. and J. L. Bennett (1990), "Groupware in Practice: An Interpretation of Work Experience," *Proceedings of the Conference on Computer Supported Cooperative Work,* Los Angeles, October.

Contractor, N. S. and E. M. Eisenberg (1990), "Communication Networks and New Media in Organizations," in J. Fulk and C. W. Steinfield (Eds.), *Organizations and Communication Technology,* Newbury Park, CA: Sage, pp. 143-172.

Culnan, M. J. (1983), "Chauffeured Versus End-User Access to Commercial Databases: The Effects of Tasks and Individual Differences," *MIS Quarterly,* 7, 1, March, 56-67.

Daft, R. L. and A. Y. Lewin (1993), "Where Are the Theories for the 'New' Organizational Forms? An Editorial Essay," *Organization Science,* 4, 4, i-vi.

Davis, G. B. and M. H. Olson (1974), *Management Information Systems,* 2nd ed., New York: McGraw-Hill.

DeSanctis, G. and M. S. Poole (1994), "Capturing the Complexity in Advanced Technology Use: Adaptive Structuration Theory," *Organization Science,* 5, 2, 121-147.

Drucker, P. F. (1988), "The Coming of the New Organization," *Harvard Business Review,* January/February, 45-53.

Eisenhardt, K. M. (1989), "Building Theories From Case Study Research," *Academy of Management Review,* 14, 4, 532-550.

Foulger, D. A. (1990), "Medium as Process: The Structure, Use, and Practice of IBM's IBMPC Computer Conferencing Facility," unpublished PhD thesis, Temple University, Philadelphia, PA.

Fujimoto, M. (1993), "Electronic Communication Technology in R&D Settings: Policy Implications for Public and Private Sectors," unpublished SM thesis, Massachusetts Institute of Technology, Cambridge.

Fulk, J., J. Schmitz, and C. W. Steinfield (1990), "A Social Influence Model of Technology Use," in J. Fulk and C. W. Steinfield (Eds.), *Organizations and Communication Technology,* Newbury Park, CA: Sage, pp. 117-140.

Giddens, A. (1984), *The Constitution of Society: Outline of the Theory of Structure,* Berkeley: University of California Press.

Howell, J. M. and C. A. Higgins (1990), "Champions of Technological Innovation," *Administrative Science Quarterly,* 35, 2, 317-341.

Johnson, B. M. and R. E. Rice (1987), *Managing Organizational Innovation: The Evolution From Word Processing to Office Information Systems,* New York: Columbia University Press.

Leonard-Barton, D. A. (1988), "Implementation as Mutual Adaptation of Technology and Organization," *Research Policy,* 17, 251-267.

Lewin, A. Y. and C. U. Stephens (1993), "Designing Postindustrial Organizations: Combining Theory and Practice," in G. P. Huber and W. H. Glick (Eds.), *Organizational Change and Redesign,* New York: Oxford University Press, pp. 393-409.

Mackay, W. E. (1990), "Users and Customizable Software: A Co-adaptive Phenomenon," unpublished doctoral dissertation, Massachusetts Institute of Technology, Sloan School of Management, Cambridge.

Maidique, M. A. (1980), "Entrepreneurs, Champions, and Technological Innovation," *Sloan Management Review,* 21, 2, Winter, 59-76.

Malone, T. M. and J. F. Rockart (1991), "Computers, Networks, and the Corporation," *Scientific American,* September, 111-117.

Miles, M. B. and A. M. Huberman (1984), *Qualitative Data Analysis: A Sourcebook of New Methods,* Beverly Hills, CA: Sage.

Orlikowski, W. J. (1992a), "Learning From Notes: Organizational Issues in Groupware Implementation," *Proceedings of the Conference on Computer Supported Cooperative Work,* Toronto, pp. 362-369.

_____ (1992b), "The Duality of Technology: Rethinking the Concept of Technology in Organizations," *Organization Science,* 3, 3, 398-427.

_____ and D. Gash (1994), "Technological Frames: Making Sense of Information Technology in Organizations," *ACM Transactions on Information Systems,* 12, 2, 174-207.

_____ and J.-A. Yates (1994), "Genre Repertoire: Examining the Structuring of Communicative Practices in Organizations," *Administrative Science Quarterly,* 39, 4, 541-574.

Poole, M. S. and G. DeSanctis (1990), "Understanding the Use of Group Decision Support Systems: The Theory of Adaptive Structuration," in J. Fulk and C. W. Steinfield (Eds.), *Organizations and Communication Technology,* Newbury Park, CA: Sage, pp. 173-193.

_____ and _____ (1992), "Microlevel Structuration in Computer-Supported Group Decision Making," *Human Communication Research,* 19, 5-49.

Rice, R. E. and E. M. Rogers (1980), "Reinvention in the Innovation Process," *Knowledge,* 1, 4, 490-514.

Rogers, E. M. (1983), *Diffusion of Innovations,* 3rd ed. New York: Free Press.

Rousseau, D. A. (1989), "Managing the Change to an Automated Office: Lessons From Five Case Studies," *Office: Technology and People,* 4, 31-52.

Schön, D. A. (1963), "Champions for Radical New Inventions," *Harvard Business Review,* 41, 2, March/April, 77-86.

Sproull, L. and S. Kiesler (1991), *Connections: New Ways of Working in the Networked Organization,* Cambridge: MIT Press.

Strassman, P. A. (1985), *Information Payoff: The Transformation of Work in the Electronic Age,* New York: Fress Press.

Straub, D. W. (1994), "The Effect of Culture on IT Diffusion: E-Mail and Fax in Japan and the U.S.," *Information Systems Research,* 5, 23-47.

Trigg, R. H. and S. Bødker (1994), "From Implementation to Design: Tailoring and the Emergence of Systematization in CSCW," in *Proceedings of the Conference on Computer Supported Cooperative Work* (October, Chapel Hill, NC), ACM/SIGGHI and SIGOIS, New York, pp. 45-54.

Tyre, M. J. and W. J. Orlikowski (1993), "Exploiting Opportunities for Technological Improvement in Organizations," *Sloan Management Review,* 35, 13-26.

_____ and _____ (1994), "Windows of Opportunity: Temporal Patterns of Technological Adaptation in Organizations," *Organization Science,* 5, 1, 98-118.

Ulfhielm, F. (1987), "Spoken Japanese: Linguistic Influence on Work Group Dynamics, Leadership, and Decision-Making," in L. Thayer (Ed.), *Organization—Communication: Emerging Perspectives II,* Norwood, NJ: Ablex.

Walsham, G. (1993), *Interpreting Information Systems in Organizations,* New York: John Wiley.

Weick, K. E. (1990), "Technology as Equivoque: Sensemaking in New Technologies," in P. S. Goodman, L. S. Sproull, and Associates (Eds.), *Technology and Organizations,* San Francisco: Jossey-Bass, pp. 1-44.

Yates, J.-A. and W. J. Orlikowski (1992), "Genres of Organizational Communication: A Structurational Approach to Studying Communication and Media," *Academy of Management Review,* 17, 2, 299-326.

6

Incentives and Computing Systems
for Team-Based Organizations

A Complementarity Perspective

ANITESH BARUA

C.-H. SOPHIE LEE

ANDREW B. WHINSTON

In an attempt to increase efficiency and flexibility, many organizations are experimenting with team-based structures and new information systems (IS) applications. Organizational design has many facets such as incentive systems, technology, organizational structure, task characteristics, and control mechanisms. The complexity of the design problems is increased due to the presence of complementarity between these design-related factors. That is, the payoff to the organization resulting from teamwork will be high when all factors pertaining to incentives, information systems, etc. are chosen in a coordinated manner rather than in isolation from each other. For example, since teams are often characterized by their task interdependencies and the nature of interaction among members, incentives and information systems designed for traditional, hierarchical organizations may not be appropriate for the flatter, team-based environment. The complexity of identifying individual contribution to team output creates difficulty in distributing rewards fairly (i.e., in proportion to one's true contribution) in a team. Along similar lines, the hierarchical supervisory structure may not work well for the

This chapter appeared originally in *Organization Science, 6*(4), July/August, 1995.

peer-to-peer nature of teamwork. However, a close relationship among team members leads to the possibility of mutual monitoring (which may be less expensive than hierarchical supervision) and peer pressure (Kandel and Lazear 1992) with significant positive impacts on team[1] productivity.

Modern information technologies (ITs) provide new means of team interaction such as media-rich synchronous or asynchronous communication. However, due to the complementarity nature of technology and other factors, systems designers must incorporate incentives and control mechanisms into IS design. For example, providing access to team members' electronic workspaces may encourage mutual monitoring (a control mechanism in a team environment). Similarly, systems design features such as anonymity and identifiability of members and their actions are expected to result in very different types of team behavior and outcomes. It can be difficult to translate social responses into electronic mail messages, and so large, geographically dispersed teams may be less able to use social influence than face-to-face teams; however, a system featuring easy communication of social response might provide incentives for members to exert social influence. Thus, the challenge faced by IS developers is to design systems which complement the chosen incentive schemes and control mechanisms in order to maximize team productivity.

The interplay between the different factors identified above is complex, and yet a thorough assessment of such interactions is crucial for providing appropriate systems support for teamwork. For instance, in the context of group decision support, an incentive system that requires close monitoring or identification of individual contribution may not work when a group decision support system (GDSS) is designed to support anonymity. Unless organizational and systems designers explicitly consider such interdependencies, large investments in sophisticated incentive systems, control mechanisms, state-of-the-art technologies, new organizational structures and task redesign are unlikely to bring forth significant productivity gains or bottom-line payoff.

In order to study the complementarity between various design choices, as an exploratory step we seek to address the following question: Given certain features of computing environments, what are the impacts of financial and social incentive systems, control mechanisms, and organizational and task characteristics on team productivity? We then ask: Knowing such interactions between technology and other factors, what implications can we derive for designing incentive systems and information systems to support team-based activities? While we clearly recognize the need to consider these design choices simultaneously, investigating what choice of, say, incentives would best complement a given set of technology features (or vice versa) is likely to provide valuable insights about the feasible design space and the organizational value associated with each design configuration. These research issues are addressed by developing an economic model of team/group interactions involving a GDSS. However, similar analysis can be done with other types of group support technologies.

In order to derive interesting propositions (testable hypotheses), we use analytical modeling as the primary research tool. The analysis relies on the qualitative properties of cost and benefit functions[2] (e.g., benefit increasing at a decreasing rate with effort), and on the premise that team members act in self-interest. We believe that this approach provides a strong theoretical basis for the hypotheses generated, which can be verified or rejected empirically. The key contribution of the study is a set of insights involving the interplay between some important organizational design factors. The specific research questions are addressed in the context of group or team interactions, and include the following:

1. Anonymity of group members' inputs may force a supervisor to divide rewards equally among group members. Does it lead to shirking of responsibilities (relative to the effort levels desired by the organization) in a team? The motivation for this question stems from the GDSS literature, where a significant body of research suggests that systems preserving the anonymity of group members may lead to better outcomes (e.g., Connolly et al. 1990, Nunamaker et al. 1987, Rao and Jarvenpaa 1991). While anonymity is used primarily in GDSS design, it plays an important role in large, dispersed groups. Our analysis focuses on the impact of this feature on group/team productivity. Other features of IS can also be analyzed in a similar way, based on their interactions with other organizational design factors.

2. How does equal sharing of reward impact individual incentives when group members differ in their productivity levels? We distinguish between group members in terms of their intrinsic abilities, as well as the effort levels they choose to apply to a particular task. While organizations rarely use equal sharing of benefits as a reward system, there is an increasing interest in team/group-based incentive systems (Applegate 1994). Furthermore, when individual contribution cannot be identified, social rewards such as praise and recognition are often directed toward an entire group or team rather than a specific team member. Does this equal sharing of social rewards have a negative impact on team output?

3. With heterogeneous group members, do low-productivity members shirk responsibility more than high-productivity members under the reward sharing system?

4. How do the level of task interdependence and the reward system affect the mutual monitoring behavior of group members?

5. Are high-productivity members monitored more or less than low-productivity members?

6. Under what organizational conditions can mutual monitoring lead to lower team productivity?

Several interesting qualitative results emerge from our analysis. Assuming that members act in their best interest, we show that equal sharing of benefits in a world of anonymity leads to shirking of responsibilities by all members. Anonymity is also shown to reduce the value of social rewards, resulting in lower effort levels. When members within a team have different productivity levels, the equal-sharing mechanism results in lower net payoff for the high-productivity members. However, high-productivity members shirk (relative to levels desired by the organization) more than the low-productivity members. We identify task characteristics and productivity thresholds for which members put in more effort under an individual contribution-based scheme. Addressing the question of whether a high-productivity member is monitored more than a low-productivity member, we find that the level of monitoring depends on the productivity factor and the effort level of the member. In investigating the negative impacts of peer pressure, we show that when an organization can benefit from diversified ideas (which may require deviation from a norm), but when members are under the pressure of an authoritarian view, anonymity can increase productivity by reducing the intensity of peer pressure. Some implications for system design in terms of optimal level of information detail are discussed.

The balance of the chapter is organized as follows. In the following section, we further discuss the interaction between various organizational design factors, and use the anonymity feature of GDSS as an illustration. We also examine the prior literature, which provides the motivation for this study. Then, we develop an analytical model of group interactions, and study the impacts of different incentive schemes, IS features, control mechanisms, and organizational and task characteristics on the group output. We also discuss the managerial implications of a set of propositions derived from the analysis. Finally, we present concluding remarks.

MOTIVATION AND PRIOR LITERATURE

Organizational structures and computing systems supporting such structures are undergoing significant changes. Many organizations with traditional, hierarchical decision authority are experimenting with flatter, team-based decision structures (e.g., see Applegate 1994). Enhancing organizational productivity is one of the key managerial concerns providing the impetus to consider flatter, team-based structures. However, empirical studies often suggest that teams are not as productive as they could be (e.g., Hymowitz 1988, Mintzberg 1973, Mosvick and Nelson 1987), and factors causing a loss in team productivity have been identified by sociologists and economists (e.g., Dashiell 1935, Olson 1965, Steiner 1972). While these factors appear to be diverse in nature, they generally relate to the design of appropriate incentive schemes and control mechanisms.

There are some key differences between hierarchical and team-based organizations which make it difficult to import incentive and IS design principles from the hierarchical to the team-based structure. In a hierarchical environment, the employee (or an "agent" in the agency theory terminology) and the employer (the "principal") enter into a contract involving some observable outcome as a basis for reward (compensation). When the outcome is accomplished by one employee, there is little problem in identifying the source of contribution. In a team-based structure, however, some observable team outcome may be used as the basis for a group reward, which is to be distributed among members. However, the interdependence between members' subtasks makes it difficult to identify the source of contribution and to distribute rewards fairly. In the classical team theory literature in economics (Marschak and Radner 1972), it is assumed that all team members have the same objective function. However, in a realistic team or group setting, different members may have different objectives (payoff functions). Since these members maximize their individual payoffs instead of the organizational payoff, and since there are, in general, interdependencies between the members' subtasks, designing team or group incentives to maximize organizational payoff is a complex problem.

The second distinguishing feature of a team is the observability of an individual's effort level by other members. In the hierarchical structure, the employee's effort level is often considered unobservable or too costly to monitor. By contrast, in a team-based organization, the interdependency of task assignments and the close working relationship among team members may make each member's effort more visible to the peers. The team structure is also unique in terms of the monitoring behavior of the members. Since a member's reward is often a function of the total group output (which depends on the performance of other members as well), the member has an incentive to monitor (and be monitored by) other members in the team (Kandel and Lazear 1992). This peer monitoring activity can have a powerful supervisory impact on the overall team productivity.

Topics relating to team productivity and observability of effort have been addressed by social psychologists. "Social loafing" occurs when team members lose motivation and become less productive (Dashiell 1935). One possible cause of social loafing is that members cannot identify their contribution and do not know how much more to contribute. Once their individual contribution is identified, their quality of work improves significantly (Szymanski and Harkins 1987, Williams et al. 1981). Another potential reason for social loafing is that members, working anonymously in a group, may feel dispensable and lose the motivation to work. When their identity is revealed, the social loafing problem is mitigated (Weldon and Gargano 1985, Weldon and Mustari 1988).

In a seminal paper, Kandel and Lazear (1992) applied microeconomic modeling to examine the effects of peer pressure on team members' effort. Peer pressure is created by monitoring other members' actions, and results in increased group effort and productivity. In this chapter, we build on Kandel and Lazear's peer pressure model and analyze the peer monitoring behavior for different incentive schemes, IS design features, and organizational task characteristics.

The move toward team-based structures has been accompanied by a rapid proliferation of network-based computing. Starting with conventional electronic mail, more sophisticated network applications are being developed to support various aspects of teamwork. For instance, computer supported collaborative work is a broad concept that involves systems supporting multiple individuals working on the same task as a team. Group editors (Ellis et al. 1990) enable team members to edit a document concurrently. GDSSs provide computer support for various phases of the group decision-making process such as issue analysis, brainstorming, resolving conflicts, and voting electronically (e.g., DeSanctis and Dickson 1987, Gray 1983, Nunamaker et al. 1987, Poole et al. 1991, Quinn et al. 1985, Steeb and Johnston 1981). One important objective of a group support system is to provide a more convenient and efficient platform for teamwork (DeSanctis and Gallupe 1987); geographically dispersed team members can interact closely over the electronic workspace, and communication can take place in either a synchronous or asynchronous mode. While there is a significant body of research on the technical aspects of group decision support, many organizational aspects of the technology are not well understood. DeSanctis and Poole (1994) investigate the appropriation of group technology using the theoretical premise of adaptive structuration. In their view, social influences play a major role (in addition to technology characteristics) in how group members use a particular technology. In this chapter, we adopt a similar viewpoint involving the interaction between various design factors.

An important implication of an electronic platform for group interaction is that many conventional features of incentive design are altered, producing both challenges and opportunities for the organizational designer. For instance, monitoring cost may be substantially lowered because it is easier to track progress when the group members have a common electronic workspace. Members can access and share information at a lower cost and exercise social influence (either praise or pressure) on others. This leads to the possibility of incorporating social rewards within the incentive system. Employee productivity records can be archived with higher precision, and supervisors can design sophisticated reward systems for group interactions. While IT can reduce the cost of monitoring peers and accessing information, it can also be designed to discourage such behavior. For example, monitoring can be made more difficult by manipulating different record access rights and access times so that one's progress can only be monitored by certain members or at certain times (e.g., when certain milestones are reached). An electronic brainstorming session can be made totally anonymous by manipulating the user interface so that monitoring individuals becomes impossible. While the technology can be easily adapted to provide such features, the influence of these features on incentive design and team productivity can be dramatic.

To demonstrate how IS design influences the incentive system (and vice versa), we consider the anonymity of comments in a GDSS session as an example. The potential benefit of anonymity is that it can reduce some negative social influences. By reducing the observability of comments, it can protect junior or shy members from being judged by their status or being intimidated (Nunamaker et al. 1987). The environment where anonymity may be favored is one where lower-status members may be reticent in expressing ideas (Huber 1984), where "group members may feel strong pressure to conform, thus stifling the input of nonconforming ideas to the decision process" (DeSanctis and Gallupe 1985, p. 7), and where "reticent individuals withholding their opinions for . . . sensitivity to disapproval, or sensitivity to the presence of high-status members" (Rao and Jarvenpaa 1991, p. 1356). For instance, when peer pressure may inhibit creativity, anonymity may be a desirable feature of the group support system.

However, from the incentive design perspective, anonymity may have a negative effect on team output. It reduces the observability of effort, and thus the supervisor has less information to distribute rewards fairly (according to an individual's contribution). In the extreme case, where all comments are made anonymous (even to the supervisor), the latter will be forced to reward each individual equally regardless of their contribution. Such equal distribution of rewards will result in shirking and free-riding behavior.

Eliminating the observability of effort makes it impossible to impose proper social influences, such as recognition and praise to high-effort members and sanctions and pressure to low-effort members. A useful concept which highlights the importance of being able to monitor group members' effort and contribution is that of public and private goods (Olson 1965). Once produced, the consumption of a private good is exclusive to the individual who has purchased it. A public good, by contrast, is consumed by many individuals. For example, a printer in a manager's home, which is not shared by anyone else, is a private good, while a printer in his or her office, which is possibly shared by many other employees, is a public good. The same good is more valuable to an individual when it is private than when it is public.

Following this distinction between public and private goods, we interpret anonymity as making a member's comments a public good instead of a private one. That is, under anonymity, an input cannot be attributed to a specific individual with certainty. By the same reasoning, the reward for the input (e.g., a felicitation letter from a senior manager) has to be collectively attributed to all members and becomes public in nature. A public good is less valuable to a member, and therefore discourages participation. The results of social loafing experiments (Weldon and Gargano 1985, Weldon and Mustari 1988) also suggest anonymity to be one factor that makes participants feel dispensable and to lose the motivation to perform.

The above interactions provide a basis for understanding the mixed findings of experimental studies involving anonymity. For example, while Nunamaker et al. (1987, 1988) find empirical support for the positive influence of anonymity, other studies (e.g., Jarvenpaa et al. 1988, Rein and Ellis 1989) do not reveal such impacts. In an open environment, where authoritarian pressure is minimum, the gain from anonymity will be neutralized by other deficiencies created by the lack of identifiability of group members. This offers a potential explanation of why studies involving more open environments may not find an association between anonymity and the quality of output.

Anonymity is only one example of how IS can play a major role in changing and enabling the incentive and control systems in team-based organizations. IS design will become even more critical as more teams rely on computer networks as their major, if not the sole, communication channel.

THEORETICAL MODEL

In this section, we analyze the performance of a group of individuals as a function of various factors, including incentive schemes, features of the supporting IS, and organizational and task characteristics. A conceptual model of interactions between various factors, and their impact on group outcomes, is shown in Figure 6.1. The organization assigns a task to a team. The benefit that each member receives by accomplishing the task is determined by the reward system of the organization. For instance, each member can receive an equal share of the team output, or each member can receive a

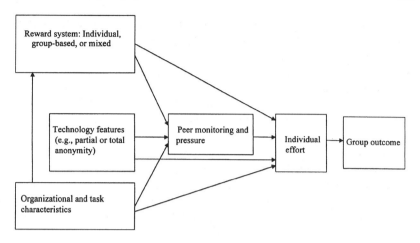

Figure 6.1. Conceptual Model Linking Design Factors to Group Interaction Outcomes

reward according to his or her marginal contribution (if it can be identified). In addition to financial benefits, a group member can also receive social rewards. IS features such as anonymity determine the suitability of a reward system and also affect the perceived value of a social reward. Alternatively, a given reward system may necessitate certain IS features. The organizational characteristics (e.g., hierarchical versus team based and authoritarian versus open) and task attributes (e.g., interdependent versus isolated) also determine the technology feature requirements. Note that the relationship between technology features and organizational and task characteristics is portrayed as unidirectional in the above model for analytical tractability. In this chapter, we do not consider reengineering efforts, which will change the organizational and task characteristics (e.g., through redesign of business processes and change in the scope of decision authority) and necessitate a bidirectional linkage. This reengineering problem of changing incentives, technology, and organizational and task characteristics in a coordinated fashion is addressed through the notion of business value complementarity by Barua et al. (1996).

The choice of individual effort levels by group members (which also determine group outcomes) depends on two sets of effects: (a) direct effects of the reward system, IS features (which may encourage or discourage shirking and free riding), and organizational and task characteristics, and (b) indirect effects of the same factors through the social control processes of peer monitoring and peer pressure. In the analytical model we develop in this section, we first consider the direct effects and derive implications for designing incentive systems. Then we study the impacts of peer monitoring and pressure on group outcomes and investigate how information systems can be designed to induce organizationally desirable behavior.

Each group member incurs a cost of putting in effort in order to accomplish the task. Under a given reward system, each member selects an effort level such that his or her net benefit—reward less cost—is maximized. On the other hand, from the organization's perspective, a desirable group behavior involves maximization of total net value (i.e., total value minus total cost). Thus, an organizational designer will use a reward system which maximizes the total net benefit after taking into account the behavior of the group members with the chosen reward system. Such a reward scheme (which considers the behavior of group members) is called "incentive compatible." It is evident that not all reward systems are incentive compatible. As an example, the number of ideas generated in a GDSS session is commonly accepted as a measure of effectiveness. However, an organization may benefit more from one high-quality idea (which requires members to devote more time with fewer ideas) than with a large number of low-quality ideas. Thus, a scheme which rewards members in proportion to the number of ideas generated may not maximize the net value to the organization. Next we characterize a team setting and analyze individual behavior under different reward systems and task characteristics.

Building on the partnership model developed by Kandel and Lazear (1992), we incorporate systems design features, incentives, and organizational and task characteristics to investigate how these factors impact team performance. A team has N members. Member i, $i = 1, 2, \ldots N$, denotes an effort level, e_i, to perform his or her task. $C(e_i)$ is the cost of effort level e_i applied by member i. Cost increases with effort, and we assume that it increases at an increasing rate. That is,

$$\frac{\partial C}{\partial e_i} > 0 \text{ and } \frac{\partial^2 C}{\partial e_i^2} > 0.$$

For simplicity, we assume that the cost function is the same for all members.

The organizational payoff, $\int$, is a function of all members' effort levels, $e = [e_1, e_2, \ldots e_N]$, or $\int = \int(e)$. We assume that the payoff increases with effort, and that it increases at a decreasing rate. That is,

$$\frac{\partial f}{\partial e_i} > 0 \text{ and } \frac{\partial^2 f}{\partial e_i^2} < 0 \text{ for all } i.$$

The net organizational payoff, π, is the benefit less the sum of all members' cost,

$$\int(e) - \sum_{i=1}^{N} C(e_i).$$

Member i's net payoff, π_i, is the individual reward less his or her cost, $C(e_i)$. An individual can be rewarded by tangible goods (task reward) and/or intangible goods (social reward). The task reward is denoted as R^T, while the perceived value of the social reward (where applicable) is denoted as R^S. R^T is some function of $\int$ but the exact form depends on the specific reward system. One such scheme is the group-based reward, where each member receives an equal share of the total group output. That is, $R^T = \int/N$, or $\pi_i = \int/N - C(e_i)$.

We assume that each member chooses an effort level to maximize his or her net payoff. This individual optimal effort level is denoted by e_i^1. However, in order to maximize the net payoff to the organization, each member should devote the organizational optimal effort level. For member i this organizational optimal level is denoted by e_i^o. Shirking is said to occur when the individual members' effort levels fall short of that required for organizational payoff maximization (i.e., when $e_i^1 < e_i^o$). In Proposition 1 below, we examine the consequences of using a group-based reward system, where the team output is divided equally among the members. Furthermore, in Propositions 1 and 2, we assume that the team members are identical. This allows us to distinguish between shirking and free-riding behavior, the latter being an outcome of equal reward sharing in a heterogeneous team.

Proposition 1. The group-based reward mechanism leads to shirking on the part of group members.

Proof. The proofs of this and all other propositions are provided in the appendix.

The group-based reward mechanism may be adopted because of the inability to identify each member's contribution. For example, when each member's performance is anonymous to other members and the performance evaluator, the latter has to assign an equal share of the team output to each member, which will result in shirking behavior. This proposition suggests that identifiability of each member to the performance evaluator is critical to increasing the group productivity. While there may be compelling reasons for a group support system to preserve anonymity among group members, a member's identity helps determine his or her contribution to group performance. Thus, identifiability (a design feature of the group support system) may provide the basis for designing reward systems to mitigate the shirking problem. It is important to note that equal sharing of financial benefits rarely exists in the pure form, but team-level performance is increasingly being used in employee evaluations;[3] for the sake of analyzing the stylized model, we are considering the extreme case of equal sharing. Since we also consider social rewards as an important determinant of members' behavior, letters or words praising a team without pointing toward specific individuals should be taken as a case of equal (social) reward sharing.

In Proposition 1, we considered only the task (financial) reward received by each member. Next, we examine how social rewards and the design of the group support system influence members' behavior. A group member may make a contribution not only for financial rewards but also for his or her perceived value of social recognition within the organization.[4] When the ownership of a good is exclusive to an individual, it is called a private good. The same good is worth more when it is private than when it is public. For instance, when a contribution (such as an important idea) is made anonymous, the recognition or praise for the contribution becomes public in nature. Under identifiability, however, the same recognition or praise is a private good, being directed to the individual making the contribution. Therefore, the social reward is higher when the member's contribution is identified than when it is anonymous. We assume that a higher effort level results in higher contribution to the team output, and that a higher contribution, when identified, receives a higher private social reward.

Definition. Member i's perceived value of a social reward, R^S, is a function of i's effort level, e_i: that is, $R^s = R^s(e_i)$.

$$\frac{\partial R^s}{\partial e_i} > 0 \text{ and } \frac{\partial^2 R^S}{\partial e_i^2} < 0 .$$

When the reward is public (private), the value of the reward is denoted as $R^{S'}(R^{S''})$. For any e_i, $R^{S''}(e_i) > R^{S'}(e_i)$.

Proposition 2. When the reward to a group member includes social rewards (in addition to the equal sharing of financial rewards), anonymity of comments reduces the member's effort level.

Proposition 2 shows the impact of anonymity on the value of social rewards. Under anonymity, a social reward becomes a public good, which has a lower value to a group member than a private good. Thus, identifiability of group members is important not only to the performance evaluator but also to peers, in order to fully implement a social reward system (such as "employee of the month"). The complementarity effects between social incentive schemes and design features of the group support system are highlighted by this proposition. We note that anonymity is less used in the design of conferencing, workflow, and groupware systems other than GDSS, but there is, nevertheless, an anonymous component to these systems as well. Communication takes on anonymity when the team size grows and when members are physically dispersed; so even if names are attached to work, the names are less meaningful in large, dispersed groups operating through groupware.[5]

In Propositions 1 and 2, we focused on the comparison between the individual and organizational choices of effort levels. However, by assuming identical group members, we did not consider how differences between the productivity of individual team members interact with different reward systems. In reality, any team will have members who have different capabilities in terms of their contribution to the organizational objectives. What are the consequences of rewarding individuals equally, regardless of their productivity and contribution to the organization? To address this question, we first define the notion of productivity in a group setting. To avoid notational complexity, we use a two-person team in the definition below. The definition can be extended to an N-person case by holding other members' effort levels constant.

Definition. For a two-person team with members i and j, let $\int_i(e_i, e_j = e)$ be the marginal contribution of member i, when e is the effort level of member j. Similarly, let $\int_j(e_i = e, e_j)$ be the marginal contribution of j, when e is the effort level of member i. The productivity of i is higher than that of j for any effort level, l, if $\int_i(e_i, e_j = e)|_{e_i = 1} > \int_j(e_i = e, e_j)|_{e_j = 1}$.

In its general form, the definition includes the possibility that the productivity of member i may depend on member j's effort level for interdependent tasks. For example, in a team presentation involving multiple speakers, the contribution of an individual to the overall quality of the presentation depends not only on the individuals' effort level but also on effort levels chosen by other team members.

However, for tasks which do not involve interdependencies among team members, an individual's contribution is independent of the effort level chosen by others. Task interdependence is an important determinant of the effort level applied by team members and hence a key factor in designing team incentives. In this chapter, we restrict our attention to two cases: (a) positive task interdependence and (b) zero task interdependence. Positive interdependence implies that the marginal contribution of member i increases with the effort level of member j, i.e.,

$$\frac{\partial}{\partial e_j} \frac{\partial J}{\partial e_i} = J_{ij} > 0.$$

When there is no task interdependence, $J_{ij} = 0$. It should be noted that the cross-partial derivative of the payoff function being nonnegative implies that the function is "supermodular" (Topkis 1978) or complementary in the effort levels of various team members. Of course, supermodularity is not limited to continuous functions, and one of the key strengths of the concept is its applicability to discrete functions. For example, Barua et al. (1996) used principles of supermodularity to rationalize the nature and direction of design changes in reengineering projects. In Propositions 3A and 3B, we study the interactions between the reward system and the heterogeneity of group members.

> **Proposition 3A.** Members with higher productivity will devote higher effort levels than lower-productivity members, both in organizational and individual payoff maximization.

> **Proposition 3B.** Under the equal-sharing mechanism, members with higher productivity will receive less net gain than lower-productivity members.

It is evident that equal reward sharing is nonequitable when group members are heterogeneous in their abilities. Free-riding by the low-productivity members is an undesirable outcome of this reward system.[6] Interestingly, however, the high-productivity members will, based on self-interest, choose an effort level that is higher than the low-productivity members. This behavior is observed in many team projects, where more capable members end up doing most of the work, and where the reward may still be equally divided among the team members. However, since effort may be equally costly for both types of members, the net payoff of the more productive members gets reduced. Thus, Propositions 3A and 3B favor identifiability as an important design feature which may enable the selection of a superior incentive system.

While the high-productivity members may choose higher effort levels than low-productivity members, both groups are expected to shirk under an equal reward-sharing scheme. Do high-productivity members shirk more than low-productivity members? In Propositions 4 and 5, we suggest that the degree of task interdependence as well as the productivity of members determine the difference in the shirking levels of the two groups. For analytical tractability we consider a two-person group (with one high- and one low-productivity member). We also assume that the benefit function for the case of zero task interdependence is given by $\int = k(e_i^{\alpha_i} + e_j^{\alpha_j})$, $(0 < \alpha_i, \alpha_j < 1)$, where $\alpha_i > \alpha_j$ (i.e., member i has higher productivity), and where k is a constant. Similarly, the benefit function for the case of positive task interdependence is given by $\int = k e_i^{\alpha} e_j^{\beta}$.

Proposition 4. With zero task interdependence, the high-productivity member shirks more than the low-productivity member. However, for positive task interdependence, both members engage in the same level of shirking.

Since the high-productivity member creates a higher marginal payoff than a low-productivity member at any effort level, the organization requires a higher effort level from the former (the cost function being the same for both members). When the subtasks are independent, a lack of distinction between the high- and the low-productivity members during the distribution of reward increases the discrepancy between the organizational and individual effort levels for the high-productivity member. However, for positive task interdependence, the group members engage in the same level of shirking (relative to the organizational requirements).

Will the effort level increase if the reward to an individual is based on his or her contribution rather than the group output? In the following sections, we examine another incentive system which determines an individual's reward by his or her marginal contribution to the team. In this reward system, a person who applies effort level e_i is paid

$$\frac{\partial \int}{\partial e_i}\bigg|_{e_i} * e_i ,$$

i.e., the marginal contribution at the effort level chosen by the member, multiplied by the effort level.

Will the members' effort levels increase by switching to the individual contribution-based reward system described above? Under what condition does the contribution-based mechanism outperform the group-based mechanism? In Proposition 5, we examine the case when the task has zero interdependence (i.e.,

$$\frac{\partial^2 \int}{\partial e_i \partial e_j} = 0$$

for $i \neq j$), while positive productivity dependence

$$\left(\frac{\partial^2 \int}{\partial e_i \partial e_j} > 0 \right)$$

is taken up in Proposition 6.

Proposition 5. Let $\int = k \sum e_i^{\alpha_i}$. For member i, whose $\alpha_i > 1/N$, the individual contribution-based system will result in higher effort level than the group-based mechanism. On the contrary, for member j, whose $\alpha_j < 1/N$, the individual contribution-based system will result in lower effort level than the group-based mechanism.

When a task has a zero interdependence, equal sharing of reward provides each member with a fraction ($1/N$) of every other member's individual contribution. Note that this portion of the reward, which can be attributed to other members, does not enter into an individual member's choice of effort level. In other words, the member chooses an effort level such that his or her marginal cost is equal to the marginal benefit that comes only from his or her own effort level. Since he or she retains a fraction $1/N$ of his or her own contribution in the equal sharing scheme, any weight greater than $1/N$ will induce him or her to put in more effort. Note that his or her productivity factor α is also the fraction of his or her contribution that he or she receives in an individual contribution-based scheme. Therefore, $1/N$ acts as a threshold value for the productivity factor.

Next we address the positive task interdependence case. Consider a team with two members i and j, and let the benefit function be given by $\int = k e_i^{\alpha} e_j^{\beta}$ ($0 < \alpha$, $\beta < 1$). Let $\alpha + \beta \leq 1$ to avoid overdivision of profits. Clearly, i's marginal contribution depends on j's effort level, e_j, and productivity factor, β. In Proposition 5, we noted that there is a threshold value ($1/N$) for the productivity factor, above (below) which a member devotes more (less) effort under an individual contribution-based scheme. Does the same result hold true for tasks that have positive interdependence? We address this issue in Proposition 6.

Proposition 6. Consider a two-person team with $\int = k e_i^{\alpha} e_j^{\beta}$ ($0 < \alpha$, $\beta < 1$) and cost function $C(e_i) = c e_i^2$. Let member i have higher productivity than member j, i.e., $\alpha > \beta$. The effort level of i under an individual contribution-based scheme will be higher than that under a group-based scheme if $\alpha > \frac{1}{2}x$, where $x > 1$.

In the positive task interdependence case, since i's contribution is dependent on j's effort level and productivity factor, i "suffers" due to j's low productivity and requires a higher threshold value (compared to the zero interdependence case) to put in more effort. Note that a productivity factor greater than 1/2 would have induced i to put more effort in the zero task interdependence case with two team members.

Propositions 5 and 6 focus on the effect of group composition, task characteristics, and the reward system on the members' choice of effort levels. As noted before, all these factors must be considered in tandem (and not one at a time) by an organizational designer to ensure high group productivity. Next we study the impact of social influence of peers on a group member's output and assess the economic and technological feasibility of using such social influences instead of more traditional hierarchical supervision.

Mutual Monitoring
and Peer Pressure

In this section, we examine the effect of a social influence, namely peer pressure, on members' effort levels under different reward systems, organizational and task characteristics. When the reward to an individual is group based, or when the task has positive interdependence, a low effort level of a member will hurt other members' rewards. Alternatively, a higher effort applied by any member will imply higher rewards for all group members. Therefore, group members may choose to apply peer pressure on each other as a mechanism to ensure high productivity. This peer pressure is often communicated through the action of peer monitoring: When an individual is monitored by peers, he or she perceives peer pressure and puts in more effort to reduce such pressure.

Kandel and Lazear (1992) model peer pressure through a function $P(e_i, a_{1i}, \ldots, a_{i-1,i}, a_{i+1,i}, \ldots a_{Ni})$, which is the peer pressure perceived by member i (with effort level e_i) and monitoring level a_{ji} of member j, $i \neq j$. Peer pressure reduces with effort and increases with peer monitoring:

$$\frac{\partial P}{\partial e_i} < 0 \ \text{ and } \ \frac{\partial P}{\partial a_{ji}} > 0,$$

for all $j \neq i$. In Kandel and Lazear's model, the purpose of i's monitoring j is not to observe how much effort j puts in but rather to exert pressure on j.

Member i's effort level depends on the monitoring action taken by other members, $1, 2, \ldots, i-1, i+1, \ldots, N$. Effort level increases with monitoring, i.e.,

$$\frac{\partial e_i}{\partial a_{ji}} > 0,$$

for all $j \neq i$. Note that this property is not an exogenously specified assumption; Kandel and Lazear (1992) show that it can be derived from the model. Monitoring incurs cost, and the cost of monitoring is denoted by $M = M(a_{i1}, a_{i2}, \ldots, a_{i,i-1}, a_{i,i+1}, \ldots, a_{iN}$. According to the group-based reward mechanism, the individual net benefit with peer pressure is given by

$$\pi_i = \frac{\int(e)}{N} - C(e_i) - M(a_{i1}, a_{i2}, \ldots, a_{i,\,i-1}, a_{i,\,i+1}, \ldots a_{iN}) -$$
$$P(e_i, a_{1i}, a_{2i}, \ldots, a_{i-1,\,i}, a_{i+1,\,i}, \ldots, a_{Ni}) \, .$$

Kandel and Lazear (1992) show that peer pressure increases effort level and the total organizational payoff. In this section, however, we investigate the impact of different reward structures and task characteristics on a member's incentive[7] to monitor others. It is intuitively evident that equal sharing of group payoff provides incentives for a group member to monitor others. However, does the member still have monitoring incentives if his or her reward is based only on individual contribution? In Proposition 7, we show that the incentive to monitor others depends on the nature of the task itself. In particular, if the task has positive interdependence, there will be mutual monitoring even when reward is individual contribution based.

Proposition 7. Under the individual contribution-based reward system, team members monitor each other's performance when the task has positive interdependence

$$\frac{\partial^2 \int}{\partial e_i \partial e_j} > 0.$$

There will be no monitoring if the task has zero interdependence

$$\frac{\partial^2 \int}{\partial e_i \partial e_j} = 0.$$

The above proposition suggests that even under individual contribution-based compensation, the nonseparability of a task helps retain the monitoring incentives of team members. Since monitoring increases task effort level, a certain level of monitoring may be required to align the objectives of the individuals with that of the organization. The proposition also shows that when the task is separable, there is no incentive to monitor under an individual contribution-based reward structure. Of course, a group-based reward system will induce monitoring behavior even for zero interdependence tasks. It is evident that there are significant complementarity effects between the nature of the task, reward system, and peer monitoring levels.

How can the benefits of individual contribution-based rewards and monitoring incentives be retained even for tasks that are productivity independent? Many organizations use a gain-sharing reward system—in addition to each individual's salary, employees receive a portion of the organization's output as reward—to address this problem. A gain-sharing reward system is a mixture of individual contribution and group-based reward,

$$w_1 \int_i e_i + w_2 \frac{\int(e)}{N},$$

where w_1 and w_2 are the individual and group weights, respectively, to be chosen by the organizational designer to achieve incentive compatibility. Formally, the designer's maximization problem is given by

$$\max_{w_1, w_2} \int(e_1, e_2,..., e_N) - \sum C(e_i) - \sum M(a_{i1}, a_{i2},..., a_{i,i-1}, a_{i,i+1},... a_{iN})$$
$$- \sum P(e_i, a_{1i}, a_{2i},..., a_{i-1,i}, a_{i+1,i},... a_{Ni}),$$

subject to

$$w_i \sum \int_i e_i + w_2 \int(e_1,..., e_N) \le \int(e_1,..., e_N),$$

for the total reward given to team members cannot exceed the total payoff generated by the team. Two other sets of constraints (arising from individual payoff maximization) need to be considered:

$$w_1 \int_{ii} e_i + w_i \int_i + w_2 \frac{\int_i}{N} - C_i - P_i = 0,$$

for all i (choice of task effort levels), and

$$w_1 \int_{ij} \frac{\partial e_j}{\partial a_{ij}} e_i + \left[w_2 \int_j \frac{\partial e_j}{\partial a_{ij}} \right] \Big/ N - M_{a_{ij}} = 0$$

for all i, j $(i \neq j)$ (members' choice of monitoring levels).

The last two sets of constraints ensure incentive compatibility between organizational and individual objectives. Through these constraints, the designer takes into account the behavior of team members as a function of w_1 and w_2. Appropriate choice of w_1 and w_2 will induce incentive compatibility. Note that as the interdependency between team members (i.e., $\int_{ij}$) decreases, the weight of the group-based component w_2 must be increased if monitoring incentives are to be retained. By increasing the weight w_2 members are encouraged to monitor each other, even when the task is not sufficiently interdependent to induce desirable levels of monitoring behavior.

Productivity Type and Monitoring

To achieve organizational and individual maximization, will a high-productivity member be monitored more or less than a low-productivity member? The answer to this question depends on the actual effort level chosen by a given member and his or her productivity factor. If the effort level of a high-productivity member is relatively high, additional peer monitoring (which incurs a cost) may not lead to significant additional benefits. However, the high-productivity factor of a member leads to the possibility that the marginal gain from monitoring a high-productivity member may be higher than that from monitoring a low-productivity member. Consider an N-person team with payoff function $\int = k \sum e_i^{\alpha_i}$. We are interested in the relationship between the productivity factor α_i and the monitoring level α_{ji}. This relationship is investigated in Proposition 8.

Proposition 8. The level of monitoring a member is subjected to increases (decreases) with his or her productivity if his or her effort level is below (above) a threshold level. For member i, this threshold level is given by

$$exp\left(-\frac{1}{\alpha_i}\right).$$

The intuition behind the threshold level is that the net gain from monitoring is positive (negative) if the equilibrium effort level of a member is lower (higher) than the threshold value. In other words, there is no monotonic relationship between the productivity factor of a member and the level of monitoring to which he or she is subjected.

Negative Impacts of Monitoring and Peer Pressure

While peer pressure can increase a team member's effort level, in certain circumstances it can have a negative impact on organizational performance. Consider a situation where a deviation from an existing norm could benefit the organization. However, members might perceive a pressure due to deviation from an "authoritative" viewpoint (the norm). This pressure (created through observability) may be so high that the team members will choose to stay with the norm (or choose a low level of deviation). In other words, anonymity may have positive impacts in highly bureaucratic organizations.

Let $d_i \geq 0$ be the degree of deviation of member i's opinion from a norm. When member i stays with the norm, $d_i = 0$. It requires effort to propose and justify a deviated view, and thus $e_i = e_i(d_i)$. The required effort increases at an increasing rate with the degree of deviation, i.e.,

$$\frac{\partial e_i}{\partial d_i} > 0 \text{ and } \frac{\partial^2 e_i}{\partial d_i^2} > 0.$$

For example, a radical deviation from the norm may require much more justification than a small variation around the status quo. The pressure felt by a member also increases at an increasing rate with his or her deviation, i.e.,

$$\frac{\partial P_i}{\partial d_i} > 0 \text{ and } \frac{\partial^2 P_i}{\partial d_i^2} > 0.$$

We assume that the organization can benefit from the deviated opinion so that

$$\frac{\partial f(d)}{\partial d_i} > 0, \text{ and that } \frac{\partial^2 f(d)}{\partial d_i^2} < 0.$$

In these circumstances, a member's payoff function is given as

$$\pi_i = f(d)N - P(d_i) - C(e_i).$$

Proposition 9. When a higher peer pressure is exerted on the members' deviated views, members will devote less effort to making such views.

Some GDSSs incorporate anonymity of comments as design feature, and as shown in Proposition 1, anonymity may produce shirking and loss of performance; but why is anonymity still favored in some organizations? It may reduce

$$\frac{\partial P}{\partial d_i}$$

since a deviation of opinions from a norm can no longer be attributed to a specific individual. In the above situation, technology incorporating anonymity can be used to mitigate the problem arising from nonconformance to existing norms in a hierarchical organization. For a more open organization, anonymity should be avoided because it may cause confusion, shirking, and loss of productivity. In such situations, the technology should be used to identify the contributions of individual members for the purpose of providing appropriate incentives for high productivity. Note that when every member deviates, anonymity cannot conceal the fact that a given member deviated from the norm. Of course, it keeps confidential the level of deviation by a given member.

The nature of the peer pressure function is an organizational characteristic and can vary from one organization to another. For example, in some organizations, a norm might be changed when a majority of group members choose to deviate. That is, a given member will feel less pressure due to deviation, when other members also depart from the norm. Thus, if a majority of members choose to deviate, the anonymity of their comments may have a less significant role. In some other organizations, however, the entire group (which deviates from the norm) may be considered as deviant, and anonymity will definitely provide protection against the level of deviation chosen by each member of the group.

Consider another example where an organization wants creativity and deviation from the status quo. In this case, a member may feel peer pressure if he or she does not deviate from the norm. Identifiability (rather than anonymity) is the required system functionality since the group supervisor would like to identify the individual contribution of each group member in creating new ideas for the organization.

Interaction Between Task Effort and Monitoring Levels

To this point, we have considered the choice of task effort and monitoring levels to be independent of each other. However, it is very likely that members have a binding time constraint (e.g., 8 hours a day), such that the choice of task and monitoring times involves a trade-off. In this section we analyze how a member's productivity type affects his or her time allocation between task effort and monitoring. When there is a time constraint, a member has to allocate each unit of time between e_i and α_{ij}, depending on which option provides a higher net benefit. Let us use the time constraint

$$\sum_{j \neq i} \alpha_{ij} + e_i = T,$$

where T is the maximum time period available to member i's and where α_{ij} and e_i are expressed in units of time. Member i's choice is given by

$$\max_{e_i, a_{ij}, i \neq j} \left[\frac{\int(e_1,...,e_n)}{N} - C(e_i) - M(a_{i1},... a_{i,i-1}, a_{i,i+1},..., a_{iN}), \right.$$

$$\left. - P(e_i,a_i,..., a_{i-1}, a_{i+1},..., a_N) + \lambda \left(\sum_{j \neq i} \alpha_{ij} + e_i - T \right) \right],$$

where λ is the Lagrangian multiplier. The first order conditions are given by

$$\int_i / N - C_i - P_i + \lambda = 0,$$

$$\frac{\int_i \partial e_j}{N \partial a_{ij}} - M a_{ij} + \lambda = 0, \text{ for } j = 1, 2, ..., i-1, i+1, ..., N \text{ and}$$

$$\sum_{j \neq i} \alpha_{ij} + e_i = T.$$

If λ is negative (i.e., if the time constraint is binding), then the marginal benefits of increasing the task effort and monitoring levels are higher than their marginal costs. In other words, the member could have increased both α_{ij} and e_i in the absence of the constraint to increase the net payoff. However, due to the time constraint, a member has to allocate each unit of time between e_i and α_{ij}. For a "high"-productivity member, it may be optimal to devote more time to the task effort than to monitoring others, while a "low"-productivity member may find it more beneficial to put more effort in monitoring others. Such a division of labor will be a very useful strategy if some members do

a better job at monitoring (i.e., have a lower monitoring cost) than those who
are better at the task itself.

Designing Information Systems
for Team-Based Organizations

As organizations move toward team-based structures, organizational computing systems evolve into networked architectures to help work groups and
teams achieve high productivity. As we have emphasized throughout the
chapter, there needs to be an integrated approach to designing incentive
schemes and computing systems for team-based organizations. Since the
appropriation of an IS depends on incentives, and organizational and task
characteristics, the design of the technology should explicitly consider complementarity effects between these factors. One of the key system design
parameters is the level of detail of information provided, which can vary
between coarsest (no information) and finest (most detailed) partitioning of
the relevant message space. For instance, in terms of information on members' effort levels, the finest partitioning provides detailed descriptions,
while a coarser system provides only categorical information (such as "high,"
"medium," or "low"). The most appropriate level of detail is one where team
members, based on such information, will apply the optimal levels of task
effort and mutual monitoring. For example, a system which provides the
coarsest information on members' effort level (e.g., due to anonymity) may
cause incentive problems such as free-riding and social loafing, while finest
information can cause problems associated with identifiability and peer
pressure. A better information system design may be one that provides a more
appropriate partitioning of information, thereby revealing the identity and
the contribution of individual members only to the supervisor who rewards
the members, but maintaining peer anonymity during intense interactions.
Such a system enables an organization to implement individual contribution-
based rewards and to avoid potential problems associated with identifiability.

Networking and related technological advances enable the monitoring of
team members' inputs and contributions to organizational performance at a
feasible cost. Such monitoring can help align the individual and organizational goals; however, too much monitoring can be harmful for both the
individual and the organization. The organizational computing system may
provide a level of detail on members' inputs so that team members engage
in an organizationally desirable level of monitoring.

We note that the use of abstraction "effort level" can be interpreted in
terms of the degree of refinement of a state space representing alternative
solutions to the organization's task. That is, the degree to which the space of
possible solutions is refined is an increasing function of the effort level.

Computing resources available to team members would enable the refinement process to proceed more effectively. Monitoring peers would then be based on reviewing the documented process of state elimination.

Several other issues relating to system design emerge from the theoretical propositions. They constitute an agenda for empirical investigation. Since our propositions have not been empirically validated, we refrain from making specific prescriptive statements about designing computing systems for teamwork.

We have shown the importance of social influence in designing group incentive systems. However, in remote, network-based communication, such influences may be difficult to convey to the group members. For example, the facial expressions and tonal effects of a face-to-face communication are likely to be lost in text-based message exchanges. While our results do not suggest specific design features which will make such social influences easier to convey, empirical research on multimedia-based group support should focus on the retention of social influences, to preserve the private nature of a social reward.

Another important implication of transmitting social messages is that the relationship between monitoring and peer pressure may be weakened in remote communication. Physical proximity can make it easier to monitor members' behavior and to exert appropriate social influence (praise or pressure). However, when two members communicate through a network, the monotonic relationship between monitoring and pressure may not exist anymore. That is, a member may monitor someone else's progress, and yet the latter may not feel a significant peer pressure. Since our propositions suggest that monitoring and social influence are important aspects of incentive design, future empirical research can focus on the design of computing environments to compensate for the potential attenuation of social influences during remote communication.

The nature of the task (e.g., the degree of interdependence) is an important determinant of the task and monitoring effort on the part of the group members. The information on task and reward dependency may not be readily available to the members, especially in the absence of a coordinator/facilitator of group activities. The computing environment can provide tools such as PERT charts and scheduling functions and update members' progress to show explicit interdependencies between different group members.

Our model suggests that the impacts of a system design feature on group productivity can be very different depending on the organizational characteristics. For instance, in a hierarchical organization where members' status or identity can be a source of pressure, the anonymity feature of a group support system may help reduce such pressure and lead to higher group productivity. However, in a flatter organization, where a member's status may have a smaller impact on peer pressure, anonymity will cause problems of identifying contribution and encourage free-riding and shirking behavior.

The chosen incentive system can be used to determine the optimal level of observability and access to be provided by the system to the group members. For example, a higher weight on the group-based component of a reward system suggests that mutual monitoring should be enabled through the design of the information system. That is, the system could make it easier for members to access information on others' activities for a successful implementation of the group-based incentive.

CONCLUSION

This chapter addresses the problem of designing incentives and information systems for enhancing group productivity. We suggest that there are significant complementarity or interaction effects between relevant factors, including incentives, IS design, and organizational task characteristics. In particular, the design of information systems should enable or reinforce the chosen incentive scheme (which itself may be based on group composition, task characteristics, and organizational objectives). Productivity gains are unlikely to be achieved unless the IS design reflects the underlying incentive scheme. We developed an analytical model of team interactions and studied the impacts of various design factors on team productivity.

Designing incentives and systems for team/group support is a rich area, and this chapter only suggests the vast potential of this line of research. For instance, peer pressure is only one form of social influence members exert on each other. Other forms of social influence such as peer recognition, team spirit, and leadership may be equally important and deserve full-scale investigation. While we treated peer pressure as an exogenously specified function for a given team, future research should focus on these social influence functions as endogenous variables which can be manipulated to increase the organizational payoff.

Technology expands the scope of incentive design. Using anonymity as an example, we showed how the design of the technology and the reward system led to different social influences on group members. IT makes a variety of scenarios feasible: identification of a member's comments for all group members including the supervisor, identification only for the supervisor or a subgroup of peers, etc. A different reward system may be appropriate for each of the above cases. Other relevant factors, such as the cost of monitoring, observability of effort, and the strength of peer pressure, can all be altered through the appropriate use of IT.

In this chapter we laid out a theoretical foundation for assessing the joint impacts of incentive and IS design on group productivity. Future research should focus on experimental validation of the theoretically derived propositions.

APPENDIX

Proposition 1. The group-based reward mechanism leads to shirking on the part of group members.

Proof. For each member, the first-order condition for payoff maximization is given by $(1/N)\int_i - C_i = 0$. For the organization, the first-order condition for payoff maximization is given by $\int_i - C_i = 0$. Let e_i^1 and e_i^0 denote the individual and organizational optimal effort levels respectively for member i. Therefore,

$$\frac{\int_i(e^1)}{N} - C_i(e_i^1) = \int_i(e^0) - C_i(e_i^0).$$

Suppose $e_i^0 < e_i^1$. Then $C_i(e_i^1) > C_i(e_i^0)$. Therefore,

$$\int_i(e^0) < \frac{\int_i(e^1)}{N} < \int_i(e^1)$$

for $N > 1$. However, $\int_i(e^0) > \int_i(e^1)$ for $e_i^0 < e_i^1$ (note that all members are assumed to be identical), which leads to a contradiction. Similarly, the supposition $e_i^0 = e_i^1$ also leads to a contradiction. Therefore, $e_i^0 < e_i^1$.

Proposition 2. When the reward to a group member includes social rewards (in addition to the equal sharing of financial rewards), anonymity of comments reduces the member's effort level.

Proof. Under anonymity, the social reward received by a member is "public" in nature and is denoted by $R^{S'}$. When each member is identified, the social reward is "private" and is denoted by $R^{S''}$. The net payoffs to member i with anonymity and identified comments are

Anonymity (public social rewards): $\pi_i' = R^T + R^{S'} - C(e_i)$

Identified (private social rewards): $\pi_i'' = R^T + R^{S''} - C(e_i)$

The first-order conditions are

(public)
$$\frac{\partial \pi_i'}{\partial e_i} = \frac{\partial R^T(e')}{\partial e_i} + \frac{\partial R^{S'}(e_i')}{\partial e_i} - C_i(e_i') = 0 \text{ and}$$

(private)
$$\frac{\partial \pi_i''}{\partial e_i} = \frac{\partial R^T(e'')}{\partial e_i} + \frac{\partial R^{S''}(e_i'')}{\partial e_i} - C_i(e_i'') = 0 .$$

Thus,
$$\frac{\partial R^T(e')}{\partial e_i} - \frac{\partial R^T(e'')}{\partial e_i} + \frac{\partial R^{S'}(e_i')}{\partial e_i} - \frac{\partial R^{S''}(e_i'')}{\partial e_i} = C_i(e_i') - C_i(e_i'') .$$

Suppose $e_i' > e_i''$. Then the RHS > 0. However,

$$\frac{\partial R^T(e')}{\partial e_i} - \frac{\partial R^T(e'')}{\partial e_i} < 0; \quad \frac{\partial R^S(e_i')}{\partial e_i} < \frac{\partial R^S(e_i'')}{\partial e_i} < \frac{\partial R^{S''}(e_i'')}{\partial e_i} . \quad \text{Therefore,}$$

$$\frac{\partial R^S(e_i')}{\partial e_i} - \frac{\partial R^{S''}(e_i'')}{\partial e_i} < 0.$$

Thus the left-hand side of the equation is less than 0, which leads to a contradiction. Similarly, the supposition $e_i'' = e_i'$ also leads to a contradiction. Therefore, $e_i' < e_i''$.

Proposition 3A. Members with higher productivity will devote higher effort levels than lower-productivity members, both in organizational and individual payoff maximization.

Proof. Let member i have a higher productivity than member j. We want to prove that $e_i^o > e_j^o$ and that $e_i^I > e_j^I$.

The organizational payoff is $\pi = \int(e) - \sum_{i=1}^{N} C(e_i)$.

The FOCs for i and j are $\dfrac{\partial \int(e)}{\partial e_i} - C_i = 0$ and $\dfrac{\partial \int(e)}{\partial e_j} - C_j = 0$ respectively.

Therefore,

(3A.1)
$$\frac{\partial \int(e^o)}{\partial e_i} - \frac{\partial \int(e^o)}{\partial e_j} = C_i(e_i^0) - C_j(e_j^0).$$

Suppose $e_i^0 < e_j^0$. Then

$$\frac{\partial \int(e^0)}{\partial e_i} - \frac{\partial \int(e^0)}{\partial e_j} > 0.$$

But the right-hand side of Eq. (3A.1) is negative, which leads to a contradiction. The supposition $e_i^0 = e_j^0$ also leads to a contradiction. So $e_1^0 > e_j^0$. Similarly, we can prove $e_i^1 > e_j^1$.

Proposition 3B. Under the equal-sharing mechanism, members with higher productivity will receive less net gain than lower-productivity members.

Proof. From Proposition 3A, $e_i^1 < e_j^1$. Therefore, $C(e_i^1) > C(e_j^1)$ and $\pi_i = \int(e^1)/N - C(e_i^1)$ is less than $\pi_j = \int(e^1)/N - C(e_j^1)$.

Proposition 4. With zero task interdependence, the high-productivity member shirks more than the low-productivity member. However, for the positive task interdependence, both members engage in the same level of shirking.

Proof

Case I. $\int_{ij} = 0$ (zero task interdependence)

The organizational maximization problem is given by

$$\max_{e_i, e_j} \left[k\left(e_i^{\alpha_i} + e_j^{\alpha_j}\right) - ce_i^2 - ce_j^2 \right].$$

For e_i, the FOC is

$$(e_i^1)^{\alpha_i - 2} = \frac{2c}{k\alpha_i},$$

where e_i^0 represents the optimal effort level from the organizational standpoint. If the reward is equally divided among the group members, then the individual maximization problem for member i is

$$\max_{e_i} \left[\frac{k\,(e_i^{\alpha_i} + e_j^{\alpha_j})}{2} - ce_i^2 \right].$$

From the FOC, we have

$$(e_i^l)^{\alpha_i - 2} = \frac{4c}{k\alpha_i},$$

where e_i^l is the individual optimal effort level of i. Taking the ratio of e_i^l and e_i^0, we have

$$\frac{e_i^l}{e_i^0} = \left[\frac{1}{2}\right]^{\frac{1}{2 - \alpha_i}}.$$

For a less productive member j, $\dfrac{e_j^l}{e_j^0} = \left[\dfrac{1}{2}\right]^{\frac{1}{2 - \alpha_j}}$.

Since $\alpha_j > \alpha_i$, $\left[\dfrac{1}{2}\right]^{\frac{1}{2 - \alpha_i}} < \left[\dfrac{1}{2}\right]^{\frac{1}{2 - \alpha_j}}$, i.e., $\dfrac{e_i^l}{e_i^0} < \dfrac{e_j^l}{e_j^0}$.

Case II. $\int_{ij} > 0$ (zero task interdependence)

$\int = k e_i^{\alpha_i} e_j^{\alpha_j}$. From the FOC, we have

$$(e_i^0)^{\alpha_i + \alpha_j - 2} = 2c \left(\frac{\alpha_i}{\alpha_j}\right)^{\frac{\alpha_j}{2}} \frac{1}{k\alpha_i} \quad \text{for organizational maximization, and}$$

$$(e_i^l)^{\alpha_i + \alpha_j - 2} = 4c \left(\frac{\alpha_i}{\alpha_j}\right)^{\frac{\alpha_j}{2}} \frac{1}{k\alpha_i}$$

for individual maximization. Therefore, $e_i^l/e_i^0 = e_j^l/e_j^0$ for $\alpha_i > \alpha_j$.

Proposition 5. Let $\int = k \sum e_i^{\alpha_i}$. For member i whose $\alpha_i > 1/N$, the individual contribution-based system will result in higher effort level than the group-based mechanism. On the contrary, for member j whose $\alpha_j < 1/N$, the individual contribution-based system will result in lower effort level than the group-based mechanism.

Proof. For an individual contribution-based reward scheme, the net payoff to i is given by

$$\pi_i = \int_i e_i - C(e_i).$$

The FOC is given by

$$\int_i + \int_{ii} e_i - C_i\,(e_i) = 0, \text{ or}$$

(5.1) $$k\alpha_i^2\, e_i^{\alpha_i - 1} = C_i(e_i).$$

For a group-based reward system, the net payoff to member i is

$$\frac{\int(e)}{N} - C(e_i),$$

and the FOC is

$$\frac{\int_i(e)}{N} - C_i\,(e_i) = 0 \text{ or}$$

(5.2) $$\frac{k\alpha_i\, e_i^{\alpha_i - 1}}{N} = C_i(e_i).$$

Denoting the optimal effort level of i under individual contribution and group-based reward systems as e_i^I and e_i^G, respectively, from Eqs. (5.1) and (5.2), we have

(5.3) $$k\alpha_i\left[\alpha_i(e_i^I)^{\alpha_i - 1} - \frac{1}{N}(e_i^G)^{\alpha_i - 1}\right] = C_i\,(e_i^I) - C_i\,(e_i^G).$$

We consider two cases: (a) $\alpha_i > 1/N$ and (b) $\alpha_i < 1/N$.

Suppose $e_i^G > e_i^I$. Then from the convexity of the cost function, the RHS of Eq. (5.3) is negative. If $\alpha_i > 1/N$, then the LHS is positive, leading to a contradiction. The supposition $e_i^G = e_i^I$ also leads to a contradiction. Therefore, for $\alpha_i > 1/N$, $e_i^I > e_i^G$. Similarly, it can be shown that for $\alpha_i < 1/N$, $e_i^I < e_i^G$.

Proposition 6. Consider a two-person team with $\int = k e_i^\alpha e_j^\beta$ $(0 < \alpha, \beta < 1)$ and cost function $C(e_i) = c e_i^2$. Let member i have higher productivity than member j, i.e., $\alpha > \beta$. The effort level of i under an individual contribution-based scheme will be higher than that under a group-based scheme if $\alpha > \frac{1}{2}x$, where $x > 1$.

Proof. For individual contribution-based reward, the FOCs for i and j are given by

(6.1) $$k\alpha^2 \, e_i^{\alpha-2} \, e_j^\beta = 2c \text{ for } i, \text{ and}$$

(6.2) $$k\beta^2 \, e_i^\alpha \, e_j^{\beta-2} = 2c \text{ for } j. \text{ Therefore,}$$

(6.3) $$\frac{e_j^I}{e_i^I} = \frac{\beta}{\alpha}, \text{ or } e_j^I = \frac{\beta}{\alpha} e_i^I,$$

where e_i^I and e_j^I denote the optimal values under the individual contribution-based system for members i and j, respectively.

Substituting the value of e_j^I (Eq. 6.3) in i's FOC (Eq. 6.1), we have

$$(e_i^I)^{\,2-(\alpha+\beta)} = \frac{k\alpha^2}{2c} \left[\frac{\beta}{\alpha} \right] \beta.$$

For group-based compensation, the FOCs for i and j are

$$\frac{k\alpha e_i^{\alpha-2} e_j^\beta}{2} = 2c \text{ for } i, \text{ and}$$

$$\frac{k\beta e_i{}^\alpha e_j{}^{\beta-2}}{2} = 2c \text{ for } j.$$

Therefore, $e_j^G = e_j^G \sqrt{\frac{\beta}{\alpha}}$, where the superscript G refers to the group-based reward scheme. Substituting the value of e_j^G in i's FOC,

$$(e_i^G)^{2-(\alpha+\beta)} = \frac{k\alpha}{4c} \left[\frac{\beta}{\alpha} \right]^{\frac{\beta}{2}}.$$

Therefore,

$$\left[\frac{e_i^I}{e_i^G}\right]^{2-(\alpha+\beta)} = 2\alpha\left[\frac{\beta}{\alpha}\right]^{\frac{\beta}{2}}.$$

If $2\alpha\left[\dfrac{\beta}{\alpha}\right]^{\frac{\beta}{2}} > 1$, then $\dfrac{e_i^I}{e_i^G} > 1$. $2\alpha\left[\dfrac{\beta}{\alpha}\right]^{\frac{\beta}{2}} > 1$

implies that

$$\alpha > \frac{1}{2}\left[\frac{\beta}{\alpha}\right]^{\frac{\beta}{2}}, \text{ i.e., } \alpha > \frac{1}{2}x, \text{ where } x \text{ is greater than } 1.$$

Proposition 7. Under the individual contribution-based reward system, team members monitor each other's performance when the task has positive interdependence

$$\left(\frac{\partial^2 \int}{\partial e_i \partial e_j} > 0\right).$$

There will be no monitoring if the task has zero interdependence

$$\left(\frac{\partial^2 \int}{\partial e_i \partial e_j} = 0\right).$$

Proof. Under the individual contribution-based reward scheme,

$$\pi_i = \int_i e_i - C(e_i) - M(a_{ij}) - P(e_i, a_{ji}).$$

The FOC for a_{ij} is given by

$$\frac{\partial \pi_i}{\partial a_{ij}} = \frac{\partial \int_i \partial e_j}{\partial e_j \partial a_{ij}} e_i - \frac{\partial M}{\partial a_{ij}} = 0, \text{ or}$$

$$\int_{ij} \frac{\partial e_j}{\partial a_{ij}} e_i = \frac{\partial M}{\partial a_{ij}}.$$

If $\int_{ij} > 0$, then $\dfrac{\partial M}{\partial a_{ij}} \neq 0$ and $a_{ij} > 0$.

However, if $\int_{ij} = 0$, then $\dfrac{\partial M}{\partial a_{ij}} = 0$ and $a_{ij} = 0$.

Proposition 8. The level of monitoring a member is subjected to increases (decreases) with his or her productivity if his or her effort level is below (above) a threshold level. For member i, this threshold level is given by

$$exp\left(-\frac{1}{\alpha_i}\right).$$

Proof. Member i's net payoff is given by

$$\pi_i = \left(\frac{1}{N}\right)k\sum_{i=1}^{N} e_i^{\alpha_i} - C(e_i) - M(a_{i1},...a_{i,\,i-1},a_{i,\,i+1},...,a_{iN}) - P(e_i,a_{1i},...a_{i-1,}a_{\,i+1,\,i},...a_{Ni})$$

The FOC for i with respect to e_i is

$$\left(\frac{k}{N}\right)\alpha_i e_i^{\alpha_i-1} - C_i - P_i = 0.$$

For $j \neq i$, $\dfrac{\partial \alpha_i}{\partial a_{ji}}$ is given by

(7.1)
$$\frac{NP_{ia_{ji}}}{k e_i^{\alpha_i-1} + k\alpha_i e_i^{\alpha_i-1}\,\textit{ln}\,(e_i)}.$$

$P_{ia_{ji}}$ is the cross-partial derivative of P with respect to e_i and a_{ji} (for $j \neq i$) and is negative. Thus expression (7.1) is negative (positive) when

$$e_i > (<)\,exp\left(-\frac{1}{\alpha_i}\right).$$

Proposition 9. When a higher peer pressure is exerted on the members' deviated views, members will devote less effort to making such views.

Proof. Member i's payoff function is given as

$$\pi_i = \frac{\int (d_1,...\,d_i,...,d_N)}{N - C(e_i) - P(d_i)}.$$

The FOC is given by

$$\frac{\partial \pi_i}{\partial d_i} = \frac{1}{n}\frac{\partial \int}{\partial d_i} - C_i\frac{\partial e_i}{\partial d_i} - \frac{\partial P}{\partial d_i} = 0.$$

Let P^A and P^B be two peer pressure functions for two groups A and B, respectively. Let d_i^A and d_i^B be the optimal deviation levels of member i for groups A and B, respectively. For the same level of deviation, let P^A exert higher pressure than P^B. That is, for any deviation x,

$$\frac{\partial P^A}{\partial d_i}\bigg|_{d_i=x} > \frac{\partial P^B}{\partial d_i}\bigg|_{d_i=x}. \quad \text{We want to show } d_i^A < d_i^B.$$

Suppose $d_i^A > d_i^B$. Then

$$\frac{1}{N}\left[\frac{\partial \int}{\partial d_i}\bigg|_{d=d^A} - \frac{\partial \int}{\partial d_i}\bigg|_{d=d^B}\right] < 0.$$

However, $C_i\bigg|_{e_i(d_i^A)}\frac{\partial e_i}{\partial d_i}\bigg|_{d_i^A} - C_i\bigg|_{e_i(d_i^B)}\frac{\partial e_i}{\partial d_i}\bigg|_{d_i^B} + \frac{\partial P^A}{\partial d_i}\bigg|_{d_i^A} - \frac{\partial P^B}{\partial d_i}\bigg|_{d_i^B} > 0,$

which leads to a contradiction. The supposition $d_i^A = d_i^B$ also leads to a contradiction. Thus, $d_i^A < d_i^B$.

NOTES

1. Traditionally, a team is characterized by a single objective function for all members (e.g., see Barua and Whinston 1991, Marschak and Radner 1972). However, in this chapter we suggest that team members make decisions to maximize their own payoffs, and that the organizational designer must select incentives and information systems such that it is in the best interest of team members to maximize the team (organizational) payoff. Accordingly, we use the terms "team" and "group" interchangeably with the understanding that members act in their best interest.

2. Occasionally we use specific functional forms for analytical tractability.

3. We thank Gerardine DeSanctis for pointing out this issue.

4. In Proposition 2, we study the impact of anonymity on the perceived value of social rewards. Later, we consider peer pressure as a form of social punishment and study its effect on group behavior.

5. We thank Gerardine DeSanctis for providing this insight.

6. Note that this free-riding occurs because of the heterogeneity of team members. In Proposition 1, we observed only shirking behavior.

7. This monitoring incentive is not exogenous to the model. It is determined by the nature of the peer pressure, cost, and benefit functions. For example, if the peer pressure function is

not significantly sensitive to the level of monitoring, and if the cost of monitoring is high, then a member does not gain from monitoring others (i.e., has no incentive to monitor others).

REFERENCES

Applegate, L. M. (1994), "Managing in an Information Age: Transforming the Organization for the 1990s," in S. Smithson, R. Baskerville, O. Ngwenyama, and J. DeGross (Eds.), *Information Technology and Emergent Forms of Organization,* New York: Elsevier North-Holland.

Barua, A., C.-H. Lee, and A. B. Whinston (1996), "The Calculus of Reengineering," *Information Systems Research,* 7, 4, 409-428.

_____ and A. B. Whinston (1991), "An Information Economics Approach to Analyzing Information Systems for Cooperative Decision Making," in *Proceedings of the 12th International Conference on Information Systems,* December, pp. 15-27.

Connolly, T., J. M. Jessup, and J. S. Valacich (1990), "Effects of Anonymity and Evaluative Tone on Idea Generation in Computer-Mediated Groups," *Management Science,* 36, 6, June, 689-703.

Dashiell, J. F. (1935), "Experimental Studies of the Influence of Social Situation on the Behavior of Individual Human Adults," in C. Murchison (Ed.), *A Handbook of Social Psychology,* Dorchester, MA: Clark University Press.

DeSanctis, G. and G. Dickson (1987, January), "GDSS Software: A Shell System in Support of a Program of Research," in *Proceedings of the 19th Annual Hawaii International Conference on Systems Sciences,* Washington, DC: IEEE Computer Society Press.

_____ and B. Gallupe (1985), "Group Decision Support Systems: A New Frontier," *Data Base,* 16, 2, 3-10.

_____ and _____ (1987), "A Foundation for the Study of Group Decision Support Systems," *Management Science,* 33, 5, 589-609.

_____ and Poole, M. S. (1994), "Capturing the Complexity in Advanced Technology Use: Adaptive Structuration Theory," *Organization Science,* 4, 4, 1-36.

Ellis, C. A., S. J. Gibbs, and G. L. Rein (1990), "Design and Use of a Group Editor," in G. Cockton (Ed.), *Engineering for Human-Computer Interaction,* pp. 13-28.

Gray, P. (1983), "Initial Observations From the Decision Room Project [DSS-83 Transactions]," in G. P. Huber (Ed.), *Proceedings of 3rd International Conference on Decision Support Systems,* Boston, June 27-29, pp. 135-138.

Huber, G. P. (1984), "Issues in the Design of Group Decision Support Systems," *MIS Quarterly,* September, 195-204.

Hymowitz, C. (1988), "A Survival Guide to Office Meeting," *Wall Street Journal,* June 21, p. 35.

Jarvenpaa, S. L., V. S. Rao, and G. P. Huber (1988), "Computer Support for Meetings of Groups Working on Unstructured Problems: A Field Experiment," *MIS Quarterly,* December, 645-666.

Kandel, E. and E. P. Lazear (1992), "Peer Pressure and Partnerships," *Journal of Political Economy,* 100, 4, 801-817.

Marschak, J. and R. Radner (1972), *Economic Theory of Teams,* New Haven, CT: Yale University Press.

Mintzberg, H. (1973), *The Nature of Managerial Work,* New York: Harper & Row.

Mosvick, R. K. and R. B. Nelson (1987), *We've Got to Start Meeting Like This,* New York: Scott Foresman.

Nunamaker, J. F., L. M. Applegate, and B. R. Konsynski (1987), "Facilitating Group Creativity: Experience With a Group Decision Support System," *Journal of Management Information Systems,* 3, 5-19.

_____, _____, and _____ (1988), "Computer-Aided Deliberation: Model Management and Group Decision Support," *Operations Research,* 36, 6, 826-848.

Olson, M. (1965), *The Logic of Collective Action,* Cambridge, MA: Harvard University Press.

Poole, M. S., M. Holmes, and G. DeSanctis (1991), "Conflict Management in a Computer-Supported Meeting Environment," *Management Science,* 37, 8, 926-953.

Quinn, R., J. Rohrbaugh, and M. McGrath (1985), "Automated Decision Conferencing: How It Works," *Personnel,* 11, 49-55.

Rao, V. S. and S. L. Jarvenpaa (1991), "Computer Support of Groups: Theory-Based Models of GDSS Research," *Management Science,* 37, 10, October, 1347-1362.

Rein, G. and C. A. Ellis (1989), "The Nick Experiment Reinterpreted: Implications for Developers and Evaluators of Groupware," *Office: Technology and People,* 5, 47-75.

Smith, W. (1980), "Experiments With a Decentralized Mechanism for Public Goods Decisions," *American Economic Review,* 70, 4, 584-599.

Steeb, R. and S. C. Johnston (1981), "A Computer-Based Interactive System for Group Decision Making," *IEEE Transactions: Systems, Man and Cybernetics,* August, 544-552.

Steiner, I. D. (1972), *Group Process and Productivity,* New York: Academic Press.

Szymanski, K. and S. G. Harkins (1987), "Social Loafing and Self-Evaluation With a Social Standard," *Journal of Personality and Social Psychology,* 53, 5, 891-897.

Topkis, D. M. (1978), "Minimizing a Submodular Function on a Lattice," *Operations Research,* April, 305-321.

Weldon, E. and G. M. Gargano (1985), "Cognitive Effort in Additive Task Groups: The Effects of Shared Responsibility on the Quality of Multiattribute Judgments," *Organizational Behavior and Human Decision Processes,* 36, 348-361.

_____ and E. L. Mustari (1988), "Felt Dispensability in Groups of Coactors: The Effects of Shared Responsibility and Explicit Anonymity on Cognitive Effort," *Organizational Behavior and Human Decision Processes,* 41, 330-351.

William, K., S. G. Harkins, and B. Latane (1981), "Identifiability as a Deterrent to Social Loafing: Two Cheering Experiments," *Journal of Personality and Social Psychology,* 40, 2, 303-311.

7

Communication Across Boundaries

Work, Structure, and Use of Communication
Technologies in a Large Organization

PAMELA HINDS

SARA KIESLER

In the early days of computers, visionaries foresaw offices and factories humming with self-propelled robots. Today, a more likely vision has the firm humming with communicating employees. Many large organizations have installed a complex network of computer-based telephone, facsimile, printing, voice mail, e-mail, and even videoconferencing technologies. These technologies increase the potential for communication in the organization. They also can support changing patterns of communication. Because technology reduces the cost and unreliability of relaying orders, management can tighten control (Casson 1994, p. 73; Sproull and Kiesler 1991, Chapter 6). The rhetoric of recent popular, business, policy, and organizational analyses, however, has emphasized a different kind of change, reflected in terms such as "self-managed teams," "computer-supported collaborative work," "flat organization," and "horizontal corporation" (e.g., *Business Week* 1993, Drucker 1988, Krachenberg et al. 1993, Quinn 1992). In this view, communication

This chapter appeared originally in *Organization Science, 6*(4), July/August, 1995.

technology is used to foster collaboration and information sharing rather than control.

We propose in this chapter that collaboration and information sharing imply employees communicate wherever and however they need to in order to solve problems and exchange know-how (e.g., Malone and Rockart 1991, Miles and Snow 1986, Nickerson 1992, Sproull and Kiesler 1991, Walton 1989). Hence, employees who need to collaborate and share information will use communication technology to communicate across organizational boundaries. Here, we define crossing boundaries as communicating nonhierarchically, that is, laterally, at the same level of the authority structure, and "diagonally," vertically outside the chain of command (Wilson 1992). Second, we propose that since technical work and workers particularly rely on collaboration and information sharing with peers, technical employees will use communication technology laterally more than will administrative employees. Finally, we propose that communication technologies can be ranked by how well they suit collaboration, particularly the intense exchange of information required for planning and technical exchange (Kraut et al. 1990). From an analysis of the attributes of three popular technologies—telephone, voice mail, and e-mail—we predict that crossing boundaries in communication, and communication by technical workers, will be associated with the use of the telephone, and secondarily, with the use of e-mail. We examine these ideas in a study of the use of these communication technologies in a large organization.

INFLUENCE OF WORK ON STRUCTURE
AND COMMUNICATION

From a large recent literature on communication and structural change in organizations has emerged a picture of a new ideal type of organization "radically different from the Weberian bureaucracy [and] characterized by relations that are based on neither hierarchical authority nor market transactions" (Nohria and Eccles 1992, p. 288). This new ideal type has been given various labels, among them "network organization" (Powell 1990, Thorelli 1986), "heterarchical organization" (Hedlund 1986), and "post-bureaucratic organization" (Heydebrand 1989). Communication in such an organization is dense, fluid, and flexible, crossing organizational boundaries of formal authority and department.

But is all network organization the same? We suggest a distinction between the networks of technical and administrative workers. We define technical workers as employees who exercise analytic or manual skills developed through extensive formal training in a specialized field (Barley

1994). Administrative workers exercise management skills, frequently developed in on-the-job training and experience (Hall 1986). In an influential paper, Powell (1990) has discussed how crafts and high-technology industries and some professions are characterized by a skilled labor force with fungible knowledge, ill-defined boundaries, overlapping work roles, and ties across teams and members of other organizations. Barley (1994) argues that firms are exploring structures and cultures of collaboration in response to technological advances and a long-term shift toward a horizontal division of labor along lines of technical expertise and occupation. These analyses suggest we take a more differentiated view of the network organization. In this more differentiated view, technical employees and administrative employees cross boundaries differently. Hence technical employees might especially communicate laterally within and across departments, reflecting their horizontal organization and need to collaborate and share know-how.

Researchers have long argued that when work is nonroutine, employees communicate both laterally and "diagonally" outside their immediate chain of command (Ancona and Caldwell 1992, Perrow 1967, Randolph and Finch 1977, Wickesberg 1968, Wilson 1992). However, technical work has been particularly associated with lateral communication both because of the nature of this work and because of the way technical workers are organized. Technical work involves "unanalyzable tasks" (Perrow 1967, Rice 1992) and is frequently complex, contextual, and interdependent with other technical work (e.g., Brooks 1987, Curtis et al. 1988, Kraut and Streeter 1990, Nohria and Eccles 1992). Mistakes or problems in one part of a complex technical system can have disastrous, unanticipated consequences (Travis 1990). Technical employees need to continually discuss nonroutine problems and integrate solutions. Doing so requires ongoing lateral coordination that may not be necessary in standardized production or administrative, bureaucratic work (Ouchi 1980).

Lateral communication among technical workers is fostered not only by the nature of technical work but also by the way technical workers are trained and organized, frequently in teams and within a strong horizontal structure.[1] Horizontally structured organizations can be traced at least to the specialized craftsmen found in medieval feudal manors and monasteries and later in crafts guilds (Kieser 1989). Professional, technical, and craftspeople have long been considered to be organized horizontally, by occupation or specialization. Collaboration and information sharing are hallmarks of horizontal structure. Consultation across specialists is not only required for coordination but also to overcome excessive specialization, which may result from hierarchy (Barley 1994, Raelin 1986). Consultation through informal lateral channels also improves individuals' ability to keep up with changes in techniques and new knowledge, and to understand and adopt innovations

(Abbott 1991, Burt 1980, Papa and Papa 1992, Rice and Aydin 1991). Finally, a strong horizontal structure tends to undercut power within the hierarchy, leaving employees in divisions and specialties with considerable autonomy (Raelin 1986).

As compared with technical work, administrative work has been associated with hierarchical communication. In its most common form in the industrialized world, the hierarchical relationship of superior and subordinate requires an authority structure, a mechanism to ensure superiors can control and monitor subordinates (Galbraith 1973). Theoretically, authority offers an efficient alternative to direct communication under conditions of complexity and interdependence (Aldrich 1979, Cyert and March 1963, Simon 1962). Rather than everybody repeatedly discussing what each person should do, management distributes and exercises control of work through layers of supervision, which in turn buffer managers from unnecessary communication (Downs 1967, March and Simon 1958). Hierarchical organization is designed to thrive on the division of labor and unity of command. That is, in order to increase efficiency and control, employees work in functional units or departments (Thompson 1967); each employee specializes in a few tasks for his or her department and reports to a single superior (Galbraith 1973). Strictly held, the division of labor into functionally specialized units and unity of command constrain communication linkages to specified vertical connections within the chain of command (Galbraith 1973).

Administrators, by virtue of their role in the hierarchy, communicate within a chain of command. However, it has long been known that administrators often face nonroutine problems and exchange information with those in functional areas outside the chain of command, and especially diagonally (Randolph and Finch 1977, Wickesberg 1968, Wilson 1992). Research on the value of weak ties (Granovetter 1982) suggests at least two reasons why administrators, especially, may engage in nonhierarchical communication. First, managers need to survey people widely in order to identify and make sense of organizational events (Kiesler and Sproull 1982). Greater diversity of weak tie contacts across levels and departments increases the probability of finding out new information and identifying problems and solutions (Burt 1983, Granovetter 1982). Second, managers might need to contact people outside their group, and especially upwardly, in order to obtain resources for their group. Lin and colleagues (e.g., Lin 1982) argue that linkages to weak ties are useful to the degree they put people in touch with those offering superior resources. If so, we would expect administrative employees to initiate communication diagonally because those at higher levels in other departments may have more resources not offered by their own superiors.

In sum, we argue that all employees will communicate across organizational boundaries using technology. However, we posit that technical employees will be distinctive in the degree to which they engage in lateral communication both because of the nature of the work they do and because of the way they are organized. Among technical workers, coordination occurs primarily through direct communication among different specialists within and across departments (e.g., Adams 1976, Allen 1977, Lave 1988, Pelz and Andrews 1966, Tushman 1977). Therefore we offer the following hypothesis.

Hypothesis 1. Technical employees, as compared with administrative employees, will have proportionately more lateral communication as compared with vertical communications.

INFLUENCE OF WORK ON USE
OF COMMUNICATION TECHNOLOGY

If employees' work influences how they communicate across boundaries, and if communication technology aids in this communication, then it follows that employees' work influences their use of communication technology (Bizot et al. 1991, Conrath 1973, Eveland and Bikson 1987, Rice and Case 1983, Rice et al. 1989). Daft and Lengel (1984, 1986) and Daft et al. (1987) have argued that people need to use "rich" channels for uncertain and equivocal communication (see also Dubin and Spray 1964, Hannaway 1985, Putnam and Sorenson 1982). Uncertainty means that data are missing; equivocality means that values, schema, or meanings for interpreting events are ambiguous or conflictful. From this argument, Daft et al. have predicted that managers at higher levels will need to use rich means of communication, face-to-face being the richest of all channels. This prediction resembles an earlier argument by Short et al. (1976) that people who must solve nonroutine complex problems perform better when communication channels convey "social presence."

To test the information richness formulation, researchers have examined the links between task characteristics and use of technology, and between managers' positions in the organization and their preferences for technology. The first relationship, that is, between task uncertainty and equivocality and technology use, has received support. People working on complex, nonroutine, "unanalyzable" problems prefer and benefit from working face-to-face or, if that is not possible, from talking by relatively rich technology such as telephone (e.g., Kraut et al. 1992, Rice 1992, Straus and McGrath 1994, Weeks and Chapanis 1976). The second relationship, that is, between managerial position and preference for technology, has received only mixed support. Managers do have many face-to-face meetings, a rich medium, but managers also advocate and use e-mail, a "poor" medium (e.g., Feldman 1987, Markus 1994, Rice et al. 1989, Trevino et al. 1987). Researchers have proposed that e-mail is not, in fact, information poor, or that other virtues of e-mail, such as its convenience or positive symbolic value, or the large number of coworkers using e-mail, can outweigh its faults (e.g., Feldman 1987, Markus 1990, Trevino et al. 1987).

Researchers have suggested that information richness (or social presence) may involve multiple dimensions (e.g., Rice 1993, Steuer 1992, Zmud et al. 1990). Two physical dimensions are bandwidth and synchrony. Bandwidth refers to the ability to exchange information from all human senses: sight, hearing, smell, and so forth (Nohria and Eccles 1992). Telephone has more bandwidth than voice mail, and voice mail more than e-mail (Fish et al. 1993). Synchrony refers to whether people can communicate at the same time. Telephone is synchronous (except when one leaves a message). E-mail and voice mail are not synchronous.

The technology attributes of bandwidth and synchrony may have different functions in communication. Bandwidth might be especially important when people need to exchange social information and social context cues, for example, when trying to establish trust with a stranger or when trying to establish dominance over a subordinate (Nohria and Eccles 1992, Zmud et al. 1990). Social information and context cues increase involvement, comprehension through back-channel cues, and social pressure (Kraut et al. 1992, Reid 1977, Siegel et al. 1986, Sproull and Kiesler 1986, Straus and McGrath 1994). We propose that telephone, voice mail, and e-mail, which differ in bandwidth, also differ in how much social information they provide. Telephone allows people to exchange more social information than voice mail. Voice mail allows people to exchange more social information than e-mail (Rice and Shook 1990). Hence people who need to convey social information will use telephone over asynchronous technology, and within asynchronous technologies, voice mail over e-mail.

Synchrony might be especially important in exchanging and discussing complex information such as the details of a technical plan, draft of a document, or interpretation of a statistical finding. Synchrony permits a great amount of information to be exchanged in a given unit of time, and ongoing feedback so that people can adjust what they say to one another, correct misunderstandings, and fill in details. People perceive rapid exchange to be important for lateral communication (e.g., Zmud et al. 1990) and collaborative planning and problem solving under uncertainty (Finholt et al. 1990, Kraut et al. 1992, Reid 1977). We propose that telephone, voice mail, and e-mail differ in how much substantive information they provide. Because telephone is synchronous, it allows people to exchange more content in a given unit of time than asynchronous technologies (Barry and Bateman 1992). But telephone not only affords synchrony; it also requires synchrony: that people be available at the same time. So, in some situations, asynchronous communication may be preferred. E-mail, because both parties can edit, store, forward, and print the same text, allows for more exchange of content in a unit of time than voice mail. Hence people who need to discuss large amounts of content, for example, in detailed technical coordination, will use telephone over asynchronous technology, and within asynchronous technologies, e-mail over voice mail.

Our arguments suggest the following hypotheses:

Hypothesis 2. Technical employees, as compared with administrative employees, will use the telephone proportionately more than administrative employees use the telephone.

Hypothesis 3. When employees use asynchronous technology, technical employees, as compared with administrative employees, will use e-mail proportionately more than voice mail.

Hypothesis 4. All employees will use the telephone rather than asynchronous technology proportionately more for lateral communication than for vertical communication.

Hypothesis 5. All employees will use the telephone rather than asynchronous technology proportionately more for communication outside the chain of command than for communication inside the chain, and more for communication outside the department than for communication inside the department.

Hypothesis 2 derives straightforwardly from the argument that telephone provides for discussion of complex content which is so essential in technical collaboration. Hypothesis 3 derives from the companion argument that e-mail allows easier discussion of complex content than voice mail. Hypothesis 4 assumes lateral communication is more likely to collaborative than vertical communication (Watson 1982). Therefore, lateral communication is likely to require more discussion; hence employees engaged in lateral communication will tend to use the telephone. Hypothesis 5 assumes that communication outside the chain of command and outside the department is more likely to connect people having weak ties than strong ties (Granovetter 1982). Establishing and maintaining weak ties requires social information exchange to establish trust (Nohria and Eccles 1992). Because telephone offers the most bandwidth, and the most exchange of social information, it should be preferred over asynchronous technologies for out-of-chain and out-of-department communication.

From our arguments on the attributes of telephone, voice mail, and e-mail technology we can derive one further hypothesis, pertaining to administrators. Substantial evidence suggests that administrators will prefer high-bandwidth technologies because these technologies allow for the exchange of social information that is important in maintaining trust, observing others' responses, and communicating dominance. For instance, people can use their voice tones to express dominance (e.g., Ferguson 1977, Meltzer et al. 1971). These behaviors are particularly related to administrators' concern with monitoring, control, and influence (e.g., Jones 1964, Kipnis et al. 1980, Watson 1982, Yates 1989, Yukl and Falbe 1990). Administrators' lives also are punctuated with a great many communications (Mintzberg 1973, Sproull 1984). Accordingly, administrators might wish to use a technology that is not only high bandwidth but also helps them control their time, namely, voice mail (Reinsch and Beswick 1990). In upward communication, particularly, administrators might favor voice mail in order to control their self-presentation and convey information without intruding. In downward communication, particularly, administrators might favor voice mail in order to broadcast messages to many people at once, delegate work and request status reports, choose their topic, limit intrusion, and avoid being sidetracked into unplanned, less important discussions (e.g., Rice and Shook 1990; see also Whitely 1984). Yet because it works through a voice channel, managers can present themselves as accessible and approachable or give a favorable but dominant self-presentation.

We propose that the need to convey social information and time pressure on administrators will exist more strongly at higher levels, and for administrators communicating vertically. Therefore we suggest the following hypothesis:

Hypothesis 6. Administrators at higher levels of authority in the organization, and administrators communicating vertically, will use asynchronous communication, particularly voice mail, proportionately more than other administrators.

OVERVIEW OF STUDY

To examine our hypotheses empirically, we collected communication data from technical and administrative employees of a large telecommunications company on the West Coast. Employees who participated in the study kept a log of all of their communication that used technology for 2 days. By matching personnel information about senders with personnel information about recipients we were able to classify each communication as lateral or vertical, and as in the chain of command, out of the chain but in the department, or outside the department. Each communication also was classified as by telephone (or voice answering), voice mail, or e-mail. We performed logit analyses to test the likelihood that a lateral communication would be sent by a technical employee (H1), that a technical employee would use the telephone or e-mail (H2, H3), that lateral, out-of-chain and out-of-department communication would be by telephone (H4, H5), and that high-level administrators and administrators communicating with subordinates would use voice mail (H6).

METHOD

Research Setting

We conducted this study in four technical departments in a technical division and three departments in an administrative division of the firm. Employees in these divisions are placed in one of two mobility tracks. Administrative employees follow a management track; when promoted, they move into higher levels of management with more authority. There are eight levels of management within the firm: Level 1, Level 2, department manager (Level 3), division manager, assistant vice president, vice president, executive vice president, and CEO. Technical employees follow a technical track whereby those with more technical expertise and experience receive more recognition and pay. Within the formal authority structure, technical employees are placed at the first level of management but do not manage others.

At the time the data were collected, the administrative division had 168 employees. This division provides support services such as contract management and procurement for the firm. The division is considered an administrative organization and has few responsibilities and employees that the firm considers technical. Employees in the administrative organization generally receive no formal training in contract management and procurement. For the most part, they learn their tasks on the job and through short training classes provided by the firm.

The second division we studied had 356 employees. This division develops and maintains computer systems used in the firm and its nonsupervisory employees are predominantly technical. Many of the technical employees have programming, mathematics, or engineering degrees. Others attend a formal, extensive training program provided by the firm to build programming skills. All technical workers are expected to analyze the needs of the firm and create software, networks, or data models for use by the firm.

There is no differentiation of technical employees along lines of authority in the technical division. In our sample, the technical employees were all at

Level 1 in the authority structure but were distributed at four levels of expertise. On average, the technical employee sample had as much seniority as the administrative employee sample. Level 2 managers in technical departments had twice the span of control ($\bar{X} = 7.0$) as did Level 2 managers in administrative departments ($\bar{X} = 3.1$). Although this is a sample of one organization, the flatter structure in the technical division fits with Barley's (1994) argument that technical workers are likely to be organized in a more horizontal structure than are administrative workers.

Technologies

We studied the use of telephone, voice mail, and e-mail.[2] All employees in the firm have access to telephone connections with other employees. The telephone system is connected with a voice mail system that provides both voice answering and voice messaging (see Rice and Danowski 1993). Voice answering, much like using an answering machine, refers to situations in which calls are forwarded to the voice mail system because the caller does not answer. Employees use voice messaging when they dial directly into the voice mail system intending to leave a message for one or more people.

Employees have access to e-mail through a computer network. Like voice mail, e-mail allows employees to send one or more messages to others. Whereas voice messages are limited to several minutes,[3] e-mail messages can be any length. Recipients can read messages, save messages, edit them, delete them, forward them to other people, or reply to the sender. Additionally, e-mail offers the option of printing the text, combining it with other computer mail or placing it in a computerized filing system.

Voice mail and e-mail are well established in this firm. Voice mail and e-mail were introduced approximately 6 and 7 years, respectively, before this study. Respondents indicated on our survey that they check for voice mail messages 6.8 times a day on average and check their e-mail messages 4.2 times a day on average. Eight respondents said they do not check their e-mail at least once a day; two of the eight employees rarely, if ever, use their e-mail account. Although both voice mail and e-mail are widely available, addressing on the e-mail system is more difficult than calling someone's voice mail. Whereas e-mail requires the sender to know the entire path of the e-mail address (including the system the recipients are using), a telephone number is all that is required to deliver a voice mail message. Even so, subjects' ratings of the ease of use of their voice mail and e-mail systems were not significantly different ($t[1, 87] = 1.64$, $p < .11$) nor were ratings of e-mail significantly different between technical and administrative employees ($t[1, 77.4] = 0.21$, $p < .84$). In contrast, ratings of the ease of use of voice mail differed significantly ($t[1, 53.3] = 2.45, p < .02$) with administrators findings voice mail easier to use.

Sample

The sample consisted of 88 employees, 33 technical employees, and 55 administrative employees. We obtained access to these employees through the vice president of each division who permitted us to approach their department heads. All three departments in the administrative division agreed to participate. Four of the five technical departments contacted in the technical division agreed to participate. (The technical department that declined to participate cited a major project with a tight deadline.) The selection of participants within each department was left to the department head (Level 3) based on our request for a sample of Level 2 managers with supervisory responsibility for at least two subordinates also included in the study. Level 2 managers then selected their subordinates. We requested department heads to treat the study as voluntary, although we offered feedback on the organization's use of communication technology. Five of the 27 Level 2 managers declined to participate or were scheduled to be on vacation. Since Level 2 managers recruited their subordinates, we have no information about individuals at Level 1 who might have declined. We told every employee who agreed to participate in the study that the study was voluntary and that all individual data would be kept confidential. All employees in the study completed all phases of data collection.

Procedure

We gathered data through a brief survey, a 48-hour (2-day) diary of all communication (see Conrath 1973, Conrath et al., 1983, Ross 1989) using any technology, and a postdiary interview. On Day 1, we met with the respondents from each department. We explained the study and the diary procedure and distributed the brief survey to obtain self reports of typical communication patterns, such as how often respondents accessed their e-mail and voice mail. The meeting and survey were intended primarily to build commitment to the study. Respondents in this study were not asked to indicate their type of job, hierarchical level, seniority, or expertise and were not told the hypotheses. Job, hierarchical level, seniority, and other demographic information was gathered from personnel records.

On Days 2 and 3, respondents completed the diary. They used booklets of forms for logging communication over 2 days. Separate booklets were provided for communications at and away from the respondent's desk. Respondents were instructed to record each of the e-mail, voice mail, facsimile, and telephone communications they sent and received during the next 2 days, including hours spent away from the office. For each communication, respondents were to indicate the technology used, the name of the sender or caller (or "me"), the name of the receiver (or "me"), and whether the communication was a reply to a previous communication. Space was provided for respondents to record the content of the communication and comments, and they were encouraged to make notes so that they would remember their communication when we interviewed them. Respondents were asked to record personal communication during work hours, but to note "private" if they wished to withhold the name of the other person(s) in the communication. (Few did so.)

To determine whether there were systematic biases in recorded communication, we attempted to match sent communications with those logged as received by other respondents in the study. Our matching procedure resulted in 166 "matched" communications of the 217 that we determined were matchable (e.g., sent by a person in the study on the same day and during office hours), a 76.5% response rate of confirmed communication by senders and receivers. By comparing "matched" and "unmatched" communication on our variables, we can estimate the bias of senders in recording their communication. The chi-square tests indicated there was only one marginally significant difference. That is, senders appear to have slightly underreported lateral communication ($\chi^2 = 2.8$, $p < .10$). A Mantel-Haenszel test of the three-way interaction between matched versus unmatched communication, technical versus administrative employee, and lateral versus vertical communication suggests that technical employees tended to underreport their lateral communication ($\chi^2 = 19.9$, $p < .001$). This bias works against our hypothesis (H1).

On Day 4, we interviewed each respondent privately. During the interview, we asked the respondent questions about each communication he or she had logged. We asked the respondent to clarify notations on the diaries, especially the names of others with whom the respondent had interacted. We also obtained measures of the importance and urgency of each communication, in order to check on potential bias in the recording of communications.

Variables

We used the corporation's formal designation of each employee to determine his or her level in the authority structure and classification in this study as technical or administrative. Supervising managers in both the technical and the administrative departments are classified as administrative. In the technical division, there were 33 technical employees, all designated as Level 1, and 18 administrative employees, 5 at Level 3, 11 at Level 2, and 2 at Level 1. In the administrative division, there were 37 participants (none of whom were technical), 3 at Level 3, 9 at Level 2, and 25 at Level 1.

A categorical variable, communication direction, was defined as whether a communication was directed from a respondent upwardly, to another employee at a higher level in the authority structure, downwardly, to another employee at a lower level in the authority structure, or laterally, to someone at the same level.

A second categorical variable, cross-cutting the communication direction variable, was communication distance. Communication distance was defined as whether a communication was directed from a respondent to another respondent in the same chain of command, out of the chain but in the same department, or out of the department. A communication was coded as "in the chain" when the communication partner was the sender's boss or subordinate, or was someone at the same level who reported to the same boss.

We did not code any communication as "hierarchical" or "diagonal" as others have done (e.g., Randolph and Finch 1977, Wickesberg 1968, Wilson 1992) because these terms have been used differently in different studies, and because such coding confounds direction and distance, two orthogonal dimensions of communication that we have proposed have different importance to administrative and technical employees. However, for comparing our data to those of others, we consider hierarchical communication to be essentially equivalent to vertical communication within the chain of command. Diagonal communication is equivalent to vertical communication outside the chain of command or the department.

All communications sent or initiated by a respondent were coded as telephone, voice mail, e-mail, or facsimile. However, we did not use facsimile communication in our analyses because there were very few such communications.

Analysis

Our analyses were performed on 848 dyadic communications sent by the respondents. To avoid double counting of communications we did not evaluate communications received by respondents. We also did not include group communication (messages to multiple addressees) because clear classification of communication direction and distance is required to test our hypotheses. Frequently group communications could not be coded for direction or distance because they were sent to recipients at multiple authority levels or in multiple departments. A chi-square test showed no difference between administrative and technical employees in the amount of group communication they initiated ($\chi^2 = 0.21$, $p < .65$). Only 3.5% of communications contained more than one addressee. Of the group communications, 46.6%

were by e-mail, 42.1% on voice mail, and 10.5% were conference calls using the telephone. Administrators and technical employees did not differ statistically in their use of technology for group communication ($\chi^2 = 1.53$, $p < .57$).

To test our predictions, we ran a series of logistic regressions. In all the analyses, we included four individual attributes as control variables: gender, minority, seniority, and total communication (all sent and received communication using technology). Ideally, a dummy variable for each individual would be used as a control to eliminate the correlation among communications caused by multiple events per respondent. But such a strategy would have prevented us from testing the effects of type of work and level in the authority structure, which are key to our predictions. Therefore, we used the control variables to approximate individual attributes.

We conducted all the analyses in pairs, first comparing technical employees to all administrators, and then comparing technical employees to administrators at Level 1 only. In this organization, technical employees have the same official authority level as Level 1 administrators, although they do not supervise other employees. Hence, in this respect at least, technical employees are more comparable to administrators at Level 1 than to all administrators.

To test predictions about communication direction, we combined upward and downward communication, and compared this vertical communication with lateral communication. To test predictions about communication distance, we made two orthogonal comparisons. First, we compared all communication inside the chain of command with all communication outside the chain of command. Then we examined only communication outside the chain of command. Within this category, we compared communication in the department (but outside the chain of command) with communication outside the department.

RESULTS

Sample Characteristics

Table 7.1, which gives descriptive data on the sample, indicates that technical and administrative employees in the sample were similar demographically. About half of each group was female, about one quarter was minority, and each group had about the same 15 plus years of experience with the firm. Goodness-of-fit tests (and *t*-tests, for continuous data) were calculated to compare the sample with the organization's population. These tests indicate that the seniority and gender of the sample and population were not significantly different. The proportions of third-level managers and

TABLE 7.1 Sample and Population Characteristics

Group	% Female	% Minority	Mean Firm Experience in Years	% Level 1	% Level 2	% Level 3
Technical sample (n = 33)	51.5	24.8	15.5	100	NA	NA
Administrative sample (n = 55)	47.3	22.2	15.8	49.1	36.4	14.5
Total sample (n = 88)	51.1	23.9	15.7	68.2	22.7	9.1
Firm population	47.3	32.7	14.7	76.1	19.9	3.2
Sample versus population p value	.45	.01	.15	.08	.50	.01

minorities in the sample are overrepresented and underrepresented, respectively. This difference mainly reflects our purposeful oversampling of managers at higher levels (who tend not to be minority). Administrators' total communication using technology (initiated and received) averaged 27.7 communications each day, whereas technical employees' total communication by these technologies averaged only 20 communications each day ($t[1, 84.7] = 2.73$, $p < .01$). This difference is consistent with the observations many others have made of managers' high frequency of communication (Sproull 1984).

Of the 1,025 sent, dyadic communications using telephone, voice mail, or e-mail, 848 could be identified by the addressee's type of work and relationship with the respondent in the authority and departmental structure. The data analyses were performed on these 848 communications.

Communication Direction and Distance

Figure 7.1 summarizes the distribution of communication within and across organizational structure by technical employees, by all administrative employees, and by administrators at Level 1. Table 7.2 shows the mean number of communications across organizational structure for each group. We hypothesized that technical employees, as compared with administrative employees, would use technology to have proportionately more lateral communication as compared with vertical communication (H1). Table 7.3 presents a series of logit analyses addressing this hypothesis. The analyses in the upper half of the table examine the likelihood that lateral communication will be initiated by a technical employee rather than an administrative

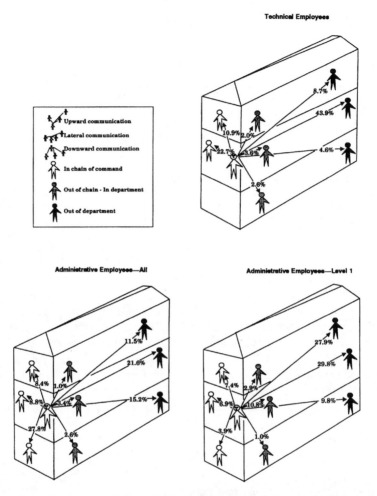

Figure 7.1. Percentage of Communication by Direction and Distance for Technical Employees, Administrators, and Level 1 Administrators

employee. Model 1a indicates that a lateral communication is more likely to be initiated by a technical employee than by an administrator. Model 1b, comparing technical employees with administrators at Level 1, shows the same result. These results support H1. Models 2a, 2b, 3a, and 3b introduce the variable, out-of-chain communication, in order to test the generality of the lateral effect for technical employees and to explore contacts involving weak ties. Comparing technical employees with all administrators in Model 2a suggests there is no difference for communication outside the chain of command between the two groups, but comparing technical employees with

Level 1 administrators (Model 2b) suggests the Level 1 administrators communicate more outside the chain of command. Models 3a and 3b show that the main effect for lateral communication of technical employees remains even with the out-of-chain variable included.

The analyses in the lower half of Table 7.3 examine only communication outside the chain of command. These analyses test the likelihood that when employees communicate outside the chain of command, lateral rather than vertical communication is more likely to be sent by a technical employee (H1). In Models 4a and 4b, there is a significant main effect such that a lateral communication (outside the chain) is more likely to be initiated by a technical employee, which supports the hypothesis. In Models 5a and 5b, there are no significant differences between technical employees and administrators in their degree of extradepartmental communication. In Models 6a and 6b, the main and interaction effects on this reduced set (out-of-chain communication only) suggest that extradepartmental communication is more likely to be initiated by an administrator at Level 1 than by a technical employee. Extradepartmental lateral communication is more likely to be initiated by a technical employee, whereas extradepartmental communication that is vertical (that is, diagonal communication) is more likely to be initiated by a Level 1 administrative employee.

Barley (1994) has suggested that both the nature of technical work and the horizontal organization of technical workers leads to their collaborative behavior. But, do technical employees communicate laterally because they must consult and collaborate with other people on technical projects or do they communicate laterally because management happens to place them in teams where they are surrounded by others at the same level of authority? Proximity effects are known to be strongly predictive of communication (e.g., Allen 1977, Kraut et al. 1990). Next to proximity, demographic and organizational similarity (Wagner et al. 1984, Zenger and Lawrence 1989) and a history of interaction (Krackhardt 1992) strongly influence communication. If people talk with others who are nearby and similar, then the lateral communication of technical employees might be explained simply by the number of other employees in the proximate peer group.

In order to evaluate the possibility that differences in the organization of employees predict their communication differences, we conducted an additional analysis. We compared the number of people that technical and administrative employees worked with at different levels in their chain of command with the number of people they contacted. The results of this analysis suggest a strong association between the number of potential connections and the number of actual connections. For instance, technical employees had an average of 8.9 other employees at the same level as them who reported to the same boss and 1.0 possible vertical connections (their

TABLE 7.2 Percentage Distribution and Mean Number of Communications Using Technology Sent During 2 Days by Technical and Administrative Employees

Technical Employees—Level 1 (n = 33 employees)

| | | Communication Distance | | | | | |
| | | Within the Chain of Command (n = 67) | | Within Dept., Outside the Chain (n = 16) | | Outside the Dept. (n = 111) | |
Communication Direction	Technology	%	Mean	%	Mean	%	Mean
Lateral (n = 138 communications)	Telephone	12.9	0.76	2.6	0.15	39.2	2.30
	Voice mail	1.0	0.06	0.5	0.03	2.6	0.15
	E-mail	9.8	0.58	0.5	0.03	2.1	0.12
	All technology	22.7	1.49	3.6	0.21	43.9	2.57
Upward (n = 42 communications)	Telephone	5.2	0.30	0.5	0.03	4.1	0.24
	Voice mail	2.1	0.12	0.5	0.03	1.0	0.06
	E-mail	3.6	0.21	1.0	0.06	3.6	0.21
	All technology	10.9	0.63	2.0	0.12	8.7	0.51
Downward (n = 14 communications)	Telephone	0.0	0.00	2.1	0.12	4.1	0.24
	Voice mail	0.0	0.00	0.5	0.03	0.0	0.00
	E-mail	0.0	0.00	0.0	0.00	0.5	0.03
	All technology	0.0	0.00	2.6	0.15	4.6	0.27

Administrative Employees—All Levels 1 (n = 55 employees)

| | | Communication Distance | | | | | |
| | | Within the Chain of Command (n = 293) | | Within Dept., Outside the Chain (n = 45) | | Outside the Dept. (n = 314) | |
Communication Direction	Technology	%	Mean	%	Mean	%	Mean
Lateral (n = 219 communications)	Telephone	4.5	0.53	1.7	0.20	16.0	1.89
	Voice mail	3.5	0.38	0.5	0.05	4.0	0.47
	E-mail	1.1	0.13	1.2	0.14	1.6	0.18
	All technology	8.1	1.04	3.4	0.39	21.6	2.54
Upward (n = 136 communications)	Telephone	2.6	0.31	0.5	0.05	8.1	0.96
	Voice mail	4.3	0.51	0.3	0.04	3.1	0.36
	E-mail	1.5	0.18	0.2	0.02	0.3	0.4
	All technology	8.4	1.00	1.0	0.11	11.5	1.36
Downward (n = 297 communications)	Telephone	11.4	1.34	1.8	0.22	10.6	1.25
	Voice mail	8.9	1.05	0.5	0.05	3.8	0.45
	E-mail	7.5	0.89	0.3	0.04	0.8	0.09
	All technology	27.8	3.28	2.6	0.31	15.2	1.79

TABLE 7.2 *Continued*

Administrative Employees—Level 1 Only (n = 27 employees)

| | | Communication Distance | | | | | |
| | | Within the Chain of Command (n = 37) | | Within Dept., Outside the Chain (n = 30) | | Outside the Dept. (n = 138) | |
Communication Direction	Technology	%	Mean	%	Mean	%	Mean
Lateral (n = 97 communications)	Telephone	4.4	0.33	5.4	0.41	25.4	1.91
	Voice mail	1.5	0.11	1.5	0.11	2.9	0.22
	E-mail	1.0	0.07	3.9	0.30	1.5	0.11
	All technology	6.9	0.52	10.8	0.82	29.8	2.24
Upward (n = 78 communications)	Telephone	1.5	0.11	1.5	0.11	22.0	1.67
	Voice mail	4.4	0.33	1.0	0.07	5.4	0.41
	E-mail	1.5	0.11	0.5	0.04	0.5	0.04
	All technology	7.4	0.55	3.0	0.22	27.9	2.12
Downward (n = 30 communications)	Telephone	3.9	0.30	1.0	0.07	8.8	0.67
	Voice Mail	0.0	0.00	0.0	0.00	0.5	0.04
	E-mail	0.0	0.00	0.0	0.00	0.5	0.04
	All technology	3.9	0.30	1.0	0.07	9.8	0.75

boss). Administrative employees at Level 1 (the same level as the technical employees) had an average of only 4.2 other Level 1 employees who reported to the same boss, less than half as many, but 2.8 vertical connections (nearly three times more). Technical people had more potential lateral contacts and administrators had more potential vertical contacts, reflecting the more horizontal structure of the technical division and technical workers.

According to a goodness-of-fit test, technical employees' and administrators' communication behavior did not vary significantly from the structure of the organization ($\chi^2 = 0.02$, $p < .11$ and $\chi^2 = 0.64$, $p < .60$, respectively). Technical employees exercised 1.6 (17.5%) of their potential lateral links and 0.6 (56%) of their potential vertical links in the chain of command, whereas administrators exercised 2.0 (44.8%) of their potential lateral links and 2.1 (38.3%) of their potential vertical links in the chain of command. These data suggest that the lateral communication of technical workers we observed may be explained in part by the way technical employees are organized. If technical employees in the firm are organized in teams at one level of the authority structure, and if people talk with coworkers, the structure has essentially institutionalized a lateral communication bias.

TABLE 7.3 Logistic Regressions Predicting Communication From Technical Employees as Compared With Administrative Employees

Variables	Technical vs. Admin. Model 1a (n = 848) Coef. (SE)	Tech. vs. Lvl. 1 Admin. Model 1b (n = 400) Coef. (SE)	Tech. vs. Admin. Model 2a (n = 1,018) Coef. (SE)	Tech. vs. Lvl. 1 Admin. Model 2b (n = 522) Coef. (SE)	Tech. vs. Admin. Model 3a (n = 846) Coef. (SE)	Tech. vs. Lvl. 1 Admin. Model 3b (n = 400) Coef. (SE)
All Communications						
Intercept	**	*		**	**	
Control variables						
Gender (male = 1)	−0.28 (0.20)	0.02 (0.29)	−0.16 (0.17)	0.21 (0.19)	−0.26 (0.20)	0.13 (0.24)
Minority	−0.57* (0.24)	−0.51 (0.27)	−0.51* (0.26)	−0.71** (0.23)	−0.55* (0.24)	−0.51 (0.28)
High seniority (> 20 years)	−1.86** (0.28)	−1.91** (0.32)	−1.57** (0.23)	−1.31** (0.27)	−1.85** (0.28)	−1.98** (0.33)
Total communications	< 0.01* (0.00)	< 0.01 (0.00)	< 0.01** (0.00)	< 0.01 (0.00)	< 0.01 (0.00)	< 0.01 (0.00)
Lateral communication	1.58** (0.19)	1.23** (0.23)		2.04** (0.32)	1.36** (0.46)	
Out of chain			0.28 (0.17)	−1.02** (0.24)	0.44 (0.30)	
Lateral × out of chain					−0.75 (0.40)	−0.11 (0.53)
Chi-square	164.61	70.41	104.37	56.87	166.48	83.98
df	5	5	5	5	7	7
p	< .01	< .01	< .01	< .01	< .01	< .01

Communications Only Out of the Chain of Command

Variables	Technical vs. Admin. Model 4a (n = 488) Coef. (SE)	Tech. vs. Lvl. 1 Admin. Model 4b (n = 296) Coef. (SE)	Tech. vs. Admin. Model 5a (n = 657) Coef. (SE)	Tech. vs. Lvl. 1 Admin. Model 5b (n = 418) Coef. (SE)	Tech. vs. Admin. Model 6a (n = 488) Coef. (SE)	Tech. vs. Lvl. 1 Admin. Model 6b (n = 296) Coef. (SE)
Intercept	**	**	**	**	**	**
Control variables						
Gender (male = 1)	-0.48* (0.24)	-0.17 (0.28)	-0.21 (0.19)	0.08 (0.21)	-0.47 (0.24)	-0.07 (0.28)
Minority	-0.62* (0.30)	-0.58 (0.33)	-0.56* (0.24)	-0.80** (0.26)	-0.58 (0.30)	-0.52 (0.34)
High seniority (> 20 years)	-2.14** (0.38)	-2.27** (0.42)	-1.60** (0.28)	-1.33** (0.31)	-2.11** (0.38)	-2.20** (0.43)
Total communications	< 0.01 (0.00)	< 0.01* (0.00)	< 0.01 (0.00)	< 0.01 (0.00)	< 0.01 (0.00)	< 0.01 (0.00)
Lateral communication	1.33** (0.24)	1.31** (0.28)			0.44 (0.65)	-.72 (0.75)
Out of department			-0.06 (0.32)	-0.06 (0.36)	-0.84 (0.47)	-1.56* (0.61)
Chi-square	86.05	61.01	60.12	34.81	87.65	69.83
df	5	5	5	5	7	7
p	< .01	< .01	< .01	< .01	< .01	< .01

*$p < 0.05$; **$p < 0.01$.

A similar argument also applies to the bias toward lateral communication of technical workers out of the chain of command and extradepartmentally. In a company with 40,000 employees, as this company employs, anyone has numerous potential connections both lateral and vertical. However, if the organization of technical workers is more horizontal throughout the firm than is the organization of administrative workers, then there are legions of technical people at Level 1 available for communication. A chi-square test examining administrative versus technical senders by administrative versus technical receivers ($\chi^2 = 139.2$, $p < .01$) indicates that, in fact, technical employees as compared to administrative employees in our sample interact proportionally more with technical recipients than with administrative recipients. Demographic and organizational similarity would tend to produce at least the appearance of lateral communication by technical workers, since they are all given the Level 1 designation. A logit analysis predicting whether or not a communicator outside the department is technical (using the same structure as in Table 7.3) indicates that technical employees communicate more laterally outside the department than do administrators (coeff. = 1.50 [0.27], $p < .01$). In short, organizational structure can account for some communication differences between technical and administrative employees.

Use of Communication Technology

Technical and administrative employees' mean use of telephone within and across structure, and the percentage distributions of use of telephone, are shown in Table 7.2. Table 7.4 presents all of the logit analyses pertaining to technical and administrative employees' use of telephone as compared with asynchronous technology (e-mail and voice mail).

Models 1a and 1b show analyses of the likelihood that a telephone call will be initiated by a technical employee rather than an administrative employee, or a Level 1 administrative employee, respectively. We predicted that technical employees would use the telephone more (H2). The main effect is not significant. We also hypothesized that when employees engaged in lateral as compared with vertical communication, they would use the telephone rather than asynchronous technology (H4). Models 2a and 2b show the increased likelihood of a telephone call being made for lateral rather than vertical communication, although the effect is not significant in Model 2b comparing Level 1 administrators with technical employees. Outside the chain of command, in Models 4a and 4b, the pattern is the same. Hence there is some support for the hypothesis. We also predicted that when employees engaged in communication outside the chain, and outside the department, they would use the telephone rather than asynchronous technology (H5). Models 2a and 2b give strong support to this hypothesis, as do Models 4a and 4b. Models 3a and 3b and 5a and 5b include interaction effects which show a significant effect for technical employees to use the telephone for lateral extradepartmental communication.

The data on the mean use of e-mail and voice mail by technical and administrative employees are described in Table 7.2. Logit analyses of the use of e-mail as compared with voice mail by employees who used asynchronous technology are summarized in Table 7.5. We hypothesized that when employees used asychronous communication technology, technical employees would use e-mail rather than voice mail proportionately more than would administrative employees (H3). The results shown in Models 1a and 1b support this hypothesis.

We argued that administrators ought to use voice mail more than do technical employees. They do. Administrators used voice mail for 29% of their total communication and administrators at Level 1 used voice mail for 17% of their communication, whereas technical employees only used voice mail for 8% of their overall communication. The difference in these percentages (between administrators and technical employees and between Level 1 administrators and technical employees) were highly significant. We hypothesized that administrative employees at higher levels in the authority structure, and administrators communicating vertically, would use asynchronous communication rather than telephone, and voice mail rather than e-mail (H6). To evaluate this hypothesis, we examined only the communication of administrators (Table 7.6). Model 1a examines the use of telephone by administrators at Level 3 in comparison to the use of the telephone by administrators at lower levels. Consistent with the hypothesis, the negative coefficient in the main effect for Level 3 shows that the higher level administrators do use asynchronous communication technology more than those at lower levels. Model 2a shows that administrators use asynchronous technology for vertical communication. Model 3a in Table 7.6 tests the hypothesis that high-level administrators use voice mail over e-mail (H6). The hypothesis is supported. Model 4a tests the hypothesis that administrators communicating vertically use voice mail rather than e-mail (also H6). This effect is not significant, mainly because administrators use voice mail extensively for both vertical and lateral communication.

DISCUSSION

Hierarchy and informal networks always existed side by side. In the past, researchers and managers emphasized the structural and operational significance of the former (Hall 1986). Informal networks were viewed as emergent ad hoc linkages formed because of physical proximity (e.g., Allen 1977,

TABLE 7.4 Logistic Regressions Predicting Use of Telephone as Compared With All Asynchronous

	Tech. and Admin.	Tech. and Lvl. 1 Admin.	Tech. and Admin.	Tech. and Lvl. 1 Admin.	Tech. and Admin.	Tech. and Lvl. 1 Admin.	Tech. and Admin.	Tech. and Lvl. 1 Admin.	Out of Chain Only	
									Tech. and Admin.	Tech. and Lvl. 1 Admin.
	Model 1a (n = 1,020)	Model 1b (n = 523)	Model 2a (n = 846)	Model 2b (n = 407)	Model 3a (n = 846)	Model 3b (n = 407)	Model 4a (n = 486)	Model 4b (n = 295)	Model 5a (n = 486)	Model 5b (n = 295)
Variables	Coef. (SE)	Coef. (SE)	Coef. (SE)	Coef. (SE)	Coef. (SE)	Coef. (SE)	Coef. (SE)	Coef. (SE)	Coef. (SE)	Coef. (SE)
Intercept	**	**								
Control variables										
Gender (male = 1)	0.18 (0.15)	0.25 (0.22)	0.11 (0.17)	−0.03 (0.25)	0.11 (0.17)	−0.04 (0.26)	0.26 (0.24)	0.20 (0.33)	0.30 (0.24)	0.29 (0.33)
Minority	−0.05 (0.17)	−0.26 (0.25)	0.07 (0.20)	−0.03 (0.29)	0.13 (0.20)	0.04 (0.29)	0.40 (0.30)	0.26 (0.37)	0.52 (0.30)	0.28 (0.38)
High seniority (> 20 years)	−0.61** (0.16)	−0.39 (0.26)	−0.54** (0.17)	−0.24 (0.29)	−0.47** (0.17)	−0.22 (0.32)	−0.56* (0.24)	−0.23 (0.39)	−0.37 (0.26)	−0.10 (0.43)
Total communications	< 0.01* (0.00)	< 0.01* (0.00)	< 0.01 (0.00)	< 0.01 (0.00)	< 0.01 (0.00)	< 0.01 (0.00)	< 0.01 (0.00)	< 0.01 (0.00)	< 0.01 (0.00)	< 0.01 (0.00)
Technical employee	0.30 (0.17)	−0.47 (0.22)								
Technical recipient					0.14 (0.47)	0.05 (0.62)			−0.46 (0.81)	−0.35 (1.00)
Lateral communication			0.44** (0.16)	0.42 (0.24)	0.44 (0.30)	0.55 (0.71)	0.42* (0.21)	−0.55* (0.31)	−0.71 (0.64)	−0.58 (0.88)
Out of chain			1.12** (0.15)	1.27** (0.25)	1.22** (0.21)	1.52** (0.51)				
Out of department						0.71** (0.29)	1.29** (0.37)	0.23 (0.48)	0.93 (0.79)	
Lateral × technical empl.					−0.12 (0.61)	−0.37 (0.88)			1.24 (1.26)	1.32 (1.39)
Lateral × out of chain					−0.35 (0.38)	−1.08 (0.76)				

Lateral × out of department									0.89 (0.69)	0.80 (0.98)
Technical empl. × out of chain					−0.71 (0.60)	−0.73 (0.82)				
Technical empl. × out of dept.									−0.09 (0.93)	−0.69 (1.22)
Lateral × technical × out of chain					1.62* (0.81)	2.10 (1.08)				
Lateral × technical × out of dept.									0.33 (1.39)	0.09 (1.55)
Chi-square	37.73	12.91	97.74	35.65	104.19	41.55	20.27	21.18	30.10	29.07
df	5	5	6	6	11	11	6	6	11	11
p	<.01	<.03	<.01	<.01	<.01	<.01	<.01	<.01	<.01	<.01

*p < .05; **p < .01.

TABLE 7.5 Logistic Regressions Predicting Use of E-Mail as Compared to
              Voice Mail

	All Employees	Level 1 Only
	Model 1a (n = 364)	Model 1b (n = 122)
Variables	Coef. (SE)	Coef. (SE)
Intercept	**	
Control variables		
Gender (male = 1)	−0.17 (0.26)	0.63 (0.45)
Minority	0.05 (0.31)	−0.87 (0.51)
High seniority (> 20 years)	0.51 (0.28)	1.37* (0.58)
Total communications	< 0.01 (0.00)	−0.01 (0.00)
Technical employee	1.94** (0.34)	1.99** (0.48)
Chi-square	37.73	30.21
df	5	5
p	< .01	< .01

*p < .05; **p < .01

Kraut et al. 1988, Monge et al. 1985), a history of prior personal relationships (Krackhardt 1992), and demographic similarity (Wagner et al. 1984, Zenger and Lawrence 1989). When informal networks were seen as "the grapevine"—unplanned, personal, and causal—neither managers nor researchers viewed them as integral to formal organization or crucial to accomplishing work (see Katz and Kahn 1978, p. 449). Today, a more deliberate "network organization" is in the offing (Nohria and Eccles 1992). Major business and technical forces are changing the nature of work, and firms are spending substantial sums on reorganization, redefinition of the role of manager, and support for technology so that lateral and diagonal ties operate efficiently and effectively (Barley 1994, Powell 1990). Our findings are consistent with Barley's (1994) idea that increasing technization of work implies an emphasis on horizontal structure and collaborative, lateral flows of communication for technical employees. Our findings also are consistent with research on network organization (Powell 1990) and technical teams (e.g., Allen 1977) and scientific collaboration (Kraut et al. 1990), which document extensive lateral and diagonal connections. Our work and that of others suggests that much of this communication is systematic and highly correlated with formal organization, not "informal" in the lay use of the term.

In our study, only 30% of employees' communication using technology was traditionally hierarchical: vertical and inside the chain of command. Of

TABLE 7.6 Logistic Regressions Predicting Use of Telephone Compared With Asynchronous and Predicting Use of E-Mail Compared With Voice Mail for Administrators Only

Variables	Predicting Telephone		Predicting E-Mail	
	Model 1a (n = 780)	Model 2a (n = 654)	Model 3a (n = 300)	Model 4a (n = 280)
	Coef. (SE)	Coef. (SE)	Coef. (SE)	Coef. (SE)
Intercept	**	**	**	**
Control variables				
Gender (male = 1)	0.29 (0.18)	0.17 (0.19)	−0.27 (0.32)	−0.30 (0.31)
Minority	−0.16 (0.20)	−0.05 (0.22)	0.22 (0.35)	0.15 (0.36)
High seniority (> 20 years)	0.61** (0.17)	−0.57** (0.19)	0.27 (0.31)	0.52 (0.31)
Total communications	< 0.01 (0.00)	< 0.01 (0.00)	< 0.01 (0.00)	< 0.01 (0.00)
Hierarchical level 3	−0.62** (0.20)		−1.55** (0.34)	
Lateral communication		0.51** (0.11)		< 0.01 (0.29)
Chi-square	43.02	29.42	27.61	4.79
df	5	5	5	5
p	< .01	< .01	< .01	< .45

*$p < .05$; **$p < .01$.

the rest, 42% was lateral and 28% was diagonal. In some respects, but not others, our data resemble patterns from the precomputer era. Wickesberg (1968) observed remarkably similar distributions as well as differences between technical and administrative employees in much the same direction as ours, though not as large. In Wickesberg's study, 30% of managers' total communication was lateral and 37% was diagonal; in our study 34% of managers' total communication was lateral and 30% was diagonal. In Wickesberg's study, 45% of professional and technical employees' total communication was lateral and 32% was diagonal; in our study 70% of technical employees' total communication was lateral and 18% was diagonal. Wickesberg's conclusion seems appropriate to our study too, that managers and nonmanagers alike seek contributors to their task effectiveness and "move wherever in the organization information, advice, counsel, and expertise may be found" (p. 267).

Our study seems to differ from earlier studies in highlighting the very large use of technology for extradepartmental communication. Both technical employees and Level 1 administrators' most frequent communication using technology was lateral and extradepartmental. But the next most frequent communication by Level 1 administrators was extradepartmental and diagonal, whereas for technical workers it was lateral communication within the work group. Hence Level 1 administrators used technology for extradepartmental communication even more than did technical employees, but the source of this difference was administrators' high frequency of diagonal communication. This finding provides some support for our argument, based on weak-tie theories (Burt 1983, Granovetter 1982, Lin 1982), that administrators seek resources unavailable locally by contacting superiors in other departments. If so, we would expect junior administrative employees to initiate extradepartmental communication upwardly because those at higher levels in other departments presumably have more resources not offered by their own superiors. Our data do show such a bias: At the first level of management, 28% of administrators' communication was upwardly diagonal whereas only 11% was downwardly diagonal, to other people's subordinates.

Our data also differ from those of others in showing some significant differences in the ways administrators and technical employees cross different boundaries to do their work. We argued that horizontally structured technical employees operating within teams and specialties across departments may particularly engage in lateral communication. Our finding of 71% lateral ties among technical employees is 25% higher than Wickesberg's pre-1970 employees, and also has precedence in a recent study by Wilson (1992) of technical military teams (including team managers). He found that employees in these teams reported having 63% lateral and 20% diagonal ties for "help or technical advice concerning work-related problems" (p. 134).

We derived hypotheses about the preferences of technical and administrative workers for different communication technologies based on analyses of the attributes of technology vis-à-vis the nature of employees' work and the way work is organized. We argued that communication technologies can be ranked by how well they suit collaboration, particularly the intense exchange of information required for planning and technical exchange. From an analysis of the attributes of telephone, voice mail, and e-mail we predicted that crossing organizational boundaries in communication, and communication by technical workers, would be associated with the use of the telephone, and secondarily, with the use of e-mail. We found that lateral and out-of-chain communication was disproportionately by telephone for all employees, not just technical employees. This finding gives support to Nohria and Eccles's (1992) argument that when people connect to weak ties (i.e., cross organizational boundaries), they must exchange social as well as substantive information. Accordingly, the superiority of the telephone over current asynchronous technologies for conveying both social information and content might outweigh the sheer convenience of asynchronous technology when people cross organizational boundaries. This balance of comfort and convenience would be expected to shift the use of technology toward asynchronous modes as people communicated with others further away and across time zones.

We found, as predicted, that when technical workers used asynchronous technology, they used e-mail rather than voice mail. This finding is consistent with our argument that e-mail is more effective than voice mail for conveying and discussing complex information. Over all, administrators were much more likely to communicate, and to use voice mail. This finding is consistent with our argument that voice mail technology would be attractive to administrators both because it is efficient and it conveys social information about the sender such as his or her status, accessibility, and dominance.

This study has a number of important limitations to both internal and external validity. For example, though we know that 50% of communication was extradepartmental, how important, consultative, or interesting is this communication? Suppose people are just ordering out for pizza? The logs of communication in this study do not contain sufficient information to allow analysis of the content of communication sent by employees. The only data that address this problem come from postdiary interviews in which we asked people to rate the importance of each communication on a scale of 1 to 10 (10 = most important), and to tell us whether or not the communication was urgent. Logit analyses predicting important communication (scores of 8, 9, or 10) indicate that administrative employees as compared with technical employees perceived more of the communication they sent to be important. Technical employees as compared with administrators indicated that more of their lateral and out-of-chain communications were important. However, there were no main effects or interactions for lateral, out-of-chain, or extradepartmental communication, suggesting that using technology to cross boundaries does not mean just talking about pizza.

In this study, we were not able to collect data on employees' face-to-face communication; hence we lack baseline statistics on overall communication of technical and administrative employees. Insofar as comparisons are possible, the similarity of our data to those of earlier studies (e.g., Wickesberg 1968) suggests that measuring face-to-face communication would not have changed our main conclusions. The logic of our argument is that telephone is much like one-to-one face-to-face communication but is done at a distance. Hence we would have predicted that, as compared with administrative employees, more of technical employees' communication would be face-to-face (though in absolute terms the administrative employees would communicate more in all venues). We also would have predicted lateral, as compared with vertical communication would be face-to-face. These hypotheses could be addressed in future research.

Ours is a case study of communication within the headquarters of one large organization in which communication partners have equal access to all three technologies, an assumption that clearly does not hold in many worldwide organizations. The corporate culture seems to promote communication within and across structure. The organization is also distinctive in having a highly observable status hierarchy reflecting the authority structure. For example, workplaces at each level of the authority structure are standardized at different levels of comfort and privacy. Just below the managerial level, people work in cubicles without doors; Level 1 and 2 managers work in slightly larger cubicles; a Level 3 manager has an office with windows looking out at the cubicles; a Level 4 manager has a larger office with better furniture, and so forth. Despite these signs of traditional hierarchy and bureaucracy, posters promoting teamwork and cooperation are placed throughout the organization, implying some institutionalization of the idea of network organization.

The firm we studied also is distinctive in that it is a telecommunications company, and views communication technology both as a critical corporate resource and as a product. In their day-to-day work, our respondents rarely dealt directly with the products of the company. Still, the firm sells communication services and its culture would seem to encourage employees to use this technology more frequently than employees might in other firms. Culture pressure and incentives will influence people's perceptions of technology and the work they do, hence how they use the technology (Fulk et al. 1990).

In future research on the use of technology to cross boundaries, the limitations of this study should be addressed by comparing face-to-face communication with communication using technology and comparing organizations of different types. One intriguing finding of our study that future research could address is that over 50% of all communication in the study was extradepartmental. Does this imply that technology can aid and abet extradepartmental communication? It might. On average, departments in the study were 0.8 floors and 1.2 wings (about 120 yards) distant from each other. (We think this underestimates overall distance between departments in the organization because we sampled only employees located at the headquarters office.) Previous research on the effects of proximity have shown that if people work in nonadjacent offices, communication drops precipitously (e.g., Monge and Kirste 1980). Allen (1977) found that contact between engineers in a research laboratory dropped to near zero at separations of 30 meters. Kraut et al. (1990) reported that communications per month dropped from over 60 for people in adjacent offices to 30 for people on different floors in the same building. Previously, investigators have argued that technology does not change this proximity effect (Allen 1986, Eveland and Bikson 1987, Mayer 1977). In this study, half of the communication using technology was extradepartmental, a distribution that does not fit the proximity model from other research. Hence we venture that both old and new communication technology used in the firm we studied does reduce the impact of proximity and encourage extradepartmental communication.

In the history of organizational studies, communication across boundaries used to be taken far less seriously than hierarchical communication. Texts warned managers to constrain informal communication, which though good for morale could undercut managerial control and disrupt smooth organizational functioning (e.g., Katz and Kahn 1978). Today, it is no longer appropriate to consider communication across boundaries as primarily social and of limited usefulness (see Ancona and Caldwell 1992). Technological change and task demands increasingly require that organizations be structured to support lateral and diagonal communication. Organizations must invest in communication technology infrastructure and the development and enforcement of policies that systematically encourage informal communication. (For example, organizations should not inhibit the use of electronic communication by allowing managers to monitor private conversations.) Recently, organizational and network theorists have extended investigations of the interplay between organizational structure and informal communication. In this research, informal structure is seen as filling important gaps in formal structure (e.g., Burt 1992, pp. 148-149). Theorists also have explored the relationship between organizational structure and communication technology (e.g., Poole and DeSanctis 1992). As researchers continue to interweave and extend these two lines of research, we will better understand communication that crosses boundaries, and how systematic changes in the use of technology for this communication changes people's work and the functioning of the organization.

NOTES

1. Although almost all organizations have a hierarchy, they do not all operate in the same manner. For instance, the locus of control need not be centralized at the top of the hierarchy. In a strong horizontal structure, the division of labor is structured along lines of expertise (such as technical specialty or profession—the accounting department, the chemical engineering department, the systems analysis department, and so forth). Doing so tends to lend greater autonomy to members of these departments as well as greater responsibility for coordinating across departments to solve problems and develop products (Raelin 1986).

2. Facsimile machines are available to all employees in a central location no more than 150 feet from any person's desk. Only 11 of the employees sent communication using facsimile.

3. Limits on voice mail minute length arbitrarily limit the exchange of large amounts of content and are not fundamental to the technology.

REFERENCES

Abbott, A. (1991), "The Future of Professions: Occupation and Expertise in the Age of Organization," in P. S. Tolbert and S. R. Barley (Eds.), *Research in the Sociology of Organizations,* Greenwich, CT: JAI, Vol. 8, pp. 17-42.

Adams, J. S. (1976), "The Structure and Dynamics of Behavior in Organizational Boundary Roles," in M. D. Dunnette (Ed.), *Handbook of Industrial and Organizational Psychology,* Chicago: Rand McNally, pp. 1175-1199.

Aldrich, H. (1979), *Organizations and Environments,* Englewood Cliffs, NJ: Prentice Hall.

Allen, T. J. (1977), *Managing the Flow of Technology,* Cambridge: MIT Press.

_____ (1986), "Organizational Structure, Information Technology, and R&D Productivity," *IEEE Transactions on Engineering Management,* 33, 212-214.

Ancona, D. G. and D. F. Caldwell (1992), "Bridging the Boundary: External Activity and Performance in Organizational Teams," *Administrative Science Quarterly,* 37, 634-665.

Barley, S. (1994), *The Turn to a Horizontal Division of Labor: On the Occupationalization of Firms and the Technization of Work,* National Center for the Educational Quality of the Workforce, University of Pennsylvania, Philadelphia. (Available from the author)

Barry, B. and T. S. Bateman (1992), "Perceptions of Influence in Managerial Dyads: The Role of Hierarchy, Media, and Tactics," *Human Relations,* 45, 6, 555-574.

Bizot, E., N. Smith, and T. Hill (1991), "Use of Electronic Mail in a Research and Development Organization," in J. Morell and M. Fleischer (Eds.), *Advances in the Implementation and Impact of Computer Systems,* Greenwich, CT: JAI, pp. 65-92.

Brooks, F. P. (1987), "No Silver Bullet: Essence and Accidents of Software Engineering," *IEEE Computer Society,* 20, April, 10-18.

Burt, R. S. (1980), "Models of Network Structure," *Annual Review of Sociology,* 6, 79-141.

_____ (1983), "Range," in R. S. Burt and M. J. Minor (Eds.), *Applied Network Analysis,* Beverly Hills, CA: Sage, pp. 176-194.

_____ (1992), *Structural Holes: The Social Structure of Competition,* Cambridge, MA: Harvard University Press.

Business Week (1993), "The Horizontal Corporation," December 20, 76-81.

Casson, M. (1994), "Why Are Firms Hierarchical?" *Journal of the Economics of Business,* 1, 47-76.

Conrath, D. W. (1973), "Communication Patterns, Organizational Structure, and Man: Some Relationships," *Human Factors,* 15, 459-470.

_____, C. A. Higgins, and R. J. McClean (1983), "A Comparison of the Reliability of Questionnaire Versus Diary Data," *Social Networks,* 5, 315-322.

Curtis, B., H. Krasner, and N. Iscoe (1988), "A Field Study of the Software Design Process for Large Systems," *Communications of the ACM,* 31, 1268-1287.

Cyert, R. M. and J. G. March (1963), *Behavioral Theory of the Firm,* Englewood Cliffs, NJ: Prentice Hall.

Daft, R. L. and R. H. Lengel (1984), "Information Richness: A New Approach to Managerial Behavior and Organization Design," in B. Straw and L. L. Cummings (Eds.), *Research in Organizational Behavior,* Greenwich, CT: JAI, Vol. 6, pp. 191-233.

_____ and _____ (1986), "Organizational Information Requirements, Media Richness and Structural Design," *Management Science,* 32, 554-571.

_____, _____, and L. K. Trevino (1987), "Message Equivocality, Media Selection and Manager Performance: Implications for Information Systems," *MIS Quarterly,* 11, 355-366.

Downs, A. (1967), *Inside Bureaucracy,* Boston: Little, Brown.

Drucker, P. F. (1988), "The Coming of the New Organization," *Harvard Business Review,* January/February, 45-53.

Dubin, R. and S. Spray (1964), "Executive Behavior and Interaction," *Industrial Relations,* 3, 99-108.

Eveland, J. D. and T. K. Bikson (1987), "Evolving Electronic Communications," *Office: Technology and People,* 3, 83-101.

Feldman, M. S. (1987), "Electronic Mail and Weak Ties in Organizations," *Office: Technology and People,* 3, 83-101.

Ferguson, N. (1977), "Simultaneous Speech, Interruptions and Dominance," *British Journal of Social and Clinical Psychology,* 16, 295-302.

Finholt, T., L. O. Sproull, and S. Kiesler (1990), "Communication and Performance in Ad Hoc Task Groups," in R. Kraut, J. Galegher, and C. Egido (Eds.), *Intellectual Teamwork: Social and Technological Foundations of Cooperative Work,* Hillsdale, NJ: Lawrence Erlbaum, pp. 291-325.

Fish, R. S., R. E. Kraut, R. W. Root, and R. E. Rice (1993), "Video as a Technology for Informal Communication," *Communications of the ACM,* 36, 48-61.

Fulk, J., J. Schmitz, and C. W. Steinfield (1990), "A Social Influence Model of Technology Use," in J. Fulk and C. W. Steinfield (Eds.), *Organizations and Communication Technology,* Newbury Park, CA: Sage, pp. 117-140.

Galbraith, J. R. (1973), *Designing Complex Organizations,* Reading, MA: Addison-Wesley.

Granovetter, M. (1982), "The Strength of Weak Ties: A Network Theory Revisited," in P. Marsden and N. Lin (Eds.), *Social Structure and Network Analysis,* New York: John Wiley, pp. 105-130.

Hall, R. H. (1986), *Dimensions of Work,* Beverly Hills, CA: Sage.

Hannaway, J. (1985), "Managerial Behavior, Uncertainty, and Hierarchy: A Prelude to a Synthesis," *Human Relations,* 38, 1085-1100.

Hedlund, G. (1986), "The Hypermodern MNC: A Heterarchy?" *Human Resource Management,* Spring, 9-35.

Heydebrand, W. V. (1989), "New Organizational Forms," *Work and Occupation,* 16, 323-357.

Jones, E. E. (1964), *Ingratiation,* New York: Appleton-Century-Crofts.

Katz, D. and R. L. Kahn (1978), *The Social Psychology of Organizations,* 2nd ed., New York: John Wiley.

Kieser, A. (1989), "Organizational, Institutional, and Societal Evolution: Medieval Craft Guilds and the Genesis of Formal Organizations," *Administrative Science Quarterly,* 34, 540-564.

Kiesler, S. and L. Sproull (1982), "Managerial Response to Changing Environments: Perspectives on Problem Sensing From Social Cognition," *Administrative Science Quarterly,* 27, 548-570.

Kipnis, D., S. M. Schmidt, and I. Wilkinson (1980), "Intraorganizational Influence Tactics: Explorations in Getting One's Way," *Journal of Applied Psychology,* 65, 440-452.

Krachenberg, A. R., J. W. Hencke, Jr., and T. F. Lyons (1993), "The Isolation of Upper Management," *Business Horizons,* July/August, 41-47.

Krackhardt, D. (1992), "The Strength of Strong Ties: The Importance of Philos in Organizations," in N. Nohria and R. Eccles (Eds.), *Organizations and Networks: Structure, Form, and Action,* Boston: Harvard Business School Press, pp. 216-239.

Kraut, R. E., C. Egido, and J. Galegher (1990), "Patterns of Contact and Communication in Scientific Research Collaborations," in J. Galegher, R. E. Kraut, and C. Egido (Eds.), *Intellectual Teamwork: Social and Technological Foundations of Cooperative Work,* Hillsdale, NJ: Lawrence Erlbaum, pp. 149-172.

_____, J. Galegher, and C. Egido (1988), "Relationships and Tasks in Scientific Collaboration," *Human-Computer Interaction,* 3, 31-58.

_____, _____, R. Fish, and B. Chalfonte (1992), "Requirements and Media Choice in Collaborative Writing," *Human-Computer Interaction,* 7, 375-407.

_____ and L. A. Streeter (1990), "Satisfying the Need to Know: Interpretational Information Access," in D. Diaper (Ed.), *Human-Computer Interaction, Interact '90,* Cambridge, UK, pp. 909-915.

Lave, J. (1988), "Situating Learning in Communities of Practice," in L. B. Resnick, J. M. Levine, and S. D. Teasley (Eds.), *Perspectives on Socially Shared Cognition,* Washington, DC: American Psychological Association, pp. 63-84.

Lin, N. (1982), "Social Resources and Instrumental Action," in P. Marsden and N. Lin (Eds.), *Social Structure and Network Analysis,* Beverly Hills, CA: Sage.

Malone, T. W. and J. F. Rockart (1991), "Computers, Networks, and the Corporation," *Scientific American,* 263, 128-137.

March, J. and H. Simon (1958), *Organizations,* New York: John Wiley.

Markus, M. L. (1990), "Toward a 'Critical Mass' Theory of Interactive Media," in J. Fulk and C. W. Steinfield (Eds.), *Organizations and Communication Technology,* Newbury Park, CA: Sage, pp. 194-218.

_____ (1994), "Electronic Mail as the Medium of Managerial Choice," *Organizational Science,* 5, 502-527.

Mayer, M. (1977), "The Telephone and the Uses of Time," in I. Pool (Ed.), *The Social Impact of the Telephone,* Cambridge: MIT Press.

Meltzer, L., W. N. Morris, and D. P. Hayes (1971), "Interruption Outcomes and Vocal Amplitude: Explorations in Social Psychophysics," *Journal of Personality and Social Psychology,* 18, 392-402.

Miles, R. E. and C. C. Snow (1986), "Network Organizations: New Concepts for New Forms," *California Management Review,* 28, 62-73.

Mintzberg, H. (1973), *The Nature of Managerial Work,* New York: Harper & Row.

Monge, R. R. and K. K. Kirste (1980), "Measuring Proximity in Human Organizations," *Social Psychology Quarterly,* 43, 110-115.

_____, L. W. Rothman, E. H. Eisenberg, K. L. Miller, and K. K. Kirste (1985), "The Dynamics of Organizational Proximity," *Management Science,* 31, 1129-1141.

Nickerson, R. S. (1992), *Looking Ahead: Human Factors Challenges in a Changing World,* Hillsdale, NJ: Lawrence Erlbaum.

Nohria, N. and R. Eccles (1992), "Face-to-Face: Making Network Organizations Work," in N. Nohria and R. G. Eccles (Eds.), *Networks and Organizations: Structure, Form, and Action,* Boston: Harvard Business School Press, pp. 288-308.

Ouchi, W. G. (1980), "Markets, Bureaucracies, and Clans," *Administrative Science Quarterly,* 25, 129-140.

Papa, W. H. and M. J. Papa (1992), "Communication Network Patterns and the Reinvention of New Technology," *Journal of Business Communication,* 29, 41-61.

Pelz, D. C. and F. M. Andrews (1966), *Scientists in Organizations: Productive Climates for Research and Development,* New York: John Wiley.

Perrow, C. (1967), "A Framework for the Comparative Analysis of Organizations," *American Sociological Review,* 32, 194-208.

Poole, M. S. and G. DeSanctis (1992), "Microlevel Structuration in Computer-Supported Group Decision Making," *Human Communication Research,* 19, 5-49.

Powell, W. W. (1990), "Neither Market nor Hierarchy: Network Forms of Organization," *Research in Organizational Behavior,* 12, 295-336.

Putnam, L. L. and R. L. Sorenson (1982), "Equivocal Messages in Organizations," *Human-Communication Research,* 8, 2, 114-132.

Quinn, J. B. (1992), *Intelligent Enterprise,* New York: Free Press.

Raelin, J. A. (1986), *The Clash of Cultures: Managers Managing Professionals,* Boston: Harvard Business School Press.

Randolph, A. W. and F. E. Finch (1977), "The Relationship Between Organization Technology and the Direction and Frequency Dimensions of Task Communication," *Human Relations,* 30, 1131-1145.

Reid, A. (1977), "Comparing Telephone With Face-to-Face Contact," in I. Desola Pool (Ed.), *The Social Impact of the Telephone,* Cambridge: MIT Press, pp. 386-415.

Reinsch, N. L. and R. W. Beswick (1990), "Voice Mail Versus Conventional Channels: A Cost Minimization Analysis of Individuals' Preferences," *Academy of Management Journal,* 33, 801-816.

Rice, R. E. (1992), "Task Analyzability, Use of New Media, and Effectiveness," *Organization Science,* 3, 475-500.

_____ (1993), "Media Appropriateness: Using Social Presence Theory to Compare Traditional and New Organizational Media," *Human Communication Research,* 19, 451-484.

_____ and C. Aydin (1991), "Attitudes Towards New Organizational Technology: Network Proximity as a Mechanism for Social Information Processing," *Administrative Science Quarterly,* 36, 219-244.

_____ and D. Case (1983), "Electronic Message Systems in the University: A Description of Use and Utility," *Journal of Communications,* 33, 131-152.

_____ and J. A. Danowski (1993), "Is It Really Just Like a Fancy Answering Machine? Comparing Semantic Networks of Different Types of Voice Mail Users," *Journal of Business Communication,* 30, 369-397.

_____, D. Hughes, and G. Love (1989), "Usage and Outcomes of Electronic Messaging at an R&D Organization: Situational Constraints, Job Level, and Media Awareness," *Office: Technology and People,* 5, 141-161.

_____ and D. E. Shook (1990), "Voice Messaging, Coordination, and Communication," in J. Galegher, R. E. Kraut, and C. Egido (Eds.), *Intellectual Teamwork: Social and Technological Foundations of Cooperative Work,* Hillsdale, NJ: Lawrence Erlbaum, pp. 327-350.

Ross, M. (1989), "Relation of Implicit Theories to the Construction of Personal Histories," *Psychological Review,* 96, 341-357.

Short, J., E. Williams, and B. Christie (1976), *The Social Psychology of Telecommunications,* London: Wiley.

Siegel, J., V. Dubrovsky, S. Kiesler, and T. W. McGuire (1986), "Group Processes in Computer-Mediated Communications," *Organizational Behavior and Human Decision Processes,* 37, 157-187.

Simon, H. A. (1962), "The Architecture of Complexity," *Proceedings of the American Philosophical Society,* 106, 467-487.

Sproull, L. and S. Kiesler (1986), "Reducing Social Context Cues: Electronic Mail in Organizational Communication," *Management Science,* 32, 1492-1512.

_____ and S. Kiesler (1991), *Connections: New Ways of Working in the Networked Organization,* Cambridge: MIT Press.

Sproull, L. S. (1984), "The Nature of Managerial Attention," in P. Larkey and L. Sproull (Eds.), *Advances in Information Processing in Organizations, I,* Greenwich, CT: JAI, pp. 9-27.

Steuer, J. (1992), "Defining Virtual Reality: Dimensions Determining Telepresence," *Journal of Communication,* 42, 73-93.

Strauss, S. G. and J. E. McGrath (1994), "Does the Medium Matter? The Interaction of Task Type and Technology on Group Performance and Member Reactions," *Journal of Applied Psychology,* 79, 87-97.

Thompson, J. D. (1967), *Organizations in Action: Social Sciences Bases of Administrative Theory,* New York: McGraw-Hill.

Thorelli, H. B. (1986), "Networks: Between Markets and Hierarchies," *Strategic Management Journal,* 7, 37-51.

Travis, P. (1990), "Why the AT&T Network Crashed," *Telephony,* 218, January 22, 11.

Trevino, L. K., R. Lengel, and R. L. Daft (1987), "Media Symbolism, Media Richness, and Media Choice in Organizations: A Symbolic Interactionist Perspective," *Communication Research,* 14, 5, 553-574.

Tushman, M. L. (1977), "Special Boundary Roles in the Innovation Process," *Administrative Science Quarterly,* 22, 587-605.

Wagner, W. G., J. Pfeffer, and C. A. O'Reilly (1984), "Organizational Demography and Turnover in Top-Management Groups," *Administrative Science Quarterly,* 29, 74-92.

Walton, R. E. (1989), *Up and Running: Integrating Information Technology and the Organization,* Boston: Harvard Business School Press.

Watson, K. M. (1982), "An Analysis of Communication Patterns: A Method for Discriminating Leader and Subordinate Roles," *Academy of Management Journal,* 25, 107-120.

Weeks, G. D. and A. Chapanis (1976), "Cooperative vs. Conflictive Problem Solving in Three Telecommunications Modes," *Perceptual and Motor Skills,* 42, 879-917.

Whitely, W. (1984), "An Exploratory Study of Managers' Reactions to Properties of Verbal Communication," *Personnel Psychology,* 38, 41-53.

Wickesberg, A. K. (1968), "Communication Networks in the Business Organization Structure," *Academy of Management Journal,* 3, 253-262.

Wilson, D. O. (1992), "Diagonal Communication Links Within Organizations," *Journal of Business Communication,* 29, 129-143.

Yates, J. (1989), *Control Through Communication: The Rise of System in American Management,* Baltimore, MD: Johns Hopkins University Press.

Yukl, G. and C. M. Falbe (1990), "Influence Tactics and Objectives in Upward, Downward, and Lateral Influence Attempts," *Journal of Applied Psychology,* 75, 132-140.

Zenger, T. R. and B. S. Lawrence (1989), "Organizational Demography: The Differential Effects of Age and Tenure Distributions on Technical Communication," *Academy of Management Journal,* 32, 353-376.

Zmud, R. W., M. R. Lind, and F. W. Young (1990), "An Attribute Space for Organizational Communication Channels," *Information Systems Research,* 1, 440-457.

8

Social Context and Interaction in Ongoing Computer-Supported Management Groups

MICHAEL H. ZACK

JAMES L. MCKENNEY

Electronic communication has been proposed as a key technology enabling new organization forms and structures, work designs, and task processes (Benjamin and Scott Morton 1988, Finholt and Sproull 1990, Hammer 1990, Hammer and Mangurian 1987, Konsynski 1993, Malone et al. 1987, Sproull and Kiesler 1991, Venkatraman 1994). These new forms include, for example, cross-functional and interorganizational teams, executive teams, networked organizations, and virtual corporations (Baker 1991, Davidow and Malone 1992, Drucker 1988, Jarillo 1988, Miles and Snow 1986, Nadler et al. 1992, Thorelli 1986). An underlying assumption is that organization structure and form can be defined in terms of communication linkages among a set of organizational units, be they individuals, departments or entire organizations. By enabling new forms or channels of communication, we enable new forms of organization. To better understand the potential for these technologies to enable fundamental organizational change, however, we must understand how existing structures and social contexts influence the adoption and adaptation of these communication technologies.

This chapter appeared originally in *Organization Science,* 6(4), July/August, 1995.

Research on computer-mediated communication (CMC) suggests that CMC can increase the range, capacity, and speed of organizational communication (cf., reviews by Culnan and Markus 1987, Kerr and Hiltz 1982, Rice and Bair 1984, Sproull and Kiesler 1991, Steinfield 1986, Williams 1977). This research, however, has assumed almost exclusively a technological imperative for predicting and explaining the organizational impacts of CMC (Markus and Robey 1988). That is, the research is framed by the belief that given an appropriate design, once the technology is implemented communication processes and patterns will ultimately change in desired and intended ways. This assumption is so embedded that the potential influence of organizational culture or social context on patterns of CMC is rarely examined. Whether or not CMC will improve or even influence organizational performance, however, may depend on the particular social circumstances under which these electronic media are employed (Fulk and Boyd 1991, Kling and Saachi 1982, Poole and DeSanctis 1990, Rice et al. 1990, Schmitz and Fulk 1991).

Markus and Robey (1988) framed the issue in terms of researchers' assumptions about causal agency. They proposed three perspectives: the technological imperative, the organizational imperative, and the emergent imperative. The technological imperative suggests that change to an organization is caused by implementing some external technology, and traditionally this has been the view adopted by implementation and impacts studies. The organizational imperative assumes that people act rationally and purposefully to accomplish their objectives. Regarding CMC, this view suggests that users' task-based information processing needs influence their usage patterns leading to rational and objective media choices (Fulk and Boyd 1991) as suggested by information processing theories such as that by Daft and Lengel (1986). The emergent imperative, in contrast, views change as emerging from the interaction of individuals, events, technology, and the organization. This view is consistent with "web models" (Kling and Saachi 1982) and other socially oriented approaches to studying CMC.

Only a small amount of CMC research has observed ongoing work groups in natural settings where history, routine, norms, social relationships, and deeply shared interpretive and behavioral context may play a large role in determining interaction patterns and choice of communication mode[1] (e.g., McKenney et al. 1992, Reder and Schwab 1989, 1990, Trevino et al. 1987, Zack 1991). However, communication is inherently a social act (Goffman 1967, Pearce 1976, Sigman 1987). Therefore any study of technologies having the potential to directly influence or alter communication patterns and processes must examine social interactions within their natural context (Hackman 1985, Schegloff 1987), and attempts to understand this phenomenon using social theories of communication should benefit from studying complete, intact social groups.

The research being reported here examined the use of electronic messaging (EM) and face-to-face communication (FTF) in two ongoing management groups performing a cooperative task. *Ongoing* means that the groups had an established culture and set of routines and held an expectation of continuing to work together for the foreseeable future. By means of an in-depth multimethod field study of the managing editorial groups of two daily newspapers, we explored the relationship between social context and the interaction patterns within each group and how these interaction patterns related to communication and performance effectiveness. We observed a variance across groups in social context, with one group displaying cooperation among its members and the other, conflict. This enabled us to compare observations across groups, strengthening the validity of our findings.

Information- and knowledge-based service organizations have been cited as potential models for new organizational forms. Therefore, understanding the use of communication technologies in this context may provide useful insight into how other types of organizations might gainfully employ these technologies to support new forms of organization.

SOCIAL INFLUENCES ON THE USE
OF COMMUNICATION TECHNOLOGY

Individuals are embedded within social systems which influenced their behaviors (Radcliffe-Brown 1940). Communication is socially and culturally situated and thus similarly influence (Pearce 1976). However, an important theme emerging from reviews of the CMC and computer-supported cooperative work literature is that this research, with few exceptions (e.g., Fulk 1993, Rice and Aydin 1991, Rice et al. 1990, Schmitz and Fulk 1991), has not adequately taken into account social influences on technology use and outcomes (Fulk and Boyd 1991, Fulk et al. 1987, Kling 1991, Kling and Saachi 1982). The bulk of the CMC and group decision support system literature, reflecting the technological imperative, generally assumes that the impact, effect, or use of CMC will be influenced by the task, technology, or functional structure of the group or organization (Fulk and Boyd 1991, Kraemer and King 1988, Pinsonneault and Kraemer 1989, Sproull and Kiesler 1991, Steinfield 1986).

To redress the focus of past research, we adopted a social network perspective (Tichy et al. 1979). This perspective proposes that a group's *social structure* is influenced by its *social context*. Social structure, a fundamental construct of social network research, refers to patterning in social relations (Freeman 1989, Radcliffe-Brown 1940, White et al. 1976). Communication researchers specifically consider social structure to represent *patterns of interaction* (i.e., who communicates with whom about what) (Jablin et al. 1987). These interaction patterns tend to persist over time, and therefore can be thought of as representing structure (Hammer 1979, Schwartz and Jacobson 1977). We defined interaction as the communication between or among group members. Social structure, then, was the overall pattern of interaction within the group.

Social structure is influenced by what we are calling *social context* (Pettigrew 1985) and is similar to what Barley (1990) referred to as social institution. Social context includes the culture, distribution of power, and the social norms, habits, practices, expectations, and preferences held by a group regarding its present and past interaction.

Structuration theory similarly accounts for the influence of social context on social structure (Giddens 1979, Ranson et al. 1980). The theory is entirely compatible with the social network perspective (Banks and Riley 1993) and, while not yet extensively tested within the CMC field, appears to offer promise is enhancing our understanding of CMC (e.g., Yates and Orlikowski 1992). Structuration theory adds a dynamic perspective by focusing on how social context constrains interaction and how interaction, in turn, defines and redefines social context.[2] Social context is considered both the medium and the outcome of interaction; therefore understanding interaction at any point in time requires taking the current and historical social context into account. Interaction patterns emerge, then, from the particular balance between the propensity to derive psychological comfort from existing routine and the propensity for social innovation. Kling (1991, p. 87), in this spirit, proposed that "the ways in which CSCW [computer-supported cooperative work] systems restructure social relationships at work, if at all, depend on preexisting patterns of authority, obligation, and cooperation and an organization's openness to change."

Poole et al. (1985), building on Giddens (1979), developed adaptive structuration theory (AST) for examining group decision making. AST has been applied to the study of computer-supported group decision-making processes (Gopal et al. 1993, Poole and DeSanctis 1990, Poole et al. 1991), and Fulk and Boyd (1991) proposed that AST might similarly offer a useful foundation for CMC research. Use of the technology is conceptualized as a socially constructed process in which the technology is "appropriated" by a group to reinforce, adapt, or reproduce a set of interaction rules and practices (Poole and DeSanctis 1990, Poole et al. 1991). Appropriation of the technol-

ogy thus becomes part of the interaction behaviors comprising social structure and, like the interaction the technology supports, influences and is
influenced by the existing social context. Therefore, the particular way group
members choose to use the technology mediates the impact of the technology
on the group: "No matter what features are designed into a system, users
mediate technological effects, adapting systems to their needs, resisting
them, or refusing to use them at all" (Poole and DeSanctis 1990, p. 177).

Rather than looking at how groups appropriate the particular structuring
mechanisms embedded in group decision support systems, we examined EM,
a form of communication technology which technologically imposes no
boundaries or constraints on patterns of interaction.[3] Pool and DeSanctis
(1990) posited that lower-structure communication technologies such as EM
provided a greater opportunity for variation in how a group would appropriate the technology. In our case, appropriation would reflect the influence of
social context on the patterns of EM and FTF interaction and how those
constraints on interaction are socially rather than technologically imposed.

Appropriation manifests at the individual and dynamic level in how EM
users employ messaging system features such as distribution (one-to-one or
one-to-many) and timing (synchronous or asynchronous exchange). Appropriation also applies to choosing from among several communication modes,
for example, based on the extent to which richness or interactivity is required
(Zack 1993). However, consistent with the social network perspective, the
influence of social context on the appropriation of EM at the network level
is best reflected in how group members employ the technology to support
interaction among themselves, and that is the approach we adopted.

While structuration theory makes provisions for both stability and change
in social context, stability appears to dominate real work groups, and this is
the aspect we emphasized. Groups and individuals require some degree of
organizational routine, order, and steady state to function properly. Stability
is sought as a means to avoid anxiety and to make sense of the world (Schein
1985). Our approach assumed that organizations move through periods of
relative stability punctuated by discontinuous interventions (e.g., implementing a new technology) which ultimately settle again into a state of
stability. These interventions initiate rounds of social and technological
adaptation (Leonard-Barton 1988), ultimately leading to some particular
appropriation of the technology within some (possibly new) social context.
The outcome may range from the technology imposing a new social context
(e.g., Barley 1990) to the social context constraining the appropriation of the
technology (e.g., Orlikowski 1992).

Communication technologies, unlike traditional production technologies,
are explicitly used to support interaction and have been designed and imple-

mented explicitly to enable changes to interaction patterns. These technologies therefore are especially subject to the constraints of the existing social context, and accounting for these constraints is important when studying CMC. Evidence of the constraints of social context on computer-supported interaction is beginning to accumulate (e.g., Norland 1992, Orlikowski 1992, Stone 1992), and calls are being made for social and cultural explanations of the institutional inertia inhibiting the intended effectiveness of CMC (Perrin 1991).

Poole et al. (1985) similarly posited that the key to understanding group behavior lay in recognizing the "essential continuity of institutions and negotiated activity" (p. 96). Actors must cope with historical precedent in the form of preexisting social context as these existing social contexts constrain later ones and perpetuate themselves through their influence on patterns of interactions (Poole et al. 1985). Guetzkow and Simon (1955) found that imposed interaction patterns could restrict a group's ability to properly communicate to organize and to create an efficient strategy for performing its task. Thus to the extent that existing context constrains the interaction comprising social structure, it might in turn constrain a group from creating a more "ideal" structure under new circumstances (new task, technology, etc.), even if that new technology itself could enable new forms of communication.

Poole et al. (1985) further posited that features of the actors' knowledge condition their actions. Tacit knowledge of how to participate in group interactions results in actors overlooking interaction choices not part of their accustomed or "legitimate" repertoire. Even talking about this knowledge is constrained by it and many limit the group only to justifying its existing practice. Therefore, we would expect that media choices and communication links would be constrained by each individual's existing socially constructed "how to's" for interaction with other individuals in the group.

Structuration theory suggests, then, that absent some significant discontinuity or external intervention, CMC technology will be appropriated in a manner that reinforces the existing social context (Kraft 1987, Poole and DeSanctis 1990). The theory further suggests that there is no particular reason, per se, to expect that the use of EM would expand the communication network or alter the patterns of communication (as assumed by the technological and organizational imperatives) beyond those which the group might consider appropriate to the existing social context of the group.[4] Studying this proposition requires comparing groups whose task, functional structure and technology (per the technological imperative), and perceptions and preferences regarding the technology (per the organizational imperative) are similar, yet whose social context is not.

This discussion leads to the following proposition.

Proposition 1. Groups with similar tasks, functional structures, electronic messaging systems, and perceptions, preferences, and practices regarding those messaging systems, but different social contexts will exhibit different patterns of FTF and EM interaction and those patterns of interaction will reflect each group's particular social context.

Social information processing theory (SIP) has offered one approach to accounting for social influences on media use (Fulk 1993, Fulk et al. 1987). SIP theory posits that significant others in an individual's social field (e.g., superiors or coworkers) influence that individual's attitudes and behaviors. Fulk and Boyd (1991), based on SIP, proposed that work groups are important sources of social support and regular interaction. They reasoned, therefore, if social influences were more important than task influences on media use, one should observe similar patterns of individual media use within work groups regardless of the task's communication characteristics, and different patterns of media use across groups. While we are proposing a different conception of social influence at the group level of analysis, the outcome should be similar, namely group-level patterns of EM and FTF interaction that are more similar within than across groups.

Theories that do not account for social context should predict organizations having the same task, functional structure, and CMC technology, yet possibly different social contexts, to exhibit equivalent patterns of interaction. Our framework, in contrast, suggests that groups with different social contexts would exhibit different patterns of interaction and that the patterned use of communication modes (in this case FTF or EM) would be expected to vary more across than within different social fields (Fulk and Boyd 1991, Fulk et al. 1987), leading to the following proposition:

Proposition 2. For groups with similar tasks, functional structures, electronic messaging systems, and perceptions, preferences, and practices regarding those messaging systems, but different social contexts, patterns of FTF and EM interaction will be more similar within groups than patterns of FTF or EM interaction across groups.

Bavelas and associates initiated a stream of experimental research studying the impact of patterns of interaction (represented as communication networks) on task-group processes and outcomes (e.g., Bavelas 1950, Bonacich 1987, Freeman et al. 1980, Guetzkow and Simon 1955, Leavitt 1951). Much of the network-task research (e.g., Shaw 1959) focused on examining the effects of communication networks which restrict communication opportunities, versus those which were more open and connected (Guetzkow 1965). The central finding of this research was that the communication requirements of a particular task determined the most appropriate communication network for the group; thus group performance depended on the fit of its interaction patterns to the task (Glanzer and Glaser 1961). For example, groups whose members had access to required information were able to solve group problems more quickly (Gilchrist et al. 1954), and structures which got information to where needed when needed improved group performance (Roby and Lanzetta 1956). An extensive review by Guetzkow (1965, p. 568) concluded that "there is clear demonstration of effects in the laboratory of the interrelations between communications and task upon performance."

Tushman (1979), studying seven departments of the R&D laboratory of a large corporation, provided real-world evidence that for high-performing units, communication structure, measured as the degree of centralization of the communication network, was contingent on the communication requirements of the units' work. The less routine and more complex the work, the more decentralized (connected) the communication network. David et al. (1989) found similar results with banks. O'Reilly and Roberts (1977) extended this line of research by examining the mediating influence of communication effectiveness (measured as communication accuracy and communication openness) on the relationship between patterns of interaction and group effectiveness using data from three real-world task groups. They found that communication effectiveness was significantly related to group interaction patterns measured as vertical and horizontal differentiation, connectedness, degree of two-way interaction, and average rank (hierarchical level) of group members. The communication effectiveness measures were, in turn, significantly related to group effectiveness. Additional field evidence for the relationship between appropriate interaction patterns and effective group performance has been provided by the group decision support system research (e.g., Jarvenpaa et al. 1988, Poole et al. 1991) and by Hackman's (1990) research on effective work groups.

We adopted group communication effectiveness as a means to link interaction patterns to outcome effectiveness (Farace et al. 1978). Given our expectation that groups performing the same task yet having different social contexts will exhibit different patterns of interaction, we would further expect those groups, therefore, to exhibit different levels of communication and performance effectiveness, leading to the following proposition:

Proposition 3. Groups with similar tasks, functional structures, electronic messaging systems, and perceptions, preferences, and practices regarding those messaging systems, but different interaction patterns, will exhibit different levels of communication and performance effectiveness.

In summary, we adopted a research framework proposing that the social context of the group influences its social structure, as reflected in its patterns of FTF and EM interaction, leading to more or less effective communication and group performance. Our goal was to show that the use of EM and FTF as described by the groups' interaction patterns was consistent with each group's social context and, in turn, influenced the groups' communication and performance effectiveness.

Blalock (1969) proposed that theoretical models or frameworks be restated in more operational terms using measurable "indicators." This operational theory links the concepts of the literature to the actual research performed. Figure 8.1 illustrates our theoretical research framework comprising the constructs' social context, social structure, communication effectiveness and performance effectiveness, and a related framework comprising a less abstract set of constructs linking the theoretical framework to the indicators actually measured. The following describes our operationalization of the theoretical constructs.

Social Context

Structuration theory proposes three modalities by which social context influences interaction: interpretive schemes for meaningful communication, facilities for the application of power, and normative schemes for the legitimization of action (Poole et al. 1985). Therefore, interaction cannot be studied without also considering the norms of power structures within which it is situated and how those influences have shaped the structuring of interaction itself (Riley 1983). The social network research, while similarly focusing on how power and control are related to interaction (Burt 1980, Freeman 1989), has also focused on "philos" (Krackhardt 1992), the level of comraderie, respect, attraction, and general spirit of cooperation among social actors. We therefore included communication norms, power and control, and philos as important descriptors of social context.

We used *communication climate* to represent the normative influences on communication. The extent to which information is shared is positively related to the strength of perceived norms supportive of information sharing (Dewhirst 1971), and perceived communication openness is strongly related to group structure (David et al. 1989, O'Reilly and Roberts 1977). Communication climate, therefore, potentially is an important contextual influence on interaction. We used *management philosophy* to capture the influence of power and control on group interaction. Poole and DeSanctis (1990) proposed that the appropriation process depended on the behavior of the group

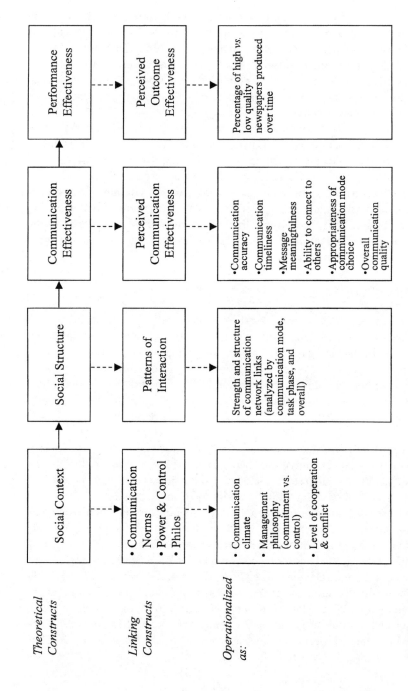

Theoretical Constructs

| Social Context | → | Social Structure | → | Communication Effectiveness | → | Performance Effectiveness |

Linking Constructs

- Communication Norms
- Power & Control
- Philos

Patterns of Interaction

Perceived Communication Effectiveness

Perceived Outcome Effectiveness

Operationalized as:

- Communication climate
- Management philosophy (commitment vs. control)
- Level of cooperation & conflict

Strength and structure of communication network links (analyzed by communication mode, task phase, and overall)

- Communication accuracy
- Communication timeliness
- Message meaningfulness
- Ability to connect to others
- Appropriateness of communication mode choice
- Overall communication quality

Percentage of high vs. low quality newspapers produced over time

Figure 8.1. Research Framework

leader, particularly the leader's willingness to act in a manner consistent with the intended spirit of the technology. Walton and Hackman (1986) proposed a framework for group leadership which could be usefully applied here. They defined two leadership strategies: control and commitment. Under a control strategy management's positional authority is emphasized in controlling the group via top-down communication and coordination. Under a commitment strategy, on the other hand, authority is derived more from competence and experience than position; coordination and control are handled through shared philosophy and goals and lateral group interaction. We used philos to denote the level of cooperation or conflict within each group.

Social Structure

For purposes of measurement and representation, the interaction patterns comprising social structure can be viewed as a network of relations (Radcliffe-Brown 1940). Social networks, a formalism representing relations as nodes and links, have been used extensively as a means for measuring or describing social structure (cf., Bavelas 1950, Burt 1980, Freeman 1989, Leavitt 1951, Tichy et al. 1979). Nodes represent the social units or actors (e.g., individuals and organizations), and the links, their relations. In our case, the social units comprising the network were the individual group members. The links were represented by group members' exchange of information. The network, then, represented the overall interaction patterns of the group. The particular network measures taken were the strength (in terms of overall interaction frequency) and the structure (in terms of the degree of hierarchy and lateral connectivity in each group).

Communication Effectiveness

We measured the perceived quality of communication in terms of accuracy, timeliness, meaningfulness, coordination, ability to communicate with whomever needed, frequency of miscommunication, appropriateness of communication mode choices, and overall quality of communication (Driver and Streufert 1969, O'Reilly and Roberts 1977, Steiner 1972).

Outcome Effectiveness

We proposed that effective communication was needed for producing a high-quality newspaper. Because of complex and emergent interactions among people, events, the task and the technology, effective groups might occasionally perform ineffectively, and ineffective groups might occasionally perform effectively, but over time we would expect effectively commu-

PROCESSES IN NEW FORM DEVELOPMENT

nicating groups to produce a high-quality newspaper more frequently than ineffective groups. That suggested measuring outcome effectiveness as a frequency over time of newspaper quality at different levels. We measured via the questionnaire the overall effectiveness of the group in terms of the perceived quality of the news section. The editors indicated the percentage of time they felt the news section was unacceptable, average, good, and great. We then summed the two lower and the two upper categories into a "good" and "bad" percentage for clarity and ease of cross-organizational comparison.

RESEARCH SITES

We studied the managing editorial group of two daily morning newspapers, one medium-sized (referred to as *The Statewide Times*) and the other large (referred to as *The Regional News*).[5] Both organizations were part of the same parent corporation. Each group comprised the senior and middle-level newsroom managers responsible for producing the "hard" news section of the newspaper. *The Statewide Times*'s editorial group had 15 members and *The Regional News*'s 14.

The task process was essentially the same at both organizations. Stories were written, transmitted, edited, and the process managed using EM together with FTF. While managers had written memo and telephone readily available, memos played little or no observed role in the day-to-day production of either paper and were reserved solely for infrequent, formal administrative communication among the top executives. Telephone accounted for just over 5% of the observed communication events at *Statewide* and less than 4% at *Regional,* almost all for communicating to others outside the newsroom and where no alternative existed (e.g., to a reporter on location or a call received from an outside party). Therefore the study focused on EM and FTF. Both groups conducted daily scheduled meetings to coordinate efforts and to negotiate newspaper content and story placement, and communicated on an ad hoc basis throughout the publishing cycle using both EM and FTF.

Researchers often make favorable assumptions about social context which may have little grounding in reality. According to Kling (1991),

> Many CSCW articles impede our understanding of the likely use and impact of CSCW since they rely on concepts with strong positive connotations such as "cooperation," "collaboration," and images of convivial possibilities to characterize workplace relationships, while understating the levels of conflict, control, and coercion—also common in professional workplaces. (p. 84)

The prediction of social theories that communication technology usage patterns will differ across groups implies the need to compare groups differing only along their social dimensions. However, evidence supporting this proposition is scarce because of the difficulty in identifying truly equivalent groups with similar tasks and media options but different norms or social context (Fulk et al. 1987). We measured contextual similarities to validate comparability of groups, and we believe that our groups met the criteria for examining this proposition. All of the contextual factors except social context were essentially the same for both groups, enabling us to explicitly examine the relationship of social context to interaction patterns and performance effectiveness.

Not only did our study explicitly address social context, but purposely compared cooperative and conflicted groups to introduce a meaningful variance in that construct. Senior management of the parent corporation nominated for our study the 2 (of approximately 30) of their newspaper organizations which, in their opinion, exhibited the greatest contrast in social context. We were introduced to the executive editors and then negotiated our entry directly with each newspaper.

As our goal was to better understand whether or not social context constrained the ultimate appropriation of the technology at a point where relative stability had been reestablished, we purposely sought our stable groups who had been using the technology for a period long enough for it to have become embedded in the routines of the group. We made our observations of each group during periods in which no major discontinuities or interventions occurred. Our repeated observations of the daily work cycle provided further evidence of stability during our data collection period.

METHODS

We employed the case study approach whereby the primary unit of analysis was the site itself (Yin 1984). That is, data, both quantitative and qualitative, were collected and analyzed on a site-by-site basis, rather than pooled, to identify convergent findings about that site. Data can be categorized as qualitative or quantitative and as objective or subjective (relative to the respondent), defining four categories. Our data collection methods addressed each category, enhancing the reliability of our findings (Jick 1979).

We used questionnaires (quantitative/subjective) to measure group members' perceptions of all constructs including perceived strength of communication ties by communication mode and phase of the task process. We computed within-group mean responses from the questionnaire data and ran two-tailed t-tests to establish significance or lack thereof in the differences between group means. We were comparing small populations; therefore achieving significant differences could be difficult. Given our small population and our use of multiple methods to validate our findings, we felt comfortable considering differences of $p \le .10$ to be "significant" and $p \le .125$ to be "moderately significant."

The questionnaire was administered to the entire, although small, population of each group. To enhance its validity, it was developed and tested at a pilot site prior to its administration in the research sites reported on in this study. The questionnaire was developed after interviewing 23 senior editors at the pilot site, and was reviewed by several editors and then revised by us prior to being administered to the pilot group. After administration to the pilot group, we conducted follow-up interviews to identify ambiguous or problematic questions. We then analyzed the data to identify anomalous results. We conducted additional follow-up interviews to understand the anomalies, and further revised the questionnaire. Threats to reliability and validity were reduced by items (e.g., tenure) being of a low level of abstraction and close to the phenomenon (Kerlinger 1986), focused on behavior (e.g., communication mode usage), focused on measuring cross-site differences rather than absolute amounts, and exhibiting small within-site variances among group members. We used multi-item scales to measure communication constructs (viz., communication climate and communication effectiveness), and the alpha reliability coefficients are presented in Table 8.1. In an attempt to keep our questionnaire to a reasonable length, we employed single-item measures for the remaining constructs, precluding our establishing their reliability individually. However, to enhance validity, we still measured many of the constructs using multiple items. While those items addressed different subconstructs and were not designed to covary for the purposes of establishing reliability, it was still possible to combine them by construct and compute reliability coefficients (Table 8.2). In this context, the reliability coefficients for these measures might therefore be somewhat lower than for true multi-item scales. The reader is cautioned to interpret the reliabilities within this context. Also, several measures (Table 8.5 [preference for FTF vs. EM], Table 8.8 [all three items addressing management philosophy], and Table 8.10 [frequency of communication breakdown and cross-shift coordination]) did not lend themselves to combination with other items, and the reader is cautioned to interpret these measures accordingly.

We used interviews (qualitative/subjective) to identify, frame, discuss, and corroborate the constructs. We used observation (qualitative/objective) to corroborate media choice rules, communication climate, communication quality, overall communication density and management style and to obtain the message content of FTF exchanges. We captured electronic messages (qualitative/objective) to obtain the content of EM. We used electronic

TABLE 8.1 Reliability Coefficients for Multiple-Item Measures

Table	Construct	α
8.7	Communication climate	.75
8.10	Communication effectiveness	
	Phase 1	.89
	Phase 2	.77
	Phase 3	.88
	Cross-shift Phase 1	.91
	Cross-shift Phase 2	.88
	Cross-shift Phase 3	.86

TABLE 8.2 Reliability Coefficients for Composites of Single-Item Measures

Table	Composite Construct	Subconstructs	α
8.3	FTF perceptions	FTF reachability	.50
		FTF meaningfulness	
		FTF restrictiveness	
		FTF efficiency	
8.3	EM perceptions	EM reachability	.81
		EM meaningfulness	
		EM restrictiveness	
		EM efficiency	
8.4	Appropriateness of use	Composite score, by communication mode, of the appropriateness of using that mode in four different real-world scenarios	
	FTF		.64
	EM		.55
	Notes		.72
	Telephone		.68
	Memo		.84
8.4	Rules of use	Various tacit rules of use derived from interviews and observation	
	FTF		.76
	EM		.63
	EM (regarding reliability)		.43
	FTF (regarding richness)		.87
	EM (regarding richness)		.64
8.10	Extent of communication breakdowns	Extent of in-shift breakdowns	.65
		Extent of cross-shift breakdowns	

message capture and structured observation of FTF communication (quantitative/objective) to describe and measure the links among group members.

The particular case design used was the multiple site replication with embedded units of analysis (Yin 1984). Replicating our study in two sites differing on the key construct of interest (i.e., social context) yet similar with regard to those constructs representing competing sources of explanation enabled us to enhance the validity of the findings (George and McKeown 1985).

While the case site represented the primary unit of analysis, other lower-level units of analysis were employed within each site. Yin (1984) referred to these secondary units as embedded units of analysis. Rogers (1986) proposed the information exchange relationship (or interaction event [Fulk and Boyd 1991, Goffman 1967, Sigman 1987]), rather than the individual, as the appropriate unit of analysis for CMC research. We used the interaction event as an embedded unit of analysis within each case site, providing the data for performing a network analysis of each group's interaction patterns.

Network analysis is central to the field of structural inquiry (Monge and Eisenberg 1987) and represents the appropriate method for guiding data collection and analysis of groups when the focus is on patterns of interaction over time (O'Reilly and Roberts 1977, Tichy 1980). Network analysis has been used in several CMC studies (Eveland and Bikson 1987, Rice and Aydin 1991, Rice and Love 1987, Rice et al. 1990), and others have called for its use with CMC research (Fulk and Boyd 1991, Rice 1990). The network paradigm is ideal for examining a socially based view of communication technologies in that it refocuses attention away from individuals as independent users of the technology to a view of users as an interconnected set of interdependent relationships embedded within organizational and social systems (Contractor and Eisenberg 1990).

Interview and general observation notes were transcribed and sorted according to our research framework. Communication events recorded during structured observation, and electronic messages captured from the electronic messaging system, were entered to a database and coded to identify the parties to the communication, the direction (from/to), the time, the mode, a summary of the content of the interaction, and the purpose of the message. Content analysis of the interactions was based on an ethnographic interpretation informed by our extended time spent in the field. We treated our interpretations as hypotheses regarding the social context of the group and its relationship to social structure, and validated our interpretations against those of the editors during follow-up interviews.

At *The Statewide Times,* 18 interviews were conducted with all but one member of the management group and with several non-group managers. The publishing process was observed (usually shadowing a central actor) for

62 hours, distributed throughout the 24-hour publishing cycle.[6] Four news meetings were attended. Electronic mail messages sent during each observation period were obtained directly from most of the editors at the end of the observation, and electronic messages corresponding to 2 days of observation were obtained directly from the editorial computer system. After conducting all interviews and observations, a questionnaire was administered, and completed questionnaires were received from 14 of the 15 editors for a response rate of 93%.

At *The Regional News,* 19 interviews were conducted with all but two members of the management group and with several non-group managers. All phases of the publishing process were observed during a total of 100 hours of observation. Again, particular editors were shadowed during most observations. Ten news meetings were attended. Electronic messages were obtained directly from participants at the end of each observation period. The questionnaire, modified slightly to reflect the particular process and jargon at this site, was administered to the 14 managers. Twelve questionnaires (85%) were returned.

In the following sections we first establish the similarity between groups regarding functional structure, task process, electronic messaging technology, and group member perceptions regarding that technology. We then establish their dissimilarities in social context. Next we present the resulting differences in their patterns of interaction, consistent with their social context (Proposition 1). We show how the patterns of interaction were more similar across modes within groups than within modes across groups (Proposition 2). Finally, we link interaction patterns to performance (Proposition 3).

CONTEXTUAL SIMILARITIES
BETWEEN GROUPS

This section establishes the similarities between the groups. In addition to controlling for the functional structure, task process, and technology as suggested by the technological imperative, we also controlled for influences on communication mode choice as suggested by the organizational imperative.

Functional Structure

Functional structure refers to the organization and assignment of occupational roles and responsibilities. Both groups used essentially the same functional structure composed of senior managers, reporting editors, news editors, and copy editors. Senior management in both groups comprised an executive editor (EE) and a managing editor (ME). The EE managed the editorial division, set the tone of the paper, influenced editorial content, and might become involved with major stories. The ME reported to the EE and was responsible for the day-to-day news gathering and editing operations. The ME made or was involved with most of the decisions on newsroom administration and editorial policy and guided or monitored the day-to-day selection of stories to run on page 1, the primary daily news decision. Reporting editors were responsible for assigning reporters, helping them to craft their stories, and monitoring their progress against deadline. Reporting editors in both groups were coordinated by an associate managing editor (AME) for reporting. News desk editors managed and coordinated the content of the news section, reviewing all copy to run in that section, and deciding which stories would run on page 1, which would run inside the news section, and would not run in the section at all. News desk editors determined story placement and specified final story length. The news desk in both groups was coordinated by an AME/News. The copy desk was responsible for giving stories a more detailed editing for grammar, spelling, and factual accuracy. They wrote headlines and trimmed stories to fit the length specified by the news desk. Senior copy editors, called slots, assigned stories to particular copy editors and reviewed their work.

Task Process

Both groups performed essentially an identical task: creating the first ("news") section of the daily newspaper. The daily publishing process at both papers could be broken into three phases: planning, decision making, and execution/production (Figure 8.2). From about 9 a.m. to 3 p.m. (Phase 1), reporting and coverage plans were being made and stories assigned and reported. Reporting desks were creating news "budgets"—a list of stories with estimated length to be offered to the news desk that evening—based on preliminary conversations with reporters and on intuition. Between 3 p.m. and 7 p.m. (Phase 2), several hours before the actual stories were filed, a preliminary decision about what would run where was made based on the news budget. This decision was formally made at a daily news meeting (4 p.m. at *Statewide* and 5 p.m. at *Regional*) attended by representatives of all four functions; however, the decision was affected by interactions occurring before and after the news meeting. Based on the budget and the preliminary placement decisions, the news desk allocated space for each budgeted story and communicated that to the copy desk. Phase 2 was especially important as this represented the transition from the day shift to the night shift and the hand-off from the planners to the producers. Communication and coordination between the day reporting editors and the night production and layout editors was essential to producing an effective news section. From about 7

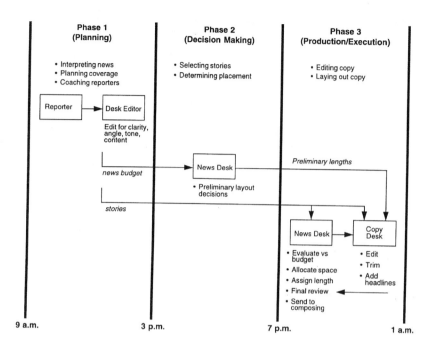

Figure 8.2 The News Editing Process

p.m. to 1 a.m. (Phase 3), late stories were filed and sent from reporting desks to the copy desk for final editing and trimming to the budgeted length assigned by the news desk. News editors monitored stories for reevaluation possibly resulting in changes to the placement decisions. The reporting editors left midway through Phase 3, once all major stories were filed and edited. The news desk spent the next few hours laying out each of several editions while making changes as stories changed or news stories were filed. The copy desk edited its backlog of stories, writing headlines and responding to changes in the budgeted length of stories it was editing. Once a story was edited and headlined by the copy desk, the news desk would do a final read, then send the story to composing for paste up and plating.

Technology

Both sites used an identical group authoring and messaging computer system. *Statewide* had been using the system for 4 years and *Regional* for 6 years. Both sites appeared to have reached an equilibrium point in the mutual adaptation of the organization and the technology (Leonard-Barton 1988).

TABLE 8.3 Communication Mode Perceptions

	Statewide		Regional			
	Ave.	SD	Ave.	SD	Diff.	2-tail p
Reachability: confidence (1 = high, 5 = low) that message will reach those it needs to via						
FTF	1.57	0.65	1.43	0.51	0.14	.523
EM	2.23	0.83	2.14	0.77	0.09	.779
Confidence (1 = high, 5 = low) that message will be understood when using						
FTF	1.50	0.52	1.57	0.65	0.07	.750
EM	2.38	0.87	2.21	0.80	0.17	.602
Restrictiveness: extent to which you feel restricted (1 = high, 5 = low) when using						
FTF	4.29	0.61	4.50	0.86	0.12	.453
EM	2.92	1.44	3.71	1.14	0.79	.129
Efficiency: extent to which mode is an efficient means for communication (reverse scored) (1 = high, 5 = low)						
FTF	3.43	1.02	4.21	0.98	0.79	.047
EM	3.77	0.73	3.86	0.86	0.09	.776

All group members were well accustomed to the technology and knowledgeable about its features.

Communication Mode Perceptions

Adopting the argument that media characteristics are perceived rather than objective or determined (Fulk et al. 1987) and thus sociocognitively influenced, different media perceptions between the two groups might account for differences in their communication patterns and outcomes. Questionnaire data (Table 8.3) showed no significant differences in how both groups perceived most characteristics of FTF and EM, the exception being that *Statewide* significantly perceived FTF to be somewhat more efficient than did *Regional*.

TABLE 8.4 Communication Mode Usage Rules and Practices

	Statewide		Regional			
	Ave.	*SD*	*Ave.*	*SD*	*Diff.*	*2-Tail p*
Appropriateness of using for four scenarios (1 = high, 5 = low)						
FTF	2.36	0.69	2.33	1.07	0.03	.920
EM	1.43	0.48	1.33	0.57	0.10	.629
Telephone	2.89	0.81	3.12	1.05	0.23	.554
Text file annotations	3.41	0.61	3.60	1.11	0.19	.602
Written memo	3.98	0.75	4.35	1.13	0.37	.350
Overall extent to which subjects agreed with a stated set of rules for using FTF (based on interactivity required, proximity, perceived reliability, richness required, and social presence required) (1 = high, 5 = low)	1.58	0.41	1.39	0.48	0.19	.270
Overall extent to which subjects agreed with a stated set of rules for using EM (based on speed required, asynchroneity required, interactivity required, and directedness of search required) (1 = high, 5 = low)	1.91	0.41	1.79	0.53	0.13	.493
Extent of agreement on rules specifically regarding EM use and perceived reliability (e.g., never use EM for important or urgent messages) (1 = high, 5 = low)	2.50	0.50	2.14	0.69	0.36	.135
Extent of agreement on rules specifically regarding FTF richness, interactivity, and social presence (e.g., use FTF in situations requiring lots of back-and-forth exchange, to create a common understanding, to influence the other person) (1 = high, 5 = low)	1.54	0.47	1.34	0.54	0.20	.315
Extent of agreement on rules specifically regarding EM richness, interactivity, and social presence (e.g., use EM in situations requiring only simple or no response, use EM when parties share common knowledge of topic, use EM to avoid personal contact) (1 = high, 5 = low)	2.03	0.44	1.81	0.62	0.22	.300

TABLE 8.5 Communication Mode Preferences

| | FTF vs. EM | |
	Ave.	SD
Statewide	2.16	1.41
Regional	1.79	0.96
Difference	0.36	
2-tail *p*	0.441	
(1 = strongly prefer FTF; 3 = neutral; 5 = strongly prefer EM)		

Communication Mode Usage
Rules and Practices

Social context, comprising rules for behavior (Poole et al. 1985), also may govern the rules for utilizing communication modes. Tacit, informal rules for using EM and FTF were derived from interview and observation data and verified by questionnaire (Table 8.4). The extent to which the editors agreed with these rules, averaged by communication mode, was strong overall (confirming the rules) and showed no significant difference between groups. This finding held for subsets of the rules specifically addressing reliability and richness.

Additionally, to confirm our findings and ensure comparability between groups, four real-world scenarios requiring a communication mode choice were presented to the editors. For each scenario they were asked to evaluate the appropriateness of five communication modes (FTF, EM, telephone, annotations embedded in text files, and written memos). The average evaluation across the five scenarios for each mode showed no significant difference between the groups. Both groups rated EM as the most appropriate communication mode, followed by FTF. Telephone received a neutral evaluation while annotated files and memos were considered inappropriate overall. Thus both groups appeared to have the same strong propensity at the microinteraction level to use EM and FTF in similar common situations, when considered apart from the macrosocial context.

Individual Preferences
Regarding Communication Modes

Regardless of a group's rules and norms, individuals may have particular preferences for one communication mode or another. Questionnaire responses (Table 8.5) showed no significant difference in the average communication mode preferences of the two groups.

TABLE 8.6 Tenure

	Statewide		Regional			
	Ave.	SD	Ave.	SD	Diff.	2-Tail p
Years in current job	4.62	5.05	5.19	4.96	0.57	.765
Years at paper	11.93	8.34	13.94	8.35	2.01	.530
Years in industry	18.93	9.42	20.79	8.98	1.86	.598

Tenure

The average tenure of the groups was not significantly different (Table 8.6).

Summary

The groups were remarkably similar in many ways. They comprised editors of similar tenure using identical technologies performing the same task using the same functional structure to perform the same process. They similarly perceived characteristics of FTF and EM communication modes and shared the same basic rules for choosing between communication modes. Despite these similarities, the groups differed significantly in social context as described in the following section.

CONTEXTUAL DIFFERENCES
BETWEEN GROUPS

This section describes the key differences between groups regarding social context, namely communication climate, management philosophy, and group philos.

Communication Climate

Questionnaire items addressing openness of communication and information sharing (Table 8.7) showed significant differences between the groups, with *Regional* the more open of the two. *Regional* clearly embraced open communication while *Statewide*'s response was more moderate. This difference was clearly observed by us, as indicated by a much greater amount of frank and open exchange of views at *Regional* than at *Statewide*.

TABLE 8.7 Communication Climate

	Statewide		Regional			
	Ave.	*SD*	*Ave.*	*SD*	*Diff.*	*2-Tail p*
Information sharing is encouraged among the group. (1 = strongly agree, 5 = strongly disagree)	2.36	1.01	1.79	0.89	0.57	.125
We share information openly among group members. (1 = strongly agree, 5 = strongly disagree)	2.64	0.84	2.07	0.73	0.57	0.06

Management Philosophy

Questionnaire data (Table 8.8) showed no significant difference in the extent to which both groups tended to follow the formal hierarchy; however, they differed significantly in their ability to transcend that structure when needed. This aspect (viz., knowledge vs. hierarchy, and flexibility) showed the largest and most significant differences between groups among contextual differences questionnaire items.

Regional's editorial group tended to let those with the relevant knowledge concerning the task at hand override the formal hierarchy to a large extent, whereas this usually did not occur at *Statewide*. At *Regional* individual knowledge and expertise were highly respected and relied on, while the editors at *Statewide* experienced a much lower level of mutual respect. *Regional* was able to operate hierarchically where needed, yet was flexible enough to transcend that structure. *Statewide* usually was not, regardless of the particular circumstances. Thus, while both organizations routinely operated in a hierarchical and structured fashion, *Regional* maintained the flexibility to transcend the formal hierarchy where needed, supported by a climate conducive to open and frank communication. *Statewide* was more rooted to its structure within an environment less conducive to the open sharing of information.

We observed the *Regional* ME routinely delegating important news decisions to the news, reporting, and copy editors. For example, the ME had little involvement in determining the content of page 1, but rather delegated this decision to the news desk in consultation with the other two functions. This was corroborated during our interviews.

Statewide showed a marked contrast. The ME inserted himself into most of the day-to-day news decisions regarding the news process. While the news

TABLE 8.8 Management Philosophy

	Statewide		Regional			
	Ave.	SD	Ave.	SD	Diff.	2-Tail p
We follow a strict and formal hierarchy for managing and controlling our work. (1 = strongly agree, 5 = strongly disagree)	2.86	0.87	3.07	1.14	0.21	.581
We let whomever has the knowledge and expertise direct the task, regardless of formal position. (1 = strongly agree, 5 = strongly disagree)	3.93	0.48	2.86	1.10	1.07	.004
The group operates in a highly flexible and fluid manner. (1 = strongly agree, 5 = strongly disagree)	2.50	1.01	1.79	0.70	0.71	.051

editor had formal responsibility for the page 1 decision, we observed him being directed and overridden by the ME on a regular basis. The news meeting, formally hosted by the news desk, typically became an opportunity for the ME to take over the meeting, query each person regarding their budget, and then impose his view of page 1 on the news editors. They regularly deferred to him, anticipating that he would make the decision anyway. We observed several instances where the news editor would seek the approval of the ME for very routine matters before making a change to the paper.

Philos and Cooperation

The reporting desks (the "artists") and the news and copy desks ("production") operated under different goals, perspectives, and time constraints. Producing a high-quality newspaper required effective coordination and communication between those who reported the news and those who determined what stories would actually run each day. At both papers, as with most newspapers, there was a natural difference in orientation between these subgroups. However, this schism ran deeper at *Statewide* than at *Regional,* particularly between the news desk and the reporting desks. The group at *Regional* exhibited a high level of philos, whereas the group at *Statewide* exhibited little philos and a moderate amount of hostility among the functional subgroups.

According to the AME/Reporting at *Statewide,*

> We tried something a couple of months ago, we call a "group grope." And I got several reporters together first thing in the morning and we said to ourselves "What's the best thing we can do tomorrow that will knock the readers' socks off?" And we had one reporter in the group who agreed that no matter what idea we came up with he would take that story and produce it for tomorrow, and we would hope it would be a page-1 story—the best story in the paper. And we did it for about 2 weeks. And every story we did, the news desk buried. And the reporters were just outraged; "Don't they know what we're trying to do? Why don't they come to this meeting if they're committed to this process too?" And I said, "Well, I agree with you."

Another *Statewide* reporting editor expressed a low opinion of the news editor: "The news editor, whom I think is a real drink, by the way, shouldn't be anywhere *near* a newspaper" (Suburban editor, *Statewide*).

The news desk often complained about finding out about reporting desk changes too late in the cycle to take appropriate action. The reporting editors countered that it was the news desk's attitude and an unwillingness to deal with the constraints of the process that was at fault:

> If we know early in the day that we've got some potentially swapable stories, we'll try to tell [the news editors], but we really don't know until later. That's one of the hard parts. You kind of have to, in my opinion, change attitudes, rather than try to fight this every day on a story-by-story basis. (Suburban editor, *Statewide*)

We observed the *Statewide* AME/Reporting querying a news desk editor to find out why several of their stories did not get in the paper. The news editor described the stories she had accepted, showing him the layout and implying that her stories were better and more important given the limited space:

AME/Reporting: Can any of these stories be reduced to briefs?

Asst. news editor: What really needs to get in?

AME/Reporting: Trim the hell out of them [the stories he wants to get in].

AME/News: (Overhearing) Why are you bringing this up now? We're 2 hours from closeout. Send them over the right length.

AME/Reporting: I'd like a lot more short stories in more often.

AME/News: Start that at *your* end.

AME/Reporting: I can't monitor that. I raise the issues at the [news] meeting.

On another occasion, the ME, bothered by a good story having been dropped from the paper, was trying to impose more interaction between the reporting and news desks:

News editor: I was in a time crunch and had no time to think about this stuff by the time I got it. I need to see the stuff before 8 p.m. to give it special treatment.

ME: Help [the reporting editors] to conceptualize it.

News editor: For special layouts, I need to get the copy with enough time— for example by 4 or 5 p.m., not 8 p.m.

ME: Often that's not possible. You should be doing *conceptualization* at that hour. Put more effort into the front end so that when it arrives late and its wrong you can slap wrists.

The ME then had a similar discussion with the AME/Reporting. The AME/Reporting rebutted that the story in question "just didn't work" and they had to make changes on deadline:

ME: You need to communicate to [the news editor] when you make a change, either face-to-face or with a[n electronic] message rather than just dropping it off on him.

AME/Reporting: We are figuring out what happened while they are at dinner. When they come back, we're in the crunch.

ME: Send a message or tape it on their screen to alert them "We need to talk when you get back."

AME/Reporting: OK. We can do that.

ME: (Exasperated) Areas do it and then shove it over and don't care how it looks or don't think about it.

It was clear in this case that even though the reporting editors simply could have sent an EM, they never even considered that option (cf. Guetzkow and Simon 1955) and that neither the reporting nor the news editors were predisposed to consider communicating with the other.

The sports editor, who fancied himself an impartial observer, offered his perspective developed from having worked at seven newspapers during his career:

There are more turf battles here than elsewhere. They hurt us day in and out. Everyone wants to protect their turf including the page-1 layout guy [news editor]. He guards that with a vengeance. The A section overall is pretty good, but it has the potential to be much better, if there were less rules and if it were not [the news desk's] job to rain on everyone's party each day, somehow.

The level of philos at *Regional* presented a clear contrast. Although *Regional*'s group members frequently negotiated their differing views and opinions, we never observed any instances of acrimony, personal argument, or hostile intent. In fact, we observed a large amount of bantering, storytelling, and joking among the editors representing all functions, and especially between the reporting desks and news desk each were highly respectful of the others' views and decisions:

The news desk has a lot of overlap of responsibility with [the reporting desk] and lots of participation. More likely we will overdiscuss something rather than miss something. Sometimes there are too many people involved in deciding page-1 heads [headlines] and stories. But having too many people involved is almost never a problem. It improves the heads and stories and tone. It is usually better to get more viewpoints. (Associate news editor, *Regional*)

According to the AME/Reporting, the news desk limited as much as possible the amount of changes they (the news desk) made to stories "so as not to surprise the reporting desks, create any error of fact or interpretation, and just out of courtesy." We observed many instances of one desk deferring to the opinion of the other and making an effort to cooperate. For example, a primary goal of each desk editor was to get their reporters' stories into the paper and especially on page 1. However, given a fixed amount of space, this often meant dropping or shortening major stories and was a potential source of hostility between the reporting desks and the news desk, as observed at *Statewide*. However, at *Regional* we observed a much higher level of cooperation. On one night of heavy news and little available space, we observed the national editor volunteering to cut a major story to allow the news editor to run additional stories from other desks. We also observed instances where the news desk volunteered to assist the copy desk when the workload became heavy. Relations between the reporting desks and the copy and news desks were so positive that the reporting editors (who usually left midway into Phase 3) informally gave their proxy on most news decisions to the copy slots and news editors, who stayed until the end of the cycle:

The night associate news editor is my alter ego after I leave. (National editor, *Regional*)

We consider the slots to be "deputy desk editors." (Foreign editor, *Regional*)

The [associate news editor] and the slots are the representatives of the [reporting] desks at night. (AME/News, *Regional*)

The level of cooperation was reflected in the day-to-day interactions of the editors. For example, at *Regional,* the night editor and reporting desk editors made it a habit to walk around the newsroom to have conversations with each other and the various reporting desks, news desk, and copy desk many times during the evening to nurture and maintain a shared context and vision of the night's paper, space issues, news events, and coordination of production and deadlines. "People maintain personal ties with each other. There is lots of informal chat with other editors when walking around. It keeps us coordinated. It's like an informal news meeting" (AME/Metro, *Regional*). Walking around rarely occurred at *Statewide* other than to announce the page-1 decision or if an editor happened to encounter another editor, for example, on the way to the snack room. As another example, at *Regional,* editors representing all four functions would usually congregate around the television to view the evening news headlines and to exchange their reactions. At *Statewide,* this opportunity to interact was replaced by a junior reporter viewing the news, typing a summary of the headlines, and broadcasting it to the editors via EM.

These findings were corroborated by our structured observation of communication events. A comparison of the messages exchanged via lateral cross-function links (reporting-news, reporting-copy, and news-copy), especially during Phase 2 when coordination among the functions was most important, revealed a much greater level of cooperation at *Regional* that at *Statewide.*

Summary

The groups differed significantly in social context. *Regional* provided a flexible, cooperative, decentralized, participatory climate supportive of open communication among the editorial functions. *Statewide,* in contrast, provided a hierarchical, fractional, relatively uncooperative climate that employed centralized decision making and did not encourage open exchange of communication among the editorial functions.

COMMUNICATION PATTERNS
AND STRUCTURES

Proposition 1 suggested that groups having different social contexts would appropriate EM differently, as reflected by different patterns of interaction. Specifically, we expected the groups to differ regarding the overall strength and structure of the prominent integrating ties among occupational roles, consistent with their respective social contexts. Proposition 2 suggested that interaction patterns would be more similar within groups across communication modes than within modes across groups, requiring us to analyze interaction patterns by communication mode. Having observed different communication requirements for the three different task phases, we compared interaction patterns by task phase as well as communication mode to see if our findings held at this greater level of detail.

We derived the social structure of interaction from the sociometric questionnaire data.[7] Editors were presented with a list of all group members and asked to indicate by task phase and communication mode (EM and FTF) the frequency of interaction (less than once per day, more than once per day but less than once per hour, or at least once per hour). We created six adjacency matrices, one for each task phase and communication mode.[8] The matrices were made symmetric, as we were primarily interested in the existence and strength of links rather than their directionality. However, this did not significantly influence the analysis, as the data showed no unreciprocated links. We assigned values to the links using an exponential function. If both editors forming a link reported high frequency, the link was scored 8. If one reported high and the other medium it was scored a 4. Both low (or one high and the other none) was scored 2. One low and the other none was scored 1, and if neither reported a link it was scored 0. These values were used in aggregating matrices by communication mode and task phase and in developing useful cutoff points for dropping low-frequency links to clarify the analysis.[9]

The network data were analyzed and groups compared by creating submatrix blocks ("blockmodels") based on occupational role and analyzing their density patterns. Blockmodels are a representational means of data reduction applied to social networks (Faust and Wasserman 1992, White et al. 1976). They are constructed by clustering members of a social network according to some measure of social distance of similarity (Burt 1980) and then rearranging the adjacency matrix or matrices so that members of the same cluster are placed next to one another in the matrix. Each cluster forms a submatrix block which can be analyzed in terms of its own within-cluster tie density (the proportion of actual links to maximum possible links among members of the block) or between block densities (the proportion of actual to possible links between members of different blocks). These densities provide a measure of tie strength or communication activity within and between blocks. Blockmodels can be thought of as hypotheses (White et al. 1976) or assumptions. Based on prior fieldwork within this context, we assumed that coordination and communication among the editorial functions in the group was required for effective performance. To reflect this assumption and to create directly comparable representations of the groups' interaction patterns, we used the blocking technique to cluster the groups by occupational role (Barley 1990, Rice and Aydin 1991). Thus each blockmodel comprised blocks representing the four primary occupational roles of the newsroom: senior management (M), reporting editors (R), copy desk slots (C), and news desk editors (N). Figure 8.3 illustrates these blockmodels with their corresponding tie densities superimposed on the links (between-block tie densities) and nodes (within-block tie densities).[10] Figure 8.3a compares the interactions aggregated across all task phases and communication modes, providing a picture of the overall social structure of the two groups. Figure 8.3b compares the groups by communication mode, with all task phases combined. Figure 8.3c shows interaction by communication mode and task phase.

Strength of Ties

We expected *Regional,* having the more collaborative social context, to exhibit stronger ties among the editorial functions, and in fact the links between blocks were stronger at *Regional.* The *Regional* group was more strongly connected overall (Figure 8.3a) and regardless of communication mode (Figure 8.3b) or task phase (Figure 8.3c). The overall connectedless of the two groups could be further compared (Table 8.9) by comparing the overall densities of the phase/mode matrices shown in Figure 8.3c. Except for Phase 1, where the networks for both groups were sparse and the network density of *Regional* was only 16% greater than that of *Statewide,* the remaining phase-by-mode network densities showed *Regional* with network densities ranging from 43% to 64% greater than *Statewide,* indicating a much greater tie strength overall at *Regional* regardless of task phase or communication mode. Compared by communication mode across all task phases, the average FTF density was 47% greater and the average EM density was 55% greater at *Regional* than at *Statewide.*

Structure of Ties

We expected *Regional* to exhibit a more integrated and less control-oriented structure than *Statewide,* again consistent with their respective

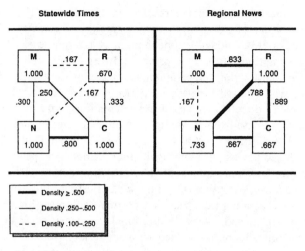

Figure 8.3a. Overall Social Structure

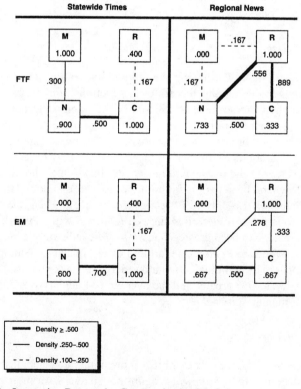

Figure 8.3b. Interaction Patterns by Communication Mode

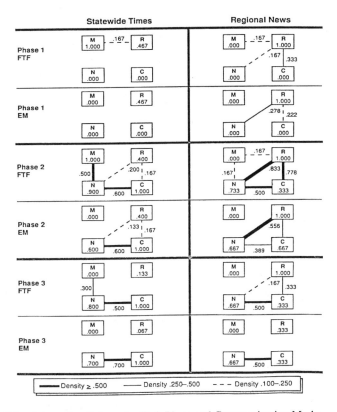

Figure 8.3c. Interaction Patterns by Task Phase and Communication Mode

social contexts. Regarding the overall structure (Figure 8.3a), *Statewide* senior management was most strongly tied to the news desk, reflecting senior management's control over news decisions, while *Regional* management showed a strong tie to the reporting desk, reflecting participatory consultation during the planning phase. Senior management was clearly more involved with the news desk and its news decisions at *Statewide* than at *Regional,* reflecting the control philosophy of the *Statewide* ME versus the delegated decision-making approach of the *Regional* senior management.

The *Statewide* network exhibited a weak senior management-news-copy (M-N-C) triangle with reporting tied into the group primarily via the copy desk, functionally the weakest of the three potential points of linkage and representative of the sequential flow of news copy (Figure 8.2). Linking via the copy desk enabled reporting to influence the process only after the fact (final editing), while linking to the news or management blocks would

TABLE 8.9 Network Densities

		Block Image Network Density		
Phase	Comm. Mode	Statewide	Regional	Ratio
1	FTF	0.095	0.110	1.16
	EM	0.067	0.110	1.64
2	FTF	0.352	0.538	1.53
	EM	0.238	0.385	1.62
3	FTF	0.219	0.330	1.51
	EM	0.162	0.231	1.43
All	FTF	0.222	0.326	1.47
	EM	0.156	0.242	1.55
	All	0.189	0.284	1.51

have provided more leverage by enabling them to influence outcomes during the earlier planning or decision-making stages. The primary link was between the news and copy desks (the production desks) who were only weakly tied to the rest of the group (the "artists" and planners). In contrast, the pattern at *Regional* showed a strong reporting-news-copy (R-N-C) triangle with senior management tied into the group primarily via reporting, a functionally strong link. The strong R-N-C triangle showed the extent to which all three functions collaborated in producing the paper.

Regardless of communication mode (Figure 8.3b), reporting at *Statewide* was relatively disconnected from the other functions, while at *Regional* the three functional groups remained strongly tied.

Examined by communication mode and task phase (Figure 8.3c), during Task Phase 1 (planning), *Statewide* showed an almost completely functionally disconnected group while at *Regional* the cross-block links were much stronger, regardless of communication mode. For example, the second strongest cross-block link among all groups and modes during Task Phase 1 was the reporting-to-news link via EM at *Regional. Regional*'s reporting editors were sending electronic messages to the news desk in preparation for the evening's production, and EM was being used to transcend time and space to coordinate these functions. While EM enabled *Statewide* to constitute this link, it did not occur.

During Task Phase 2 (decision making/transition) a difference between groups in their use of hierarchy was apparent. At *Statewide,* senior management was strongly tied into the news decision-making structure via FTF. The news and copy desks were strongly tied to each other via both communication modes, while reporting was only weakly linked via either communication mode. At *Regional,* the reporting, news, and copy functions were strongly linked via both modes as they collaborated to make the news decisions. Senior management was kept weakly in the loop via FTF ties with reporting and news for status updates once or twice each evening.

During Task Phase 3 (production/execution) senior management at *Statewide* continued to interact with the news desk via FTF, directing news decisions, and the news and copy desks continued their multiplex (EM and FTF) link in support of production, while reporting was essentially disconnected at this point. At *Regional,* reporting continued to be tied into the process, weakly to the news desk and moderately strongly to the copy desk. Similar to *Statewide,* the copy and news desks were strongly tied by both modes at this time.

These findings were corroborated by our structured observation of communication events. We sorted our notes describing the observed interactions by task phase, communication mode, and the six possible role-block linkages. These data showed essentially the same structural patterns as the analysis of sociometric questionnaire data. The message content of our Task Phase 2 and 3 observations in particular found that senior management at *Statewide* was much more directive and control oriented, while at *Regional* the senior management was more "hands-off," delegating decisions and allowing the other three functions to coordinate among themselves. Interaction was more intense and cooperative within and among the functions at *Regional* than at *Statewide.*

Similarity of Ties

Comparing the groups by communication mode (all task phases combined) (Figure 8.3b), the pattern of EM interaction resembled the pattern of FTF interaction in both groups and was almost identical when senior managers (who made relatively little use of EM overall) were disregarded. Examined by communication mode and task phase (Figure 8.3c), again except for the senior managers, EM patterns continued to reflect the strongest FTF links in each task phase for both sites. Additionally, ties were more similar within group than across group within mode.

Summary

In support of Proposition 1, our network analysis of the interaction patterns of both groups clearly showed that (a) the functional subgroups at *Regional* were much more integrated and connected, (b) the density of connections and level of communication involvement was much greater at *Regional,* and (c) *Regional* was a much more lateral organization, while

Statewide was much more hierarchical and less integrated or interconnected. These findings were consistent with the social context of the groups and held regardless of the communication mode. In support of Proposition 2, the patterns of EM communication were highly similar to FTF within both groups and dissimilar within communication mode between the groups.

PERFORMANCE EFFECTIVENESS

Proposition 3 was that outcome effectiveness would depend on the effectiveness of communication within each group and would differ between groups having similar functional structures, task processes, and communication technologies, but different interaction patterns.

Communication Effectiveness

Based on questionnaire responses (Table 8.10), perceived communication by task phase and overall was rated significantly more effective at *Regional.* The largest difference was specifically for cross-shift communication. The Phase 1 to 2 cross-shift communication, primarily the communication of the morning news plans from the reporting editors to the production (news and copy) editors who would eventually execute them, and again, a key link to producing a successful paper, was rated much less effective at *Statewide.* Cross-shift communication during the other two phases showed smaller, nonsignificant differences. Information tended to be more factual, focused, and logistics-oriented at these points in the process and its exchange was more routine. *Regional* also perceived a significantly lower extent of communication breakdowns across shifts and lower frequency of breakdowns overall than *Statewide.* While both groups received favorable coordination scores, overall *Regional* was perceived to be significantly better coordinated during the planning and decision-making phases (1 and 2) and when coordinating across shifts.

These findings were corroborated by the structured observation data, especially during the Phase 2 cross-shift transition, and by interview data where many of the *Statewide* editors volunteered that day-to-day communication was not effective, while most of the editors at *Regional* felt that day-to-day communication was generally effective.

Outcome Effectiveness

Regional had a higher rate of good or great papers than did *Statewide,* as expected (Table 8.11). *Statewide* was good or great a bit over half the time,

TABLE 8.10 Communication Effectiveness

	Statewide		Regional			
	Ave.	SD	Ave.	SD	Diff.	2-Tail p
Communication effectiveness *by phase* (1 = high quality, effective; 5 = low quality, not effective)						
Phase 1	2.78	0.75	2.03	0.54	0.75	.42
Phase 2	2.57	0.60	2.12	0.47	0.45	.049
Phase 3	2.75	0.82	2.02	0.37	0.73	.014
Between-shift communication *effectiveness* (1 = high quality, effective; 5 = low quality, not effective)						
Phase 1	2.84	0.81	1.82	0.55	1.02	.014
Phase 2	2.93	0.67	2.50	0.85	0.43	.187
Phase 3	2.94	0.69	2.56	0.80	0.38	.285
Overall communication effectiveness Overall communication patterns are effective; overall communication detracts from quality of work (reverse scored) (1 = effective, 5 = not effective)	2.71	0.80	1.92	0.51	0.79	.005
Miscommunication Extent of within-shift communication breakdowns (1 = large extent, 5 = small extent)	3.07	0.83	3.57	0.94	0.50	.147
Extent of between-shift communication breakdowns (1 = large extent, 5 = small extent)	2.36	0.84	2.93	1.00	0.57	.114
Frequency of communication breakdowns (1 = almost never, 2 = 1/month, 3 = 1/week, 4 = 1/day, 5 = >1/day)	3.79	0.70	2.86	1.10	0.93	.014
Coordination (1 = high coordination, 5 = low coordination)						
Phase 1	2.48	0.56	1.79	0.43	0.69	.012
Phase 2	2.67	0.47	2.15	0.62	0.52	.035
Phase 3	2.56	0.39	2.22	0.75	0.34	.246
Extent to which activities and tasks between or across shifts are well-timed and coordinated (1 = large extent, 5 = not at all)	3.14	0.36	2.61	1.00	0.53	.078

TABLE 8.11 Outcome Effectiveness

News Section Quality	Statewide Ave.	SD	Regional Ave.	SD	2-Tail p
% Good or great	55.2	17.6	71.2	25.3	.72
% Unacceptable or average	44.8	17.6	28.8	25.3	.72

while *Regional* was considered good or great over two thirds of the time. These results were corroborated by our interview data, and the rank order of quality and effectiveness reflected the opinions and beliefs of the parent corporation, enhancing validity of the findings.

DISCUSSION

Our research examined the relationships between social context and patterns of FTF and EM interaction in two similar ongoing management groups. It is the only published field study we know of that examined simultaneously both FTF and EM communication patterns, and their content as well as structure.

News editing, the task context of this study, would appear to be an ideal situation for CMC technology to flourish. The work is rapidly paced and communication intensive, uncertainty concerning breaking news is high, interaction is intense, the group must respond quickly to changing events, and coordination is crucial. In this sense, the newsroom is potentially an appropriate model for new organizational forms supporting knowledge-based teamwork.

Technological and organizational imperatives regarding information technology suggest that EM, implemented in groups as similar as the editorial groups reported on here, should exhibit similar patterns of use; namely an integrated, lateral, and responsive network for information exchange. However, the evidence presented here showed that two similar groups can have very different patterns of EM use depending on the social context within which that EM interaction takes place.

Kling (1991) called for a more substantial shift from "technological utopianism to social realism" by engaging in *in situ* research with real groups, especially in less "euphoric" circumstances than connoted by the terms cooperation and collaboration and which include control and hierarchy as viable elements. In our study, *Statewide* was clearly managed under a control strategy and held a climate that was less conducive to open sharing of information, while *Regional* operated under a commitment strategy and a climate generally supportive of information sharing, providing a clear and useful social comparison.

Adopting the perspective of adaptive structuration theory (Poole et al. 1985), we proposed that the groups' appropriation of EM would reflect the social context of each group (Poole and DeSanctis 1990). This would be reflected by observing different patterns of EM and FTF for each group, and by observing a greater similarity of interaction within group across communication mode than within communication mode across group. Furthermore, we proposed that group outcomes would be mediated by the groups' interaction patterns and, given the same task requirements but different patterns of interaction, we would expect the communication and outcome effectiveness of the groups to differ.

Our findings strongly supported these propositions. The two groups were extremely similar on many measures of context but differed sharply regarding cooperation, communication openness, and management philosophy. *Regional,* a cooperative, open, participatory group, integrated their use of EM into a responsive and tightly connected interaction network enabling effective communication and coordination. *Regional* exhibited little vertical or lateral constraint on interaction. They enjoyed a much more participatory climate, and senior executives delegated almost all of the day-to-day decision-making responsibility of reporting and production to those functions themselves. Laterally, the functions at *Regional* enjoyed a culture of trust, collaboration, and information sharing, and by working together and communicating to enact a shared context concerning each day's news developed a shared worldview as well. *Statewide,* in contrast, was a much less cooperative and more fractionalized group operating under a hierarchical control philosophy. Their social context constrained them from appropriating either EM or FTF to form the communication links necessary for effective and coordinated action. *Statewide*'s interaction was organizationally constrained both vertically and laterally. Vertically, they were under the leadership of an autocratic management with a centralized decision-making philosophy and hierarchical culture. Laterally, they were socially constrained by a culture of low trust and a history of conflict between functions. Those functions held very different worldviews and employed no means to reconcile them. Ultimately, *Regional* produced a higher-quality newspaper than did *Statewide.*

Although we were able to describe a scenario for the effective use of EM applied to one particular cooperative group task, we did not expect those particular findings to generalize much beyond that context. Our primary intent was neither to identify particular conditions for success or failure of EM nor to propose any normative or prescriptive measures for making effective use of EM, but rather to raise awareness that social context counts when implementing technologies that support group interaction. The social context of every organization is in some ways unique and that uniqueness makes a difference to technology-related outcomes. While any set of initial conditions within either group could have given rise to a very different set of outcomes, our sites provided an opportunity to show clearly that the existing social context must be reckoned with, as it represents the vehicle by which the group adopts and adapts new communication technologies. We must take into account the unique social conditions within which groups operate to better understand the way in which technologies like EM, group decision support systems, and groupware will be appropriated by the group. The impact of CMC technology on group outcomes is mediated by social context and related interaction patterns. Social context influences how a communication technology is appropriated (Poole and DeSanctis 1990), directly influencing the group's interaction patterns via that technology and in turn influencing the group's performance. We believe these results are quite useful, given the small amount of research on this topic (Poole et al. 1991).

Our findings also suggested that communication effectiveness operates on the micro- and macrolevel of interaction, and both must be dealt with for successfully employing CMC or other technologies affecting interaction. Producing meaningful messages between particular individuals at the microlevel of interaction says nothing about the use of EM and communication effectiveness at the macrolevel of interaction and the appropriateness of the resulting communication network. Although the group might understand how to employ EM to render particular microinteractions meaningful, and although establishing new communication links might be easier or more convenient using EM, those potential links might not, in actuality, be realized. First, as we observed at *Statewide,* communicators are limited by their learned repertoire of interactions. Recall the situation where *Statewide*'s AME/Reporting never even considered sending an EM to the news desk to alert them to an important change in a story, even though that communication link was "obviously" crucial to the effective performance of the group and simple to perform. Second, basic economics tells us that a transaction requires the ability and the willingness to transact on the part of both parties. EM provides the ability but the social context provides the willingness, therefore media choices may not be objectively determined by task requirements, per the organizational imperative. We observed many cases at *Statewide* where even though a potential link might be salient, it would not be made because the communicators plainly did not want to interact with each other, for political, personal, or normative reasons.

This finding has important methodological implications. Findings at one level do not necessarily generalize to the next level. Ignoring the levels problem invites misleading and confounded interpretation of results. For example, our context-free, microlevel questionnaire items regarding rules for using communications modes showed no intergroup differences, yet the study clearly revealed significant macrolevel differences regarding EM and FTF. Therefore, if we relied only on context-free questionnaires at the microlevel, our results would be misleading unless interpretations were strictly contained to the microlevel. Network data collection and analysis offers a useful means to bridging these levels when investigating interaction (Fulk and Boyd 1991, Rice 1990).

The two levels influence each other as well. For example, Zack (1994) found that, at the microinteraction level, shared interpretive context was required for the effective coordination of meaning (Pearce 1976) using EM. But in particular (macro) social contexts, communicators may not want to be understood. We observed *Statewide* editors intentionally choosing EM because they knew that their message would be sufficiently equivocal to enable them to be duplicitous yet appear not to be. Second, the macrosocial context influences who controls the cognitive frameworks and premises used for interpreting microlevel interactions. At *Regional,* interpretation and context building was a collaborative and consensual process. At *Statewide,* the ME was attempting to impose his vision and worldview on others, while the reporting and production functions were attempting to defend and impose their own perspectives on each other. These findings suggest that both micro- and macrointeraction levels must be investigated when studying information technologies and that we not bound our studies, a priori, by level of analysis, but by the phenomenon we are investigating.

Despite the obvious benefits of doing extensive in-depth case analysis, our study had its limitations. We looked at a snapshot in time and did not identify the way in which the structuration and appropriation processes unfolded within each group over time. We did not do a pre/poststudy of an implementation but merely provided evidence that different communication structures and appropriations of communication technology can emerge in apparently similar groups employing identical technologies and tasks. Our lack of explicit time-sequenced measure limits our ability to identify strict causal relationships. In traditional experimental research, groups would be formed, tasks assigned and other treatments applied, the process set in motion, and measures taken or observations made in the appropriate time sequence. Rather than studying many groups performing a one-time task, we studied two ongoing groups performing the same task over and over. In our case, it was not possible to say where the process began. It was in motion when we arrived and continued after we left. In cases like this, we can only take "averages" of the groups' behavior and see how these constructs relate. This is especially true for structuration research. In our case, we do not know what events "caused" the social context of each group. All we can say is that each group's social context appears to be reflected in their patterns of interaction. We believe that longitudinal research is essential to expanding what we know about structuration and technology appropriation. Future research might also focus on different tasks, technologies, genders, and cultures: any dimension which might influence or be influenced by the social context of the group.

Our findings suggest a responsibility for CMC technology researchers to explicitly assess, describe, and, if applicable, control for the social context within which they collect their data. For example, questionnaires should include items addressing social, political, and communication climate. Beyond that we would call for researchers to consider social context as a key construct to be explicitly examined and varied. To this end, information technology researchers may benefit from cross-disciplinary research teams comprising, for example, technologists, sociologists, organizational behaviorists, and anthropologists.

Our findings have implications for the groups and organizations employing the technology as well. Groups with shared history, culture, and social context must explicitly acknowledge, describe, and diagnose their existing social context and patterns of interaction related to that context before attempting a direct intervention on those patterns as occasioned by EM or other groupware technologies. The most difficult part of implementing groupware or other technologies to support new organizational forms effectively will be the implementation of social interventions (i.e., to culture, norms, interaction habits and practices, and leadership style) to align the social context with the technological and organizational intentions.

While implementation of communication technologies must be viewed as a social as well as organizational and technological intervention, social context is rarely addressed when implementing these technologies. Organizations should diagnose their existing social context to determine if the spirit of the technology (Poole and DeSanctis 1990) fits the social context of the group. Requirements analyses should focus on social and interactional requirements and constraints as well as technical flows of information. Training should be modified or expanded beyond the traditional approach focusing on the technology and task to including socially oriented training such as team-building exercises. This suggests an entirely new skill set for technology implementers and trainers. Additionally, technology development and implementation projects, similar to research teams, should have sociologists, social psychologists, and organizational development specialists as central members to benchmark existing social context and to design appropriate interventions.

We believe that the strategic advantages associated with these technologies will not derive from having the technical skills to evaluate and implement these technologies, or even from being the first mover (especially if the social climate for appropriation is not favorable), but rather will come from having the appropriate social context, norms, politics, reward systems, and leadership to take advantage of electronic communications technologies for enabling new organizational forms. As organizations attempt to adopt new forms, especially those which cross functions, departments, and traditional organizational boundaries, social context will become even more important and influential.

NOTES

1. *Communication mode* refers to the combination of communication channel and medium. In this study, we focused on the modes electronic messaging (electronic channel, textual medium) and face-to-face (interpersonal channel, multisensual medium).

2. While network theory is concerned with the relationship between social context and social structure, structuration theory focuses primarily on what we are calling social context, yet which they call social structure. Social structure in structuration theory refers to the rules and resources used in interaction, similar to our definition of social context, which result in "regularized relations of interdependence" (Poole et al. 1985), similar to our definition of social structure. To avoid confusion, we will continue to use the terms social context and social structure consistent with the network perspective described earlier.

3. While electronic messaging can place technological constraints on interaction at the microlevel, for example, by regulating the ability to send graphics as well as text, it typically poses no constraints at the network level of interaction. That is, typically there are no design constraints preventing anyone from connecting to anyone else having access to the mail system.

4. This is not to say that EM could not expand or alter communication networks, but rather those new patterns of communication would be expected to be considered socially legitimate by the group. We would not expect those who for socially based reasons *chose* not to communicate with one another before the availability of CMC to want to communicate merely because a new communication mode was now available. Our thesis is that existing research has not sufficiently examined the influences of social context on CMC.

5. Pseudonyms.

6. The task process at both newspapers exhibited three phases: planning, decision making, and execution. These phases were initially developed as a result of a literature review and interviews and observations at a pilot site. They were confirmed for both research sites via interview and observation. At *Regional,* the planning phase was observed 4 times, the decision-making phase 11 times, and the execution phase 7 times. At *Statewide,* the planning phase was observed 5 times, the decision-making phase 7 times, and the production phase 4 times. During each observation, a central actor was shadowed, and the time, mode, participants, and content of all observed interactions were recorded. An ongoing record of the context of exchange was also kept.

7. Network analysis was performed using UCINET 3.0 (MacEvoy and Freeman 1987).

8. An adjacency matrix is one whose columns and rows list all nodes (i.e., people) in the network (i.e., the group). Each cell represents a relation *from* the row *to* the column, and the value of each cell is a measure of the strength of the link between the group members represented by that cell. Consequently, adjacency matrices are often called "who-to-whom" matrices. Thus the value in cell (1, 2) of the matrix represents the strength of the link from person 1 to person 2 and is usually interpreted as 1's perception of 1's relationship to 2. In a symmetric matrix, the strength of the link is the same in both directions, and one half of the matrix mirrors the other.

The density of the matrix is the percentage of possible ties actually made (i.e., the percentage of cells with nonzero values) and is a measure of group connectivity or cohesiveness. Rows and columns are often sorted (e.g., by placing next to each other in the matrix all those who in some way are similar). The new matrix can then be divided into meaningful submatrices or "blocks" by assigning all those considered sufficiently similar to the same block. The density of these submatrix blocks then can be computed and compared.

9. Thus, the maximum tie strength within any phase/mode matrix was 8. The maximum tie strength for matrices combining both communication modes for a particular phase was 16 (2 × 8). The maximum tie strength for matrices combining all three phases for a particular communication mode was 24 (3 × 8). The maximum tie strength for matrices combining all modes and phases was 48 (6 × 8).

10. Blockmodels were constructed using binary matrices dichotomized to highlight the primary interaction patterns of the groups.

REFERENCES

Baker, W. E. (1991), "The Network Organization in Theory and Practice," in N. Nohria and R. G. Eccles (Eds.), *Networks and Organizations: Structure, Form, and Action,* Cambridge, MA: Harvard Business School Press, pp. 397-429.

Banks, S. R. (1990), "Structuration Theory as an Ontology for Communication Research," *Communication Yearbook,* 16, 167-196.

Barley, S. R. (1990), "The Alignment of Technology and Structure Through Roles and Networks," *Administrative Science Quarterly,* 35, 61-103.

Bavelas, A. (1950), "Communication Patterns in Task-Oriented Groups," *Journal of the Acoustical Society of America,* 22, 725-730.

Benjamin, R. I. and M. S. Scott Morton (1988), "Information Technology, Integration, and Organization Change," *Interfaces,* 18, 3, May/June, 86-98.

Blalock, H. M., Jr. (1969), *Theory Construction: From Verbal to Mathematical Formulations,* Englewood Cliffs, NJ: Prentice Hall.

Bonacich, P. (1987), "Communication Networks and Collective Action," *Social Networks,* 9, 389-396.

Burt, R. S. (1980), "Models of Network Structure," *Annual Review of Sociology,* 6, 79-141.

Contractor, N. S. and E. M. Eisenberg (1990), "Communication Networks and New Media in Organizations," in J. Fulk and C. Steinfield (Eds.), *Organizations and Communication Technology,* Newbury Park, CA: Sage, pp. 143-171.

Culnan, M. J. and M. L. Markus (1987), "Information Technologies," in F. M. Jablin, L. L. Putnam, K. H. Roberts, and L. W. Porter (Eds.), *Handbook of Organizational Communication: An Interdisciplinary Perspective,* Newbury Park, CA: Sage, pp. 420-443.

Daft, R. L. and R. H. Lengel (1986), "Organizational Information Requirements, Media Richness and Structural Design," *Management Science,* 32, 5, May, 554-571.

David, F. R., J. A. Pearce II, and W. A. Randolph (1989), "Linking Technology and Structure to Enhance Group Performance," *Journal of Applied Psychology,* 74, 2, 233-241.

Davidow, W. H. and M. S. Malone (1992), *The Virtual Corporation,* New York: HarperCollins.

Dewhirst, H. D. (1971), "Influence of Perceived Information Sharing Norms on Communication Channel Utilization," *Academy of Management Journal,* September, 305-315.

Driver, M. J. and S. Streufert (1969), "Integrative Complexity: An Approach to Individuals and Groups as Information-Processing Systems," *Administrative Science Quarterly,* 14, 2, 272-285.

Drucker, P. F. (1988), "The Coming of the New Organization," *Harvard Business Review,* January/February, 45-53.

Eveland, J. D. and T. K. Bikson (1987), "Evolving Electronic Communication Networks: An Empirical Assessment," *Office: Technology and People,* 3, 103-128.

Farace, R. V., J. A. Taylor, and J. P. Stewart (1978), "Criteria for Evaluation of Organizational Communication Effectiveness: Review and Synthesis," *Communication Yearbook,* 2, 271-292.

Faust, K. and S. Wasserman (1992), "Blockmodels: Interpretation and Evaluation," *Social Networks,* 14, 5-61.

Finholt, T. and L. S. Sproull (1990), "Electronic Groups at Work," *Organization Science,* 41-64.

Freeman, L. C. (1989), "Social Networks and the Structure Experiment," in L. C. Freeman et al. (Eds.), *Research Methods in Social Network Analysis,* Fairfax, VA: George Mason University Press.

_____, D. Roeder, and R. R. Mulholland (1980), "Centrality in Social Networks II: Experimental Results," *Social Networks,* 2, 119-141.

Fulk, J. (1993), "Social Construction of Communication Technology," *Academy of Management Journal,* 36, 5, 921-950.

_____ and B. Boyd (1991), "Emerging Theories of Communication in Organizations," *Journal of Management,* 17, 407-446.

_____, C. W. Steinfield, J. Schmitz, and J. G. Power (1987), "A Social Information Processing Model of Media Use in Organizations," *Communication Research,* 14, 5, October, 529-542.

George, A. L. and T. J. McKeown (1985), "Case Studies and Theories of Organizational Decision Making," *Advances in Information Processing in Organizations,* 2, 21-58.

Giddens, A. (1979), *Central Problems in Social Theory,* Berkeley: University of California Press.

Gilchrist, J. C., M. E. Shaw, and L. C. Walker (1954), "Some Effects of Unequal Distribution of Information in a Wheel Group Structure," *Journal of Abnormal Social Psychology,* 49, 554-556.

Glanzer, M. and R. Glaser (1961), "Techniques for the Study of Group Structure and Behavior: II. Empirical Studies of the Effects of Structure in Small Groups," *Psychological Bulletin,* 58, 1-27.

Goffman, E. (1967), *Interaction Ritual,* New York: Pantheon.

Gopal, A., R. P. Bostrom, and W. W. Chin (1992/1993), "Applying Adaptive Structuration Theory to Investigate the Process of Group Support Systems Use," *Journal of Management Information Systems,* 9, 3, Winter, 45-69.

Guetzkow, E. (1965), "Communication in Organizations," in J. G. March (Ed.), *Handbook of Organizations,* Chicago: Rand McNally, pp. 534-573.

_____ and H. A. Simon (1955), "The Impact of Certain Communication Nets Upon Organization and Performance in Task-Oriented Groups," *Management Science,* 1, 233-250.

Hackman, J. R. (1985), "Doing Research That Makes a Difference," in E. E. Lawler, A. M. Mohrman, S. A. Mohrman, G. E. Ledford, and T. G. Cummings (Eds.), *Doing Research That Is Useful for Theory and Practice,* San Francisco: Jossey-Bass, pp. 126-149.

_____ (Ed.) (1990), *Groups That Work (and Those That Don't): Creating Conditions for Effective Teamwork,* San Francisco: Jossey-Bass.

Hammer, M. (1979/1980), "Predictability of Social Connections Over Time," *Social Networks,* 2, 165-180.

_____ (1990), "Reengineering Work: Don't Automate, Obliterate," *Harvard Business Review,* 90, 4, July/August, 104-112.

_____ and G. E. Mangurian (1987), "The Changing Value of Communications Technology," *Sloan Management Review,* Winter, 65-71.

Jablin, F. M., L. L. Putnam, K. H. Roberts, and L. W. Porter (1987), "Structure: Patterns of Organizational Relationships," in F. M. Jablin et al. (Eds.), *Handbook of Organizational Communication,* Newbury Park, CA: Sage, pp. 297-303.

Jarillo, J. C. (1988), "On Strategic Networks," *Strategic Management Journal,* 9, 31-41.

Jarvenpaa, S. L., V. Srinivasan Rao, and G. P. Huber (1988), "Computer Support for Meetings of Groups Working on Unstructured Problems: A Field Experiment," *MIS Quarterly,* December, 645-665.

Jick, T. D. (1979), "Mixing Qualitative and Quantitative Methods: Triangulation in Action," *Administrative Science Quarterly,* 24, December, 602-611.

Kerlinger, F. N. (1986), *Foundations of Behavioral Research,* 3rd ed., New York: Holt, Rinehart & Winston.

Kerr, E. B. and S. R. Hiltz (1982), *Computer-Mediated Communication Systems,* San Diego: Academic Press.

Kling, R. (1991), "Cooperation, Coordination and Control in Computer-Supported Work," *Communications of the ACM,* 34, 12, December, 83-88.

_____ and W. Saachi (1982), "The Web of Computing: Computer Technology as Social Organization," in *Advances in Computers,* San Diego: Academic Press, Vol. 21, pp. 1-90.

Konsynski, B. R. (1993), "Strategic Control in the Extended Enterprise," *IBM Systems Journal,* 32, 111-142.

Krackhardt, D. (1992), "The Strength of Strong Ties: The Importance of Philos in Organizations," in N. Nohria and R. Eccles (Eds.), *Networks and Organizations,* Cambridge, MA: Harvard Business School Press, pp. 216-239.

Kraemer, K. L. and J. L. King (1988), "Computer-Based Systems for Cooperative Work and Group Decision Making," *ACM Computing Surveys,* June, 115-146.

Kraft, P. (1987), "Computers and the Automation of Work," in R. E. Kraut (Ed.), *Technology and the Transformation of White-Collar Work,* Hillsdale, NJ: Lawrence Earlbaum, pp. 99-111.

Leavitt, H. J. (1951), "Some Effects of Certain Communication Patterns on Group Performance," *Journal of Abnormal and Social Psychology,* 46, 38-50.

Leonard-Barton, D. (1988), "Implementation as Mutual Adaptation of Technology and Organization," *Research Policy,* 17, 251-267.

MacEnvoy, B. and L. Freeman (1987), *UNICET Version 3.0,* Irvine: University of California, School of Social Sciences, Mathematical Social Science Group.

Malone, T. M., J. Yates, and R. I. Benjamin (1987), "Electronic Markets and Electronic Hierarchies," *Communications of the ACM,* 30, 6, June, 484-497.

Markus, M. L. and D. Robey (1988), "Information Technology and Organizational Change: Causal Structure in Theory and Research," *Management Science,* 34, 5, May, 583-598.

McKenney, J. L., M. H. Zack, and V. S. Doherty (1992), "Complementary Communication Media: A Comparison of Electronic Mail and Face-to-Face Communication in a Programming Team," in N. Nohria and R. Eccles (Eds.), *Networks and Organizations,* Cambridge, MA: Harvard Business School Press, pp. 262-287.

Miles, R. E. and C. C. Snow (1986), "Organizations: New Concepts for New Forms," *California Management Review,* 28, 3, Spring, 62-73.

Monge, P. R. and E. M. Eisenberg (1987), "Emergent Communication Networks," in F. M. Jablin et al. (Eds.), *Handbook of Organizational Communication,* Newbury Park, CA: Sage, pp. 305-342.

Nadler, D. A., M. S. Gerstein, R. B. Shaw, and Associates (1992), *Organizational Architecture: Designs for Changing Organizations,* San Francisco: Jossey-Bass.

Norland, K. E. (1992), "Lotus Notes Implementation Factors," in D. D. Coleman (Ed.), *Group-Ware '92,* San Mateo, CA: Morgan Kaufmann, pp. 312-314.

O'Reilly, C. A., III and K. H. Roberts (1977), "Task Group Structure, Communication and Effectiveness in Three Organizations," *Journal of Applied Psychology,* 62, 6, 674-681.

Orlikowski, W. J. (1992), "Learning From NOTES: Organizational Issues in Groupware Implementation," in J. Tuner and R. Kraut (Eds.), *Proceedings of the AMC 1992 Conference on Computer-Supported Cooperative Work,* Toronto: ACM Press, October 31-November 4, pp. 362-369.

Pearce, W. B. (1976), "The Coordinated Management of Meaning: A Rules-Based Theory of Interpersonal Communication," in G. R. Miller (Ed.), *Explorations in Interpersonal Communication,* Beverly Hills, CA: Sage, pp. 17-35.

Perrin, C. (1991), "Electronic Social Fields in Bureaucracies," *Communications of the ACM,* 34, 12, December, 75-82.

Pettigrew, A. M. (1985), "Contextualist Research and the Study of Organizational Change Processes," in E. Mumford et al. (Eds.), *Research Methods in Information Systems,* New York: Elsevier, pp. 53-78.

Pinsonneault, A. and K. L. Kraemer (1989), "The Impact of Technological Support on Groups: An Assessment of the Empirical Research," *Decision Support Systems,* 5, 197-216.

Poole, M. S. and G. DeSanctis (1990), "Understanding the Use of Group Decision Support Systems: The Theory of Adaptive Structuration," in J. Fulk and C. Steinfield (Eds.), *Organizations and Communication Technology,* Newbury Park, CA: Sage, pp. 173-193.

_____, M. Holmes, and G. DeSanctis (1991), "Conflict Management in a Computer-Supported Meeting Environment," *Management Science,* 37, 8, August, 926-953.

_____, D. R. Seibold, and R. D. McPhee (1985), "Group Decision-Making as a Structuration Process," *Quarterly Journal of Speech,* 71, August, 74-102.

Radcliffe-Brown, A. R. (1940), "On Social Structure," *Journal of the Royal Anthropological Society of Great Britain and Ireland,* 70, 1-12.

Ranson, S., B. Hinings, and R. Greenwood (1980), "The Structuring of Organization Structures," *Administrative Science Quarterly,* 25, March, 1-17.

Reder, S. and R. C. Schwab (1989), "The Communicative Economy of the Workgroup: Multi-Channel Genres of Communication," *Office: Technology and People,* 4, 3, 177-198.

_____ and _____ (1990), "The Temporal Structure of Cooperative Activity," *Proceedings of the Conference on Computer-Supported Cooperative Work,* October, pp. 303-316.

Rice, R. E. (1990), "Computer-Mediated Communication System Network Data: Theoretical Concerns and Empirical Examples," *International Journal of Man-Machine Studies,* 32, 627-647.

_____ and C. Aydin (1991), "Attitudes Toward New Organizational Technology: Network Proximity as a Mechanism for Social Information Processing," *Administrative Science Quarterly,* 36, 219-244.

_____ and J. H. Bair (1984), "New Organizational Media and Productivity," in R. E. Rice (Ed.), *The New Media,* Beverly Hills, CA: Sage.

_____, A. Grant, J. Schmitz, and J. Torobin (1990), "Individual and Network Influences on the Adoption and Perceived Outcomes of Electronic Messaging," *Social Networks,* 12, March, 27-55.

_____ and G. Love (1987), "Electronic Emotion: Socioemotional Content in a Computer-Mediated Communication Network," *Communication Network,* 14, February, 85-108.

Riley, P. (1983), "A Structurationist Account of Political Culture," *Administrative Science Quarterly,* 28, 414-437.

Roby, T. B. and J. T. Lanzetta (1956), "Work Group Structure, Communication, and Group Performance," *Sociometry,* 19, 105-113.

Rogers, E. M. (1986), *Communication Technology: The New Media in Society,* New York: Free Press.

Schegloff, E. A. (1987), "Between Macro and Micro: Contexts and Other Connections," in J. C. Alexander, B. Giesan, R. Munch, and N. J. Smalser (Eds.), *The Micro-Macro Link,* Berkeley: University of California Press, pp. 207-234.

Schein, E. H. (1985), *Organizational Culture and Leadership,* San Francisco: Jossey-Bass.

Schmitz, J. and J. Fulk (1991), "Organizational Colleagues, Media Richness, and Electronic Mail," *Communication Research,* 18, 4, August, 487-523.

Schwartz, D. F. and E. Jacobson (1977), "Organizational Communication Network Analysis: The Liaison Communication Role," *Organization Behavior and Human Performance,* 18, 158-174.

Shaw, M. E. (1959), "Acceptance of Authority, Group Structure and the Effectiveness of Small Groups," *Journal of Personality,* 27, 196-210.

Sigman, S. J. (1987), *A Perspective on Social Communication,* New York: Lexington Books.

Sproull, L. and S. Kiesler (1991), *Connections: New Ways of Working in the Networked World,* Cambridge: MIT Press.

Steiner, I. D. (1972), *Group Process and Productivity,* San Diego: Academic Press.

Steinfield, C. W. (1986), "Computer-Mediated Communication Systems," *Annual Review of Information Science and Technology,* 21, 167-202.

Stone, D. (1992), "Groupware in the Global Enterprise," in D. D. Coleman (Ed.), *GroupWare, '92,* San Mateo, CA: Morgan Kaufmann, pp. 312-314.

Thorelli, H. B. (1986), "Networks: Between Markets and Hierarchies," *Strategic Management Journal,* 7, 37-51.

Tichy, N. M. (1980), "Networks in Organizations," in P. G. Nystrom and W. Starbuck (Eds.), *Handbook of Organization Design,* London: Oxford University Press, pp. 225-247.

_____, M. L. Tushman, and C. Fombrun (1979), "Social Network Analysis for Organizations," *Academy of Management Review,* 4, 507-519.

Trevino, L. K., R. H. Lengel, and R. L. Daft (1987), "Media Symbolism and Media Choice in Organizations: A Symbolic Interactionist Perspective," *Communication Research,* 14, 553-574.

Tushman, M. L. (1979), "Work Characteristics and Subunit Communication Structure: A Contingency Analysis," *Administrative Science Quarterly,* 24, 82-97.

Venkatraman, N. (1994), "IT-Enabled Business Transformation: From Automation to Business Scope Redefinition," *Sloan Management Review,* 35, 2, Winter, 73.

Walton, R. E. and J. R. Hackman (1986), "Groups Under Contrasting Management Strategies," in P. S. Goodman (Ed.), *Designing Effective Work Groups,* San Francisco: Jossey Bass, pp. 168-201.

White, H. C., S. A. Boorman, and R. L. Breiger (1976), "Social Structure From Multiple Networks. I. Blockmodels of Roles and Positions," *American Journal of Sociology,* 81, 4, January, 730-780.

Williams, E. (1977), "Experimental Comparisons of Face-to-Face and Mediated Communication: A Review," *Psychological Bulletin,* 84, 5, 963-976.

Yates, J. and W. J. Orlikowski (1992), "Genres of Organizational Communication: A Structurational Approach to Studying Communication and Media," *Academy of Management Review,* 17, 2, 299-326.

Yin, R. K. (1984), *Case Study Research: Design and Methods,* Beverly Hills, CA: Sage.

Zack, M. H. (1991), "Some Antecedents and Consequences of Computer-Mediated Communications Use in an Ongoing Management Group: A Field Study," in *Proceedings of the Twelfth International Conference on Information Systems,* December, pp. 213-227.

_____ (1993), "Interactivity and Communication Mode Choice in Ongoing Management Groups," *Information Systems Research,* 4, 3, September, 207-239.

_____ (1994), "Shared Context and Communication Effectiveness in a Computer-Supported Work Group," *Information and Management,* 26, 4, April, 231-241.

9

Constructing the Networked Organization

Content and Context in the Development
of Electronic Communications

MARTIN LEA

TIM O'SHEA

PAT FUNG

Despite the recent trend away from deterministic analyses of communication technology impacts in favor of studies that examine the influence of a wide range of contextual factors, the debate about how context is constituted in relation to organizational electronic communications has only just begun (e.g., Fulk and Steinfield 1990, Lea 1992, Sproull and Kiesler 1991). In addressing this issue, Fulk et al. (1992) identified two major inadequacies with current approaches. One is the tendency for studies to view context as a static and stable entity and so assume that it can be adequately measured by cross-sectional studies of media use in organizations. The other is the failure to examine the complex reciprocal interaction between context and action wherein social context affects and is affected by communication technology and behavior. Fulk et al. (1992) argue that context should be seen as having its own evolving history and recommend that studies of electronic communication explore the dynamic reciprocal relationship between context and action as it evolves over time.

This chapter appeared originally in *Organization Science,* 6(4), July/August, 1995.

In this chapter we respond to these challenges by presenting an approach based on *actor-networks* (e.g., Callon and Law 1989, Latour 1991, Law and Callon 1992), which uses a network metaphor to describe and explain the simultaneous reciprocal relationship between context and content in the design of technology. Here, however, we extend the approach to what is classically defined as the implementation or adoption phase of a technology and explore its utility in relation to the development of organizational electronic communications. As will become clear, this approach has little in common with traditional structural analyses of social network influences on media adoption (e.g., Rice and Aydin 1991, Rice et al. 1990). Instead, it is positioned within the relativist program of the social construction of technology and therefore provides an alternative perspective from which to study the adoption of communications technology in organizations that avoids some of the problematic assumptions on which diffusion of innovations theory is based (Rice 1987, Rogers 1986).

Whereas traditional approaches to studying communication technology in organizations tend to make strong distinctions between the (technical) content of technology and the (social) context into which it is introduced (e.g., Caswell 1988, Rice 1987, Rogers 1986), we consider that there are a number of problems with the definition and distinction between these concepts that undermine our understanding of the reciprocal influence between communication technology and organizational change. Using the actor-network framework, we suggest how some of the dualities that currently frame contextualized studies of electronic communications in organizations—that is, between the technical and the social, and between the content and context of technology—might be transcended. We argue for definitions of content and context that recognize the technical and social composition of both and which are sensitive to their essentially constructional nature. That is to say, the composition of content and context is not predetermined by technological design or by the prior existence of certain social groups, and nor should the boundary between the two be legislated a priori by the analyst. Instead we argue that the heterogeneous composition of both content and context is variable and constructed *in situ* by the relevant actor-networks in the process of developing an organizational electronic communications project. A further corollary of this approach is that the boundary of contextual influences on the communications project does not map on to the boundary of the organization in which it is situated, but may extend far wider as the actors engaged in the project mobilize the necessary resources to develop the project.

Our application of the actor-network approach centers around a 4-year case study of a medium-sized organization.[1] In the latter stages of the study the company was engaged in the process of restructuring from being five independent, national companies to becoming a single, integrated, "networked organization" poised for the new Single European Market of the 1990s. We contrast this phase with the earlier foundations of electronic communications within the company and analyze the interplay between the company's electronic mail project and the developing organizational form. Due to considerations of space we necessarily exclude from our present analysis some of the many structural, cultural, and technological changes that occurred within the organization during this period. Rather than attempt a comprehensive analysis here, our aim is to illustrate the actor-network approach and to use it to address the issues that we have identified.

We begin therefore by briefly discussing content and context in relation to electronic communication networks and introduce social constructionism as our metatheoretical orientation. We then outline the main features of the actor-network approach (A-N) before moving on to present our case study. In the concluding section we reconsider the theoretical implications of our approach for contextualized studies of communication technology and contrast it with another recent approach advocated by Fulk et al. (1992), which is based on contextualism (Georgoudi and Rosnow 1985, McGuire 1983) and structuration theory (Giddens 1984, Poole and DeSanctis 1990).

SOCIAL CONSTRUCTIONISM AND COMMUNICATION TECHNOLOGY

Our approach to studying communication technology in context is based on recent developments in the social study of technology that are in turn informed by ideas and approaches from the sociology of scientific knowledge. The social construction of technology views the development of technology not just as the purely technical product of design, or as shaped by social factors; rather it proposes that technology is grounded in and constituted by social forces. A cornerstone of the social constructionist approach is the proposal that technology exhibits interpretive flexibility. That is, technology is open to more than one interpretation; it can mean different things to different individuals or different groups. This flexibility is frequently (though not always) transient however, and after "closure" occurs (e.g., because a consensus emerges or one particular group wins the debate), the memory of the original process by which the design was "fixed" may be lost. The goal of social constructionism is to follow this process and to expose how and why closure occurs and technology comes to assume one particular form from a range of possible alternatives (e.g., Bijker et al. 1987, Bijker and Law 1992, Law 1991).

At first sight it may not be clear how an historical approach that was developed in order to study the relationship between technology and society might contribute to our understanding of contemporary implementation projects of electronic communications within organizations. However, from a social constructionist perspective design is not fixed in the traditional development stage; instead the interpretive flexibility of technology means that its design continues to evolve even during diffusion, implementation, and usage (e.g., Bijker 1992). Consequently, the functions of a new commu-nication medium are not pregiven but are negotiated during the course of its development and through its manner of adoption by users. This process is clearly seen in the case of the telephone whose early developers perceived it variously as a broadcast medium rather than for interpersonal communica-tion, or else as a tool of commerce rather than for social use (Fischer 1988, Marvin 1988). A more recent example can be found in the development of the French videotex system (Télétel) which, although originally designed as an information service linking French households to on-line databases, was subsequently reinvented during use to become primarily a notoriously suc-cessful computer-based messaging system for interpersonal communication between users themselves (Feenberg 1992).[2]

The social constructionist perspective seeks to account for both success and failure of technology within the same theoretical framework. Thus, the success of videotex in France and the contemporary failure of similar systems in Britain and many other countries are explained in terms of the relevant (social) actors and the kinds of social and technical issues that were negotiated and renegotiated during the development and use of the respective systems.[3] In this case the functions of videotex followed from the interpre-tations that were agreed on through the negotiations of governments, PTTs, manufacturers, the press, the public, and eventually the users themselves, over issues such as the mode of connection of databases to the system, the means of providing access to the system, the definition of services and service providers, the kind of user interface, the system of tariffs, the communication infrastructure, the place of the technology in national politics and ideology, and so on. "Technical problems" and their resolution had profound implications for relations between relevant social actors. However, a stable technology only emerged once solutions to the relational issues were themselves resolved (Feenberg 1992, Thomas et al. 1992).

While the social construction of technology (SCOT) has done much to undermine more deterministic analyses of technology design and adoption, one further contribution of A-N has been to extend the constructionist approach beyond its primary concern with the influence of prior social groups on technology development. SCOT (e.g., Bijker et al. 1987) focuses on tracing the development of the forms and functions of technology through the construction of different meanings by preexisting relevant social groups, such as different categories of end user. A-N on the other hand argues that these social groups are themselves constructed in part by the technology; that the process of constructing technology and its users is a reflexive one in which both technology and social groups mutually elaborate each other.

Latour (1991) has demonstrated this co-constructionist process in the simultaneous development of the Kodak camera by the Eastman Company in the late nineteenth century and the building of a new mass market of amateur photographers. This new form of end user who sent away their used film to be developed by Eastman's laboratories did not exist prior to Eastman. At the same time, the preexisting professional amateurs, who were used to developing their own photographic plates and were not interested in the inferior quality of the roll film camera, were nevertheless interested in using Eastman's newly developed photographic paper and modified their own laboratories to accommodate it. In addition to these social changes, the form and functions of Eastman Company were also transformed simultaneously with these new social and technical developments.

Latour (1991) argues that what is observed in such cases is an innovatory path in which all the actors co-evolve in a process of translation of technology and social group by each other. This is in contrast to the notions of introduction, rejection, resistance, and adoption of new technology by end users that characterize more traditional approaches to technology study. Similarly, in the case study presented below, we show how a single organization and some of the relevant social groups that comprise it reconstruct themselves through a process of mutual elaboration together with the development of organizational communication technology.

CONTENT AND CONTEXT IN ORGANIZATIONAL ELECTRONIC COMMUNICATIONS

The process of socially constructing technology takes place whenever different relevant groups are linked by their interests in a technology whose form and function are still open to debate. In the case of videotex, these negotiations took place largely between organizations operating in national arenas. However, the same process can be identified within organizations that are engaged in technological change. The interpretive flexibility of electronic communications in organizations, that is, their "openness" to different constructions by different groups, is perhaps most readily seen during the "implementation" phase which is traditionally regarded merely as the point when the designers' original intentions for the technology are implemented for a particular group of users.

In the case of computer-mediated communications, this openness manifests itself through the diverse set of elements that are brought together to
form the communications network. These include the cabling (e.g., twisted
pair, thick coax), network design protocols (e.g., Token Ring, Appletalk),
communication software (e.g., Microsoft Mail, The Coordinator), and communication structures supported by the software (e.g., conferencing, electronic mail). Even if we were to restrict our definition of electronic
communication technology to the physical-technical realm (e.g., Caswell
1988), the choice of elements available to the end-user organization and the
variety of possible arrangements of these different elements guarantee a
fluidity of form to network design that is far from being fixed in the R&D
laboratory, or even at the moment of installation, but is capable of being
redesigned at any moment by the substitution or addition of yet other
elements.

Moreover, an adequate definition of technology refers not only to these
physical objects and artifacts but also to the activities, processes, and knowledge that go into its design and operation (MacKenzie and Wajcman 1985).
Electronic communication networks therefore comprise social actors too,
such as manufacturers, suppliers, network managers, computer support personnel, and end users. These should not be regarded merely as the contextual
backdrop to technology use, nor as the passive recipients of technology
impacts; they are all necessary elements if the system is to function and do
work for the organization. Technology is interpreted and formed through the
interactions between these social and technical actors. It follows then, that
communication systems such as electronic mail are not merely technical, but
are better viewed as sociotechnical systems. That is, the content of the
technology is both technical and social. Moreover, the heterogeneous technical and social elements can be combined and recombined at any time, e.g.,
through the choice and configuration of technical elements, the socialization
of new users, and the evolution of communication practices. Electronic
communication systems are therefore never technologies whose design is
fixed; instead their design continues to be developed simultaneously with
their implementation and use. Indeed, their design is in part constituted by
these practices and only when a "snapshot" of the design is taken at a
particular point in time through the lens of a cross-sectional study does the
system design appear to be fixed.

Just as the content of technology consists of both technical and social
elements so too does the context in which technology is designed and used.
In the case of electronic communications the organization provides a rich
social context comprising individuals (e.g., the director, the internal systems
manager), groups (e.g., the technical support group, the senior management
team), and divisions (e.g., the marketing division) whose practices of inter-

action and behavior form organizational culture and shape the technology. However, approaches that place great emphasis on the social context of technology use tend to overlook the technical factors that also go to make up the context. These include the presence and type of cabling already *in situ,* the kinds of communication systems that are already installed, the compatibility and incompatibility of different systems, the available technical knowledge and prior user experience, the availability of national and international networks, and so on. Furthermore, the elements that make up the context (and the content) of organizational electronic communications are not only contained within the organization but also extend outwards beyond the organizational boundaries to include, for example, equipment suppliers, "information superhighways," government policy, and so on.

If both the content and context of technology—traditionally defined— consist of a heterogeneous mixture of technical and social elements, how are we to distinguish between the two? As Woolgar (1991) points out, the two are essentially indefinite and reflexively linked. Descriptions and other determinations of what the technology is are derived from descriptions of the technology context, and similarly, descriptions of the context are dependent on a sense of the technology in its content. Both content and context mutually elaborate each other (Woolgar 1991, p. 68). In other words, design decisions involve making decisions about the allocation of roles between the technology and its environment. These decisions are both technical and social in nature and the definition of the technology is also the definition of its sociotechnical context (Callon 1991). Together these form the configuration of electronic communications within an organization.

The proponents of the A-N approach argue that the boundary between content and context is not one that should be legislated by the analyst then, but is instead a division that is negotiated and renegotiated by the actors themselves (Callon and Law 1989). An understanding of the process by which technological projects are conducted can be gained by "following the actors" in their interactions as they construct and elaborate the technology, the context, themselves, and each other (Latour 1987). In order to do so we need a framework that avoids legislating a priori the boundaries between content and context, or between different types of actors (cf. social network analysis). A-N aims to transcend these distinctions by adopting a network metaphor to make sense of the myriad of heterogeneous technical and social elements that make up both content and context. In our presentation of the implementation of electronic communications which follows, we use A-N to trace the process by which actors set about building electronic communications within an organization. In order to do so, however, we must first introduce some of the main concepts in A-N. These are intended to form a neutral vocabulary of description that avoids privileging technology on the one hand or the social on the other in accounting for the construction of technical artifacts in context (e.g., Callon 1991, Callon and Law 1989).[4]

THE ACTOR-NETWORK APPROACH

Unlike diffusion theory or social network analysis, A-N considers that relevant actors are co-constructed through their interactions with each other, rather than being defined prior to the technology by the structural boundaries of organizations, divisions, and work groups. Neither are actors constrained to particular types for the purpose of analysis. Instead A-N recognizes that in practice actors tend to be varied and can take the form of associations between humans and nonhumans. An actor speaks for the network of associations that it fronts; hence actor-network (Akrich 1992, Callon 1991).

A *network* is a set of relations between an actor and its neighbors on the one hand, and between those neighbors on the other. In the present case it is a coordinated set of heterogeneous actors which interact more or less successfully to design, install, promote, and maintain communications technology within an organization. The composition of the networks is not predetermined but is an empirical matter achieved through the negotiations of actor-networks with one another. A successful innovation is one that draws resources from existing networks and builds a novel network that is able to sustain a two-way exchange of resources with these networks. A practical distinction can be drawn between a *global* network (consisting of relatively dependable, *performing* networks), and a *local* network. Preforming a network refers to the reciprocal process by which well-established networks are mobilized to provide support for a project and at the same time are themselves reworked or reshaped by the project. The successful construction of a global network by a set of actors generates a *negotiation space*; that is, a space, period of time, and set of resources that are provided for a project by the global network in anticipation of a future return. The conduct of the project is achieved through the building and stabilizing of a local network of actors in this negotiation space (Callon and Law 1989, Law and Callon 1992).

Actor-networks are subject to continual processes of definition and re-definition by the actors themselves. The construction and transformation of these sociotechnical networks is achieved through the process of *translation* whereby sets of relations between separate projects, interests, goals, and objects are proposed and built. This process of translation involves the production of intermediaries. An intermediary is anything passing between actors that defines the relationship between them. They include texts (such as reports, manuals, training materials, help files, and so on), technical artifacts (the relatively stable technical elements which combine to form the technology), and human beings and the skills and knowledge that they incorporate. Actors put intermediaries into circulation. They take the last generation of intermediaries and transform them to create the next generation. The difference between an actor and an intermediary is not predetermined by, for example, the distinction between humans and machines; it is an entirely practical matter concerning agency and authorship. Finally, the act of translation is achieved through a series of investments of form whereby objects that are numerous, heterogeneous, and difficult to manipulate are rendered less numerous, more homogeneous, and more easily controlled while nevertheless remaining sufficiently representative of the former as to facilitate their control also (Callon 1986, 1991, Callon and Law 1989).

The actor-network framework was applied to our study of the implementation and development of an electronic mail system project in an organization that was fundamentally restructured during this time. In the next section, we trace how the project was positioned in a global network that provided the resources to build and stabilize the local network of heterogeneous actors that shaped the electronic communication system. We highlight, for example, how local and global networks were extended in pragmatic fashion across structural boundaries such as the boundaries of the organization, and how such networks comprised both social and technical actors. We note the interpretive flexibility of the design at different points and discuss the strategies and constraints that led to the creation of global and local networks, highlighting their reciprocal influence and comparing the shapes of these networks at different stages of system development. The process of translation, the investments of form that were made, and the intermediaries that were exchanged in the process are also identified. Finally, we describe the relative success and failure of the electronic communication project at different points in terms of the extent to which the project was able to attach itself to the global networks to obtain resources and mobilize the local network to carry out the project (Law and Callon 1992).

CASE STUDY

Our chosen organization is the European arm of a large independent professional services company in the information industry. Its services range from management education and consulting in the strategic use of information technology through the design, engineering, building, integration, and operation of computer-based systems and communication networks. It has offices in five European countries and employs around 2,000 people, most of whom are consultants working at client sites. We refer to this organization as "SoftCo."[5]

From its foundation some 20 years earlier until 1991, SoftCo. in the United Kingdom operated largely independently of its sister companies in neighboring European countries. For much of this time it maintained two offices in England, eventually expanding to six, and employed around 550 staff. Several of these branches were quite small and functioned mainly as resource bases and coordination centers for consultants who were frequently employed for long periods at client sites and needed to maintain contact with the company. From 1989 the company engaged in a major expansion by acquisition that continued into 1992. This activity was designed to broaden the range of services that it could offer and increase its market share in preparation for the Single European Market. We begin by charting the introduction of a PC network some 4 years earlier that laid the foundations for electronic mail and in a later section explore some of the ways in which these organizational changes shaped the development of electronic communications.

During 1991 and 1992 we made a series of visits to the SoftCo. offices in England. Our general research strategy began with a prior contact who negotiated our entry into the organization and thereafter we "followed the actors" (Latour 1987), an informal procedure not unlike snowball sampling. That is, after interviewing our contact, we noted which actors were mentioned during conversation and followed up by initiating conversations with these actors in turn, and so on. Thus we obtained data from "consultants" (the main workforce), technical support personnel, and management. Conversations ranged across various topics to do with the organization generally or else focused specifically on the introduction and use of the new communication technologies. In practice, we exercised some judgment about whether to hold an interview, an informal conversation, or to bypass someone altogether according to the degree to which individuals appeared from our data to be representative of a particular actor-network. Nine hours of formal interviews were recorded during this period and later transcribed in full, and potentially useful information arising from informal conversations was noted afterwards. These conversations were supplemented by data from two earlier projects involving the first author. These included the full transcripts of 6 hours of unstructured interviews with managers conducted in 1988 that focused on communication practices in the organization at that time. In addition, an internal survey of communication practices carried out among 50 employees shortly after the introduction of the electronic mail system in 1989 provided answers to questions about the use of the new e-mail system. We also had access to an independent consultant's report of communications within SoftCo. based on 20 interviews carried out in 1990. These interviews were intended to ascertain the kinds of communication that staff engaged in, the technologies being used in the process, and the main communication problems they encountered. Collectively these data sources extended the time frame of our observations over a period of about 4 years between 1988 and 1992.

Conversations were only one way in which the actor-networks spoke to us; we also collected documentation about the organization and the communication technologies. There were two main reasons for this. First, it enabled us to identify actors and events through an analogous process of "historical snowballing" (Bijker 1992), noting which actors were described in which documentation and following these in turn. Organizations speak through their publicity and sales literature, their training materials, their organizational charts and telephone directories, annual reports, and press releases. We collected dozens of such documents including 63 reports and articles about SoftCo. that had appeared in the national press and specialist computer journals. Together, these provided us with a rich impression of the organization itself and of the events that were spoken about in conversations.

A second reason for going beyond the interview data is that technical actors cannot be interviewed as such. However, technology does speak; not only through peripheral actors such as sales and technical support personnel but also through its own performance (for example, what functions it permits and doesn't permit, its reliability, and usability considerations), and the documentation, manuals, training materials, and training courses that accompany the technology (Bijker 1992, Latour 1992, Woolgar 1991). Therefore, in addition to interviewing technical staff, we arranged to receive guided tours and demonstrations of the technology and we collected technical documentation produced both in-house and by the equipment manufacturers.

INTRODUCING ELECTRONIC COMMUNICATIONS

The introduction of electronic communications cannot be pinned down to any one determining factor or to the influence of one particular individual or social group within the company. Rather, it depended on a variety of actors, some social, some technical, that together shaped the communications infrastructure. The chief actors were the senior management team (SM), who controlled company policy and the budget and the Internal Systems department (IS), responsible for the procurement, installation, and maintenance of information technology (IT) systems within the organization. However, these were not the only ones involved and, in the course of the negotiation between the IS department and the SM various other actors were also mobilized to shape electronic communications within SoftCo. Initially, these included equipment suppliers, a large, heterogeneous group of consultants, a small group of individuals interested in office automation and computer-supported cooperative work systems, the marketing division, and the Novell network system itself.

During 1988 the company took the first few hesitant steps into PC networking. These were initiated by the IS, partly because it foresaw that a costs saving could be achieved by sharing software over a network. A network of shared printers would also be an improvement on the inconvenience of moving printers around on trolleys to serve stand-alone PCs, which was the existing practice. Moreover, a network would enable the IS to standardize software and to maintain better control of its systems. However, the promise of eventual cost savings was outweighed by the initial costs of cabling the offices and installing the network system, and neither the IS nor the costs arguments were sufficiently persuasive for the senior management. Neither were the management team wholly convinced that e-mail would achieve any significant improvement in internal communications. One of the two offices was quite small and a high degree of face-to-face communication was possible. An internal mail system already operated in the larger of the two offices and a daily courier service relayed mail between the offices.

It was also clear that it would prove very expensive to provide the consultants, who formed the bulk of the workforce, with access to the network. At SoftCo. consultants worked for long periods of time at client sites and used the office only on an irregular basis. However, consultants were not only responsible for carrying out the work on contracts won by the marketing people but were also frequently required to contribute a substantial technical input to project proposals to win new business from clients. Frequently, these proposals had to be worked up at very short notice, and involved exchanging draft documents and holding urgent meetings between various technical, sales, marketing, and legal personnel.

Efficient communication between office staff and consultants in the field could sometimes be crucial for winning new business. However, this depended to some extent on the particular consultants, the kind of projects they were working on, and the level of demand for their particular expertise, all of which necessarily varied according to many factors both within and outside the control of the company. Some consultants were involved in long-standing government agency projects and for all practical purposes acted as (and sometimes regarded themselves more as) the client's employees rather than as outside consultants, even though they were ultimately responsible to their line manager back at the SoftCo. central office. Other consultants maintained much stronger links with SoftCo., were much more mobile between projects, and managed their projects more as a "partnership" between SoftCo. and their clients. Consultants were thus a very heterogeneous group and their working arrangements were similarly very varied. Many of the consultants worked on their client's mainframe systems and had no access to a PC. Attaching the consultants to the network would require a substantial investment in hardware and software (to provide home workstations) and the IS had no success in convincing the senior managements team—who generally did not have previous experience of computer networking and electronic mail—that there would be an eventual return on their investment in terms of improved communications.

From the perspective of the IS there were benefits to be obtained just from installing small local networks in each of the central offices even if the offices were not interconnected. However, this did not translate into an immediate cost saving and the IS made little headway with the networking project until they joined forces with a small group of consultants—specifically those involved in office automation systems and with an interest in the embryonic field of computer-supported cooperative work—who provided the argument that the IS could use to make some progress. They could see the personal benefits to be derived from electronic communications and had another reason for wanting to develop a network system which proved to be a very effective argument. The consultants effectively mobilized a much larger and more powerful group to further their aim: the company's clientele. They argued that it was difficult to acquire new business in the field of office automation (a field that statistics indicated had vast growth potential) because SoftCo. lacked a demonstrable commitment to networking for its own communications. Thus, in A-N terms, the local network of actors turned toward actors in the global network to convince their opponents to look beyond the issue of cost savings. This won the IS some limited negotiation space to come up with a design for the computer network, and they assembled a "task force" consisting of representatives from various parts of the company to look into the issue of computer networking and to identify their requirements. At the same time a small team within the IS began to evaluate the different networking products on offer.

Over a period of 6 months a number of investments of form were made. The IS consulted with suppliers, the task force, and with their counterpart in the U.S. parent organization where they had substantial experience of using PC networks. They also set up a miniature network of six workstations to evaluate different products and eventually settled on a client-server architecture and the Novell Netware network operating system. At the end of this period they submitted a planning report (an *Intermediary* in A-N terms) to the senior management that proposed the installation of a thin Ethernet cable at each of the two branch offices with a 64-kbp kilostream route leased from British Telecom to link the offices together. The system became operational in December 1988.

The choice of an e-mail product was fairly limited in 1988 and was shaped by a number of factors both social and technical. File transfer capability was an important adjunct to e-mail communication to handle interoffice transfer of formal documents such as spreadsheets to the accounts/finance department and draft client contracts to and from the legal department. The Novell Netware was also seen to place an important constraint on the e-mail system. Whichever system was chosen would have to be fully compatible with the Netware to ensure reliability and low maintenance overhead. This was especially important as the e-mail would have to work with the network bridges to filter the traffic destined for the other office over the kilostream route. The Novell suppliers as well as the IS were keen to settle on a Novell certified product, and the IS, who were very satisfied with the existing suppliers, were keen to stay with them.

Once again, however, the company's existing and intended clients were mobilized by those consultants and marketing personnel who were members of the task force and who sought to represent not only consultants as a group and the marketing division but also actors from the global network: the company's clients. Specifically, they were concerned that a suitable image should be projected to these clients by the adoption of an appropriate advanced e-mail system and that the company should acquire experience of operating such a system. At the time the Coordinator, which had just made its entry into the office systems market, embodied the most advanced concepts in social and technical engineering. In terms of a feature count, Coordinator was way ahead of its competitors and all importantly, the Coordinator was Novell certified and was backed by the existing suppliers. Implementation of the Coordinator e-mail system went ahead in early 1989, beginning with the pilot system set up in the IS department and fanning out over a few months to include management, support staff, operational divisions, recruitment, personnel, and accounts.

ANALYSIS: MOBILIZATION, TRANSLATION, AND INVESTMENT OF FORM

To begin with, we note that an electronic communication network meant different things to different groups; that is, it possessed a high degree of *interpretive flexibility*. For the senior management it would provide an improvement in the efficiency of intraoffice and interoffice communications and the acquisition of new office automation business. For the IS department, it was the means by which resources could be shared and technical support could be provided remotely. For staff working in the central offices, it meant better access to company databases and printers and an alternative means of intraoffice and interoffice communication. For the consultants it meant more efficient exchange of project proposal drafts and consequently reduced travel to the central offices. For those involved in selling office automation systems, it was a demonstration to clients of the company's own commitment to network systems.

The development of electronic communications up to this point can be viewed from the actor-network perspective as a process in which the IS first struggled to position the project within the global network from which resources would emanate and then set about creating and stabilizing a local network to design and implement the system. At first, arguments about productivity and cost saving were not in themselves sufficient to persuade the SM to finance the project and the IS was only successful in its efforts when it mobilized the company's client group (both potential and existing) whose interests were spoken for by consultants and marketing personnel within the company. The successful positioning of the project led to the creation of a limited negotiation space in which the IS could begin to mobilize a temporary local network consisting of actors that would constitute the electronic communications network. The local network included potential suppliers, representatives from the company divisions, and consultants knowledgeable about office automation who formed a task force that was able to speak for a range of actors. In A-N terms, independent projects pursued by existing actor-networks (e.g., development of an internal network system, winning of new clients, and selling equipment) were translated by the process of proposing and building sets of relations between these separate projects, interests, goals, and objects. Their initial task was to produce a report expressing recommendations for the design of the system and the provision of funds for its implementation was dependent on the production of that intermediary. As the system began to take shape, the local network grew to include technical as well as social actors, such as the chosen Novell Netware operating system. The choice of e-mail system was then influenced by the desire to maintain a stable local network of actors while keeping the project positioned in the global network. The maintenance of a stable network for the project was a matter of staying with the same supplier, retaining the support of consultants, and choosing a Novell-compatible e-mail product.

A-N lays emphasis on the work done by translators to convert objects that are numerous, heterogeneous, and manipulable only with difficulty into a smaller number of more easily controlled and more homogeneous elements. Two examples of these *investments of form* performed by the local network can be identified from the above: (a) the work of representing numerous heterogeneous company clients as a potential office automation market in order to secure funding for the project and (b) the work of representing a small pilot network of interconnected PCs as a simplified but workable representation of the full network system in order to establish the feasibility of converting numerous stand-alone machines into a single homogeneous network.

Another important point is the range of resources that were mobilized in forming a global network. Although the communication system was to be used wholly for internal communications, the actors crossed the organizational boundary when it came to mobilizing their resources to persuade the SM to finance the project. Specifically, they mobilized the large and powerful group of clients and potential clients—who would themselves never use the system—to bring about the project and to shape the form of the system as a substantial interoffice network. However, the IS was less successful in mobilizing the U.S. parent company in its attempts to define a sociotechnical context for the project. Communication with the United States was an issue that reemerged later in the history of the e-mail system, at which point relevant actors were successfully mobilized. However, at this stage integration with the U.S. e-mail network was seen to be impossible to achieve because the internal network used by the U.S. company was shared with the (military) client for whom it was initially developed who for security reasons imposed restrictions on its accessibility from other countries. The important point however, as we shall see, is not that integration presented a technically insurmountable problem or that it was actively resisted, but that the relevant actors in the global network were not effectively mobilized.

Unfortunately, a range of groups was not spoken for by the local network responsible for the design and implementation of the system, and the mobilization of a relatively limited local network influenced the success of the project. Most important, "end users" of the system were excluded, for while the task force represented the various divisions in the company, no one spoke for the individual user at his or her terminal. That is, the investment of form required to translate numerous heterogeneous users into a more homogeneous yet representative subset was neglected. Partly as a result the issue of usability of the software was not fully considered and Coordinator turned out to be complex and unintuitive to master and this was to limit its use in the company. Once again, the failure to mobilize all the relevant actors was to have further implications for development of the network at a later stage.

SHAPING THE USE
OF ELECTRONIC MAIL

The composition of the global and local networks, the negotiations between the various actors in these networks, and the various compromises that were worked out shaped the form of the network system, and the design

TABLE 9.1 Two Shapes of Electronic Communications in a Changing Organization

Electronic Communication		Actor's Definitions
Shape A	IS:	Shared printing
PC & Ethernet		File transfer
Novell Netware		Cheaper computing
Limited implementation		Installation hard
Easier maintenance	C:	Office automation/CSCW
Coordinator		Easier work on draft proposals
Support for divisions		Easier communication with office
Support for project groups	M:	Demonstrate commitment to networking
Informal support & maintenance	SM:	Office automation expensive
		Increase office automation business
Shape B		
Full implementation	IS:	Installation hard
Microsoft mail		Maintenance high
Formal maintenance procedures		Standardization high
Pan-European network	C:	Support problem sharing and mutual interests
Trans-Atlantic link	M:	Demonstrate commitment to formal network management practices
Software database	SM:	Support mobility of resources
Distribution groups		Improve communication with European offices

IS, internal systems; C, consultants; M, marketing; SM, senior management.

decisions that were taken in turn helped shape its subsequent use (Table 9.1, Shape A). In this first attempt to design electronic communications within SoftCo. the form owed much to the views of office automation prevalent at that time. That is, it would be used for the transfer of formal documents between departments through a faster, paperless medium, connecting those directly involved in the hands-on preparation of these documents. The choice of Coordinator seemed to fit well with this view. Coordinator provided a highly structured e-mail environment, based on speech/act theory, in which interaction takes the form of one of a number of predefined conversations. Selection of a particular conversation type (e.g., a request, a promise, or an offer) commands the system to constrain the conversation by automatically filling in various text fields, offering certain reply options, defining completion of the conversation, and filing completed conversations (Winograd 1986, Winograd and Flores 1986).

Coordinator's influence as an actor in the electronic communications project was very strong since the highly structured form of communication that it provided turned out to be too inflexible in everyday use. Furthermore, the user interface for the package was complex and difficult to master. The effects of Coordinator were therefore to discourage widespread use of the system. This was further reinforced by the choice of communication link between the two offices. The network bridge worked too slowly to allow on-line use so interoffice communication was asynchronous and provided solely through Coordinator.

The manner of establishing initial use of the system may also have been crucial in shaping its subsequent use. Use of the new e-mail system was voluntary and informal one-to-one training was provided on request by users. New users were issued with guidelines by the IS that encouraged initially frivolous and social use of the system. Although many users developed more serious uses for the system, only a proportion came to see it as essential to their work. This initial construction of the technology as peripheral was reinforced by the attitudes and behavior of the SM and by the pattern of diffusion of the network system outwards from the technical IS department rather than downwards from the top management.

By 1991, all staff who regularly worked at one of the company's offices (around 65 at one site and 20 at the other) had access to the network and new staff at either site were routinely registered to use it and given brief training. At this time, two and a half years after its introduction, an external consultant's report on company communications found e-mail to be used almost entirely for sending messages to elicit technical information while carrying out a project for a client, to request and obtain technical assistance from the IS, and for informal memos and social messaging. E-mail and file transfer were not generally used by support departments for administrative tasks such as contractual discussions and notification of meetings. More important still, for the construction of project proposals which involved rapid communication among project managers, heads of divisions, and legal and accounts departments, electronic communications were not being used in preference to face-to-face communication, even when staff had to travel long distances to attend meetings.

The same report found that users were unwilling to rely on e-mail for critical and urgent communications because of the perceived unreliability of the system, particularly for interoffice communication. Although the IS established a number of distribution lists for group e-mail, these initially corresponded to the structural divisions in the company and distribution lists for project groups were only later added and then only in response to users' requests. In addition, the fact that only a proportion of staff were registered to use the network and the difficulty in establishing who had access to e-mail (and who actually used it) acted as disincentives to staff to widen their electronic communications beyond their immediate coworkers.

DEVELOPING THE NETWORK

Between 1989 and 1991 the negotiation space for developing the network of electronic communications was quite limited. The go-ahead for the e-mail project had been won largely because a return on the investment was perceived from the symbolic value of a network that could be represented to the company's potential clients. Limited improvements in internal communications and eventual cost savings were also hoped for and the acquisition of technical knowledge about networks was another gain, but these were not seen as critical returns. Generally speaking, further large-scale development of the system was resisted by the SM; no capital funds were available and each improvement or addition to the network had to be fought for and justified either as a cost saving or else to remove clearly identifiable bottlenecks in the system. E-mail was extended to consultants by justifying each individual case and the manner of purchasing software licenses also contributed to the stepwise progression of the PC network as access to the system for new users tended to be postponed until there was sufficient demand to justify bulk-buying new licenses. More important still were the falling costs of computer hardware: a perennial situation which financially rewarded the IS for holding off requests for hardware and so encouraged a generally cautious approach to purchasing decisions. The IS department was also progressively reduced in size during this time from 11 people, who not only installed and maintained the system but also produced documentation and training, to a complement of only 5 (4 technical and 1 clerical) staff. From an A-N perspective, this reflected the difficulties experienced in preforming dependable networks for the electronic communications project. Over this time, development of the electronic communications ebbed as the project was no longer engaged in the global network and the local network involving the task force disintegrated.

In order to extend its business opportunities beyond mainframe systems, SoftCo. acquired in 1991 a business that installed point-of-sale computer networks for retailers. The new office was already cabled to allow PC networking and some small networks were already in place so that laser printers and other peripherals could be shared. Once again, the company's clients were mobilized in various ways to shape the electronic communications network, even though these clients would never themselves become users of the system. First, managers of the new office argued that in order to convince their clients of the need to implement formal network management methods for the systems which they installed and maintained for them, SoftCo. first had to be able to demonstrate a commitment to such procedures within the company. Second, the company was attempting to obtain BS5750 certification for quality management systems from the British Standards Institute and its European equivalent, IS9000. Certification would provide "unrivaled customer reassurance" for SoftCo.'s clients but first required the IS to fully document and audit their internal procedures.

A support agreement was negotiated with the IS that specified staffing levels, response times, documentation, and change control procedures. Maintenance and development of the network at the remote site were carried out by stationing two IS personnel there. In order to integrate the office with the SoftCo. network (which would double in size) an upgraded version of Coordinator was installed. This again formed the basis for between-office communications, this time using public telephone lines with gateway access between the two networks for file exchange every 15 minutes. In A-N terms, the expanding network project developed through a process of translation whereby a set of relations between the electronic communications project and the project to sell maintenance contracts to SoftCo.'s clients was proposed and built. This involved actors (IS, SM, and Marketing) putting in place new generations of intermediaries (e.g., documentation, training manuals, telephone lines, gateways, and support staff). At the same time the global actor-network of SoftCo. clients and their systems began to be reshaped or preformed by the introduction of formal network management methods for their own systems.

Around this time SoftCo. was also preparing for the new Single European Market which was created when trade barriers and other restrictions between European Member States were removed on December 31, 1991. The removal of border controls would bring not only substantial new business opportunities but also strong new competitors from other countries. The construction of a single European organization was therefore seen to be an essential strategy if the company was to become a major player in the new market. This would enable the company to reap the benefits of scale of a large organization in every member country. It would involve turning a group of hierarchical national companies that up until then had been operating independently into a single, tightly woven, networked organization operating transnationally across Europe.

The new organizational form that emerged during 1991 was predicated on the concepts of "dispersed centralization" and "integrated diversity." SoftCo. saw little value in a headquarters coordinating transnational activities. Rather than centralizing expertise in a single location the headquarters was disbanded and its functions were dispersed across Europe. Thus, while an office in Brussels had previously housed the European headquarters, as the reengineering of SoftCo. began to gather pace specialists throughout the organization were encouraged to network with others in their work. "Act locally and think globally" became a slogan for the new organization.

Although it would remain the local company's responsibility to meet the customer's needs, the entire resources of SoftCo. in Europe were now potentially available to meet those needs. From this point onwards the form that electronic communications took within SoftCo. was substantially shaped by these new concerns, while the successful shaping of the new organization relied in turn on a dependable electronic communications network that would support dispersal and integration and provide a powerful symbol of the new networked organization. Relatively dependable networks such as the organization and the IS were to be once again preformed by the translation of the networked organization project and the electronic communications project and this involved mobilizing new actors and proposing and building a new generation of intermediaries.

As a part of the new policy of "scaling up" there was a pressing need to take more advantage of the knowledge and expertise residing in the American parent company. For example, although SoftCo. had long been concerned with the problem of how to encourage pooling of knowledge and software reusability among their consultants, this issue now became part of a much larger concern: how to ensure that globally distributed resources within the company could be assembled locally in order to meet a client's requirements. The U.S. software library, set up as a separate organization by the parent company to address this formidable problem, organized a presentation in the United Kingdom which led to the immediate purchase of 50 modems locally in order to provide consultants in the field with direct access to the library via transatlantic toll-free telephone lines paid for by the library. In this way, consultants in Europe barred from directly accessing the American e-mail network were able to take advantage of items of software code and technical advice placed on the databases by their American counterparts. Another consequence, however, was that more consultants now had the technical capability to remotely access SoftCo.'s internal e-mail network in the United Kingdom and so maintain better contact with their peers at other client sites and their line managers at the company's offices. At this point, SoftCo.'s e-mail network was directly shaped by additional actors in both the local and the global networks that stretched beyond the company's walls.

Compared to its European counterparts, SoftCo. in England had more extensive experience of developing internal electronic communications. A formal presentation (another intermediary) by the IS to the top management of the European companies successfully established the IS in the role of expert adviser and coordinator for further, transnational growth of the e-mail network. Around this time the decision was made to assign more people to the IS team which doubled in size over the next few months. In actor-network terms the IS was positioned as an *obligatory point of passage* between the local network of actors that built the European electronic communications and the global network of resource providers (the five national SoftCo. companies).

The selection and standardization of technical components was a crucial task in this development for which a series of investments of form were made. A new actor-network consisting of a task force of IS members and representatives from the new European partners was constructed which put into circulation an intermediary consisting of a single terminal at each company location configured to match the UK communication protocols, which was intended to represent the possible form of a European network system. The difficulties with matching the UK system in different sites led to the adoption of Microsoft Mail as the e-mail platform, which in turn paved the way for full compatibility of the communication protocols between the UK and Continental network systems. In A-N terms, the investment of form had failed in its function of sufficiently representing the existing communication network and facilitating its control while at the same time rendering the developing networks more homogeneous, and more easily controlled, and was replaced by a more successful one. Once again, relatively well-established networks were translated by the construction of relations between initially independent projects, the production of intermediaries, and by a series of investments of form.

THE PROJECT TRAJECTORY

By 1992 around 46% of all staff in the United Kingdom (including 27% of consultants) were users of the e-mail network, and although the development of the network was far from complete we can already see how a number of changes in the social and technical composition of the global and local networks were reshaping the form of the electronic mail system (see Table 9.1, Shape B). In this second phase of development, actors in the global network now included the European partners and the U.S. software library as well as a client group mobilized by the managers of the newly acquired office. We have also suggested that the development of the local network depended on the positioning of the project as one that was relevant to each of these actors and, most crucially of all, essential to the construction of a networked organization. In this way the e-mail project emerged as a concrete manifestation of the new company objectives and mode of operation and gave it the capability of reciprocally acting on the global network. For example, it enabled the networking of the software tools library and other databases and the setting up of e-mail distribution lists to link consultants with knowledge and interests in the same technical issues and cultural groups consisting of staff with particular knowledge of the customs and languages of countries in which the company was as yet unestablished but seeking to expand.

In the development of the electronic communications project in SoftCo. we see the shaping and reshaping, or preforming, of networks. The IS contracted, expanded, and adapted its function. Groups that had previously failed to join the local network, such as the SM, were eventually successfully mobilized. New technical components substituted for old ones as part of the process of building the project, and like the social actors, the technical elements were changed by the project. The organization as a whole, previously the context for the development of electronic communications, was foregrounded and the European "networked organization" became part of the content of the project. In short, the composition of the content and context of the project was negotiated and renegotiated by the actors themselves in the course of mobilizing and stabilizing networks and making investments of form.

According to A-N, the relative success and failure of a project is determined by the degree of control exerted over the local and global networks. The positioning of a project on these two dimensions at different time points can be represented by a two-dimensional graph which also describes the trajectory of the project (Law & Callon, 1992). Figure 9.1 presents the trajectory of the e-mail project in SoftCo. where the vertical axis measures the degree of attachment of actors in the global network and the horizontal axis measures the degree of mobilization of the local network.

Beginning at the center of the graph, then, the e-mail project at first failed to win approval on the grounds of cost savings alone (A), but was successful in obtaining resources after mobilizing the company's clients (B). Mobilization of a local network consisting of the project "task force," external suppliers, and development of a pilot system culminated in a report to the SM (C) which resulted in funds to implement the network system (D). Up until this point the project had followed a fairly straightforward linear path after a hesitant start. However, further development of the system was thwarted by a lack of resources and the project team actions became more reactive than proactive (E). The future development of e-mail was at risk when the e-mail project initially failed to be positioned in the company's reorganization plans (F). However, a newly acquired office was networked (G) and negotiations with this office, which included mobilization of the company's clients, together with the drive for BSI certification increased pressure on the overstretched local network to develop formal network management procedures (H). Encouragement to utilize the U.S. software tools databases and improved accessibility led to expansion of external links to the network (I). A presentation by the IS to the European partners positioned the IS as an obligatory point of passage in the development of a

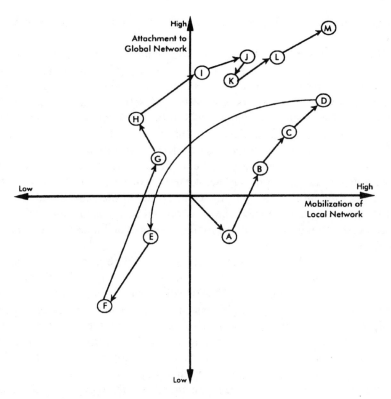

Figure 9.1. Trajectory of the Electronic Mail Project

European network and European access routes were forged (J). The IS failed
to convince European partners to adopt Coordinator and was in danger of
losing its pivotal position (K), but a decision was made to drop Coordinator
in favor of a windows product compatible with European partners (L).
Expansion of the IS prefaced acceleration of the development of the new
network systems (M).

Precise positioning of the points on the graph is necessarily subjective
and not based on any quantifiable data, but nonetheless they meaningfully
represent the relative success or failure of the project at a given time in terms
of the degree of control that it exercised over the global and local networks.
To the extent that the project is located in the top right quadrant, the project
can be described as successful at that time, as reflected in the availability of
resources from the global network and the local assembly of required social
and technical actors to implement the project. In contrast, its location in the
bottom left quadrant indicates a weak, disintegrating project starved of

resources and lacking the required local capability. A project located in the top left quadrant is one whose desirability is recognized by resource providers, but which lacks the local network of actors that would secure the resources to implement it. Finally, a project located in the bottom right quadrant is one for which the required social and technical actors are assembled locally, but which is failing to mobilize the appropriate combination of resource providers.

CONCLUSIONS

What conclusions does this case study offer for defining and studying content and context in relation to the implementation of electronic communications in a changing organization? First, our observations are intended to contribute to dispelling technological or economic determinisms, but the cataloging of historical detail unique to a single organization has only limited utility without a conceptual framework that allows some generalization and comparability between cases. Here then, we have employed actor-networks as a framework for identifying patterns in our data that would permit generalization while avoiding the reductionism characteristic of more deterministic approaches. A-N attempts to provide a neutral vocabulary that avoids privileging either the technical or the social in the analysis of sociotechnical design and a method of analyzing the simultaneous reciprocal influences between context and content without legislating the composition of either. The analysis has therefore been in terms of global networks, local networks, and obligatory points of passage that are argued to shape the form of technological projects. We have also briefly illustrated some of the investments of form carried out by translators that constitute the work of the project. We have noted the different ways in which the networks were mobilized and how their shapes changed over time as different actors came to be included or excluded. The trajectory of the project has been drawn in terms of the degree to which the project was able to position itself between these networks. Viewed in this way, the development of electronic communications did not follow a simple linear path, but instead was shaped and reshaped erratically and somewhat haphazardly as a host of different actors and events came into play.

The actor-network approach also differs in a number of ways from other contextualized studies of communication technology. For example, the context-behavior approach proposed by Fulk et al. (1992) advocates the development of context-specific hypotheses in preference to generalized hypotheses in order to make sense of the apparently conflicting conclusions suggested by previous research in the technological determinist tradition. In order to overcome problems that arise from relying on level of analysis (e.g., group, organization, and community) as a mechanism for defining and measuring the social context in contradistinction to individual action—a process that denies the contribution of individuals in forming the social context—Fulk et al. (1992) invoke the theory of structuration (Giddens 1984, Poole and DeSanctis 1990). Context is therefore viewed as being composed of structures of generative rules and resources that provide constraints on individual action. While structures guide and influence behavior, they are at the same time continually altered by social action so that social systems are formed and reformed by the interplay of structure and action. Such an approach allows for the influence of individuals' action in the formation of context as well as the simultaneous reciprocal link between context and action.

In common with Fulk et al. we regard the structural approach that presents context merely as the backdrop against which technology has its effects to be flawed. We also concur with their observations regarding the tendency to exclude individual action from the analysis of context. In our own observations we saw how the forms and functions of the communications project, various groups (the IS and the consultants), and the organization itself were worked and reworked through a process of reciprocal influence. However, the analysis of context-behavior in interactions that Fulk et al. propose raises its own problems and at the same time does not confront some of the more fundamental problems of research in the positivist tradition. One problem is how to maintain a prior distinction between the content and the context of the project when the composition of both is recognized to be mutually elaborated *in situ*. A tendency which is characteristic of contextualized studies of computer-mediated communication in general in seeking to avoid the reification and rationalistic thinking that is characteristic of the technological determinist tradition is to neglect the technology in favor of a full exposition of the rich social context in which it is embedded. Thus, while social groups, norms, and practices, for example, may be unpacked to demonstrate their prior effects on implementation strategies or technology use, the technology itself often remains "black-boxed." This tendency toward simplification and obfuscation of the technology in social studies of technology has been referred to in another context as a "curious case of vanishing technology" (Button 1993). However, unless a full elaboration of context is made that includes the technical as well as the social, the (social) contextualized approach is in danger of becoming as much a tyranny as the technological determinism that it wishes to replace. In the context-behavior approach, as elsewhere, we identify a tendency to equate the social with the context and the technology with content, whereas the actor-network approach and the data we present here argue both conceptually and empirically for the consideration of both content and context as socially and technically constituted.

A second distinction between content and context in the context-behavior approach appears to hang on the distinction between individual action and social influence and the researcher/analyst is privileged to decide what constitutes action and what constitutes its context. In contrast, the actor-network approach argues that instead of the distinction being legislated by the analyst, we should consider the boundary between content and context as one that is continually negotiated and renegotiated by the actors themselves in the course of building a project. Actors of all kinds are at work in constructing content and context, and in practice they pay no heed to the boundaries between individuals, groups, or organizations—or distinctions drawn between the social and the technical—in their elaboration of both. Instead the work of translator leads to a local definition of context (in the shape of performing, global networks) and content, as investments of form placed within the negotiation space created by the local actor-networks.

A third potential problem with the context-behavior approach is at the operational level where, in the interest of developing causal models of context effects, the duality of structure is untied and replaced with analytical dualism in which the interaction between context and action is conceived in terms of temporal cycles of alternating cause and effect (cf. Archer 1982). Such an approach is forced by a positivistic metatheoretical orientation. In doing so, however, some of the analytic power of structuration theory, with its emphasis on the complex, simultaneous interweaving of structural attributes and individual action is lost, no matter how temporarily the links between the components of the system are severed. An alternative to this reductionism is to focus instead on the "shifting assemblies of associations and substitutions" in the project (Latour 1991, p. 113). Such an approach has the advantage of making the passage of time a consequence of these associations rather than a fixed framework onto which the analyst charts development.

In sum, using actor-networks as a framework, the present study has sought to illustrate how the "entirely pragmatic, permeable, and revisable boundary between content and context" (Callon and Law 1989, p. 74) was formed and reformed throughout the development of organizational electronic communications.

NOTES

1. This study was carried out as part of the "Implications of Technological Change in Communications" (Project Number F93302) funded by the Joint (ESCR/SERC) Committee of the U.K. Science and Engineering Research Council. The authors are grateful to Ruth Finnegan and Ray Thomas for their assistance and advice during the project. In developing the chapter, the first author also gratefully acknowledges the financial assistance of a fellowship from the Joint

Council (MRC/SERC) Initiative in Cognitive Science/Human Computer Interaction, the facilities and support of the Computing Department, University of Lancaster made possible by Ian Sommerville, together with the comments on previous drafts made by the editors and their anonymous reviewers.

2. For example, in the summer of 1985 the new French packet switching network, Transpac, crashed due to the volume of messaging services estimated to account for over 40% of all network traffic (e.g., Feenberg 1992).

3. Of course, definitions of success and failure for a particular technology are themselves open to negotiation. For example, Télétel is viewed as a success by some because it has attracted over 6 million subscribers but as a failure by others since the export of Minitel terminals to other countries was not achieved and the system failed to influence emerging international standards for database design. In the case of the equivalent British Prestel system, closure can be said to be complete since the system is generally regarded as belonging to the list of great IT disasters (Feenberg 1992, Miles 1992, Thomas et al. 1992).

4. See Akrich and Latour (1992) and Latour (1992) for additional proposals not covered here.

5. The identities of the participating organization and of the individual employees have been kept confidential.

REFERENCES

Akrich, M. (1992), "The De-scription of Technical Objects," in W. E. Bijker and J. Law (Eds.), *Shaping Technology/Building Society: Studies in Sociotechnical Change,* Cambridge: MIT Press.

_____ and B. Latour (1992), "A Summary of a Convenient Vocabulary for the Semiotics of Human and Nonhuman Assemblies," in W. E. Bijker and J. Law (Eds.), *Shaping Technology/Building Society: Studies in Sociotechnical Change,* Cambridge: MIT Press.

Archer, M. (1982), "Morphogenesis Versus Structuration: On Combining Structure and Action," *British Journal of Sociology,* 33, 455-483.

Bijker, W. E. (1992), "The Social Construction of Fluorescent Lighting, or How an Artifact Was Invented in Its Diffusion Stage," in W. E. Bijker and J. Law (Eds.), *Shaping Technology/Building Society: Studies in Sociotechnical Change,* Cambridge: MIT Press.

_____, T. P. Hughes, and T. J. Pinch (Eds.) (1987), *The Social Construction of Technological Systems: New Directions in the Sociology and History of Technology,* Cambridge, MA: MIT Press.

_____ and J. Law (1992), *Shaping Technology/Building Society: Studies in Sociotechnical Change,* Cambridge: MIT Press.

Button, G. (1993), "The Curious Case of the Vanishing Technology," in G. Button (Ed.), *Technology in Working Order: Studies of Work, Interaction, and Technology,* London: Routledge.

Callon, M. (1986), "Some Elements of a Technology of Translation: Domestication of the Scallops and the Fishermen of St. Brieuc Bay," in J. Law (Ed.), *Power, Action and Belief: A New Sociology of Knowledge?* London: Routledge.

_____ (1987), "Society in the Making: The Study of Technology as a Tool for Sociological Analysis," in W. E. Bijker, T. P. Hughes, and T. P. Pinch (Eds.), *The Social Construction of Technological Systems: New Directions in the Sociology and History of Technology,* Cambridge: MIT Press.

_____ (1991), "Techno-Economic Networks and Irreversibility," in J. Law (Ed.), *A Sociology of Monsters: Essays on Power, Technology and Domination*, London: Routledge.

_____ and J. Law (1989), "On the Construction of Sociotechnical Networks: Content and Context Revisited," *Knowledge and Society*, 8, 57-83.

Caswell, S. A. (1988), *E-Mail*, Boston: Artech House.

Feenberg, A. (1992), "From Information to Communication: The French Experience With Videotex," in M. Lea (Ed.), *Contexts of Computer-Mediated Communication*, London: Harvester-Wheatsheaf.

Fischer, C. (1988), "Touch Someone: The Telephone Industry Discovers Sociability," *Technology and Culture*, 29, 32-61.

Fulk, J., J. A. Schmitz, and D. Schwarz (1992), "The Dynamics of Context-Behaviour Interactions in Computer-Mediated Communication," in M. Lea (Ed.), *Contexts of Computer-Mediated Communication*, London: Harvester-Wheatsheaf.

_____ and C. C. Steinfield (Eds.) (1990), *Organizations and Communication Technology*, Newbury Park, CA: Sage.

Georgoudi, M. and R. L. Rosnow (1985), "The Emergence of Contextualism," *Journal of Communication*, 35, 76-88.

Giddens, A. (1984), *The Constitution of Society: Outline of the Theory of Structuration*, Chicago: Polity.

Latour, B. (1987), *Science in Action: How to Follow Scientists and Engineers Through Society*, Milton Keynes, UK: Open University Press.

_____ (1991), "Technology Is Society Made Durable," in J. Law (Ed.), *A Sociology of Monsters: Essays on Power, Technology and Domination*, London: Routledge.

_____ (1992), "Where Are the Missing Masses: The Sociology of a Few Mundane Artifacts," in W. E. Bijker and J. Law (Eds.), *Shaping Technology/Building Society: Studies in Sociotechnical Change*, Cambridge: MIT Press.

Law, J. (1991), *A Sociology of Monsters: Essays on Power, Technology and Domination*, London: Routledge.

_____ and M. Callon (1992), "The Life and Death of an Aircraft: A Network Analysis of Technical Change," in W. E. Bijker and J. Law (Eds.), *Shaping Technology/Building Society: Studies in Sociotechnical Change*, Cambridge: MIT Press.

Lea, M. (1992), *Contexts of Computer-Mediated Communication*, London: Harvester-Wheatsheaf.

MacKenzie, D. and J. Wajcman (1985), *The Social Shaping of Technology*, Milton Keynes, UK: Open University Press.

Marvin, C. (1988), *When Old Technologies Were New: Thinking About Electric Communication in the Late Nineteenth Century*, Oxford, UK: Oxford University Press.

McGuire, W. J. (1983), "A Contextualist Theory of Knowledge: Its Implications for Innovation and Reform in Psychological Research," in L. Berkowitz (Ed.), *Advances in Experimental Social Psychology*, New York: Academic Press, Vol. 16.

Miles, I. (1992), "When Mediation Is the Message: How Suppliers Envisage New Markets," in M. Lea (Ed.), *Contexts of Computer-Mediated Communication*, London: Harvester-Wheatsheaf.

Poole, M. S. and G. DeSanctis (1990), "Understanding the Use of Group Decision Support Systems: The Theory of Adaptive Structuration," in J. Fulk and C. Steinfield (Eds.), *Organizations and Communication Technology*, Newbury Park, CA: Sage.

Rice, R. E. (1987), "Computer-Mediated Communication and Organizational Innovation," *Journal of Communication*, 37, 4, 65-94.

_____ and C. Aydin (1991), "Attitudes Towards New Organizational Technology: Network Proximity as a Mechanism for Social Information Processing," *Administrative Science Quarterly*, 36, 219-244.

_____, A. Grant, J. Schmitz, and J. Torobin (1990), "Individual and Network Influences on the Adoption and Perceived Outcomes of Electronic Messaging," *Social Networks,* 12, 27-55.

Rogers, E. M. (1986), *Communication Technology: The New Media in Society,* New York: Free Press.

Sproull, L. and S. Kiesler (1991), *Connections: New Ways of Working in the Networked Organization,* Cambridge: MIT Press.

Thomas, G., T. Vedel, and V. Schneider (1992), "The United Kingdom, France and Germany: Setting the Stage," in H. Bouwman and M. Christoffersen (Eds.), *Relaunching Videotex,* London: Kluwer.

Winograd, T. (1986), "A Language/Action Perspective on the Design of Cooperative Work," in *Proceedings of the Conference on Computer Supported Cooperative Work, CSCW '86, Austin, Texas,* New York: ACM.

_____ and F. Flores (1986), *Understanding Computes and Cognition: A New Foundation for Design,* Norwood, NJ: Ablex.

Woolgar, S. (1991), "Configuring the User: The Case of Usability Trials," in J. Law (Ed.), *A Sociology of Monsters: Essays on Power, Technology and Domination,* London: Routledge.

PART III

SHAPING INTERORGANIZATIONAL
RELATIONSHIPS AND COMMUNITIES

How are information and communication technologies affecting interorganizational relationships and the formation of larger social communities? Whereas the prior chapters focused almost exclusively on the small group, work unit, or firm level, here we broaden our focus beyond traditional organizational boundaries. In the information age, consideration of larger, less formally defined social groups becomes relevant, even within the study of organizational form. Communities are collections of people whose common characteristics are determined more by general social identity than by an organizational reporting structure and whose membership can extend outside the firm.

Boland and Tenkasi (Chapter 10) employ models of language, communication, and cognition to propose how electronic communication systems can be designed to support knowledge-intensive firms. They provide a riveting exploration of the knowledge production process within and between communities. They distinguish between perspective making, which is communication that strengthens unique knowledge of a given community, and perspective taking, which takes the knowledge of other communities into account. The authors emphasize that the role of technology is more than providing media or a conduit for connection. Rather, technology should support the nurturing of emergent communities of knowing and respect for the uniqueness of a local community's distinctiveness. New organizational forms are processes of distributed cognition, defined less by formal organizational structure and more by membership in a knowledge community. Technologies can facilitate knowledge work by providing support for narratives, information interpretation, theory building, and sense making both within and between communities of knowing.

Lind and Zmud (Chapter 11) provide a unique empirical study of voice mail effects. They take great care to link the specific functionality of the technology to specific organizational processes and reveal both direct and indirect effects of communications technology on interorganizational effectiveness. Researchers will find their method for mapping technical functionality with organizational process to be helpful in studies of electronic communication impacts on outcomes. They show how technology can enhance interorganizational relationships both directly, through specific features that can affect interpersonal behaviors, and indirectly, through the ongoing communication dynamics among members inside and outside the firm.

Pickering and King (Chapter 12) follow with a stimulating essay outlining the forces encouraging growth of interorganizational computer-mediated communication. They argue that the long-predicted shifts away from hierarchical to market forms of organization are being bootstrapped via two strong forces—the professionalism of key occupational communities seeking autonomy and a persistent desire by organizations to reduce fixed costs and organizational size. These forces are operating to "hardwire" what are otherwise weak social ties, thus spurring real movement toward new organizational forms.

Weak ties are relationships between acquaintances or strangers. Constant, Sproull, and Kiesler (Chapter 13) examined the practice of distant employees (strangers) exchanging technical advice through a large organizational computer network. They surveyed advice seekers and those who replied in the exchange of technical advice and found that information providers gave useful advice despite lack of a personal connection with the information seekers. Organization culture was critical to sustaining the useful information exchange through these weak ties. The authors conclude that computer networks offer more opportunities to see others contributing than would be available in face-to-face interactions; this may reinforce norms of contribution within a culture that values it. In this sense, computer networks can provide a means for leveraging the "kindness of strangers."

Together, the chapters in this section show how technology, woven within the rich rubric of organizational incentives, culture, and knowledge exchange, can play an important role in shaping relationships inside and outside the firm. Advanced communication technologies, such as groupware, voice mail, bulletin boards, and discussion-based networks, are important to the evolution of new connections within traditional forms of organizing.

10

Perspective Making and Perspective Taking in Communities of Knowing

RICHARD J. BOLAND, JR.

RAMKRISHNAN V. TENKASI

Organizations are developing innovative products and services on faster cycle times (Lawler 1992, Purser and Pasmore 1992), causing an increase in knowledge work (Pava 1983) and a gradual replacement of capital and labor-intensive firms by knowledge-intensive firms (Starbuck 1992). Knowledge work creates new understandings of nature, organizations, or markets and applies them in valued technologies, products, or processes. Knowledge-intensive firms are composed of multiple communities with highly specialized technologies and knowledge domains (Purser et al. 1992). In the pharmaceutical industry, for example, developing new products requires integration of knowledge from a broad array of disciplines such as molecular biology, physiology, biochemistry, synthetic chemistry, pharmacology, and even esoteric specialties such as molecular kinetics (Henderson 1994). A similar pattern is observable in other industries. The first generation of cellular telephones used 5 subtechnologies, but their third generation incorporated 14 distinct subtechnologies (Grandstrand et al. 1992). The increasing proliferation of specialized and distinct knowledge communities and the need for their integration has also resulted in the emergence of new organizational forms, among them the lateral-flexible form of organization (Galbraith 1994, Galbraith and Lawler 1993). The lateral-flexible organizational form

---

This chapter appeared originally in *Organization Science,* 6(4), July/August, 1995.

relies on peer-to-peer collaboration (as opposed to a vertical hierarchy) in achieving organizational objectives.

It is our contention that all organizations are becoming more knowledge intensive across the service, industrial, and governmental sectors. It is easiest to see the fundamental importance of knowledge work in firms involved with new product development in leading-edge technologies, but the relentless pace of change in market expectations means that all organizations will increasingly rely on creating new knowledge and adopting lateral organizational forms. The major issue for such firms is to find creative ways for representing and integrating knowledge across their lateral units (Galbraith 1994, Weick and Roberts 1993).

Knowledge production involves communication within and between a firm's multiple communities of knowing. We refer to communication that strengthens the unique knowledge of a community as perspective making, and communication that improves its ability to take the knowledge of other communities into account as perspective taking. In this chapter we employ models of language, communication, and cognition to propose how electronic communication systems can be designed to support perspective making and perspective taking in knowledge-intensive firms.

We argue that perspective making and perspective taking are achieved by narrating our experience as well as by rationally analyzing it. These processes are like playing games with language as well as like transmitting messages through a conduit, and they involve heightened levels of reflexivity. The narrating of experience is a critically important but often overlooked element of knowledge production in knowledge-intensive firms, even though it is recognized that scientific reasoning is often conducted through narratives and that scientists' interpretive practices are embodied in their conversation (Knorr-Cetina 1981, Mulkay et al. 1983). Similarly, the importance of playful situated action for strengthening one's own perspective and the importance of reflexivity for appreciating the perspective of another is not sufficiently recognized in communication system design. After analyzing the processes of perspective making and perspective taking, we describe an idealized knowledge-intensive firm to highlight some of the features of an electronic communication system that would support those processes.

We first present the concept of a community of knowing as an open system and provide a brief overview of models of language, communication, and cognition that can guide the design of electronic communication systems. The language games model of Wittgenstein (1974) and Bruner's (1986, 1990) model of narration as a cognitive mode are presented as supplements to the dominant organizational models of language as message transmissions and cognition as information processing. Science is used as an example of knowledge work to draw implications for applying these models to the communication requirements in knowledge-intensive firms. We then explore the dynamics of perspective making and perspective taking and some potential breakdowns in the perspective-taking process. This allows us to summarize the strengths and weaknesses of the language game and the conduit models of communication for designing electronic communication systems, and to emphasize the importance of reflexivity and boundary objects in perspective taking. Finally, we present our admittedly utopian vision of some future applications of electronic communication for supporting knowledge work in a hypothetical firm with a lateral-flexible form.

COMMUNITIES OF KNOWING
AS OPEN SYSTEMS

Organizations are characterized by a process of distributed cognition in which multiple communities of specialized knowledge workers, each dealing with a part of an overall organizational problem, interact to create the patterns of sense making and behavior displayed by the organization as a whole (Boland et al. 1994).

Organizations are necessarily characterized by distributed cognition because their critically important processes and the diversity of environments and technologies to be dealt with are "too complex for one person to understand in its entirety" (Brehmer 1991, p. 4; Nersessian 1992). This problem is especially acute in knowledge-intensive firms that rely on multiple specialties and knowledge disciplines to achieve their objectives. Each such community of specialized knowledge workers is what we term a "community of knowing."

A number of scholars, such as Fish (1980), Fleck (1979), Barnes (1983), and Brown and Duguid (1991), have commented on the way that communities develop unique social and cognitive repertoires which guide their interpretations of the world. Fleck's (1979) concept of "thought collective" is one such notion that emphasizes the unique interpretive repertoires of a distinct community of knowing. A thought world evolves in a community of knowing as a "readiness for directed perception." Thought worlds with different funds of knowledge and systems of meaning cannot easily share ideas and may view one another's central issues as esoteric, if not meaningless. Other terms which echo our concept of community of knowing include "interpretive community" (Fish 1980), "context of learning" (Barnes 1983), and "community of practice" (Brown and Duguid 1991, Lave and Wenger 1990, Orr 1990). However, given our focus on knowledge-intensive firms, and our concern with the interaction of different expert knowledge groups in the process of knowledge creation, we feel "community of knowing" is the most appropriate label for our purposes.

The multiple communities of knowing in knowledge-intensive firms overlap in complex and shifting ways. There is a rich structural hierarchy (Smith 1981) of communities of knowing within the firm and between the firm and its environment. Divisions, functional areas, product lines, professional specialties, project teams, issue-based committees, and so on are all possible sites for communities of knowing that interweave with each other across various levels of the organization. Individuals will find themselves as members of several communities of knowing operating within a firm and its environment.

In science, the interaction of communities of knowing has been viewed as an open system by Star (1993) and a similar notion has been expressed by Barnes (1983) and Hesse (1974), who characterize each community as a knowledge net within an institution or culture. Even in settings where communication appears unproblematic and knowledge homogeneous, the nets of individual communities differ. It is through the dynamic interactions between such communities that new configurations of the knowledge net emerge by creating new meanings, new linguistic routines, and new knowledge. Maintenance and refinement of the existing knowledge in a community can be attributed to feedback processes operating within established routines and policies. The creation of new knowledge in an organization, however, is often the result of an open system transformation of that organization's communities of knowing as they question and revise routines and create new processes and relationships among themselves (Argyris and Schön 1978, von Bertalanffy 1968, Wiener 1954). We argue that perspective making and perspective taking are the basis for transformations within and between communities of knowing and thereby the basis for open system control in knowledge work. Our principal contention is that designing electronic communication systems for knowledge-intensive firms requires an appreciation of how they can mediate the transformation and changing relationships among communities of knowing by affecting perspective-making and perspective-taking capabilities.

ASSUMPTIONS ABOUT LANGUAGE COMMUNICATION AND COGNITION IN KNOWLEDGE WORK

The knowledge work of perspective making and perspective taking requires individual cognition and group communication. Our understanding of language, communication, and cognition is centrally important in designing electronic communication systems, and below we supplement the dominant model for each with an alternative that we believe necessary for creating more effective designs.

Supplementing a Conduit Model of Communications With a Language Games Model

In considering how electronic communication can be designed to support knowledge work in organizations, two models of language and communication are important to consider. One is the conduit model inspired by the work of Shannon and Weaver (1949), which we see as the dominant model in management literature; the other is the language game model of Wittgenstein (1974). Each of these theoretical orientations is useful for thinking about language and communication in an organization when it is viewed as an open system of communities of knowing. Each is good for certain purposes, but not for all, and we will employ them for different needs in our analysis.

The conduit model is the most familiar in organizational studies and portrays communication as a message-sending and message-receiving process through a transmission channel with a limited channel capacity. A conduit model suggests that communication can be improved by reducing noise in the channel, with noise defined as the possibility for error contaminating the message on its route from sender to receiver. Noise can be reduced by increasing the channel capacity, by refining the procedures for encoding and decoding messages, by providing more reliable data storage and retrieval facilities, or by making the channel of communication more universally available. A central limitation of the conduit model is its unproblematic treatment of a message (Redding 1972, Reddy 1979) in which the symbolic or interpretive character of messages in language is not considered. The encoding and decoding activities are treated as discrete selections of messages from a predefined set and the problem of human meaning in language is avoided. In management studies we see this model being used in organization design (Allen 1986, Galbraith 1973, Tushman 1978) as well as in research and development and innovation (Allen and Cohen 1969, Allen et al. 1980, Davis and Wilkof 1988). Attempts to expand the conduit model to address ambiguity in language can be seen in studies of media richness (Daft and Lengel 1984) and the interpretation of noise (Ciborra et al. 1984), but they remain within a message-transmitting framework.

As an alternative model we will consider Wittgenstein's image of language and communication as games in forms of life (Astley and Zammuto 1992, Wittgenstein 1974). His image of communication appreciates language as fundamentally and inexorably embedded in the situated action of our immediate communities, or our "forms of life." Action in our immediate communities is the locus for language development and use. Conversations and activity in our forms of life are language games, and through our language games we create the meaning of particular words and forms of speech, and we continuously evolve new ways of talking and acting together.

Wittgenstein spent the first part of his life trying to define the essence of language, searching for a stable, ideal meaning for words and sentences, and the principles of logic that could be relied on to provide unambiguous and coherent knowledge (Wittgenstein 1961). He later rejected the notion of an ideal language in which words pictured objects, and meaning was uniquely identifiable and stable. Instead, he came to see how language cannot be understood apart from its rootedness in life experience, nor can words stand apart from situated use with unambiguous meaning. Language games in forms of life are the basis for all we know. Through action within communities of knowing we make and remake both our language and our knowledge. Unlike the conduit model, in a language game there is no fixed set of messages or meanings from which to choose in communicating:

> 23. But how many kinds of sentences are there? . . . There are *countless kinds*: countless different kinds of use of what we call "symbols," "words," "sentences." And this multiplicity is not something fixed, given once for all; but new types of language, new language-games, as we may say, come into existence, and others become obsolete and become forgotten.
>
> Here the "language game" is meant to bring into prominence the fact that the *speaking* of language is part of an activity, or a form of life. (Wittgenstein 1974, p. 11)

Supplementing an Information Processing Mode of Cognition With a Narrative Mode of Cognition

Bruner (1986, 1990) has proposed that we recognize there are at least two distinct modes of cognition, the information processing (or paradigmatic) mode and the narrative mode. We believe that explicitly recognizing the narrative mode of cognition is important for understanding how perspective making and perspective taking occur. The dominant way of understanding cognition today is to emphasize its paradigmatic mode, as reflected in information processing models of cognition (Simon 1977). Bruner (1986, 1990) has proposed that this information processing view of cognition, emphasizing the rational analysis of data in a mental problem space and the construction of deductive arguments, be supplemented by recognizing that humans also have a narrative cognitive capacity. We narrativize our experience almost continually as we recognize unusual or unexpected events (the noncanonical) and construct stories which make sense of them (restore canonicality). Bruner argues persuasively that the narrative capability of humans is a fundamental cognitive process through which our cultural world and sense of self are constructed and maintained over time.

Good arguments and good stories are equally important for understanding human cognition in knowledge work, but the two modes are judged by different criteria. Whereas an argument is judged to be good if it is logical, coherent, consistent, and noncontradictory, a narrative is judged to be good if it is interesting, plausible, and believable. An argument proves something about the world to be true, but a narrative shows how events or features in the world are sensible and fit within our shared cultural field. It is well recognized that surfacing and challenging the often implicit assumptions that underlie a paradigmatic argument is an important element for innovative knowledge work. Narrative serves an important role in this regard. By bringing the apparently noncanonical into relief alongside the canonical, the narrative mode of cognition provides access to the implicit assumptions and interpretive structures that characterize a community of knowing. We will give an example of such an analysis later in the chapter, when we describe some of the electronic communication systems we envision.

There are several points of similarity in the underlying assumptions of these models of communication and cognition, particularly between the conduit and paradigmatic, and between the language game and narrative (see Table 10.1). Both the conduit model of communication and the paradigmatic mode of cognition are based on information processing images in which words point at things, meanings are not problematic, and the power of deductive logic is emphasized. Similarly, both the language game model of communication and the narrative mode of cognition are based on social constructionist images in which words gain sense only through actual use in a community, meanings are symbolic and inherently ambiguous, and the power of social processes, storytelling, and conversation is emphasized. In spite of this family resemblance among the models of communication and cognition being drawn upon, they will not be combined. Whereas the language games model is philosophical and proposed as a more accurate depiction of human language and communication, the conduit model is technical and proposed as the necessary requirements for a communication system. One focuses on human language, the other focuses on communication technology. The narrative and paradigmatic modes of cognition, on the other hand, are meant by Bruner (1990) as complementary functions of the same whole, each being capacities of the human being. We will not collapse them, and will treat all four as having a separate tradition and use. We will employ each to serve different purposes in understanding the processes of perspective making and perspective taking among communities of knowing.

TABLE 10.1

Key assumptions behind conduit model of communication and paradigmatic mode of cognition
* There is underlying objective knowledge in the world that has universal applicability.
* Language can be a medium for representing objective knowledge and words have fixed meaning.
* Human beings can achieve universality of understanding since fixed meanings of words can be communicated objectively from one person to another.
* Realization of objective knowledge is a rational process. Knowledge evolves and progresses through the systematic application of logic and principles of the scientific method.

Key assumptions behind language games model of communication and narrative mode of cognition
* Knowledge as well as methods for realizing knowledge are objective only to the extent they are ratified as objective by a specific community's interpretive conventions.
* Words can have consensus of meaning only within a specific community of knowing. However, even within a unique community, the meanings of words change and are never fixed in time or space.
* Language is not a medium for representing our thoughts and objective underlying knowledge but language is thought and knowledge. The limits of our language are the limits of our knowledge since we can explain the world only through language and narrative forms.
* Knowledge evolves by inventing new language and narrative forms. Renarrativizing the familiar or coming up with narratives that explain the unfamiliar is the primary activity by which new knowledge comes about.

We will now look to science for insights on how communities of knowing develop and change through communication. We will then draw implications for designing electronic communication systems for knowledge work in organizations and also consider how multiple communities of knowing interact.

SCIENCE AS KNOWLEDGE WORK
IN COMMUNITIES OF KNOWING

Considering science as organized knowledge work has many insights to offer for understanding perspective making and perspective taking in knowledge-intensive firms and for speculating on how electronic communication can be designed to support knowledge work in lateral organizational forms. A central source for these insights is provided by Thomas Kuhn (1970) as he describes the historical process of scientific work. Readers are no doubt familiar with Kuhn's argument of how normal science within paradigms leads to crisis and revolution. For Kuhn, a paradigm is a shared sense of what the metaphysical nature of the world is, what problems are important, and what serve as good exemplars for a domain of concern.

There are many difficulties with Kuhn's notion of paradigm. It is often taken to be totalizing, unitary, and almost religiously held. As Masterman (1970) has noted, Kuhn (1962) used the term paradigm in many different ways in the first edition of *The Structure of Scientific Revolutions*. In the revised edition Kuhn (1970) acknowledged the concept's ambiguity and added further refinements, but debates about just how a paradigm is to be defined or isolated for further study in its own right will not concern us here. We believe his basic insight is valid and is in keeping with Polanyi's (1967) idea of "tacit knowledge," Boulding's (1956) discussion of "the image," Pepper's (1942) notion of "world hypotheses," and numerous others who point out that perception is only accomplished through a perspective (Bartunek 1984, Burrell and Morgan 1979).

Kuhn's (1970) insights are particularly relevant for understanding how knowledge is produced in a community of knowing by refining and clarifying the perspective of the community. Development of knowledge in a community is a process of posing and solving puzzles, thereby elaborating and refining the vocabulary, instruments, and theories that embody the perspective. Agreement that knowledge is progressing is agreement that the perspective is strengthening. Unexpected events or findings can only be recognized as such from within a perspective. Without a strong perspective the community cannot tell an anomaly from noise; a challenge to their knowledge from an irrelevancy.

Collins (1983) makes some interesting observations on the dynamics of knowledge development and the different kinds of competence required of the scientist. Working within a perspective has well-established methods for externalizing its objects, and the scientist should be competent in those respects. Collins terms this "native competence." It is the kind of competence that makes meanings, perceptions, and acts of the native member follow naturally as a matter of course. However, changing or overturning the taken-for-granted rules or replacing them with a completely new set requires "interpretive competence" on the part of the scientists. It lies in perspective taking: being able to reflect on and renarrativize the familiar to open up new insights and understandings.

The stronger and more well developed a community's perspective is, the more useful a conduit model of communication and feedback becomes. As theories, puzzles, measures, and accepted results are clarified and institutionalized within the community, the more likely it is that messages can be thought of as selections from a predefined set. The process by which new communities of knowing begin to form, however, and the processes of questioning and changing perspectives are not as well handled by a conduit model. Work that questions a perspective is of a different logic type than work within a perspective and is primarily controlled by the dynamics of change in an open system rather than simple feedback (Bateson 1972, von Bertalanffy 1968, Wiener 1954). For this second-order knowledge work, the language games communication model is more helpful than the conduit model. Previously accepted understandings, measurements, and logics are in a sense "up for grabs." The perspectives behind ways of knowing of the organizational communities are being made in real time by the communities' members. The language of their communication is changing as their practices in forms of life are changing. Messages cannot be separated from the evolving context of making and using them as in the conduit model.

Two final themes from Kuhn that we will consider before drawing implications for knowledge work in organizations are the incommensurability between perspectives and the emergence of new perspectives. If members of a community create a strong perspective and do distinctive and important knowledge work, it will of necessity approach becoming incommensurable with other perspectives. They may use the same words as other communities of knowing, but they will use them to see things in different ways (Knorr-Cetina 1981). They will look at the same phenomena as another community, but will see different problems, different opportunities, and different challenges (Czarniawska-Joerges 1992). As Kuhn puts it, they will live in a different world from those in other communities of knowing. Data important to one are irrelevant to another or are used for entirely different purposes. Arguments that persuade convincingly in one community of knowing have little or no weight in another. And the more developed and refined the community of knowing becomes, with an increasingly elaborate and detailed perspective, the more nearly incommensurable it becomes with others (Brown and Duguid 1991, Dougherty 1992, Fleck 1979). If the members' language games within one community of knowing fully understood and appreciated the positions of another, they would not be different communities and would not be doing distinct knowledge work.

Knorr-Cetina (1981) presents some grounded examples of how local communities of knowing develop their unique paradigmatic worlds and are resistant to changing them. In her sociological study of different research units, she found that research laboratories developed local interpretations of methodical rules, or a local know-how with regard to how to make things work best in actual research practice. Criteria for what mattered and what did not matter were neither fully defined nor standardized throughout the research community. Nor were the rules of official science exempt from local interpretations. Many important selections of the research process were locally driven, including questions of ingredients, instrumentation, and duration of experiments.

Implications of Kuhn and Knowledge Work in
Science for Understanding Knowledge-Intensive Firms

A first implication of Kuhn for thinking about knowledge-intensive firms is that the primary unit of analysis should be the community of knowing. The individual does not think in isolation and is not an autonomous origin of knowledge. A community of knowing is a language game and neither the language nor the knowledge created within it comes from the actor alone.

Second, a community of knowing requires perspective making in order to do knowledge work. Without a strong perspective it cannot produce important knowledge. A community's perspective develops by refining its vocabulary, its methods, its theories and values, and its accepted logics through language and action within the community of knowing. This means that the community must, of necessity, have a space for conversation and action isolated from the larger organization.

Third, the ability of one community of knowing to work jointly with another requires an ability to overcome the degree of incommensurability between them. This, of course, must be done without sacrificing the integrity and distinctiveness of their own perspective. Below we will explore this process of perspective taking in which the perspective of another can be taken into account as part of a community's way of knowing.

Fourth, the conditions for change in the perspective of a way of knowing come from both the inside and the outside. Inside the perspective, conditions of change come from the accumulation of anomalies as it is tested and elaborated. From outside the perspective, pressure for change comes from adherents drawn to a promise of the aesthetics, power, or excitement of a new perspective. This suggests that memories of errors and anomalies are important to maintain and review openly, and that the isolation of communities necessary for their development should be punctuated by periods of interaction between communities.

Finally, new perspectives need to be nurtured and given protection from strong demands for performance. Of necessity, they will not be able to compete with an established perspective in another community's way of knowing.

For a knowledge-intensive firm, then, we look to its ecology of communities of knowing to understand its possibilities for doing knowledge work. Electronic communication can mediate how the open system of communities emerge, develop, elaborate, suffer crisis, and transform within it. Electronic communication can also mediate how communities of knowing interact and their capacity for perspective taking. It is to these processes of perspective making and perspective taking that we now turn.

PERSPECTIVE MAKING AND PERSPECTIVE
TAKING IN COMMUNITIES OF KNOWING

The Process of Perspective Making

Perspective making is the process whereby a community of knowing develops and strengthens its own knowledge domain and practices. As a perspective strengthens, it complexifies and becomes better able to do knowledge work. Complexification is achieved cognitively through the use of paradigmatic analysis within a narrative framing of experience. It is a process of developing finer language games and, from a paradigmatic standpoint, more precise causal laws. Complexification signifies a movement from a global, undifferentiated naming to a more precise explication of constructs, where more coherent meaning structures are developed than preceding ones (Waddington 1957, Werner 1957). Knorr-Cetina (1981) proposed that scientific conceptual systems have to progressively complexify themselves over a period of time to successfully solve scientific problems. This implies the ability to respond to shifts and fluctuations in the novelty of the scientific problem domain by modeling the shifts themselves (Rubinstein et al. 1984).

A good example of complexification in perspective making is presented by Bradshaw (1992) in his analysis of the Wright brothers' invention of the airplane. He also illustrates the interweaving of narrative framing and paradigmatic analysis in the perspective-making process. Bradshaw asks why the Wright brothers were so successful in conquering the challenge of manned flight, while many of their competitors with better training and resources failed? He answers that first, the Wright brothers narratively framed the phenomenon of flying using a different metaphor than their competitors, and second, they employed finer problem-solving procedures. Whereas their competitors narrated flight with a "chauffeurs of the air" metaphor, telling how flying was akin to driving a car into the air, a group that included the Wright brothers narrated flight as being like "flying a kite." Many of the unsuccessful inventors had a propensity to construct complete aircrafts and then to test them by measuring distance and time in flight. To these designers, the airplane as a vehicle to be chauffeured was an assemblage of parts (wings, fuselage, propulsion, etc.) and developing an aircraft meant exploring possible designs for configuring these parts.

However, for the Wright brothers, the major concern was to understand how a kite flew and to achieve its functions (lateral control, sufficient lift, reduced drag, etc.) in the airplane. They first isolated these functional problems and then proceeded to solve them one at a time. The pattern in their work was to explore solutions to subproblems using directed experiments.

For example, a kite was built to explore lateral control and wind tunnel experiments explored lift and thrust. Through extensive testing of models, the Wright brothers "discovered an important error in aerodynamics overlooked by other investigators" (Bradshaw 1992, pp. 246-247). Only when each separate problem was understood and solved did the Wright brothers invest time and energy in building a new craft. The Wright brothers employed both narrative and paradigmatic modes of cognition in their perspective making, as they modeled and developed more complex and finer understandings of the workings of aerodynamic laws. In contrast, their competitors were exploring the possibility of flight with minimal understandings of aerodynamic laws and relied on trial and error, hoping one of their models would fly, without having any conception of why. They lacked the strong perspective necessary to do important knowledge work.

The Importance of Narrative in Perspective Making

Perspective making within communities of knowing is a social practice in a form of life. For insight into how this process takes place in a community of knowing, we will return to Jerome Bruner's work on the role of narrative in constructing knowledge of self and world (Bruner 1986, 1990). Bruner argues that we must look to how actors make meaning of their experience through narrative if we are to understand the process of perspective making. Bruner, synthesizing studies of child development, language acquisition, and concept formation, proposes an innate narrative capacity as the engine for our cognitive activity. "The typical form of framing experience (and our memory of it) is in narrative form. What does not get structured narratively is lost in memory" (Bruner 1990, p. 56). Paradigmatic thinking is an important part of our cognitive repertoire, but only a part. Narrativizing our reflexive monitoring and rationalization of conduct is not ruled by an abstracted logic. Within a community of knowing, a narrative explanation works not only because it is logically acceptable but also because it is life-like and plausible; it fits the culturally bound demands of a form of life.

In parallel with Giddens' structuration theory (Giddens 1976), Bruner emphasizes that when we narrativize experience, we also construct and validate the self. The narrator's perspective as an essential element in any story assures this. The self is always at stake in the individual's narrativizing of experience because the self is at least the narrator (recognizing the canonical, indicating and explaining the anticanonical, determining how the world should be) and often part of the story (being herself delineated as a causal agent with motives, intentions, and values).

The importance of narrative has not gone unnoticed in organizational research. Clark (1972) explored the importance of sagas and Mitroff and

Kilmann (1976) recognized the importance of myth. Myth and saga are important, but they can distract our attention from the way that human cognition operates almost continuously in a narrative, storytelling mode. We wish to emphasize that narrative is fully equal to paradigmatic analysis in the construction, maintenance, and change of perspectives in an organization. We see them in a type of figure-ground relation in which paradigmatic, rational-analytic thought takes place in a context provided by narrative, and narratives are constructed against a backdrop of paradigmatic understandings in a kind of "genuine union" of the two modes (Boland and Pondy 1983). The rational analytic elements of a perspective in a community of knowing are a product of storytelling as much as they are a medium for it.

The role of stories and storytelling in the day-to-day functioning of organizations has been addressed by Boje (1991). The constructive, changing quality of stories documented by Boje in his focus on situated practice is a major step toward the position we argue for here. He moves beyond the mythic view of the story as an "object," found in Martin and Meyerson (1988), McConkie and Boss (1986), and Gabriel (1991), and turns our attention to the community-dependent process of producing the story.

When scientists experience anomalies within a perspective they often turn to narrative in an attempt to make sense of the noncanonical observation. Science, and scientific papers documenting experiments and theories, in retrospect, always seem paradigmatic, linear, and certain. This is partly dictated by the social conventions of what good science is (Knorr-Cetina 1981). However, an examination of the informal discourse of scientists presents another picture altogether. Highly variable and inconsistent accounts of action and belief are very much the norm. Actors continually construct and reconstruct the meaning of their scientific world through the formulation of divergent narrative accounts. As Mulkay et al. (1983) summarize,

> Unless we understand how actors socially construct their accounts of action and how actors constitute the character of their actions primarily through the use of language, we will continue to fail . . . to furnish satisfactory answers to the long-standing questions about the nature of action and belief in science. (pp. 195-196)

Others such as Nersessian (1992) and Eysenck and Keane (1990) have also pointed out the important role of narrative in scientific reasoning. Thought experiments are a prevalent form of scientific reasoning in which the scientist imagines a sequence of events and then narrativizes the sequence in order to communicate the experiment to others. Einstein is supposed to have performed thought experiments based on stories about riding on a light beam and traveling in elevators. Rutherford in his investigations of the structure of the atom is reputed to have imagined the electrons as revolving around the nucleus in the same way as planets revolve around the sun (Gentner 1983). Galileo (Gallilei 1638; cited in Nersessian 1992) likewise used a thought experiment in arguing against the Aristotelian theory that heavier bodies fall faster than lighter ones.

The Process of Perspective Taking

In knowledge-intensive firms, competitive advantage and product success are a result of collaboration in which diverse individuals are able to appreciate and synergistically utilize their distinctive knowledge through a process of perspective taking (Brown 1991, Dougherty 1992, Henderson 1994, Nonaka 1994, Purser et al. 1992). Duncan and Weiss (1979, p. 86) summarize this process as one in which "the overall organizational knowledge base emerges out of the process of exchange, evaluation, and integration of knowledge. Like any other organizational process . . . [i]t is comprised of the interactions of individuals and not their isolated behavior." It requires a process of mutual perspective taking where distinctive individual knowledge is exchanged, evaluated, and integrated with that of others in the organization (Nonaka and Johansson 1985, Shrivastava 1983).

Much of social behavior is predicated upon assumptions an actor makes about the knowledge, beliefs, and motives of others. This is the beginning of the process of perspective taking and is fundamental to communications. In any communication, the knowing of what others know is a necessary component for coordinated action to take place (Bakhtin 1981, Clark 1985, Krauss and Fussell 1991). As Brown (1981) observed, effective communicating requires that the point of view of the other be realistically imagined. Others such as Rommetveit have affirmed this point: "An essential component of communicative competence in a pluralistic social world . . . is our capacity to adopt the perspective of different others" (Rommetveit 1980, p. 126). The fundamental importance of taking the other's point of view into account is seen in Mead (1934) who referred to it as taking the attitude of the other and equated our ability to be fully human with our ability to maintain an inner conversion with a generalized other.

In order for perspective taking to proceed, the diverse knowledge held by individuals in the organization must be presented in its uniqueness and made available for others to incorporate in a perspective-taking process. Valuing diversity of knowledge by enabling each type of expertise to make unique representations of their understandings, and assisting actors with different expertise to better recognize and accept the different ways of knowing of others, is the foundation for perspective taking. It can be encouraged by communication systems that include an emphasis on supporting the distinctive needs of separate communities of knowing.

The task of taking each other's knowledge and background into account is a complex process and can frequently break down. For example, Purser et al. (1992) did a comparative study of two knowledge-intensive product development projects of equal technical complexity in a high-technology firm. One project succeeded while the other failed. Two essential factors accounted for the differences in results between the two projects. The first was a higher incidence of barriers to knowledge sharing among the members on the failed project team. But behind this first factor was a second, causal factor of failed perspective taking. Team members were unable to surface and reconcile dissimilarities in their knowledge and cognitive frames of reference. Failure to achieve perspective taking through depicting and exchanging representations of their unique understanding dramatically reduced their possibilities for successful team knowledge work.

Perspective taking involves a variety of inferential and judgmental processes. Individuals may utilize an assortment of techniques including stereotypes and inference heuristics to estimate what others know. Such heuristics can induce systematic errors and biases (Kahneman et al. 1982, Nisbett and Ross 1980). The ready availability of the actor's own perspective may lead the actor to overestimate the likelihood that the perspective will be shared by others (Steedman and Johnson-Laird 1980). This false consensus effect, in which subjects assume that others are more similar to themselves than is actually the case (Ross et al. 1977), is a form of bias particularly relevant to the perspective-taking process. This heuristic leads to overestimates of the extent to which a person's knowledge is shared by others, and studies support the existence of such a bias (Dougherty 1992, Krauss and Fussell 1991).

Dougherty (1992) provides an insightful analysis of breakdowns in the perspective-taking process due to actors' inability to surface and examine their differing interpretive schemes. She found that in unsuccessful cases of new product development, the key players interpreted and understood issues around technology-market linking and new products in qualitatively different ways from each other and were not able to reconcile these differences. The differences in interpretation centered around three themes. The first theme was what people see when they look into the future, including which issues are seen as most uncertain. What they saw seemed uncertain, while what they did not see, did not seem particularly uncertain or even noteworthy. The business planner worried about positioning against competition while the field person worried about identifying the right potential customers. A second theme characteristic of failed teams involved people's understanding of the development process itself. People not only ignored the activities of others and failed to argue over relative priorities, they glossed over the concerns of others, and tended not to appreciate their complexities. A third theme characteristic of failed teams involved the different "thought worlds" of team members. For new product development, different departmental thought worlds were coherent and consistent within themselves. This reduced the possibility for creative perspective taking since members of a department thought that they already knew everything (Dougherty 1992). As lucidly worded by Dougherty (1992),

> Nor is the problem like the proverbial set of blind men touching a different part of an elephant. It is more like the tales of eye witnesses at an accident, or of individuals in a troubled relationship—each tells us a complete story, but tells a different one. (p. 191)

In summary then, the problem of integration of knowledge in knowledge-intensive firms is not a problem of simply combining, sharing, or making data commonly available. It is a problem of perspective taking in which the unique thought worlds of different communities of knowing are made visible and accessible to others. Making explicit representations of one's knowledge and understandings to exchange with others enables one to better appreciate the distinct ways of knowing that those others will attempt to communicate. In order to integrate knowledge through perspective taking, communication systems must first support diversity of knowledge through the differentiation provided by perspective making within communities of knowing. Only after a perspective is differentiated and strengthened can it be reflected upon and represented so the actors in other communities of knowing have something to integrate through a perspective-taking communication.

IMPLICATIONS FOR ELECTRONIC
COMMUNICATION SYSTEMS AND POLICIES

The design of electronic communication systems affects how organization members are able to engage in perspective making and perspective taking and thus build communities of knowing. In knowledge-intensive firms, the problem of designing systems and policies for electronic communication is a problem of providing an environment in which an ecology of communities of knowing can develop through complexification over time. In perspective making, a community of knowing complexifies by enriching and refining its distinct perspective and way of knowing. Its categories for partitioning the world become more numerous and subtle; the distinctions it makes as to the appropriateness of problem statements, measures, tests, and logics for a given situation become more esoteric and precise. In perspective taking, complexification involves an increased capacity for communities of knowing to take each other into account within their own language games and to construct new language games for their interaction. The development of complexified perspective taking represents the integrative capacity of the ecology of communities.

These two dynamics, perspective making and perspective taking, are instantiated only through speaking and acting in a community. Electronic communication media provide an important part of the physical and symbolic environment available for engaging in the forms of life of the organization's communities of knowing, but only a part. Other concerns such as task, technology, structure, culture, reward systems, and leadership style all play a role in mediating the type of language games that will emerge. Although the entire set of these issues is beyond the scope of this chapter we will discuss some of the issues further in the next section when we describe some examples of communication systems that would support these processes. Here, we will concern ourselves with presenting a certain sensibility as a way of thinking about how electronic communication media provide conditions for the two dynamics of perspective making and perspective taking.

A first element in the sensibility we propose is to recognize the strengths and weaknesses of the models of communication and cognition we are drawing upon in designing these systems. The conduit model, with its assumption of messages that carry unambiguous meaning if they are coded and decoded error free, is a good model for thinking about the communication of well-established elements in a community of knowing's vocabulary and methods of practice. Communication within established community routines can and should be addressed with a conduit model. The knowledge is semifixed and reliably interpretable within the community, so the assumptions of a conduit model match the communication needs well. The organizationwide community where culture and identity are acted out and a sense of institution is developed is also well suited to a conduit model. It is appropriate for questions of broadcast bandwidth and for development of a firmwide vocabulary. Research in corporate strategy emphasizing the importance of shared interpretive schemes (Bartunek 1984, Ranson et al. 1980), common visions (Bennis and Nanus 1985, Collins and Porras 1991), or shared strategic image (Bertado 1990, Hamel and Prahalad 1991) are examples of this type of communication at the level of the organization as a whole.

The symbolic quality of this culture-building communication, with its reliance on evocative images rather than precise language, is somewhat at odds with the conduit model but can generally be adequately handled by redundancy or repetition. The conduit model can support activities that broadcast and reinforce important symbols, stories, and exemplars which become commonly available to members of the community as a whole and incorporated in their language games. Very little in the way of distinctive, organizational knowledge work is accomplished at the cultural level of the community as a whole. It is better thought of as a backdrop against which the more esoteric language games of more locally situated forms of life are played out.

The conduit model, however, does have some distinct weaknesses. The perspective-making process requires a nurturing of emergent communities of knowing, and requires a respect for the uniqueness of a local community's distinctive form of life. The conduit model stands in opposition to this requirement with its emphasis on developing data models, decision models, and communication formats that are common and shared across the organization. Current research in information technology often reflects this inappropriate use of the conduit model with its emphasis on enterprise modeling and data architecture with a single, unified data structure (Chen 1976, Deng and Chaudhry 1992, Richardson et al. 1990, Scheer 1992, Targowski 1988). Similarly, model management systems concern themselves with unifying the diversity of knowledge in management decision models through a variety of meta-level integrative techniques (Dolk 1988, Elam and Konsynski 1987, Geoffrion 1987). Finally, it seems that a principal concern with end-user computing is the reduction of diversity and the establishment of standards and common structures for data and models (Brown and Bostrom 1989, Munro et al. 1987, Rivard and Huff 1988). We disagree with these calls for commonality in vocabulary and knowledge practices, and call instead for recognizing the importance of strong perspective making and differentiation of knowledge among a firm's communities of knowing.

Electronic media based on the wrong model of communication can hinder perspective making and taking in interactions among communities of knowing. An example from research on new product development processes will illustrate the point. The task for this new product development team was to choose a nonhuman analog such as a rat, rabbit, or primate model with which to conduct tests of a new drug compound they were developing for certain afflictions associated with the human intestine. The team had members representing different disciplines such as life sciences, chemistry, toxicology, and biopharmaceutics. There were differences of opinion as to the nonhuman analog most appropriate for the task. As a result, the team members resorted to a popular groupware product and its voting system to reach a consensus. Based on the voting procedure, a rat analog was chosen. Unfortunately, the rat was not suitable for the task of representing the human intestine, but the team only found that out at the human clinical trials. The poor choice had by then cost the company considerable expense and 3 years of development time. The groupware voting system, with its emphasis on finding consensus, hampered the team members from first strengthening and representing their own perspective and then engaging in a dialogue of perspective taking with each other. The groupware helped reduce noise in the communication and provided an illusion of certainty. What was required, however, was a language games model of communication to complexify the unique understanding of each through dialogue within their community of knowing. Then, they should have employed a technology that would support reflexivity and creation of a visible representation of their unique knowledge that would have enabled perspective taking among them.

The language games model also has its strengths and weaknesses. One strength is helping us think through issues of perspective making with its insistence on the primacy of speaking and acting in a local community. Electronic communication media may reduce bounds of space and time for such communities (Giddens 1991), but the language games model can help us to recover the importance of enabling and protecting local logics, practices, and vocabularies (Jönsson 1992), even within dispersed communities. The language games model is also useful for emphasizing the need for isolation to create identity in a community of knowing. Time for participating in communities is limited, and identified spaces for members to engage the community's language games and develop its perspective is an important condition for its persistence and development.

Schön (1979) provides a vivid example of the need to respect the importance of communication in local communities from the history of town planning. When town planners saw their task as a need to cure a blighted area, they intervened with all manner of planned renewals to tear down and remake whole sections of a city, often disturbing the patterns of communication within neighborhoods. But their efforts went terribly wrong, again and again, until they came to see such areas of town not as blighted, but as folk communities with a strong network of communication and support that sustained them quite well in the face of substantial difficulty. The problem for the town planners then became how to design systems and policies that would enable that emergent capacity of the local communities of knowing to strengthen and self-organize. We hope to build such an awareness into our approach to thinking about electronic communication from the start.

The language games model is also a good basis for thinking about narrative in a community of knowing. It emphasizes that narrative is experientially grounded and that it is a search for ways to make issues and events of interest to the community sensible within its way of knowing. The causal implications and action sequences in narrative are the source of perspective making for the community, as members reflect on the underlying logics, values, and identities of the community of knowing.

A major limitation of the language games model is the "epistemic inhibitions of its own paradigm" (Rubinstein et al. 1984). The stronger a community of knowing is supported by communication systems reflecting a language game model of communication, the stronger is perspective-making complexities, and the less able it may become to allow for other ways of seeing. A vivid example of this dynamic is presented in Dougherty's (1992) field study. The various functions involved in the product development process agreed on the need for the product to be market oriented. However, in the language games of the research and development group, market orientation meant product specifications and technical features: The market is what the product can do. For the manufacturing people, on the other hand, a market-oriented product was a durable and reliable one. Lowering the number of features and specifications would improve its market orientation. Furthermore, the marketing group considered customer needs on a customer by customer approach. For the planning group, to be market oriented meant to position the product in the right market niche. They did not worry about product features, customer needs, or reliable product performance. This is where the reward systems and culture of the organization become important in maintaining a balance between perspective making and perspective taking. One important design element in this regard is the establishment of an issue-specific space for perspective taking between strong communities of knowing to take place. Isaacs (1993) refers to this space as a container for dialogue, and we will think of it as a forum within an electronic communication system.

As we have seen, both models have strengths and weaknesses that primarily relate to their role in perspective making, but both models alone have distinct weaknesses with respect to perspective taking (see Table 10.2). The conduit model, with its emphasis on a commonly available and exhaustive set of messages and coding techniques, denies the importance of perspective taking. A common vocabulary and set of decision models presumes that each member of the organization participates in the same way of knowing and needs no special support for opening a space within the dialogue of their own local community for taking the perspective of another. The language game model, as we have just seen, also does not help in thinking about perspective taking because of its emphasis on speaking and acting within a form of life and its increasingly specialized language games. Another aspect of communication must be considered for thinking about perspective taking, one that is absent or overlooked in the conduit and language games models. This aspect concerns how the richness of representations and the reflexive capacity of a communication system enables the creation and exchange of boundary objects (Star 1989, 1993), which we will discuss in the next section.

TABLE 10.2 Two Models of Communication and Their Relative Merits for Supporting Electronic Media in Systems of Knowledge Work

Conduit model

Strengths

  * Reliable and precise channel for communicating well-established elements in the vocabulary of a community of knowing and techniques of practice.
  * Can facilitate culture building, organizationwide integration activities through shared and common images.

Weaknesses

  * Does not value diversity; emphasis on uniform data and decision models and communication format across the organization can hamper the emergence of unique communities of knowing.
  * Inappropriate for supporting the narrative forms of cognition that are central to the perspective-making process.
  * Common vocabulary and set of decision models denies the importance of perspective taking.

Language game model

Strengths

  * Facilitates perspective making by virtue of its insistence on primacy of speaking and action in a community of knowing.
  * Underscores the importance of enabling and protecting local logics, local practices, and local vocabularies.
  * Implicates the importance of narrative in a community of knowing.
  * Emphasis on narratives enables reflection on underlying logics, values, and identities of the community of knowing.

Weaknesses

  * Increasingly specialized language games results in epistemic inhibitions (imposed by each community's unique paradigm) and comes in the way of perspective taking.
  * May heighten conflict among communities.

REFLEXIVITY, BOUNDARY OBJECTS, AND PERSPECTIVE TAKING

In our discussion of perspective making in communities of knowing, we saw the individual speaking and acting within the community's form of life. For perspective taking we need a shift in emphasis, to focus on the individual's ability to make his or her own understanding visible for self-reflection. Once a visible representation of an individual's knowledge is made available for analysis and communication, it becomes a boundary object and provides a basis for perspective taking.

Representations of ways of knowing from members in one community can then be exchanged with members of another, who, having themselves engaged in an effort to make rich representations of their understandings, can now engage in communication about the perspectives of another. This taking of the other into account, in light of a reflexive knowledge of one's own perspective, is the perspective-taking process.

Perspective taking is never a one-to-one mapping of meanings. Members of the same community of knowing will not have full consensus, and members of different communities cannot simply adopt the meanings of another. But as Star (1989, 1993) has observed, scientists within and between communities do find a way of bringing their distinctive perspectives into dialogue through the construction and discussion of boundary objects. An indexed collection of items, a map, an idealized image, or a label can all serve as boundary objects around which sense making can take place. Such boundary objects do not convey unambiguous meaning, but have instead a kind of symbolic adequacy that enables conversation without enforcing commonly shared meanings. Boundary objects can, of course, be a center of intense conflict as easily as one of cooperative effort. Creating and reshaping boundary objects is an exercise of power that can be collaborative or unilateral. Nonetheless, in the absence of boundary objects, the possibility of perspective taking is limited and the opportunity for knowledge work in the firm is reduced.

Reflection on our own perspectives is difficult and often not attempted. As Rubinstein et al. comment, "If practicing scientists were more conscious of the processes of science, it would go a long way toward circumventing the epistemological inhibitions imposed by paradigms" (1984, p. 138). Collins (1983) also notes the hidden nature of such processes. He argues that many times it is only when the rules go wrong that the scientist questions the nature of his or her interpretation. "Otherwise, our giving of meaning to objects—our interpretive practices are so automatic that we do not notice that any interpretation is involved" (Collins 1983, p. 90). In Schutz's (1964) terms, reflexivity is the ability to periodically suspend our natural attitude and notice the matter-of-course, taken-for-granted ways in which our communities of knowing are constructed and interpreted, which can open possibilities to change them (Collins 1983). Rubinstein et al. (1984) posit that becoming aware of, evaluating, and modifying perspectives is required for maintaining adaptive knowledge. There are many possible forms for boundary objects that can represent knowledge from one community for perspective taking by another, including physical models, spreadsheets, or diagrams. We will present two examples that could be incorporated in communication systems: cognitive maps (Axelrod 1976, Boland et al. 1994, Eden 1992, Huff 1990, Weick 1990, Weick and Bougon 1986) and narrative structures (Knorr-Cetina 1981, Mulkay et al. 1983, Tenkasi and Boland 1993).

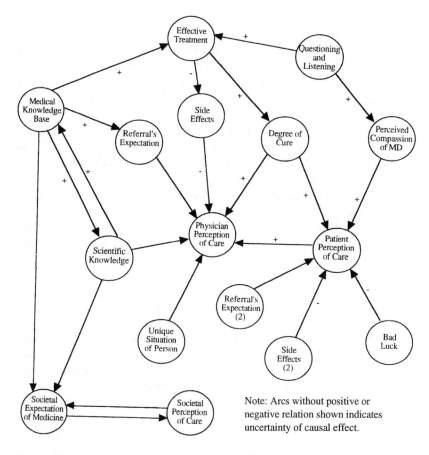

Figure 10.1. A Physician's Map of Quality in Medical Care

A cognitive map is a directed graph whose nodes represent concepts or factors in the actor's decision domain, and whose arcs represent cause-and-effect relationships between source and destination nodes (Boland et al. 1992, Burgess et al. 1992). Figure 10.1 presents an example of a cause map depicting a physician's understanding of quality in medical care. Creating this map is an exercise in perspective making, and exchanging it with actors from other communities of knowing within the hospital makes it a boundary object and opens the possibility for perspective taking in the search for quality in medical care. Building such a map can be evocative for the map creator as well as informative to its recipient. Creating cognitive maps can reveal personal cause-and-effect logic, which in turn forces the individual to confront the reasonableness and validity of previously tacit cause-effect assumptions (Fiol and Huff 1992, Weick and Bougon 1986). Creating maps of one's understanding of a problem domain and reflecting on them can also facilitate new and more complex understandings of the situation at hand, improving the chances for scientific success (Weick 1990).

Cognitive maps are a good beginning for making rich representations of an understanding within a perspective. But a key ingredient for communicative success is a way to link elements and relations in a map, as well as the map itself, to unstated elements and assumptions of the perspective. That is, the knowledge representation grows richer as context is added, layer by layer, to individual elements in the cognitive map. This suggests a hypertext or hypermedia communication environment in which actors find a self-reflective space to build rich knowledge representations whereby factors in a cause map are linked to underlying beliefs, values, or assumptions in the form of spreadsheets, notes, or graphs or other cause maps (Boland et al. 1992, 1994).

Another kind of boundary object that can serve as a focal point for perspective taking is a narrative structure. Narratives, if bracketed and approached for analysis with an interpretive stance, can also provide elements of the reflexive quality we see as necessary for perspective taking. Narrative analysis can reflexively give access to the implicit and unstated assumptions that are guiding perspective making, and in so doing help enable a perspective-taking process. We will demonstrate this by first presenting a narrative from an actual incident collected during fieldwork in a pharmaceutical company and then analyzing and interpreting its narrative structure.

THE STORY OF NORMAN, A CHEMIST

Norman stood up from his workbench in midmorning and went to the men's toilet where he used the urinal. Shortly after returning to his workbench, Norman felt a numbness in his penis. He was startled, but he immediately thought that trace amounts of the XV75 hypertension compounds he had been working with that morning had been on his hands and may just be a powerful topical anesthetic.

He told two colleagues about this potential discovery and created an informal team to explore its possibilities. After about 6 weeks, he obtained formal approval from the assistant director for this project and his team. At this stage, the idea was to go for a topical application of the compound. After several weeks, Norman went to see the assistant director to inform him of a metabolic study of the compound in a cell culture that showed some indications of toxicity. He learned from the assistant director that a market study had just been completed showing that an oral form of the drug would be very successful and highly profitable, whereas the topical version would actually have a very limited market potential.

The assistant director told Norman that the toxicity report was uncertain and that he should reorient his team toward an oral form of the compound. "Think positive," he told Norman. "We have to move on and we have to take risks if we expect to reap rewards." Market projections of the proposed oral form of the drug were presented to the executive committee of the corporation and were enthusiastically received.

Chatman (1978) presents an elaborate framework for diagramming narrative structure, and we can use some of his techniques in a simplified form to show how narrative analysis can surface assumptions and aid reflexivity in perspective making. In diagramming the structure of events in a story plot, Chatman (1978) distinguishes between major and minor events. He calls major events kernels and shows them as a square in his diagrams. Chatman refers to minor events as satellites (1978, p. 54) and shows them as circles in his diagrams. Satellites are events which enrich the story aesthetically but are not crucial to the plot. Satellite events "necessarily imply the existence of kernels, but not vice versa" (Chatman 1978, p. 54). Figure 10.2 is a partial diagram of the plot of Norman's story.

In diagramming the first part of this story, we have identified two kernels, treating the other elements as satellites. Other readers might interpret the structure differently, but that is what keeps an interpretive conversation lively. The two kernels we isolate are the trip to the toilet and the initial toxicity report. For purposes of an example, we will provide a brief analysis of the two kernels.

First Kernel: A Trip to the Toilet. From this kernel, the story could have taken several different paths. First, Norman could have simply returned to his workstation and waited for the numbness to go away. Eventually it would have and this episode would be over. Or, Norman might have become enraged that no one had warned him that the XV75 compounds could have this effect. After much finger-pointing and the establishment of stricker chemical handling policies, this story would also eventually end without a new project being instituted. Instead, Norman used the event of the numbness to engage in perspective taking, looking at XV75 and his own experience from a perspective other than that of hypertension or personal discomfort. In so doing, much about the canonicality of the world of the lab is revealed.

First, the way the kernel is resolved shows that it is canonical to be open to the meaning of an unexpected event, that science will take strange twists and the seemingly irrelevant could be the basis for an important new discovery. It is canonical in this lab for a scientist to take any event, no matter how bizarre or personal, and view it as a potential for creating new knowledge. Second, we learn that it is canonical to see the event of numbness as an

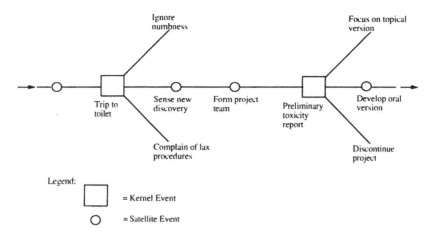

Figure 10.2. Narrative Structure of the Story of Norman

experiment on oneself. This lesson of the narrative is supported by fieldwork which confirmed that self-experimentation is a frequent practice among the lab workers. The first kernel, then, can tell us much about the values and lab practices in this community.

Second Kernel: The Preliminary Toxicity Report. In this kernel, we can imagine several alternatives that did not happen; the project could have been focused on a topical version only, because of the risk of toxicity, or the project could have been dropped altogether. Instead, canonicality is restored by a call for positive thinking and the lure of a large profitable market for an oral version. The tension between the market/profit-seeking perspective in product innovation and the toxicology perspective is lopsidedly made canonical in favor of the market. In this kernel there is a distinct failure of perspective taking on the part of the assistant director. As a result, the possibilities for knowledge creation in this network are diminished, the framing of the problem is constrained, and opportunities for a complex exploration of how risk, rewards, toxicity, and efficacy can become a topic of open dialogue are diminished.

There is obviously more that could be done in reading the canonicality of the lab in these kernels, but these examples should suffice. The important point is that the kernel is a "hinge" in the structure of the story and interpretation of the kernel gives access to what is canonical in a community that may be difficult to surface otherwise.

Implications

Perspective taking through boundary objects is a relatively unexplored frontier in electronic communication. One can expect that tools and media to support reflexivity, representation of knowledge structures, and their exchange with others in a perspective-taking process will increase over time. Paradoxically, it is a kind of communication with others that grows out of an improved communication with self. Communication with one's self is the basic stance of reflexivity; an inner conversation that builds and reflects on a representation of one's understanding of a situation. Being able to do so implies that the perspective making in a community of knowing has progressed far enough to provide a sufficiently strong perspective to reflect on. Having had this type of communication with one's self, the actor is equipped to enter into a new kind of communication with others, that of perspective taking. We now present some examples of the types of electronic communication systems suggested by our analysis thus far, by describing an idealized firm that displays strong capacities for perspective making and perspective taking.

SOME EXAMPLES OF DESIGNING COMMUNICATION SYSTEMS TO SUPPORT PERSPECTIVE MAKING AND PERSPECTIVE TAKING

The implications of using information technologies to provide support for perspective making and perspective taking are best understood as the interrelationship of organizational, cultural, and technological elements. This insight was evident in the first experiences with industrial research laboratories (Carlson 1992, Marcson 1960), in the Manhattan project (Davis 1969), and also in studies of new product innovation (Carlson 1992, Dougherty 1992, Law and Callon 1992). In keeping with an emphasis on how a narrative and language game orientation can be interweaved with paradigmatic reasoning, this section will present a plausible but admittedly utopian form of a knowledge-intensive firm. In this idealized firm, a reflexive hermeneutic attitude (Boland 1993, Boland et al. 1994, Gadamer 1975) and an open recognition of language games and the process of perspective taking is assumed to be well established. We will first describe the technological, organizational, and cultural backdrop for such a hypothetical knowledge-intensive firm of the near future. We will then describe some applications of information technologies that could be employed for perspective making and perspective taking by its communities of knowing.

Technologically, we expect to see that computing, imaging, and communication devices have become ubiquitous. The information environment in this hypothetical firm is a seamless integration of multimedia devices for collection, storage, processing, and display. The organization is replete with systems based on the conduit model and language games model. Once certain kinds of knowledge are established and the perspective of a community of knowing becomes mature, the decision routines are embedded in project management and other kinds of software, although such decision premises are always subject to question and revision. Graphics, texts, models, audio and video applications are all radically tailorable to a user's needs. Hyperlinks from an element in any one application to elements in any other application are fully supported, making contextually rich, complexly layered representations the norm. Groupware is highly developed, with multimedia meetings and discussion groups in a wide variety of issue forums. A sophisticated vocabulary of electronic forms for initiating, replying, or commenting on decisions models and discussion topics has emerged through an open process of structuration (Giddens 1979).

Organizationally, the firm is characterized by a critical density of interdependent knowledge communities. There is a postmodern (Harvey 1989) quality to the organization, and groupware communication processes are marked by multiple voices with shifting patterns of interest, giving a sense of a fragmented, almost chaotic communication environment compared to the predominantly hierarchical one of the late 1980s. The organization uses lateral teams extensively in which the vertical authority structure plays a muted role while the principal value-adding activities of knowledge creation and knowledge application are carried out in a changing mosaic of lateral project teams. Because of the firm's strong lateral form and collaboration-based reward structure, parochial interest groups and fiefdom-like power bases which used to subvert efforts at free and informed communication have largely disappeared. Individuals who play important liaison roles between strong communities of knowing use their newly developed skills as "semiotic brokers" (Lyotard 1984) to help facilitate the perspective-taking process.

Culturally, the idea that doing work in a knowledge-intensive firm means perspective making and perspective taking in communities of knowing has taken hold and has shaped both individual and group identities. Individuals have a reflexive awareness of their paradigmatic as well as their narrative modes of cognition. The culture reinforces an awareness of the individual's capacity to step outside of a message stream and engage in meta-communicative analysis (Bateson 1972). Members of the firm are used to taking an interpretive stance, playing with possible meanings, searching for underlying structures, and questioning the social construction of new nouns and verbs in their language games. They enter into and make readings of communication episodes with an open awareness of the hermeneutic circle in which they tack back and forth from an interpretation of the larger context of a perspective to an interpretation of the detailed elements of the message at hand (Palmer 1969). Their hermeneutic attitude means they avoid debate in favor of dialogue unless compelling reasons call for a dialectic communicative process. They realize that debate is a win-lose polarizing strategy that rarely results in true synthesis or creative insights. Dialogue, in contrast, is a mutually reinforcing, working together through language. It is a realization that we can assume a perspective-taking orientation and benefit from opening ourselves to the horizon of another.

Within the organizational, cultural, and technological environment sketched above, communities of knowing are using advanced groupware facilities to conduct meetings, construct multiauthor documents, and coordinate their promises and deadlines, all with the capability to access data and knowledge through a worldwide network of knowledge repositories. As is true today, the groupware systems are composed of a series of forums which serve as "containers" for dialogue on certain topics, issues, concerns, projects, or tasks. Forums reflect the way the knowledge work is being focused and the kinds of knowledge structures that are emerging in the firm, and are thus one avenue into its communities of knowing. Individuals participate in many forums in an evolving pattern. The lateral groups to which they belong and their unique expertise defines the types and kinds of forums in which they participate.

What takes place in these forums are language games. The mode of cognition is a mixed one in which paradigmatic reasoning is interwoven with stories and narration. The applications of advanced information technologies for perspective making and perspective taking that we describe below depend on there being a higher level of reflexivity in knowledge-intensive firms than is presently the case. These communication systems depend not only on talking about issues and problems within a groupware environment but on talking about how they are talking (Bateson 1972). It depends on a critical hermeneutic attitude in which the strangeness and multiple possibilities for making meaning in our conversations are constantly in our awareness (Boland 1993, Gadamer 1975, Ricoeur 1981).

As groups form and reform in a knowledge-intensive firm employing a lateral organization structure, we anticipate five new classes of electronic communication forums as examples of ones that would enhance the processes of perspective making and perspective taking. Within each class there would be several different types of forums as we will discuss below. The five new classes of forums we propose as examples are

1. Task narrative forums
2. Knowledge representation forums
3. Interpretive reading forums
4. Theory-building forums
5. Intelligent agent forums

Task Narrative Forums

This type of forum has been envisaged by Brown and Duguid (1991) and Galbraith (1994) among others and is an implicit recognition of the importance of narrativizing our experience and sharing the narratives with others in our community. Through narrative, the community constructs its practices and its social world by building and restoring its sense of the canonical. Narrative, by making the implicit and the tacit inferable to the reader or the listener, is a critically important first step in achieving perspective taking within and among communities of knowing. Because these task narratives would be multimedia, and include video and audio, they enable the benefits of learning by experience to extend beyond normal constraints of space and time.

Task-narrative forums serve as perspective making for those creating the narratives and also serve as a perspective-taking experience for those reading the narratives. The narrative is always incomplete and the reader must "read into" the story in making it sensible. Bruner (1990) refers to this "reading into" as a subjunctive process and is a primary vehicle for opening oneself up to the perspective of another and making real its possibilities for seeing the world differently.

Knowledge Representation Forums

Current groupware enables linking from a text document to a spreadsheet, decision model, graphic depiction, or picture. Once a document is hyper-linked in this way, the context it carries with itself is enriched and its possibilities for interpretation are increased. So we are already used to seeing a message with other documents linked to or embedded within it. A knowledge representational forum, in contrast, is one which focuses on the understanding that lies behind such complex documents. It is a forum that captures a community's cooperative efforts to reflect on, interpret, and depict an understanding of their situation to themselves.

It is not a problem-solving or task-practice forum so much as a sense-making forum in which the objects of discussion are visual representations

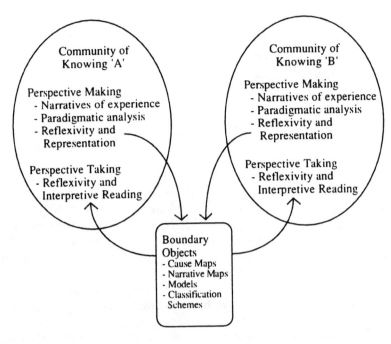

Figure 10.3. Perspective Making and Perspective Taking

of their understanding of a situation, a problem, or an objective. It is an openly reflexive forum in which communities of knowing explicitly talk about their understandings. Such forums could use storyboards in which still or animated pictures are assembled in a sequence, in a kind of visual depiction of an understanding, or these forums could use cause maps as in Figure 10.1 or other diagrams and models for representing an understanding.

Like narrative forums, representational forums serve as a perspective-making experience for those constructing, revising, or commenting on an emerging representation within a community of knowing. They also serve as a perspective-taking experience for those who read them with a hermeneutic attitude of engaging the horizons of another thought world (see Figure 10.3).

Interpretive Reading Forums

Whereas representation forums are overtly reflexive in that participants are trying to reflect on their current state of understanding of some issue, interpretive reading forums are a space for reflecting on the assumptions and meanings revealed by the communications in other forums. In this forum, participants are subjecting other texts to rereadings in hopes of portraying the tacit and implicit meanings characterizing a community of knowing, their own or others' (Czarniawska-Joerges and Guillet de Monthoux 1994).

Discussions in this forum could resemble dialogues of literary criticisms in which critical-reflexive readings are made of the streams of entries in other forums. Eventually, rereadings could even be made of the dialogues in the interpretive reading forum itself, as layers of reflexivity begin to compound (Ashmore 1989).

In addition to interpretive essays, such a forum would also be used for discussing the narrative structures in the task narratives forum and in the narrativization that is evident in all other forums as well. Here, the diagramming of narrative structures, the isolation of kernels, and the unpacking of how the canonical and noncanonical are revealed for different communities of knowing would take place.

Another type of forum within this class could be focused on words and might be known as a word-talk forum. This would be another type of reflexive analysis in which words (new words, especially nouns and verbs, as well as familiar ones) were systematically considered as to their changing meanings and uses, their shifting contexts and connotations, and the implicit and tacit assumptions they reveal.

The interpretive reading forums discussed above are the most explicitly hermeneutic-interpretive ones we envision and have the greatest dependence on the supportive organizational and cultural qualities discussed above. Without a widely shared sense of the importance of perspective making and perspective taking in knowledge creation, and a well-established sense of the value of a hermeneutic attitude, these forums would not be possible.

Theory-Building Forums

These forums would most closely reflect the dialogue of theory that is woven throughout scientific practice. We envision this as a series of forums in which different communities of knowing articulate, critique, extend, and explore the theories that do or should guide their work. Theory-building forums are not just for science work, however, and we would anticipate that in a knowledge-intensive firm the ethos of perspective making and perspective taking also would be held by the financial, marketing, and other nonscientific fields of discourse within the organization, and between the organization and its many environments.

In addition to "Theory Corners," or forums dedicated to dialogue on theories within and across specific communities of knowing, we would also expect theory-building forums to include "Thought Experiment" forums, where individuals played with theories and their implications by narrativizing thought experiments. Thought experiments entail the construction of mental models by a scientist who imagines a sequence of events and then uses a "narrative" form to describe the sequence in order to communicate the experiment to others (Nersessian 1992). Thought-experiment forums would also include the construction and playful exploration of simulation models, especially multimedia simulations and virtual reality systems.

Once again, we see this class of forums playing an important role in perspective making and also perspective taking. Constructing theories and conducting thought experiments in dialogue within a community of knowing is essential for strong forms of perspective making. Participating in these forums from the fringes of the community, or reading and interpreting the theory building from outside the community, is a powerful means of perspective taking.

Intelligent Agent and
Expert System Forums

The final class of conversational forums we will present have to do with intelligent agents and expert systems. By intelligent agents we mean personal assistants in the form of software systems that can roam the network of forums within a firm as well as libraries, repositories, and information sources outside the firm. These agents help an individual to direct his or her attention within the burgeoning field of forums that could be of importance and interest to him or her, and also help assemble contextual materials for building cross-document links in complexly layered representations.

We see these intelligent agents as well as expert systems as another important form of reflexivity within the firm. Both are classes of software systems where expertise and interests have been reflected on, made visible, and embodied within these artificial agents. In the forums we envisage, individuals would develop and share insights into how these systems can best be constructed and deployed and how their results can best be interpreted. The forums would thus be directly concerned with thinking about thinking, especially as thought processes are embodied in the active agents and expert systems.

Summary

The applications described above are not intended as an exhaustive listing, nor as a taxonomy of ways in which perspective making and perspective taking can be supported by electronic communication. Rather, we intend merely to open a discussion of some possibilities for appreciating language games, narrative cognition, and reflexivity in the design of electronic communication systems. No doubt, many of these kinds of activities are already being explored in nascent form by those organizations that are installing extensive groupware capabilities.

CONCLUDING THOUGHTS

Any design of an electronic communication system implies a model of human communication and of human cognition. We have explored how principles and policies for the design of electronic communication systems are affected by incorporating a language games model of communication and an awareness of the narrative mode of cognition. In so doing, we have argued that perspective making and perspective taking in the science work of knowledge-intensive firms and in firms generally using lateral organizational forms would benefit from systems designed with this sensibility in mind. We have also provided some examples of computer-based applications which embody these ideas and the types of organizational, cultural, and technological preconditions for them to succeed.

Behind all the arguments and examples we have presented is an interest in strengthening the possibilities for perspective making and perspective taking in communities of knowing. Making a strong perspective and having the capacity to take another perspective into account are the means by which more complexified knowledge and improved possibilities for product or process innovation are achieved. Our discussion has necessarily emphasized narrative cognition at the expense of paradigmatic, and reflexivity at the expense of action. This was necessary, we believe, in order to open a space for dialogue on these often overlooked features of social life that are nonetheless central to creating knowledge in communities and organizations.

Some of our assumptions about organization culture and power as well as our proposed applications may seem optimistic about the chances of overcoming deeply entrenched fears and resistance to change in organizations and their communities of knowing. We believe, however, that designing electronic communication systems with a language game model of communication that explicitly incorporates a narrative mode of cognition and heightened levels of reflexivity is an important means to achieve just those organizational qualities we are assuming.

REFERENCES

Allen, T. J. (1986), "Organizational Structure, Information Technology, and R&D Productivity," *IEEE Transactions on Engineering Management,* EM-33, 4, 212-220.

_____ and S. Cohen (1969), "Information Flows in R&D Laboratories," *Administrative Science Quarterly,* 12, 12-19.

_____, L. Tushman, and D. Lee (1980), "Technology Transfer as a Function of Position in the Spectrum Research Through Development to Technical Services," *Academy of Management Journal,* 22, 4, 694-708.

Argyris, C. and D. Schön (1978), *Organizational Learning: A Theory of Action Perspective,* Reading, MA: Addison-Wesley.

Ashmore, M. (1989), *The Reflexive Thesis: Wrighting Sociology of Scientific Knowledge,* Chicago: University of Chicago Press.

Astley, W. G. and R. F. Zammuto (1992), "Organization Science, Managers, and Language Games," *Organization Science,* 3, 4, 443-460.

Axelrod, R. (1976), *Structure of Decision,* Princeton, NJ: Princeton University Press.

Bakhtin, M. M. (1981), "Discourse in the Novel," in M. Holquis (Ed.), *The Dialogic Imagination,* Austin: University of Texas Press.

Barnes, B. (1983), "On the Conventional Character of Knowledge and Cognition," in K. D. Knorr-Cetina and M. Mulkay (Eds.), *Science Observed,* London: Sage.

Bartunek, J. (1984), "Changing Interpretive Schemes and Organizational Restructuring: The Example of a Religious Order," *Administrative Science Quarterly,* 29, 355-372.

Bateson, G. (1972), *Steps to an Ecology of Mind,* New York: Random House.

Bennis, W. and B. Nanus (1985), *Leaders: The Strategies for Taking Charge,* New York: Harper.

Bertado, R. (1990), "Implementing a Strategic Vision," *Long Range Planning,* 23, 5, 22-30.

Boje, D. M. (1991), "The Storytelling Organization: A Study of Story Performance in an Office-Supply Firm," *Administrative Science Quarterly,* 36, 106-126.

Boland, R. J. (1993), "Accounting and the Interpretive Act," *Accounting, Organizations and Society,* 18, 2/3, 125-146.

_____ and L. R. Pondy (1983), "Accounting in Organizations: Toward a Union of Rational and Natural Perspectives," *Accounting, Organizations and Society,* 8, 2/3, 223-234.

_____, D. Schwartz, R. V. Tenkasi, A. Maheshwari, and D. Te'eni (1992), "Sharing Perspectives in Distributed Decision Making," *Association of Computing Machinery Conference on Computer Supported Cooperative Work,* Toronto, Ontario, Canada, pp. 306-313.

_____, R. V. Tenkasi, and D. Te'eni (1994), "Designing Information Technology to Support Distributed Cognition," *Organization Science,* 5, 3, 456-475.

Boulding, K. E. (1956), *The Image: Knowledge in Life and Society,* Ann Arbor: University of Michigan Press.

Bradshaw, G. F. (1992), "The Airplane and the Logic of Invention," in R. N. Giere (Ed.), *Cognitive Models of Science: Minnesota Studies in the Philosophy of Science,* Minneapolis: University of Minnesota Press, Vol. 15.

Brehmer, B. (1991), "Distributed Decision Making: Some Notes on the Literature," in Rasmussen et al. (Eds.), *Distributed Decision Making: Cognitive Models in Cooperative Work,* New York: John Wiley.

Brown, C. V. and R. P. Bostrom (1989), "Effective Management of End-User Computing: A Total Organization Perspective," *Journal of MIS,* 6, 2, Fall, 77-92.

Brown, J. S. (1991), "Research That Reinvents the Corporation," *Harvard Business Review,* January/February, 102-111.

_____ and P. Duguid (1991), "Organizational Learning and Communities-of-Practice: Toward a Unified View of Working, Learning, and Innovation," *Organization Science,* 2, 40-57.

Brown, R. (1981), *Social Psychology*, New York: Free Press.

Bruner, J. S. (1986), *Actual Minds, Possible Worlds*, Cambridge, MA: Harvard University Press.

_____ (1990), *Acts of Meaning*, Cambridge, MA: Harvard University Press.

Burgess, G. M., T. D. Clark, Jr., R. D. Hauser, Jr., and R. W. Zmud (1992), "The Application of Causal Maps to Develop a Collective Understanding of Complex Organizational Contexts in Requirements Analysis, *Accounting, Management and Information Technologies*, 2, 3, 143-164.

Burrell, G. and G. Morgan (1979), *Sociological Paradigms and Organizational Analysis*, London: Heinemann.

Carlson, W. B. (1992), "Artifacts and Frames of Meaning: Thomas A. Edison, His Managers and the Cultural Construction of Motion Pictures," in W. Bijker and J. Law (Eds.), *Shaping Technology/Building Society*, Cambridge: MIT Press.

Chatman, S. (1978), *Story and Discourse in Fiction and Film*, Ithaca, NY: Cornell University Press.

Chen, P. P. S. (1976), "The Entity Relationship Diagram—Toward a Unified View of Data," *ACM Transactions on Database Systems*, 1, 9-36.

Ciborra, C., P. Migliarese, and P. Romano (1954), "A Methodological Inquiry of Organizational Noise in Sociotechnical Systems," *Human Relations*, 37, 8, 565-588.

Clark, B. R. (1972), "The Organizational Saga in Higher Education," *Administrative Science Quarterly*, 17, 178-184.

Clark, H. H. (1985), "Language Use and Language Users," in G. Lindzey and E. Aronson (Eds.), *Handbook of Social Psychology*, New York: Random House.

Collins, H. M. (1983), "An Empirical Relativist Programme in the Sociology of Scientific Knowledge," in K. D. Knorr-Cetina and M. Mulkay (Eds.), *Science Observed*, London: Sage.

Collins, J. C. and J. I. Porras (1991), "Organizational Vision and Visionary Organization," *California Management Review*, 34, 30-42.

Czarniawska-Joerges, B. (1992), *Exploring Complex Organizations*, Newbury Park, CA: Sage.

_____ and P. Guillet de Monthoux (Eds.) (1994), *Good Novels, Better Management: Reading Organizational Realities*, Reading, UK: Harwood Academic.

Daft, R. and R. Lengel (1984), "Information Richness: A New Approach to Managerial Behavior and Organizational Design," in L. L. Cummings and B. M. Staw (Eds.), *Research in Organizational Behavior*, Greenwich, CT: JAI, Vol. 6, pp. 191-223.

Davis, N. P. (1969), *Lawrence and Oppenheimer*, London: Jonathan Cape.

Davis, P. and M. Wilkof (1988), "Scientific and Technical Information Transfer for High Technology: Keeping the Figure in Its Ground," *Research and Development Management*, 18, 45-55.

Deng, P. S. and A. Chaudhry (1992), "A Conceptual Model of Adaptive Knowledge-Based System," *Information Systems Research*, June, 127-149.

Dolk, D. R. (1988), "Model Management and Structured Modeling: The Role of Information Resource Directory System," *Communications of the ACM*, June, 704-718.

Dougherty, D. (1992), "Interpretive Barriers to Successful Product Innovation in Large Firms," *Organization Science*, 3, 2, 179-202.

Duncan, R. and A. Weiss (1979), "Organizational Learning: Implications for Organizational Design," in L. L. Cummings and B. M. Staw (Eds.), *Research in Organizational Behavior*, Greenwich, CT: JAI, Vol. 1.

Eden, C. (1992), "On the Nature of Cognitive Maps," *Journal of Management Studies*, 29, 3, 261-265.

Elam, J. J. and B. Konsynski (1987), "Using Artificial Intelligence Techniques to Enhance the Capabilities of Model Management Systems," *Decision Sciences*, 18, 487-501.

Eysenck, M. W. and M. T. Keane (1990), *Cognitive Psychology: A Student's Handbook,* London: Lawrence Erlbaum.

Fiol, C. M. and A. S. Huff (1992), "Maps for Managers: Where Are We? Where Do We Go From Here?" *Journal of Management Studies,* 29, 3.

Fish, S. (1980), *Is There a Text in This Class?* Cambridge, MA: Harvard University Press.

Fleck, L. (1979), *Genesis and Development of a Scientific Fact,* in T. J. Trenn and R. K. Merton (Eds.), Chicago: University of Chicago Press. (Original work published in German, 1935)

Gabriel, Y. (1991), "Turning Facts Into Stories and Stories Into Facts: A Hermeneutic Exploration of Organizational Folklore," *Human Relations,* 44, 8, 857-876.

Gadamer, H. G. (1975), *Truth and Method,* New York: Seabury.

Galbraith, J. (1973), *Designing Complex Organizations,* Reading, MA: Addison-Wesley.

Galbraith, J. R. (1994), *Competing With Flexible Lateral Organizations,* Reading, MA: Addison-Wesley.

_____ and Lawler, E. E. (1993), *Organizing for the Future,* San Francisco: Jossey-Bass.

Gentner, D. (1983), "Structure-Mapping: A Theoretical Framework for Analogy," *Cognitive Science,* 7, 155-170.

Geoffrion, A. M. (1987), "An Introduction to Structural Modeling," *Management Science,* 33, 5, 547-588.

Giddens, A. (1976), *New Rules of Sociological Method,* New York: Basic Books.

_____ (1979), *Central Problems in Social Theory,* London: Macmillan.

_____ (1991), *Modernity and Self-Identity,* Stanford, CA: Stanford University Press. •

Granstrand, O., E. Bohlin, C. Oskarsson, and N. Sjöberg (1992), "External Technology Acquisition in Large Multi-Technology Corporations," *Research and Development Management,* 22, 2, 111-133.

Hamel, G. and C. K. Prahalad (1991), "Corporate Imagination and Expeditionary Marketing," *Harvard Business Review,* 69, 4, July/August, 81-92.

Harvey, D. (1989), *The Condition of Postmodernity,* Oxford, UK: Basil Blackwell.

Henderson, R. (1994), "Managing Innovation in the Information Age," *Harvard Business Review,* January/February, 100-105.

Hesse, M. (1974), *The Structure of Scientific Inference,* Berkeley: University of California Press.

Huff, A. S. (1990), *Mapping Strategic Thought,* Chichester, UK: Wiley.

Isaacs, W. N. (1993), "Taking Flight: Dialogue, Collective Thinking, and Organizational Learning," *Organizational Dynamics,* 22, 2, 24-39.

Jönsson, S. (1992), "Accounting for Improvement: Action Research on Local Management Support," *Accounting, Management and Information Technologies,* 2, 2, 99-116.

Kahneman, D., P. Slovic, and A. Tversky (1982), *Judgment Under Uncertainty: Heuristics and Biases,* New York: Cambridge University Press.

Knorr-Cetina, K. D. (1981), *The Manufacture of Knowledge: An Essay on the Constructivist and Contextual Nature of Science,* Oxford, UK: Pergamon.

Krauss, R. M. and S. R. Fussell (1991), "Perspective-Taking in Communication Representation of Others Knowledge in Reference," *Social Cognition,* 9, 2-24.

Kuhn, T. S. (1962), *The Structure of Scientific Revolutions,* Chicago: University of Chicago Press.

_____ (1970), *The Structure of Scientific Revolutions* (2nd ed.), Chicago: University of Chicago Press.

Lave, J. and E. Wenger (1990), "Situated Learning: Legitimate Peripheral Participation," *IRL Report No. 90-0013,* Palo Alto, CA: Institute for Research on Learning.

Law, J. and M. Callon (1992), "The Life and Death of an Aircraft: A Network Analysis of Technical Change," in W. Bijker and J. Law (Eds.), *Shaping Technology/Building Society,* Cambridge: MIT Press.

Lawler, E. E. (1992), *The Ultimate Advantage,* San Francisco: Jossey-Bass.

Lyotard, J. F. (1984), *The Postmodern Condition: A Report on Knowledge,* Minneapolis: University of Minnesota Press.

Marcson, S. (1960), *The Scientist in American Industry,* New York: Harper & Brothers.

Martin, J. and D. Meyerson (1988), "Organizational Cultures and the Denial, Channeling, and Acknowledgment of Ambiguity," in L. R. Pondy, R. J. Boland, and H. Thomas (Eds.), *Managing Ambiguity and Change,* New York: John Wiley, pp. 93-125.

Masterman, M. (1970), "The Nature of a Paradigm," in I. Lakatos and A. Musgrave (Eds.), *Criticism and the Growth of Knowledge,* London: Cambridge University Press.

McConkie, M. L. and W. R. Boss (1986), "Organizational Stories: One Means of Moving the Informal Organization During Change Efforts," *Public Administration Quarterly,* 10, 2, 189-205.

Mead, G. H. (1934), *Mind, Self and Society,* Chicago: University of Chicago Press.

Mitroff, I. I. and R. H. Kilmann (1976), "On Organization Stories: An Approach to the Design and Analysis of Organizations Through Myth and Stories," in R. H. Kilmann, L. R. Pondy, and D. P. Slevin (Eds.), *The Management of Organization Design,* New York: North Holland.

Mulkay, M., J. Potter, and S. Yearley (1983), "Why an Analysis of Scientific Discourse Is Needed," in K. D. Knorr-Cetina and M. Mulkay (Eds.), *Science Observed,* London: Sage.

Munro, M. C., S. L. Huff, and G. Moore (1987), "Expansion and Control of End-User Computing," *Journal of MIS,* 4, 3, Winter, 5-27.

Nersessian, N. J. (1992), "How Do Scientists Think? Capturing the Dynamics of Conceptual Change in Science," in R. N. Giere (Ed.), *Cognitive Models of Science: Minnesota Studies in the Philosophy of Science,* Minneapolis: University of Minnesota Press, Vol. 15.

Nisbett, R. E. and L. E. Ross (1980), *Human Inference: Strategies and Shortcomings of Social Judgment,* Englewood Cliffs, NJ: Prentice Hall.

Nonaka, I. (1994), "A Dynamic Theory of Organizational Knowledge Creation," *Organization Science,* 5, 14-37.

_____ and J. Johansson (1985), "Japanesse Management: What About the 'Hard' Skills?" *Academy of Management Review,* 10, 2, 181-191.

Orr, J. (1990), "Sharing Knowledge, Celebrating Identity: War Stories and Community Memory in a Service Culture," in D. S. Middleton and D. Edwards (Eds.), *Collective Remembering: Memory in Society,* Newbury Park, CA: Sage.

Palmer, R. E. (1969), *Hermeneutics,* Evanston, IL: Northwestern University Press.

Pava, C. (1983), *Managing New Office Technology,* New York: Free Press.

Pepper, S. C. (1942), *World Hypotheses,* Berkeley: University of California Press.

Polanyi, M. (1967), *The Tacit Dimension,* Garden City, NY: Doubleday.

Purser, R. E. and W. A. Pasmore (1992), "Organizing for Learning," in R. Woodman and W. A. Pasmore (Eds.), *Research in Organizational Change and Development,* Greenwich, CT: JAI, Vol. 6.

_____, _____, and R. V. Tenkasi (1992), "The Influence of Deliberations on Learning in New Product Development Teams," *Journal of Engineering and Technology Management,* 9, 1-28.

Ranson, S., R. Hinings, and R. Greenwood (1980), "The Structuring of Organizational Structures," *Administrative Science Quarterly,* 25, 2, 1-17.

Redding, C. W. (1972), *Communication Within the Organization,* New York: Industrial Communication Council.

Reddy, M. J. (1979), "The Conduit Metaphor," in A. Ortony (Ed.), *Metaphor and Thought,* Cambridge, UK: Cambridge University Press, pp. 284-324.

Richardson, G. L., B. M. Jackson, and G. W. Dickson (1990), "A Principles Based Enterprise Architecture: Lessons From Texaco and Star Enterprise," *MIS Quarterly,* December, 385-403.

Ricoeur, P. (1981), *Hermeneutics and the Human Sciences,* J. Thompson (Ed. and Trans.), Cambridge, UK: Cambridge University Press.

Rivard, S. and S. L. Huff (1988), *Communications of the ACM,* 31, 5, 552-561.

Rommetveit, R. (1980), "On 'Meanings' of Acts and What Is Meant by What Is Said in a Pluralistic Social World," in M. Brenner (Ed.), *The Structure of Action,* Oxford, UK: Blackwell & Mott, pp. 108-149.

Ross, L., D. Greene, and P. House (1977), "The False Consensus Phenomenon: An Attributional Bias in Self-Perception and Social Perception Processes," *Journal of Experimental Social Psychology,* 13, 279-301.

Rubinstein, R. A., C. D. Laughlin, and D. McManus (1984), *Science as Cognitive Process: Toward an Empirical Philosophy of Science,* Philadelphia: University of Pennsylvania Press.

Scheer, A.-W. (1992), *Architecture of Integrated Information Systems: Foundations of Enterprise-Modelling,* Berlin: Springer-Verlag.

Schön, D. (1979), "Generative Metaphor," in A. Ortony (Ed.), *Metaphor and Thought,* Cambridge, UK: Cambridge University Press.

Schutz, A. (1964), *Studies in Social Theory,* Collected Papers II, The Hague, The Netherlands: Martinus Nijhoff.

Shannon, C. and W. Weaver (1949), *The Mathematical Theory of Communication,* Chicago: University of Illinois Press.

Shrivastava, P. (1983), "A Typology of Organizational Learning Systems," *Journal of Management Studies,* 20, 9-25.

Simon, H. A. (1977), *The New Science of Management Decision,* 2nd rev. ed., Englewood Cliffs, NJ: Prentice Hall.

Smith, C. S. (1981), "Structural Hierarchy in Science, Art and History," in J. Wechsler (Ed.), *On Aesthetics in Science,* Cambridge: MIT Press.

Star, S. L. (1989), "The Structure of Ill-Structured Solutions: Boundary Objects and Heterogeneous Distributed Problem Solving," in M. Huhns and L. Gasser (Eds.), *Readings in Distributed Artificial Intelligence 2,* Menlo Park, CA: Morgan Kaufmann.

_____ (1993), "Cooperation Without Consensus in Scientific Problem Solving: Dynamics of Closure in Open Systems," in S. Easterbrook (Ed.), *CSCW: Cooperation or Conflict,* London: Springer.

Starbuck, W. H. (1992), "Learning by Knowledge-Intensive Firms," *Journal of Management Studies,* 29, 6, 713-740.

Steedman, M. J. and P. N. Johnson-Laird (1980), "The Productions of Sentences, Utterrances and Speech Acts: Have Computers Anything to Say?" in B. Butterworth (Ed.), *Language Productions: Speech and Talk,* London: Academic Press.

Targowski, A. S. (1988), "Strategic Planning for the Enterprise-Wide Information Management Complex: The Architectural Approach," *Journal of MIS,* 5, 2, Fall.

Tenkasi, R. V. and R. J. Boland (1993), "Locating Meaning Making in Organizational Learning: The Narrative Basis of Cognition," in R. W. Woodman and W. A. Pasmore (Eds.), *Research in Organizational Change and Development,* Greenwich, CT: JAI, Vol. 7, pp. 77-103.

Tushman, M. L. (1978), "Information Processing as an Integrating Concept in Organizational Design," *Academy of Management Review,* 3, 3, 613-624.

von Bertalanffy, L. (1968), *General System Theory,* New York: George Braziller.

Waddington, C. H. (1957), *The Strategy of the Genes,* London: Allen & Unwin.

Weick, K. E. (1990), "Cognitive Processes in Organizations," in L. L. Cummings and B. M. Staw (Eds.), *Information and Cognition in Organizations,* Greenwich, CT: JAI.

_____ and M. K. Bougon (1986), "Organizations as Cognitive Maps: Charting Ways to Success and Failure," in H. Sims and D. Goia (Eds.), *The Thinking Organization,* San Francisco: Jossey-Bass.

_____ and K. H. Roberts (1993), "Collective Minds in Organizations: Heedful Interrelating on Flight Decks," *Administrative Science Quarterly,* 38, 357-381.

Werner, H. (1957), "The Concept of Development From a Comparative and Organismic Point of View," in D. Harris (Ed.), *The Concept of Development,* Minneapolis: University of Minnesota Press.

Wiener, N. (1954), *The Human Use of Human Beings,* New York: Avon Books.

Wittgenstein, L. (1961), *Tractatus Logico-Philosophicus,* London: Routledge Kegan Paul (First edition, with a translation, 1922)

_____ (1974), *Philosophical Investigations,* New York: Macmillan (First edition, 1953)

11

Improving Interorganizational
Effectiveness Through Voice Mail
Facilitation of Peer-to-Peer Relationships

MARY R. LIND

ROBERT W. ZMUD

The quality of an organization's interactions with key entities of its external
environment has long been recognized as an important factor in organizational performance (Adams 1976, 1980, Katz and Kahn 1978). Particularly
critical interorganizational relationships for a manufacturing organization
are those nurtured and maintained by its field marketing representatives,
who, through their interactions with stakeholders in the organization's first-
order environment (distributors, retailers, etc.), facilitate the marketing,
selling, and outbound logistics of products and services to stakeholders in
the organization's second-order environment (the end-consumers who purchase and use the manufacturer's products and services). The importance of
the relationships between a manufacturer's field marketing representatives
and the sales representatives of the distributors and/or retailers carrying the
manufacturer's products increases with both the products' technological
complexity and the extent to which the products are custom manufactured to

This chapter appeared originally in *Organization Science,* 6(4), July/August, 1995.

end-consumer specifications. It is this dyadic relationship between the manu-facturer's field marketing representatives and the sales representatives of its distributors/retailers that is the specific focus of this study.

Structural mechanisms enabling and enhancing such dyadic relationships represent potentially important vehicles for improving organizational per-formance (Aldrich and Whetten 1981, Laumann et al. 1978). In their discussions of developmental processes associated with interorganizational relationships (IORs), Ring and Van de Ven (1994) argue that it is through enactment processes, like collective sensemaking, that participants in IORs achieve congruent interaction. A primary mechanism for carrying out this convergent sensemaking is the nature of the communication pathways provided to participants to enable the communication exchanges (Lind and Zmud 1991, Neale and Northcraft 1991, Weick 1979). These exchanges produce psycho-logical contracts across the interacting parties regarding the acceptable norms of behavior both with each other and with customers (Argyris 1960, Kotter 1973).

Field marketing representatives and sales representatives have available numerous communication channels for carrying out their communication exchanges. Nonetheless, this facet of the sales/marketing arena has been and continues to be a focus of complaints regarding communication ineffective-ness (Mohr and Nevin 1990). Computer-mediated asynchronous media (Rice and Associates 1984, Rogers 1986), such as electronic mail and voice mail, have the potential to enhance dramatically the communication exchanges which form the basis of effective IORs (Allen and Hauptman 1990, Contrac-tor and Eisenberg 1990). This field study examines an initiative by one manufacturing firm to improve its dealers' sales performance by providing its field marketing representatives with a voice mail capability.

The following section builds a conceptual framework linking together interorganizational communication behaviors with effectiveness of the IOR. Next, the study's research model and hypotheses are developed. Then, the research context and methodology are described. The study concludes with a discussion of findings and their implications to both research and practice.

THE STUDY'S CONCEPTUAL FRAMEWORK

Building on work by Wieck (1979), Pfeffer (1981), and Huber and Daft (1987) which posits that organizations can be viewed as systems of shared meaning, Ring and Van de Ven (1994) argue that it is the convergent interactions of participants within IORs that ultimately provide for the delivery of product and service to end-consumers. Furthermore, Ring and

Van de Ven (1994) state, "communication among the (interorganizational) parties produces this shared interpretation" (p. 99). Thus, in an interorganizational context, it is the nature of the communication exchanges among key actors that largely determines the effectiveness of the IOR which, in turn, contributes significantly to enhanced organizational performance.

Much research (Boulding et al. 1993, Bullard et al. 1993, Fuchsberg 1992) has focused on the quality of service delivered to customers through interorganizational relationships; however, little is understood about how the communication interactions among participants in these interorganizational relationships influence service performance. Furthermore, the service delivery research examining interorganizational relationships has typically relied on perceptual appraisals of performance rather than objective performance measures (Bullard et al. 1993, Edvardsson and Gustavsson 1991, Mattson 1993, Provan and Skinner 1989). Finally, few of these prior studies sufficiently control for contextural factors in service delivery through embedding the data gathering activity tightly within a field setting (Bolton and Drew 1991, Haynes 1993, Vandermere 1993). A notable exception is the electronic data interchange (EDI) research that has provided needed interorganizational research by showing that EDI reduces business transaction costs, reduces order cycles, improves partner relationships, improves the flow of data, and improves planning and forecasting (Zaheer and Venkatraman 1994).

In this study's interorganizational context, then, augmenting the communication milieu enveloping an IOR is expected to positively enhance effectiveness of the IOR by both improving the communication capabilities of key participants in an IOR and improving the quality of the dyadic interactions of these participants (see Figure 11.1). Enhancing individual communication behaviors should enable participants in the IOR to both obtain and provide better information; enhancing dyadic relationships within the IOR should enable participants in the IOR to operate out of a common set of beliefs and norms regarding the nature and objectives of the IOR. Together, improved information and the existence of a common understanding across participants in the IOR should result in a higher quality of service being provided to end-consumers of the IOR.

One of the mechanisms for improving individual communication behaviors involves enlarging the portfolio of pathways through which these communicating partners interact. Voice mail, the focal technology in this study, is one of a class of store-and-forward communication technologies that have been shown to reduce communication barriers associated with time zone differences, geography, partner unavailability, and social/organizational status (Culnan and Markus 1987, Hiltz and Turoff 1978, Rice and Bair 1984, Sproull and Kiesler 1986). Additionally, voice mail is generally considered

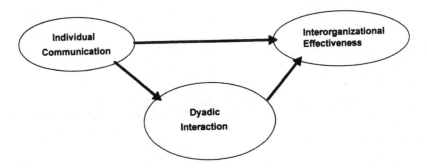

Figure 11.1. Conceptual Framework

the most "accessible" of this class of communication technologies as access to it is generally provided through keys on the omnipresent touch-tone phone.

When considering the influence of voice mail or any communication technology on interorganizational communication processes, it must be noted that any newly introduced communication medium will both engender and be affected by media substitution (Rice and Bair 1984); thus, it is important not to overstate voice mail's singular impact on communication behaviors in organizational settings (Picot et al. 1982). Newly introduced communication media compete with existing media and contend with deeply entrenched organizational and individual norms and routines (Contractor et al. 1986, Ebadi and Utterback 1984, Fulk et al. 1987, Kling and Scacchi 1982). Just as important, the various media available in a particular setting also complement one another's use. For example, Zack (1993) has shown that electronic mail is most effective when it is complemented with face-to-face contact. While computer-mediated communications technologies such as voice mail raise the potential for individuals to engage in new forms of interaction (Culnan and Markus 1987, Rice and Associates 1984, Steinfield 1986), their introduction into an organization must contend with and eventually blend within the organization's overall communication milieu (Foster and Flynn 1984, Palme 1981, Rice and Case 1983, Sproull and Kiesler 1986).

Finally, any study examining the impact of an information technology on organizational performance must contend not only with technological substitution and complementary effects but must also recognize that technologies are used for many purposes, both intended and unintended, and can affect organizational performance directly (immediate and manifest casual effects) or indirectly (distant and diffuse causal effects). While a number of empirical studies have attempted to assess the impact of information technology on organizational performance (Alpar and Kim 1990, Bender 1986, Chismar and Kriebel 1985, Cron and Sobol 1983, Harris and Katz 1991, Kauffman and Weill 1989, Roach 1988, Weill 1992), the findings have tended to be either mixed or inconclusive and have often proven difficult to interpret (DeLone and McLean 1992). Given (a) that a wide variety of information technologies and business activities exist across all organizations, (b) that the impact of these technologies on specific activities is often indirect, and (c) that at least some of the applications are outdated, poorly designed, or poorly implemented, then it should not be surprising that research designs involving aggregation of either information technologies or business activities, or both, often show, at best, weak associations between investment in information technology and organizational performance.

As a consequence, empirical investigations of the relationship between information technology and organizational performance should strive to ensure that research designs are as cohesive as possible regarding the information technology involved, the business domain involved, and the relative advantage of the information technology within the business domain. Without a well-conceived research design, noise in any collected data is likely to obscure or confound an existent relationship. Consider, for example, the nicely conceived study by Banker et al. (1990). By focusing at the store level (fast-food chain) and studying a narrow range of information technologies (point-of-sale hardware and order management software), a quasi-experimental design found that the most efficient stores were those having both the information technology and a more complex product mix. By capturing in the research design a tightly bounded technology-task-situational context, one can increase the likelihood that a significant effect, if present, is observed.

THE STUDY'S
RESEARCH CONTEXT

The U.S. headquarters for a multinational firm served as the site for this research. This manufacturing firm produced heavy trucks used in interstate transport; these trucks were sold and serviced by independent dealerships located throughout the United States. End-consumers of the manufacturer's trucks included both self-employed truck drivers and firms either in the transportation business or that used the trucks to handle their own distribution of supplies and products. As the very largest of these end-consumers were handled through national accounts, the independently owned dealerships handled sales to individuals and to small- and medium-sized firms. The manufacturer used three types of field representatives to support the dealerships: sales representatives, parts representatives, and warranty service representatives.

The firm's CEO had reservations about using voice mail and did not allow voice mail at headquarters because of the threat that "the headquarters staff might hide behind their voice mail and not return customer calls." This was a major complaint voiced about one of the firm's major competitors. While this CEO has since retired and voice mail is now in use at the company headquarters, at the time of this study, the CEO only permitted the firm's field representatives to use voice mail that was obtained through a third party. Field representatives having access to voice mail were provided a voice mail telephone number which dealership personnel could call and leave verbal messages. The objective, quite obviously, was to make it easier to get messages to the highly mobile field representatives, each of whom supported multiple dealerships and many of whom supported dealerships within a market territory that often spanned several states and two time zones.

For parts and service, voice mail had been in use nationwide for 12 to 18 months prior to this research project, which collected its data in the fall of 1989. The national parts and service managers worked closely together, and the service manager was a very strong advocate of information technology. The national sales manager, however, was technologically conservative and, as he was not located in the same building as were the national parts and service managers, did not interact much with these two individuals. Still, the national sales manager did agree to experiment with voice mail for 1 year in two sales regions. If the experiment went well, voice mail was to be implemented in all five of the sales regions. The southeastern region was selected as a site for the voice mail experiment because the national headquarters was located in the southeast and thus could easily be monitored in the experiment. The southwest region was selected as the second site because the national sales manager anticipated visiting the southwest quite often during the year-long experiment. Depending on the timing of the voice mail implementation in a sales territory, study participants has used voice mail for 6 to 10 months prior to their completion of the survey instrument.

The researchers were introduced by the manufacturer's senior information systems manager to the parts, sales, and service managers after the voice mail implementation decisions were made and did not engage in any consulting activities with the firm. In following up on an opportunity to explore the effects of voice mail on organizational performance, the researchers' sole commitment to the truck manufacturer was the provision of an early analysis of these findings.

DEVELOPMENT OF
RESEARCH HYPOTHESES

As Allen and Hauptman (1990) argue, certain organizational tasks are more amenable than others to productivity improvements through information technologies. An interorganizational arrangement involving a manufacturing organization selling technologically complex products to end-consumers through independent dealerships poses particularly daunting communication problems both for keeping dealership personnel informed regarding the products and for responding to questions from these personnel. Typically, in such situations, a field representative serves as the primary liaison between the manufacturer and one or more dealerships (Mohr and Nevin 1990). In carrying out their duties for a dealership, each of the field representatives establishes a dyadic relationship with a designated member of the dealership; and the effectiveness of this dyadic relationship is a key determinant of the quality of the services provided to a dealership's end-consumers and, hence, the dealership's sales performance.

An obviously crucial aspect influencing the effectiveness of the dyadic relationship is the nature of the communication exchanges that occur between the field representative and the sales managers. Voice mail has the potential to significantly enhance these communication exchanges by reducing instances of communication failure due to communication-partner unavailability when communication is required. Such communication failures are likely to have detrimental effects on dealership performance. For example, if a sales manager needs to contact the field representative in order to answer a customer's technical question and the field representative cannot be reached, customer dissatisfaction is likely to result. If such occurrences are frequent, dealership sales performance is likely to suffer. This rationale leads to the first research hypothesis:

Hypothesis 1. Sales regions having access to voice mail will outperform sales regions not having access to voice mail.

As discussed earlier, the impacts of information technologies on organizational performance can occur through both direct and indirect casual pathways. Fulk et al. (1990) have shown that the use of any communication media, such as voice mail, occurs within a complex web of social relationships, where the introduction of any new technology both shapes and is shaped by prevailing social structures (Contractor and Eisenberg 1990, Orlikowski and Robey 1991). With the availability of voice mail, it is anticipated that the dyadic partners, the field representative-sales manager pairs, will find themselves revising their communication rituals such as their selection of communication media in ways which improve their overall communication effectiveness. It is expected that organizational performance as determined by dealership sales performance will improve along with overall communication effectiveness.

It is further expected that such improvement will be observed for both verbal and written communication, as both forms of communication exchange are particularly salient for interorganizational arrangements involving manufacturers of complex, technical products and dealerships that sell and service these products. Verbal media, such as face-to-face and telephone, facilitate the rich communication exchanges (Daft and Lengel 1986, Daft et al. 1987, Lind and Zmud 1991) required to resolve technical ambiguities arising in negotiating with end-consumers regarding, for example, customized product orders or service contracts. Such episodes, if handled satisfactorily, result in more effective interorganizational service delivery relationships enabling more units of the product to be sold (Chase and Bowen 1991, pp. 157-178). On the other hand, written media, such as printed documents and facsimile, are necessary in this interorganizational service context to confirm and expedite the handling of special customer requests. In particular, purchases requiring customized manufacturing entail considerable paperwork both to place the order and to document its progress through the manufacturing process. Again, if such episodes are handled satisfactorily, more effective interorganizational service delivery relationships will exist. These ideas result in the following two research hypotheses:

Hypothesis 2. A stronger positive relationship will exist between the frequency of verbal communication exchanges by dyadic partners and dealership sales performance in those sales regions having access to voice mail than will exist in those sales regions not having access to voice mail.

Hypothesis 3. A stronger positive relationship will exist between the frequency of written communication exchanges by dyadic partners and dealership sales performance in those sales regions having access to voice mail than will exist in those sales regions not having access to voice mail.

Furthermore, to better understand how voice mail might be impacting effectiveness of the IOR, the convergent sensemaking processes of the dyadic partners should also be assessed (Chase and Hayes 1991, Juran and Gryna 1989). In particular, the extent to which each dyadic partner is satisfied with the other partner's interactions provides a transaction-specific evaluation of the quality of the service being provided by the dyad (Bitner 1990, Bolton and Drew 1991). If voice mail availability does, in fact, enhance the overall communication effectiveness of each of the dyadic partners, then the satisfaction of each with the other's interactions should also increase. Stated simply, with the more robust set of communication alternatives available to dyads in the sales regions with voice mail, each partner should be better able to react in a timely and complete manner in meeting the other dyadic partner's requests. As argued earlier, these relationships should hold for both verbal and written communication. Thus, the following two hypotheses are proposed:

Hypothesis 4. A stronger positive relationship will exist between the frequency of verbal communication exchanges by dyadic partners and their satisfaction with the dyadic interactions in those sales regions having access to voice mail than will exist in sales regions not having access to voice mail.

Hypothesis 5. A stronger positive relationship will exist between the frequency of written communication exchanges by dyadic partners and their satisfaction with the dyadic interactions in sales regions having access to voice mail than will exist in sales regions not having access to voice mail.

Finally, improvements in effectiveness in the IOR characterized by greater dealership sales performance should accompany these increases in the effectiveness of dyadic interaction. When each of the dyadic partners believes the other dyadic partner is responsive in facilitating the delivery of high-quality customer service, it is likely that higher-quality customer service is, in fact, being provided. As a consequence, effectiveness of the IOR should increase. And, if such beliefs occur within organizational contexts providing for more effective communication behaviors, both the validity of the beliefs and the actual quality of service being provided should be greater. This relationship leads to the final research hypothesis:

Hypothesis 6. A stronger positive relationship will exist between satisfaction with the dyadic interactions and dealership sales performance in sales regions having access to voice mail than will exist in sales regions not having access to voice mail.

Figure 11.2 summarizes the relationships described as Hypotheses 2 through 6.

RESEARCH METHODOLOGY

The study's unit of analysis is the dyadic relationship between a field representative and the sales manager at a dealership supported by that field

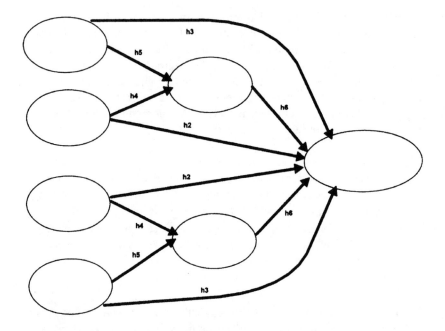

Figure 11.2. Indirect Causal Pathways

representative. In total, 71 dealerships were located in sales regions having access to voice mail, while 173 dealerships were located in sales regions not having such access. Note, a field representative worked solely in a voice mail or a non-voice mail region; there was no crossover. Responses were collected from each dyadic partner regarding communication media usage, satisfaction with each respondent's dyadic partner's interaction, and attributes of the task context. As the field representatives each supported 10 to 12 dealerships, each field representative completed a separate questionnaire regarding each dealership's sales manager. Given the limitations of validity in field contexts (Cook and Campbell 1979), the means of the collective responses for all the dealerships served by a single field representative were compared across all the field representatives with no systematic differences evident. Thus, the field representative appeared to be responding in terms of dyadic relationship with a specific sales manager. Each of the questionnaires given to a field representative was transcribed with that dealership's name and relevant questionnaire items were framed in terms of the field representative's relationship with this dealership's sales manager.

Since the completion of the questionnaires was requested by the national sales manager, a high response rate was observed: 63 of the 71 voice mail

TABLE 11.1 Items Used to Assess Media Usage With Dyadic Partner[a]

Sales manager media usage

Sales manager verbal media usage
> Extent to which the sales manager uses face-to-face contact in communicating with the field rep
> Extent to which the sales manager uses the telephone in communicating with the field rep
> Extent to which the sales manager uses voice mail in communicating with the field rep[b]
> $\alpha = .85$

Sales manager written media usage
> Extent to which the sales manager uses facsimile in communicating with the field rep
> Extent to which the sales manager uses written or printed documents in communicating with the field rep
> $\alpha = .87$

Field rep media usage

Field rep verbal media usage
> Extent to which the field rep uses face-to-face contact in communicating with the sales manager
> Extent to which the field rep uses the telephone in communicating with the sales manager
> Extent to which the field rep uses voice mail in communicating with the sales manager[b]
> $\alpha = .85$

Field rep written media usage
> Extent to which the field rep uses facsimile in communicating with the sales manager
> Extent to which the field rep uses written or printed documents in communicating with the sales manager
> $\alpha = .85$

a. Cues: 1, no extent; 2, little extent; 3, some extent; 4, great extent; 5, very great extent.
b. This item was only used for the regions with voice mail.

dealership dyads and 139 of the 173 non-voice mail dealership dyads. The field representatives returned their completed questionnaires to the national sales manager and delivered a questionnaire to each of the sales managers he or she supported. Then, each sales manager completed this questionnaire, placed it in a sealed envelope, and mailed it to the national sales manager. The national sales manager collected the questionnaires and delivered them to the first author.

Communication media usage was collected in the specific context of this communication dyad. That is, each respondent was asked to indicate the extent to which various media—face-to-face, telephone, voice mail (where available), printed documents, facsimile—were used in communicating with a dyadic partner. Table 11.1 gives the specific items used. Factor analysis of the responses resulted, as expected, in two media forms: verbal and written. The results of this factor analysis can be obtained from the first author.

TABLE 11.2 Items Used to Assess Satisfaction With Dyadic-Partner Interactions[a]

Sales manager satisfaction with the quality of interaction with the field representative
1. Field rep assists you in calling on potential customers
2. Field rep provides sales training for your dealership
3. Field rep provides assistance in setting sales goals
4. Field rep provides quick and accurate response to problems
   $\alpha = .87$

Field representative satisfaction with the quality of interaction with the sales manager
1. Sales commitments made by the dealership are carried out
2. Sales issues can be resolved without the sales manager referring to higher management levels
3. Sales manager uses innovative selling techniques
4. Sales manager is cooperative in developing sales marketing plans
5. Sales manager consistently meets new truck sales goals
   $\alpha = .85$

a. A five cue "Faces" scale (Taulbee 1977) was used.

Additionally, open-ended questions were used to ascertain what each respondent liked best and least regarding their efforts to communicate with a dyadic partner.

Satisfaction with dyadic partner interaction was determined in a similar manner using 5-point Likert scales. Distinct items (shown in Table 11.2) were used to reflect the perspectives of the field representatives and the sales managers. These items reflect the national sales manager's performance objectives for his field representatives and dealerships. The face validity of these items and those in Table 11.1 were assessed in a pretest.

Dealership sales performance as determined by the number of new trucks sold by each dealership was obtained from archival sources for the year of the voice mail trial as well as for the prior year. These sales amounts were each standardized for the prior year of 1990 and the trial year of 1991 through the application of the Buying Power Index (*Survey of Buying Power* 1990, 1991), reflecting the demographic and economic profile of each dealership's sales territory. A description of the Buying Power Index is provided in Appendix 1.

Finally, in order to control for the nature of the task context of respondents, items assessing the routineness of the work context and the equivocality of the information being exchanged were included in the questionnaires. While the wording of these items (see Appendix 2) captures this specific work context, the items were similar to those developed and used by Van de Ven and Ferry (1980). Appendix 2 also contains analytical results showing that this work context was similar for both the voice mail and non-voice mail sales regions.

DISCUSSION OF RESULTS

Tables 11.3 and 11.4 provide descriptive statistics and intercorrelations for the study's variables for the voice mail regions and for the non-voice mail regions. These correlations are not multicollinear since the tolerance factors (Hair et al. 1992, p. 48) are well above the .10 cutoff threshold for multicollinearity; a tolerance of .10 indicates a correlation of .95 or higher. As Hair et al. (1992) discuss, tolerance is a common measure of pairwise and multiple variable collinearity where it represents the amount of variability of selected independent variables not explained by other independent variables.

Table 11.5 displays the results of an analysis of covariance to determine if sales regions having access to voice mail outperformed their non-voice mail counterparts. As hypothesized, controlling for the previous year's sales, the presence of voice mail did produce a main effect on performance. An analysis of variance on the prior year's sales performance indicated no differences between the voice mail and non-voice mail sales regions. Taken together, these results provide strong support for Hypothesis 1.

The structural modeling technique LISREL (Joreskog and Sorbom 1986) was used to examine the theoretical model shown as Figure 11.2 and, hence, to test Hypotheses 2 through 6. Note that LISREL controls for the intercorrelations of the model variables. As with the analysis of covariance model used to assess Hypothesis 1, dealership sales performance measures are standardized using the Buying Power Index and the prior year's sales performance is used as a control variable.

The LISREL results for the sales regions with voice mail are given in Figure 11.3. The goodness-of-fit index (GFI) was 0.934, suggesting a reasonably good fit of the model to the data, and the Bentler and Bonett (1980) normed index was 0.93. As the sample size was only 63, these results must be treated with caution (Harris and Shaubroeck 1990). To address this concern, the noncentralized normed fit index (NCNFI) was calculated:

$$NCNFI = \frac{(\chi_n^2 - df_n) - (\chi_t^2 - df_t)}{(\chi_n^2 - df_n)}$$

Here, n represents the null model, t the target model, and df the degrees of freedom. Recent research on fit indexes indicates that the NCNFI removes the bias that can occur for small samples (McDonald and Marsh 1990) and other LISREL studies have successfully used this index (Bagozzi et al. 1991, Judge and Zeithaml 1992). For this model, the NCNFI was 0.92, an acceptable fit. As the causal model shown as Figure 11.3 fits the data reasonably well, an iterative modification process was not necessary (Joreskog and

TABLE 11.3 Intercorrelations Among the Study's Variables for Sales Regions With Voice Mail

	Field Rep Verbal Media Use	Field Rep Written Media Use	Sales Manager Verbal Media Use	Sales Manager Written Media Use	Field Rep Satisfaction With Sales Manager Interaction	Sales Manager Satisfaction With Field Rep Interaction	Dealership Sales Performance
Field rep verbal media use	1						
Field rep written media use	0.24*	1					
Sales manager verbal media use	0.36**	0.25*	1				
Sales manager written media use	0.27*	0.33**	0.42***	1			
Field rep satisfaction with interaction	0.32**	0.12	0.20	0.32*	1		
Sales manager satisfaction with interaction	0.36**	0.34**	0.38**	0.34*	0.24*	1	
Dealership sales performance	0.42***	0.19	0.18	0.17	0.21	0.39**	1
Mean	3.98	3.42	3.89	2.90	3.98	3.24	0.69
Standard deviation	0.62	0.78	0.97	1.01	0.83	0.76	0.23

*p < .01; **p < .001; ***p < .0001; n = 63.

TABLE 11.4 Intercorrelations Among the Study's Variables for Sales Regions Without Voice Mail

	Field Rep Verbal Media Use	Field Rep Written Media Use	Sales Manager Verbal Media Use	Sales Manager Written Media Use	Field Rep Satisfaction With Sales Manager Interaction	Sales Manager Satisfaction With Field Rep Interaction	Dealership Sales Performance
Field rep verbal media use	1						
Field rep written media use	0.27*	1					
Sales manager verbal media use	0.31**	0.26*	1				
Sales manager written media use	0.19*	0.34**	0.33**	1			
Field rep satisfaction with interaction	0.29**	0.20	0.32**	0.31**	1		
Sales manager satisfaction with interaction	0.36**	0.37**	0.29**	0.35**	0.28*	1	
Dealership sales performance	0.07	0.16	0.21	0.30*	0.11	0.10	1
Mean	3.12	3.01	3.23	3.03	3.18	3.09	0.35
Standard deviation	0.52	0.61	0.96	0.67	0.57	0.89	0.32

$*p < .01$; $**p < .001$; $n = 139$.

TABLE 11.5 Results of Analysis of Covariance[a]

Sources	Dependent Variable df	Performance Quasi-Experimental Year	
		MS	F
No covariate			
Main effect			
Voice mail vs. no voice mail	1	1185.31	20.76***
Error	200	57.09	
Covariate			
Performance base year	1	7278.64	288.61****
Main effect			
Voice mail vs. no voice mail	1	305.24	12.10***
	199	25.22	

a. Controlling for economy and demographics in dealership area. Barlett's test indicates homogeneity of variance across treatment and control groups. For the base year performance measure there was not a significant difference across the voice mail (mean = 0.345) vs. non-voice mail sales regions (mean = 0.369). ***$p < .001$; ****$p < .0000$.

Sorbom 1986). While communication media use is not observed as having a direct effect on sales performance, significant associations are seen with the dyadic-partner's satisfaction with dyadic interaction (except for the sales manager's use of verbal media). Furthermore, one indirect path can be seen to relate communication media use with sales performance:

Field representative media use → sales manager satisfaction with field representative interaction → dealership sales performance

The LISREL results for the three sales regions without voice mail did not produce a good fit (a GFI of 0.86, a Bentler and Bonett of 0.81, and a NCNFI of 0.84). However, after a model trimming exercise which dropped sales performance from the model shown as Figure 11.3, a stable model was obtained for the sales regions with (see Figure 11.4) and without (Figure 11.5) voice mail. Given the absence of a comparative LISREL model examining a direct effect of dyadic-partner media use on dealership sales performance in the regions without voice mail, simple correlations between these variables (shown in Table 11.6) are used to assess Hypotheses 2, 3, and 6. Significant differences in correlation coefficients (in the hypothesized directions) are observed for the associations between the field representative's verbal media use and dealership sales performance, and the sales manager's satisfaction with the field representative's interactions and dealership sales

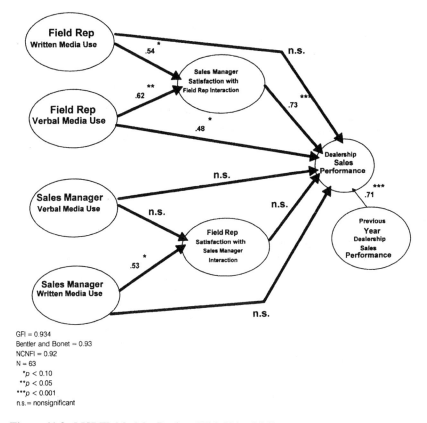

GFI = 0.934
Bentler and Bonet = 0.93
NCNFI = 0.92
N = 63
 *p < 0.10
 **p < 0.05
 ***p < 0.001
n.s. = nonsignificant

Figure 11.3. LISREL Model—Regions With Voice Mail

performance. These results provide partial support for Hypotheses 2 and 6 but no support for Hypothesis 3.

Comparisons of the respective path coefficients of Figures 11.4 and 11.5 enable assessments of Hypotheses 4 and 5. Mixed results were observed regarding Hypothesis 4 as significant relationships were observed with the field representative's verbal media use and the sales manager's satisfaction with field representative interactions (sales regions with voice mail) and with the sales manager's verbal media use and the field representative's satisfaction with sales manager interactions (sales regions without voice mail). Apparently, the availability of voice mail enabled effective field representative verbal communication with the sales manager. Hypothesis 5 was strongly supported by these data, with the availability of voice mail enabling more effective written communication by both the field representative and

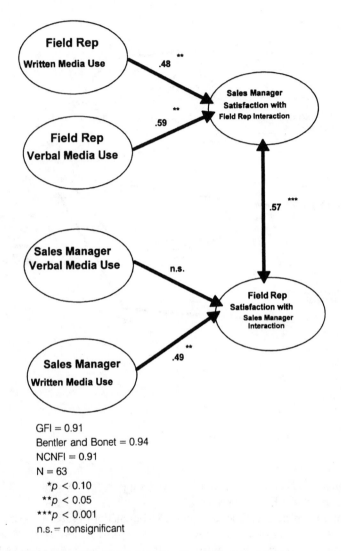

Figure 11.4. Trimmed LISREL Model—Regions With Voice Mail

the sales manager. A summary of the outcomes regarding each of the study's research hypotheses is given as Table 11.7.

Finally, in order to demonstrate the presence of both direct and indirect voice mail effects, an additional LISREL analysis was undertaken which included voice mail as a categorical independent observed variable (Bentler

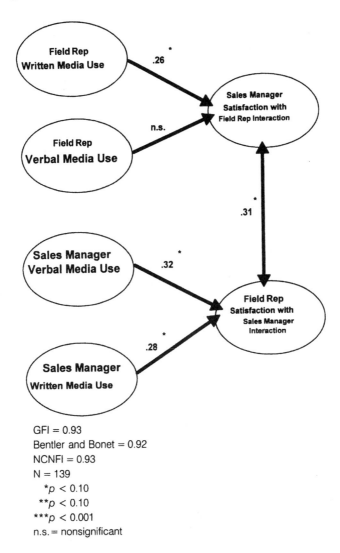

GFI = 0.93
Bentler and Bonet = 0.92
NCNFI = 0.93
N = 139
   *p < 0.10
  **p < 0.10
 ***p < 0.001
n.s. = nonsignificant

Figure 11.5. Trimmed LISREL Model—Regions Without Voice Mail

and Chow 1987, p. 87). The stable model which resulted (GFI = 0.934, Bentler and Bonet index = 0.99, NCNFI = 0.99, $n = 207$) demonstrated the existence of both a significant direct effect (voice mail → dealership sales performance) and a significant indirect effect (voice mail → field representative's written media use → sales manager's satisfaction with field repre-

TABLE 11.6   Tests of Significance for H2, H3, and H6 Using Simple
Correlations Across the Voice Mail and Non-Voice Mail Regions

Simple Correlations	Dealership Sales Performance	
	Regions With	Regions Without
Hypothesized Sales	Voice Mail	Voice Mail
Performance Predictors	(n = 63)	(n = 139)
Field rep verbal media use	.42**[!!]	.07[!!]
Sales manager verbal media use	.18	.21
Field Rep written media use	.19	.16
Sales manager written media use	.17	.30*
Sales manager satisfaction with field rep interaction	.39**[!]	.10[!]
Field rep satisfaction with sales manager interaction	.21	.11

$*p < .05; **p < .01.$
[!]Significant difference between the correlation coefficients for the two subgroups (voice mail regions, non-voice mail region) (Kleinbaum and Kupper 1978, pp. 106-108); [!]$p < .03;$ [!!]$p < .01.$

sentation interactions → dealership sales performance). Details regarding this analysis can be obtained from the first author.

DISCUSSION OF
THE STUDY'S RESULTS

The research design had three limitations which were addressed prior to our interpreting the study's findings. First, data were gathered in the context of a single interorganizational context characterized by a durable goods manufacturer and its associated dealerships. Clearly, these findings need to be examined in other contexts in order that the findings can be readily generalized. Second, criticism might be legitimately raised regarding the sufficiency of the sample sizes for the "with voice mail" and "without voice mail" LISREL analyses. However, after examining this issue using the noncentralized normed fit index (McDonald and Marsh 1990), it appears that one can feel confident regarding the stability of the LISREL results. Third, criticism might also be raised regarding the use of subjective cues to assess communication media usage. However, given the internal consistency of these measures (see Table 11.1) as well as their means and standard deviations (see Tables 11.3 and 11.4), obvious deficiencies do not appear to exist.

TABLE 11.7 Results of Assessing the Study's Research Hypotheses

Hypothesis	Results	Commentary
1	Strong support	Dealerships in sales regions with voice mail exhibited higher sales performance than did dealerships in sales regions without voice mail, controlling for market potential and prior years' sales.
2	Partial support	Verbal media use by field representatives in sales regions with voice mail was more positively associated with dealership sales performance.
3	No support	
4	Mixed support	The association between verbal media use by field representatives and sales managers' satisfaction with field representative interactions was strongest in sales regions with voice mail.
		Verbal media use by sales managers in sales regions without voice mail was positively associated with field representatives' satisfaction with their sales manager's interactions.
5	Strong support	The association between written media use by field representatives and sales managers' satisfaction with their field representative's interactions was strongest in sales regions with voice mail.
		The association between written media use by sales managers and field representatives' satisfaction with their interactions with their sales manager was strongest in sales regions with voice mail.
6	Partial support	Sales managers' satisfaction with their field representative's interactions was positively associated with dealership sales performance in sales regions with voice mail.

As anticipated, the introduction of a voice mail capability appears to have both directly and indirectly—and positively—influenced sales performance for this interorganizational (manufacturer-dealership) relationship. The direct effect seems rather straightforward: Voice mail apparently enabled the dyadic partners to exchange messages with one another in a more convenient and more timely manner. As a result, it is likely that problems and opportunities were dealt with more successfully, resulting in an increase in dealership sales performance. That this, in fact, may have occurred is supported through two additional evidence sources. First, the sales managers were asked, using a single-item question, their level of communication satisfaction with regard to the communication nuisance factors: ring but no answer, person called in a different time zone, and person called but not available. Respondents in sales regions with voice mail reported significantly ($p < .01$) higher communication satisfaction than did respondents in sales regions without voice mail. Second, respondents were also asked to list those aspects regarding communication with a dyadic-partner which they liked least. For sales regions with voice mail, the sales managers in total listed 5 such aspects, and the field representatives in total listed 8. For sales regions without voice mail, the sales managers in total listed 31 negative aspects and the field representatives in total listed 21. Even considering the larger respondent sample size for the sales regions without voice mail, these complaints do indicate a greater degree of communication dissatisfaction by respondents in the sales regions without voice mail.

The nature of the indirect effects is much less clear. However, the LISREL results do provide insight into the nature of effective communication processes for this specific IOR. Written media appear to serve a very important role in this particular context, likely because they provide an effective vehicle for substantiating requests, confirmations, and situational circumstances, and, as a consequence, communication accuracy and timeliness are increased. Note the importance of written media use in Figures 11.3, 11.4, and 11.5: Written media use consistently increases respondents' interaction satisfaction with a dyadic-partner.

However, as these results show, the key variable with this indirect pathway is not written media use per se but rather the sales manager's satisfaction in interacting with a field representative. In retrospect, this is not surprising as it is the sales manager who coordinates the dealership's relationships with its end-consumers. The sales manager's capability to fully service end-consumers successfully, however, is dependent on the ability of the field representative to answer questions, provide commitments, or otherwise facilitate the handling of customer requests. What variable seems to most influence a sales manager's satisfaction with his or her interaction with a field representative? It seems clear from the study's results that the field representative's use of written media is the primary determinant. But, in order for the field representative to exchange written media with a sales manager, the need to commence such a dialogue must be recognized. It is here, we believe, that the benefits of voice mail are felt, since often a voice mail message (a) signals the need for a communication episode to occur and (b) enables the dyadic partners to interact asynchronously using written media, either in current or archived form, as a basis for resolving the business event which precipitated the need. We followed up our study with interviews with a small sample of sales managers and field representatives in an effort to validate this interpretation. In these interviews, voice mail was consistently raised as an important vehicle for improving the effectiveness of the field representatives in reacting to specific customer requests.

IMPLICATIONS AND CONCLUSIONS

In response to Ring and Van de Ven's (1994) call for research on interorganizational relationships, this study has produced two contributions for both research and practice. The first contribution is the demonstration that the introduction of a communications technology into an interorganizational relationship affects communication behaviors and, hence, organizational performance through dual pathways. The first pathway reflects the distinctive asynchronous communication attribute of the technology providing organizational members communications capabilities previously not available. If these new communication capabilities dramatically improve certain communication processes, such as timely reaction to an end-consumer's service requests, and if these processes are closely associated with member actions producing valued organizational outcomes, such as truck sales, then the introduction of the communications technology can directly improve interorganizational effectiveness. The second pathway reflects the capability of the introduced communications technology to enrich the portfolio of communication options made available to an organization's members. If the new technology dramatically improves members' ability to apply previously available media like the written media and these media improve members' communication processes closely associated with actions producing valued organizational outcomes, then the introduction of the communications technology can be said to indirectly improve interorganizational effectiveness. The message to both researchers and practitioners is clear: Efforts to assess, in either an ad hoc or post hoc fashion, the impacts of a new communications technology must consider both how the technology's attributes themselves add value and how the new technology might embellish the use of already in-place communication technologies.

The study's second contribution lies in its demonstration of the necessity, when examining the impacts of an information technology, to devise data gathering procedures which tightly link the functionality of the newly introduced technology to those organizational activities whose outcomes are expected to be beneficially affected. Here, for example, the introduction of voice mail was examined in the context of an interorganizational relationship which crossed sizeable geographical and temporal boundaries and, hence, could benefit from the asynchronous communications aspects of voice mail. Furthermore, data were collected on aspects of this relationship such as communications exchanges between dyadic partners and satisfaction with dyadic partner interactions which were expected to be affected directly by an asynchronous communications capability. This study's generally supportive findings suggest that the general lack of strong results characterizing much prior research examining the organizational impacts of information technology may be due to the difficulty of, first, isolating and then capturing the beneficial effects of the technology's functionality within the targeted organizational context.

As Weill (1992) has indicated, the information technology construct may suffer in a fashion similar to the technology construct (Scott 1987, Woodward 1959) in organization theory and be too broad a construct to be explored successfully as a homogeneous entity. As just mentioned, it is quite likely that one of the primary reasons why research examining the organizational impact of information technology has often produced mixed or inconsequential findings is that such studies have been unable to isolate these technology-induced organizational restructuring events where for example a single technology is targeted at a well-defined process or relationship. When research designs, such as that applied in this study, are able to capture both the nature and outcomes of specific restructuring episodes with a dynamic analysis over time, then it becomes more likely that significant relationships will be observed among a study's variables. We hope this study will result in future research which more tightly and more appropriately focuses on such phenomena.

APPENDIX 1
Buying Power Index

Research on buying trends indicates that consumers with the same demographics and economic profiles and with access to similar channels of distribution will normally buy the same quantity and quality of product. The Buying Power Index (BPI) (*Survey of Buying Power* 1990, 1991) is used to equitably compare markets across these three factors (demographics, economic profile, and channels of distribution). The BPI weights the total population, income, and retail sales data for metropolitan areas and counties in the United States. The buying potential for the United States as a whole is 100.00. To calculate the performance index for an area (county or metropolitan area), take the annual sales for the entire company (truck manufacturer) and multiply that figure by the BPI for that market. This yields the sales measure (SM) for that particular territory. Then divide the actual number of trucks sold in that market by the SM figure which yields a performance index. A performance index above 1 indicates that actual sales have exceeded the sales potential and conversely for results below 1.

APPENDIX 2

TABLE A.1   Comparison of Task Context Across Treatment and Control Groups

| | | Non-Voice Mail | |
Task Context[a]	Voice Mail Regions Mean (SD)	Regions Mean (SD)	p Value (t-Test, 1 Tailed)
Field rep—To what extent is your sales work with this dealership routine.	3.024 (0.651)	3.133 (0.683)	.389
Field rep—To what extent are sales issues and activities performed dissimilar from day-to-day.	2.951 (0.740)	2.980 (0.746)	.419
Field rep—To what extent is there variety in your sales work with this dealership.	3.122 (0.842)	3.156 (0.730)	.405
Sales manager—To what extent must sales issues be dealt with in an urgent manner.	3.839 (0.898)	8.309 (0.976)	.440
Sales manager—To what extent in sales problems does more than one satisfactory solution arise.	3.258 (0.855)	3.271 (0.732)	.468
Sales manager—To what extent can information for your sales issues be interpreted differently leading to different but acceptable solutions.	2.968 (0.836)	3.065 (0.692)	.261
Sales manager—To what extent in your sales decisions does the information used mean different things to those involved in the decision.	3.206 (1.031)	3.121 (0.917)	.346

a. Cues: 1, no extent; 2, little extent; 3, some extent; 4, great extent; 5, very great extent.

REFERENCES

Adams, J. S. (1976), "The Structure and Dynamics of Behavior in Organizational Boundary Roles," in M. D. Dunnette (Ed.), *Handbook of Industrial and Organizational Psychology,* Chicago: Rand McNally, pp. 1175-1199.
_____ (1980), "Interorganizational Processes and Organization Boundary Activities," in L. L. Cummings and B. Staw (Eds.), *Research in Organizational Behavior,* Greenwich, CT: JAI, Vol. 2, pp. 321-355.

Aldrich, H. E. and D. A. Whetten (1981), "Organization-Sets, Action-Sets, and Networks: Making the Most of Simplicity," in P. C. Nystrom and W. H. Starbuck (Eds.), *Handbook of Organizational Design,* New York: Oxford University Press, pp. 385-408.

Allen, T. J. and O. Hauptman (1990), "The Substitution of Communication Technologies for Organizational Structure in Research and Development," in J. Fulk and C. Steinfield (Eds.), *Organizations and Communications Technology,* Newbury Park, CA: Sage, pp. 275-294.

Alpar, P. and M. Kim (1990), "A Microeconomic Approach to the Measurement of IT Value," *Journal of Management Information Systems,* 7, 2, 55-70.

Argyris, C. (1960), *Understanding Organizational Behavior,* Homewood, IL: Dorsey.

Bagozzi, R. P., Y. Yi, and L. W. Philipps (1991), "Assessing Construct Validity in Organizational Research," *Administrative Science Quarterly,* 36, 421-458.

Banker, R. D., R. J. Kauffman, and R. C. Morey (1990), "Measuring Gains in Efficiency From IT," *Journal of Management Information Systems,* 7, 2, 29-54.

Bender, D. H. (1986), "Financial Impact of Information Processing," *Journal of Management Information Systems,* 3, 2, 22-32.

Bentler, P. and D. G. Bonett (1980), "Significance Tests and Goodness of Fit in the Analysis of Covariance Structures," *Psychological Bulletin,* 88, 588-606.

Bentler, P. M. and C. Chow (1987), "Practical Issues in Structural Modeling," *Sociological Methods and Research,* 16, 78-117.

Bitner, M. J. (1990), "Evaluating Service Encounters: The Effects of Physical Surroundings and Employee Responses," *Journal of Marketing,* 54, 2, 69-82.

Bolton, R. N. and J. H. Drew (1991), "A Longitudinal Analysis of the Impact of Service Changes on Customer Attitudes," *Journal of Marketing,* 55, January, 1-9.

Boulding, W., A. Kalra, R. Staelin, and V. Zeithaml (1993), "Process Model of Service Quality: From Expectations to Behavioral Intentions," *Journal of Marketing Research,* 30, February, 7-27.

Bullard, W. R., J. J. Cronin, and D. J. Shemwell (1993), "The Effects of Strategic Customer Service Levels on Corporate Performance," in R. Johnston and N. D. C. Slack (Eds.), *Service Superiority,* Warwick, UK: Warwick Printing, pp. 155-162.

Chase, R. B. and D. E. Bowen (1991), "Service Quality and the Service Delivery System," in S. W. Brown, E. Gummersson, B. Edvardsson, and B. Gustavasson (Eds.), *Service Quality: Multi-Disciplinary and Multi-National Perspectives,* Lexington, MA: Lexington Books.

_____ and R. H. Hayes (1991), "Beefing Up Operations in Service Firms," *Sloan Management Review,* 32, Fall, 15-26.

Chismar, W. C. and C. H. Kriebel (1985), "A Method for Assessing the Economic Impact of Information Systems Technology on Organizations," in *Proceedings of the Sixth International Conference on Information Systems,* Indianapolis, IN, December, pp. 45-56.

Contractor, N. S. and E. M. Eisenberg (1990), "Communication Networks and New Media in Organizations," in J. Fulk and C. Steinfield (Eds.), *Organizations and Communications Technology,* Newbury Park, CA: Sage, pp. 143-172.

_____, J. Fulk, P. R. Monge, and A. Singhal (1986), "Cultural Assumptions That Influence the Implementation of Communication Technologies," *Vikalpa,* 11, 4, 287-300.

Cook, T. D. and D. T. Campbell (1979), *Quasi-Experimental: Design and Analysis Issues for Field Settings,* Boston: Houghton Mifflin.

Cron, W. L. and M. G. Sobol (1983), "The Relationship Between Computerization and Performance: A Strategy for Maximizing the Economic Benefits of Computerization," *Journal of Information and Management,* 6, 171-181.

Culnan, M. J. and M. L. Markus (1987), "Information Technologies," in F. M. Jablin, L. L. Putnam, K. H. Roberts, and L. W. Porter (Eds.), *Handbook of Organizational Communication,* Newbury Park, CA: Sage, pp. 420-443.

Daft, R. L. and R. H. Lengel (1986), "Organizational Information Requirements, Media Richness and Structural Design," *Management Science,* 32, 5, 554-572.

_____, _____, and L. K. Trevino (1987), "Message Equivocality, Media Selection, and Manager Performance: Implications for Information Systems," *MIS Quarterly,* 11, 3, 355-366.

DeLone, W. H. and E. R. McLean (1992), "Information Systems Success: The Quest for the Dependent Variable," *Information Systems Research,* 3, 60-95.

Ebadi, Y. and J. Utterback (1984), "The Effect of Communication on Technological Innovation," *Management Science,* 35, 5, 572-585.

Edvardsson, B. and B. Gustavsson (1991), "Quality in Services and Quality in Service Organizations: A Model for Quality Assessment," in S. Brown, E. Gummeson, B. Edvardsson, and B. Gustavsson (Eds.), *Service Quality: Multidisciplinary and Multinational Perspectives,* Lexington, MA: Lexington Books, pp. 319-340.

Foster, L. W. and D. M. Flynn (1984), "Management Information Technology: Its Effects on Organizational Form and Function," *Management Information Systems Quarterly,* 8, 229-236.

Fuchsberg, G. (1992), "Quality Programs Show Shoddy Results," *Wall Street Journal,* May 14, VCCXIX, No. 95, pp. B1-B8.

Fulk, J., J. Schmitz, and C. W. Steinfield (1990), "A Social Influence Model of Technology Use," in J. Fulk and C. Steinfield (Eds.), *Organizations and Communications Technology,* Newbury Park, CA: Sage, pp. 117-140.

_____, C. W. Steinfield, J. Schmitz, and J. G. Power (1987), "A Social Information Processing Model of Media Use in Organizations," *Communication Research,* 14, 5, 529-552.

Hair, J. F., R. E. Anderson, R. Tatham, and W. C. Black (1992), *Multivariate Data Analysis With Readings,* New York: Macmillan.

Harris, M. M. and J. Schaubroeck (1990), "Confirmatory Modeling in Organizational Behavior/Human Resource Management: Issues and Applications," *Journal of Management,* 16, 337-360.

Harris, S. E. and J. L. Katz (1991), "Firm Size and the Information Technology Investment Intensity of Life Insurers," *MIS Quarterly,* 15, 3, 333-352.

Haynes, R. M. (1993), "Service Quality Models: Reality in Airline Management," in R. Johnston and N. D. C. Slack (Eds.), *Service Superiority,* Warwick, UK: Warwick Printing, pp. 461-466.

Hiltz, S. R. and M. Turoff (1978), *The Network Nation,* Reading, MA: Addison-Wesley.

Huber, G. P. and R. L. Daft (1987), "The Information Environments of Organizations," in F. M. Jablin, L. L. Putnam, K. H. Roberts, and L. W. Porter (Eds.), *Handbook of Organizational Communication: An Interdisciplinary Perspective,* Newbury Park, CA: Sage, pp. 130-164.

Joreskog, K. and D. Sorbom (1986), *LISREL VI: User's Guide,* Mooresville, IN: Scientific Software.

Judge, W. Q. and C. P. Zeithaml (1992), "Institutional and Strategic Choice Perspectives on Board Involvement in the Strategic Decision Process," *Academy of Management Journal,* 35, 4, 766-794.

Juran, P. and F. Gryna (1989), *Juran's Quality Control Handbook,* New York: McGraw-Hill.

Katz, D. and R. Kahn (1978), *The Social Psychology of Organizations,* 2nd ed., New York: John Wiley.

Kauffman, R. J. and P. Weill (1989), "An Evaluative Framework for Research on the Performance Effects of Information Technology Investment," *Proceedings of the Tenth International Conference on Information Systems,* Boston, December, pp. 377-388.

Kleinbaum, D. G. and L. L. Kupper (1978), *Applied Regression Analysis and Other Multivariable Methods,* Boston: Duxbury.

Kling, R. and W. Scacchi (1982), "The Web of Computing: Computer Technology as Social Organization," *Advances in Computers,* 21, 2-60.

Kotter, J. P. (1973), "The Psychological Contract: Managing the Joining Up Process," *California Management Review,* 15, 3, 91-99.

Laumann, E. O., J. Galaskiewicz, and P. Marsden (1978), "Community Structure as Interorganizational Linkages," *Annual Review of Sociology,* 4, 455-484.

Lind, M. R. and R. W. Zmud (1991), "The Influence of a Convergence in Understanding Between Technology Providers and Users on Information Technology Innovativeness," *Organization Science,* 2, 2, 195-217.

Mattson, J. (1993), "How Managers Cope With Crude Performance Systems: A Multiperspective Case Study," in R. Johnston and N. D. C. Slack (Eds.), *Service Superiority: The Design and Delivery of Effective Service Operations,* Warwick, UK: Warwick Printing, pp. 493-499.

McDonald, R. P. and H. W. Marsh (1990), "Choosing a Multivariate Model: Noncentrality and Goodness of Fit," *Psychological Bulletin,* 107, 247-255.

Mohr, J. and J. R. Nevin (1990), "Communication Strategies in Marketing Channels: A Theoretical Perspective," *Journal of Marketing,* October, 36-51.

Neale, M. A. and G. B. Northcraft (1991), "Behavioral Negotiation Theory: A Framework for Conceptualizing Dyadic Bargaining," in L. L. Cummings and B. M. Staw (Eds.), *Research in Organizational Behavior,* Greenwich, CT: JAI, Vol. 13, pp. 147-190.

Niederman, F., J. C. Brancheau, and J. C. Wetherbe (1991), "Information Systems Management Issues for the 1990s," *MIS Quarterly,* 15, 4, 475-502.

Orlikowski, W. J. and D. Robey (1991), "Information Technology and the Structuring of Organizations," *Information System Research,* 2, 2, 143-169.

Palme, J. (1981), *Experience With the Use of the COM Computerized Conferencing System,* Stockholm: Forsvarets Forskningsanstalt.

Pfeffer, J. (1981), "Management as Symbolic Action: The Creation and Maintenance of Organizational Paradigms," in L. L. Cummings and B. M. Staw (Eds.), *Research in Organizational Behavior,* Greenwich, CT: JAI, Vol. 3, pp. 1-52.

Picot, A., H. Klingenberg, and H. P. Kranzle (1982), "Organizational Communication: The Relationship Between Technological Development and Socioeconomic Needs," in L. Bannon, U. Barry, and O. Holst (Eds.), *Information Technology Impact on the Way of Life,* Dublin: Tycooly, pp. 114-132.

Provan, K. G. and S. J. Skinner (1989), "Interorganizational Dependence and Control as Predictors of Opportunism in Dealer-Supplier Relations," *Academy of Management Journal,* 32, 202-212.

Rice, R. E. and Associates (1984), *The New Media: Communication, Research, and Technology,* Beverly Hills, CA: Sage.

_____ and J. H. Bair (1984), "New Organizational Media and Productivity," in R. E. Rice and Associates (Eds.), *The New Media: Communication, Research, and Technology,* Beverly Hills, CA: Sage, pp. 185-216.

_____ and D. Case (1983), "Computer-Based Messaging in the University: Description of Use and Utility," *Journal of Communication,* 33, 131-152.

Ring, P. S. and A. H. Van de Ven (1994), "Developmental Processes of Cooperative Interorganizational Relationships," *Academy of Management Review,* 19, 90-118.

Roach, S. S. (1988), "Technology and the Service Sector: The Hidden Competitive Challenge," *Technological Forecasting and Social Change,* 34, 4, December, 387-403.

Rogers, E. M. (1986), *Communication Technology,* New York: Free Press.

Scott, R. E. (1987), *Organizations Rational, Natural, and Open Systems,* 2nd ed., Englewood Cliffs, NJ: Prentice Hall.

Sproull, L. and S. Kiesler (1986), "Reducing Social Context Cues: Electronic Mail in Organizational Communication," *Communication Research,* 14, 479-490.

Steinfield, C. W. (1986), "Computer-Mediated Communication Systems," in M. Williams (Ed.), *The Annual Review of Information Science and Technology,* White Plains, NY: Knowledge Industry, Vol. 21, pp. 167-202.

Survey of Buying Power (1990), Sales and Marketing Management, New York.

Survey of Buying Power (1991), Sales and Marketing Management, New York.

Taulbee, E. S. (1977), *The Minnesota Multiphasic Personality Inventory (MMPI): A Comprehensive Annotated Bibliography (1940-1965),* Troy, NY: Whitston.

Vandermere, S. (1993), "Service Quality: The Soft Side Is Harder," in R. Johnston and N. D. C. Slack (Eds.), *Service Superiority: The Design and Delivery of Effective Service Operations,* Warwick, UK: Warwick Printing, pp. 265-272.

Van de Ven, A. H. and D. L. Ferry (1980), *Measuring and Assessing Organizations,* New York: John Wiley.

Weick, K. (1979), *The Social Psychology of Organizing,* 2nd ed., Reading, MA: Addison-Wesley.

Weill, P. (1992), "The Relationship Between Investment in Information Technology and Firm Performance: A Study of the Valve Manufacturing Sector," *Information Systems Research,* 3, 4, 307-333.

Woodward, J. (1959), *Management and Technology,* London: Her Majesty's Stationary Office.

Zack, M. H. (1993), "Interactivity and Communication Mode Choice in Ongoing Management Groups," *Information Systems Research,* 4, 3, 207-239.

Zaheer, A. and N. Venkatraman (1994), "The Impact of Electronic Data Interchange on Operations Performance: Technological Factors and Interorganizational Relationships," *Management Science,* 40, 5, 549-566.

12

Hardwiring Weak Ties

Interorganizational Computer-Mediated Communication, Occupational Communities, and Organizational Change

JEANNE M. PICKERING

JOHN LESLIE KING

Computer-mediated communication refers to person-to-person communication, often in text or graphic form, over computer networks. Organizational computer-mediated communication (OCMC) in the form of proprietary, within-company electronic mail systems, has been around since the 1970s (Hiltz and Turoff 1978). Interorganizational computer-mediated communication (ICMC) systems, such as the broad "Internet" family of networks, started out as experiments supporting rudimentary, interorganizational communication and have expanded rapidly to incorporate utilities such as Gopher systems, the World Wide Web, and interactive multimedia. The government-subsidized experimental era of these ICMC networks is closing as support by commercial firms and private individuals grows (DeLoughry 1994, McGarty 1992, Smarr and Catlett 1992). Pricing of the Internet and

This chapter appeared originally in *Organization Science, 6*(4), July/August, 1995.

399

other ICMC services is well under way (Faulhaber 1992), and the complex regulatory issues involved in merging various networks and utilities into the larger communications infrastructure are becoming apparent (Branscomb 1992).

ICMC technologies have long been expected to bring serious challenges to organizational leaders (Cash and Konsynski 1985, Jonscher 1994, Keen 1986, Malone and Rockart 1991, Nolan and Croson 1995, Nohria and Eccles 1992). Two challenges are of special import for this chapter. One concerns the organizational payoffs from use of expensive ICMC technologies that most clearly benefit individual-level communications (Giridharan and Mendelson 1994). The other concerns the use of new communications technologies to change the form and function of organizations in a manner similar to that seen from use of older communication technologies (Beniger 1986, Chandler 1977, Yates 1989). A considerable literature has evolved arguing the importance of information technologies such as ICMC to organizational success in the future (Applegate et al. 1988, Davenport 1993, Hammer and Champy 1993). These accounts provide a workable logic of explanation regarding why the technology is important, but with few exceptions (e.g., Markus 1994), they seldom attempt to provide a detailed explanation of the mechanisms by which the postulated changes actually occur. Until such mechanisms can be postulated and studied in detail, much of the rhetoric surrounding the transformational power of ICMC technologies remains superficial.

This chapter provides one explanatory mechanism for the growth of ICMC as seen to date: the exploitation of ICMC infrastructure by individuals seeking to establish and maintain interpersonal social ties, and particularly so-called "weak ties." In this argument, organizations that depend on employees with highly developed weak tie networks can be expected to provide and maintain ICMC infrastructure more readily than organizations with no such dependence. The use of ICMC is likely to be especially rapid in organizations dependent on what Van Maanen and Barley (1984) call "dispersed occupational communities" that are dependent on maintenance of weak social ties. Such organizations are also likely to face early the challenges of organizational change resulting from heavy ICMC use. Maintenance of weak social ties is not the only mechanism one might use to explain ICMC growth, but it is effective at explaining at least part of the extraordinary growth seen in such ICMC initiatives as the Internet, and it provides an instructive example of the mechanism-based argument required for further understanding of a complex sociotechnical evolution (King and Kraemer 1984, Van Parijs 1981).

WEAK TIES AND
COMPUTER-MEDIATED COMMUNICATION

Computer-mediated communication technologies are new to many organizations, although the roots of the notion reach back to the 1960s (Hiltz and Turoff 1978, Kraemer and King 1988). The technology that best illustrates the computer-mediated communication vision is interorganizational electronic mail (Jonscher 1994, Kraut 1990). Individuals who use interorganizational electronic mail claim the technology reduces their costs for carrying out certain kinds of communications activities, thereby supplementing the full array of communications modalities available. Electronic mail enables asynchronous communication, rapid and felicitous response and forwarding capabilities, easy broadcast distribution, and so on. Electronic mail users often claim their overall level of communication goes up as they become facile in its use. What is not clear from the early studies done on the electronic mail is what motivates individuals to use electronic mail beyond lessened costs that, in themselves, do not bring benefits. The benefit, we suggest, comes through changes in personal social tie networks computer-mediated communication users can effect.

Social ties are the links that bind individuals to other individuals, as manifested in the frequency and kinds of communications among individuals. Granovetter (1973) differentiated between strong and weak social ties on four dimensions: time, emotional intensity, mutual confidence, and reciprocity. Strong ties are maintained through frequent and emotionally intense communication, often entailing the sharing of confidences and, over time, the establishment of reciprocity between the parties. Individuals maintain strong ties with spouses, children, close friends, and coworkers with whom they share mutual dependencies in the execution of work-related tasks. Weak ties are maintained through less frequent and less emotionally intense communication, in relationships that do not require or encourage sharing of confidences or establishment of strong reciprocities. Weak ties are maintained among extended family members, coworkers not central to an individual's task domain, and everyday acquaintances made in connection with work, social activities, and mutual friendships. Granovetter theorized (1973) and subsequently demonstrated (1983) that weak ties are important in work-related contexts.

CMC technologies such as electronic mail can play a role in maintenance of strong ties, as seen in cases of rapid spread of electronic mail among close coworkers for mutual communication even when their offices are adjacent to one another. This support is exemplary of OCMC. OCMC marginally improves communication in such strong tie networks, but such networks are generally in place for reasons not affected by marginal changes in communication costs, and such strong ties will seldom be weakened by lack of OCMC access. As partial support for this, Krackhardt (1992), while demonstrating that work-related strong ties are quite important, noted that they seemed to be reinforced mainly through direct, face-to-face interaction. This finding is consistent with other studies (Culnan and Markus 1987, Eccles and Crane 1988, Sproull and Kiesler 1991).

The effects of CMC capability on weak ties is another matter altogether. Feldman (1987) has argued that interorganizational electronic mail would greatly facilitate establishment of weak ties through use of distributed lists that enable individuals to post electronically a message to a large number of individuals and thereby discover others with common interests. The astonishing proliferation of communications through distributed lists since Feldman's prediction is seen in Usenet, a conglomeration of newsgroups or electronic bulletin boards accessible from the Internet community. In just a few years Usenet grew from a small enterprise to a huge network of hundreds of newsgroups accessed regularly by millions of users (Quarterman 1990).

The Usenet phenomenon is instructive, but it does not fully engage the role of ICMC with respect to weak ties. Many communications to Usenet are strictly "read only," and the newsgroups are known to be heavily populated by "lurkers" who never post anything but who read the messages posted there (Eveland and Bikson 1987, Finholt and Sproull 1990). Lurkers are no more "tied" to the network than viewers of broadcast television are "tied" to the stations they view. Such communication elicits no dialogue, much less confidences or reciprocity among the individuals involved (Denning 1982, Mackay 1988). Individuals who read the communications delivered via distributed lists obviously get something from doing so, but their minimal level of engagement is enabled by the very low cost of participation due to the ICMC infrastructure. As impressive as Feldman's conjecture proved to be with respect to the subsequent growth of Usenet, this example of computer-mediated communication use does not make a compelling argument for organizational support of ICMC infrastructure for employee use.

A more persuasive argument for organizational support of ICMC infrastructure is informational. ICMC supported weak ties are probably often maintained to gather information and facilitate problem solving. A motivation for Feldman's prediction about the growth of weak ties through distribution lists was the argument that an increase in information diffusion via electronic distribution lists would improve problem solving for problems not well structured or well aligned with the organization's problem-solving structures. Many of the messages posted to Usenet newsgroups are requests for particular information and assistance with problem solving, and the more popular groups maintain lists of frequently asked questions and answers to those questions (Quarterman 1990).

A different incentive for organizations to support ICMC infrastructure can be constructed from Granovetter's (1983) finding that weak ties serve as links between strong tie networks. In principle, employees' weak tie links to other strong tie networks provide access to organizationally useful information. Such links can also facilitate mobilization of like organizations (e.g., an association of speciality manufacturers) to respond to a common problem. However, there is a potential tension between the interests of individuals and the interests of the organization in exploitation of these weak ties, and the empirical evidence that organizations benefit directly from their employees' use of ICMC infrastructure is shaky at best (Sproull and Kiesler 1991). ICMC systems also have been convenient targets for cost cutting when organizations get into financial trouble (Fanning and Raphael 1986).

The dramatic 15% average monthly growth of Internet connections over the past several years attests that organizations are linking to ICMC infrastructure (SRI International 1994). While impressive in the aggregate, growth in Internet connections is not uniform across organizations. As Figure 12.1 shows, growth of host connections among educational and commercial institutions (with extensions .edu and .com in the Internet naming convention) has been much more significant than that shown in government (.gov), military (.mil), and organizational (.org) domains. Growth in ICMC activity is occurring mainly among organizations that already support weak tie networks for their employees because they are dependent on the expertise of "occupational communities" (Van Maanen and Barley 1984) that are, by their nature, weak tie networks.

WEAK TIES AND
OCCUPATIONAL COMMUNITIES

Occupational communities are groups of people engaged in work with such a high professional content that the norms of the professions transcend the norms of the organizations that employ them. This work is often a "central life interest" of community members (Dubin 1958). Members of occupational communities share values, norms, and perspectives, and their contacts with one another frequently extend beyond their work life. Some occupational communities consist of members who live and work in close proximity to one other, but physical proximity is not a necessary condition for an occupational community. Members can be widely separated geographically and still see themselves as part of the community. Such dispersed occupational communities face difficulty in developing and maintaining close

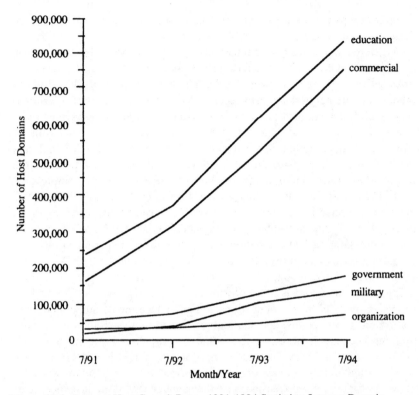

Figure 12.1. Internet Host Growth Rates, 1991-1994 Statistics: Internet Domain Survey, *http://www/nw/com*

community bonds, and thus make use of conferences, conventions, newsletters, journals, and other means of keeping members in contact with one another. Some make use of professional associations to accredit educational programs in their profession, bar from practice individuals not sanctioned by the association, and discipline members for misconduct or malpractice. Other occupational communities are very loosely coupled, as with the invisible colleges of academics enmeshed in weak tie networks of shared research pursuits.

The facilitation of weak tie maintenance in an occupational community by use of ICMC can be seen readily in the case of the academic research community, from which the Internet emerged. The academic research world is organized into occupational communities whose members are widely dispersed throughout many geographically separated organizations (Crane

1972). The need for an individual researcher to maintain ties with other members in the discipline is great. Traditionally, these ties are kept via journal publications, conference attendance, sabbaticals, and other relatively expensive mechanisms. Availability of a lower-cost ICMC infrastructure to support research would be a strong incentive for organizational investment in ICMC infrastructure to emerge, and evidence suggests that such investment is under way. The growth of the education domain on the Internet provides a hint, but more persuasive evidence is seen in studies of ICMC use by researchers. Oceanographers are using ICMC networks for joint writing of papers, reviewing manuscripts, committee work and other organizational activities, in addition to making new contacts within their discipline (Hesse et al. 1993). Similarly, molecular biologists studying the nematode worm *C. elegans* have come to depend heavily on ICMC infrastructure to coordinate their efforts on a large, highly dispersed genome sequencing endeavor (Star and Ruhleder 1994).

Research universities have traditionally borne the costs incurred by their faculty in the maintenance of weak ties within respective disciplines because research universities serve multiple missions that create practical conflicts. Strong research programs in particular fields require the hiring of numerous faculty to provide "critical mass," but such a strategy works against the need to provide adequate expert teaching coverage for all the academic disciplines required to form solid instructional programs. By underwriting the maintenance of weak ties among faculty in their research work through mechanisms such as conference trips, research visits, sabbaticals, and leaves of absence, the research university can build a diverse faculty for its instructional mission and at the same time have "virtual" critical mass for research. Support for ICMC infrastructure is merely an extension of this tradition. Similar behavior has been seen in large organizations with divisions similar to separate organizations. For example, IBM and Digital Equipment Corporation were early pioneers in intracompany networking through proprietary data communications networks. OCMC networks can thus function in large, dispersed organizations as ICMC networks do, linking together members of key occupational communities within the broader organization.

There are inherent tensions that mitigate against uncritical organizational support of ICMC infrastructure for employees who are members of occupational communities. Occupational communities are potential rivals to managerial control (Perin 1991), capable of directing employee loyalties outside the organization. They are also sources of values and norms over which management may have little influence. ICMC technology in the hands of occupational community members can be used to provide information about job opportunities and salaries that employees can use as leverage with management or to share valuable organizational information with individuals outside the organization in ways that greatly concern managers. Equally important, questions of privilege vital to occupational communities quickly arise in the context of both OCMC and ICMC networks, as seen in the recent controversies in universities about the posting of what some view as sexually and racially biased material to university-owned electronic communication networks (Earnest et al. 1991). University leaders are accountable for ensuring that the university's resources are used in socially and politically acceptable ways, but university faculty hold freedom of expression as such a crucial community value that they resist any form of censorship as a direct attack on the autonomy of their community.

The tension observed in ICMC networks is not strictly limited to conflicts of principle and power between occupational communities and organizational leadership. IBM management long refused to open its OCMC V-NET gateways to other networks because of fear of information leakage, and only opened such gateways in the past few years after realizing that failure to do so was costing them access to valuable information from the outside. In contrast, the military arm of the Internet, MILNET, pulled away from the Internet environment out of concern over excessive public proximity to military communications. As the capabilities and price/performance characteristics of CMC technologies improve, we expect to see explosive growth in use of these technologies both within organizations and between organizations. But because of tension between the welfare of individuals and the organizations they work for, growth of ICMC use is not likely to be uniform across classes of organizations. Organizational support for ICMC infrastructure should grow among organizations that are already dependent on flows of information over weak tie social networks linking members of occupational communities found in research and education, engineering, software development, health science, law, journalism, and so on.

ICMC GROWTH IN CONTEXT:
EVIDENCE AND CONTINGENCIES

It would be useful to compare organizations pursuing rapid development of ICMC infrastructure against organizations that are not supporting such infrastructure. This would at least offer inferential information regarding the patterns of adoption. Organizations aggressively pursuing ICMC infrastructure development and granting employees broad discretion in use should exhibit strong dependencies on employee weak-tie networking, while organizations that are significantly further behind in development, support, and encouragement in use of ICMC infrastructure should be those that do not depend on effective maintenance of external weak ties among employees.

That being said, strengthening of weak ties among occupational communities is likely to be only one of several complementary factors stimulating use of ICMC. Geographical dispersion of operations and integration of production are also likely to play important, interacting roles. Organizations with geographically dispersed operations are dependent already on long-distance intraorganizational communications, and as shown by companies like IBM and DEC, can exploit OCMC to meet this need. OCMC capability is usually required before ICMC can be exploited effectively because it provides the "last mile" connection between individuals within the organization and the external network supporting ICMC. In a similar vein, an organization may support ICMC infrastructure in order to reduce the burden of transaction costs incurred in the coordination required to integrate various facets of production (Piore 1994, Williamson 1981). Organizations that depend on outside organizations for crucial inputs to production or for downstream distribution are likely to benefit from use of ICMC infrastructure to facilitate interorganizational coordination (Malone and Crowston 1994). We can therefore assume that strong incentives to underwrite ICMC infrastructure use will occur among organizations with high dependency in distributed occupational communities, geographically dispersed operations, and a need to coordinate production among dispersed suppliers and distributors. Table 12.1 provides a summary of these contingencies.

IMPLICATIONS OF ICMC
GROWTH FOR ORGANIZATIONS

The capabilities embodied in ICMC infrastructure already figure prominently in speculation about the transformation of organizational form and function (Malone and Crowston 1994, Malone et al. 1987, Nolan and Croson 1995, Piore 1992, 1994). These speculations build on earlier theory and historical analysis of the relationship between communication and the organization of productive enterprise (Chandler 1977, Leavitt and Whisler 1958, McKenney 1995, Yates 1989), often updated from the perspective of transaction cost theory. The basic notion in these speculations is that changing communication capability alters the efficiency and effectiveness of the processes whereby organizational coordination of production occurs. Disaggregated and loosely coordinated production prior to the advent of electric communication technologies such as the telegraph and telephone gave way to highly integrated and hierarchically organized production manifested in

TABLE 12.1 Possible Contingencies in ICMC Infrastructure Support

Organizational Characteristics	Scope of Organizational, CMC Infrastructure Support, and Employee Use
Organizational dependence on dispersed occupational communities	
None or dependence only on occupational communities internal to the company	ICMC weekly supported and employee use restricted. OCMC might be highly supported and widely used if strong internal occupational communities are present.
High dependence on dispersed occupational communities	Strong support of ICMC infrastructure and unrestricted use, likely support of OCMC at least as complement to ICMC.
Geographic Characteristics of the organization's operations	
Geographically consolidated operations	Limited ICMC infrastructure and restrictions on use. An exception could be geographically remote location requiring ICMC to provide employee contact with other important centers of activity.
Geographically dispersed operations	ICMC infrastructure and use supported as needed to facilitate occupational community communication and environmental scanning. OCMC might be highly developed to support internal occupational communities.
Integration of organizational production	
Vertical integration of production	ICMC support and use limited to environmental scanning and relatively noninteractive information retrieval purposes. OCMC infrastructure likely to be highly developed and employee use unrestricted.
Unintegrated, depending on external sourcing and/or distribution	Heavily developed ICMC infrastructure and generally unrestricted use. Possibly OCMC development and use as complement to ICMC activity.

the large multidivisional firm or government bureaucracy (Chandler 1977). The long dominance of this form of organization was dependent on high communication costs and limited access to information on the part of organizations and individuals alike (Malone et al. 1987). As new communications technologies and other elements of information infrastructure become available and ubiquitous, the costs of communication will drop and access to information will grow dramatically. In consequence, the coordination advantages held by integrated and hierarchical production will diminish and the advantages of flexibility and responsiveness inherent in market modes of coordination will rise. Eventually, we can expect to see a shift from hierarchical to market coordination in many sectors (Allen and Hauptman 1994, Malone and Crowston 1994).

The logic behind these conjectures is sound, and there is meager but interesting empirical evidence that a shift might be under way. For example, Brynjolffson et al. (1994) report that firms investing heavily in information technology that can facilitate ICMC are significantly smaller in staff size while holding other measures of size (e.g., revenues) constant. What is missing from this emerging theory of organizational transformation is articulation of the "bootstrap" mechanism required to initiate and sustain the shift—the explicit pathway of actions and outcomes necessary to make the logical presumption real. ICMC, in light of the incentives discussed above, might provide such a mechanism in industries dependent on occupational communities. ICMC technology alone will not perform the bootstrapping role, but in the larger constellation of relevant factors surrounding the relationships between technology, occupational communities, and organizations dependent on occupational communities, the bootstrapping can take place.

The bootstrap mechanism we posit depends on the assumption that ICMC technology plays a catalytic role in the presence of two circumstantial conditions. One is the professionalized nature of occupational communities in which community members move from job to job in search of better compensation, terms of employment, and professional challenge. These occupational community members are likely to exhibit a relatively low level of organizational loyalty and relatively strong search behavior among social networks in their professional community to facilitate a career of itinerant or self-employment. The other condition is the prevailing bias of organizations toward reducing costs, downsizing, and streamlining operations in the face of intense fiscal and competitive pressures (Nolan and Croson 1995). Such firms seek opportunities to outsource key elements of their productive capacity, even at a higher unit cost, as long as they are able to obtain reliable performance on needed tasks in a timely fashion and reduce their fixed cost base. Under these conditions, a highly accessible and felicitous ICMC infrastructure could catalyze a shift from hierarchical to market relations in four ways:

- Providing the means for notification and negotiation among organizations shopping for professional services and the members of the relevant occupational communities

- Providing occupational community professionals with access to essential information resources required to carry out the contracted-for tasks, whether those resources be located in the buying organization or some other information utility

- Providing a wide and supportive conduit through which task coordination and ongoing renegotiation of the work can occur

- Providing mechanisms whereby contracted-for information products are delivered to the buyer and compensation is delivered to the supplier through electronic funds transfer

ICMC support of weak-tie networking among professionalized occupational communities is not the only mechanism by which the shift from hierarchies to markets might be bootstrapped. It is at best complementary to other factors such as geographically dispersed organizational operations, organizational requirements for coordinating a diverse group of suppliers and distributors, and pressures to outsource professional services due to cost cutting and competition. However, it is one of the more potent mechanisms we can identify at this time to explain the adoption patterns seen in researcher participation in the Internet, which itself has served as a powerful signifier of the evolving concept of "cyberspace." Our purpose in this chapter is not to explain, in theory or in fact, the full story behind the growth of ICMC. That is not going to be possible until much later, when careful historical analysis reveals what cannot be seen in the turbulence of the present. Rather, we offer one example of how focused application of one, robust theoretical construction—the role of weak social ties in distributed occupational communities—can be used in concert with other reasonable theoretical constructions to build a plausible, if limited, explanation for the growth of ICMC use to date.

REFERENCES

Allen, T. J. and O. Hauptman (1994), "The Influence of Communication Technologies on Organizational Structure: A Conceptual Model for Further Research," in T. J. Allen and M. S. Morton (Eds.), *Information Technology and the Corporation of the 1990's: Research Studies,* New York: Oxford University Press, pp. 475-483.
Applegate, L. M., J. I. Cash, and D. Q. Mills (1988), "Information Technology and Tomorrow's Manager," *Harvard Business Review,* 66, 6, November/December.
Beniger, J. (1986), *The Control Revolution,* Cambridge, MA: Harvard University Press.

Branscomb, L. M. (1992), "Information Infrastructure for the 1990's: A Public Policy Perspective," in B. Kahin (Ed.), *Building Information Infrastructure: Issues in the Development of the National Research and Education Network,* New York: McGraw-Hill, pp. 15-30.

Brynjolffson, E., T. Malone, V. Gurbaxani, and A. Kambil (1994), "Does Information Technology Lead to Smaller Firms?" *Management Science,* 40, 12, 1628-1644.

Cash, J. and B. Konsynski (1985), "IS Redraws Competitive Boundaries," *Harvard Business Review,* 63, 134-142.

Chandler, A. (1977), *The Visible Hand: The Managerial Revolution in American Business,* Cambridge, MA: Harvard University Press.

Crane, D. (1972), *Invisible Colleges: Diffusion of Knowledge in Scientific Communities,* Chicago: University of Chicago Press.

Culnan, M. J. and M. L. Markus (1987), "Information Technologies," in F. M. Jablin, L. L. Putnam, K. H. Roberts, and L. W. Porter (Eds.), *Handbook of Organizational Communication,* Newbury Park, CA: Sage, pp. 420-443.

Davenport, T. (1993), *Process Innovation: Reengineering Work Through Information Technology,* Boston: Harvard Business School Press.

DeLoughry, T. J. (1994), "Science Foundation Scales Back Its Management of the Internet," *Chronicle of Higher Education,* February 23, p. A23.

Denning, P. (1982), "Electronic Junk," *Communications of the ACM,* 23, 3, 163-165.

Dubin, R. (1958), *The World of Work,* Englewood Cliffs, NJ: Prentice Hall.

Earnest, L., J. McCarthy, and J. Hollombe (1991), "Risks-Forum: Digest Contributions," in C. Dunlop and R. Kling (Eds.), *Computerization and Controversy: Value Conflicts and Social Choices,* San Diego: Academic Press, pp. 376-378.

Eccles, R. G. and D. Crane (1988), *Doing Deals: Investment Banks at Work,* Boston: Harvard Business School Press.

Eveland, J. D. and T. K. Bikson (1987), "Evolving Electronic Communication Networks: An Empirical Assessment," *Office: Technology and People,* 3, 103-128.

Fanning, T. and B. Raphael (1986), "Computer Teleconferencing: Experience at Hewlett Packard," in *Proceedings of the CSCW '86,* December 3-5, Austin, TX: Conference Committee for CSCW '86, pp. 291-306.

Faulhaber, G. (1992), "Pricing Internet: The Efficient Subsidy," in B. Kahin (Ed.), *Building Information Infrastructure: Issues in the Development of the National Research and Education Network,* New York: McGraw-Hill, pp. 271-296.

Feldman, M. S. (1987), "Electronic Mail and Weak Ties in Organizations," *Office, Technology and People,* 3, 83-101.

Finholt, T. and L. S. Sproull (1990), "Electronic Groups at Work," *Organization Science,* 1, 41-64.

Giridharan, P. S. and H. Mendelson (1994), "Free Access Policy for Internal Networks," *Information Systems Research,* 5, 1-22.

Granovetter, M. (1983), "The Strength of Weak Ties: A Network Theory Revisited," in R. Collins (Ed.), *Sociological Theory 1983,* San Francisco: Jossey-Bass.

Granovetter, M. S. (1973), "The Strength of Weak Ties," *American Journal of Sociology,* 78, 6, 1360-1380.

Hammer, M. and J. Champy (1993), *Reengineering the Corporation: A Manifesto for Business Revolution,* New York: Harper Business.

Hesse, B. W., L. S. Sproull, S. B. Kiesler, and J. P. Walsh (1993), "Returns to Science: Computer Networks in Oceanography," *Communications of the ACM,* 36, 8, 90-101.

Hiltz, S. R. and M. Turoff (1978), *The Network Nation: Human Communication via Computer,* Reading, MA: Addison-Wesley.

Jonscher, C. (1994), "An Economic Study of the Information Technology Revolution," in T. J. Allen and M. S. Morton (Eds.), *Information Technology and the Corporation of the 1990's: Research Studies,* New York: Oxford University Press, pp. 5-42.

Keen, P. G. W. (1986), *Competing in Time: Using Telecommunications for Competitive Advantage,* Cambridge, MA: Ballinger.

King, J. L. and K. L. Kraemer (1984), "Evolution and Organizational Information Systems: An Assessment of Nolan's Stage Model," *Communications of the ACM,* 27, 5, 466-475.

Krackhardt, D. (1992), "The Strength of Strong Ties: The Importance of Philos in Organizations," in N. Nohria and R. G. Eccles (Eds.), *Networks and Organizations: Structure, Form and Action,* Boston: Harvard Business School Press, pp. 216-239.

Kraemer, K. L. and J. L. King (1988), "Computer-Based Systems for Cooperative Work and Group Decision Making," *ACM Computing Surveys,* 20, 2, 115-146.

Kraut, R. (1990), Comments in "How Can We Make Groupware Practical?" A Panel Discussion, in J. C. Chew and J. Whiteside (Eds.), *Empowering People: CHI '90 Proceedings,* Reading, MA: Addison-Wesley, p. 88.

Leavitt, H. J. and T. L. Whisler (1958), "Management in the 1980's," *Harvard Business Review,* 36, 41-48.

Mackay, W. E. (1988), "Diversity in the Use of Electronic Mail: A Preliminary Inquiry," *ACM Transactions on Office Information Systems,* 6, 7, October, 308-397.

Malone, T. and K. Crowston (1994), "The Interdisciplinary Study of Coordination," *ACM Computing Surveys,* 26, 87-119.

_____ and J. Rockart (1991), "Computers, Networks, and the Corporation," *Scientific American,* 265, 3, 128-136.

_____, J. Yates, and R. I. Benjamin (1987), "Electronic Markets and Electronic Hierarchies," *Communications of the ACM,* 30, 484-497.

Markus, M. L. (1994), "Electronic Mail as the Medium of Managerial Choice," *Organization Science,* 5, 4, November, 502-527.

McGarty, T. P. (1992), "Alternative Networking Architectures: Pricing, Policy and Competition," in B. Kahin (Ed.), *Building Information Infrastructure: Issues in the Development of the National Research and Education Network,* New York: McGraw-Hill, pp. 218-270.

McKenney, J. L. (1995), *Waves of Change: Business Evolution Through Information Technology,* Boston: Harvard Business School Press.

Nolan, R. L. and D. C. Croson (1995), *Creative Destruction: A Six-Stage Process for Transforming the Organization,* Boston: Harvard Business School Press.

Nohria, N. and R. G. Eccles (1992), "Face-to-Face: Making Network Organizations Work," in N. Nohria and R. G. Eccles (Eds.), *Networks and Organizations: Structure, Form and Action,* Boston: Harvard Business School Press, pp. 288-308.

Perin, C. (1991), "Electronic Social Fields in Bureaucracies," *Communications of the ACM,* 34, 12, December, 75-82.

Piore, M. J. (1992), "Corporate Reform in American Manufacturing and the Challenge to Economic Theory," in T. J. Allen and M. S. Morton (Eds.), *Information Technology and the Corporation of the 1990's: Research Studies,* New York: Oxford University Press, pp. 43-60.

_____ (1994), "Fragments of a Cognitive Theory of Technological Change and Organizational Structure," in N. Nohria and R. G. Eccles (Eds.), *Networks and Organizations: Structure, Form and Action,* Boston: Harvard Business School Press, pp. 430-444.

Quarterman, J. S. (1990), *The Matrix: Computer Networks and Conferencing Systems Worldwide,* Bedford, MA: Digital Press.

Ruhleder, K. and J. L. King (1990), "Computer Support for Work Across Space, Time and Social Worlds," *Journal of Organizational Computing,* 1, 4, 341-356.

Smarr, L. and C. Catlett (1992), "Life After the Internet: Making Room for New Applications," in B. Kahin (Ed.), *Building Information Infrastructure: Issues in the Development of the National Research and Education Network,* New York: McGraw-Hill, pp. 119-143.

Sproull, L. and S. Kiesler (1991), *Connections: New Ways of Working in the Networked Organization,* Cambridge: MIT Press.

SRI International (1994), Merit Network Information Systems Center On-Line Internet Statistics Utility *(ftp.merit.edu).*

Star, L. and K. Ruhleder (1994), "Steps Toward an Ecology of Infrastructure," in *Proceedings of the 1994 Computer Supported Cooperative Work Conference,* New York: Association for Computing Machinery.

Van Maanen, J. and S. R. Barley (1984), "Occupational Communities: Culture and Control in Organizations," *Research in Organizational Behaviour,* 6, 287-365.

Van Parijs, P. (1981), *Evolutionary Explanations in the Social Sciences: An Emerging Paradigm,* Totawa, NJ: Rowman & Littlefield.

Williamson, O. E. (1981), "The Economics of Organization: The Transactions Cost Approach," *American Journal of Sociology,* 87, 548-575.

Yates, J. (1989), *Control Through Communication: The Rise of System in American Management,* Baltimore, MD: Johns Hopkins University Press.

13

The Kindness of Strangers

The Usefulness of Electronic Weak Ties for Technical Advice

DAVID CONSTANT

LEE SPROULL

SARA KIESLER

In geographically dispersed organizations, employees cannot always get useful advice from their local colleagues. If expertise is not available locally, simply finding out who has it may be difficult. Inducing those who have it to share it may be even more difficult. People in organizations usually prefer to exchange help through strong collegial ties, which develop with physical proximity (e.g., Allen 1977, Kraut et al. 1988, Monge et al. 1985), group membership (Crane 1971, Zurcher 1965), a history of prior relationships (Krackhardt 1992, 1994), and demographic similarity (Wagner et al. 1984, Zenger and Lawrence 1989). Depending on unknown employees at distant locations for technical advice requires depending on the kindness of strangers.

Computer networks, which are being used by growing numbers of organizations, make it relatively easy and inexpensive to ask distant acquaintances for advice via e-mail. They also make it possible to ask strangers for advice. A person can post a query of the form, "Does anybody know . . .?" to a large electronic distribution list, electronic conference, or computer bulletin board without knowing who might read it. People who read the query can reply without having to know the person who posted it. Computer networks can

This chapter appeared originally in *Organization Science, 7*(2), March/April, 1996.

link people in the absence of acquaintance, physical proximity, group membership, a history of prior relationships, and demographic similarity. This chapter explores the process of giving and receiving technical advice over an organizational computer network. We draw upon theories of weak ties and prosocial motivation to suggest how this process can lead to useful advice and we use data from one multinational firm to illustrate the process.

THEORETICAL FRAMEWORK
AND PREDICTIONS

A theory of "the strength of weak ties" proposed by Granovetter (1973) suggests that relative strangers could offer an advantage over friends and colleagues in obtaining useful information. Granovetter (1973, 1982) argues that strong-tie relationships occur among people who are similar in many respects; similar people are likely to know the same things and are unlikely to know dissimilar things. When information is unavailable through strong ties, people may obtain it through weak ties: relationships characterized by absent or infrequent contact, lack of emotional closeness, and no history of reciprocal services. Weak ties serve as information bridges across cliques of strong ties and can offer people access to resources that are not found in their strong-tie relationships. Subsequent research has given some support to this "strength-of-weak-ties" hypothesis (Granovetter 1982, Brown and Reingen 1987, Stevenson and Gilly 1991, Weenig and Midden 1991).

Weak-tie theorists have proposed three arguments for why weak ties are useful. One argument is simply that weak ties comprise more numerous potential helpers than do strong ties (Friedkin 1982). Statistically, if weak ties are more numerous than strong ties, then calling on weak ties increases the probability that at least one contact will have useful information. If an employee broadcasts a request for technical information on a computer network, many people will see the request. Numerous replies increase the probability of finding one correct answer. If the problem is additive, that is, the solution is made up of many parts, numerous replies could increase the total usefulness of contributions. This argument leads to our first hypothesis: Advice from more people will be more useful than advice from fewer people.

There are some reasons for arguing that numerous weak ties might not result in more useful advice, however. A bigger sample of weak ties is likely to increase bad advice as well as good advice. Very poor advice might be especially costly, causing confusion, uncertainty, or "information overload." Numerous weak ties, therefore, will be useful only to the extent that the benefits of more good advice outweigh the costs of more bad advice.

Perhaps it is not the number of people giving advice, per se, that makes weak ties useful but the range or diversity of those ties. Burt (1983) points out that if all of a person's weak-tie contacts are themselves members of the same strong-tie group, then the expertise offered by those ties will be redundant. He suggests that it is the extent to which weak-tie contacts tap diverse groups that makes weak ties useful. A diverse range of ties increases the probability of finding a useful answer if expertise is heterogeneously distributed across groups but homogeneously distributed within groups. Group diversity also could increase alternative solutions (people offer different answers) or provide pieces to a multipart solution (people offer partial advice that can be combined into a solution). This argument leads to our second hypothesis: Advice from more diverse ties will be more useful than advice from less diverse ties.

Useful weak ties might draw on not merely diverse resources, but superior resources. Lin, Ensel, and Vaughn (1981) argue that those using weak ties will solicit help from people having desirable resources: wealth, status, prestige, power, or access to others (see also DiMaggio and Mohr 1985, Lin 1982, Lin and Dumin 1986, Lin et al. 1981, Marsden and Hurlbert 1988). Investigations evaluating this idea have been concerned primarily with job mobility. Referrals to attractive jobs come from people who have more seniority, higher job status, or more desirable employers. Useful weak-tie contacts therefore tend to have resources that are superior to those of seekers. In this view, the number and range of ties are important only insofar as they tap superior resources.

In the context of technical advice, superior resources are ones that increase the probability of a contact's offering correct or otherwise useful advice. In an organization, a contact's personal resources and social resources derived from his or her organizational position, department, or location might be differentially helpful (e.g., Krackhardt 1992). Personal resources important in technical help might be the contact's technical expertise, industry experience, and firm experience. The more technical expertise and experience a contact has, the more likely that contact will provide useful technical advice. Resources relevant to technical help that depend on job or position are the contact's physical proximity to the technical center of the organization and the contact's hierarchical status. Physical proximity to other experts has been shown to be important for the exchange of technical information (Allen 1977, Finholt 1993, Kraut et al. 1990, Lave 1991). Thus proximity to the technical center of the organization can be viewed as a useful resource.

The relationship of hierarchical position to useful technical help is problematic. Hierarchical position is an important social resource for organizational power (Krackhardt 1990). However, power may not be relevant to technical advice. An organizational cliché is that people whose technical knowledge is outdated are promoted into management. In this view, a contact's hierarchical status would be negatively related to useful technical knowledge. Alternatively, even though managers may no longer have useful technical information themselves, they may know who does have it. In this case, a contact's hierarchical status would be positively related to useful technical knowledge. Because we had no way of gauging which organizational resources would be most important for giving useful advice, we posed the following general resource hypothesis: Advice from people with more resources will be more useful than advice from people with fewer resources.

The Problem of Motivation

The usefulness of computer network help from strangers is problematic. The help seeker has no direct way of assessing the provider's reliability, expertise, possible strategic motives for misinformation, or knowledge about the seeker's situation. The seeker also has no control over the provider's incentives. The provider has little information about the seeker and therefore may misunderstand the request for help or advice, use inappropriate assumptions in generating a response, or formulate that response using language or concepts not shared by the seeker. These difficulties should increase with the weakness of the tie, i.e., with the physical and social distance of the information provider from the seeker. Some theorists suggest that if help is offered in the absence of direct reciprocity, it may not be very useful (e.g., Thorn and Connolly 1987). In this view strangers who could offer high-quality help will find it too costly do so. Only those who have "nothing better to do" may offer assistance, which is likely to be of poor quality.

Even when weak ties are potentially helpful, the motivation of strangers to help may be poor. People provide help to people they know, people they like, people who are similar, and people who have helped them (e.g., Amato 1990, Dovidio 1984, Festinger et al. 1950, Fulton et al. 1977, Heimer 1992, Kelley and Thibaut 1978, Krackhardt 1992, Williamson and Clark 1989). In personal relationships, benefactors themselves benefit from providing help, either through increasing the beneficiary's obligation to reciprocate or through receiving the beneficiary's esteem or both.

Generalized requests for help over a computer network do not meet the requirements of personal connection. Why would someone respond to a request for help from a stranger when the likelihood of direct personal benefit is low? Friendship and similarity are unlikely explanations. Personal friendships are uncommon across the geographic distances spanned by computer networks (Feldman 1987). Computer networks offer few cues to make demographic similarity salient to a potential benefactor (Sproull and Kiesler

1986). Also, computer networks do not provide a very rich medium for proffering esteem and gratitude (Daft and Lengel 1986).

Theories of prosocial motivation suggest two alternative processes that could lead people to provide useful technical help to strangers, even when this help is personally costly. First, some theorists have posited that people are not only pragmatic but also expressive of feelings, values, and self-identities (Bandura 1986, Schlenker 1985, Shamir 1991). If technical expertise is important in self-identity, experts can gain personal benefits from helping strangers on a computer network with technical problems. Helping others can increase self-esteem, personal identification with the organization, self-respect, respect from others, and feelings of commitment (e.g., Orr 1989). This reasoning suggests that personal benefits can lead experts to offer technical help even in the absence of personal acquaintance, similarity, or the likelihood of direct reciprocity. However, the usefulness of advice from experts motivated by personal benefit is questionable since such advice may be provided idiosyncratically or without close attention to the requirements of information seekers.

A second theoretical argument is that instead of direct personal benefit, help on a computer network is founded on organizational citizenship (Bateman and Organ 1983, Brief and Motowidlo 1986) and norms of generalized reciprocity (Berkowitz and Daniels 1964, Mauss 1925/1967, Titmuss 1971). Faced with a request for help, those who are organizationally motivated would be concerned with such things as how much they are needed, how they can be useful to others, and how their advice might solve organizational problems. People who have a strong organizational orientation are likely to be sensitive to the needs of help seekers and to adjust their advice to the requirements of those asking for help. Accordingly, we offer a fourth hypothesis: Advice from people who are more organizationally motivated will be more useful than advice from people who are less organizationally motivated.

Generalized reciprocity emerges when people have positive regard for the social system in which requests for help are embedded and show respect for it through offering help. Their regard may have an indirect basis in personal experience. For instance, they may have been helped by others on the computer network in the past or they may expect that someone on the network would help them in the future if they had a question.

Alternatively, their regard might stem from a more abstract view of the computer network as an organizational resource and worthy institution. In either case offering help is unrelated to direct reciprocity and more related to maintaining the social institution of the network as an organizational resource. Hence in opposition to the prediction developed from an economic rational theory of exchange (e.g., Thorn and Connolly 1987) that help providers will be unmotivated people who have nothing better to do and not much to offer, we offer a fifth hypothesis: On average, information providers will represent a pool of people whose resources for helping are at least as good as and perhaps better than those of information seekers.

Methodological Perspective

Previous research on weak ties has been conducted mainly through studies using retrospective accounts of the search for a successful outcome. These studies do not provide base rate data on all the weak ties that seekers of help tried and do not include ties that proved useless (see Nohria 1992 for one exception). Lacking within-search comparisons of individuals' useful and useless contacts, we cannot estimate the true association between weak-tie connections and the outcome of seeking help through weak ties. Furthermore, retrospective accounts often produce "good stories" (Ross 1989). Retrospective survey research on the search process may be biased in favor of stories that inflate the usefulness of weak ties.

Previous research also has not addressed the liabilities of weak-tie searches. Although weak ties potentially draw on resources that are more numerous, diverse, or better than strong ties do, they also could generate wasted effort and useless information. By collecting data from information seekers and each of their subsequent information providers, our study provides a way to estimate the overall value of search.

METHOD

Research Setting

The study was conducted at Tandem Computers Incorporated, a *Fortune* 500 computer manufacturer whose headquarters and main technical organization are located in Silicon Valley. Tandem employs over 11,000 people worldwide in the manufacture and sales of its products. Virtually all employees use a corporate computer network, which allows employees to send and receive mail messages from computer terminals on their desks. The system is used extensively: Employees from all levels of the company and from all locations feel free to (and in fact do) send messages to the president, to managers not in their direct chain of command, or to people outside their subunits; tens of thousands of messages are sent and received each day.

The e-mail system at Tandem organizes messages into first-class, second-class, and third-class mail. First-class mail is for person-to-person messages and for work-related distribution lists (e.g., All_Sales_Reps). Second-class mail is for work-related broadcast messages that go to the entire organization, including announcements from headquarters, industry news, and requests for information. Third-class mail is for extracurricular broadcast messages such as restaurant reviews or "want ads." The focus of this research is broadcast requests for information appearing on second-class mail. About 30% of the second-class messages on the network contained such requests. An example of a query and responses found in second-class mail is given in the appendix.

Study Design and Data Collection

The study used an event-driven survey methodology, whose triggering event was a request for information broadcast in second-class mail. During the 6-week research period, 82 employees broadcast one or more questions and announced they would make the replies available in public reply files on the network. When each question appeared, we sent survey questionnaires electronically to the information seeker who broadcast the question and to the information providers who replied to the question.[1] Information seekers received two surveys: The first asked them about themselves and requested that they keep all replies to their question; the second survey, sent 1 week later, asked them to evaluate each reply they had received. The survey sent to information providers asked them for information about themselves and about why they replied to the information seeker. We also captured the text of each question and all replies that had been placed in public reply files. We used Tandem's on-line organizational database to gather data on respondents' geographic location and hierarchical level.

For purposes of comparison we also collected data from an additional 67 employees who broadcast requests for information but did not create public reply files. We captured the text of their questions and sent them both surveys but we did not collect data from their providers because their providers' replies had not been made public.

Independent and Dependent Variables

Strength of Ties and Relationship Variables

We measured the strength of ties by asking information providers how well they knew the information seeker on a 10-point scale (1 = "don't know at all" and 10 = "know very well"). We measured network history by asking how many questions they had posed and replies they had given in the past year on second-class mail. We evaluated the demographic similarity of seekers to providers using difference scores on headquarters location (1 = seeker or provider at headquarters; 0 = both or neither at headquarters), managerial position (1 = seeker or provider is a manager; 0 = both or neither), hierarchical level (difference in the number of levels from the CEO), firm experience (difference in years of experience), and industry experience (difference in years of experience). Our measures of firm and industry experience similarity are roughly equivalent to demographic similarity variables used in prior research (Zenger and Lawrence 1989).

Resources

We used years of firm experience and years of experience in the computer industry as measures of resources for both seekers and providers. We estimated the expertise of information providers by asking them on a 10-point scale: "How informed are you on the subject matter of this question?" (1 = novice; 10 = expert). We also used three measures of resources associated with a person's organizational position. One was location at headquarters, the site of most engineering and product development (0 = no; 1 = yes). Another was whether or not the person held a managerial position. A third was hierarchical level, coded as lower when the employee reported through fewer levels to the CEO.

We used two estimates of the range or diversity of the social groups to which information providers belonged. Diversity is a group-level variable, a characteristic of the group of information providers who reply to the information seeker's request for advice. The measure of group diversity should be relevant to the usefulness of technical advice. Because Tandem has field offices all over the world, we operationalized diversity for each information seeker's set of providers as the number of different countries where information providers were based. Since the firm's products and clients differ across countries, and since field offices in each country have staff who were educated in their native land, the more countries represented in a set of replies, the more those replies would be expected to reflect differences in people's resources for technical advice. We also operationalized diversity for each information seeker's providers as the number of different hierarchical levels of information providers. People at different levels often have different perspectives on a firm's approach to problems: for example, on whether a machine is worth fixing, or whether one should rely on experts at headquarters. The more hierarchical levels represented in a group of replies, the more perspectives the information seeker receives.[2]

Provider Motivation

We measured providers' motivations by asking them to allocate 100 points among several reasons that they might have had for replying to the information seeker. We listed four reasons associated with personal benefits and four reasons associated with organizational motivation.

Usefulness and Content of Aid

To measure the usefulness of advice, we asked information seekers to "please 'award' $0 to $25 to each answer based on how helpful it was to you." We asked information providers to award themselves $0 to $25 according to how useful they thought their reply was to the information seeker. We also asked information seekers to impose a "fine" of as much as $25 on any answer that wasted their time. And we asked information seekers an open-ended question: "What have you done or what do you intend to do as a result of each reply?" We coded the responses to indicate whether one or more of the replies solved the seeker's problem (solved problem = 1; did not solve problem = 0).

A coder blind to the research hypotheses analyzed the texts of replies to determine their content using the following categories: technical content, story of personal experience, pointer to a person, document, database, or customer, inclusion of a document or e-mail from others, request for clarification, and expression of interest in seeing replies from others. The first author coded a subset of the responses to check for reliability. Scott's Pi for intercoder agreement ranged from 0.75 to 1.0, with the exception of the story category, which had a Pi of 0.45 and was dropped from analysis.

Analyses

The data are grouped, with each group consisting of data about (a) an information seeker, (b) the question broadcast by the seeker, (c) the information providers who responded to that information seeker, and (d) the replies given by the information providers. We tested hypotheses involving individual characteristics, such as the resources of information providers, at the individual level controlling for group (information seeker). This procedure controls for dependence among providers and replies to the same question.

We tested hypotheses involving group characteristics, such as diversity of contact resources, at the group level.

RESULTS

Response Rates and Sample Characteristics

We collected 100% of the 82 question texts and sent two questionnaires sequentially to the 82 information seekers who posted them, 55 of whom completed both (67% response rate). These information seekers reported receiving 429 replies to their broadcast questions, an average of 7.8 replies per question. They gave us the names of 365 repliers to whom we sent surveys. We received 295 completed surveys from the repliers (80% response rate) and obtained the text of 263 replies. We obtained on-line organizational employee data for 92% of information seekers and providers.

For analyses combining data from different sources (seeker and provider characteristics, and question and reply characteristics), we used a core sample of information exchanges with no missing categories of data. These exchanges include the seeker's question, two completed questionnaires from the information seeker, a text file of public replies to the question, and questionnaires from the repliers. Full data were available for 48 of the 82 questions broadcasted, leaving an effective response rate of 58%: 48 information seekers, their 48 questions, their 263 information providers, and the 263 public replies they gave.

To explore possible effects of missing data, we compared the similarity of our research sample to (a) information seekers who kept their replies private, (b) public replies archived over the previous year, and (c) the general population of employees in the firm. We had data on the office location, hierarchical level, industry experience, firm experience, and self-reported experience with second-class e-mail of both public and private information seekers. They differed only in their reported experience with second-class e-mail; information seekers in our research sample had replied to others more, $p < .05$. Because we did not survey private information providers, we could not compare them with public information providers. However, insofar as we could determine, private and public transactions did not differ; there were no differences between the two in number of replies, usefulness of replies, or whether replies solved the information seeker's problem.

Our research sample was similar to the population of employees who use second-class mail. Sample employees are predominantly male professionals, proportionally the same as those who use second-class mail generally and the same as in the company as a whole. However, significantly more of our sample and of second-class e-mail users are in sales and field support positions than in the company as a whole, and more are located in smaller sites, in offices more distant from headquarters, and outside the United States.

Questions Asked and Information Received

Information seekers asked primarily technical questions that averaged nearly half a page (mean = 12.1 lines of text, SD = 8.7). They did not pose their questions lightly: 91% of information seekers reported querying at least one other information source before broadcasting their question. Information providers, on average, estimated they spent 9 minutes (SD = 4.1) on their replies. Replies averaged about three quarters of a page (mean = 19.1 lines, SD = 81.3). Fifty-four percent of the answers contained technical information, and 53% contained a referral to another source of information, such as a specific person or computer file.

Information seekers valued the usefulness of the average reply they received at $11.30 ($SD$ = $8.70; min. = $0, max. = $25). (See the appendix for an example of values given by one information seeker to the replies she received.) The value of the best reply was highly correlated with the value of the mean reply ($r[48]$ = .79, $p < .0001$). This correlation suggests a "halo" response effect by information seekers, or that replies were additive. Information seekers used fines so infrequently—only 8.4% of replies were assigned any fine—that we did not use fines in the analysis. On average, information providers valued their own replies at $13.20 ($SD$ = $8.00; min. = $0, max. = $25).

Half of the information seekers (49%) said that the replies they received solved their problem. The mean usefulness of information seekers' replies was positively but not significantly correlated with whether or not information seekers said their problem was solved (r = .18). The value of the best reply also was not significantly correlated with whether or not the problem was solved (r = .20). Since we cannot evaluate the comparative validity of these measures, we used both the dollar value of usefulness and whether or not the problem was solved as dependent variables in our analyses. Usefulness can be used in both individual-level and group-level analyses, whereas problem solution can be used only in group-level analyses.

If weak ties for technical help actually do provide useful advice, this usefulness should be reflected in the technical content of replies. To address the question of how the content of advice is related to its usefulness, we regressed the usefulness of information on the presence or absence of technical content and referrals to other sources of information, controlling for information seeker and the resources of providers. This analysis was performed at the individual level so that the content and usefulness of each reply could be matched.[3] The model is significant (F[46, 159] = 2.60, $p <$ .0001, R^2 = .429) as is the improvement over a model with only provider resources and information seeker (ΔR^2 = .034, F[2, 159] = 5.50, $p <$ .005). The unstandardized coefficients for technical content and referrals are 2.74 (SE = 1.27, p = .03) and 3.36 (SE = 1.27, p = .009), respectively.

Strength of Ties and Basis of Relationship

As we had expected, people did not have a personal connection to the person they helped. Information providers did not know their seekers; 81% of the providers said they did not know the seekers at all; an additional 10% said they were barely acquainted. Acquaintance was uncorrelated with the number of replies ($r = -.11$), with the usefulness of replies ($r = .07$), or with the solution of the seekers' problems ($r = .05$). A history of posting or answering questions on second-class e-mail was uncorrelated with acquaintance ($rs = 0$) nor did this history predict the number of replies ($rs = 0$) or their usefulness ($r = .06$, $r = .03$, respectively) or whether or not seekers' problems were solved ($r = -.07$, $r = .03$). Providers did not help based on the friendliness, social content, or tone of the questions they saw. We used three "sociability" measures: whether the question included a greeting, a closing, or named the company. The presence of a personal opening or closing or both in the question was negatively correlated with the number of replies, r[48] $= -.30$, $p < .05$. The social content of questions did not predict the usefulness of replies or whether or not the problem was solved.

Information providers generally did not help based on their similarity to the person needing help. On only one measure of similarity, whether both or neither person worked at a headquarters location, were information providers more similar to their "own" information seeker than they were to the mean of all the information seekers. There was no similarity effect for managerial status, hierarchical level, firm experience, and industry experience. Group-level correlations between the usefulness of replies and the similarity of information seekers to their information providers indicated that similarity of managerial status and similarity of firm tenure were negatively related to the usefulness of replies ($r = -.12$, $p < .07$ and $r = -0.12$, $p < .05$, respectively) and similarity of industry tenure was related positively ($r = .13$, $p < .05$). However, adding similarity variables to a regression of usefulness on information provider did not improve the model (R^2 without similarity variables = .34; with similarity variables = .37, change F = 1.64, n.s.). The similarity of information providers to their information seeker also was not correlated with whether or not the seeker's problem was solved; none of the individual correlations was significant and a logistic regression of problem solution on information provider and similarity variables was not significant.

In sum, the data reported above do not describe a system of direct social exchange whereby people give useful help to those with whom they have a personal relationship, to those who are similar, or to those who have helped them. Neither acquaintance, a history of reciprocity using the network to exchange advice, nor similarity was very important in predicting the incidence or usefulness of replies.

The Usefulness of Information

We examined three hypotheses about the usefulness of weak-tie information: The number of replies will predict the usefulness of replies; the range or diversity of groups from which providers come will predict the usefulness of replies; and the resources of information providers will predict the usefulness of replies. (See Table 13.1 for a correlation matrix of all variables used in these analyses.) In each analysis we used hierarchical regression to estimate the contribution of separate groups of variables to the overall model. At the individual level we can test hypotheses about how the number of replies and the resources of information providers predict usefulness. At the group level we can test hypotheses about how the number of replies and resource diversity predict problem solutions as well as usefulness.

Number of Replies

We regressed the usefulness of replies on the number of replies controlling for information providers' resources. This regression is significant at $p < .01$ and the coefficient for the number of replies is negative (Table 13.2). This result does not support the hypothesis that the number of weak ties statistically increases the likelihood of obtaining good advice.

We explored this relationship further by investigating if the number of replies was positively related to the most useful reply, reasoning that more replies might offer more opportunity to find one truly useful answer. Regressions of the most useful reply on the number of replies were carried out at the group level since each information seeker can have only one best reply (or several replies receiving a tie score for most usefulness). The coefficients are positive but not statistically significant, with and without controls for resources (bivariate $r = .22$, $p = .14$). The number of replies is more strongly related to the least useful reply (bivariate $r = -.30$, $p < .04$). This relatively big drop in the usefulness of the worst reply when there were more replies could explain why mean usefulness declined with more replies. The same result was obtained in analyses using information providers' own assess-

TABLE 13.1 Correlations Among Measures of Replies and Information Providers' Resources

	2	3	4	5	6	7	8	9	10	11
Individual level[a]										
1. Usefulness of reply	-.05	.08	.08	.17	.11	-.06				
Resources										
2. HQ location		.01	.04	.04	-.13					
3. Manager			-.43	-.09	.13					
4. Hierarchical level[b]				-.11	-.17	-.10				
5. Expertise					.16	.21				
6. Firm experience						.27				
7. Industry experience										
Group level[c]										
1. Usefulness of replies	.18	-.10	-.03	.26	.16	.22	.41	.04	-.11	-.34
2. Solved the problem		-.02	.03	-.24	.00	.28	.22	.13	.06	.01
3. Number of replies			.53	.11	-.18	-.01	.10	.08	.45	.66
Resources										
4. Mean providers at HQ location				.02	-.46	.01	.14	.02	.06	.61
5. Mean providers who are managers					.19	-.35	-.01	.27	.19	.02
6. Mean hierarchical level of providers[b]						-.10	-.01	-.21	.13	-.33
7. Mean expertise of providers							.28	-.03	-.26	-.06
8. Mean firm experience of providers								.22	-.09	.08
9. Mean industry experience of providers									.00	-.06
Diversity										
10. Number of different countries										.28
11. Number of different levels										

a. Correlations of .12 and greater are significant at the individual level, $p < .05$. Ns = 249-286.
b. Hierarchical level is coded as levels from the CEO; a smaller integer = higher hierarchical level.
c. Correlations of .28 and greater are significant at the group level, $p < .05$. Ns = 45-48.

TABLE 13.2 Regressions Predicting Reply Usefulness From the Number of
Replies and Information Providers' Resources (Individual Level)

	Models	
Variables	β *(SE)*	β *(SE)*
Information seeker[a]		**
Number of replies[b]	−0.24** (0.06)	
Resources	0.55 (1.33)	1.19 (1.35)
HQ location		
Manager	3.51* (1.65)	2.37 (1.60)
Hierarchical level[c]	1.20* (0.60)	0.97 (0.62)
Expertise (1-10)	0.45* (0.23)	0.59** (0.23)
Firm experience	0.32[+] (0.18)	0.22 (0.18)
Industry experience	−0.12 (0.09)	−0.12 (0.09)
R^2	0.119	0.414

NOTE: The table contains unstandardized coefficients. Both models are significant, $p < .01$. $N = 242$.
a. A model using information seeker ($df = 47$) alone as a predictor variable explains 39% of the variance in usefulness ($F[44, 233] = 2.72, p < .01$).
b. Number of replies is automatically controlled when information seeker is controlled in the second model.
c. Hierarchical level is coded as levels from the CEO; a smaller integer = higher hierarchical level.
[+]$p < .10$; *$p < .05$; **$p < .01$.

ments of the usefulness of their replies which, unlike seekers' assessments, are not affected by their evaluations of other replies.

The number of replies also did not predict whether or not information seekers' problems were solved. In sum, for these information seekers, more replies did not improve the net benefit of weak ties.

Information Provider Resources

As Table 13.2 shows, resources of information providers were positively related to seekers' usefulness ratings.[4] At the individual level, controlling for the number of replies, there are significant coefficients at the .05 level for the resources of being a manager, hierarchical level, and expertise. In a similar analysis controlling for information seeker instead of number of replies, the only significant coefficient is the resource of expertise. These analyses generally support our hypothesis that weak ties for technical advice in an organization are useful to the degree they tap people with superior resources.

At the group level we used mean usefulness of replies as the dependent variable (Table 13.3) to test effects of groups of replies rather than of individual replies. A model with resources, controlling for number of replies,

TABLE 13.3 Regressions Predicting Mean Reply Usefulness from the Number
of Replies, the Mean of Information Providers' Resources, and the
Diversity of Ties (Group Level)

	Models			
Variables	β (SE)		β (SE)	
Number of replies	−0.21	(0.13)	−0.01	(0.16)
Mean resources				
Mean providers at HQ location	1.39	(4.47)	4.33	(4.53)
Mean providers who are managers	12.08[+]	(6.26)	12.91*	(6.03)
Mean hierarchical level of providers[a]	1.91	(1.86)	1.91	(1.86)
Mean expertise	0.41	(0.67)	0.62	(0.68)
Mean firm experience	1.27*	(0.55)	1.05[+]	(0.53)
Mean industry experience	−0.01	(0.25)	−0.19	(0.23)
Diversity of ties				
Number of different countries from			−0.05	(0.72)
which providers come				
Number of different hierarchical levels			−2.15*	(0.94)
from which providers come				
R^2	0.29		0.38	
F	2.18		2.44	
df	7.45		9.45	
p	0.06		0.03	

NOTE: The table contains unstandardized coefficients. $N = 46$.
a. Hierarchical level is coded as levels from the CEO; a smaller integer = higher hierarchical level.
[+]$p < .10$; *$p < .05$.

is significant at the .06 level. It contains significant coefficients at the .10
level for the resource of being a manager and at the .05 level for the resource
of firm experience.

Diversity

We used the number of different countries and the number of different
hierarchical levels represented in a group of replies as proxies for diversity.
We regressed mean usefulness on number of replies, resources, and diversity.
(See second column of Table 13.3.) Diversity contributes to the prediction
of usefulness but in a direction opposite to the hypothesis. In the combined
model the resources of being a manager and firm experience, but fewer levels
of the hierarchy represented in replies, contribute to usefulness. Adding
diversity to a model containing number of replies and resources increases

TABLE 13.4 Logistic Regressions Predicting Whether or Not the Problem Was Solved From the Number of Replies, the Mean of Information Providers' Resources, and the Diversity of Ties (Group Level)

	Models			
Variables	β (SE)		β (SE)	
Number of replies	-0.12	(0.08)	-0.17	(0.10)
Mean resources				
Mean providers at HQ location	8.00*	(3.15)	11.00**	(4.15)
Mean providers who are managers	-4.61	(2.92)	-6.36*	(3.73)
Mean hierarchical level[a] of providers	1.85	(1.02)	1.79	(1.15)
Mean expertise	0.47	(0.34)	0.71[+]	(0.40)
Mean firm experience	0.13	(0.25)	0.15	(0.27)
Mean industry experience	0.08	(0.11)	0.06	(0.12)
Diversity of ties				
Number of different countries from which providers come			0.84[+]	(0.43)
Number of different hierarchical levels from which providers come			-0.49	(0.57)
χ^2	17.25		22.10	
df	7		9	
p	.02		.01	

NOTE: The table contains unstandardized coefficients. $N = 47$.
a. Hierarchical level is coded as levels from the CEO; a smaller integer = higher hierarchical level.
[+]$p < .10$; *$p < .05$; **$p < .01$.

the R^2 by .09 ($p < .10$). This analysis suggests that advice from a less hierarchically diverse (rather than more diverse) set of ties increases usefulness.

Solving the Problem

A group-level model regressing solving the problem on resources, controlling for number of replies, is significant ($\chi^2 = 17.25, p = .02$) (Table 13.4). Within this model the coefficient for working at the technical center of the organization is significant at the .05 level.

In contrast to the findings for mean usefulness, the diversity of ties contributes positively to the model when problem solution is the dependent variable. Generally, the coefficients are positive in this analysis. In the full model, the resources of working at the technical center ($p < .01$) and being an expert ($p < .10$), but not being a manager ($p < .05$), and having more

TABLE 13.5 Information Providers' Reasons for Replying

Reasons	Mean (SD) Number of Points Given to Reason		Percentage of Information Providers Choosing This as a Most Important Reason[a]
Personal benefits			
I enjoy helping others.	16.0	(15.3)	23
I enjoy solving problems.	9.5	(11.9)	15
I enjoy earning respect.	4.8	(7.7)	8
The company rewards information sharing.	0.9	(3.0)	1
Total personal benefits	31.2	(30.0)	
Organizational motivation			
Being a good company citizen.	17.8	(18.5)	27
The problem is important to the company.	14.0	(17.8)	21
It's part of my job to answer questions like this one.	12.6	(18.8)	21
I expect others to help me, so it's only fair to help them.	11.8	(13.0)	17
Total organizational motivation	56.2	(27.8)	
"Other"	12.6	(23.2)	23

NOTE: $N = 263$.
a. The most important reason is the reason given the most points, or the reasons tied for the most points.

countries represented in the replies ($p < .10$) predict solving the problem. Diversity alone, controlling for number of replies, does not predict problem solution. The full model with resources and diversity, controlling for number of replies, is an improvement over a model without diversity ($\Delta\chi^2 = 4.85$, $p < .10$).

Effects of Motivation

When asked, "Why did you answer this question?" information providers gave reasons of personal benefit as well as reasons related to general organizational benefit, but they gave more of the latter than the former (paired-t [262] $= 8.75$, $p < .01$). That is, they favored reasons such as "Answering questions like this is part of being a good company citizen" over "I enjoy helping people" or "I enjoy solving problems" (Table 13.5). We found little evidence that providers' personal history of giving or receiving

TABLE 13.6 Regressions Predicting Reply Usefulness From Information
Providers' Resources and Self-Reported Motivations for Replying
(Individual Level)

Variables	β (SE)		β (SE)	
		Models		
Information seeker	***	***		
Resources				
HQ location			1.32	(1.40)
Manager			2.04	(1.63)
Hierarchical level[a]			0.80	(0.63)
Expertise (1-10)			0.32	(0.24)
Firm experience			0.08	(0.18)
Industry experience			−0.18*	(0.09)
Personal benefits motivation				
Enjoy helping others	−0.01	(0.03)	−0.01	(0.03)
Enjoy solving problems	−0.03	(0.05)	−0.04	(0.05)
Earn respect	0.14+	(0.07)	0.14+	(0.07)
Firm rewards sharing	−0.23	(0.19)	−0.22	(0.19)
Organizational motivation				
Good organizational citizen	0.01	(0.03)	0.02	(0.03)
Important firm problem	−0.02	(0.03)	−0.02	(0.03)
Part of my job to help	0.07*	(0.03)	0.07*	(0.03)
It's only fair to help	0.07	(0.04)	0.08+	(0.04)
R^2	0.46		0.48	
F	2.93		2.80	
df	49,221		55,221	
p	<.01		<.01	

NOTE: The table contains unstandardized coefficients.
a. Hierarchical level is coded as levels from the CEO; a smaller integer = higher hierarchical level.
+$p < .10$; *$p < .05$.

help over the network or their acquaintance with information seekers predicted the reasons they gave for helping.[5]

Table 13.6 shows individual-level analyses regressing usefulness of advice on personal benefits and organizational motivations for answering
questions. The regressions are shown with and without controls for resources. Column 1 shows that the personal benefit of earning respect ($p <$
.05) and the organizational motivations of "it's part of my job to help" ($p <$
.05) and "it's only fair to help" ($p < .10$) predict the usefulness of replies.
Change statistics indicate that adding personal benefits to the model does not
improve the model, but adding organizational motivation to the model does

TABLE 13.7 Mean Resources of Information Seekers and Information Providers

Resources	Information Seekers (n = 48)	Information Providers (n = 281)	t Statistic
HQ location (yes = 1, no = 0)	14%	31%	2.88**
Manager (yes = 1, no = 0)	2%	12%	3.23**
Hierarchical level[a]	6.0 (0.8)	5.6 (1.0)	2.50*
Firm experience (years)	4.0 (2.7)	4.3 (3.0)	0.71
Industry experience (years)	12.2 (6.2)	13.8 (6.8)	1.52

a. Hierarchical level is coded as levels from the CEO; a smaller integer = higher hierarchical level.
*$p < .05$; **$p < .01$.

improve it ($p < .05$). Column 2 adds resources and shows slightly stronger results in the same direction.

The results shown in Table 13.6 support our hypothesis that organizational motivations of information providers can predict the usefulness of their technical help. The personal benefit of earning respect also predicted usefulness. Self-reports of motivation may be suspect, particularly when they emphasize socially desirable items. However, there is no reason that providers' social desirability would be expected to have a positive relationship with seekers' usefulness ratings. Our results show that providers' organizational motivation items, and an item probably less socially desirable, "earning others' respect," predicted how seekers rated the usefulness of replies. Hence we have some cause to take providers' self-reported reasons at face value.

If information providers help simply because they have nothing better to do, their resources and the quality of their help is likely to be inferior. If, instead, information providers are motivated by a communal orientation to the needs of others and to the problems of the organization, they may represent a pool of helpers whose resources are as good or superior to those of information seekers. We argued that in a community where generalized reciprocity is a norm, people generally should be motivated to help others.

Therefore, the pool of information providers should offer as good or better resources as the pool of information seekers. To examine this hypothesis, we compared the resources of information providers with those of information seekers. Providers did not have significantly more firm or industry experience than did seekers. Providers did have significantly more resources of managerial and hierarchical status and location at the technical center of the organization. We could not directly compare seekers and providers on expertise because we did not measure seekers' level of expertise (Table 13.7).

DISCUSSION

In this study, weak ties established through a computer network offered information seekers technical information or referrals. Information providers gave useful advice and solved the problems of information seekers despite their lacking a personal connection with the seekers. Weak ties with superior resources provided more useful information. Controlling for those resources, the number of replies was not positively related to the average usefulness of replies, to the most useful advice, or to the solution of problems. The diversity of ties as well as the resources of information providers contributed to whether or not seekers' problems were solved. Finally, replies from people responding out of organizational motivation were rated as more useful.

In this study, expertise contributed both to the usefulness of advice and to problem solving. But replies could be deemed useful without actually solving problems. Information seekers obtained advice they considered very useful (but that did not necessarily solve the problem) from ties with managers (being a manager is negatively related to expertise, $r = -.35$, $p < .05$ at the group level; see Table 13.1) and from ties having more firm experience (positively correlated with expertise; $r = .28$, $p < .05$ at the group level). By contrast, information seekers' problems were solved through diverse ties from different countries (negatively correlated with expertise, $r = -.26$, $p = .06$) and by having more ties at the technical center and more ties with lower-level people (both unrelated to expertise). Apparently information providers who solved people's problems and those who gave very useful advice were somewhat different groups; the type of information they offered may have been different too. For instance, it seems consistent with our data that repliers who solved the seeker's problem gave site-specific technical answers (which would be tapped more easily at the technical center as well as through more diverse ties), whereas those who gave especially useful advice gave broader firm-specific knowledge (which managers and people with longer firm experience would have).

We found that diversity of countries from which information providers came contributed to solving information seekers' problems. However, diversity did not contribute to ratings of usefulness. These findings are consistent with a process in which diversity does not increase the likelihood of finding the best experts (in general) but might increase the likelihood of obtaining site-specific advice (for example, advice about a product used in only one or a few countries). The value of diversity might be especially high when experience is very widely and unevenly distributed in an organization and people encounter rare problems.

Our results are consistent with the theory that weak ties' usefulness is due to their bridging capacity as Granovetter (1982) and Burt (1983) have hypothesized, rather than to their sheer number, as has been suggested by Friedkin (1982). The computer network used to draw on weak ties linked people across distance, time, country, and hierarchical level and organizational subunit. Consistent with the resource arguments of Lin and colleagues (e.g., Lin 1982), these links were useful to the degree they put people in touch with those offering superior resources; they were not useful nor did they have a greater likelihood of solving the information seeker's problem when they were simply greater in number. People who received more replies did get replies of high quality; they also received replies of very low quality. Perhaps many replies caused confusion or uncertainty, which detracted from potentially beneficial information.

Our results extend the superior resources formulation of weak ties to the domain of technical information exchange and suggest that the event-driven survey of information seekers and their information providers can be used to evaluate aspects of weak ties. In general, the results support the idea that the usefulness of weak ties for obtaining technical advice depends on the help seeker's access to providers' resources. Information providers in this study had somewhat superior resources to those of information seekers, and those who had better resources gave more useful advice. Provider resources, however, must be evaluated in terms of the particular kind of information sought. For example, in this study, industry experience was not related to providing useful technical advice. By contrast, if help seekers had been looking for competitor information or for job information, industry experience might well have been positively associated with usefulness of advice.

Ours is a case study of weak-tie sharing within one geographically dispersed organization. The firm we studied views the computer network as a critical corporate resource, encourages employees to use it, and rewards them for devising software that improves communication. We have no data on employees who did not help—the baseline statistics on the motivations or expertise of employees in general—so our inferences must be cautious. Yet it seems unlikely that, in the absence of a culture that supports information sharing and considers the network to be an organizational resource, the kinds of information exchanges among weak ties we observed could be sustained for long. The form of exchange we observed had been established more than 6 years before the data were collected, evidence of considerable stability. Technology alone will not impel this kind of weak-tie sharing over time; an organizational culture that fosters it also is necessary. In this organization strangers incur the costs of "kindness" because they can perform as experts and meet important needs of others. Norms of generalized reciprocity sustain kindness as a social institution and lead people who can provide useful help to do so.

Given a corporate culture that promotes information sharing, we suggest three probable scope conditions for our findings related to kind of information, degree of slack in employee time, and intensity of usage. Technical information is relatively more likely to be exchanged in a computer network weak-tie environment than are other kinds of information such as strategic, political, or personal information. For example, we never saw any broadcast questions of the form, "Does anybody know who will be named as the next engineering vice president?" or "Does anybody know what X is like as a boss?" Undoubtedly people used the computer network to search for non-technical information, but they probably did so within their strong-tie relationships rather than through weak ties. Although answering questions had relatively low costs, it was not costless; information providers had to have enough slack in their workday so that the 9 minutes (on average) they reported it took them to produce a reply was not viewed as excessive. By contrast, in professional organizations that require employees to account for their time to the tenth of an hour for billing purposes, 9 minutes of "free" help could be viewed as costly to the provider. The number of questions asked per day must be governed by self-limiting processes. We saw about seven questions a day; if there had been 700 or 7,000 the system would have been swamped and, presumably, would not have continued to yield useful answers.

Broadcasting requests for help over a computer network can be viewed as a public goods problem in which it is in no one's best interest to respond and in which people rich in resources will be particularly disinclined to respond (Thorn and Connolly 1987). Others have noted that a small "critical mass" can overcome this problem (e.g., Marwell et al. 1988). The models generally assume a situation where free riders cannot be excluded but neither increase the net cost to providers nor decrease the net benefit to recipients. The characteristics are true of the situation we studied, since neither information providers nor information seekers would notice free riders who read the public reply files. A remaining problem, however, is that a person's contribution may be inconsequential or redundant. Why would someone take the time to give advice when someone else could do it? Our data do not show that inconsequentiality was a problem. Information providers with more expertise tended to believe fewer others replied ($r[205] = -.21, p < .01$). However, 73% of the information providers could give us the name of a least one other person who could answer the question. And the average provider estimated that 15.4 other people replied to the question to which they replied. These findings suggest that many providers, including experts, replied despite their apparent inconsequentiality.

Macy (1990) has argued that group members can learn to contribute despite their marginal significance or inconsequentiality when they observe others contributing and see rewards to the public good. Once a critical mass of contributors is achieved, the legitimacy and value of contributing can be self-reinforcing. Computer networks with public reply files and other facilities for public information exchange, like those at the company we studied, may contribute to the creation of a critical mass by increasing the visibility of prosocial behavior (Cialdini et al. 1990). Computer networks make it physically easy to reach large numbers of people and make weak-tie contacts, and they also make it relatively easy to respond to information requests. They also offer more opportunities to see others contributing than would be available in face-to-face interactions. By facilitating social observation of technical information exchange, computer networks may encourage people to contribute for personal benefits such as pride, and they may reinforce norms of contribution within a culture that values it. Hence computer networks can provide a means for leveraging the kindness of strangers.

APPENDIX
Broadcast Question and Replies on the Computer Network

(This example is verbatim from our sample, except that the proper names of employees and products have been changed. The "Value to Information Seeker" of each reply is the actual rating "Nadia" made of the usefulness of her replies.)

Question

SENT: 89-06-12 15:44
FROM: BOULANGER_NADIA
TO: DL.ALL_TANDEM@SLC
SUBJECT: 2:?? 2311 at 7 but still too dim??
Hi all,
    I am sure I'm not the first to ask this question but I can find no help in Quest [on-line database of previous public questions and replies] so I'm copying the world to see if I can get any answers.
    I have a number of 2311's [computer terminals] (50+) installed at ABC Co. and many of them are starting to get too dim even at the max brightness setting. Is there any way to increase the brightness on these monitors or is the solution a replacement.
    Any info would be greatly appreciated. Replies if any at \SLC.$CE.DIM2311. REPLYS [location of public replies file].
    Regards, Nadia

Replies

SENT: 89-06-13 09:06
FROM: REICH_STEVE@AUSTIN
   In Reply To: 89-06-12 15.44 FROM BOULANGER_NADIA 2:?? 2311 at 7 but still too dim ??
   How long have these 2311s been installed? What is the duty power- on cycle (5 days/10 hrs, 7 days/24 hrs, etc.)? Are they/were they using screensaver? If so, what was the value?
Value to Information Seeker = $5.00

SENT: 89-06-13 08:37
FROM: GLASS_Phil@AUSTIN
   In Reply To: 89-06-12 15.44 FROM BOULANGER_NADIA 2:?? 2311 at 7 but still too dim ??
   Hi,
   Try tweaking the potentiometer inside the monitor. I've had to do the same with the terminals and Agelbars (no comments please) when I worked in the private sector. I've never taken a 2311 apart, so I can't tell you the location of the pot, but you should see something on or near it to indicate that it controls brightness.
   My only word of warning is to be damn careful when you stick a screwdriver in there. You may want to cover the shaft in a layer of electrical tape. Good luck.
   Regards, Phil Glass
Value to Information Seeker = $5.00

SENT: 89-06-13 01:18
FROM: SCHOENBERG_ARNIE@BELGIUM
   In Reply to: 89-06-12 15.44 FROM BOULANGER_NADIA 2:?? 2311 at 7 but still too dim ??
   Hallo Nadia,
   No problem. With two screws you can easily remove the top cover of the 2311. Under the cover you will find the monitorboard and on that board the two potmeters for brightness and contrast.
   Greetings, Arnie
Value to Information Seeker = $25.00

SENT: 89-06-12 18:01
FROM: CAGE_JOHN@PRUNE
   In Reply to: 89-06-12 15.44 FROM BOULANGER_NADIA 2:?? 2311 at 7 but still too dim ??
   Nadia,

We had a few of 'em that we took apart and tweeked up a pot labeled "brite" or "brightness" or some such. They're still working!

jc

Value to Information Seeker = *$20.00*

SENT: 89-06-13 12:01
FROM: PENTLAND_BARBARA@ORCA
In Reply to: 89-06-12 15:44 FROM BOULANGER_NADIA 2:?? 2311 at 7 but still too dim ??

THE COST TO MAINTAIN THESE UNITS WOULD GREATLY EXCEED THE PRICE IN WHICH WE BOUGHT THEM FOR. THE BEST SOLUTION IS TO THROW THESE UNITS OUT AND PURCHASE NEW ONES. BESIDES THAT REPLACEMENT PARTS ARE SLIM TO NONE.

Value to Information Seeker = *none given*

SENT: 89-06-14 10:11
FROM: SCHAEFFER_MURRAY@EASY
TO: BOULANGER_NADIA@SLC
SUBJECT: ?? 2311 at 7 but still too dim ??
In Reply to: 89-06-12 15:44 FROM BOULANGER_NADIA 2:?? 2311 at 7 but still too dim ??

Nadia,

There is probably an adjustment inside the monitor. You should ask your CE [customer engineer] about adjusting the range with the internal pot.

Murray

Value to Information Seeker = *$5.00*

SENT: 89-06-15 07:14
FROM: THEBERGE_PAUL@PITT
SUBJECT: 2311 BRIGHTNESS
HI THERE,

THERE IS AN INTERNAL BRIGHTNESS POT THAT CAN BE ACCESSED BY OPENING UP THE MONITOR. I HAVE ADJUSTED QUITE A FEW TER-MINALS THIS WAY. I DON'T KNOW IF THIS IS THE PRESCRIBED METHOD BUT IT WORKS! HOPE THIS HELPS!

PAUL THEBERGE

Value to Information Seeker = *$20.00*

SENT : 89-06-17 19:27
FROM: LEVERKUHN_ADRIAN@OMAHA
In Reply to: 89-06-12 15:44 FROM BOULANGER_NADIA 2:?? 2311 at 7 but still too dim ??

Nadia, I had a couple of the Beta units and that was one of the problems, only it occurred after a week. I tried getting inside and adjusting, just as I have done with 2316s with about the same results. You can crank up the brightness a bit but then you start to lose your contrast and get complaints of "fuzzy" characters. We have found that the units, being FRUs [field-replaceable units] in-toto are not worth the effort.

Adrian

Value to Information Seeker = $15.00

NOTES

1. In the case of 17 people who broadcast more than one question during the research period, we asked only about the first question. In the case of people who replied to more than one question, we sent a separate survey about each reply they sent up to three.

2. Because diversity is a group-level variable in our study, we could not use measures of demographic diversity that assess how individuals differ from one another within a group (Tsui et al. 1992). Other measures such as Blau's index of heterogeneity (1977) depend on distributional assumptions that are untestable in this context. Our measures, while simple, are unbiased and relevant to technical advice and therefore are useful in this context (D. Krackhardt, personal communication).

3. In cases where the overlapping of dyadic data is pronounced, the violation of independence assumptions can be serious (Krackhardt 1988). In our case the number of overlapping dyads (those with a common seeker and/or replier) is small relative to the total number of dyads.

4. We used hierarchical regression to separately examine the effects of two blocks of resource variables: personal resources (expertise, firm experience, and industry experience) and social resources attached to location or job position (location near headquarters, being a manager, and hierarchical position). Because we did not obtain consistent differences between these blocks of variables, we do not discuss them separately further.

5. Of 24 correlations examined, 3 were significant at the .05 level. A history of replying in second-class mail was correlated with the personal benefit, "I gain respect from others" ($r = .14$, $p < .05$). Acquaintance was positively correlated with saying "It's part of my job" ($r = .22, p. < 001$) and negatively with "It's part of being a good citizen" ($r = -.12, p < .05$).

REFERENCES

Allen, T. J. (1977), *Managing the Flow of Technology,* Cambridge: MIT Press.

Amato, P. R. (1990), "Personality and Social Network Involvement as Predictors of Helping Behavior in Everyday Life," *Social Psychology Quarterly,* 53, 31-43.

Bandura, A. (1986), *Social Foundations of Thought and Action: A Social Cognitive Theory,* Englewood Cliffs, NJ: Prentice Hall.

Bateman, T. S. and D. W. Organ (1983), "Job Satisfaction and the Good Soldier: The Relationship Between Affect and Employee 'Citizenship,' " *Academy of Management Journal,* 26, 586-595.

Berkowitz, L. and L. R. Daniels (1964), "Affecting the Salience of the Social Responsibility Norm: Effects of Past Help on the Response to Dependency Relationships," *Journal of Abnormal and Social Psychology,* 68, 275-281.

Blau, P. M. (1977), *Inequality and Heterogeneity,* New York: Free Press.

Brief, A. P. and S. J. Motowidlo (1986), "Prosocial Organizational Behaviors," *Academy of Management Review,* 10, 710-725.

Brown, J. J. and P. H. Reingen (1987), "Social Ties and Word-of-Mouth Referral Behavior," *Journal of Consumer Research,* 14, 350-362.

Burt, R. S. (1983), "Range," in R. S. Burt and M. J. Minor (Eds.), *Applied Network Analysis,* Beverly Hills, CA: Sage, pp. 176-194.

Cialdini, R. B., R. R. Reno, and C. A. Kallgren (1990), "A Focus Theory of Normative Conduct: Recycling the Concept of Norms to Reduce Littering in Public Places," *Journal of Personality and Social Psychology,* 58, 1015-1026.

Crane, D. (1971), *The Invisible College,* Chicago: University of Chicago Press.

Daft, R. and R. Lengel (1986), "Organizational Information Requirements, Media Richness and Structural Design," *Management Science,* 32, 554-571.

DiMaggio, P. and J. Mohr (1985), "Cultural Capital, Educational Attainment, and Marital Selection," *American Journal of Sociology,* 90, 1231-1261.

Dovidio, J. F. (1984), "Helping and Altruism: An Empirical and Conceptual Overview," in L. Berkowitz (Ed.), *Advances in Experimental Social Psychology,* New York: Academic Press, Vol. 17.

Feldman, M. S. (1987), "Electronic Mail and Weak Ties in Organizations," *Office: Technology and People,* 3, 83-101.

Festinger, L., S. Schachter, and K. Back (1950), *Social Pressures in Informal Groups: A Study of Human Factors in Housing,* New York: Harper.

Finholt, T. (1993), "Outsiders on the Inside," unpublished doctoral dissertation, Carnegie-Mellon University, Pittsburgh, PA.

Friedkin, N. (1982), "Information Flow Through Strong and Weak Ties in Intraorganizational Social Networks," *Social Networks,* 3, 273-285.

Fulton, J., R. Fulton, and R. Simmons (1977), "The Cadaver Donor and the Gift of Life," in R. Simmons, S. Klein, and R. Simmons (Eds.), *Gift of Life: The Social and Psychological Impact of Organ Transplantation,* New York: John Wiley, pp. 338-376.

Granovetter, M. (1973), "The Strength of Weak Ties," *American Journal of Sociology,* 78, 1360-1380.

_____ (1982), "The Strength of Weak Ties: A Network Theory Revisited," in P. Marsden and N. Lin (Eds.), *Social Structure and Network Analysis,* New York: John Wiley, pp. 105-130.

Heimer, C. (1992), "Doing Your Job and Helping Your Friends: Universalistic Norms About Obligations to Particular Others in Networks," in N. Nohria and R. G. Eccles (Eds.), *Networks and Organizations: Structure, Form, and Action,* Boston: Harvard Business School Press, pp. 143-164.

Kelley, H. H. and J. W. Thibaut (1978), *Interpersonal Relations: A Theory of Interdependence,* New York: John Wiley.

Krackhardt, D. (1988), "Predicting With Networks: A Multiple Regression Approach to Analyzing Dyadic Data," *Social Networks,* 10, 359-381.

_____ (1990), "Assessing the Political Landscape: Structure, Cognition, and Power in Organizations," *Administrative Science Quarterly,* 35, 342-369.

_____ (1992), "The Strength of Strong Ties: The Importance of Philos in Organizations," in N. Nohria and R. Eccles (Eds.), *Organizations and Networks: Structure, Form, and Action,* Boston: Harvard Business School Press, pp. 216-239.

_____ (1994), "Constraints on the Interactive Organization as an Ideal Type," in C. Heckscher and Anne Donnelan (Eds.), *The Post-Bureaucratic Organization,* Thousand Oaks, CA: Sage, pp. 211-222.

Kraut, R. E., C. Egido, and J. Galegher (1990), "Patterns of Contact and Communication in Scientific Research Collaborations," in J. Galegher, R. E. Kraut, and C. Egido (Eds.),

Intellectual Teamwork: Social and Technological Foundations of Cooperative Work, Hillsdale, NJ: Lawrence Erlbaum, pp. 149-172.

_____, J. Galegher, and C. Egido (1988), "Relationships and Tasks in Scientific Collaboration," *Human-Computer Interaction,* 3, 31-58.

Lave, J. (1991), "Situating Learning in Communities of Practice," in L. B. Resnick, J. M. Levine, and S. D. Teasley (Eds.), *Perspectives on Socially Shared Cognition,* Washington, DC: American Psychological Association, pp. 63-84.

Lin, N. (1982), "Social Resources and Instrumental Action," in P. Marsden and N. Lin (Eds.), *Social Structure and Network Analysis,* Beverly Hills, CA: Sage.

_____ and M. Dumin (1986), "Access to Occupations Through Social Ties," *Social Networks,* 8, 365-385.

_____, W. M. Ensel, and J. C. Vaughn (1981), "Social Resources and Strength of Ties: Structural Factors in Occupational Status Attainment," *American Sociological Review,* 46, 393-405.

_____, J. C. Vaughn, and W. M. Ensel (1981), "Social Resources and Occupational Status Attainment," *Social Forces,* 59, 4, 1163-1181.

Macy, M. (1990), "Learning Theory and the Logic of Critical Mass," *American Sociological Review,* 55, 809-826.

Marsden, P. V. and J. S. Hurlbert (1988), "Social Resources and Mobility Outcomes: A Replication and Extension," *Social Forces,* 66, 1038-1059.

Marwell, G., P. Oliver, and R. Prahl (1988), "Social Networks and Collective Actions: A Theory of Critical Mass III," *American Journal of Sociology,* 94, 502-532.

Mauss, M. (1967), *The Gift,* New York: Norton, 1st ed., 1925.

Monge, P. R., L. W. Rothman, E. M. Eisenberg, K. L. Miller, and K. Kirste (1985), "The Dynamics of Organizational Proximity," *Management Science,* 31, 1129-1141.

Nohria, N. (1992), "Information and Search in the Creation of New Business Ventures: The Case of the 128 Venture Group," in N. Nohria and R. G. Eccles (Eds.), *Networks and Organizations: Structure, Form, and Action,* Boston: Harvard Business School Press, pp. 240-261.

Orr, J. E. (1989), "Sharing Knowledge, Celebrating Identity: War Stories and Community Memory Among Service Technicians," in D. S. Middleton and D. Edwards (Eds.), *Collective Remembering: Memory in Society,* Newbury Park, CA: Sage.

Ross, M. (1989), "Relation of Implicit Theories to the Construction of Personal Histories," *Psychological Review,* 96, 341-357.

Schlenker, B. R. (1985), "Identity and Self-Identification," in B. R. Schlenker (Ed.), *The Self and Social Life,* New York: McGraw-Hill.

Scott, J. (1991), *Social Network Analysis: A Handbook,* Newbury Park, CA: Sage.

Shamir, B. (1991), "Meaning, Self and Motivation in Organizations," *Organization Studies,* 12, 405-424.

Sproull, L. and S. Kiesler (1986), "Reducing Social Context Cues: Electronic Mail in Organizational Communication," *Management Science,* 32, 1492-1512.

Stevenson, W. B. and M. C. Gilly (1991), "Information Processing and Problem Solving: The Migration of Problems Through Formal Positions and Networks of Ties," *Academy of Management Journal,* 34, 918-928.

Thorn, B. K. and T. Connolly (1987), "Discretionary Data Bases: A Theory and Some Experimental Findings," *Communication Research,* 14, 512-528.

Titmuss, R. M. (1971), *The Gift Relationship: From Human Blood to Social Policy,* New York: Pantheon.

Tsui, A. S., T. D. Egan, and C. A. O'Reilly (1992), "Being Different: Relational Demography and Organizational Attachment," *Administrative Science Quarterly,* 37, 549-579.

Wagner, W. G., J. Pfeffer, and C. A. O'Reilly (1984), "Organizational Demography and Turnover in Top-Management Groups," *Administrative Science Quarterly,* 29, 74-92.

Weenig, M. W. and C. J. Midden (1991), "Communication Network Influences on Information Diffusion and Persuasion," *Journal of Personality and Social Psychology,* 61, 734-742.

Williamson, G. and M. Clark (1989), "The Communal/Exchange Distinction and Some Implications for Understanding Justice in Families," *Social Justice Research,* 3, 77-103.

Zenger, T. R. and B. S. Lawrence (1989), "Organizational Demography: The Differential Effects of Age and Tenure Distributions on Technical Communication," *Academy of Management Journal,* 32, 353-376.

Zurcher, L. A. (1965), "The Sailor Aboard Ship: A Study of Role Behavior in a Total Institution," *Social Forces,* 43, 389-400.

PART IV

CONTROVERSIES AND DIRECTIONS

Will the newer organizational forms be more effective than their older counterparts? Will organizations and the people within them find the new forms to bring improvements in productivity and quality of life? Are there downsides to new forms and, if so, how can the negative effects of new forms be minimized? We explore these questions in this section.

Victor and Stephens (Chapter 14) observe that any far-reaching organizational change involves destruction and creation. Just as new organizational forms bring enamoring advances, they also can bring painful downsides: displaced workers, greater disparities in distribution of wealth between rich and poor, more part-time work, fear of job loss, excessive travel, and potential for alienation and boredom. They explore concepts such as "virtual occupations" and the "virtual wage slave," which are by-products of the incessant demand for innovation in a growth-oriented, uncertain workplace.

Poole (Chapter 15) examines new challenges brought on by new structural characteristics in firms and the physical and social changes that limit firms' ability to deliver promised benefits. For example, the tight coupling of operational processes across an otherwise disaggregated organizational form can lead to greater potential for technology-enabled disaster. A problem in one process can multiply its effects in connected processes. Few individuals may fully understand the entirety of a complex, interconnected set of structures such that problems will be difficult to detect, correct, and contain from affecting other systems or organizations. Related challenges of new organizational forms include managing complexity, blending new with old system components, and providing for adequate security within a highly complex network. There are the challenges of maintaining cohesion in temporary organizations without tradition or common culture, fostering commitment and loyalty in the face of fluid personnel assignments, and forming and maintaining trust among various entities of an organizational network. Furthermore, technology may well be a Trojan horse, which promises to facilitate change but sneaks in old values that ultimately undermine transformation. Managers and researchers should think about these possibilities as they enter the age of new organizational forms.

Dutton (Chapter 16) concludes this section with a discussion of "tele-access," which he views as the key mechanism by which information and communication technologies facilitate changes in organizations. By providing tele-access, information and communication technologies reshape communication patterns (access to people), how organizations conduct their business (access by suppliers or customers), and the equipment, techniques, and know-how available to the firm (access to technology). Various forms of distributing work—telework, telecenters, mobile work, and distributed firms—are enabled by the ability of new technologies to support tele-access. Advances in tele-access are lessening the constraints of telecommunications on the location of jobs and functions and make possible the virtual form of organization. The virtual organization does not provide a model for all organizations to emulate, but it does illustrate one approach to a more general strategy for using technology to improve access to information, people, services, and other technology. In exploring the potential of virtual organizations, Dutton also warns us to be careful not to overestimate the ability of tele-access to bring change because social and organizational constraints can limit the impacts of new technologies. He explores both the potentialities and the constraints for technology to shape organizational forms.

14

The Dark Side of the
New Organizational Forms

BART VICTOR

CARROLL STEPHENS

> I suppose one might have persuaded oneself that this was but the replacement of
> an ancient tranquility, or at least an ancient balance, by a new order. Only to my
> eyes, quickened by my father's imitations, it was manifestly no order at all. It was
> a multitude of uncoordinated fresh starts, each more sweeping and destructive
> than the last, and none of them ever worked out to a ripe and satisfactory
> completion. Each left a legacy of products—houses, humanity, or whatnot—in its
> wake. It was a sort of progress that had bolted; it was change out of hand, and
> going at an unprecedented pace nowhere in particular.
>
> —H. G. Wells from *New Machiavelli* (1910)

The field of organization theory is rife with discussion of new organizational forms (Daft and Lewin 1993). So is the popular business press. It is no exaggeration to claim that the emergence of the organizational form variously termed postindustrial, postbureaucratic, network, cluster, and perpetual matrix has rejuvenated organization theory. Not only do scholars have a panoply of novel challenges facing turn-of-the-millennium organizations to address, but—as evidenced by coverage in magazines including *Fortune,*

This chapter appeared originally in *Organization Science,* 5(4), November, 1994.

Forbes, and *Business Week,* and the best-seller status of books such as *Reengineering the Corporation* (Hammer and Champy 1993)—practitioners actually seem to care about organization design.

As we career into the brave new world of the twenty-first century organization—networked, information rich, delayered, lean, hypercompetitive, and boundaryless—an unanticipated, undesirable, and indirect consideration has been overlooked. Radical redesign of organizations throughout the society—indeed globally—necessarily entails losses as well as gains. We believe that the time is right to break the silence about the dark side of the new organization forms. In this chapter, we wish to call attention to moral as well as pragmatic questions about the new forms.

These fundamental alterations in the nature of organizational forms are occasioned by changes of a magnitude that have not been seen since the industrial revolution and the consequent emergence of bureaucracy. New organizational forms tend to arise in response to social and technological advances (Chandler 1962, 1977, Weber 1910/1978). Particular forms of organizations arise at particular times, within particular sets of conditions. Bureaucracy evolved in response to post-enlightenment rational thought, the weakening of primary institutions such as family and church, and the technological advances of the industrial revolution (Lewin and Stephens 1993, p. 400). The mechanization of the industrial revolution led many former artisans, craftspeople, and farmers to leave the sphere of community and self-sufficiency (Gemeinschaft) in order to enter the labor markets of the large modern organization (Gesellschaft). This shift was propelled by the laborpower demands of the industrial organization, which created net economic gains for society at large. Yet even a cursory review of the literature from the time that the bureaucratic organization was dawning reveals at least as much trepidation as heralding. Writers as disparate as Kafka, LePlay, Orwell, Durkheim, Huxley, Marx, Tonnies, and Michels powerfully depicted the social and human costs of modernization. Nowhere is this expressed more poignantly than by Weber himself—simultaneous chronicler and critic of bureaucracy:

> It is as if we were deliberately to become men who need order and nothing but order, who become nervous and cowardly if for one moment the order wavers, and helpless if they are torn away from their total incorporation in it. That the world should know no men but these: It is in such an evolution that we are already caught up, and the great question is therefore not how we can promote and hasten it, but what we can oppose to this machinery in order to keep a portion of humankind free from this parcelling-out of the soul, from this supreme mastery of the bureaucratic way of life. (in Mayer, 1944)

Although chroniclers of and apologists for the new organizational forms are multitudinous, critics are rare—at least in the organization theory literature. Yet a juxtaposition of the flossy "new org form" language—empowerment, high commitment, downsizing, restructuring, and reengineering—against the hard economic data presents a jarring image. The lean, flexible organization has far-reaching consequences for the downsized worker, and hence for society. One third of all American workers now hold temporary, part-time, or short-term contract jobs (U.S. Bureau of Labor Statistics). The number of temporary workers tripled between 1982 and 1990. Although the U.S. economy is, by conventional measures, in recovery following the recession of the late '80s and early '90s, a record number of companies announced layoffs in 1993. More than 90% of new jobs being created are part-time. After the four previous recessions, nearly half of all laid-off workers returned to their original jobs; the current figure is 15%.

These figures, taken together, suggest that the U.S. economy and workplace are undergoing profound structural alterations, not merely cyclical ups and downs. This is not necessarily a bad thing. According to theories of modernization (Schumpeter 1934, Weber 1910/1978), economic progress generally brings about both a bigger pie for all to share and a more equitable distribution of that pie, even when changes involve cataclysmic dislocations such as the shift from an agrarian to an industrial economy. Furthermore, arguments can be made that trimming the workforce—downsizing—is necessary to succeed in today's hypercompetitive environment. However, in contrast to earlier economic upheavals, the postindustrial changes have led to heightened income disparities rather than shared benefits. Between 1980 and 1990, the richest 1% of the U.S. population became 50% wealthier while the poorest 20% found themselves 8% more disadvantaged. Over the past decade, America's CEOs stretched their pay advantage over production workers from 40/1 to 93/1.

Of course, any far-reaching organizational change involves destruction as well as creation. As Durkheim (1893) wrote,

> What is in fact characteristic of our development is that it has successively destroyed all the established social contexts: One after another they have been banished either by the slow usury of time or by violent revolution, in such a fashion that nothing has been developed to replace them.

The destructive aspects of the industrial revolution were well reported. Those of the post-industrial revolution and the concomitant new organizational forms seem to be passing almost unobserved. Over 20 years ago a few prescient scholars such as Herbert Marcuse (1968) and Daniel Bell (1973) posed the seemingly science-fiction question of how organizations, society, and economy would be restructured once technological advances rendered the full-time industrial employment of the majority of adults obsolescent. This is precisely the eventuality that we believe has come to pass at the turn of the millennium.

If quantum leaps in technology have enabled organizations to become leaner, thus leading to widespread job loss that our society has yet to address in a systematic manner, so too have technological changes had profound impact on those who remain members of the organization. Sophisticated computer-mediated telecommunications have permitted the development of the "virtual office"; where organizational boundaries begin and end is unclear. And, as Burns and Stalker warned in 1961 when they first described the flexible organic organization, postbureaucratic organization forms carry the hazard of blurring the boundaries of the demands that may be placed on workers.

Looking ahead, the new organizational forms are supplanting jobs with what amount to virtual occupations. Total quality organizational cultures would have workers perform whenever tasks are required to satisfy the customer, or reach the quality wishdream of continuous improvement. Instead of a role anchored by the organization and codified in a job description, the new forms are offering a role defined by the task of the moment and location of the worker. Time, space, and shifting group membership are becoming the primary definers of responsibility and accountability for the virtual wage slave. Traditional indicators of status are becoming blurred as a result of obligations that are networked and diffused, and rights that are increasingly ephemeral in this new world of ours. At just the time that organizational commitment to the employee has been thoroughly violated, the employee is expected to exhibit feverishly enhanced commitment to the organization. And, fearing job loss, many are compliant despite the increasing onesideness of the deal.

There is much discussion about the empowering, challenging, and equalizing advantages of the new organizational form. But there is also a justified fear and loathing. Bureaucracy may have led to alienation and anomie; we tend to overlook the fact that bureaucracy also fostered procedural if not substantive justice for workers. Furthermore, not every person will be at ease with the free-floating demands of the hyperflexible workplace. As Erich Fromm (1941) pointed out, many if not most people thrive on predictability and routine.

The boundaryless, adaptive, learning organization will extract a price from everyone involved. One notable and distinctly unromantic consequence of the transformation from the craft form to the new bureaucracy was the impact on traditional know-how and skill. Confidence gained from inheritance and apprenticeship was stripped away by the machines and procedures of the new factory. As Elton Mayo (1945) described the fate of the Welsh workers in the newly mechanized coal mines of Pennsylvania,

> These men, many in late middle age, found themselves without an avocation and without means of continuing to support themselves and their families in the way of life to which they had become accustomed. This was for them a personal calamity of the first magnitude; as former pillars of society they did not lapse readily into revolutionary attitudes. They drifted downwards toward unemployment as their savings became exhausted and toward profound personal depression.

In the new organizational form, the periodic deskilling that comes with technical progress in bureaucracy is replaced with an incessant demand for innovation and adaptation. To accommodate this, the new "learning organization" insists that everyone become a self-motivated, continuous learner. Absent this obsession with learning about work, workers are threatened with rapid obsolescence—and little hope of getting back on the treadmill of continuous progress.

This impact of new forms extends to our social selves as well. Flat organizations force interpersonal relations in more demanding and intrusive modes than ever before. Private self, benign eccentricities, and social warts become new terms of employment, even as we hope for a more diverse and unbiased workplace. Teams and networks call for new levels and kinds of cooperation. No one can expect to escape the demands to interact and be interactive. Even the values of the employee are offered up as fodder to be transformed by management for organizational ends. Yet these high-velocity, high-commitment workplaces—flash in the pan collectives—offer no ongoing relationships, no safe haven, no personal space.

Concepts such as loyalty, dedication, and belonging have at best a radically new place in the emerging workworld. We still wax nostalgic about the concept of family in a fashion that harkens to a lost (and mostly fictitious) past. How much more distant will the future take us? Concepts such as the expropriation of surplus value, rate busting, union busting, impression management, careerism, and dehumanization emerged from the bureaucratic form, along with the work ethic, affordable luxuries, corporate social responsibility, and meritocracy. In the discussion of the new organizational form we hear a great deal about valuing diversity, empowerment, and customized solutions. But what of the potential negative values and consequences? Perhaps it is our time to think critically enough of the future to warn our descendants of some of the potential dangers.

We cannot stop the emergence of the new form, just as the critics of bureaucracy could not stem the ineluctable reach of the iron cage. Less all its ills, the emergence of bureaucracy has probably been a net benefit for humankind. The same may be true of the new form. Organizational scholars are eagerly examining the implementation of the new forms. Perhaps we should expand our research agenda to address questions that have far-reaching moral as well as economic consequences: How can companies assist surviving workers in making the transition to the brave new Workplace? How can stress be minimized, rather than accentuated, in the ambiguous new form? And, most important, what is to become of the superfluous downsized workers? It is worth repeating for our times the moral exhortation that Durkheim (orig. 1893; Trans. 1933, Free Press) issued:

> Science can help finding the direction in which our conduct ought to go, assisting us to determine the ideal that we gropingly seek. But we shall only be able to raise ourselves up to that ideal after having observed reality, for we shall distill the ideal from it.

REFERENCES

Bell, D. (1973), *The Coming of Post-Industrial Society: A Venture in Social Forecasting,* New York: Basic Books.

Burns, T. and G. Stalker (1961), *The Management of Innovation,* London: Tavistock.

Chandler, A. (1962), *Strategy and Structure in the History of Industrial Enterprise,* Cambridge: MIT Press.

_____ (1977), *The Visible Hand: The Managerial Revolution in American Business,* Cambridge, MA: Harvard University Press.

Daft, R. and A. Lewin (1993), "Where Are the Theories for the Organizational Forms? An Editorial Essay," *Organization Science,* 4, 4, i-vi.

Durkheim, E. (1893), *Suicide,* New York: Avon.

_____ (1933), *The Division of Labor in Society,* New York: Free Press. (Original work published 1893)

Fromm, E. (1941), *Escape From Freedom,* New York: Avon.

Hammer, M. and J. Champy (1993), *Reengineering the Corporation: A Manifesto for Business Revolution,* New York: Harper Business.

Lewin, A. and C. Stephens (1993), "Designing Post-Industrial Organizations: Combing Theory and Practice," in G. Huber and W. Glick (Eds.), *Organizational Change and Redesign,* Oxford, New York, pp. 393-409.

Marcuse, H. (1968), *Negations: Essays in Critical Theory,* London: Penguin.

Mayer, P. (1944), *Max Weber and German Politics,* London: Faber & Faber.

Mayo, E. (1945), *The Social Problems of an Industrial Civilization,* Boston: Harvard Business School Press.

Schumpeter, J. (1934), *The Theory of Economic Development,* Cambridge, MA: Harvard University Press.

Weber, M. (1978), *Economy and Society* (G. Roth and C. Wittich, Trans.), Berkeley: University of California Press. (Original work published 1910)

15

Organizational Challenges
for the New Forms

MARSHALL SCOTT POOLE

New organizational forms present exciting possibilities. The dynamic network (Miles and Snow 1986, Powell 1990), virtual organization (Nohria and Berkley 1994), postbureaucratic ideal (Heckscher 1994), and others promise greater flexibility, adaptability, and interactivity than traditional structures. They have the potential to serve customer and client needs better, to enhance employees' skills and control over their work, and to increase democracy and participation in the workplace.

This exciting potential should not blind us to problems in the new forms. It is easy to identify the problems with traditional structures, such as the bureaucracy and the matrix, because they have been explored for decades. It is more difficult to discern potential challenges for new forms because we know relatively little about them. Every type of organization, however, has particular problems and limitations that may neutralize its benefits and decrease its effectiveness. Effective implementation of new organizational forms requires us to find ways to cope with unanticipated problems and to surmount the limitations that inevitably emerge in practice.

Many organizational challenges that face new organizational forms are discussed in this chapter. The chapter is focused not on the social problems that new forms may create (see Chapter 14) or on problems in implementing new forms (Venkatraman 1991); rather, this chapter examines challenges internal to the new organizations—challenges engendered by the defining qualities of the new forms. These challenges are of two types. First, there are problems born of their structural characteristics. Second, there are physical and social limitations that affect the new forms by circumscribing their ability to deliver promised benefits.

The chapter is organized as follows: The next section considers defining characteristics of the new organizational forms. The majority of the chapter is devoted to discussion of five sets of potential challenges: problems due to tight coupling, challenges stemming from fluid structures, limits on interaction in networks, stresses on individuals in new organizations, and technology as a limiting factor. For each challenge, I describe the challenge and its causes and effects, discuss possible solutions, and define a research agenda. The goal of this chapter is not to argue that new organizational forms are inherently flawed. Rather, I aim to identify potential problem areas and limitations in the hope of stimulating research into how best to minimize them. Before exploring the five challenges, it is important to consider some of the characteristics of the new forms that breed them.

NEW ORGANIZATIONAL FORMS

New forms are composed of one or more of the following characteristics:

1. They use information technology to integrate across organizational functions, reengineer production and service processes, and create increased interdependence among activities. This speeds up production and response time and enables the organization to adapt to customer needs and environmental demands in highly specific ways.

2. They use flexible, modular organizational structures that can be readily reconfigured as new projects, demands, or problems arise. These structures may be composed of units of a single larger organization, or they may be composed of different organizations joined through various types of interorganizational alliances. Accounting and information systems play important roles in the creation and maintenance of flexible structures, substituting for traditional hierarchical control (Child 1987).

3. They use information technology to coordinate geographically dispersed units and members. In the extreme case, there may be a virtual organization whose dispersed members are linked primarily through telecommunications and information technology.

4. They are team-based work organizations, which emphasize autonomy and self-management. This is generally combined with a strong emphasis on quality and continuous improvement.

5. They have relatively flat hierarchies and a reliance on horizontal coordination among units and personnel.

6. They use intra- and interorganizational markets to mediate transactions such as the assignment and hiring of personnel for projects and the formation of interorganizational networks. The market mechanism is used as an alternative to hierarchy when many comparable individual units or actors are involved.

These are the modal qualities found in a range of descriptions of new organizations (Child 1987, Eccles and Crane 1987, Hammer and Champy 1993, Heckscher 1994, Jarvenppa and Ives 1994, Konsynski and Sviokla 1994, Lucas and Baroudi 1994, Nohria and Berkley 1994, Powell 1990, Scott Morton 1991), although not every new organization embodies all six qualities. Organizations have created these structures for their advantages, but hidden within them are potential problems and limitations that may prevent new forms from living up to their billing.

PROBLEMS DUE TO TIGHT
COUPLING OF COMPLEX SYSTEMS

Through integration across functions, designers of new forms often seek to achieve efficiencies, improved response time, and more effective control of work. Reengineering and business network redesign emphasize this strategy (Hammer and Champy 1993, Venkatraman 1991). Information technology is used to reorganize work to create a tightly connected system of complex activities. This system has one or more of the following attributes: Jobs are consolidated so that one position performs functions previously distributed among several; information technology is used to coordinate and integrate activities through a common nexus; units and individuals outside the focal organization are integrated into the information system and production activities; and checks and controls are reduced to enable faster response.

The benefits of integrated, reengineered organizations are challenged by the possibility of accidents inherent to tightly coupled systems. In *Normal Accidents* (1984), an incisive exploration of failures in complex systems, Charles Perrow defined an accident as a "failure in a subsystem or system as a whole that damages more than one unit and in doing so disrupts the ongoing or future output of the system" (p. 66). Perrow analyzed accidents and near-accidents in nuclear power plants, chemical processing plants, the air transportation industry, and other complex organizational systems. He concluded that severe failures were a "normal" part of the operation of such systems—by-products of their tightly coupled designs. His analysis points to several features of complex systems that enhance their propensity to sudden, catastrophic failure.

First, these systems typically have multiple interconnected processes that operate simultaneously, often in the same unit. This tight coupling creates nonlinear interactions among processes whereby a problem in one process multiplies its effects in connected processes; once a disruption is initiated, it runs out of control because it reverberates through other processes and units integrated with the site of the original problem. As a result, the disruption rapidly grows to unmanageable proportions; moreover, it is hard to trace the origin of the problem (if this is possible in a complex interconnected system) because so many parts of the system are disrupted.

A second property of complex systems is the need for indirect control by operators. Because complex systems are managed mostly through information technologies, operators have no direct contact with the processes being controlled. Hence, operators must learn to judge what is happening through surrogate measures, such as gauge readings or system reports (Zuboff 1988). Moreover, the complex interconnections between system parts dictates that nonlinear interactions must be controlled indirectly because interventions can only be made in a particular part of the interaction. Hence operators often do not understand what is going on in the system because they have access only to indirect indicators of critical events. This problem may be heightened in reengineering because there is often an emphasis on downsizing, leaving fewer operators to monitor the indirect indicators.

Third, these systems are open to environmental perturbations that can disrupt their operation. Even nearly closed systems, such as nuclear power plants, are subject to earthquakes, floods, labor unrest, and other environmental jolts. New organizational forms, which often build in connections to customers or suppliers, are especially subject to perturbations from without. In tightly coupled, nonlinear systems, such perturbations can spread rapidly, and even relatively small ones may result in major disruptions.

A fourth problem implied by Perrow's (1984) analysis is the unwieldy, sedimented information systems used to control complex processes. Major information systems have a history of late delivery and problematic introductions across many industries. The complicated, interconnected information systems necessary to manage complex systems, however, introduce several problems. They tend to grow gradually, accreting layers of code on top of old code and new modules designed to enhance performance and fix problems. They are tightly coupled and subject to nonlinear interactions mediated by commonly used modules or functions. Whether new additions will work with old components is never clear; often, complicated "kluges" must be set into place to make the new and old work together. In short, they become complex systems in their own right, subject to the same types of reverberating disruptions that derail the larger systems in which they are a part. Hardware problems and security problems due to the openness of the organization to its environment are additional strains on the complex system.

The similarity between many new organizational forms and the description of organizations subject to normal accidents is striking. Ironically, some of the same characteristics that promise to yield great benefits in the new forms—their integration, use of information technology, tight coupling, and interconnection with their environments—may be an Achilles' heel that causes unexpected disruptions in organizational functioning. Examples of such disruptions include the shutdown of the Chicago Board of Exchange due to the power outage during the flood of 1992 and the 1990 shutdown of the AT&T long-distance network (which emphasized survivability; Neumann 1992). These incidents were triggered by propagation through the system of environmental events, relatively minor human errors, or software problems. The benefits of linkage for new organizations can be immense, but there is also an increase in the fragility of operations (Osterman 1991).

This challenge implies several research issues. First, to what extent are new forms vulnerable to normal accidents? Are they likely only in very large networks or in networks that depend heavily on information technology? Are some types of configurations or design more likely to fall prey than others? Second, are there ways of protecting against systemwide disruptions in new forms? Are some work designs more effective than others in helping to head off disruptions? Can operators be taught nonlinear thinking and, if so, how can it be employed to best effect? Are different sorts of training and education needed? Although normal accidents may be inevitable, it is hoped that they can be made sufficiently rare that complex systems can yield a great excess of benefits to costs.

CHALLENGES OF FLUIDITY

New organizational forms are often described as more "fluid" than traditional forms. Fluidity is discussed at two different levels. New forms may be more fluid in terms of their overall design, which refers to the number and composition of the units, their configuration, and how they are coordinated and controlled. To varying degrees, new forms strive to be project or customer centered and change their configuration, makeup, and practices to meet situational demands. For perhaps the most fluid model of new organizations, Miles and Snow (1986) discuss brokers who assemble temporary network organizations from smaller, more specialized units. Although not all new forms are temporary, and although the rate of change may differ across organizations, the concept is the same: The organization recognizes the need to redesign itself so that it can be effective in light of current exigencies.

New forms may also be more fluid in terms of personnel assignment. Personnel move from project to project and firm to firm relatively rapidly rather than remaining with firms or a group of peers for relatively long periods of time. This implies great differences in career paths, human resource policies, and management methods for new and traditional forms (Jarvenpaa and Ives 1994).

For these two types of fluidity, there are several challenges for new organizational forms. These challenges are based on the fact that the traditional foundation for developing relationships with organizations and co-workers—proximate interaction over relatively long periods of time—no longer exists in many new forms (Handy 1995).

First, there is the challenge of maintaining a sense of mission in a temporary organization with little or no tradition or common culture. A fluid organization composed of an aggregation of different units for a time-limited project will encounter difficulty in building a community that can anchor common resolve. Certainly, the project gives the organization a goal, but it is also important that the goal be infused with a sense of mission, which makes the uniqueness of organization clear, gives direction to efforts to meet the goal, and energizes members to give their utmost (Hackman and Walton 1986). Gordon (1994) argues that a limitation of the interactive organizational form is diffusion of responsibility across networks of actors. He believes that strong and inspirational leadership is needed for an interactive organization to be effective. This implies that the broker role may often extend beyond merely assembling and coordinating units to providing leadership.

The diffuseness of networked organizations, however, may militate against the effective exercise of leadership. If units communicate mostly for purposes of coordination and do not develop a common culture, the leader is fighting an uphill battle. Leaders have the best chance to exert influence in richer social systems that rise above mundane considerations of work and coordination. Additionally, there is a question of whether units in a dynamic network would have sufficient time to attend to a leader or to develop a sense of mission. In the fast-changing world of the new forms, units in dynamic networks are likely to be involved in multiple projects, often in more than one network. Their attention is likely to be diffuse and focused on their immediate work rather than on larger issues such as mission. Although a leader could in principle provide mission, in practice focusing attention may prove difficult.

An alternative to leadership is the development of communities of small firms that are familiar with and trust each other. The components of networked organizations can be drawn from this pool, and their common acquaintance can substitute to some extent for common culture. For example, Kingston Electronics has constructed "a tightly knit 'family' of independent companies that, for many purposes, functions as one . . . sharing capital, know-how, and markets" (Meyer 1993, p. 40). Kingston does business in this network on a "handshake" basis, with no contracts or legal ties. It helps related firms grow to keep up with its needs and forms extremely tight relationships of mutual trust with suppliers and sales reps. Still at issue, however, is the question of whether Kingston is the exception rather than the rule and of whether networks could regularly provide the foundation for shared resolve and an inspirational mission.

This implies several research questions. What are the conditions for the exercise of effective leadership in dynamic networks? Is a leader necessary to develop an effective sense of mission in new organizational forms or can other mechanisms achieve this? Can professionalism substitute for mission in ensuring high-quality, devoted performance? What other substitutes for leadership are available in this context?

A second challenge due to fluidity stems from interunit conflicts of interest. In new forms that are composed of a network of smaller independent organizations or units, coordination is a primary task. At least two dynamics militate against smooth coordination, however. First, if the organization experiences setbacks, failures, or crises, some units may blame others, fomenting conflict. Blaming may occur because units wish to shift possible sanctions or penalties for problems onto other units. Blame may also be placed as a result of the common tendency to scapegoat groups that are less known and trusted or groups that have histories of problems or failure. The resulting conflict may be displaced throughout the network as blame is passed around (Smith 1989).

Second, powerholders in component units may actively promote interunit conflicts to give their units identity and to solidify their own positions. As Coser (1956) observed in his study of the functions of conflict, conflict between social units serves to reinforce and reiterate the identity of each as an independent functioning whole; members are galvanized into action by the conflict and stress loyalty to the unit. Units or organizations undergoing internal difficulties may unconsciously welcome such conflicts, even at the price of effective networking. Interunit conflict encourages members to pull together behind their leadership, temporarily forestalling leadership challenges. Hence, leaders in shaky positions, or units in trouble, may actively undermine coordination to strengthen themselves.

If the organization and the units are functioning properly, these problems are not likely to arise. It seems more likely than not, however, that setbacks will occur, units will not trust each other equally, and some units will have internal problems. Under such conditions, dynamics that challenge the integrity of the new forms are likely to arise.

Gordon (1994) thought it very likely that these problems would emerge in new forms. He suggested that "socialized rivalry" be promoted in the place of integrated, interactive configurations. In socialized rivalry, groups compete for resources and rewards and top management evaluates their contributions and effectiveness. Although of limited value for many projects and tasks, this model may work for tasks with pooled interdependence, such as sales or new product innovation.

Research issues implied by this challenge include the following: How severe must the setbacks or internal problems be to set these processes in motion? What measures can be taken to set up networked forms that do not promote unequal familiarity and blame passing? Child (1987) describes how full-disclosure information systems can be used in cocontracting and coordinated contracting arrangements to track responsibilities in networks of organizations. Kingston also uses an open-books policy to ensure trust and alleviate possible resentments (Jarvenpaa and Ives 1994, Meyer 1993). These observations, however, are based largely on anecdotal evidence.

A third challenge concerns problems with commitment and loyalty in the face of fluid personnel assignments. In many new organizational forms, personnel are shifted regularly through temporary assignment to projects, assignment to more than one project, and movement between different organizations in the same network. Such movement is envisioned to increase as these forms are perfected (Jarvenpaa and Ives 1994). Continuous movement can cause problems with role conflicts and loyalty such as those documented for employees who move from government regulatory agencies into the industries they regulate and back again repeatedly.

In many new forms, employees may be encouraged to work on different assignments and in different positions so that they learn many aspects of the organization. The advantage of this is that it helps employees gain a big picture of the company. Not residing in a single unit, however, may engender only shallow loyalty, especially when moves are among very different units or different organizations and when the employee knows that his or her tenancy will not be long.

If the trust important to the functioning of new forms is to be maintained, it is important to be able to count on the loyalty of members to the goals of the organization as a whole rather than the goals of individual units. If members place greater store in personal interests or if their loyalties are so shallow as to undermine commitment, it is difficult for the network to move decisively.

One corrective is to put stringent controls on the system to prevent betrayals and to enable monitoring of effort levels. Such controls, however, may create resentment and impede the initiative that flexible organizations require. Klein (1994) frames the problem as one of maintaining commitment while maintaining control. She recommends that this be achieved by fostering direct ties among network members through mutual sacrifice, by making it clear to employees that they are valued for their skills and knowledge, and by elevating the interest level of the work. The feasibility of these measures when members are regularly shifting from position to position is not clear. Researcher questions related to this issue include the following: Do frequent transfers and reassignments result in less than adequate loyalty? Is loyalty to the firm as a whole sufficient to counteract loyalties to immediate units and coworkers? Is professionalism and involvement in work a substitute for loyalty? and What are other possible substitutes?

A final challenge due to fluidity is the maintenance of trust in new forms. Several scholars commented that relationships in new forms are based primarily on trust (Handy 1995, Jarvenpaa and Ives 1994). Trust takes the place of well-defined structures, roles, and rules in ensuring effective performance in virtual organizations and networks. This enables new forms to attain the flexibility and adaptability they desire.

Heckscher (1994) observes that trust in the new forms is based more on the idea that all are seeking mutual benefit than on traditional grounds for interpersonal trust (for a different view, see Handy 1995):

> Though relationships of trust are a critical ingredient in [interactive organizations], these are not the warm *gemeinschaft* solidarities of traditional communities, or even of the communal version of bureaucracy. Relationships in such a system are formalized and specialized to a high degree: It is a matter of "knowing who to go to" for a particular problem or issue, rather than a matter of building a stable network of friendship relations. (p. 27)

Similarly, Barber (1983) defines trust in the public arena as being composed of two expectations: (a) the expectation of technically competent role performance by the other in his or her relationships with us and in his or her work and (b) the expectation that others will carry out "their fiduciary obligations and responsibilities, that is, their duties in certain situations to place others' interests before their own" (p. 9). This definition captures the expectations that members of new forms must have for others if these forms are to operate smoothly and effectively.

A key challenge for new forms is the cultivation of trust. Barber (1983) cites numerous cases in which public institutions—charity, business, and professions—have lost the trust of their constituents. Building and maintaining trust in these terms is no easy undertaking. The fluidity of new forms makes the usual route to building trust—prolonged experience and interaction—less feasible than it would be in traditional organizations. Other routes have been suggested, such as creating and maintaining repositories of peer ratings or reputational data of various types. Investment banks studied by Eccles and Crane (1987) are one example of how this might be done. Reputational rating systems would have the advantage of leveling the playing field in labor or bid markets, but it is unclear who would maintain these systems. Professional certification is another possibility, but as Barber (1983) points out this is subject to question because professional organizations have traditionally been loathe to sanction or discipline members who violate their standards. An additional possibility is the use of information technology to foster trust. Electronic media-based communication can provide the basis for the development of relationships between participants through electronic mail, the Internet, and conference systems. Over time, the relationships formed and maintained over computer-mediated communication grow as strong as those formed face-to-face (Walther 1995).

As Barber (1983) argues, distrust is the functional equivalent of trust. Therefore, it may be possible to develop new forms based on distrust and competition. Relationships in such forms would be based on verification of technical performance and fiduciary responsibility rather than on the assumption that these would occur. Comprehensive information systems to monitor participants' behavior and to provide verification to all involved could be one way to implement this form (Child 1987). Electronic markets such as the commodity exchange bear some resemblance to these arrangements. A barrier to the establishment of organizations based on this principle, however, is that it is impossible to monitor everything. At some point, it is necessary to depend on others.

How trust can be developed and maintained in new organizational forms is therefore a pressing research issue. More thought and research is needed regarding the very nature of trust in organizations (Hosmer 1995). Is distrust as effective as trust in forging new forms? What types of information exchange are necessary to build trust? Can organizations initially founded on distrust evolve into those premised on trust? If trust is indeed a cornerstone of the new forms, much more attention must be devoted to it.

LIMITS ON INTERACTIVITY

An often-discussed benefit of the new forms is the enhancement of organizational learning and creativity through increased interconnections among members. An emphasis on lateral linkages, fluid structures, and intensive use of communication technology have the potential to open communication in new organizations, bringing people from different units and strata into contact. Potential results include a more free flow of ideas, synergistic thinking, and empowerment of members.

These benefits accrue only if the ideal of increased interaction can be achieved. As Krackhardt (1994) argues, however, there may well be limits on the level of interactivity that even completely connected forms can achieve. He spells out two "laws" of networks that limit their interactivity. The law of N^2 states that as the number of nodes (people and units) in a network increases, the number of possible connections increases by approximately the square of the nodes. Therefore, for 10 nodes there are approximately 90 possible links (10^2 – one link for each of the 10 nodes), for 20 there are approximately 380, and for 50 there are approximately 2,400. In large organizations, the finite time and energy of participants precludes using all these links, imposing an inherent limitation on the degree of connectedness that can be achieved. Also, when communication is aided by technology that removes temporal barriers to contact, such as electronic mail, another problem may emerge: Popular nodes may receive so many messages that they become overloaded. Either way, the law of N^2 imposes limits on the openness of communication.

The second dampening force is the law of propinquity, premised on the fact that there are strong preferences to communicate with those in close physical proximity via the face-to-face mode. Allen (1977) found an exponential decay in the rate of communication as a function of the receiver's distance from the sender. One might think that technologies such as electronic mail would dampen this effect, but it seems to persist (Krackhardt 1994). Why is this so? There is considerable evidence that people seek to maintain their level of contact with others in a range optimal for their needs (Cappella 1994). If they do not have enough contact, people seek out others. If they have more that their optimal level of contact, they avoid others. It is possible that the physically proximate people "use up" the limited contact time most individuals have available, and that as a result individuals are less motivated to communicate with distant others. It is important to realize, however, that the spread of electronic mail and other convenient, fast modes of electronic communication may undermine this "law" in the near future.

Electronic mail is already the medium of choice for many people, and it is becoming the norm in many organizations.

Together, the law of N^2 and the law of propinquity may place limits on the degree to which interactivity can be realized in new organizational forms. Questions needing research include the following: Does becoming accustomed to new technologies that support distal communication erode propinquity effects over time? Will the results of proximity continue to hold up as broadband technologies that provide greater social presence, such as videoconferencing, spread? Are there ways to limit contact among those physically proximate to make "room" for communication with dispersed colleagues? and Can technological advances in filtering and handling messages mitigate overload problems?

STRESSES ON INDIVIDUALS

The new forms offer numerous benefits for their members, including the chance for continuous learning and development, freedom from becoming "stuck" in a backwater of the hierarchy, empowerment, and the chance to exercise creativity. Along with these benefits, however, are challenges for the new forms.

One problem arises due to the tensions arising from the individualistic motivation traditional in Western societies. In traditional organizations, rewards have been thought of in terms of upward movement for the individual, and status and large pay raises have been tied to upward promotions. For decades, organizational behavior scholars have observed that it is difficult to implement team-based organizations if individual meritocratic reward systems remain in place. Although many organizations have attempted to install team-based rewards, their efforts have generally been partial, and participants have been slow to adapt to a team as opposed to individualistic orientation.

Many of the new forms, however, have relatively flat hierarchies. Indeed, the hierarchy is unclear in many fluid networked organizations. Many new forms also base much of their work on teams. These characteristics have little to offer in the way of motivation for members steeped in the reward-as-upward-movement philosophy. Donnellon and Scully (1994) considered many measures that organizations have taken to move away from traditional reward systems. They concluded that most of these are unlikely to work because of the fact that most traditional organizations keep individual reward systems in place beside team-based systems and retain hierarchies. Given the value that U.S. society places on individualism and on upward mobility, presumption always tends to be given to the traditional reward systems.

Donnellon and Scully (1994) offer an alternative prescription: Take advantage of the flexibility of new forms and scrap the entire individual-based reward structure. They recommend three steps: (a) Stress professionalism and the intrinsic interest of work, but maintain an income floor so that people feel some security; (b) reward excellence with status and "fame" and also with material compensation, but maintain an income ceiling so that stars do not become an elite. Base rewards on effort and dedication as much as on exceptional performance based on natural ability; and (c) keep the concept of merit out of the organization's discourse as much as possible. Together, these measures are meant to redirect member attention from the meritocracy to rewards based on working for the common good.

Although an intriguing proposal, Donnellon and Scully's (1994) scheme faces constant erosion from two facts. First, the values of the larger society are still stacked against it. Although we may be in the midst of an information revolution that will bring a fundamental change in how we view ourselves and our world, for the short term we are stuck in an individual-centered society. There will be continuing pressures toward a meritocratic model. Second, many of the new organizational forms have components that are hierarchically organized, such as mass production facilities and various other line organizations. Hence, pressures arise from the internal contradictions among forms and desires to return to individualistic reward systems.

Research regarding the feasibility of Donnellon and Scully's (1994) suggestions is needed. Also needed is investigation of the degree to which professionalism and market mechanisms can motivate members of new forms. A related question is how novel reward systems can survive in the face of the general expectation that meritocracy is the appropriate system. New employees will tend to expect individual-based reward systems, and it may take considerable work to socialize them to team rewards. Moreover, an organization that attempts to break new ground by using novel reward schemes runs the risk of losing its institutional legitimacy in the view of other important organizations.

A second challenge for the new forms is burnout. Early studies of communication-intensive matrix organizations allude to stress and exhaustion as problems (Delbecq and Filley 1974). The new forms may build in stressors: They emphasize quality, they stress speed of response time and quick adaptability, they may require members to deal with heavy communication loads, they may not offer job security, and members may be dealing with multiple projects and networks simultaneously.

These characteristics clearly related to several components of an integrated model of job burnout developed by Cordes and Dougherty (1993). They posited that burnout was a function of emotional exhaustion, a depersonalization of others that was augmented by the exhaustion, and an accompanying feeling of diminished personal accomplishment. Factors contributing to the development of these three states were individual stressors (high achievement expectations, high organizational expectations, and high job involvement) and organizational stressors (role overload, role conflict, and high levels of interaction with clients). These factors may result from many new organizational forms; therefore, burnout seems likely to be a danger. Burnout, however, may be mitigated by another characteristic of new forms—communication openness. The ability to find supportive others is a great help to those facing burnout (Albrecht et al. 1994). Finding support may be easier in new forms than in traditional organizations because of their emphasis on openness and connectivity.

The following are key research questions related to burnout in new organizations: How can organizations foster communication networks that provide needed support? What types of support are most effective in high-speed organizations? What types of supportiveness are still compatible with maintaining high quality and high responsiveness? and Can supportive communities be maintained in fluid organizational structures?

TECHNOLOGY AS TROJAN HORSE

A key theme in the new organization forms is that business will not be conducted as usual. New forms emphasize novel, flexible arrangements for work and work relations. They often seek to empower members to enhance both quality of work and quality of work life and to develop members' knowledge and skills. Information technology is a key driver in this case, supporting fast, flexible operations and giving workers the information and support they need to work independently and to learn as they work.

Successful use of technology to achieve these ends, however, depends on its tractability. The organization and its members must be able to make technology serve them. This is consistent with the popular view of technology as neutral, as something sufficiently pliable to be used for whatever ends humans select. A good argument can be made that this view is overly simplistic. Adaptive structuration theory (DeSanctis and Poole 1994) contends that unintended and unsought consequences often ensue as technologies are employed in practical relationships. Technology use and implementation involves a complex interaction whereby user and technology redefine and shape each other. This process is not wholly under the control of the user or others and may ultimately undermine original plans.

Numerous studies suggest that technology in general and information technology in particular incorporate a thrust toward control and disempowerment of human agents (Beniger 1986, Perrolle 1991, Weizenbaum 1976). Studies of supposedly neutral technologies such as machine tools have shown them to be shaped early in their development by managerial intentions to control workers. As a result, limitations on worker choice were incorporated into the tools designs (Edwards 1979, Noble 1984), and these limitations shaped the nature of their technological trajectories. Information technology is certainly not immune. Garson (1988) details cases of the use of information technology to restructure work to control workers. Zuboff (1988) distinguishes the more common strategy of automating (the use of information technology for control) from informating (the use of information technology to redefine work and to empower workers). Bloomfield (1995) gives a compelling example of control via information technology that is informed by recent work on the social construction of technology (Bijker et al. 1987). According to this school of thought, technology and society are indistinguishable because society accomplishes its work using technology. As a result, "technology does not *impact* on organizations or society; a change in social relations, tasks, skills, and knowledge is already prefigured in the way the technology is conceived of and constructed" (Bloomfield 1995, p. 497).

Hence, technologies introduced by old orders may hide built-in assumptions about control and about how things should be done. These are built in so tightly and subtly that the value direction of the technology is not immediately evident; the values are part of the artifact and therefore are inherent in its operation. The controlling aspects of technology become apparent only after it has been introduced, and then only with some reflection and analysis.

As a case in point, Bloomfield (1995) discusses the introduction of information technology into the British National Health Service (NHS) to support monitoring of resources in various health care areas, with the goal of making the system more efficient and responsive to its members. The system was designed to enable hospitals to compete for NHS funds through a market-like mechanism similar to those in many new organizational forms. The result, however, was that the system shifted the emphasis in the NHS (Bloomfield 1995):

> The change has been marked by an adjustment away from a technology orientated toward doctors and managers, toward a technology for enabling the mechanisms of internal market transactions; from IT as the promise of future efficiency and rationality vis-à-vis resource allocation and usage, to IT as the underpinning of the efficiency and rationality of the market. (p. 511)

Bloomfield shows how this shift stemmed from the social pressures (toward increased business control of the NHS) that the technology embodied as it was selected, designed, and implemented.

The point here is not that technologies are always premised on control or domination but rather that the values of previous social orders lie implicit in technology and may reassert themselves in current situations. Organizations that attempt to use information technology to escape previous ways of working and to "free" themselves from previous assumptions may be frustrated in their efforts precisely because the technology implicitly incorporates old values. For example, American Airlines' Sabre system enables a different, more cooperative work arrangement to emerge in the travel business, but it still made it possible for American to engage in cutthroat competition and to deny competitors access if they were too aggressive or successful vis-à-vis American (Rotenberg and Saloner 1991). Technology may well be a Trojan horse that promises to facilitate change but sneaks in old values that ultimately undermine transformation.

This suggests several research avenues. First, it is not at all clear that the social construction or control analyses are entirely correct. Empirical research similar to Attewell's (1991) is needed to sort out the degree to which the envisioned influences actually materialize. Second, to what extent are new technologies "reformable" in the sense that they can be developed to incorporate new values about organizations and organizing? It may be possible to create new paradigms for information technology that parallel new organization forms. Some argue that this is already occurring (Konsynski and Sviokla 1994, Venkatraman 1991). Finally, can reinvention during implementation counteract conservative forces operating in information technologies?

CONCLUSION

Table 15.1 summarizes the problems and challenges discussed in this chapter. Several qualifications should be mentioned. First, currently several of these problems and challenges should be considered plausible hypotheses rather than proven facts. It is a question for research whether they will in fact emerge as significant problems or limitations in actual organizations. Second, not all new organizational forms are equally subject to all challenges. For example, problems due to fluidity are probably more likely to emerge in a temporary joint venture among six small software firms than in a large corporation with a stable workforce that attempts to use dynamic networks to manage several projects. Third, there are "solutions" or countermeasures for many of the challenges. Their degree of effectiveness is a matter for

TABLE 15.1 Challenges for New Organizational Forms and Their Effects

Challenge	Effects
Tight coupling of complex systems: due to nonlinear interactions, indirect control of processes, tight coupling, vulnerability to environmental perturbations, and sedimented information systems	Unexpected disruptions that reverberate through system Collapse of interconnected organizations
Fluidity	Problems maintaining a sense of mission due to personnel movement Interunit conflict of interests Problems with commitment and loyalty
Limits on interactivity	Problems maintaining cohesiveness and a sense of mission Inability to attain benefits due to freer flow of ideas, empowerment, and synergistic thinking
Stresses on individuals	Tensions due to individualistic motivation undermine team and organizational orientation Burnout that undermines the ability of members to effectively carry out their jobs
Technology as Trojan horse	Undermine empowerment allowed by flexible forms Reinforce traditional values that virtual organization forms are meant to change

research. Fourth, the list of challenges is incomplete. Research will undoubtedly uncover more as these forms become more common.

The spate of novel organizational forms that has emerged during the past 20 years may offer the first chance to really break the bureaucratic mold. It is important, however, that we do not allow our enthusiasm for these innovations to blunt our critical faculties. As Diderot remarked, "Skepticism is the first step toward truth."

REFERENCES

Albrecht, T. L., B. R. Burleson, and D. Goldsmith (1994), "Supportive Communication," in M. L. Knapp and G. R. Miller (Eds.), *Handbook of Interpersonal Communication,* Thousand Oaks, CA: Sage, 2nd ed., pp. 419-449.

Allen, T. J. (1977), *Managing the Flow of Technology: Technology Transfer and the Dissemination of Technology Information Within the Research and Development Organization,* Cambridge: MIT Press.

Attewell, P. (1991), "Big Brother and the Sweatshop: Computer Surveillance in the Automated Office," in C. Dunlop and R. Kling (Eds.), *Computerization and Controversy: Value Conflicts and Social Choices,* Boston: Academic Press, pp. 236- 256.

Barber, B. (1983), *The Logic and Limits of Trust,* New Brunswick, NJ: Rutgers University Press.

Beniger, J. R. (1986), *The Control Revolution: Technological and Economic Origins of the Information Society,* Cambridge, MA: Harvard University Press.

Bijker, W. E., T. P. Hughes, and T. Pinch (Eds.) (1987), *The Social Construction of Technological Systems: New Directions in the Sociology and History of Technology,* Cambridge: MIT Press.

Bloomfield, B. P. (1995), "Power, Machines, and Social Relations: Delegating to Information Technology in the National Health Service," *Organization,* 2, 489-518.

Cappella, J. N. (1994), "The Management of Conversational Interaction in Adults and Infants," in M. L. Knapp and G. R. Miller (Eds.), *Handbook of Interpersonal Communication,* Thousand Oaks, CA: Sage, 2nd ed., pp. 380-418.

Child, J. (1987), "Information Technology, Organization, and the Response to Strategic Challenges," *California Management Review,* 29, 33-50.

Cordes, C. L. and T. W. Dougherty (1993), "A Review and Integration of the Research on Job Burnout," *Academy of Management Review,* 18, 621-656.

Coser, L. (1956), *The Functions of Social Conflict,* New York: Free Press.

Delbecq, A. and A. Filley (1974), *Program and Project Management in a Matrix Organization: A Case Study,* Monograph No. 9, Madison: University of Wisconsin, Graduate School of Business, Bureau of Business Research.

DeSanctis, G. and M. S. Poole (1994), "Capturing the Complexity in Advanced Technology Use: Adaptive Structuration Theory," *Organization Science,* 5, 2, 121-147.

Donnellon, A. and M. Scully (1994), "Teams, Performance, and Rewards: Will the Post-Bureaucratic Organization Be a Post-Meritocratic Organization?" in C. Heckscher and A. Donnellon (Eds.), *The Post-Bureaucratic Organization: New Perspectives on Organizational Change,* Thousand Oaks, CA: Sage, pp. 63-90.

Eccles, R. G. and D. B. Crane (1987), "Managing Through Networks in Investment Banking," *California Management Review,* 30, 176-195.

Edwards, R. (1979), *Contested Terrain: The Transformation of the Workplace in the Twentieth Century,* New York: Basic Books.

Garson, B. (1988), *The Electronic Sweatshop,* New York: Penguin.

Gordon, F. M. (1994), "Bureaucracy: Can We Do Better? We Can Do Worse," in C. Heckscher and A. Donnellon (Eds.), *The Post-Bureaucratic Organization: New Perspectives on Organizational Change,* Thousand Oaks, CA: Sage, pp. 195-210.

Hackman, J. R. and R. E. Walton (1986), "Leading Groups in Organizations," in P. S. Goodman and Associates (Eds.), *Designing Effective Work Groups,* San Francisco: Jossey-Bass, pp. 72-199.

Hammer, M. and J. Champy (1993), *Reengineering the Corporation,* New York: HarperCollins.

Handy, C. (1995), "Trust and Virtual Corporations," *Harvard Business Review,* 73, 40-48.

Heckscher, C. (1994), "Defining the Post-Bureaucratic Type," in C. Heckscher and A. Donnellon (Eds.), *The Post-Bureaucratic Organization: New Perspectives on Organizational Change,* Thousand Oaks, CA: Sage, pp. 14-62.

Hosmer, L. T. (1995), "Trust: The Connecting Link Between Organizational Theory and Philosophical Ethics," *Academy of Management Review,* 20, 379-403.

Jarvenppa, S. L. and B. Ives (1994), "The Global Network Organization of the Future: Information Management Opportunities and Challenges," *Journal of Management Information Systems,* 10, 25-57.

Klein, J. A. (1994), "The Paradox of Quality Management: Commitment, Ownership, and Control," in C. Heckscher and A. Donnellon (Eds.), *The Post-Bureaucratic Organization: New Perspectives on Organizational Change,* Thousand Oaks, CA: Sage, pp. 178-194.

Konsynski, B. and J. J. Sviokla (1994), "Cognitive Reapportionment: Rethinking the Location of Judgment in Management Decision-Making," in C. Heckscher and A. Donnellon (Eds.), *The Post-Bureaucratic Organization: New Perspectives on Organizational Change,* Thousand Oaks, CA: Sage, pp. 91-107.

Krackhardt, D. (1994), "Constraints on the Interactive Organization as an Ideal Type," in C. Heckscher and A. Donnellon (Eds.), *The Post-Bureaucratic Organization: New Perspectives on Organizational Change,* Thousand Oaks, CA: Sage, pp. 211-222.

Lucas, H. C. and J. Baroudi (1994), "The Role of Information Technology in Organizational Design," *Journal of Management Information Systems,* 10, 9-23.

Meyer, M. (1993), "Here's a 'Virtual' Model for America's Industrial Giants," *Newsweek,* August 23, 40.

Miles, R. E. and C. C. Snow (1986), "Organizations: New Concepts for New Forms," *California Management Review,* 28, 62-73.

Neumann, P. G. (1992), "Inside Risks: Survivable Systems," *Communications of the ACM,* 35, 130.

Noble, D. (1984), *The Forces of Production: A Social History of Industrial Automation,* New York: Knopf.

Nohria, N. and J. D. Berkley (1994), "The Virtual Organization: Bureaucracy, Technology, and the Implosion of Control," in C. Heckscher and A. Donnellon (Eds.), *The Post-Bureaucratic Organization: New Perspectives on Organizational Change,* Thousand Oaks, CA: Sage, pp. 108-128.

Osterman, P. (1991), "The Impact of IT on Jobs and Skills," in M. Scott-Morton (Ed.), *The Corporation of the 1990s: Information Technology and Organizational Transformation,* New York: Oxford University Press, pp. 220-239.

Perrolle, J. A. (1991), "Intellectual Assembly Lines: The Rationalization of Managerial, Professional, and Technical Work," in C. Dunlop and R. Kling (Eds.), *Computerization and Controversy: Value Conflicts and Social Choices,* Boston: Academic Press, pp. 221-235.

Perrow, C. (1984), *Normal Accidents: Living With High Risk Technologies,* New York: Basic Books.

Powell, W. W. (1990), "Neither Market nor Hierarchy: Network Forms or Organization," in L. L. Cummings and B. M. Staw (Eds.), *Research in Organizational Behavior,* Westport, CT: JAI, Vol. 12, pp. 295-336.

Rotenberg, J. J. and G. Saloner (1991), "Interfirm Competition and Collaboration," in M. S. Scott-Morton (Ed.), *The Corporation of the 1990s: Information Technology and Organizational Transformation,* New York: Oxford University Press, pp. 95-121.

Scott-Morton, M. (Ed.) (1989), *The Corporation of the 1990s: Information Technology and Organizational Transformation,* New York: Oxford University Press.

Smith, K. K. (1989), "The Movement of Conflict in Organizations: The Joint Dynamics of Splitting and Triangulation," *Administrative Science Quarterly,* 34, 1-20.

Venkatraman, N. (1991), "IT-Induced Business Reconfiguration," in M. Scott-Morton (Ed.), *The Corporation of the 1990s: Information Technology and Organizational Transformation,* New York: Oxford University Press, pp. 122-158.

Walther, J. (1995), "Computer-Mediated Communication: Impersonal, Interpersonal, and Hyperpersonal," *Communication Research,* 23, 3-43.

Weizenbaum, J. (1976), *Computer Power and Human Reason,* San Francisco: Freeman.

Zuboff, S. (1988), *In the Age of the Smart Machine: The Future of Work and Power,* New York: Basic Books.

16

The Virtual Organization

Tele-Access in Business and Industry

WILLIAM H. DUTTON

During the 1990s, global competition, recession, regulatory change, and revolutionary advances in information and communication technologies (ICTs) have influenced major transformations in the structure and geography of the firm.[1] One organizational form that has been closely associated with advances in ICTs has been the virtual organization. Charles Handy (1996) notes,

> We are beginning to see more signs of these "virtual organizations," organizations that do not need to have all the people, or sometimes any of the people, in one place in order to deliver their service. The organization exists, but you can't see it. It is a network, not an office. (p. 212)

This chapter provides an overview of the virtual organization, focusing on the assumptions that underpin discussion of this new organizational form, and places it in the context of prevailing perspectives on the technology and structure of organizations. This overview argues that virtual organizations represent only one approach to realizing the benefits of "tele-access"—a concept that provides a more general perspective on ICTs. Innovations in ICTs create the infrastructure of tele-access, building the virtual highways and barriers that will influence personal and electronic access. This chapter also illustrates how tele-access choices, such as moves toward a virtual organization, are being shaped by four general sets of factors: new ICT paradigms and practices, the transformation of organizational structures and processes, the changing geography of the firm, and the conceptions and responses of the users of ICTs.

Managers and the producers, users, and consumers of ICTs are likely to reconsider many policies and practices if and when they become involved in the process of shaping tele-access. Large or small—integrated or distributed—forward-looking organizations should

- Understand how ICTs can be used to shape access to people, including customers and suppliers, and information and services
- Question whether their organization is structured and networked with other organizations in ways that take full advantage of ICTs
- Challenge any taken-for-granted assumptions about the geographical distribution of people and activities of the firm
- Train personnel to use ICTs effectively, as an enhancement of interpersonal communications, while challenging optimistic stereotypes to gain more realistic conceptions of the end users of ICTs—consumers and personnel

THE VIRTUAL ORGANIZATION

A *virtual organization* is composed of private firms or public agencies that have employed ICTs to transform business processes within the organization or among themselves and other organizations so as to enable new kinds of joint ventures, alliances, or outsourcing arrangements. Networking is so central to this new form of organization that a virtual organization is often referred to as a "networked organization" (Murray and Willmott 1997).

The virtual organization is a social and organizational innovation as well as a technical one. Some management consultants refer to virtual linkages primarily as cross-functional linkages, as in virtual teams (Hammer and Champy 1993/1994, p. 67). Others use the term to denote linkages across companies (Johansson et al. 1993, p. 9). Both are important, particularly because the boundaries of the organization and the units that compose them are becoming increasingly permeable. Essential dimensions of this organizational form include (a) networking through the use of ICTs, (b) restructuring into a decentralized network of companies, and (c) building a team culture (Table 16.1).

TABLE 16.1 The Virtual Organization: A Technical, Structural, and Cultural
Vision

Networking through information and communication technology
  Substitution of electronic media for paper and face-to-face communication
  Focusing face-to-face communication on building cohesion and trust
  Changing business processes to take advantage of computer-based networks and their
    enabling technologies such as the Internet

Restructuring to form a decentralized network of companies versus integrated firm
  Using networks rather than rational planning to organize structures of communication
  Emphasizing horizontal coordination across functional, divisional, and firm boundaries
    through task forces, project teams, and informal networks in lieu of vertical control, central
    monitoring, and management surveillance
  Creating jobs that span separate functions and geographical locations

Building a team culture of trust and responsibility
  Pushing authority and initiative down with managers acting as coaches and facilitators
  Instilling trust and cooperation among employees as team players
  Valuing learning, change, and reorganizing rather than rules and procedures

---

SOURCE: Adapted from Hammer and Champy (1993), Nohria and Berkley (1994, p. 115), Fulk and
DeSanctis (1995, p. 340), and Murray and Willmott (1997).

Executives view the virtual organization as a technical fix to key social
and organizational problems confronting management, from the difficulty of
exercising management control to the expense of office space. The virtual
organization provides a strategy for downsizing, outsourcing, and transforming the business processes of the firm. It presents a structural approach to
managing the changing geography of the firm.

Enthusiasm for the virtual organization, however, is drawn from a few
anecdotal success stories. Also, several aspects of this vision, such as the
paperless office and the substitution of telecommunications for travel, are
problematic. The paperless office has been promoted and sought for decades
in the face of escalating uses of paper (Uhlig et al. 1979). The use of ICTs as
a substitute for face-to-face communications has also been an elusive goal
and is a controversial strategy (Elton 1985).

Moreover, no single prototype is likely to help all organizations realize
the benefits of ICTs. Also, the inappropriate use of ICTs can create new
problems for management and business strategy, as evident in growing
concerns regarding information overload and the management of electronic
documents. The potential loss of management control over vital business
processes is another possible pitfall.

The virtual organization does not provide a model for all organizations to
emulate, but it does illustrate one approach to a more general strategy for
using ICTs to improve access to information, people, services, and other

ICTs. Also, it highlights the potential that exists for organizations to use ICTs to enable major change in the structure, location, and composition of the firm in ways that could enable productivity improvements and extend electronic access not only within and among firms but also to markets.

PERSPECTIVES ON TECHNOLOGICAL
AND ORGANIZATIONAL CHANGE

Most work on the relations between organizational structure and technology can be grouped within one of three general perspectives: technological, organizational, or emergent (Sampler 1996, pp. 6-12). A technological perspective emphasizes the influence of ICTs on the structure of organizations, such as centralization and decentralization of control (Negroponte 1995) or the improvement of information (Huber 1990). At the extreme, this perspective is technologically deterministic, viewing new organizational forms arising from technological change such as the growth of the Internet.

An organizational perspective places emphasis on how characteristics of organizations will influence the design and use of ICTs. For example, large integrated firms might employ ICTs to reinforce centralized management control, whereas a decentralized firm might use ICTs to distribute information and control (Danziger et al. 1982). Management strategies become more critical than characteristics of the technology (Child 1987).

Those who take an emergent perspective argue that both organizational and technological change unfold in unpredictable ways as a consequence of ongoing interactions—a "dialectic of alternative possibilities"—among multiple actors and institutions (Mansell and Silverstone 1996). Actors are constrained by existing technologies and structures, but they are also actively interpreting and using them to influence others and pursue their own values and interests.[2]

These perspectives—technological, organizational, and emergent—have contributed to an understanding of the ways in which technology can shape organizations and how organizations can constrain technical change and its implications. The resulting intellectual puzzles about technology and organizational structure, however, have focused attention on the interplay between technological and organizational change and deflected attention from the difference these changes make on the bottom line. For example, how do organizational and technological changes together influence the productivity of the firm? In addition, a debate focused on technology and organization ignores the geography of the firm, which is a strategic resource of growing importance in a globally competitive economy (Goddard and Richardson 1996).

TABLE 16.2 Four Dimensions of Tele-Access

Information: ICTs not only change the way those in a firm get information but also change the whole corpus of what people know and the information available to them at any given time and place. ICTs play a role in making some firms information rich, but they can also make others comparatively information poor—by accident or design.

People: ICTs not only provide new ways to communicate with others but also influence who people meet, talk to, stay in touch with, work with, and get to know and with whom they do business. ICTs can connect or isolate people and firms.

Services: ICTs do not simply change the way individuals consume products and services but also influence what products and services people consume and from whom they purchase them. ICTs can render obsolete a local business or an entire industry but also create new businesses and industries.

Technologies: ICTs interconnect and depend on one another in so many ways that access to particular technologies shapes access to others. The Internet can provide access to millions of computers throughout the world. Firms need ICTs such as personal computers, however, to access the Internet.

Adapted from Dutton (1999, Chapter 1).

Tele-Access in Organizational Settings: A New Perspective

In discussing the role of theory in organizational research, Karl Weick (1987, pp. 98-99) has argued that we "prefigure what we see" and, therefore, we should intentionally choose the theoretical frameworks we use to "improve the quality of understanding." He explains, "If believing affects seeing, and if theories are significant beliefs that affect what we see, then theories should be adopted more to maximize what we will see than to summarize what we have already seen" (p. 99). It is in this sense that I suggest a new perspective on ICTs in organizations that moves away from the debate regarding the relationship between technology and organization and the limited things one will see from this vantage point.

First, it is important to focus on the role of ICTs in shaping access to information, what I call "tele-access." The concept of tele-access is central to distinguishing this perspective from conventional views of the impact of ICTs. By providing tele-access, ICTs reshape an individual's or firm's access to information, people, services, and technologies (Table 16.2).

The links between the revolution in ICTs and organizational design are often presented as a straightforward increase in information and communication (Fulk and DeSanctis 1995, Huber 1990, Leidner and Elam 1995). As Earl (1996, p. v) noted, ICTs create "more information" and "more flexibility" in organizational design.

ICTs, however, do not always provide more information. ICTs can reduce, screen, and change the content and flow of information—by accident or design. Similarly, ICTs do not provide access to more people as much as they provide access to a different set of people than accessible in others ways. Nor do ICTs necessarily create more flexibility in organizational design. To achieve the economic payoffs of ICTs, such as increases in productivity, firms need to reorganize business processes to take full advantage of ICTs (Scott Morton 1991). Economic imperatives may then constrain the flexibility of organizations. In fact, information systems have evolved in such complex and interdependent ways within some organizations that they can become a major brake on organizational change (Quintas 1996, pp. 85-89).

A focus on tele-access recognizes that ICTs are involved in a process of shaping electronic access. ICTs do not simply provide more information and more flexibility. They change the content and flow of information. They can wire firms in and out of networks. Also, as shown in Table 16.2, ICTs do not simply reconfigure access to "information" (information access) but also change communication patterns (access to people), how organizations conduct their business (access by suppliers or customers), and the equipment, techniques, and know-how available to the firm (access to technology).

Technological change has provided the potential to reshape access in business and industry. Teleconferencing systems can change the composition of meetings—who participates—and permit meetings to occur that might otherwise not have been held. Corporate communication systems can give top managers and executives direct access to every employee within the firm. ICTs allow employees in different locations to collaborate on a day-to-day basis. Networks such as the Internet give companies the opportunity to redistribute jobs and functions throughout the world while simultaneously providing electronic products and services more directly to the consumer.

Advances in ICTs have become bound not only with how an organization accomplishes its tasks but also with the nature of its products and services (Coombs and Hull 1996, Scott Morton 1991). The use of ICTs in business and industry not only enhances the productivity of organizations but also creates new information products and services (Penzias 1995, Zuboff 1988). One effect of this shift to electronic services and to information as a product is that the ICT function within the organization becomes more critical to the business strategy of the firm and a matter of more relevance to top executives (Bloomfield et al. 1997).

It can be argued that the telegraph and telephone were the most radical innovations supporting tele-access and the viability of a virtual organization. As John Carey (1989, p. 203) pointed out, the telegraph "permitted for the first time the effective separation of communication from transportation." That said, more incremental developments during the past several decades

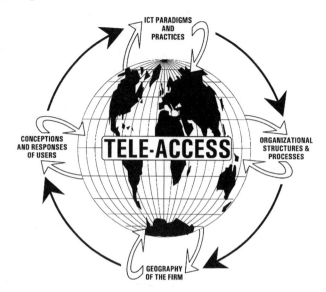

Figure 16.1. Factors Influencing Tele-Access in Business and Industry

have provided a significantly greater infrastructure for tele-access. For example, networking technologies, such as call distribution systems, have increased the utility and convenience of telephone links with consumers by offering 24-hour access to offices distributed throughout the world (Richardson 1994). In such ways, ICTs are reshaping access to "people" and to information. Firms are placing information, people, and products of the firm "on-line" and thereby making them accessible over electronic networks. This has, in turn, allowed firms to locate people and functions in locations that are not determined by the need to see the corporate headquarters or the customer in person.

FACTORS SHAPING TELE-ACCESS IN BUSINESS AND INDUSTRY

The design and use of ICTs in organizations is the principal way in which business and industry shape tele-access. This is often done by design, but because access is not a primary concern of many managers and executives it is often shaped by accident. The design and use of ICTs for tele-access, however, are constrained by four sets of factors: ICT paradigms and practices, organizational structures and processes, the geography of the firm, and the conceptions and responses of users (Figure 16.1).

ICT Paradigms and Practices

The virtual organization is a vision steeped in much rhetoric about the future of organizations. Visions matter, however, when they are taken seriously and sustained over time. They can change the beliefs and attitudes of the firm and the users of ICTs (Bloomfield et al. 1997, Dutton 1996).

Visions of the virtual organization are built on two interrelated paradigms. One is a new ICT paradigm that has been central to achieving the gains in productivity promised by ICTs (Freeman 1996). Another is what might be called a telecommunications-substitution paradigm.

The New "Techno-Economic" ICT Paradigm

During the past 20 years, ICTs have been associated with what Chris Freeman (1994, 1996) has called a new techno-economic paradigm, in contrast to the "Fordist" paradigm that dominated mass production-oriented organizations. The virtual organization is in line with many characteristics associated with the new ICT paradigm (Table 16.3). It is information intensive in that it relies heavily on ICTs. It seeks to create more flexibility by being anchored in networks rather than ownership—a single firm. A virtual organization promises to reduce hierarchical patterns of communication in favor of a flatter organization with project and ad hoc teams that cut across departmental boundaries.

For example, during the 1990s, many successful organizations across the economy as a whole have become more committed to and dependent on the use of ICTs; more specialized, through such mechanisms as the spin-off of noncore businesses (Whitman 1994, p. 33); smaller, with a decreasing number of full-time and larger proportion of part-time or temporary employees, particularly in companies spending proportionately more on ICTs (Whitman 1994, p. 33); more dependent on contract employment across skill levels (Whitman 1994, p. 36); less hierarchically organized through flatter management structures and creation of project teams (Commission on Management Research 1994); and more geographically distributed (Goddard and Richardson 1996). These trends explain why the concept of a virtual organization is taken seriously by management consultants, researchers, and top executives (Handy 1996, Penzias 1995).

The Telecommunications Substitution Paradigm

A telecommunication-transportation substitution paradigm has been prominent for decades, despite continued debate regarding its empirical validity. An implicit assumption is that ICTs will be an adequate substitute for a large

TABLE 16.3 Changing Paradigms and the Virtual Organization

	Fordist	*Post-Fordist ICT Paradigm*	*Examples of Virtual Organization*
Technology	Low technology, energy intensive	High technology, information intensive	Organization is a network
Focus of ICTs	Automation, mechanization	Systematization	Electronic data interchange (EDI)
Design and production process	Sequential	Concurrent	Collaborative work, screen sharing
Production	Standardized mass production of fixed product lines	Customized production of changing products	Organized for innovation, mass customization
Plant and equipment	Dedicated plant and equipment	Flexible production systems	Outsourcing production to maintain flexibility
Ownership	Single large integrated firm	Networks, profit centers, internal markets	Outsourcing, spin-offs to maintain lean organization
Management control structures	Hierarchical, vertical chain of command	Flat horizontal structures, lateral communication	Coordination through the marketplace, competition
Work	Departmentalized	Integrated in teams across departments	Project and ad hoc teams
Knowledge, learning, memory	Centralized	Distributed intelligence	Strategic protection of core tacit knowledge
Job skills	Specialized, bureaucratic	Multiskilling, professional, entrepreneurial	Employees involved in more aspects of the business

Adapted from Perez (1983), Miles and Robins (1992), and Freeman (1994).

proportion of face-to-face, person-to-person communication and therefore impact the structure and location of organizations, primarily by supporting their dispersal (Dickson 1973, pp. 114-141; Harkness 1973; Nilles et al. 1976; Tapscott 1996). Others have argued that telecommunications is most often used to enhance rather than substitute for person-to-person communication (Dutton 1995b, Elton 1985).

Social psychological research on the impact of electronic communications on the outcome of group interaction is far from conclusive (McGrath and Hollingshead 1994). Research has long found, however, that mediated communications can be as effective as face-to-face meetings for many tasks, such as getting and receiving information, and are often more efficient (McGrath and Hollingshead 1994, Short et al. 1976). Despite the uncertainty surrounding its effects, the logic of substitution is accepted as a current reality and not a future prospect. As Handy (1996, p. 212) stated, "It becomes cheaper and quicker to communicate with people electronically than face to face in a room."

The economic logic of substitution, moving "bits" instead of "atoms" as Negroponte (1995) argued, is compelling. Nevertheless, many management and communication researchers have challenged the appropriateness of substitution, for example, in arguing that face-to-face meetings and the media that more closely emulate them are better for situations in which there is a need for getting immediate feedback and reactions of the participants (Daft and Lengel 1984).

Most research on the virtual organization has been conducted within the management field. As a consequence, communication issues have not been a major focus of attention. As increasing numbers of firms embrace the new organizational paradigms such as the concept of the virtual organization, there is a risk of ICTs being poorly applied or implemented. The inappropriate substitution of electronic communications for face-to-face communication could diminish access, trust, understanding, leadership, and motivation—all critical within groups and organizations.

Organizational Structures and Processes

Advances in ICTs have become bound with particular kinds of structural change in organizations (Coombs and Hull 1996, Sampler 1996, Scott Morton 1991). Changes in organizational structures and processes are seen as important to realizing the productivity payoffs of ICTs (Scott Morton 1991). Likewise, the increasing centrality of ICTs is argued to be enabling transformations in organizational design, such as the virtual organization (Hammer and Champy 1993). Tele-access has encouraged the transformation of organizational structures and processes, but it is also the case that existing organizational structures and processes influence the adoption and design of ICTs and influence how tele-access is used in particular firms.

Since the earliest decades of computer use in organizations, management researchers forecasted dramatic changes in organizational design as a consequence of information technology. Until the 1980s, computers were widely perceived to be a tool for enhancing centralized control (Kraemer et al. 1981), even as research highlighted the stability of organizational structures (Danziger et al. 1982). Since the 1980s, however, a decentralization thesis has become dominant within the management literature, both as a description

TABLE 16.4 Dimensions of Change in Organizational Forms Tied to ICTs

---

Intraorganizational: vertical control
    Decentralized, less hierarchical control over decisions
    Delayering or flattening of hierarchies: eliminating layer of middle managers
    Reducing administrative intensity, proportion of administrative support staff
    Decreasing formalization of behaviors and requirements of jobs

Intraorganizational: horizontal coordination
    Electronic workflow, collocating work electronically versus physically
    Concurrent engineering: simultaneous design by distributed teams
    Stockless production, such as American just-in-time (JIT) systems

Organization and unit size
    Downsizing, as associated with flattening of hierarchies
    Spinning off or outsourcing activities
    Creating federated organizations that centralize and decentralize

Interorganizational coordination
    Interorganizational coupling, such as in electronic data interchange (EDI)
    Strategic alliances across industries to share information or networks
    Interstitial linkages, such as coordinating associations or electronic *keiretsu*

Adapted from Jablin (1987), Fulk and DeSanctis (1995), and Rice and Gattiker (1995).

of trends (Zuboff, 1988) and as a prescription for management that is in line with the new ICT paradigm (Murray and Willmott 1997).

Syntheses of research on ICTs and the structure of organizations, such as provided by this book, illuminate the complex variety of organizational changes tied to ICTs (Table 16.4). Within the organization, ICTs have been linked to moves away from tight vertical control structures. In the 1990s, ICTs are seen as a means for supporting the flattening of organizational hierarchies by short-circuiting intermediaries and supporting increased horizontal coordination. Delayering and the reduction of administrative control structures enable the downsizing of organizations, which is further facilitated by spinning off and outsourcing activities that might otherwise be done in-house.

Users of computer-mediated communications such as e-mail are critical to organizations because they can increase the frequency and change the patterns of dialogue among managers (Charan 1991, Rice 1984). For example, networks help managers develop new connections as individuals meet others on-line (Sproull and Kiesler 1991); generate more communication across, up, and down the organizational hierarchy; engage in more open and honest dialogue (Charan 1991, Hiltz and Turoff 1978, Rice 1984); and create an opportunity for those plugged into computer networks to become new gatekeepers between the world on the line and the "off-line" world within the organization (Culnan and Markus 1987, Sproull and Kiesler 1991). In supporting these patterns of communication, ICTs can be used purposively to create new cross-functional linkages within companies that span traditional departmental boundaries or to enable improved linkages across firms.

Despite the thrust of these trends in organizational design, ICTs do not necessarily push firms toward decentralizing control structures. In fact, some ICTs might enable greater centralized control over far-flung activities and personnel. Business television is one example of media that enable central management to communicate with one voice and more directly to employees located throughout the world. The telephone and enhancements in its use, such as through voice mail and wireless telephones, permit more centralized control of distributed activities. In such ways, geography can be more independent of control structures than it was in the past.

Also, ICTs facilitate coordination among organizations, such as in the use of electronic data interchange between a manufacturer and a supplier (Hart and Saunders 1997). Interorganizational networking generates the potential for multiple suppliers and customers, which lessens an organization's dependence on any one firm or on in-house staff while creating the competition among firms that is a market incentive for higher levels of performance. It is hoped that competition and market forces will replace direct management control and supervision. This does not mean that management control is extended through space over sophisticated telecommunication networks. To the contrary, management structures such as outsourcing enable local management control.

ICTs have been linked to the movement of multinational firms toward "relationship enterprises," which Marina Whitman (1994, pp. 35-36) describes as "temporary networks of strategic alliances that shift among firms in different industries, locations, and even countries, linked by information technology and common goals that enable and encourage them to behave like a single entity." There are also incentives for cooperation among organizations within any given chain for supplying a particular product or service because they do indeed comprise a virtual organization. In addition, electronic networks and services create new opportunities for cooperation and strategic alliances across organizations in formerly distinct industries.

The Geography of the Firm

Geography might matter more rather than less as tele-access permits some firms to be more competitive and efficient through the strategic distribution of jobs and functions across locations (Goddard and Richardson 1996, Hepworth 1989). Geographically dispersed organizations have a greater need for tele-access, but the increasing ease and lower costs of tele-access can be an incentive for organizations to redistribute—centralizing or decentralizing—jobs and functions to different areas of a locale, region, or the world to gain the particular advantages of each location.

There are many prominent strategies for using tele-access to the advantage of the firm, including the use of telework, telecenters, mobile work, and what can be called distributed work. Each employs different configurations of technologies and has unique advantages and problems.

Telework encompasses many forms of working at a distance from one's employer, whether a person or organization. Most people in an organization use a telephone and, in a broad sense, have been viewed as teleworkers by some authors. Most studies, however, adopt a narrower definition and use it to refer to "electronic home work undertaken remotely from a central office" (Gillespie and Feng 1994). Defined in this way, telework accounts for up to 6% of the total workforce in the United States (Parliamentary Office of Science and Technology 1995, p. 6). Estimates vary widely because telework has been expanding and encompasses a wide variety of situations (Haddon and Silverstone 1993). A company might purchase equipment to enable talented software developers to work at home as one incentive to attract and retain them. A manager might use a fax machine at home to keep in touch with the company on evenings and weekends. A firm might place a computer in the home of a lone parent, who might transcribe audiotapes for a set price per page. Advantages to the firm can include increased productivity, higher morale among employees, a reduction or more efficient use of office space, and the ability to hire personnel who might otherwise be unavailable or attracted to more flexible jobs elsewhere.

Telecenters or telecottages are local centers that make personal computers, printers, copiers, facsimile, and other equipment available to individuals and firms. Some are supported by public funds or private corporations, and many charge users for the time and equipment used. Telecenters offer an alternative to working at home but are also a resource for those who work at home.

Mobile workers have been around as long as the traveling salesman. They can also be supported by ICTs, however. Cellular phones, portable computers, and paging systems, for example, have enabled individuals to do a greater variety of work on the road and to do it more efficiently. Organizations have been able to marry developments in information technology such as case management systems with advances in telecommunications, such as cellular telephones and facsimile, to extend the firm to the car.

The most significant impact of ICTs on remote work might be the "distributed firm" in that ICTs facilitate the "spatial reorganization" of the functions and personnel of the firm (Goddard and Richardson 1996). An early form of this type of redistribution of jobs and functions was the move of many back-office clerical functions, such as those at many banks and

financial institutions, outside the central business districts and into the
suburbs of major cities. The relocation of the back-office enabled firms to
reduce the cost of facilities and gain access to skilled clerical personnel in
the suburbs who could work for equivalent or lower wages than those
required in central business districts.

Another form of job redistribution has extended well beyond the bounds
of any single metropolitan area to encompass broader regions, sometimes
extending beyond national borders. For example, the increasing capacity and
standardization of national and international telecommunication networks
can support centralized or geographically distributed call centers to handle
telephone sales and inquiries as if they were in one place. Many companies
have centralized routine operations, such as billing processes, in ways that
achieve enormous economies of scale.

All these forms of distributing work—telework, telecenters, mobile work,
and distributed firms—are enabled by the ability of ICTs to support tele-
access. Advances in tele-access are lessening the constraints of telecommunications on the location of jobs and functions. This permits individuals and
functions to be located in the most strategic locations. This makes geography,
such as the particular advantages of a locale, more rather than less important
to a firm's locational decisions.

Conceptions and Responses of Users

A fourth set of factors shaping approaches to tele-access entails the
conceptions and responses of users (Woolgar 1996). Virtual organizations,
for example, are anchored in an information-centric conception of managers,
employees, and consumers. Some of the most serious constraints on the
development and use of ICTs in business and industry, however, have been
tied to a lack of acceptance by users, whether they be executives expected to
type or meet using videoconferencing systems or consumers expected to
shop over interactive television. Tele-access strategies must be mindful of
the following kinds of constraints:

1. Users in business and industry have rejected major ICT innovations: There are
   many managers, professionals, and other personnel who are enthusiastic about
   the use of ICTs. The users of ICTs in the firm (employees and increasingly the
   consumer), however, are not always as agile and positive about ICTs as conceived by the proponents of the virtual organization. Videoconferencing, for
   example, diffused less rapidly and has become far less pervasive than expected, largely due to the responses of users (Johansen 1984, 1988). Likewise,
   many employees have rejected telework for fear that being away from the
   office can isolate a person from informal communication and undermine their

career advancement. Others might not have the physical space, equipment, peace and quiet, or desire to mix work with their family life.

2. Managers are often unwilling to abandon traditional control structures: There has been much resistance to virtual forms, such as telework, due to top management concern for maintaining control and oversight of employees. Despite the economic rationality for substituting telecommunications for travel, the virtual organization poses a threat to management control. Decentralized organizational structures, such as those embodied in the virtual organization, are linked with innovation, whereas large integrated companies that they replace are more often identified with management control. For instance, the ongoing struggle between IBM and Microsoft stemmed in part from IBM's decision to outsource the provision of its IBM personal computer (PC) microprocessor from Intel and operating system from Microsoft (Chesbrough and Teece 1996). The same approach, however, was credited with the speed with which IBM was able to bring the PC to market. Therefore, deciding when and if to go virtual depends on whether the circumstances surrounding the product or service require greater control over all phases of the production, such as in the case of a highly "systemic innovation" that is dependent on a series of interdependent innovations (Chesbrough and Teece 1996), or an activity central to a company's long-term business strategy.

3. ICTs can distance the user from colleagues and customers: The success of ICTs creates the potential for individuals and firms to rely too heavily on mediated communications with their colleagues and their customers—using ICTs to replace rather than augment communications. There are signs that business and industry are seeking to redress the balance by, for example, attempting to get in closer human touch with their customers. For example, McDonald's restaurants are experimenting with the use of two-way video communications to create a closer and more personal link with drive-through customers and the staff who take the customer's order. Banks have experimented with the use of video communications associated with ATMs and creative ways to entice customers to enter the bank.

4. Inappropriate uses of ICTs could undermine trust and commitment: Management must be responsible and in control of organizations—virtual or real. The mechanisms for effective management control, however, are likely to change with distance. One change may be a greater dependence on trust as opposed to day-to-day oversight and supervision of people one does not see (Handy 1995, 1996, p. 212; Murray and Willmott 1997). Another shift would be toward management by the achievement of objectives rather than process, such as in moves toward more performance-based pay schemes and "team-based rewards" (Mankin et al. 1996, pp. 217-252). Researchers have pointed out the potentially conflicting nature of these expectations placed on employees in the

networked organization (Hart and Saunders 1997, Murray and Willmott 1997).
On the one hand, they are expected to assume more responsible, autonomous,
and self-directed roles as team players rather than "employees." On the other
hand, in increasingly competitive times, employees must be viewed as expend-
able resources in the context of a virtual organization, which is constantly
assessing the value of downsizing, outsourcing, and restructuring. At some
point, moves to restructure business processes must be limited by the need for
teamwork and trust within the organization.

5. The designers of ICTs need to respect the human limits of users: Emerging
   ICT paradigms reflected in trade magazines targeted to the new managers and
   entrepreneurs of the virtual organization emphasize the need for highly skilled
   personnel who are able and willing to multitask, cross functional divides, and
   move quickly. This emphasizes the need to recruit well-educated and skilled
   personnel as well as the need to create continuing opportunities for motivating
   and training personnel across the management and professional ranks. This
   developing image of the new employee counters early forecasts that organizations would use ICTs in ways that would deskill employees. Empirical research is mixed but generally counters the deskilling thesis (Attewell and Rule
   1984, Kraemer et al. 1981, Webster 1996). A need for new skills is not limited
   to the top managerial and professional ranks. For example, the increased use
   of electronic mail and other computer-based information systems in organizations has been widely attributed to a rise in information overload at many
   levels. Notable ICT disasters have been linked to systems that overwhelm
   end-users with too much information (Peltu et al. 1996). Developers of ICTs
   need to respect human limits, but users in organizations must also recognize
   the need for skills, routines, and technological approaches to screening information and communication (Culnan and Markus 1987, Peltu et al. 1996).

6. ICTs can threaten privacy and increase the surveillance of individuals: Computers and telecommunication systems have generated concerns regarding electronic surveillance in two respects—within the work setting (Zuboff 1988, pp.
   319-337) and the collection and disclosure of information about customers
   (the public at-large; Laudon 1986, Westin and Baker 1972). The thrust of much
   empirical research has been the degree to which electronic surveillance has
   not been practiced either in the workplace or in society as a whole. In the
   workplace, fears of electronic surveillance tend to underestimate the ability
   of employees to undermine and block systems designed to monitor and control
   their work (Attewell 1986). Also, a seminal study of computers and privacy
   in the United States found that computers did not tend to change the record-
   keeping practices of organizations in ways that threatened the privacy of the
   public (Westen and Baker 1972). There are ICTs, however, that are aimed at

extending the capability of managers and others to know where people are and what they are doing. An example is the development of personal location devices, such as the Active Badge System, which track the movement and location of individual badges across "infrared cells" to permit every individual of a company to determine the location, movement, and availability of every other member (Weiser 1991, p. 69). Personal communication services—linking a telephone number to a person rather than a place—are another set of innovations designed to improve the portability of the telephone but that also increase the potential for surveillance. Unfortunately, as ICTs enhance tele-access they create a greater potential for the abuse of systems designed to improve the coordination and services of the firm. Users—consumers and personnel—are likely to underestimate these threats until an abuse occurs, creating a real risk for the firm.

7. Conceptions and responses of users are culturally varied: An executive committee of faculty at a university in Brazil found it difficult to envision the use of computer mail and conferencing systems as even an enhancement to their face-to-face meetings. It was a marked departure from a culture that places great value on face-to-face interpersonal communication (Asper et al. 1996). This is but one example of how cultural traditions can constrain tele-access strategies such as the virtual organization. Combined with the dominance of the English language on the Internet, national cultures could create opportunities for some firms to move toward the virtual organization more rapidly than others. In a global economy, increasingly dependent on tele-access, it might become important for firms to reduce these cultural barriers by recruiting and training skilled gatekeepers—individuals who can create an interface between the firm and the on-line virtual organization.

TELE-ACCESS AND ORGANIZATIONAL FORM: DIRECTIONS FOR MANAGEMENT AND RESEARCH

The rhetoric surrounding the virtual organization has exaggerated the significance and novelty of this new organizational form and has been overgeneralized from some exceptional success stories. Nevertheless, the concept of a virtual organization captures the growing centrality of tele-access to the management and business strategies of the firm and presents a vision appropriate for many organizations.

Forward-looking managers need to critically examine the role of tele-access in business and industry. This synthesis of theory and research highlights five main points related to the central themes of the chapter:

1. Tele-access: ICTs are being used to shape electronic access. User organizations need to think strategically about shaping access to information, skilled personnel, and markets as opposed to imitating a particular strategy or organizational structure such as the virtual organization. Many of the most important ICT developments are tied to the telephone and electronic mail rather than to more exotic technologies that have yet to reach a critical mass of users.

2. ICT paradigms and practices: Top executives of firms across every sector of the economy need to recognize the role that ICTs can play in business and industrial strategy. ICTs are influencing what organizations do and not just how they do it. Top managers and executives must understand tele-access as one element of an emerging ICT paradigm. Organizations should employ ICTs to shape access as one central feature of their business strategies, using ICTs to enhance rather than to substitute for face-to-face communication.

3. Organizational structures and processes: ICTs will not determine new organizational forms and they should not do so. Organizations will want to structure communication in ways that enhance innovation and improve the speed of business processes while also maintaining the ability to make decisions, manage operations, and keep proprietary information secure. ICTs and organizational structures should be used in complementary ways to shape access.

4. Geography of the firm: Tele-access permits firms to consider more strategically the location of jobs and functions. Most industries are local or regional, such as in the case of the film and automotive industries in the United States. It is likely that ICTs will make local and regional economies more significant in the global economy rather than less significant. The firm will be far from rootless. The virtual organization, however, illustrates the potential for locational decisions to provide competitive advantages to a firm. Managers should understand tele-access and its potential to increase competition for their customers. The geographical boundaries of their competitors' firms—not just their own—are extended by ICTs (Ilinitch et al. 1996).

5. Conceptions and responses of users: The virtual organization and other new organizational forms will be shaped by the users of ICTs within the firm, including suppliers and consumers. The users of ICTs in some of the showcase virtual organizations are not necessarily typical of users in most other firms. The assumption that most personnel and consumers will embrace all advances in ICTs has been mistakenly made in the past. Education, recruitment, and training are likely to be increasingly important across all ranks of the firm. The systems most likely to support the firm are those that are designed with a strong and accurate conception of the user. This will entail changes in the production and manufacturing of ICTs and applications that create a closer link between producers and users and that are sensitive to variations across cultures.

This is a time in which fascinating organizational transformations are taking place regarding the use of emerging and off-the-shelf technologies and services, such as the Internet and World Wide Web. Nevertheless, the effective management and use of ICTs is not inevitable. In the process of creating virtual organizations, managers can and must erect virtual boundaries, install new gatekeepers, and create a new set of constraints on access. With a sustained program of research on electronic communications and new organizational forms, there could be an improved understanding of how management practices and new ICT products and services can enhance tele-access in business and industry.

NOTES

1. The concept of tele-access is drawn from the author's synthesis of research undertaken by the Programme on Information and Communication Technologies that is developed and compared with alternative perspectives on the information revolution in Dutton (1999). The author's research on virtual organizations was conducted through the generous support of the Fujitsu Research Institute for Advanced Information Systems & Economics, Tokyo, Japan.

2. Many researchers taking this perspective, such as Mansell and Silverstone (1996), anchor their views in structuration theory developed by Giddens (1984). Other streams of work in this area are anchored in the social construction of reality (Bloomfield et al. 1997), a social influence model of media use (Fulk et al. 1990), or an "ecology of games" (Dutton 1995a, Dutton and Mackinen 1987).

REFERENCES

Asper, G., W. Dutton, M. E. M. Nascimento, and M. de Lourdes Teodoro (1996), "Perspectivas de Implementaçao da Technologia de Reunioes Electronicas na Câmara de Pesquisa e Pós-graduaçao da Universaidade de Brasília, No Contexto da Difusao de Inovaçoes," paper presented at the National Meeting of Graduate Schools of Administration, Angra Bos Reis, Rio de Janero, Brazil, September 22-25.

Attewell, P. (1986), "Imperialism Within Complex Organizations," *Sociological Theory,* 4, 115-125.

_____ and J. Rule (1984), "Computing and Organizations: What We Know and What We Don't Know," *Communications of the ACM,* 27, 12, 1184-1192.

Bloomfield, B. P., R. Coombs, D. Knights, and D. Littler, (Eds.) (1997), *Information Technology and Organizations: Strategies, Networks, and Integration,* Oxford, UK: Oxford University Press.

Carey, J. W. (1989), *Communication as Culture: Essays on Media and Society,* Boston: Unwin Hyman.

Charan, R. (1991), "How Networks Reshape Organizations—For Results," *Harvard Business Review,* 69, 5, 104-115.

Chesbrough, H. W. and D. J. Teece (1996), "When Is Virtual Virtuous?" *Harvard Business Review,* 73, January/February, 65-73.

Child, J. (1987), "Managerial Strategies: New Technology and the Labour Process," in R. Finnegan, G. Salaman, and K. Thompson (Eds.), *Information Technology: Social Issues,* London: Hodder & Stoughton, pp. 76-97.

Commission on Management Research (1994), *Building Partnerships: Enhancing the Quality of Management Research,* Swindon, UK: Economic and Social Research Council.

Coombs, R. and R. Hull (1996), "The Politics of IT Strategy and Development in Organizations," in W. H. Dutton (Ed.), *Information and Communication Technologies—Visions and Realities,* Oxford, UK: Oxford University Press, pp. 159-176.

Culnan, M. J. and M. L. Markus (1987), "Information Technologies," in F. M. Jablin, L. L. Putnam, K. H. Roberts, and L. W. Porter (Eds.), *Handbook of Organizational Communication: An Interdisciplinary Perspective,* Newbury Park, CA: Sage, pp. 420-443.

Daft, R. L. and R. H. Lengel (1984), "Information Richness: A New Approach to Managerial Behavior and Organizational Design," in L. L. Cummings and B. M. Staw (Eds.), *Research in Organizational Behavior,* Greenwich, CT: JAI, Vol. 6, pp. 191-233.

Danziger, J. N., W. H. Dutton, R. Kling, and K. L. Kraemer (1982), *Computers and Politics,* New York: Columbia University Press.

Dickson, E. M. (1973), *The Video Telephone: Impact of a New Era in Telecommunications,* New York: Praeger.

Dutton, W. H. (1995a), "The Ecology of Games and Its Enemies," *Communication Theory,* 5, 379-392.

_____ (1995b), "Driving Into the Future of Communications? Check the Rear View Mirror," in S. J. Emmott (Ed.), *Information Superhighways: Multimedia Users and Futures,* London: Academic Press, pp. 79-102.

_____ (Ed.) (1996), *Information and Communication Technologies—Visions and Realities,* Oxford, UK: Oxford University Press.

_____ (1999), *Society on the Line: Information Politics in the Digital Age,* Oxford, UK: Oxford University Press.

_____ and H. Mackinen (1987), "The Development of Telecommunications: The Outcome of an Ecology of Games," *Information & Management,* 13, 255-264.

Earl, M. J. (Ed.) (1996), *Information Management: The Organizational Dimension,* Oxford, UK: Oxford University Press.

Elton, M. C. J. (1985), "Visual Communication Systems: Trials and Experiences," *Proceedings of the IEEE,* 73, 4, 700-705.

Freeman, C. (1994), "The Diffusion of ICT in the World Economy in the 1990s," in R. Mansell (Ed.), *Management of Information and Communication Technologies: Emerging Patterns of Control,* London: Aslib, pp. 8-41.

_____ (1996), "The Factory of the Future and the Productivity Paradox," in W. H. Dutton (Ed.), *Information and Communication Technologies—Visions and Realities,* Oxford, UK: Oxford University Press, pp. 123-141.

Fulk, J. and G. DeSanctis (1995), "Electronic Communication and Changing Organizational Forms," *Organization Science,* 6, 4, 337-349.

_____, J. Schmitz, and C. Steinfield (1990), "A Social Influence Model of Technology Use," in J. Fulk and C. Steinfield (Eds.), *Organizations and Communication Technology,* Newbury Park, CA: Sage, pp. 117-140.

Giddens, A. (1984), *The Constitution of Society: Outline of the Theory of Structuration,* London: Polity.

Gillespie, A. and L. Feng (1994), "Teleworking, Work Organisation, and the Workplace," in R. Mansell (Ed.), *Management of Information and Communication Technologies: Emerging Patterns of Control,* London: Aslib, pp. 261-272.

Goddard, J. and R. Richardson (1996), "Why Geography Will Still Matter: What Jobs Go Where?" in W. H. Dutton (Ed.), *Information and Communication Technologies—Visions and Realities,* Oxford, UK: Oxford University Press, pp. 197-214.

Haddon, L. and R. Silverstone (1993), *Teleworking in the 1990s: A View From the Home,* SPRU/CICT Report No. 10, Brighton, UK: University of Sussex, Science Policy Research Unit.

Hammer, M. and J. Champy (1994), *Reengineering the Corporation: A Manifesto for Business Revolution,* London: Nicholas Brealey. (Original work published 1993)

Handy, C. (1995), "Trust and the Virtual Organization," *Harvard Business Review,* 73, 3, 40-48.

_____ (1996), *Beyond Certainty: The Changing World of Organizations,* Boston: Harvard Business School Press.

Harkness, R. (1973), "Telecommunications Substitutes for Travel," unpublished doctoral dissertation, University of Washington, Seattle. (University Microfilms)

Hart, P. and C. Saunders (1997), "Power and Trust: Critical Factors in the Adoption and Use of Electronic Data Interchange," *Organization Science,* 8, 23-42.

Hepworth, M. (1989), *Geography of the Information Economy,* London: Belhaven Press.

Hiltz, S. R. and M. Turoff (1978), *The Network Nation: Human Communication via Computer,* Reading, MA: Addison-Wesley.

Huber, G. (1990), "A Theory of the Effects of Advanced Information Technologies on Organizational Design, Intelligence, and Decision Making," *Academy of Management Review,* 15, 47-71.

Ilinitch, A. Y., R. A. D'Aveni, and A. Y. Lewin (1996), "New Organizational Form and Strategies for Managing in Hypercompetitive Environments," *Organization Science,* 7, 3, 211-220.

Jablin, F. M. (1987), "Formal Organization Structure," in F. M. Jablin, L. L. Putnam, K. H. Roberts, and L. W. Porter (Eds.), *Handbook of Organizational Communication: An Interdisciplinary Perspective,* Newbury Park, CA: Sage, pp. 389-419.

Johansen, R. (1984), *Teleconferencing and Beyond: Communications in the Office of the Future,* New York: McGraw-Hill.

_____ (1988), *Groupware: Computer Support for Business Teams,* New York: Free Press.

Johansson, H. J., P. McHugh, A. J. Pendlebury, and W. A. Wheeler, Jr. (1993), *Business Process Reengineering: Breakpoint Strategies for Market Dominance,* New York: John Wiley.

Kraemer, K. L., W. H. Dutton, and A. Northrop (1981), *The Management of Information Systems,* New York: Columbia University Press.

Laudon, K. C. (1986), *Dossier Society: Value Choices in the Design of National Information Systems,* New York: Columbia University Press.

Leidner, D. E. and J. L. Elam (1995), "The Impact of Executive Information Systems on Organizational Design, Intelligence, and Decision Making," *Organization Science,* 6, 6, 645-664.

Mankin, D., S. G. Cohen, and T. K. Bikson (1996), *Teams and Technology: Fulfilling the Promise of the New Organization,* Cambridge, MA: Harvard Business School Press.

Mansell, R. and R. Silverstone (Eds.) (1996), *Communication by Design: The Politics of Information and Communication Technologies,* Oxford, UK: Oxford University Press.

McGrath, J. E. and A. B. Hollingshead (1994), *Groups Interacting With Technology,* Thousand Oaks, CA: Sage.

Miles, I. and K. Robins (1992), "Making Sense of Information," in K. Robins (Ed.), *Understanding Information: Business Technology and Geography,* London: Belhaven, pp. 1-26.

Murray, F., and H. Willmott (1997), "Putting Information Technology in Its Place," in B. P. Bloomfield, R. Coombs, D. Knights, and D. Littler (Eds.), *Information Technology and*

Organizations: Strategies, Networks, and Integration, Oxford, UK: Oxford University Press, pp. 160-180.

Negroponte, N. (1995), *Being Digital,* London: Hodder & Stoughton.

Nilles, J., F. R. Carlson, Jr., P. Gray, and G. J. Hanneman (1976), *The Telecommunications-Transportation Tradeoff,* New York: John Wiley.

Nohria, N. and J. D. Berkley (1994), "The Virtual Organization: Bureaucracy, Technology, and the Implosion of Control," in C. Heckscher and A. Donnelon (Eds.), *The Post-Bureaucratic Organization: New Perspectives on Organizational Change,* Thousand Oaks, CA: Sage, pp. 108-128.

Parliamentary Office of Science and Technology (1995), *Working at a Distance—UK Teleworking and Its Implications,* London: Author.

Peltu, M., D. McKenzie, S. Shapiro, and W. H. Dutton (1996), "Computer Power and Human Limits," in W. H. Dutton (Ed.), *Information and Communication Technologies—Visions and Realities,* Oxford, UK: Oxford University Press, pp. 177-195.

Penzias, A. (1995), *Harmony: Business, Technology, and Life After Paperwork,* New York: Harper-Collins.

Perez, C. (1983), "Structural Change and the Assimilation of New Technologies in the Economic and Social System," *Futures,* 15, 5, 357-375.

Quintas, P. (1996), "Software by Design," in R. Mansell and R. Silverstone (Eds.), *Communication by Design: The Politics of Information and Communication Technologies,* Oxford, UK: Oxford University Press, pp. 75-102.

Rice, R. E. (1984), "Mediated Group Communication," in R. E. Rice and Associates (Eds.), *The New Media: Communication, Research, and Technology,* Beverly Hills, CA: Sage, pp. 129-154.

_____ and U. E. Gattiker (1995), "Computer-Mediated Communication and Organizational Structuring," paper presented at the Programme on Information and Communication Technologies (PICT) International Conference, Westminster, London, May 10-12.

Richardson, R. (1994), "Back-Officing Front Office Functions: Organizational and Locational Implications of New Telemediated Services," in R. Mansell (Ed.), *Management of Information and Communication Technologies: Emerging Patterns of Control,* London: Aslib, pp. 309-335.

Sampler, J. (1996), "Exploring the Relationship Between Information Technology and Organizational Structure," in M. J. Earl (Ed.), *Information Management: The Organizational Dimension,* Oxford, UK: Oxford University Press, pp. 5-22.

Scott Morton, M. S. (Ed.) (1991), *The Corporation of the 1990s: Information Technology and Organizational Transformation,* Oxford, UK: Oxford University Press.

Short, J., E. Williams, and B. Christie (1976), *The Social Psychology of Telecommunications,* London: Wiley.

Sproull, L. and S. Kiesler (1991), *Connections: New Ways of Working in the Networked Organization,* Cambridge: MIT Press.

Tapscott, D. (1996), *The Digital Economy: Promise and Peril in the Age of Networked Intelligence,* New York: McGraw-Hill.

Uhlig, R. P., D. J. Farber, and J. H. Bair (1979), *The Office of the Future: Communication and Computers,* Amsterdam: North-Holland.

Webster, J. (1996), "Revolution in the Office? Implications for Women's Paid Work," In W. H. Dutton (Ed.), *Information and Communication Technologies—Visions and Realities,* Oxford, UK: Oxford University Press, pp. 143-157.

Weick, K. E. (1987), "Theorizing About Organizational Communication," in F. M. Jablin, L. L. Putnam, K. H. Roberts, and L. W. Porter (Eds.), *Handbook of Organizational Communication: An Interdisciplinary Perspective,* Newbury Park, CA: Sage, pp. 97-122.

Weiser, M. (1991), "The Computer for the 21st Century," *Scientific American,* 265, 66-75.

Westin, A. F. and M. A. Baker (1972), *Databanks in a Free Society: Computers, Record-Keeping and Privacy,* New York: Quadrangle.

Whitman, M. V. N. (1994), "Flexible Markets, Flexible Firms," *American Enterprise,* May/June, 27-37.

Woolgar, S. (1996), "Technologies as Cultural Artefacts," in W. H. Dutton (Ed.), *Information and Communication Technologies—Visions and Realities,* Oxford, UK: Oxford University Press, pp. 87-102.

Zuboff, S. (1988), *In the Age of the Smart Machine: The Future of Work and Power,* New York: Basic Books.

Conclusion

Research Issues and Directions

GERARDINE DESANCTIS

JANET FULK

Early on, when electronic communication systems first arrived on the scene, the study of technology design and technology impacts occurred, for the most part, as separate research activities. In recent years, researchers have recognized the dynamic nature of technology and form, and research focus has broadened to consider the interplay of these two phenomena. This book aims to deepen the study of technology-form relationships by providing theoretical and empirical consideration of both the role of organization in technology development and the role of technology in organizational form development. We hope that greater attention will be given to technology-form relationships and to discovering ways in which technologists and organizational designers can jointly shape positive organizations and communities for the future.

Each chapter in this book suggests potential avenues for research:

* The nature of authority and control structures in light of technological advances
* How the development of global communication networks within and between firms pushes designers to new technological frontiers
* The relative power of technology vis-à-vis other social forces to shape and be shaped by changes in organizational forms
* The use of intermediaries to direct the consequences of new technologies as they are introduced into organizational settings
* The combinatorial effects of technology and incentive systems design on organizational behavior

* Communication patterns that emerge within and between various organizational communities

* The coevolution of technology and form over time

* The relative power of strong and weak electronic ties to influence shifts in organizational behavior

* How organizational norms and cultures influence design and implementation of new communication systems

* The degree to which unanticipated, negative, or destructive impacts can result from managerial choices regarding technological implementation

The wealth of research possibilities is at once energizing and daunting. As a conclusion, we highlight four major directions that we view as especially critical for the future. The first two extend traditional research on technology design and technology impacts to consider the technology-form dynamic. The third focuses on technology-form articulation, suggesting a new domain for study wherein technology and form become the same phenomenon. The fourth attends to dissenting situations in which technology is deliberately removed from organizational form or otherwise omitted altogether from its evolution.

ORGANIZATIONAL FORM DEVELOPMENT

A host of long-standing research questions are becoming increasingly important, particularly in light of recent technology advances and continual shifts in the structure and operations of the business enterprise. Questions include the following: How does communication technology facilitate or impede transformation of organizations? How does organizational transformation, in turn, affect technology use, including the ongoing organizational discourse that surrounds technology (Miller 1990, Tushman and Romanelli 1985)? How can organizational members effectively use communication technology to shape organizational communities in positive ways (Boland 1991, DeSanctis and Poole 1994, Hinds and Kiesler, Chapter 7)? As we enter the twenty-first century, economic, social, and geopolitical dynamics will compel researchers to shed new light on these basic questions.

A critical corequisite is the development of refined typologies of organizational form (Rich 1992). Study of organizational form today tends to be dominated by such dichotic concepts as market versus hierarchy or bureaucratic versus postbureaucratic. A multilevel taxonomy would provide a basis for identifying an array of new organizational forms that differ in observable ways in memberships, relationships, groupings, adaptation styles, competencies, boundaries, and so on. Until we have a meaningful taxonomy that systematically differentiates organizations of past, present, and future along common dimensions of research interest, comparative study remains difficult.

COMMUNICATION TECHNOLOGY
DEVELOPMENT

A variety of questions address the technology-form relationship from the perspective of the impacts of form on technology, examining the ways in which organizations influence technological advances and modifications (Kling 1991). What is the nature of the sociotechnical evolution of systems in organizations? How do broader societal forces affect technology developments in organizational settings? By what processes do organizations shape development of communication technology? Though there has been substantial scientific advance with regard to these issues during the past decade, further understanding of the processes by which communication technologies are developed in organizational contexts may facilitate more precise alignment of technology and form in organizations of the future. These issues become particularly important as communication technology becomes more content laden, flexible, and customizable during its implementation.

A popular approach to the study of communication technology development has been to compare new media for their effects on the frequency, content, and quality of communication in organizations (Chapanis 1972, Hollingshead et al. 1993, Trevino et al. 1987). Within the study of technology-form relationships, situated studies are needed that compare the relative effectiveness of alternative media systems for supporting specified, new organizational arrangements (Zack 1993). In the future, it is also important for research to consider multifunctional systems rather than single media (e.g., electronic mail or videoconferencing) detached from the overall media system (Fulk and Collins-Jarvis 1998, Marshall and Novick 1995). New, integrated media systems are multifunctional, and alternative technical configurations may support similar dimensions of organizational forms.

Of related importance is research on the processes of defining standards and protocols for organizational communication (Kambil and Short 1994). Technical advances can outpace organizational capacity to incorporate technical changes, so research that sheds light on the mutual development of technical and social protocols is of significant organizational relevance. Additionally, there are a host of possible research questions related to development of technologies to support alliances, partnerships, and other interorganizational relationships as well as a need for research on developmental tools that aim to justify and evaluate such relationships (Meade et al. 1997). Finally, there is the issue of whether certain technologies or organizational forms are "effective" or not (Marshal and Novick 1995) and which organizational environments are able to yield relatively effective development of communication technology over time.

INSTANTIATION OF
TECHNOLOGY IN FORM

The chapters presented in this book suggest that managerial action that focuses exclusively on organizational form development or exclusively on communication technology development as mechanisms to shape communities of the future will miss the opportunity to manage at the juncture between technology and form. In the past, communication technology was less pliable or customizable and therefore issues of technology selection or technology impact were paramount. Organizations had to either select the right technology to "fit" existing needs or engage in organizational change programs to meet capabilities brought on by new technology. Today, both technology and form are far more pliable than in the past. As a result, they more readily can be incorporated into one another. Today, technology and form often become inseparable such that when managers ask, "How shall we design the organization," the question is—de facto—a consideration of technology design as much as organization design (Beniger 1990). So-called electronic organizations, virtual communities, groupware, and organizational networks conflate technology and organization to the point where they are nearly one and the same.

One area in which the instantiation of technology in form is gaining the interest of researchers is in the study of communication infrastructure. Jarvenpaa and Ives (1994) note the presence in corporate information architectures of values, attitudes, and behavioral requisites concerning information sharing. Star and Ruhleder (1996) have demonstrated the relational properties of technology infrastructure, observing that the properties of a communication system in an organization are evident simultaneously both in electronic media and in human behavior. They argue that infrastructure is increasingly a relational property that requires both technology and behavior and, moreover, that the two are for the most part one and the same from the point of view of development, use, and evaluation. In a similar vein, Davenport (1997) discusses information ecology as a multidimensional landscape in which technology and organizations evolve together and become inseparable over time. Increasing interest in electronic commerce would seem to beckon researchers to develop theories, models, and methods that can account for the instantiation of communication technology into organizational form or vice versa.

TECHNOLOGY REJECTION

A final set of research issues concerns the deliberate efforts by some organizations to remove technology from organizational form or to restrict its instantiation. In the information age wherein communication technology permeates nearly every aspect of organizational life, attempts by some organizations to restrict use of electronic communication or to actively remove it from situations in which it once thrived should be of interest to researchers. Why is it that organizations that provide electronic mail for nearly every formal and informal conversation then decide to ban its use for discussion of, for example, performance evaluation information? Why do companies that have invested heavily in groupware technologies decide not to provide computers inside of meeting rooms or certain meeting rooms? Why do some banks remove automatic tellers from their lobbies following large rollouts of such systems in earlier decades? These are instances in which technology has become instantiated in form, and the organization then takes formal or informal action to "undo" their melding, bringing the single phenomenon of an electronic organization back to its original duality of two phenomena, technology and form. What happens to organizational structures and processes when technology whose use has been deeply embedded in the organization is then separated from it?

In previous decades, researchers concerned themselves with the phenomenon of "user resistance" and attended to methods for overcoming such resistance and coopting users to adapt to new technologies. In the twenty-first-century organization, in which communication technology will penetrate nearly every aspect of social life, the question, "Why do organizations resist technology change?" may be replaced with the following: "Why, when, and how do organizations rescind technology choices and revert to more human methods of work?" What effects do such reversals have on technological development, organizational functioning, human systems, and social factors? Rather than consider the impact of technology on form or the impact of form on technology, researchers might juxtapose situations of technology instantiation with situations of technology rejection.

These four major research directions provide a wealth of possibilities for research on communication technology and changing organizational forms. Together with the chapters in this book, they suggest an important research agenda for the future.

REFERENCES

Beniger, J. R. (1990), "Conceptualizing Information Technology as Organization, and Vice Versa," in J. Fulk and C. Steinfield (Eds.), *Organizations and Communication Technology,* Newbury Park, CA: Sage.

Boland, R. J., Jr. (1991), "Information System Use as a Hermeneutic Process," in H.-E. Nissen, H. K. Klein, and R. Hirschheim (Eds.), *Information Systems Research: Contemporary Approaches and Emergent Traditions,* New York: Elsevier North-Holland, pp. 439-458.

Chapanis, A. (1972), "Studies in Interactive Communication: The Effects of Four Communication Modes on the Behavior of Teams During Cooperative Problem Solving," *Human Factors,* 14, 487-509.

Davenport, T. (1997), *Information Ecology,* New York: Oxford University Press.

DeSanctis, G. and M. S. Poole (1994), "Capturing the Complexity in Advanced Technology Use: Adaptive Structuration Theory," *Organization Science,* 5, 121-147.

Fulk, J. and L. Collins-Jarvis (1998), "Mediated Meetings in Organizations," in F. Jablin and L. Putnam (Eds.), *New Handbook of Organizational Communication,* Thousand Oaks, CA: Sage.

Hollingshead, A. B., J. E. McGrath, and K. M. O'Connor (1993), "Group Task Performance and Communication Technology: A Longitudinal Study of Computer-Mediated Versus Face-to-Face Work Groups," *Small Group Research,* 24, 3, 307-333.

Jarvenpaa, S. L. and B. Ives (1994), "The Global Network Organization of the Future: Information Management Opportunities and Challenges," *Journal of Management Information Systems,* 10, 4, 25-57.

Kambil, A. and J. E. Short (1994), "Electronic Integration and Business Network Redesign: A Roles-Linkage Perspective," *Journal of Management Information Systems,* 19, 4, 59-83.

Kling, R. (1991), "Computerization and Social Transformations," *Science, Technology, and Human Values,* 16, 3, 342-367.

Marshall, C. and D. Novick (1995), "Conversational Effectiveness and Multi-Media Communications," *Information Technology and People,* 8, 54-79.

Meade, L. M., D. H. Liles, and J. Sarkis (1997), "Justifying Strategic Alliances and Partnering: A Prerequisite for Virtual Enterprising," *Omega, International Journal of Management Science,* 25, 29-42.

Miller, D. (1990), "Organizational Configurations: Cohesion, Change, and Prediction," *Human Relations,* 43, 8, 771-789.

Rich, P. (1992), "The Organizational Taxonomy: Definition and Design," *Academy of Management Review,* 17, 4, 758-781.

Star, S. L. and K. Ruhleder (1996), "Steps Toward an Ecology of Infrastructure: Design and Access for Large Information Spaces," *Information Systems Research,* 7, 111-134.

Trevino, L. K., R. H. Lengel, and R. L. Daft (1987), "Media Symbolism, Media Richness, and Media Choice in Organizations," *Communication Research,* 14, 5, 553-574.

Tushman, M. L. and E. Romanelli (1985), "Organizational Evolution: A Metamorphosis Model of Convergence and Reorientation," *Research in Organizational Behavior,* 7, 171-122.

Zack, M. H. (1993), "Interactivity and Communication Mode Choice in Ongoing Management Groups," *Information Systems Research,* 4, 3, 207-239.

Index

Academic research world, 404-405
Access to data, 47
Accounting systems, 454
Acorn project, 138
  See also Computer-mediated
    communication (CMC)
Actor-network framework (A-N), 296, 297,
    301-303, 309
  See also Content/context in development
    of electronic communications
Adaptive structuration theory (AST),
    250-251, 285, 466
Adhocracy, 35
Adjustment and computer-mediated
    communication technologies,
    150-152, 161, 163, 165
Administrative workers, 213-215
  See also Communications across
    boundaries
Advice from strangers. *See* Weak ties
Age of Unreason, The (Handy), 115
Airline industry, 91
Alliance capitalism, 79
Alliances, strategic, 23-24, 92-93
American Hospital Supply (AHS), 22, 90-91
Anonymity and team interactions, 175, 179,
    180, 184-186, 199-200
Apple, Inc., 89
Appropriation of the technology, 250-251
Articulation of technology and
    organizational form, 7

  See also Communication technology and
    organizational form
Asian network organizations, 79, 80
AT&T, 457
Authority systems and structures, redefining,
    50-59

Bandwidth, 216
Banks, 487
Barnevik, Percy, 35
Blockmodels, 276-277
Boundaries, communications across
    organizational, 6, 56, 59, 83, 348-354
  See also Communications across
    boundaries
British National Health Service (NHS),
    467-468
Bureaucracy, 51, 450, 451
Burnout, 465-466
Business process engineering, 61
Buying power index (BPI), 392-393

Causal agency, assumptions about, 248
Cellular telephones, 327
Centralization, dispersed, 314
Centralization-decentralization debate, 14-17
Challenges facing new organizational forms,
    453

503

About the Editors

Gerardine DeSanctis is Professor of Management at Duke University. She received her PhD from Texas Tech University in 1982. Her research interests are in the general areas of electronic communication, distributed work arrangements, and management of information technology. Since 1990, she has been a senior editor for *Organization Science.* She has served as senior editor for *Management Information Systems Quarterly* and currently is a member of the editorial review board. She is on the advisory board of *Information Systems Research.*

Janet Fulk is Professor of Communications in the Annenberg School for Communication, University of Southern California. She earned her MBA and PhD from Ohio State University. Her research focuses on the interplay of communication technology and social systems. Her publications have won several awards and include *Organizations and Communication Technology* (with Charles Steinfield) and "Social Construction of Communication Technology" (*Academy of Management Journal*). She is a fellow of the Academy of Management.

About the Contributors

Lynda M. Applegate is a professor at Harvard Business School. She is also on the board of directors of MicroAge, Inc., and the strategic advisory boards for Mainspring Communications and the Alliance Analyst. She is also a member of the strategic advisory board for the U.S. GAO and was a member of a roundtable of advisers to President Clinton's Commission on Critical Infrastructure Protection. Her research and recent publications focus on the impact of information technology on organizations and industries. She is author of two books and more than 25 articles on this subject. She is a senior editor of *Management Information Systems Quarterly* and an associate editor for the *Journal of Organizational Computing and Electronic Commerce.*

Anitesh Barua is Associate Professor of Information Systems and Spurgeon Bell Fellow at the Graduate School of Business, the University of Texas at Austin. He received his PhD from Carnegie Mellon University. Research interests include the business value of information technology and reengineering, team-based organizations, and electronic commerce. More than 25 of his papers have appeared (or are scheduled to appear) in journals and refereed conference proceedings.

Richard J. Boland, Jr. is a professor at Case Western Reserve University. He has held visiting positions at Gothenburg University (Sweden), UCLA Graduate School of Management, and Oxford University (United Kingdom). He teaches in the areas of system analysis, philosophy of science, and research methods. His research interests include qualitative analysis of the design and use of information systems, and he is particularly interested in organization and human consequences of information technologies. He is editor-in-chief of the research journal *Accounting, Management and Information Technologies.*

David Constant is a partner in Process Inc., a firm providing consulting services in software process improvement. He holds degrees in systems design engineering from the University of Waterloo (Canada) and in organization theory from Carnegie Mellon University. His industrial experience includes management consulting in information systems and software development in real-time communications systems. His research interests include information and communications technologies in organizations, group behavior in organizations, and perceptions of ownership of information.

William H. Dutton is Professor in the Annenberg School for Communication, University of Southern California. He has edited or coedited several books related to computing and information systems, including *Computers and Politics* (with J. Danziger, R. Kling, and K. Kraemer, 1982), *The Management of Information Systems* (with K. Kraemer and A. Northrop, 1981), and *Information and Communication Technologies—Visions and Realities* (1996). His most recent book is *Society on the Line.*

Masayo Fujimoto is a senior researcher at the Sumitomo Marine Research Inst. Inc. (Japan). She does research and consulting for governmental organizations and companies. She received her master's degree in technology and policy from the Massachusetts Institute of Technology and is pursuing her doctorate at the Tokyo Institute of Technology. Her current interests are in technology innovation and diffusion in society, focusing especially on the technology developed by heterogeneous groups and organizations such as government, companies, and users (e.g., medical informatics, such as telemedicine and medical record systems, and electronic commerce technologies).

Pat Fung is an honors graduate of Bristol Polytechnic (United Kingdom), where she studied modern languages. After following a conversion course in computing and studying for a master of science in knowledge-based systems at Sussex University, she undertook her doctoral studies at the Open University. She is currently a lecturer in educational technology at the Open University, with research interests in the introduction and use of computing technologies and electronic communications in learning environments.

Pamela Hinds is on the faculty of Industrial Engineering at Stanford University, where she studies the relationship between people, groups, and technology. She received a PhD in organization science and management from Carnegie Mellon University. Her research interests include media effects on cognitive processing and social perception, the effects of expertise on cognitive biases, and the relationship between social networks and the diffusion of innovation.

Sara Kiesler is Professor of Social and Decision Sciences at Carnegie Mellon University. She is coauthor of *Connections: New Ways of Working in the Networked Organization* and editor of *Culture of the Internet.* She has published more than 45 research papers on electronic communication and has served on five National Academy of Sciences panels concerned with technology. Recently, she has been working with the HomeNet project, a longitudinal study of residential Internet use. She is also studying anthropomorphism of computer agents and electronic support groups.

John Leslie King is Professor of Information and Computer Science and Management at the University of California at Irvine. His work focuses on the role of information technology in the social organization production, especially in highly institutionalized contexts. Current projects include a study of the evolution of cellular telephony standards in Europe, the use of computer-supported cooperative work technology in felony courts, and coordination without process integration in complex logistics systems. He has published in a variety of fields related to information technology and organizations, and he was recently editor-in-chief of *Information Systems Research.*

Martin Lea is Research Fellow in Psychology at the University of Manchester (United Kingdom). He received a PhD from the University of Lancaster. His main research interest is in the social psychology and sociology of communication technologies. He recently held research fellowships in information technology from the United Kingdom Science and Engineering Research Council and in cognitive science-human computer interaction from the United Kingdom Joint Research Council Initiative. His current work is focused on the implications of computer-mediated communication for social identifications and the self, personal relationships, intragroup behavior, and intergroup relations. He is editor of *Contexts of Computer-Mediated Communication.*

C.-H. Sophie Lee is Assistant Professor of Information Systems at the College of Management, University of Massachusetts at Boston. She received her MBA and PhD in information systems from the University of Texas at Austin. Her research interests are in the area of complementarity of technology, incentive, and organizational design, including the business value of process-oriented technology, mass customization, and telecommuting. Her work has appeared in *Organization Science* and *Information Systems Research.*

Mary R. Lind is Associate Professor of Management Information Systems in the School of Business and Economics at North Carolina A&T State University. She received a PhD in business administration from the University of North Carolina at Chapel Hill. Prior to graduate school, she worked for 10 years as a systems analyst in the management information systems field. Her current research interests are in the areas of innovation, computer-mediated communication channels, and the impact of technology on firm performance and service quality.

James L. McKenney is Professor of Business Administration Emeritus at Harvard University, Graduate School of Business Administration. He received his PhD from the University of Californian at Los Angeles. He served as director of the Senior Management Program at Templeton College, Oxford. His research focuses on computer-mediated communication, knowledge-based systems, and the design and management of private communication systems. He is currently conducting a multiyear study of the impact of information technology on the grocery industry. His articles have appeared in many journals. His most recent book is *Waves of Change: Business Evolution Through Technology* (1995).

Peter Monge is Professor of Communication at the Annenberg School for Communication, University of Southern California. He has published *Communicating and Organizing* (with Vince Farace and Hamish Russell), *Multivariate Techniques in Human Communication Research* (coedited with Joe Cappella), and *Policing Hawthorne* (with Janet Fulk and Greg Patton). His research on organizational communication networks, collaborative information systems, globalization and communications processes, and research methods has been published in numerous leading communication and organizational journals, handbooks, and book chapters. He served as editor of *Communication Research* from 1986 to 1993 and as president of the International Communication Association 1997-1998. He is currently writing a book on globalization and theories of communication networks.

Kazuo Okamura is a senior researcher at Matsushita Electric Industrial Company, Japan. He has worked as a visiting scientist at MIT's Center for Coordination Science. His research interests include group communication systems in multimedia interactive environments and socioclutural differences in the usage of communication technologies.

Wanda J. Orlikowski is Associate Professor of Information Technologies and Organization Studies at MIT's Sloan School of Management. She received her PhD in information systems from New York University. Her research focuses on the ongoing interaction between information technologies and organizational elements such as structure, culture, communication, social cognition, and work practices. Recently, she has been studying the implementation and use of groupware technologies in organizations. She is working with Professor JoAnne Yates, also of the Sloan School, to develop a genre perspective on the role and use of electronic communication technologies in organizations.

Tim O'Shea is a professor and Pro-Vice Chancellor for Quality Assurance and Research at the Open University. He received a PhD in computer science from the University of Leeds (United Kingdom). He has carried out research on the educational applications of computers at the Universities of Texas at Austin and Edinburgh. He has published nine books, more than 100 articles, and six BBC programs on information technology and education. His current research projects include work on portable computing in education, ordering effects in human learning, and the design of interactive learning environments for hard mathematical and scientific concepts.

Jeanne M. Pickering is a research associate in information and computer science at the University of California at Irvine. She is studying software system requirements definition in the interactive game industry.

Marshall Scott Poole is Professor of Speech-Communication at Texas A&M University. He received a PhD from the University of Wisconsin. He has conducted research and published extensively on the topics of group and organizational communication, computer-mediated communication systems, conflict management, and organizational innovation. He has coauthored or edited four books, including *Communication and Group Decision-Making, Working Through Conflict,* and *Research on the Management of Innovation,* and has published in many journals. He is currently a senior editor of *Information Systems Research* and *Organization Science.*

Lee Sproull is Professor of Business at New York University. She has published extensively on topics related to electronic communication and the impact of new media on individuals, groups, and organizations. Her publications appear in a variety of journals across the disciplines of psychology, sociology, management science, and education. In 1991, she published (with Sara Kiesler) *Connections: New Ways of Working in the Networked Organization.*

Carroll Stephens is Assistant Professor of Management at Virginia Tech, where she teaches organization theory, business ethics, and a seminar on critical theories of organization. Her research interests include economic sociology, neo-institutionalism, postbureaucratic organization forms, and the effects of organizations on macrosocial structures. She focuses particularly on normative evaluation of the new organization forms and their social impact.

S. Lynne Taylor is Assistant Professor of History in the Department of History at the University of Waterloo, Canada. She received a PhD in history from the University of Michigan. She researches the social history of World War II and its immediate aftermath. Recent work has focused on black markets and the post-World War II refugee crisis.

Ramkrishnan V. Tenkasi is Assistant Research Professor in the School of Business Administration, University of Southern California. He received his PhD in organizational behavior from Case Western Reserve University. His research examines learning and sensemaking in complex and nonroutine task environments such as new product development and organizational change. Recent publications have appeared in *Organization Science, Employee Relations,* and *Advances in Interdisciplinary Study of Work Teams* (Vol. 2).

Bart Victor is Professor at the Institute for Management Development in Luzanne, Switzerland. He received his PhD in organization theory from the University of North Carolina-Chapel Hill. His research interests focus on ethical climates in organizations and the applications of social psychological theory to problems in organization design. He is especially interested in the social implications of globalization. His work has been published in many journals.

Andrew B. Whinston is the Hugh Roy Cullen Centennial Chair in Business Administration, Professor of Information Systems, Computer Science and Economics, Jon Newton Centennial IC^2 Fellow, and Director of the Center for Information Systems Management at the University of Texas at Austin. He is editor of *Decision Support Systems* and the *Journal of Organizational Computing* and coauthor or coeditor of 20 books and more than 275 articles. His current research interests include economic issues in electronic commerce and the pricing of Internet services.

Susan J. Winter is a member of the faculty of decision and information systems at Florida Atlantic University. She received her PhD from the University of Arizona. Her research focuses on the nonfunctional aspects of information technology and has included work on the role of technology in the organization of work, the symbolic nature of computer technology, and the evaluation of electronic meeting systems.

JoAnne Yates is Associate Professor of Managerial Communication and Information Studies at the Alfred P. Sloan School of Management, Massachusetts Institute of Technology. Her research, which includes both contemporary and historical studies, focuses on understanding how the use of communication and information within firms shapes and is shaped over time by its changing organizational, managerial, and technological contexts. During the past several years, she has worked jointly with Professor Wanda Orlikowski, also of the Sloan School, on studies using a genre perspective to illuminate the initial and ongoing use of electronic communication technologies.

Michael H. Zack is Associate Professor and the Joseph G. Riesman Research Professor in the College of Business Administration at Northeastern University. His research and teaching focus on managing information and information technology to enhance organizational performance. He has been a research fellow of the Lotus Institute since 1994, where he has studied the use of information technology to support teams and to codify and share organizational knowledge. He also has worked extensively in the areas of electronic commerce, information brokerage, and information products and services. His current research examines the relationships among corporate strategy, information technology, and the creating, sharing, and leveraging of knowledge within and among organizations.

Robert W. Zmud is Professor of Management Information Systems in the Information and Management Science Department at the College of Business, Oklahoma University. His current research interests focus on the impact of information technology in facilitating a variety of organizational behaviors and on organizational efforts involved with planning, managing, and diffusing information technology. He is outgoing editor-in-chief of *MIS Quarterly* and serves on the editorial boards of *Management Science, Information Systems Research,* and *Accounting, Management & Information Technology.* He is also the research director for the Advanced Practices Council of the Society for Information Management, International.